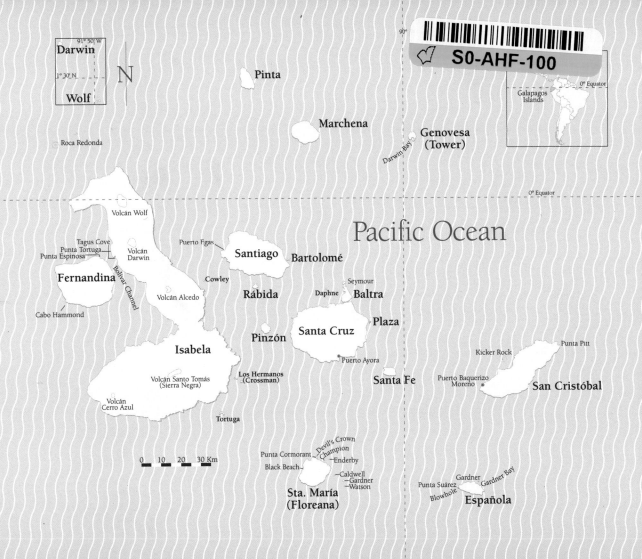

Darwin
91° 50' W
1° 30' N
Wolf

N

Pinta

Marchena

Roca Redonda

Darwin Bay

Genovesa
(Tower)

0° Equator

S0-AHF-100

Galapagos
Islands

0° Equator

Pacific Ocean

Volcán Wolf

Tagus Cove
Punta Tortuga
Punta Espinosa

Volcán
Darwin

Puerto Egas

Santiago

Bartolomé

Fernandina

Bolívar Channel

Cowley

Seymour

Daphne

Baltra

Cabo Hammond

Volcán Alcedo

Rábida

Plaza

Pinzón

Santa Cruz

Kicker Rock

Punta Pitt

Isabela

Volcán Santo Tomás
(Sierra Negra)

Los Hermanos
(Crossman)

Puerto Ayora

Santa Fe

Puerto Baquerizo
Moreno

San Cristóbal

Volcán
Cerro Azul

Tortuga

0   10   20   30 Km

Devil's Crown
Champion

Punta Cormorant

Enderby

Black Beach

Caldwell
Gardner
Watson

Gardner

Gardner Bay

Punta Suárez

Blowhole

Española

Sta. María
(Floreana)

GALAPAGOS
The Untamed Isles

imagine!
New York
www.imaginebks.com

We dedicate this book to all people whose aim is to live in a better world, where Nature is still in charge.

GALAPAGOS

The Untamed Isles

Pete Oxford & Reneé Bish

Galapagos: The Untamed Isles By Pete Oxford and Reneé Bish
E-mail: pete@peteoxford.com
www.peteoxford.com

Photo Captions

Front Cover: Male marine iguana in breeding colors, Española Island.
Spine: Male great frigatebird with pouch inflated, Tower Island.

Back Cover: Volcanic eruption - Cabo Hammond, Fernandina Island 1995.

Page # 1: A frigatebird mobbing a blue-footed booby, Punta Pitt, San Cristóbal Island.

Page # 2 & 3: Volcanic eruption - Cabo Hammond, Fernandina Island 1995.

Page # 5: Marine iguana, Fernandina Island.

Page # 7: Swallow-tailed gull in flight, South Plaza Island.

Page # 9: Galapagos flycatcher, Santa Cruz Island.

Design: Juan Lorenzo Barragán & Lorena Zurita / Azuca

The publication of the map of the Galapagos Islands has been authorized for this book by the Instituto Geográfico Militar - Autorización No. IGM - 9907008, del 7 de Julio de 1999, Quito, Ecuador.

For information about custom editions, special sales, premium and corporate purchases, please contact Imagine Publishing, Inc. at specialsales@imaginebks.com

imagine!
New York
www.imaginebks.com

Published by Imagine Publishing, Inc.
25 Whitman Road, Morganville, NJ 07751

Text and Photography © 2009 Pete Oxford and Reneé Bish

Distributed in the United States by:
BookMasters Distribution Services, Inc.
30 Amberwood Parkway
Ashland, OH 44805

Distributed in Canada by:
BookMasters Distribution Services, Inc.
c/o Jacqueline Gross Associates
165 Dufferin Street
Toronto, Ontario, Canada M6K 3H6

Distributed in the United Kingdom by:
Publishers Group U.K., 8 The Arena, Mollison Avenue, Enfield, EN3 7NL, U.K.

ISBN 13: 978-0-9822939-0-4
ISBN 10: 0-9822939-0-9
Library of Congress Control Number: 2009922011

Printed in China

Contents

Foreword

We are entering a critical time for the future of the biodiversity of Galapagos. Island archipelagos act as barometers for change in the world. The global human population is increasing, economies are growing, marine and forest resources are being depleted, wilderness areas are decreasing, and pollution is increasing. In the Galapagos, human population is increasing, tourism is increasing rapidly, marine resources are being depleted, pressures are growing on the terrestrial and marine protected areas, and pollution events are becoming sadly more frequent. The Galapagos of the next fifteen years could resemble the Hawaii and Caribbean of the present; including the continuing battles against invasive species, large hotel developments, and the extinction of large percentages of the famous Galapagos endemics. However, if we act now we could possibly avoid this future and ensure the conservation over the long term of the extraordinary biodiversity of these enchanted islands.

The purpose of Pete and Renee's book is to present the views and realities of Galapagos today. Pete's photographs are an artist's representation of the extraordinary wildlife of the Galapagos; they not only capture the wildlife as many have seen it, but each photograph is set with a master's eye. The text describes the situation in the archipelago and is based on over 20 years of experience with the islands. Key within the book is the recognition that the people of the Galapagos represent the future solution for the conservation of the islands. As such the book is a unique view of the archipelago based on photographs of the wildlife that are often seen on a typical cruise but with a text based on a behind the scenes understanding of the islands.

The Galapagos Islands face urgent challenges to a sustainable and conservation oriented future. Latterly, human population growth and economic growth have been exponential and the present development model appears unsustainable. There are substantial and limiting conflicts in fisheries management which contribute to a lack of collaborative local action in the islands. In addition, historical and potential new invasive species continue to be a major threat to the native biodiversity. The solutions to these challenges will require strengthened local institutions to work cooperatively to ensure informed decision making resulting in equitable and sustainable development. Local institutions will only be able to work together when conflicts are reduced and managed effectively and local residents begin to work together for a shared common vision. Part of this vision for the future must include building an island culture that understands natural resource limits; conserves energy, water and essential resources; and critically builds a local constituency for long term sustainability.

I hope that this book will remind you of these extraordinary islands and will also encourage you to take joint action with the institutions of the Galapagos to ensure a sustainable future that balances the needs of people and biodiversity and where the biodiversity of the islands is conserved over the long term.

Dr. Graham Watkins
Director,
Charles Darwin Research Station
Puerto Ayora, Galapagos

9

Sea lion mother and young, Española Island.

Authors' Preface

In this book we have attempted to consider the Galapagos Islands as a whole, without burdening the reader with loads of facts and figures, or with long, complicated biological life histories of the plants and animals. A book this size could never hope to be a complete treatise of the islands. This is not a wildlife guide, nor did we intend it as such. Other works are already available, many of them excellent, and these we have included in the bibliography.

With this portfolio of photographs, in an unashamed celebration of the Galapagos, we have tried to capture the essence and the spirit of this remarkable group of islands. We have attempted to inspire a sense of awe and simple pleasure as the reader shares with us momentary and common-place events in the everyday lives of the animals and plants, which we have captured on film. In addition, we have included a record of the volcanic eruption of Fernandina in February 1995, which we have also interpreted as a regular event (albeit on a geological time scale), fundamental to the soul and character of the archipelago.

We have divided the text and photographs into four geographical regions, namely, the western, northern, southern and central isles, in which we have included representative typical sites within the groups.

We have not attempted to offer an 'indepth' underwater coverage of the islands, although a few shots have been included for the benefit of the thousands of visitors every year who experience as much joy underwater with mask and snorkel as with camera and binoculars above.

Our greatest hope is that the reader be able to pick up this book at any time and open it to any page and simply enjoy. We hope that it will release a flood of memories to those who have visited the islands, and create a desire to do so in those who have not. We have also tried to create a sense of understanding of the archipelago without having dwelt too heavily on the serious threats facing the national park. Instead, we have attempted to highlight the beauty and uniqueness of the islands and, in this way, contribute to efforts to conserve their sanctity.

Sally lightfoot crabs and marine iguanas, Santiago Island.

Introduction

The Galapagos Islands are, without question, one of the most important natural history sites in the world. Straddling the equator in the mid-Pacific Ocean 1000 kilometers west of mainland South America, the group is made up of thirteen major islands, each at least fourteen kilometers square. There are also six smaller islands greater than one square kilometer and over forty rocks and islets. Almost entirely volcanic in origin, the islands have risen directly from the ocean floor. In order to understand the composition of the fauna and flora of the archipelago, it is critical to keep in mind that the islands have never been connected to a mainland source of colonization.

Hailed as a living laboratory, the archipelago rose to fame through the writings of British naturalist Charles Darwin. Significantly, today they have been declared a World Heritage Site by UNESCO and have become a mecca for nature-loving visitors.

The age of the archipelago is uncertain. Using potassium-argon dating methods, geologists have been able to determine that the oldest emergent rocks came into being between three and five million years ago. These are to be found on the island of Española in the extreme southeast. The westernmost island of the group (excluding Darwin and Wolf Islands), the island of Fernandina, is much younger, however, and has been dated at only 700,000 years. Indeed, there is a general progression of age towards the east. This age differential between the islands is very well explained by the "hot spot" theory proposed by geologists. The Galapagos archipelago is situated at the confluence of three tectonic plates, the Nazca, Pacific and Cocos. Consequently, as these plates move, the islands which rest on them move as well. The three plates are moving in different directions at different rates. The net movement of the Galapagos Islands is about seven centimeters per year southeast, towards the mainland. However, geologists propose that there is a weakness in the earth's crust more or less where the island of Fernandina lies today. Intermittently, for reasons as yet unknown, boiling magma breaks through this weak point, or hot spot. The result is a volcanic eruption. Lava is spewed from the vent, first underwater. It then builds up into a submarine cone until

Sea lions, Fernandina Island.

finally the tip of the volcano emerges into the air, cools, and solidifies. This newly formed island, sitting on the Nazca plate, then heads southeast, as if it were on a conveyer belt. An empty space forms over the hot spot and, in time, the process is repeated to form another new island, younger and to the west of the previous one. This is, in reality, a simplistic view of events as it seems that the Galapagos hot spot is relatively weak and horseshoe shaped, and its volcanic plume does not always break the surface in the same position.

One problem for evolutionary biologists was to explain how the Galapagos marine iguana, for example, could have evolved from the common green iguana, yet be so different after the relatively short lapse of three to five million years, the age claimed by geologists for the islands on which it lives. It was evolutionary biologists who suggested to geologists that the Galapagos Islands must be older. When geologists began investigating on the sea bed, they discovered that, in a direct line between the archipelago and the mainland, the sea bed is raised in what is called the Carnegie Ridge. Rock samples from the ridge have revealed that some of the rocks were formed in air rather than underwater. This evidence supports the fact that these eroded submarine

mountains were once Galapagos Islands themselves. As they traveled eastwards towards the mainland, the islands were eroded to the point where they disappeared below sea level and out of sight. This was the evidence evolutionary biologists needed and, although not conclusive as yet, does suggest that the original Galapagos Islands were formed a very long time ago and are thus much older than the originally proposed three to five million years.

However old the islands actually are, what we do know is that every new island first emerged from the sea as red-hot lava. The Galapagos Islands are indeed one of the most volcanically active sites on earth belonging, as they do, to the 'Pacific Ring of Fire'. There have been many eruptions over the past two decades, including two in 1979 and one in 1982, 1984, 1987, 1998 and 2005. Even today, the young volcanoes in the west continuously blow steam into the air, smell of sulfur and threaten to erupt. And sometimes they make good on that threat, as evidenced by a recent eruption on the Island of Fernandina which we were able to document in 1995.

Once the new lava has cooled to form an island, the result is nothing more than a barren, inhospitable environment, the canvas on which the paint-

Magnificent frigatebird female in flight, South Plaza Island.

ing will take shape. Onto this raw material begins the long, erratic process of colonization. There are two important stages to the appearance of life on remote oceanic islands: arrival of the organism, followed by subsequent establishment. Many organisms may arrive, but whether they are able to establish themselves or not is an entirely different matter. Consider the case of the iguana. The ancestor of both land iguanas and marine iguanas in Galapagos is thought to be the green mainland species, *Iguana iguana*. It must have arrived on a raft of vegetation, which floated from somewhere like the Guayas River in Ecuador. After 1000 kilometers at sea, the dehydrated and hungry iguana arrives to the barren, rocky shore of one of the islands. In order to survive it must eat. Iguanas are vegetarian, therefore it must find plants to feed on. Not so difficult, one might imagine. But remember that for there to be plants, they, too, must have previously arrived and established themselves. Only very few plants are able to colonize bare lava; these include

Brown noddy, Baltra Island.

the lava cactus, *Brachycereus nesioticus*, and *Mollugo* sp., an herb species. The roots of these "pioneer" plants are able to crack the lava and extract nutrients from it. Together with weathering by wind and rain, the lava is very slowly broken down. As parts of the pioneer plants die, their dead leaves and stems are blown into small crevices in the lava. These tiny pockets of organic material provide for the survival of the secondary colonizers. The process advances slowly and, gradually, the breakdown of the secondary colonizers forms more humus and, eventually, the beginnings of a soil for tertiary colonizers and so on, and so on. Therefore, in order for our iguana to find enough to eat, there must already have occurred an important succession of events on the island on which the reptile happened to become marooned. Without any plant life on the island, the iguana would die. The second vital step is that of establishment. In order for the iguana to establish itself as a viable species, this new arrival must then, somewhere, find another

iguana! Not only that, but it must be another iguana of breeding age and of the opposite sex! Unless the iguana which arrives in the first place is a pregnant female, in which case she has a whole new problem: finding a soft substrate in which to bury her eggs. One begins to understand the incredible degree of chance involved in any form of colonization of remote oceanic islands such as the Galapagos.

Certain factors play an important role in determining the diversity of successful colonizers. These include the distance the islands lie from the mainland, i.e., the nearest source of potential candidates for colonization, the direction of the prevailing winds and marine currents, the amount of rainfall, the topography, the diversity of habitats and the age of the islands. The Galapagos Islands have a paucity of species due to the fact that they have proved relatively difficult to colonize. They may also be said to have a disharmonic fauna with respect to the mainland. What this means is that, although perfect niches are available in the Galapagos for certain animals which live on the mainland, these animals are not represented in the islands. Amphibians and terrestrial mammals are prime examples. There are no natu-

Giant tortoise, Charles Darwin Research Station.

rally occurring amphibians, despite plenty of lush habitat in the highlands of some of the islands, and only nine species of native terrestrial mammals have been able to colonize, including seven rat species (some – nobody is sure how many – are now extinct) and two bats. Both amphibians and terrestrial mammals have a low rate of long-distance dispersal. Amphibians, unlike reptiles such as our iguana, have soft, permeable skin which, in a marine environment (i.e.,1000 kilometers of open ocean), means that the animals dehydrate and die due to osmosis. For most terrestrial mammals this salt-water barrier has also proved too much. Even if they found themselves on a floating raft rather than swimming, they would surely die of thirst en-route. Bats, on the other hand, can fly, while rats are small enough to have occasionally survived the journey, probably on large rafts where sufficient liquids could be obtained by eating the foliage of the raft itself. Rats also happen to be versatile and highly adaptable animals.

Examples of disharmony among plants also abound. Several species may continuously arrive but be unable to establish. Orchid seeds, for example, are minute and very likely often arrive wind-borne to the islands. It seems, however, that orchids have a problem, in that most of them need either a highly specific insect pollinator or a symbiotic mychorrhizal fungus, or both, in order to establish. Since neither of these seems to precede the orchid, its seeds are condemned to certain doom. Presently, only eleven species of orchid have managed to establish in the islands, while thousands of species exist on the mainland. Given time, however, surely more will make the grade. It has been calculated by Wiggins and Porter (1971) that less than four hundred chance instances of arrival and subsequent establishment, over the millions of years in the history of the islands, were sufficient to account for the full complement of the present-day native flora of the archipelago. Of the approximately five hundred and fifty native plant species in the islands, roughly two hundred and fifty are endemic.

It seems incongruous to find penguins and iguanas sharing the same few meters of coastline, or albatross sharing an island with giant tortoises. Many of such apparent anomalies can be explained by the complex systems of marine currents which bathe the archipelago. Driven by both the offshore southeast trade winds and the Coriolis force, surface waters off the coast of Chile and Peru are blown north and west. Deflected by the Coriolis force along the equa-

tor, the water heads west towards the Galapagos. The coastal waters of Chile and Peru can not simply all be blown west, however, without being replaced. This water is replaced by Antarctic water, cold, deep and nutrient-rich, that upwells off the coast of Peru and Chile. The trade winds persist and the cold fertile water continues towards the Galapagos, forming the Humboldt and South Equatorial currents. Water cannot be shunted incessantly west, to the shores of Indonesia and the Far East, without being displaced as well. As it is, the water tends to pile up in the west and is often almost a meter or so higher than in the east Pacific. Some of this water returns as the submarine Cromwell current, the first obstacle which the current encounters impeding its flow is the island of Fernandina. As the current collides with the island, cool, rich, water upwells to the surface, flowing around the island into the Bolívar Channel and also around Isabela Island. Likewise, the relatively cool westerly flowing currents, driven by the Humboldt, also upwell locally. The upwellings are determined by the contours of the bottom topography. The flow of water glances upwards predictably off the submarine rises to reach surface waters in key

Sea lion, Española Island.

20

areas of the archipelago. When these nutrient-rich waters move upwards into depths to which solar radiation penetrates (known as the photic zone), then the process of photosynthesis kicks in, forming huge algal blooms and the beginnings of the food chain. These areas of local upwelling support the highest concentrations of marine-based life forms and it is in such areas that penguins and iguanas feed side by side.

Darwin was the first to publicize the fact that on neighboring islands with similar conditions, closely related, yet different, species existed. It was this observation, and the realization that there had been a divergence of species within the archipelago, that steered him on his way to propose the revolutionary theories of natural selection. How has this process of evolution, resulting in unique species on the islands, occurred? There have been basically two processes at work. First, a simple "drift" by an errant colonizer towards a single new species and, second, the process of adaptive radiation, whereby two, or more, species are formed from the original colonizer. Any individual, or small group of colonizers, represents only a fraction of the genetic diversity contained

Sea lion chasing crabs, Santiago Island.

Adult, juvenile and chick flamingos, Floreana Island.

within the original parent population. Within such small, genetically simple populations, there is much more susceptibility to change and the influence of chance. For example, if a gene were to mutate, as happens at random under natural conditions anyway, this gene would represent a relatively much larger percentage of change within the small founder population of individuals than it would within its parent population of millions of individuals. In a parent population of finches, for example, the mutated gene would be so 'diluted' in the gene pool that it would not 'express itself', whereas it may represent the difference between a small beak or a large beak in ten percent or more of a colonizing population. These changes, which are more rapid in small founder populations, due to random change alone, are referred to as 'genetic drift'. This 'genetic drift', if it continues in isolation without the influx of new genetic material from the parent population (i.e. more colonizers of the same species arriving), will eventually lead to colonizers so distinct that they become a new species.

Displaying flamingos, Floreana Island.

Adaptive radiation essentially takes genetic drift one step further. That is, after a founder population has arrived and established itself on an island, an errant individual (or individuals) migrates to a neighboring island. This small sub-population has an even more limited degree of genetic diversity than the original colonizers. Therefore, the same process of 'genetic drift', away from the original colonizing population, begins. Eventually, the two populations become so different from each other that even if some of the secondary colonizers return to the orig-

inal island they continue as two separate species. This process may happen repeatedly over the millennia such that, as in the case of Darwin's finches, thirteen different species evolved from an original finch ancestor on the islands. Apart from random 'genetic drift', there may also be active processes of selection acting on the populations. For example, a typical ancestral finch stock arriving to a young island will normally encounter a situation of low predation and low inter-specific competition. The finches will also encounter a wide variety of poten-

tial resources at their disposal. In a hypothetical and simplistic situation, where there are different sized plant seeds available, some small, some large, and only very few of intermediate size, then the finches born with small beaks as well as those born with larger beaks will have an advantage over finches with intermediate-sized beaks. Gradually, the genes for small-sized beaks and large-sized beaks become more dominant than those for intermediate-sized beaks and the two populations diverge, eventually becoming so different that they no longer interbreed and two distinct species are formed. This example grossly over-simplifies the situation. In real terms, one must consider a combination of mechanisms for reproductive isolation by which speciation occurs.

The barriers to reproduction which develop may, for example, be geographical, where a small group of individuals colonizing a neighboring island, or indeed, a different part of the same island, do not encounter each other and therefore cannot mix. Behavioral differences may develop such that groups evolve different songs or different sexually attractive displays, so that one group eventually may not recognize and respond to the other. Temporal

Penguin and Pinnacle rock, Bartolomé Island.

separation, where breeding cycles become out of phase, also leads to genetic isolation. Even physical differences may develop and the two stocks may diverge sufficiently to become physically incompatible. Even if cross-breeding does occur, gene counts may be different and any hybrids which form will usually be sterile or less 'fit'.

Through one or more of the processes mentioned, the Galapagos Islands have become home to a fascinating array of plants and animals found nowhere else on the globe. The islands continue to be extremely important to scientists due, primarily, to the simplicity of the ecosystems. The apparent relative youth of the archipelago, combined with barren terrain and difficult access, has not allowed a large diversity of organisms to colonize the islands and so the various niches remain fairly open. The raw processes of evolution can almost be seen to be working, and are certainly well within the bounds of painstaking and careful scientific study.

When first discovered, the uniqueness of the archipelago was not appreciated. On March 10th, 1535, the Bishop of Panama, Fray Tomás de Berlanga, discovered the Galapagos. He and his crew

Iguana swimming (seen from underwater), Bartolomé Island.

Painted locust, Santiago Island.

were blown off course and found themselves in a perilous, life-threatening situation. Although he did comment on the tameness of some of the animals, and was the first to mention the giant tortoises, the bishop was rather preoccupied with his main goal, which was to find water. Indeed, the scarcity of water on these arid islands has proved to be one of the greatest hardships to overcome for all arriving life forms. Some of his horses and several sailors died of thirst.

Once discovered, various ships repeatedly visited the islands. The archipelago soon became known as the "Encantadas" - the "Enchanted Isles". Due to the strong inter-island currents, unpredictable winds and thick banks of fog which tend to suddenly blanket the archipelago, sailors at the mercy of the winds actually believed that the islands moved in order to deliberately confuse them. When the fog lifted, the vessels would find themselves in different positions relative to the islands, due to the action of unseen currents. This was a little too disconcerting for the superstitious men who thus described the archipelago as "enchanted", that is, bewitched. Coupled with the fact that the Galapagos became a pirate stronghold, the islands were feared rather than revered as they are today.

By the late 1500s, pirates were regularly hiding out in the archipelago, and even using some of the beaches to careen their ships. They used the islands as a refuge and a source of meat and fresh water before setting off on raids, pillaging the coastal towns of Ecuador and Peru. It was the pirates and buccaneers who first began the concerted harvest of the endemic tortoises. They discovered that these giant reptiles would remain alive, stored upside down on top of each other in the holds of their ships, for up to a year without food, a welcome source of fresh meat for the crew for whom anything was better than the traditional fare of salted pork and weevil-ridden biscuits. Over the next few hundred years, between one and two hundred thousand tortoises were subsequently removed for food. The pirates were also the first to introduce non-native mammals. Today this legacy of various introduced mammal species is one of the most serious problems facing the well being of the ecosystems within the islands.

Ecuador officially claimed the archipelago in 1832, and a penal colony was quickly established on Floreana. Only three years later, the HMS Beagle from England made its historic visit. The two distinguished personages on board not only put the Galapagos on the map, so to speak, but also revolutionized the whole of modern thinking. Charles Darwin and Captain Robert FitzRoy R.N. spent a mere five weeks in the archipelago, from September 15th to October 20th, 1835. Darwin visited only Santiago, San Cristóbal, Isabela and Floreana, yet, from such a limited stay, he not only drew examples from the islands on which to base his theories of evolution, but also remarked extensively on their geology and formation. FitzRoy, meanwhile, was so accurate in mapping the coastline that his charts were not improved upon for over one hundred years.

Since Darwin's visit, various colonizers and scientists have come to the islands and, over the years, five islands have become permanently colonized. In 1959 the Galapagos was declared a national park, except for those areas already colonized, and the Charles Darwin Foundation was established. In 1964, the Charles Darwin Research Station was launched. In 1968, the first two conservation officials were sent to the islands and thus began the

Pelican, Isabela Island.

Galapagos National Park administration. Already by 1970 major tourism had begun. A 58-passenger ship, the Lina-A, arrived, and several concrete docks were built at various visitor sites around the archipelago.

Human population growth in the islands has continued, virtually unchecked, to the present day. Most of the increase has been in one way or another a direct result of the huge tourism industry which has developed. Thousands of immigrants have arrived from mainland Ecuador, many because they already have family who superceded them to the islands, the effects of population pressure are mounting and even farms in the highlands of Galapagos are being turned in to condos to accomodate the population which now threatens to pass the 30,000 mark.

Those who make up this huge influx of generally unskilled labor, with their attendant families, are looking to reap some reward from the pot of tourist gold. When no work can be found, the immigrants often find themselves in a worse position than that which they held on the mainland. Hope turns to despondency, and the once-inspired immigrants find themselves in a hand-to-mouth situation as they try to feed their families. Others arrive specifically to fish the lucrative sharks, lobsters and sea cucumbers and, often in disregard for the negative effects which their efforts may cause the national park, over-exploitation of the marine stocks becomes the norm.

As the Galapagos is a province of Ecuador, every citizen of the Republic had, until recently, an equal birthright to reap hoped-for rewards from the high paying foreign tourists. In practice, of course, most of the money does not filter down the social ladder, having been creamed off at source, often not even reaching Ecuador. The last several decades have also seen many people born on the islands, people who, now in early adulthood, are defensive of their rights as Galapagueños. This new generation considers it natural to harvest the marine resources. They did not immigrate to the archipelago with a frontier mentality, knowing its international importance as a wildlife refuge, but were simply born there in a quirk of fate. Understandably, some are angry when restrictions are placed on their fishing activities, and it is no surprise in an underdeveloped country that the rules are broken. Perhaps the real blame lies with immigration policies. Indeed, until recently, there has existed not only a distinct lack of interest in curbing population growth on the islands, but also active encouragement of immigration. Increased air services, gasoline stations, satellite communications and banks as well as government sponsored electricity and propane have all been added for the comfort of any would-be colonizer. Galapagos is no longer the hardship post it used to be and, as more and more people come to live there, the human population pressure is being felt by the unique fauna and flora of the archipelago. The time has come to recognize that the human population is permanent and to empower the residents to protect and become proud of their resource. To treat it as finite, use it sustainably and for them to become their own guardians of their future by keeping out the negative and non sustainable impacts. However, in an encouraging move, the National Congress has recently approved a bill – the Special Law for Galapagos – that provides for certain restrictions on further immigration to the islands. Also, a further step in the right direction has been the initiation of an inspection and quarantine program to reduce to a minimum the introduction of aggressive alien species.

For the visitor, the islands remain a truly magical destination. The enchantment lies in the extreme approachability and tameness of the wildlife. There can be few natural experiences more rewarding than quietly sharing a beach with sea lions, especially when one decides to waddle over, flop its body across your outstretched legs, and go to sleep. Mockingbirds scamper down the beach to greet newcomers to their home as finches fly into nearby bushes and investigate the proceedings. The marine iguanas, meanwhile, snort plumes of salt from their nostrils and look on in disdain. One may approach to within a few feet a male great frigatebird with his bright red gular sac, or throat pouch, inflated to the size of a football. Regardless of your presence, he will stretch his wings to their full span of more than two meters, throw his head back, and, quivering with anticipation, let out his shrill, reverberating call to every female flying overhead. Should he be up-to-scratch, passing the female's scrutiny, she will alight next to him and he will lay a huge protective wing across her back to seal the bond. The list of potential interactions to be experienced with the wildlife is endless. One may swim with sea lions in a face to

Swallow-tailed gull, South Plaza Island.

face encounter, snorkel with sharks and manta rays, watch turtles return to the sea after a night of egg-laying, sit with albatross or stay quietly adrift, surrounded by a pod of forty sperm whales, a whale shark or a hundred leaping dolphins cavorting around the vessel in play. Indeed, the islands are nothing short of a wildlife paradise.

The Galapagos National Park Service and the Charles Darwin Research Station are together going to great lengths to restore the natural balance of the archipelago to that existing before the intervention of human beings. In an effort to protect the habitat, most official visitor sites are serviced by narrow trails which the licensed guides accompanying each group ensure are strictly adhered to. Some of the islands, sadly, are riddled with introduced plants and animals. Many are seriously affected. Isabela, for example, has herds of wild cattle, horses, donkeys and goats roaming the volcanoes. Cats, dogs, pigs and rats are also at large and prey at will on the native fauna.

Red-billed tropicbird, South Plaza Island.

The populations of many of the native Galapagos species are extremely small. Such populations are fragile and need protection from the ravages of the introduced predators. The island of Santiago is another seriously affected island. It is thought that there were once up to 100,000 goats and 10,000 pigs on the island! The national park's funds, however, are seldom adequate; thus, until now the costly eradication programs have not always been feasible. In any event, the situation regarding introduced animals is complicated. Pigs, for example, being rather intelligent animals, have become nocturnal and extremely shy. They must be eliminated before the goats because, with no goats, the denuded vegetation will regenerate, rendering it impossible to find and eliminate the pigs. Another example of the complexity of the situation was illustrated on the north of Santa Cruz Island where packs of feral dogs were attacking the limited numbers of land iguanas. The park decided to act. The dogs were locally erad-

icated in an effort to save the iguanas. Subsequently, however, it was noticed that the cat population increased and this, in turn, reduced the local rat population. Perhaps surprisingly, the cattle population was also seen to increase somewhat as a result of eliminating predation pressure from dogs. The net result is that the introduced animals are in their own state of equilibrium. Rats are extremely damaging and almost impossible to eradicate. Unless all of the introduced animals could be eradicated overnight, which is clearly unachievable, it is almost a blessing that there are a few cats to control the rats. On the other hand, one needs a few dogs to control the cats, and so it goes. The situation is probably permanent and indicates the importance of maintaining unaffected islands free from all introduced fauna and flora.

In recent years, the human impact from fishermen has come to rival that from introduced animals. Lobsters, endemic groupers and sharks have been caught in enormous quantities. The lobsters and grouper are for the home market, while huge numbers of large adult sharks have been killed for the sake of a few square centimeters of fin to satisfy the

Bottlenose dolphins bow riding.

Far-Eastern palate. Sea cucumber fishing has also reached calamitous proportions, satisfying the same insatiable markets. Nobody yet understands the biological consequences of the monumental harvests of sea cucumbers from the archipelago but, as with all uncontrolled exploitation, it is bound to create an imbalance somewhere in the food chain. Today sea cucumber exploitation is close to the point of commercial extinction. A major subsidiary problem to the industry has been that fishermen set up illegal camps in sensitive areas such as Fernandina Island. These camps usually involve a high degree of infrastructure. Already Fernandina, perhaps the world's largest (almost) pristine island, has had escaped hunting dogs roaming free over the island, and live goats have been brought on as food. The risk of their subsequent introduction, or of rats and fire ants from these uncontrolled visits, is grave. It certainly does not seem fair that while tourists who pay high fees are controlled to the point that even a step off the path is seen as an invasion of the sanctity of the park, some of the fishermen, despite their conspicuous disregard for the rules and ecology of the islands, have proven hard to control due to political pressures. Since a park guard was shot in the line of duty in March 1997, however, the pressure has apparently increased to control illegal activities. Ecotourism, where conducted in a controlled manner, seems to us the only viable, long-term solution to the continued vitality of the Galapagos Islands. At recent rates of extraction and population growth, the Galapagos National Park has a limited future. What was once the paragon of national parks in the world has sadly been in a steady state of decline. We sincerely hope, however, that the implementation of the Special Law for Galapagos, combined with a general change in attitude from a frontier extractive mentality, to a proud, sustainable, conservationalist attitude among the population will lead to a reversal of this deterioration. Our hopes lie with the Ecuadorians themselves, a people with a growing ecological awareness. Fortunately, today there is hope in the form of the many young Ecuadorians who have already joined the ranks of those fighting for the continued well being of this natural resource. We salute them and wish them well - a true victory must come from within.

Perhaps the recent eruptions on Fernandina and Isabela are a message that the power of nature is a force still to be reckoned with and Nature will one day be able to heal her wounds.

Lava flow - Cabo Hammond, Fernandina Island 1995.

Western Isles

In this chapter, the area of coverage includes principally the islands of Fernandina and Isabela, although some of the satellite rocks and islets are also mentioned. Isabela is the largest of all the Galapagos Islands, accounting for more than half of the total land area.

In excess of 4500 square kilometers, Isabela stretches more than 130 kilometers in length and is over 75 kilometers at its widest point. Whereas most of the other islands in the group represent the emergent tip of a single, largely submarine volcano, Isabela is actually a coalescence of six different volcanoes, each probably formed separately but close together, both temporally and spatially. The result is a wonderfully dramatic skyline, each volcano sitting proudly next to its sibling. The five main volcanoes, namely Cerro Azul, Sierra Negra, Alcedo, Darwin and Wolf stand 1100 meters or more in height. Volcán Ecuador, which straddles the equator along with Volcán Wolf, is largely eroded, half of it having fallen into the sea.

Across the Bolívar Channel to the west, the island of Fernandina is the youngest in the archipelago. Certainly one of the most important islands, it is also perhaps the most impressive. As one stands on the fresh black lava at the edge of the 'aa' lava field ('aa' pronounced 'ah ah', is an Hawaiian word meaning pain, and has come to refer to very jagged and broken lava) at Punta Espinoza on the northeast of the island and looks southwest towards the volcano, one looks out over a dark, barren, dramatic landscape. The volcano rises from the ocean to form what geologists refer to as the 'upturned soup plate' shape of classic basaltic, oceanic shield volcanoes. It sits in a somber mood against the sky, reminding us of the power of the natural forces responsible for its creation. Behind the green facade of mangroves which line the shore, the outlook across the island to the summit of the volcano is indeed hostile. The 'aa' field in the foreground, of sharp and twisted clinker plates, jutting two meters or more into the air, creates an imposing terrain. The more stable areas of lava have, incredibly, become host to one or two isolated plants, principally grasses, the herb *Mollugo* sp. and the endemic lava cactus

Dripping lava - Cabo Hammond,
Fernandina Island 1995.

Brachycereus nesioticus. As mentioned in the introduction, these pioneer plants are incredibly important in the initial stages of soil formation and animal colonization of the islands. Apart from the few such specialized plants, very little other life manages to survive on the 'aa', and not until the gaze falls upon the slopes of the cone itself can a few sparse trees be seen clinging to an existence, relying largely on condensation and mist to satisfy their 'thirst'.

The visitor arriving by boat usually concludes that vegetation is lush on the island after noticing the dense stands of green mangroves lining the shore. These hardy plants, however, derive all their sustenance directly from the sea and use the island only as a point of anchorage. The red mangrove, particularly, is of great importance for its complex system of roots grows seaward forming baffles to dissipate wave action. As the force of the wave is diminished, the more slowly moving water is able to support less particulate matter which

Erupting parasitic cone, Cabo Hammond, 1995.

therefore sediments out. Mud builds up behind the roots and, subsequently, the mangroves also advance. Land reclamation is only one important service provided by these root systems; they also play host to an infinite number of larval marine species. Fish fry, young shrimp and molluscs all use the still water areas created by the mangroves as nurseries. In addition, given that the spaces between the roots are too small to allow the entry of large fish, the root system can be likened to a giant sieve which strains out the predators allowing the larvae to grow in relative safety. On Fernandina the mangroves appear to be growing slightly inland in certain areas due to the fact that the ocean has channeled through the lava cracks to form pools of full strength sea water which allow the growth of the salt-tolerant plants. None of the four mangrove species in Galapagos are endemic. Their seeds are highly salt tolerant and, once having fallen into the ocean, will remain afloat for weeks until, through

Cowley Island.

the action of the wind and currents, they are washed up on another shore, possibly thousands of kilometers away, where they eventually germinate. Due to their very high tendency for long distance dispersal, mangroves are often some of the first colonizers on newly formed foreign shores.

The southwestern coastline of Fernandina also recently extended towards the sea, this time not due to the actions of mangroves but to a dramatic few months of volcanic eruption. In early 1995 hundreds of visitors were lucky enough to witness this incredible, primeval display of Nature's power. As small tourist boats bobbed humbly on the ocean in front of the spectacle, dense pillars of white steam billowed skyward to block out the sun. The long, slow swell from the Pacific lazily crashed over the glowing red river of molten lava, causing hideous explosive reactions. During this eruption, the poor creatures in the area had no idea of the significance of the huge pyroclastic displays around them and would walk across the lava onto a red-hot floe and burst into flames. Truly a

Common dolphins, Bolívar Channel.

spectacular site, it was a parasitic cone on the southwestern flank of the volcano which erupted. For several months, molten lava and volcanic bombs were flung eighty to one hundred meters into the air. The red-hot lava spewed over the edge of the cone and ran in a fast flowing river, more than thirty meters wide in places, towards the sea. Everything in its path was destroyed. Trees exploded into flame on contact, while various animals and birds were also engulfed. On reaching the sea, numerous fingers of the main floe poured into the ocean. As has happened many times before in the history of the islands, the red-hot lava hissed on contact with the water while the sea boiled and turned to clouds of steam. Only a kilometer or so away, a large colony of Galapagos fur seals and the rare Galapagos flightless cormorants, like the iguanas, were oblivious to the enormous forces of both destruction and creation going on all around them. Slowly the island grew.

Fernandina is still incredibly active. It is the youngest island of the archipelago and the closest

Male Galapagos flightless cormorant offering seaweed to female, Fernandina Island.

Galapagos flightless cormorant on nest,
Fernandina Island.

41

Galapagos flightless cormorant and chicks, Fernandina Island.

to the proposed hot spot explained earlier. Due to its youth, it has not yet undergone sufficient colonization to be as diverse as its motherly neighbor, Isabela. Luckily for the island, when Fernandina rose from the sea it did not quite become large enough to close the gap of the Bolívar Channel and fuse with Isabela. It is only this isolation which has prevented the colonization of Fernandina by introduced mammals, the fate of many other islands. To this day, Fernandina still remains relatively pristine - but for how long?

The Galapagos populations of birds and animals are generally very small. Although stable, many species are extremely fragile. Their very existence hangs precariously in the balance so that the slightest intervention by man could tip the scales and quickly render the species extinct - forever. Two vulnerable populations that quickly come to mind are those of the flightless birds in the archipelago. Galapagos is host to the most northerly penguin population in the world.

Flightless cormorant drying wings.

The only entirely tropical penguin species, and the only one which actually breeds just into the northern hemisphere, it is naturally enough called the Galapagos penguin; its total population is less than 1,000 breeding pairs.

The other flightless bird in the archipelago is a cormorant. This unique bird, known as the Galapagos flightless cormorant, numbers only seven to eight hundred pairs. The population is centered in the western isles, around both Fernandina and Isabela. Neither species is capable of rapid dispersal in case of hard times, or rapid escape in case of predation, as neither can fly. They require, therefore a rather simple life with relatively few external pressures. Isabela is an island overrun with introduced animals, many have now crossed the notorious Perry isthmus, an extensive 'aa' field lying between Volcán Alcedo and Volcán Sierra Negra, which for some time was hoped to prove an impenetrable barrier to non-native fauna. Rats, cats, goats and donkeys

Sierra Negra volcano's crater, Isabela Island.

are all now beyond the barrier, having followed the coastline and migrated north from the centers of human population in the southeast. The New Scientist Magazine stated (15 April 1995) that the number of feral goats on Alcedo increased from about 10 in 1982 to a staggering 100,000 in 1995. The goats, of course, are a serious threat to the tortoises. They browse the vegetation to beyond the reach of the reptiles and seriously deplete their food supplies. We were even told recently of a guide sighting a goat actually standing on a tortoise, using it as a platform in order to increase its reach - the height of audacity. Project Isabela however is in the process of a huge, concerted effort to eradicate the goat population. The big problem for the birds, however, is the predatory rats and cats. Unable to escape, the Isabela populations of flightless birds are particularly vulnerable. Being unaccustomed to any threat of terrestrial predation, the birds are oblivious to the dangers and take little action in their own defense when at risk. We have watched, on more that one occasion, a cat walk across the backs of marine iguanas to reach a blue-footed booby chick which did nothing to defend itself and was eaten. Fernandina remains the last safe bastion for many species where such threats are nil. The island's importance in this respect cannot be overstated.

Although most of the penguins live around the western isles, some do occur also in the central islands, notably, a small population around Bartolomé island where they are actually more easily seen. Penguins are cold water species, which is why they concentrate in the west where the ocean water is coldest and richest in nutrients. It seems incongruous, nevertheless, to see penguins at home on bare, black lava (side by side with cactus), directly under the equatorial sun. They are *Spheniscid* penguins, related to the Jackass, Humboldt and Magellanic species. Like all *Speniscids*, they are black and white, diminutive in size, bray rather like donkeys, and live and nest in burrows. In the case of the Galapagos penguins, as there is little suitable soil at sea level around their breeding areas in which to burrow, they have taken to using lava crevices for shelter and nesting. Said to be flightless, penguins really do fly underwater. Their wings have adapted to become true flippers and, on close inspection, the tiny feathers with which they are covered are visible. The body feathers of penguins are strongly curved so that they lay neatly on top of one another with

Marine iguana head bobbing, Fernandina Island.

Marine iguana, Fernandina Island.

Marine iguana, Fernandina Island.

a large degree of overlap, like the tiles of a roof. This arrangement helps to trap air, which acts as an insulation layer to keep the penguin warm when it dives. To overcome the added buoyancy of the trapped air, however, penguins often swallow stones to act as counter-weights.

Of the 29 species of cormorant in the world, the Galapagos flightless cormorants are the largest and the only species without the power of flight. Underwater their vestigial wings are held close to their sides, and they paddle with their very muscular legs and webbed feet. They are not pursuit feeders but make a living by foraging in the submarine cracks and crevices between rocks. Their favorite prey is the moray eel and the octopus, which they capture with a swift strike of their powerful head and neck, using the sharply hooked bill to retain the prey. The cormorants are highly local in their distribution, barely ranging more than a kilometer from their natal shores. They have a variable nesting season, but the courtship, if witnessed, is something to remember. In the water, the cormorant uses a rattling call to attract a mate and then the two entwine their necks and rotate energetically on the surface until the pair-bond is formed. The nest is built on the bare rock close to the water's edge and is a scruffy construction comprised mostly of seaweed. At each reunion with his mate at the nest, the male brings an offering of more seaweed which, with great ceremony, is accepted by the female and added to the nest. After laying, both adults incubate the three eggs and raise the young. One of the most characteristic images of the Galapagos Islands is the sight of a cormorant, having returned to land after a spell at sea, with its vestigial wings 'hanging out to dry'. Although useless for flying, the cormorant's wings still serve a slight function as balance organs used when the bird hops from one rock to the next. Cormorants do not produce sufficient oil to waterproof all of their feathers and so do not suffer increased buoyancy from trapped air as do penguins. Therefore, the wing, as it is not waterproofed, must be properly dried out or the feathers will be damaged. Another remarkable characteristic of the flightless cormorant is the piercing gaze of its intensely turquoise eyes.

As unique as they may be, the cormorants are upstaged by perhaps the most quintessentially Galapagos species of them all, the marine iguana. The only truly marine lizard in the world, visitors to the islands are reminded of miniature versions

Great blue heron preying on marine iguana, Fernandina Island.

of the dragons of fairy tales. Of all visitor sites in the archipelago, Punta Espinoza, on Fernandina Island, is the marine iguana capital. On early morning arrival to the site, one finds densely packed marine iguanas 'spread-eagled' over the rocks. Darwin's 'Imps of Darkness', the iguanas lounge over huge areas and blend imperceptibly with the rock itself. As one approaches, a sporadic burst of sneezes issues from the prostrate iguanas. In a 'fight-or-flight' response to a potential threat, the large reptiles clear their nasal passages of a concentrated salt solution enabling them to breathe more deeply if need be. The solution is expelled explosively as two jets of salty spray, one from each nostril. A marine iguana, like a seabird, has a special salt gland in its head which is able to rid the body of excess salt ingested by the animal as part of its daily life. Better adapted than kidneys for the job, the salt gland is equipped with an osmotic pump to extract salt up to twenty parts per thousand more concentrated than seawater.

Marine iguana swimming, Fernandina Island.

The iguanas, particularly the large ones, go out to sea to feed. They dive down many feet underwater and, while clinging to the rocks with their strong, sharp claws, graze the marine algae. Being poikilothermic, or cold-blooded, they must regularly return to shore, however, to recharge their solar battery. The iguanas prefer grazing at low tide so they don't have to immerse their bodies in the frigid waters around the western isles and, in so doing, increase the time of their feeding. They have slightly protruding tricuspid teeth which enable the animals to crop the 'sea lettuce', *Ulva* sp., very close to the rock surface. Iguanas will unhesitatingly swim from one grazing area to the next if necessary, a behavior for which they are admirably evolved. During swimming, the limbs are held passively at the sides of the body while the full propulsion of the animal is derived from the undulating tail which describes a series of sinusoidal curves. The tail itself is dorsoventrally flattened, that is, from back to belly, to present a large surface area to the paddle-like organ.

Male iguanas are larger than females and, during the breeding season in the hot summer months, they aggressively defend a small territorial area of rock favored by females. The males display their might with frequent deep head bobs. Dominance is achieved by vigor, and similarly matched individuals compete in a trial of strength by shoving. The raised scales on the crown of the iguanas' heads interlock as one male tries to push the other out of the disputed area. After the breeding season is over, the females also become antagonistic towards each other. They retire to a sandy area where they dig a tunnel in which they lay two to four leathery eggs. They then aggressively defend the nest site from other females who otherwise might destroy the eggs during an excavation of their own. Once the danger has passed and all the females have laid their eggs, the nests are abandoned and the young are left to their own devices with no further parental care.

The young are constantly in peril after hatching. They hide in lava cracks where they try to remain undetected. Galapagos snakes and herons, particularly the great blue heron, are their main

Galapagos tortoise sleeping on Alcedo volcano.

predators; an experienced great blue heron can eat many hatchling iguanas in a single day. Endemic Galapagos hawks also take young iguanas and will, on occasion, also tackle an adult, particularly the females exhausted after nesting. In general, however, once having reached adulthood, the iguanas are free from predation and actually welcome visitations from birds, such as finches and mockingbirds which, along with Sally lightfoot crabs and lava lizards, prey upon any infestations of ticks and external parasites as well as feeding on molting skin.

The western isles are also home to the second major group of reptiles inhabiting the archipelago, huge animated boulders living on the volcano rims. More Galapagos giant tortoises live on the island of Isabela than on any other in the Galapagos. Each volcano has effectively become an island in its own right. The tortoises do not cross from their native volcano to another, not even to volcanoes on the same island. Due to this relative remoteness and isolation, the tortoise populations on each volcano have gradually drifted apart over the millennia, so that the gene pools have changed and individual groups have become subspecies of one another. Today it is estimated that the total Galapagos giant tortoise population stands at about fifteen thousand individuals divided into eleven subspecies.

Galapagos tortoise on Alcedo volcano.

The largest population is on the volcano of Alcedo, numbering approximately three thousand individuals reaching up to 225kgs (500 lbs) in weight. Some of the individuals alive today may even have been around when Darwin made his visit to the Galapagos. Many individuals have also died since then. Hundreds of thousands of these dinosaurs were removed over the years by pirates, buccaneers and whalers for whom they were a source of fresh meat. The original population probably stood in the order of two hundred and fifty thousand. As the visitor climbs Alcedo, he or she will begin to encounter the tortoises half way up the slopes

Galapagos hawk, Isabela Island.

towards the rim. Thanks to their dome-shaped carapaces, they can bulldoze their way easily through the dense vegetation in which most of them live. With a relatively slow metabolism, however, they spend a lot of time at rest and, in the warm months, particularly during the heat of the day, under shade. Tortoises love water and mud. When it is available they will spend hours at a time in a wallow which also helps in the removal of ectoparasites. Surprisingly, mosquitoes and ticks can bite even through the shell of the tortoise where they tap into the growing edges of the scutes which have a large blood supply. All along the trail to the rim of Alcedo one can see evidence of tortoises: paths of flattened vegetation, large grassy scat and tortoise-sized sandy pits where the animals have spent the night. Every now and again a tortoise is encountered in the middle of the trail, slowly and deliberately feasting on the lowly plant life. Rhythmic dull thumps and the sounds of 'snoring' can be heard occasionally. Apart from a sudden hiss which the tortoise expels as it quickly retreats into its shell in defense, these sounds are its only vocalizations. The thumping is the bump of the male's concave plastron banging against the rear of the female's carapace as he mounts her. The 'snoring' is actually a grunt, an expression of the effort involved in the act. Matings may last several hours if undisturbed. When the female is ready to lay her eggs, she will wander off on her own looking for a suitable spot. There she will dig a hole with her hind legs, deposit up to sixteen large spherical eggs the size of tennis balls, and then urinate over the covered nest to create a muddy layer which hardens to a solid, protective cap. Like most reptiles, she subsequently abandons the eggs and young who must fend for themselves. Though they seem passive, tortoises will sometimes become quite aggressive towards one another. Males, in particular, compete over females and food resources. A typical display of aggression is a head-on approach with necks outstretched. Once face-to-face, the contenders raise themselves up as high as possible in a threatening posture with mouths agape. He who is tallest is the winner and the shorter animal backs down.

Once reopened the effort of the climb up Alcedo to see the tortoises is definitely worthwhile. There is something very special about sitting a few feet from such a creature, a window on the past, especially in its natural environment, that of a huge volcanic crater. Of course, tortoises

Green turtle, Fernandina Island.

are not the only animals one might see. While walking up the path, the visitor will be accompanied by mockingbirds and hundreds and hundreds of endemic Galapagos finches of many different species. In fact, Isabela boasts ten of the thirteen Darwin's finches, while Fernandina is home to nine. The two islands are also the only home of the rare mangrove finch which today is possibly under threat from over-exploitation of mangrove wood used illegally for fuel by fishermen. This dead wood is the habitat of the wood boring insects the mangrove finch feeds on. Though diminutive and dull in appearance, the finches are very curious little birds, often gathering in large flocks to watch unusual comings and goings.

The habitats on the hike are varied. The path winds through areas of *Opuntia* cactus and *Scalesia* sp., then lush forests of *Bursera* sp. and *Pisonia* sp. festooned with lichens like old men's beards. The endemic Galapagos flycatcher is another attractive bird to look out for, while its cousin, the vermillion flycatcher, cannot be missed. The male vermillion flycatcher will often be seen calling from the high point of a tree or energetically trying to attract a mate with its acrobatic display flight. The brilliant red of the male is indeed striking, while the female is dressed in a pale lemon yellow. Galapagos hawks are in evidence throughout the walk, often flying down for a closer inspection of passers by. They have even been known to land on tourists' heads, so tame are they! Spiders, grasshoppers and endemic carpenter bees are also common. The black female bees vastly outnumbering the rarely seen orange-colored males.

On returning to the arid areas of the coast, the visitor sees snake-like trails crossing the path. These tracks are made by the tails of rambling iguanas. Land iguanas live mostly in this region, foraging on the succulent vegetation of the area. Of the two species of land iguana in the Galapagos Islands, the most wide-

Lava heron hunting.

Land iguana, Isabela Island.

spread is *Conolophus subcristatus* which is also both the largest and most brightly colored. Like their marine iguana relatives, the land iguanas are also vegetarian. They are stockier animals, however, and their color ranges from yellow to brick red. The nose is longer and more typical of the *Iguanidae* family than is that of the marine iguana, while the tail, which does not function as a paddle, is simply round in cross-section. The crest is shorter than its cousin's, and not nearly so ominous. Although there are many land iguanas on both Isabela and Fernandina Islands, Plaza and Santa Fe in the central isles are both much easier sites in which to see them.

The coastlines of the islands are where most of the biological activity occurs, and Fernandina is a favorite area for combing the shore. A magnificent frigatebird will occasionally sit on a dead mangrove, on the lookout for any opportunity to feed. Lava herons stalk the strand, freezing to a motionless statue at the first sign of

Sea lion mother and pup, Fernandina Island.

small fish (staring into a tide pool in absolute concentration, its neck held sprung at full recoil, ready for a lightening strike at its prey). Green turtles inhabit the same waters. Trapped in tidal lagoons as the ocean recedes, they lie a few feet below the surface under rock ledges.   When forced to breathe, they gently rise, push their head through the skin of viscous water into the air, extend their neck backwards and inhale deeply. With complete grace and a sense of deliberation, they once again return to their submarine slumber. Sea lions have nursery areas under the mangroves, and the young pups are left to cavort and play under the direction of just one or two mothers during a receding tide, while the others go out to sea to feed. The tide pools offer the pups a perfect playground in which to learn the skills of coordination needed for hunting on their own. Completely isolated from the sea before the tide returns, they are safe in the knowledge that no large marine predators, such as sharks, can attack.

Sea lion mother and newborn pup with afterbirth, Fernandina Island.

Sea lion pups playing in tide pool, Fernandina Island.

Juvenile pelican, Isabela Island.

The adult females return one by one and it is very rewarding to watch the reunion of the mother with her pup. First she calls and immediately a single pup from the playground sits bolt upright and starts bleating back in her direction. The two come closer, scrambling over the rocks just like a scene from Gone with the Wind, until they finally make contact. Final recognition is established by an elaborate process of nuzzling and whisker touching to confirm one another's smell. When satisfied that the pup is indeed her own, the mother finds herself a comfortable spot on the lava, rolls over and lets her offspring suckle.

The western isles also happen to be home to breeding groups of sperm whales. World renowned whaling grounds in years gone by, the waters off Fernandina have now been declared a protected habitat and the whales revel in the security of their sanctuary. The waters are also known for whale sharks, dolphins and sun fish, while hammerhead sharks concentrate in large numbers around 'Roca Redonda', a lonely outpost to the north. There is something eerie about Roca Redonda (Round Rock): rising out of the deep, dark gray waters, and often clothed in mist, the massive rock looks like a castle, a towering monolith, a monument to itself. Many times, while snorkeling in the area, we have had the privilege of sharing the water with bottlenose dolphins who approach for an appraisal and disappear. Close to the rock, we have also swum with huge hammerhead sharks gliding silently past on outstretched hydrofoils. Despite these wonderful encounters, the waters around the rock somehow hold a sense of foreboding. Perhaps it is their sheer depth. At over two thousand meters, one knows one is in deep water. Perhaps it is also the knowledge that large pelagic tiger sharks are known to inhabit the area. Nevertheless – or perhaps therefore – for us it is Fernandina which holds the most mystery and best embraces the essence of Galapagos.

Adult pelican, Isabela Island.

Tower Island seen from Prince Phillip's Steps.

Northern Isles

In the northern isles of the Galapagos, we have included the remote islands of Darwin, Wolf, Pinta, Marchena and Tower (or Genovesa). The only one, however, with a terrestrial visitor site is Tower, and this is our justification for considering it alone in this chapter. This is truly a spectacular location, and one which, along with Fernandina and Española, should not be missed. Tower is best described, simply, as 'bird island'. Unfortunately most tours to the Galapagos do not include all three of the above islands on a standard visit because each lies at the furthest extremity of the archipelago and the distances involved are great. A typical day on a cruise consists of two visits, either to different islands or to distinct areas of the same island. Once having arrived to Tower, however, changing anchorage and going on to another island for a second visit the same day is out of the question. Luckily, there are two excellent visitor sites available from the same anchorage.

The approach to Tower Island from the south is usually under the cloak of darkness. This is a beautiful pre-dawn experience if the seas are calm and the visitor able to wander around on deck and soak in the ocean's special ambience. Swallow-tailed gulls, the only nocturnal gulls in the world, flit in and out of range of the vessel's navigation lights. Appearing as ghostly apparitions for a few seconds, they quickly disappear. As the boat approaches the island, more and more gulls become apparent, with the curious hovering long enough alongside to display their scarlet eye-ring. The gulls' general progression is shoreward, for they have done their night's work and are returning home to rest and digest their catch of squid. They hurry to return home before daylight, so avoiding the threat of the piratical frigatebirds which swarm in clouds overhead as day breaks.

A cloudless night reveals a plethora of stars from the top deck. Away from artificial lights, the city dweller will be astounded by the sheer number and brightness of the stars in the firmament. Even from above the equator at Tower's position in the northern hemisphere, it is a delight to

Bottlenose dolphin.

spend a few hours and trace the arc described by the Southern Cross as the constellation rises and sets. On a morning with little or no moon, a look over the bow is a revelation: the bow-wave is inevitably alive with bright spots of a cold blue-green light, not the reflection of the stars but light from below, a light produced by planktonic organisms. Many such organisms are able to produce this so called bioluminescence or phosphorescence. Biochemically, the process occurs when, due to a physical disturbance, an enzyme called luciferase is released by the organism. This is a catalyst which acts on a compound produced by the plankton, called luciferin, producing light. It is a process similar to that used by fireflies and glowworms of the terrestrial environment. As the vessel progresses through the water, it causes a huge disturbance to these small planktonic organisms, and they 'fire' their lights in response. The effect is breathtaking. Schools of fish are also 'threatened' by the boat and suddenly scatter in all directions to escape. They too cause the plankton to light up and the result is like a private fireworks display of light guiding the bow. Most impressively, as one arrives close to the island (still before daylight), a pod of dolphins – residents, apparently – often joins the ship. They suddenly appear from several directions, like huge illuminated torpedoes aiming for the bow. Instantly they take up position below the observer, who by now is hanging over the bow in earnest for a closer look at the magnificent phantom performers. Side by side, the dolphins maintain a dynamic formation, keeping just ahead of the turbulent prow, their outlines continuously illuminated by the ghostly light of the plankton. With effortless grace, the dolphins switch positions, roll over and occasionally leap out of the water to almost eye level with the observer, landing with a splash in a seemingly deliberate attempt to soak their private audience and thus include them in the fun. At the first light of day, an orange blush shimmers over the water, and the cold glow of bioluminescence from the plankton dims as the warmth and light of the sun out-compete them in brilliance. By now scanes of red-footed boobies are dipping low over the ocean on their way far out to sea to their favored fishing

Bottlenose dolphins, Tower Island.

Juvenile red-footed booby, Tower Island.

grounds. The shapes of the dolphins can now be clearly made out and even the rake marks from the teeth of fellow dolphins stand out against the uniform gray of the upper body. These are bottlenose dolphins, large – up to three and a half meters in length and 650 kilograms in weight – highly social and intelligent. They come from miles away to play at the bows of passing ships and boats, the dolphins' equivalent of surfing. The movement of the vessel ploughing through the sea pushes water ahead of it. It is in this pres-

sure wave that the dolphins ride. They are not actually being pushed by the vessel as many onlookers have imagined. The officer on watch slows the engines as the vessel approaches the island. The cetaceans instantly respond and miraculously disappear.

The island looms ahead. A narrow break in the volcano wall allows cautious access by sea into the once active crater, known as Darwin Bay. The range markers on the far shore are lined up and the vessel steams above the eroded barrier into the

Great frigatebird male, Tower Island.

calm enclosed waters of the bay. Audubon shear-waters zig zag across the wake while storm petrels gently patter on the surface. More and more of the adult red-footed boobies are leaving their roosts in the mangroves and heading out in search of flying fish on the open ocean. The frigatebirds take to the air, but leave the boobies unmolested knowing not to waste their energy attacking an unproductive target. As the boat comes to anchor close to the north wall of the bay, juvenile red-footed boobies land clumsily on the rails and rigging, staring inquisitively with an apparently dumbfounded and shortsighted gaze at almost anything, whether of interest or not. With prehensile feet they are the only Galapagos boobies which are able to properly perch and it is not long before many individuals have graced the boat with their presence. Despite their slightly ungainly and silly appearance when at rest, boobies are magnificent flyers. Even though they far outnumber the other two Galapagos boobies, the red-foots are the least often seen by visitors. But Tower Island is the largest red-

footed booby colony in the world, boasting one hundred and forty thousand pairs. Rather than coming into the center of the archipelago to feed, red-footed boobies fly a long way offshore, which explains why they only breed on the out-lying islands in the first place. They are the world's smallest booby and, because of the distances they fly to catch fish, can only bring back enough food to raise a single chick from each brood, indeed they lay only one egg. Red-footed boobies catch a lot of squid near the surface of the water but seem to have specialized in flying fish as prey. Many times – not only in Galapagos but in all the tropical oceans we have witnessed red-footed boobies swoop down with the swiftness of an arrow in front of the bow of a ship and pluck a flying-fish from midair. The boobies often hang in the air level with the ship on the updraught caused by its forward motion. The instant the vessel disturbs a school of flying fish at the surface, the fish take to the air, accelerating low over the water, like exocet missiles, in a truly remarkable escape response. With its tailfin's lower lobe, the fish paddles violently to create forward thrust while the grossly

White morph red-footed booby, Tower Island.

enlarged pectoral (and sometimes pelvic) fins are extended to maintain the fish airborne. The sharp-eyed booby, however, swoops down on the unfortunate victim and, to its complete surprise, snatches it from the air. Adult red-footed boobies exhibit two color morphs, going through life either as a dull brown-bodied bird or a white one. In the Galapagos Islands, only a small percentage of the birds are white, whereas elsewhere in the world the ratio is reversed. Nevertheless both color types of adults have brilliantly red feet together with an exquisitely decorated face. Both the blue skin surrounding the eyes and the pink tinge at the base of the pastel blue bill look as if the bird had applied make-up before leaving the house. The bill's attractive black border adds a finishing touch. The juveniles are less attractive, an ashy brown with dark legs and bill for their first two to three years.

No matter what the age or color of the boobies, they continue to be the universal targets for the scores of marauding frigatebirds patrolling the skies. On their homeward journey before dusk, the returning boobies maintain contact by calling. Incredible as it may seem, the pugnacious frigate-

Red-footed booby perching, Tower Island.

71

Nesting red-footed booby, Tower Island.

bird can detect the difference in the call made by a booby with a full gullet and one without, as the fish pressing on the throat of the former distorts the sound of its call. They home in on the defenseless boobies, besieging them in dramatic, swashbuckling aerial combat. While the challenged birds fly the gauntlet in a dash for home, the attacks are relentless. Those frigatebirds which have not joined in the chase hang effortlessly on the wing casting an ominous shadow on the scene below. Their silhouettes are reminiscent of competition bows, with arrows at full cock ready to fly. With a span of more than two meters and only weighing in at a kilo or so, frigates have the largest wingspan-to-body-weight ratio of any seabird - the secret to their supreme maneuverability. And with its powerful, strongly hooked bill to complete the arsenal, the frigatebird is arguably the ultimate flying machine. When swooping on a booby, the frigate invariably goes for the tail. With a firm grip it simply shakes the

Galapagos dove, Tower Island.

unhappy victim like a rag-doll in the air. Rather than risk injury from its attacker, the anxious booby has no option but to disgorge its hard-won prize. The frigate releases its grip and swoops to catch the falling fish before it hits the water. Impressive though they are at flying, the frigatebirds cannot either land on, or immerse themselves in, the water as their feathers quickly waterlog and they would drown. The unfortunate booby, meanwhile, returns to its partner empty-handed after a hard day's fishing.

Due to the extremely complicated techniques of food gathering, young frigatebirds are dependent for a long time on their parents, up to one year or more. The young spend a lot of their time sitting forlornly on the small pad of guano encrusted twigs, which was once the nest, waiting for the adults to return. Spread far and wide on the tops of the salt bushes sit other youngsters amid adults in full courtship regalia. There are two species of frigatebird in the

Male great frigatebird with fully inflated pouch, Tower Island.

Male and female great frigatebird together on nest site, Tower Island.

Eagle ray, Tower Island.

Galapagos Islands. The adult male great frigatebird is all black except for the long metallic green scapular feathers flowing off its back, while the female has a white throat and breast and sports a red eye ring. The magnificent frigatebird male, on the other hand, wears purple scapular feathers while the female is distinguished by a black throat and blue eye ring. The *pièce de résistance* of the male of both species, however, is his ability to inflate his brilliant scarlet, grossly oversized gular pouch. The effect is dazzling. During the first half of the year, scores of expectant males display throughout the area of Darwin Bay. In response to an inquisitive female flying low overhead, the unattached males unanimously throw back their heads to maximize the visibility of the pouch; then, with wings at full stretch and shaking with excitement, they pierce the air with their rattling call. The female alights alongside her successful suitor whereupon he jealously embraces her as proof of his prowess.

Great frigatebird chick, Tower Island.

The subsequent nest building is a labor intensive endeavor. The nest itself is a scruffy assemblage of twigs perched a few meters off the ground on a low bush. Red-footed boobies have mastered the ability to break off fresh twigs for their own nests whereas frigates have not. Yet, despite the apparent over-abundance of suitable twigs scattered throughout, they, too, are seriously contested by the frigatebird. Once again, the boobies must suffer the harassment of aerial dog fighting for possession of their hard earned resource. So piratical are the frigatebirds that they will without hesitation steal nesting material even from the nests of other frigates. Indeed, one of the major causes of frigatebird mortality is nests so badly raided that the eggs fall through the gaps and smash soon after they've been laid.

Of the many other avian species which nest on the island, the most attractive are the aforementioned swallow-tailed gulls. These stunning birds

Swallow-tailed gull, Tower Island.

have been described by many as the most beautiful gull in the world. Their instantly distinctive feature is the bright red fleshy ring encircling the large dark eye. Nobody fully understands its function, but the ring probably plays a role in the nocturnal feeding habits of the gull, aiding the bird in detection of the soft bioluminescent light produced by squid and other prey. Many of the world's gulls have a red tip to the bill, a stimulus for the chicks who peck at the red spot, an action that serves as a counter stimulus for the adult birds to regurgitate food. Red, however, is one of the first colors lost at night, so the swallow-tailed gull, a nocturnal bird, not only has a highly visible white tip but also a white base to the bill which serves the same purpose. The nest is a simple accumulation of small stones and coral laid on

Lava gull calling, Tower Island.

the beach or lava. Once hatched, the single chick, which is extremely cryptic in coloration, spends its time under the bushes, or in cracks in the lava, away from the murderous beak of the frigatebird.

One of the greatest revelations of the biology of the swallow-tailed gull is the fact that it may use a primitive form of echo-location to help accurately relocate a landing spot, thereby avoiding a crash landing into the rock face in darkness.

Also living on Tower Island is a relative of the swallow-tailed gull, the endemic lava gull, the rarest gull in the world. The bird is oblivious of its unenviable status and appears locally common. It is not unusual for one gull or a pair of them to spend the greater part of the day either resting on the bow of a moored vessel or quietly sitting on the outboard engine of a *panga*. Their patient demeanor underlies their scavenging behavior as a result of which lava gulls are also doing fairly well around the growing human populations in the islands. Akin to the laughing gull of mainland America, this species' most memorable and unmistakable trait is to suddenly break into raucous 'laughter', revealing the bright orange pigment on the inside of its throat. Normally a territo-

rial display, a pair of gulls often lock into a duet for several minutes, leaving the onlooker in no doubt as to ownership of that particular patch.

Nocturnal yellow-crowned night herons stand stoically on lava ledges around the landing site pretending to be asleep as we, in turn, politely pretend not to see them. When their eyes are open they seem to be in a state of perpetual surprise, perhaps bewildered at seeing strange creatures wandering around in broad daylight.

Tower Island's paucity of faunal and floral species is due to its remoteness: for many species, the island is too distant to be successfully colonized. The shrubby prickly pear cactus, *Opuntia helleri*, unlike the *Opuntias* on the other islands, has soft, hairlike spines which serve no protective role at all. Peter Grant has reasoned that, due to the absence of the Galapagos carpenter bee on

Juvenile yellow-crowned night heron sunbathing.

the island (the cactus flower's usual pollinator), the plant has had to lower its defenses to allow access to birds, particularly Galapagos doves, which pollinate the flowers when feeding on them. Nor have the finches been very successful colonizers of Tower: only four species have succeeded there, namely, the large ground finch, which can often be observed cracking seeds; the large cactus finch, usually with its head probing a cactus flower; the diminutive and almost ubiquitous warbler finch; and the unusual sharp-billed, or vampire, finch. The so called vampire finch has developed a noteworthy trait on Darwin and Wolf Islands where, to sustain its need for liquid, it has taken to pecking wounds at the elbow or cloaca of nesting boobies and drinking the blood! Apparently unperturbed by this blatant act of parasitism, the boobies suffer the assault without complaint. The sharp-billed ground finches on Tower have not yet learnt the tricks of their northern counterparts; indeed, they may never do so. Thus far, they haven't experienced the shortages of fresh water that are prevalent on the more northerly islands.

Another major bird absent from the avian species list is the Galapagos hawk. At the top of the natural food chain in the islands, the hawk is missing not only on Tower Island but on Darwin and Wolf as well. The short-eared owl, on the other hand, has triumphed and managed to settle on all but Wolf. With the absence on Tower of competition from the more dominant Galapagos hawk (perhaps the rarest non-threatened raptor in the world), the short-eared owl has become diurnal. It seems strange to be walking along the eastern plateau above Prince Phillip's steps and come face-to-face with a beautiful yellow-eyed owl in the middle of the day. The resident owls have become expert at preying on the huge numbers of storm petrels sharing the island. Hundreds of thousands of both Galapagos storm petrels and band-rumped storm petrels nest and breed in the area. During the day, mostly Galapagos storm petrels are visible at the colony. They can often be seen in enormous flocks, like clouds of mosquitoes, flitting above their nest sites in the lava cracks. The owls are extremely adept at catching these little storm petrels and have developed a most 'un-owl-like' technique; instead of pursuing them in flight low over the lava, as one might expect, they wait patiently at the entrance to one of the nest burrows wedged between the plates of lava. When a bird emerges

Lava cactus, Tower Island.

Opuntia cactus, Tower Island

Masked boobies' mutual preening, Tower Island.

Masked booby, Tower Island.

to within range, the owl plunges its whole leg into the crevice and seizes the bird in its talons. Luckily for the storm petrels, the small number of owls on the island does not seem to be anywhere close to making a dent in their enormous population. These diminutive birds (tube-nosed creatures related to albatross) fly above their nest sites in a seemingly chaotic and erratic fashion. Amazing though it seems, with thousands of nest sites in the lava crags, they recognize their own nest by smell!

Tower and Darwin are also unusual due to being the only major islands without any terrestrial reptiles. No lizards, snakes, geckos, tortoises or land iguanas live there. Once again, it seems that the relative remoteness of the islands have proved too much for any successful establishments.

The visitor to Tower will, however, encounter many marine iguanas on the shoreline, though they are often overlooked initially because of their small size. It seems that the relatively tropical conditions of Tower are less than conducive to the growth of their preferred algal food species, resulting in an average iguana body

Masked booby, Tower Island.

86

size which is the smallest for any population in the archipelago. The warmer waters from the Panama Basin which affect the northern isles do, on the other hand, lend themselves to more tropical species of fish than are able to survive in the colder upwelling waters bathing the remaining islands of the archipelago. Large schools of king angelfish can be seen during a snorkel along the crater walls, while enormous bumphead parrot fish rise into view from the murky green waters. Gold-rimmed surgeon fish and convict tangs verify the northerly distribution of the island and flash past regardless. Schools of eagle rays are also commonly seen close to shore and, with care, a snorkeler can join the school, working his or her way to the middle and watch the rays swimming all around.

Short-eared owl with storm petrel prey.

Nor should one be alarmed if large moray eels, hammerhead sharks or manta rays are encountered while swimming. All are common in the bay but none has so far proved to be dangerous. The northern isles of Darwin and Wolf have become internationally recognised in recent years as a mecca for scuba divers interested in intimate encounters with large schools of hammerhead sharks which congregate in dense groups of up to two hundred individuals. Whatever the individual experiences of visitors to Tower Island, the time will have been inevitably well spent. At the end of a full day, as the boat sails out of the bay entrance en route to the next adventure, the dolphins once again are waiting. Even baleen whales seem to spend a disproportionate amount of time in the vicinity of the island and can often be spotted in the evening glow as their falcate dorsal fins break the surface. The first clue that usually betrays their presence is a puff of vapor forcibly expelled with each breath. The sun sets on the marine mammals as the vessel leaves them in its wake, on course for somewhere new in the Southern Hemisphere.

Large cactus finch on Opuntia cactus, Tower Island.

Swallow-tailed gull chick with parent.

Cliffs and waves on Española Island.

The Southern Isles

In this chapter the three main islands to be considered are San Cristóbal, Floreana and Española, as well as many satellite rocks and islets of each. In contrast to the young, dramatic islands of the west, with high volcanic peaks and smoldering fumaroles, these southern isles are old, cold, eroded and dormant. The southeastern group, being the oldest present day islands, probably represents the first stepping stones of some of the life forms arriving to the Galapagos from their distant shores of origin. Española is now so eroded that there no longer remains any evidence at all of a volcanic cone.

Two of the three islands are now inhabited by human beings. During the period of human association, particularly in the last two centuries, non-native mammals such as pigs and goats were deliberately introduced to provide future food stocks. Other species, such as rats, were accidental introductions, simply jumping ship and swimming ashore or escaping while the vessels were being caulked and repaired on the beaches. During this period, scientists also took an interest in the archipelago. A scientific mission of exploration sent out from Spain in 1790 was followed shortly by a mission of exploration under the command of English whaling captain James Colnett aboard the vessel HMS Ratter in 1793. Colnett had a commercial interest in the stocks of whales in the area. During this era in Europe and North America, whale oil had become a very valuable product used to fuel street lamps in the cities. Subsidiary products were also coveted, including spermaceti from sperm whales used as a fine lubricant, while the baleen plates of the rorqual whales were used in the manufacture of chique body corsets for ladies of the period. Colnett discovered healthy whale stocks and, at about the same time, the commercial harvest of fur seals for their pelts began. Over the next century, the hunting pressures were so great that not only the fur seals but also some of the whale species were brought to commercial extinction.

Captain Colnett has also been credited with the establishment of the Post Office Barrel on the island of Floreana. It served as a receptacle for mail for crews of whaling and fur-sealing vessels. The

mail was collected by homeward bound ships and, on arrival, was delivered to anxious recipients, predictably more than a year after its deposit in the barrel. To this day the tradition continues as tourists regularly leave mail in the Post Office Barrel which is collected and delivered by subsequent visitors to the bay. Often quicker than the national postal system, the tradition now continues more for fun than out of necessity.

In the 1830s there was an attempt to colonize on Floreana. The settlement quickly turned into a penal colony, an institution more in tune with the harsh environmental conditions prevailing. In 1858 Manuel J Cobos and an associate, José Monroy, set up a company on San Cristóbal to harvest the epiphytic *orchilla* moss used in the dye industry. After this effort failed, Cobos went into the sugar business, planting many hectares of sugar cane and building a sugar mill. As he owned the only boat going to and from the mainland, and the only shop on the island, he had a complete monopoly on the comings and goings of his workers. They were paid not in cash but in tokens, which could be traded only in the shop for goods

Flamingo, Punta Cormorant, Floreana Island.

at inflated prices. Due to the absence of an official law enforcement entity, Cobos quickly reverted to a maniacal tyrant responsible for executing and deliberately marooning people on waterless islands. Unsurprisingly, a bloody revolt ended with his murder and the escape of the enslaved work force. Various other colonization attempts were made around the archipelago throughout the last century, resulting in five islands with permanent human inhabitants today.

The Galapagos has attracted an eclectic mix of visitors in its history. The most famous, of course, was Charles Darwin, who visited four of the islands. He first set foot ashore somewhere in Steven's Bay on San Cristóbal, an area whose appearance has changed very little in the interim. Darwin noted the event as follows: "In the morning we landed on Chatham Island [San Cristóbal], which, like the others, rises with a tame and rounded outline, broken here and there by scattered hillocks, the remainder of former craters. Nothing could be less inviting than the first appearance. A broken field of black basaltic lava, thrown into the most rugged waves and crossed by

Adult greater flamingo, Floreana Island.

Mocking bird attacking turtle hatchling, Española Island.

great fissures, is everywhere covered by stunted, sun-burnt brush wood, which shows little signs of life." After his stay in the islands, Darwin continued on his voyage aboard HMS Beagle, taking with him many rocks and biological samples, together with the seeds of new ideas which, once having flowered, were set to change the course of scientific thinking. Contemporary colonization stemmed mostly from Europe, with Ecuadorian residents not arriving in any significant numbers until much later. During the 1930s a strange mixture of Europeans settled on Floreana at Black Beach near Post Office Bay. The group included Heinz Wittmer and his wife Margaret (she died at the age of 95 in 2000) who arrived with their son Harry. Dr Friedrich Ritter and his mistress Dore Strauch, having arrived before the Wittmers, had already molded a distinctive way of life for themselves in their own personal Eden. Friedrich and Dore had met in Berlin and managed to convince their respective spouses to

Mocking bird with turtle hatchling.

cohabit while they eloped to the Galapagos. In preparation for the sojourn, Friedrich and Dore saw fit to have their teeth removed as a precaution against dental emergencies, but prudently packed a single set of stainless steel dentures which they would share when eating something requiring mastication. A third party to arrive and join the bickering assembly was headed by the Baroness von Wagner who disembarked with three lovers. Many unexplained deaths and disappearances occurred over the next few years, when members of the three parties were the sole inhabitants of the island. Sadly the delightful Margaret Wittmer passed away recently but her daughter and granddaughter, still run both the post office and a modest boarding house. There is now also a naval base at Black Beach on Floreana and a small agricultural community which farms in the highlands.

Although not the largest town in the archipelago, Puerto Baquerizo Moreno, on the island of

Exhausted female green turtle ready to lay eggs, Floreana Island.

San Cristóbal, is the site of the capital of the Galapagos province. Having rapidly expanded in the last two decades, aided by the construction of an airport and increased air services, the town now sprawls a long way up the hill towards the crater. San Cristóbal is the only island in the province which can be considered to have a large permanent fresh water supply which comes from the rain-filled lake known as El Junco. As such, living conditions have always been less harsh than on the other inhabited islands. There is also a naval base on the island, much larger than the one on Floreana. The town's folk rely primarily on tourism and fishing to support their way of life and, apart from serving as an administrative center, the island is an excellent base for both day-tripping tourism and a starting point from which to join a live-aboard yacht tour.

As wildlife viewing in the southern isles is superb, both Floreana and Española islands rank high on the list of sites to be seen. Floreana has

Green turtle hatchlings emerging from nest.

several places of interest, both above and below the water. For the snorkeler, a sea lion fantasia awaits at the small islet of Champion. It is simply heavenly to swim there, close to the steeply shelving shoreline, while a multitude of young, curious sea lions, with exquisite grace and agility, frolic playfully, interacting with their awkward audience. Approaching closely for an intimate inspection of the face behind the mask, or an inquisitive nibble of the snorkeler's flippers, the sea lions suddenly shoot off, like living torpedoes, out of view into the depths. A few minutes later they return to continue the inspection and once again disappear. One is never certain who is appraising whom as contact is made underwater with a pair of wide, bright, intelligent eyes.

Devil's Crown, lying just off Punta Cormorant, on the northern shore of Floreana, is an old, eroded parasitic cone. It, too, is a favorite visitor's site. One can swim in shallow, protected areas within the cone, surrounded by

brightly colored tropical fish or, outside, in the current with sharks. The beautiful markings of the stylish Moorish idol, a tricolored reef fish of black, white and yellow adorned with a pennant-like streamer from the dorsal fin, compete with the blacks and yellows of sergeant-majors, or the pastel shades of parrot fish and king angelfish which also abound. The serenity of their watery world is only occasionally disturbed by the large form of a sea lion streaming through the field of view, vying for some of the attention. Outside of the crown, the snorkel starts at the eastern mouth of the cone's broken wall. A steady current carries the passive snorkeler over the bottom. The topography is uneven, with dramatic pinnacles of rock rising from a depth of fifteen meters or so. Large shoals of grunts and creolefish hang mid water, huddled together for protection as the current and swell buffet them to and fro. *Bacalao* (an endemic grouper) and large snappers patrol the rock faces, and schools of barracuda cruise through the water column. Six or seven harmless white-tipped reef sharks slide under an overhanging rock close to the bottom when, suddenly, the adrenaline starts

Pelican, Gardner Bay, Española Island.

pumping as the exact shape of the large dark objects flowing over the sea bed is deciphered by the brain - hammerhead sharks! The novice snorkeler's first thoughts are to return to the attendant dinghy. On the other hand, there is nothing better than to swim down to the group of maybe twenty individuals and have a closer look. Sharks, of course, should always be highly respected, especially large ones such as these scalloped hammerheads of up to three meters or more in length. However, with caution and an understanding of the behavioral cues of aggression, they can readily be approached. Free diving with these huge marine predators is indeed a wonderful experience and accentuates the magic and tameness of the Galapagos fauna. We have even had sea lions follow us down and tease the sharks by nipping their dorsal fins, something they would never dare to do at night when the sharks have the advantage. As the drift continues, green turtles are also commonly encountered lazily flapping their large front flippers, maintaining their course to nowhere in particular. Once having satisfied a curiosity for that which lives underwater off Floreana, the visitor is

Galapagos hawk, Española Island.

Sally lightfoot crab, San Cristóbal Island.

Female lava lizard, Española Island.

Young sea lions, Punta Pitt, San Cristóbal Island.

naturally drawn to explore the remarkable area of Punta Cormorant itself.

The landing beach has a subtle greenish hue imparted to it by the high content of volcanic crystal olivine. After forming in the magma chamber under conditions of extremely slow cooling, olivine is released to the surface during the following eruption. It is subsequently broken down to the consistency of coarse sand by wave action, and sorted onto particular beaches around the archipelago. A short walk behind the green beach leads to a large, saline lagoon. On either side of the path grow some fascinating plants. *Lecocarpus pinnatifidus*, or cutleaf daisy, grows as an erect shrub to about two meters in height. It is a member of the composite family, with large yellow, daisy-like flowers which are in bloom for the greater part of the year. It represents one of seven endemic genera of plants on the islands. A second of these is the *Scalesia* genus, examples of which grow amongst the *Lecocarpus*. At Punta Cormorant, the species *Scalesia villosa* is locally common. *Scalesia* is important for, like Darwin's finches, it provides excellent examples of adaptive radiation (there are an impressive fourteen species with an additional sextet of subspecies). Also known as daisy trees, the various species range from small, isolated shrubs to dense stands up to fifteen meters in height. Another composite, the flowers vary in complexity but are always white. As many of the *Scalesia*s occur in the arid and transition zones, they have evolved a coating of delicate hairs on the leaves which are able to trap the fine mist which falls in the *garúa* season.

At the end of the short path, the shallow lagoon offers a perfect flamingo habitat. Numbers range from a few individuals to almost two hundred flamingos at a time which stand out in prominent pinks against the muted background of *palo santo* trees on the slopes of the volcanic cone behind. There are, however, only an estimated four hundred or so individuals in the whole archipelago, making the population rather fragile. They move in groups to various brackish lagoons between the islands in response to the levels of food available in each area. Flamingos are filter feeders. Similar in some ways to the great baleen whales, flamingos actually filter out minute inver-

Bull sea lion, Española Island.

Blue-footed booby, Española Island.

tebrate organisms from the shallow waters and fine silts. The piston-like tongue has a rapid pumping action which draws the water in and out of the beak. In so doing, the prey items, such as brine shrimp and larval crustaceans, are trapped by the fine grooves in the bill. The tongue, armed with a row of spines, serves to rake the food into a bolus prior to swallowing. Although highly specialized, the feeding technique is not particularly efficient and flamingos spend a large part of their day with their heads down in the water, swaying from side to side in their attempt to glean enough sustenance to see them through. The unusual down-curved bill is designed to be used in this manner upside down, so that when flamingos are in the feeding position, the active area of the bill is actually horizontal to the water which, of course, is exactly where it wants to be. The beautiful coloration of the flamingos is enhanced by the pigments contained in the food items. Many flamingos in zoos fade to white unless the high levels of carotenoids are maintained in their diet during molting. The flamingos found in the lagoon at Punta Cormorant also breed there and, looking into the distance with binoculars, one can often spot small volcano-like cones made of mud. These elevated nests, which the flamingos make for themselves under normal circumstances, serve as ideal platforms on which to raise their single chick. As they are low on the ground, however, they are susceptible to heavy flooding (particularly during an El Niño year) and, unfortunately, raids by feral pigs. The birds sometimes wander out onto the beachfront and feed in the shallow surf zone. Visitors delight in watching such handsome creatures meander, unconcerned, about their business among the onlookers. The chicks and young occasionally follow the adults down to the shore, but seem somewhat ungainly alongside their resplendent parents.

On the far beach, through a forest of *palo santo* and *palo verde* trees, the atmosphere is very different. The beach itself is known locally as the "Flour Beach" and is remarkable for the texture of the sand. Most visitors are encouraged to shed their footwear in order to fully appreciate the phenomenon. The instant the bare feet come into contact with the cool, extremely fine coralline sand is almost sensual. It is a sheer pleasure to walk on, an

Blue-footed boobies diving, San Cristóbal Island.

105

experience not to be missed. On the white sandy areas grow more endemic plants, particularly an unusual endemic succulent called *Nolana*. The top of the beach is deeply pitted with excavations made by nesting female green turtles with an occasional carcass of one of them biodegrading slowly on the shore, a testament to the effort involved in egg laying. At the water's edge the ocean laps a long way up the sand as each small wave breaks on the shore. By carefully shuffling out to a position knee-deep in water, visitors will find hundreds of stingrays sharing the sand with them. They are carried up the beach with each action of the swell, where they feed on buried molluscs and other invertebrates. Some of the rays come to such shallow waters that their backs actually break the surface. Potentially dangerous, these fish, with a wing span of less than one meter, are not aggressive and, like the sharks, if approached with caution are no threat whatsoever. Towards evening, frigatebirds congregate over the turtle nests, patrolling the line of depressions in the sand. With their extremely acute vision, they are able to detect the slightest movement of an emerging turtle.

Dancing blue-footed booby, Española Island.

Sometimes the timing of the baby reptiles goes array and all of the hatchlings break out while still daylight, condemning most of them to death.

On the neighboring island of Española to the east, another fantastic wildlife destination, there are also large areas of turtle nesting beaches. It is the southernmost island of the group and, in many ways, the most unusual. One important turtle beach in particular is the spectacular expanse of Gardner Bay. Many tens, probably hundreds, of female green turtles nest on the narrow beach each year. Thousands of their young also die there. Pelicans sit patiently waiting for hatching time. Frigates keep vigil overhead. Galapagos hawks patrol by walking up and down along the line of salt bushes at the top of the beach. Mockingbirds, however, actively dig them up. At least a score of times we have carefully followed the birds and watched them unearth hatchling turtles. The Española mockingbird is endemic to the island and has the longest dagger-like beak of all Galapagos mockingbirds. It is used with brutal efficiency, serving as the perfect lethal weapon. With its bill, the mockingbird digs in the sand after detecting a slight movement below the

surface. It flicks sand in all directions as it energetically digs down as far as four inches below the surface. Suddenly, with a violent tug, the forcep-like beak grips the baby turtle's head and jerks it out of the sand. Taken under the bushes out of reach of the frigatebirds, the struggling baby is repeatedly flipped onto its back as the mockingbird incessantly stabs it in the soft umbilical area. The fellow gang members of the mockingbird clan quickly descend on the turtle

Blue-footed booby coming in to land, Española Island.

107

Juvenile pelican, San Cristóbal Island.

Blue-footed booby, Española Island.

Waved albatross, Española Island.

and, eventually, after a harrowing struggle, it is killed. The turtle body is too tough for the mockingbirds to break open so they are able to eat only that which they can reach through the umbilical hole. The carcass is left for ants or hawks, and another turtle is uncovered.

Sharing the fabulous beach with birds and turtles lie lazy, relaxed sea lions. Outstretched on the golden sands at the edge of turquoise waters, like the humans beside them, they seem to have found a certain paradise. A subspecies of the Californian sea lion of circus fame, our Galapagos cousin is every bit as endearing. The females and juveniles tend to congregate in clumps along the beach and, being thigmotactic, they enjoy body contact. Lying on their fore flippers with their hind flippers tucked in under their sausage shaped, hydrodynamic bodies, they orientate themselves with several heads coming together in a point, whiskers touching, or head-to-tail in pairs, with both animals lying slightly on

Waved albatross incubating egg.

their sides maximizing the area of skin-to-skin contact. Sea lions seem to be very efficient hunters, preying largely on fish, but also occasionally tackling octopus and crustaceans. So efficient are they, in fact, that a large part of their day is spent on a beach at rest. With no pressures to find food, they have time to express their curiosity and, as stated earlier, it is not unusual for a patient observer to become the subject of that curiosity. The young sea lions are particularly inquisitive, often approaching an observer to sniff the face or feet and sometimes playfully even taking the toes gently in their mouths. Nor is it unusual, if the object of interest remains calm, for the sea lion to decide that it is not under threat and lay gently alongside or on top of the legs of its human companion for a nap.

The main visitor site of Española Island, however, is not Gardner Bay but the westernmost tip, Punta Suárez. This area is home to large numbers of birds and animals and gives a good overview of

Bull sea lions fighting, Gardner Bay, Española Island.

Waved albatross, Española Island.

the islands of Galapagos. The first major attraction on landing are the marine iguanas. Even though the visitor may have seen these reptiles on other islands in the archipelago, none are quite like those of Española. They are of average size and similar shape to their contemporaries, but their coloration is quite different. During the breeding season, in the warm months around Christmas time, the iguanas stray dramatically from the dull blacks of their brethren and become gloriously technicolored. The bulk of their body is imbued with a bright red while their forelimbs and a median area of the back and crest become a garish turquoise, the color of oxidized copper (see cover). The overall effect, however, is very pleasing as the iguanas become conspicuous against the dark lava background. Even outside of the breeding season, the Española iguanas retain a lot of the red base color, setting them apart from those of other islands.

For an as yet unexplained reason, the endemic lava lizards of the island are also the

Waved albatross gamming, Española Island.

reddest of the archipelago. Unusual among animals, to the human eye at least, the female lava lizards of Galapagos are more attractive than their male counterparts, sporting varying degrees of red around the head and neck. The female lava lizards on Española have not only a large red area on the head and neck, but also spreading over the throat, chest and forelegs. As the lizards scuttle over the rocks defending their territories or searching for food, they are naturally drawn to the nests of their feathered neighbors where the hunting for flies is better than average.

Two species of boobies nest on Española island, both on the ground. The larger of the two, the masked booby, a startlingly white bird trimmed in stylish black, tends to nest in colonies on edges of islands close to the sea. In contrast to the red-footed boobies mentioned in the chapter on the northern isles, masked boobies are referred to as inshore feeders. They fly away from the islands but do not leave the confines of the archipelago when they go hunting. Like all members of their family, the *Sulidae*, masked boobies are spectacular plunge divers. They shoot like arrows, from fifteen meters or more in the air, onto their

Waved albatross gamming, Española Island.

Galapagos hawk feeding on marine iguana, Española Island.

Galapagos snake, Española Island.

fish prey below. Due to the high impacts suffered at the moment of hitting the water, boobies have some specially adapted features to avoid potential damage. Not only do they have a series of small air-sacs in the head and chest area, but their nostrils are shielded to prevent the force of the dive sending two powerful jets of water into the brain. They have heavy, sharply pointed bills to streamline their entry into the water, and forward pointing eyes providing stereoscopic vision and therefore the ability to judge the distance of their prey. One of the largest birds in the Galapagos Islands, the masked boobies have a wingspan in excess of a meter and a half. The most notorious element of the masked booby's behavior concerns the rearing of offspring. The female invariably lays two eggs over the course of several days, though only one chick will be raised. The nest of the booby is merely a shallow scrape in the ground, which is almost always surrounded by a white guano ring. This ring is formed by incubating adults who, as they rotate on the nest following the sun's motion, squirt guano randomly in all directions. The ring delin-

Blue-footed booby, Española Island.

eates the boundary of the nest. The first chick to hatch has an immediate size advantage over the later arrival. If it is healthy and grows normally, it will quickly become much more powerful than its younger sibling. As soon as it is strong enough, it simply pushes the weaker chick out of the nest beyond the guano ring, whereupon it will be disowned by its parents and killed by predators. Should anything happen to the first chick, the insurance policy kicks in and the second chick descends from death row to grow normally, rather than suffer the consequences of the bizarre so-called 'Cain and Abel syndrome'.

The second booby species to breed on Española is the comical blue-footed booby. They appear to be everywhere on the island, so tame that they have built their nests in the middle of trails, forcing visitors to step over them. When looked at head on, boobies appear to have a very quizzical expression, explaining in part, the derivation of their name, which originates from the Spanish word 'bobo' – which translates as "clown". This species is known as a coastal feeder and rarely leaves sight of the shoreline when

Female sea lion, Española Island.

hunting. They, too, are spectacular plunge divers and often hunt in large groups. As aerial predators, they rely on large predatory fish trapping the smaller prey species against the water surface and therefore putting them within reach of the relatively shallow-diving birds. Without the larger predators the bait fish will naturally favor deeper depths, out of reach of the aerial assault by the boobies (a message that over exploitation of one species can drastically affect another, apparently unrelated species in the food chain). Feeding so close to the nest site, blue-footed boobies, on the other hand, are able to make many feeding forays during the day and therefore bring back enough food to raise up to three offspring if conditions are good. Their most striking feature, however, is their webbed blue feet. When asked, "Why have these boobies got blue feet?", scientists simply reply, "Why not!" They are obviously important as sexual stimuli to mates, but why they should be blue nobody knows. Blue-foots are perfect showmen and a delight to watch. When flying in to a prospective mate or established partner, the males throw back their wings and raise their

Blow hole, Española Island.

splayed leathery blue webs in a flag-like salute just before landing. Courtship begins with rather a lot of vocalization between the smaller, whistling male, and his beefier partner who honks. Apart from size and call, she is easily recognized by an apparently larger pupil. Actually, it is not larger than the male's pupil but there is a dark staining of the iris which gives it this effect. The two birds coyly offer presents, a twig, a stone (something symbolic of nest building), and may also touch bills. A few sideways glances, some ritualistic high-stepping, showing off the blue feet, and the bond is strengthened. The culmination of the courtship is expressed in a series of dramatic, simultaneous skypoints, with beak, tail, wingtips, and everything else that is pointed, on both partners stretched skyward as the two birds face each other and vocalize. In the grand finale and climax of the show, he steps onto her back to bring his cloaca into contact with hers, and they mate.

Once having walked through the large blue-footed booberie on the plateau area inland from the shore, the trail takes the visitor through another, uniquely Galapagos, phenomenon.

Blue-footed booby chick, San Cristóbal Island.

Masked booby pair, Española Island.

There exists on Española a colony of some fifteen thousand pairs of Galapagos waved albatross. Considered endemic to the islands, they spend most of their lives at sea, only returning to land to breed. This is an exquisite bird with the apparent texture of porcelain. The chest area of the adult is delicately marked with a fine, wavy pattern, hence the derivation of its name. Weighing in at an impressive three or four kilograms, with a wingspan of over two meters, it ranks as one of the archipelago's largest birds. The path skirts the outer edge of one of the colonies, offering the visitor superb close-up views of the magnificent birds. Albatross begin returning to the island towards the end of March, usually the males first, ready to start breeding. They spend their non-breeding period off the coast of Peru and northern Chile, where we have seen hundreds at any one time. They pair for life in a monogamous relationship lasting perhaps half a century; it is not thought, however, that they travel with their mate while at sea. On returning to Española, each albatross, must once again find its partner amongst all the other individuals on the island. They do so by gamming (dancing). Amazingly, despite the lapse of time between their last meeting and the present one, they remember how the other partner danced. For the male to reunite himself with his spouse, he must wander through the colony and dance for the females until there is recognition. Needless to say, the dance itself is very complex, highly stylized and immaculately choreographed. It involves a series of behaviors such as 'fencing', 'gaping', the 'shy look', 'swaggering' and a bolt upright stance, the true significance of which is only fully understood by the pair involved. Part of the albatross elegance is a pale, straw-colored area on the head which is offset by the rather large, erectile eyebrows, unusual among albatross and perhaps serving to shade the eyes of the world's only truly tropical species from the intense sunlight. Like all albatross species, these lay only a single egg, weighing approximately two hundred and fifty grams. After two months of incubation, a dark brown chick emerges. The offspring is regularly fed by its parents who, over a series of months, eventually end up feeding it two kilograms of food at a sitting, a quantity that requires foraging over hundreds of miles for days at a time. Such a large meal is almost grotesque. It fills the chick to bursting such that all it can do is sit and digest, looking

like nothing so much as an oily sack of feathers. The food, called chick oil, is formed of partly digested squid and crustaceans, a highly nutritious substance manufactured by the adults in the proventriculus of the stomach. This food gathering and delivery system allows the parents to collect and preserve large quantities of prey without having to return to the nest each time an item is caught. The maiden flight of the newly fledged chick occurs around December. The young bird must walk to the cliff edge at the end of the 'runway' and leap off in an impressive show of confidence. If luck is with it, it will disappear into the distance only to return four or five years later, ready to think about finding a mate.

On leaving the albatross, the trail winds along the cliff edge to overlook the famous blow-hole, a fissure in the lava which, when it receives the full force of the large Pacific swell, deflects an explosive burst of spray and water which funnels impressively, high into the air. Accompanied by a thunderous roar, the larger the swell which crashes against the island the greater the height of spray which gushes from the hole. Like staring into a

Kicker rock and roosting birds, San Cristóbal Island.

fire, there is something hypnotic about watching powerful waves beating relentlessly against a rocky shore, all the while seated at the edge of a cliff. Tourists pose to have their photographs taken while the marine iguanas and boobies look on unimpressed, having seen it all before.

Another dramatic natural feature of the southern isles is a gigantic rocky outcrop lying off the north shore of San Cristóbal Island. Kicker rock, or 'León Dormido' (Sleeping lion), as it is called in Spanish, is often the last of the visits made by passengers on a cruise from the Puerto Baquerizo Moreno airport. It is a fascinating structure, an old eroded tuff cone which glows orange in the morning light. The fascination lies in its shape, different from every angle, and its surface, home to hundreds of seabirds. With deep water all around, vessels are able to approach extremely close, with smaller yachts able to pass between the huge monoliths. The oldest of the present day Galapagos Islands, these southern isles, like those before them, will one day move further southeast and they, too, will submerge into oblivion, making room in the west for newer islands in their wake.

Masked booby, Española Island.

Kicker Rock, San Cristóbal Island.

Sunset, Punta Cormorant Lagoon, Floreana Island.

Pinnacle rock, Bartolomé Island.

Central Isles

The central isles of this chapter represent both the hub of tourist activity and the administrative and conservation nerve center in Galapagos. The principal islands we have concentrated on are Santiago, Sante Fe, Santa Cruz, South Plaza and lastly Bartolomé which, along with the Charles Darwin Research Station, is one of the most visited sites in the archipelago. The area around pinnacle rock, one of the classic Galapagos landmarks, also happens to be the best area of all in which to see the diminutive penguins so accustomed to our presence that they virtually ignore anybody in the water with them. It is a rare experience indeed to swim with penguins, and one reserved only for the brave in a penguin's more normal latitudes. That's not to say the water does not get cold. A thin wetsuit is actually a real pleasure in the islands and allows you to be much more comfortable for longer periods when snorkeling. Bartolomé is also a great area for white-tipped reef sharks and green turtles which use the beaches for nesting. Most of the other central isles also have very good snorkeling areas, including the beautiful bay at Santa Fe, Puerto Egas of

Santiago and North Plaza Island. Although Baltra, which is administered by the armed forces, has no official visitor site, it is probably visited by as many people as any other island. Tourists, having arrived at the island, are always eager to meet their boat and leave to begin their cruise, not really appreciating that they have made it to the archipelago. Baltra airport was first built as a US Air Force base in 1942 and maintained as a strategic point during World War II. Today it remains the principal airport serving the Galapagos, though only a few military personnel live on the island.

Anyone who has traveled to Santa Cruz via Baltra will remember that it is not an entirely straightforward process. After jostling for position in the scrum to receive luggage (unless you are travelling with a professionally escorted group), you must board a bus which will take you, for a small charge, to the Itabaca Channel. The last section of the road is somewhat worrying as the bus negotiates hairpin bends on a very steep incline. With luck, the ferry is waiting and, for another small fee and but a few minutes travel, you set foot onto the northern

One of the 'Gemelos' craters, Santa Cruz Island.

Spider, Santiago Island.

shores of Santa Cruz. There is no human habitation on the north of the island, and the town of Puerto Ayora, which is the main metropolis of the entire archipelago, lies on the far side to the south. This necessitates a bus journey which varies both according to the condition of the road and the bravado of the driver. In previous years, during a heavy El Niño season, the road has all but completely washed away, making access very difficult. Latterly however the well paved road now seems permanent. No matter how anxious the chauffeur is to return to town, one should count on at least an hour's drive. Some of the journey may at least be spent reading the stickers above the windscreen. Translated, they include such sayings as "God guides my way", "Daddy don't drive fast, we are waiting for you at home" and "Be cultured, throw your garbage out of the window".

The remainder of the journey is more profitably spent noticing the change in the vegetation zones which one must pass when traversing the island to the south. At sea level down near the channel, the vegetation is dominated by mangroves and salt-bush, an area of mostly evergreen plants that pro-

Vermillion flycatcher and Spanish moss, Santa Cruz Island.

vide a false sense of lushness. Not determined so much by climatic factors, the strip of coastal plants are essentially those with a high salt tolerance. These areas are often of less interest to the botanist than other vegetation zones of the islands as the plants themselves show low levels of endemism.

As soon as the bus pulls away from the coast on its climb towards the center of the island, the greens of the mangroves dramatically disappear and the first of the climatically controlled vegetation zones becomes apparent - the arid zone. This is the most abundant vegetation type in the Galapagos and, along with the coastal strip, is the area in which most of the visitor-site trails are set. It is a semi-desert area covered in deciduous forest dominated by the *Bursera* sp. or *palo santo* (holy stick) trees. They, like all the plants of the arid zone, are drought resistant, with small leaves and deep roots. The *palo santos* spend much of the year with no leaves in a ghostly, deathlike, appearance. Their regular spacing, when seen from a distance, highlights the competition between individual trees for the scant water available. Interspersed among the *palo santos* are the characteristic dry zone plants; cacti such as *Opuntia* sp., or

Male yellow warbler, Bartolomé Island.

prickly pear, sprawl over the rocky soil while the elegant candelabra cactus, *Jasminocereus* sp., towers gracefully above the substrate. More prickly plants thrive in the area, including the gorse-like *Scutia pauciflora*, a dense, spiny green bush, along with one of the most attractive trees of the Galapagos, the *palo verde* (green stick). Although protected by heavy spines, the long sweeping green boughs, covered in compound leaves and tiny leaflets, distract the mind from the heavy armor. Growing with majestically arching branches reminiscent of a willow, even the trunk of this tree is green and capable of photosynthesis. The flowers are also attractive, being a rather showy yellow and orange in color.

With a slight increase in altitude as the bus continues on its journey, the plants begin to change. Like most things in nature, the transition is gradual. The aforementioned species slowly disappear to be replaced by a more heterogeneous mix of robust trees and thick tangled shrubs also deciduous in character. The increase in elevation brings with it greater levels of precipitation and even epiphytic plants, such as lichens, begin to appear. The

Saddle-back tortoise from Española Island, Charles Darwin Research Station, Santa Cruz Island.

Galapagos are essentially desert islands with two main seasons, a warm, wet season from January to June, and a cool, dry (or *garúa*) season from July to December. The prevailing trade winds in the Galapagos are from the southeast and, as they sweep over the ocean towards the islands, they pick up water. When the moisture-laden air meets an island of certain relief, it is forced upwards and over the island. As the air rises, it cools and, in cooling, its capacity to hold water diminishes, causing precipitation which either condenses to a fine mist called *garúa* or falls as rain. The southern sides of the islands are therefore the first to receive this bounty of fresh water and support lush vegetation growth. By the time the trade winds have pushed over the island to the northern side, most of the water is spent and the region is more arid due to this 'rain shadow' effect. As such, the arid and transition zones on the northern side of Santa Cruz are extended in area and altitude when compared with the equivalent regions in the south. Not only that, but fewer climatic and vegetation zones are present due to the more restricted water supply. Nevertheless, the transition zone,

Galapagos tortoise head, Charles Darwin Research Station, Santa Cruz Island.

containing such trees as the endemic *pega pega* (*Pisonia floribunda*) and *guayabillo* (*Psidium galapageium*), gives way, on the northern slopes of the island, to the *Scalesia* zone. This lush area of tall, spindly evergreen trees, related to sunflowers, is only present on the higher Galapagos Islands. *Scalesia* forms a forest, rather homogeneous in character, of a closed canopy up to fifteen meters in height. The understory is fairly open and contains many epiphytes as well as birds such as finches and flycatchers which also relish the habitat. Sadly, it is a seriously threatened ecosystem. Being such a fertile environment, it has been extensively cut by man and replaced with pasture on which to range livestock such as cattle and horses.

Driving out through the other side of the *Scalesia* zone, the vegetation opens up to an area of low growing ferns, sedges and grasses. This pampa zone at the top of the island receives more than two meters of precipitation in some years. At the summit of Santa Cruz the view looks out over a scene of lushness as the island dips south towards the coast. The pampa suddenly gives way to dense stands of an attractive, endemic shrub, *Miconia robinsoniana*,

Santa Fe land iguana, Santa Fe Island.

which in turn is surpassed by an area of vegetation dominated by *Zanthoxylum fagara*, or cat's claw, heavily draped with thick brown beards of epiphytic mosses and liverworts. As the bus continues careering down the hill, once again it passes through a thick stand of *Scalesia pedunculata*, the daisy tree, which tries to conceal two fabulous pit craters, one on either side of the road. The *Gemelos*, or twins as the craters are called, are huge in area and many tens of meters deep. The best theory as to their formation is that they were created by a series of collapses along circumferential fissures when magma from a large subterranean chamber was diverted to another area of the volcano via the immense system of underground lava tunnels throughout the island. As the now empty chambers could no longer support the heavy roof of rock, they proceeded to collapse. Surrounded by verdant growth, the *Gemelos* are a very pretty area, worth a visit by those with time on their hands while in Santa Cruz. A walk to the lookout point at the far end of the larger pit-crater is very rewarding. *Lycopodiums* line the cliff edge like minute Christmas trees while more endemic plants, *Scalesia* and *Darwiniothamnus*,

Galapagos land iguana, South Plaza Island.

Galapagos penguin hunting, Bartolomé Island.

Galapagos penguin, Bartolomé Island.

Sally lightfoot crabs mating, Santiago Island.

Oystercatcher eating Sally lightfoot crab, Santiago Island.

line the path. The keen observer may also be lucky enough to spot a short-eared owl which is often present in the area. Continuing down the hill, the ocean comes in and out of view as the bus negotiates fearsome corners. Fenceposts appear, occasionally decorated by a distinctive male vermillion flycatcher perched on their tops. The endemic plants give way to farmland and huge trees brought in from the mainland. They now line the road. Small towns appear and civilization instantly is upon you.

The sprawling town of Puerto Ayora begins a long way up the road, lining either side of its main artery. Before you know what has happened, the bus brakes to a dusty halt and people and bags begin spewing out onto the pavement. The heat of the town is somewhat oppressive after the misty cool of the highlands. There is a vibrant hustle-bustle of activity as people come to meet and greet the day's new arrivals. The town of Puerto Ayora is the largest of the Galapagos, with possibly as many as 16,000 residents. The commercial center comprises one main street and is lined almost its entire length with places to eat and T-shirt shops. In only the last decade, the growth of the town has been incredible.

White-tipped reef sharks in shallows, Bartolomé Island.

Since I went to guide in the islands in 1987 I have been saying that the Galapagos of tomorrow will resemble the Hawaii of today. Ten years ago there were just a few cars, trucks and buses which slowly negotiated the dusty dirt road. Gasoline was stored at people's homes in fifty-five gallon drums and replenished each time the ship came to port. The atmosphere was casual and people seemed happy. They had only come in the first place because they wanted to be there. Today, as progress has swept through the community like a tidal wave, attitudes have changed, the roads are paved to accommodate the large volume of traffic, including 700 taxies, fueled by modern gasoline facilities, which race around the one way circuit hurrying to do business. Monetary transactions are now facilitated by satellite banking communications. Instead of the once laid back lifestyle the air is now filled with a palpable electricity. The exponential population growth is putting pressure on natural and human resources alike, discontent and social unrest is rife as the lower classes struggle to make a living. Recent instability in local government institutions has done little to help the situation. Tourism is by far the mainstay of the economy within the islands, except for the huge clandestine wealth being generated by a few in illegal fishing and other illicit industries. The harbor hums to the sound of outboard engines ferrying tourists from their live-aboard yachts to shore. One of the most important things on their minds while in Santa Cruz seems to be to stock up on a collection of souvenir T-shirts with which to impress friends back home. The second, and more important, reason for visiting the town is to visit the Charles Darwin Research Station. Here, in a recently upgraded facility, visitors are led by their guide through an excellent series of educational displays. The main thrust of the section open to the public is to highlight the extremely successful and long standing tortoise repatriation program. Since its early beginnings, more than 3,000 young tortoises have been reintro-

Sea cucumber, Bartolomé Island.

Galapagos fur seal, Santiago Island.

Galapagos fur seal, Santiago Island.

Inset: Green turtle laying eggs, Baltra Island.
Green turtle digging nest pit, Baltra Island.

duced to their original habitats – an impressive effort. After having been reared in the station's facilities, they are rat or dog proof (dependent on the particular threat on their native island), and are deemed ready for reintroduction. It has been to date a fabulous success. One story especially worthy of mention is the case of the Española population which was reduced at one point to only fourteen individuals (2 males and 12 females) so thinly spread out on the island that they probably seldom, if ever, met to breed. It was decided to bring them all into the station for breeding purposes. Eventually, with the aid of a third, particularly vigorous, stud male repatriated from San Diego Zoo, more than 1,300 individuals have been released back onto Española, leaving us with the hope that one day we will be watching courting albatross and suddenly be surprised by a healthy giant tortoise lumbering through as it always should have been.

Turtle returning to sea after egg laying.

As mentioned in the introduction, introduced flora and fauna pose some of the most serious threats to the health of the park. Both the Charles Darwin Research Station (CDRS) and the Galapagos National Park Service (GNPS) are tremendously committed to reversing the legacy of human intervention. Both institutions have traditionally been so strapped for cash that nothing was easy. (The economics have improved lately, with the national park now retaining a higher percentage of the entrance fee.) Nevertheless, a momentous breakthrough in 2004 was the complete eradication of pigs and donkeys on Santiago Island. In a near superhuman effort, the national park guards, with their teams of male-only dogs (to prevent accidental introductions of viable populations), have overcome the rough lava terrain, the hordes of introduced fire ants, tangled, spiny vegetation and extreme heat and lack of water to reduce the total island pig population to zero. The next challenge will be the final phase of the removal of the goat population, another daunting prospect. With their extremely rapid

Sea lion in long green grass, El Niño 1998, South Plaza Island.

Lava lizard eating scorpion, Santiago Island.

Bull Galapagos fur seal, Santiago Island.

reproduction rates, goats are a nightmare to extirpate totally. An introduction of only three goats on Pinta in the late 1950s, for example, led to a population of over 400,000 by 1970! However with cutting-edge technology, including the use of Judas goats, GIS tracking and helicopters the efforts are well on the way to becoming completely successful. (Currently there is an extensive campaign, Project Isabela, to not only rid Alcedo volcano of its huge, recent goat population but also to restore the entire island to a more natural state. Again, a combined GNPS and CDRS project.) There are innumerable other projects on the go, such as land iguana breeding and repatriation programs, exotic plant eradication programs and also a heavy emphasis on local environmental education programs. Both institutions are doing a fabulous job, particularly considering their means. The CDRS relies heavily on foreign donations and it is here that you are able to help. A list of organizations receiving donations towards Galapagos conservation projects appears in Appendix B.

Giant Opuntia cactus, Santa Fe Island.

Glossary

Careen

To haul a vessel onto a beach or dry area where it is turned on its side for maintenance and repair.

Cloaca

Opening in birds, reptiles and amphibians of genital and excretory organs.

Coriolis force

The force exerted on fluids (in this case) due to the rotation of the earth.

Endemic

An animal or plant is endemic to a specified area if it occurs naturally in that area and nowhere else.

Garúa

Local name for a fine mist forming in elevated portions of the Galapagos usually between July and December.

Morph

A variant.

Niche

The specific role of an organism within its environment.

Osmosis

The transfer of a concentrated solution to a less concentrated solution through a semi-permeable membrane.

Panga

Local Galapagos term for a small dingy.

Parasitic cone

A volcanic cone forming on the flank of a larger volcano.

Pelagic

Organisms of open ocean.

Photosynthesis

The process whereby plants use sunlight to convert carbon dioxide into organic compounds in order to grow.

Pinniped

Mammals of the seal family which includes walruses, seals, sea lions and fur seals.

Tectonic Plate

A rigid section of the earth's crust or ocean floor which drifts in relation to other tectonic plates in response to convection currents within the mantle of the earth.

Thigmotactic

Seeking body contact.

Female magnificent frigatebird, Fernandina Island.

Bibliography

Anhalzer, J.J. National Parks of Ecuador. Quito, Ecuador: Imprenta Mariscal.

Beebe, W. 1924. Galapagos - World's End. London, New York: C.P. Putman.

Boyce, B. 1994. A Traveller's Guide to the Galapagos Islands. Galapagos Travel, San Jose, CA.

Castro, I and A. Phillips. 1996. A Guide to The Birds of the Galapagos Islands. Princeton University Press.

Constant, P. 1992. Marine Life of the Galapagos. A Guide to the Fishes, Whales, Dolphins and other Marine Mammals. Production House.

Corral, C., Corral, P., Oxford, P. 1998. Ecuador Spaces of Light. Quito, Ecuador: Imprenta Mariscal.

Cribb, J. 1986. Subtidal Galapagos, Exploring the Waters of Darwin's Islands. Camden House Publishing Ltd.

Darwin, C. 1845. The Voyage of the Beagle. Journal of researches into the Natural History and Geology of the Countries visited during the Voyage round the World of H.M.S. 'Beagle' under command of Captain FitzRoy, R.N. John Murray. London.

Darwin, C. 1859. On the Origin of Species. John Murray. London.

De Roy, T. and M. Jones, 1990. Portraits of Galapagos. Quito, Ecuador: Imprenta Mariscal

De Roy, T. 1998. Galapagos: Islands Born of Fire. Quito, Ecuador: Libri Mundi.

Grant, P.R. 1986. Ecology and Evolution of Darwin's Finches. New Jersey: Princeton University Press.

Grant, B.R. and P.R. Grant. 1989. Evolutionary Dynamics of a Natural Population. The Large Cactus Finch of the Galapagos. The University of Chicago Press.

Grove, J.S., S. García and S. Massey. 1984. Lista de los peces de Galápagos. Guayaquil, Ecuador: Boletín Científico Y Técnico, Instituto Nacional de Pesca.

Grove, J.S., R.J. Lavenberg, 1997. The Fishes of the Galapagos Islands. Standford University Press.

Harris, M.P. 1974. A Field Guide to the Birds of the Galapagos. London: Collins.

Harrison, P. 1983. Seabirds an Identification Guide. Christopher Helm. London.

Hickman, J. 1985. The Enchanted Islands. The Galapagos Discovered. Anthony Nelson Ltd.

Hickin, N.E., Animal Life of the Galapagos.

Horwell, D., P. Oxford. 1999. Galapagos Wildlife. Bucks, England: Bradt Publications.

Humann, P. 1993. Reef Fish Identification. Galapagos. Quito, Ecuador: Libri Mundi.

Jackson, M. H. 1993. Galapagos, a Natural History. Calgary: The University of Calgary Press.

Lack, D.1947 Darwin's Finches. London: Cambridge University Press.

Leatherwood, S., R.R. Reeves. 1983. The Sierra Club Handbook of Whales and Dolphins. San Francisco: Sierra Club Books.

Merlin, G. 1988. A Field Guide to the Fishes of Galapagos. Quito, Ecuador: Imprenta Mariscal

Moore, A., and T. Moore. 1980. Guide to the Visitor Sites of Parque Nacional Galápagos. Servicio Parque Nacional. Galápagos, Ecuador.

Moore, T. 1980. Galapagos Islands Lost in Time. New York: Viking Press.

Moorhead, A. 1971. Darwin and the Beagle. Harmondsworth, Penguin, England.

Nelson, J.B. 1978. The Sulidae. London: Oxford University Press.

Nelson, B. 1968. Galapagos. Islands of Birds. Longmans Green and Co. Ltd.

Patzelt, E. 1989. Fauna del Ecuador. Quito, Ecuador: Ediciones del Banco Central.

Perry, R. 1984. Galapagos. - (Key Environments). Oxford: Pergamon Press Ltd.

Quammen, D. 1997. The Song of the Dodo. New York: Touchstone.

Reeves, R.R., B.S. Stewart, S. Leatherwood. 1992. The Sierra Club Handbook of Seals and Sirenians. San Francisco: Sierra Club Books.

Ryan, P.R. 1987. Oceanus, the International Magazine of Marine Science and Policy. Vol 30. Number 2. Woods Hole Oceanographic Institute.

Schofield, E.K. 1970. Field Guide to Some Common Galapagos Plants. Columbus: Ohio State University Research Foundation.

Schonitzer, K. Galapagos Plants. Contribution Number 172 of the Charles Darwin Foundation.

Shaw, J. 1984. The Nature Photographers' Complete Guide to Professional Field Techniques. New York: Amphoto, American Photographic Book Publishing. Ltd.

Steadman, D.W. and S. Zousmer. 1988. Galapagos Discovery on Darwin's Islands. Smithsonian Institution Press.

Thornton, I. 1971. Darwin's Islands; A Natural History of the Galapagos Islands. Garden City, New York: Natural History Press.

Treherne, J.E. 1983. The Galapagos Affair. London: Jonathan Cape.

The Charles Darwin Foundation for the Galapagos Islands. Annual Report, 2004.

Wellington, G.M. 1975. The Galapagos Coastal Marine Environments. Ph.D. Thesis. Galapagos: Charles Darwin Research Station.

Weiner, J. 1995. The Beak of the Finch. A Story of Evolution in Our Time. England: Vintage.

Wiggins, I.L., and D.M. Porter. 1971. Flora of the Galapagos Islands. Stanford University Press.

Wittmer, M. 1989. Floreana. Quito, Ecuador: Libri Mundi.

Yépez, V., P. Díaz, L. S. Rodríguez, (INEFAN-GEF). 1998. Guía de Parques Nacionales y Reservas del Ecuador. Quito, Ecuador: INEFAN.

APPENDIX A

Rules and Guidelines of the National Park

1. Do not remove or disturb any plant, rock or animal on the islands.
2. Be careful not to transport any live material to the islands or from island to island. Check your clothing for seeds and insects before disembarking the ship for shore.
3. Do not touch the animals.
4. Do not feed the animals.
5. Always remain on the path where designated.
6. Always remain with your guide where required.
7. Do not startle or chase any animal from its nest or resting place. Be extremely careful in and around breeding colonies.
8. Do not force your way through dense bush or thickets. This will destroy the plant life and seeds may become lodged on your person.
9. Do not litter on land or from the vessel whilst at sea.
10. Do not buy souvenirs made from any native animal part, coral or plant except certain wood.
11. Do not write graffiti or deface rocks and plants on the islands.
12. Do not hesitate to show your conservationist attitude and explain to others the rules. Notify the National Park Service if you see any damage being done.

Galapagos hawk, Española Island.

Appendix B

Institutions

Charles Darwin Foundation, Inc.
407 North Washington Street, Suite 105
Falls Church, VA 22046, USA.
tel: +1 703 538 6833
e-mail: *darwin@galapagos.org*
www.galapagos.org

Zoologische Gesellschaft Frankfurt
Alfred-Brehm-Platz 16
D-60316 Frankfurt, Germany.
Spenden mit dem Hinweis "Galapagos" an: Frankfurter
Sparkasse BLZ 500 502 01, Kontonummer: 80002.
e-mail: *info@zgf.de*
www.zgf.de

Stichting Vrienden van de Galapagos Eilanden
c/o Mevr. E. Boele-de Jong
Mendelssohnstraat 13
3281 VH Numansdorp, The Netherlands.
tel: +31 186 651590
e-mail: *secr.galapagos@hetnet.nl*
www.galapagos.nl

The Charles Darwin Research Station
Puerto Ayora, Isla Santa Cruz,
Galapagos, Ecuador.
tel: +593 5 2526651
e-mail: *infocdrs@fcdarwin.org*

Nordic Friends of Galapagos
Korkeasaari
00570 Helsinki, Finland.
tel: +358 50 5644279
e-mail: *k.kumenius@kolumbus.fi*
www.galapagosnordic.fi

Galapagos Conservation Trust
5 Derby Street
London W1Y 7AD, UK.
tel: +44 (0) 20 7629 5049
e-mail: *gct@gct.org*
www.gct.org

The Galapagos Darwin Trust
Banque Internationale à Luxembourg
2, Boulevard Royal
L-2953 Luxembourg.
Donations marked "For the Galapagos" may be made
to Account No. 1-100/9071.

Freunde der Galapagos Inseln (CH)
c/o Zoo Zürich
Zürichbergstr. 221
CH-8044 Zürich, Switzerland.
tel: +41 (0) 1 254 26 70
e-mail: *galapagos@zoo.ch*
www.galapagos-ch.org

Acknowledgements

When first arriving to take a job on the coast of mainland Ecuador in 1985, it was with a sense of longing that I looked west across the ocean towards the distant and magical Galapagos Islands beyond the horizon. In 1987 I moved to the Galapagos to become a naturalist guide. It is during that time that I made many valued friends. I would like to express my deepest gratitude to the following people, Carmen Angermeyer, Fiddi Angermeyer, Eliécer Cruz, Felipe Cruz, Georgina Cruz, the late Gayle Davis Merlen, David Day, Jacqueline De Roy, Tui De Roy, Andy Drumm, Sylvia Harcourt, Mark Jones, Godfrey Merlen, Jack Nelson, the Schiess family, Graham Watkins, the Galapagos National Park Service and the Charles Darwin Research Station.

As a couple, Reneé and I would like to thank our loyal friends on mainland Ecuador. They include Dorothy Albright, Beny Ammeter, Juan Lorenzo Barragán, María Elena Barragán, Colleen Berlin, Jean Brown, Ximena Benavides, Andrés & Andrea Bustamante, Ben Dodd, Patricio and Ivette Jiménez, László Károlyi, Julian Larrea, Belen Mena, Lisanne Newport, Gary Parkin, Tom Quesenberry, Ana Lucía Sosa, Clarice Strang, Lucho Suarez, Andrea Tamayo, Mariela Tenorio, Kristina Tronstad, Sally Vergette, Charlie and Sherry Vogt, Andy Watkins, Ellen and Phil Whitaker and Guillermo and Roxana Zaldumbide.

Our special thanks also go to Marcela Garcia of Libri Mundi, Paco Valdivieso of Imprenta Mariscal and also to his team, particularly Andy Valdivieso, Gustavo Moya, and Jaime Mosquera; Juan Lorenzo Barragán and Lorena Zurita of Azuca, for an excellent design; Mary Ellen Fieweger, for her red pen and grammatical mangle through which she squeezed the text and to Graham Watkins for his vision and dedication to the islands.

As always our love goes out to our families who continue to encourage our endeavors from their farflung corners of the planet.

Pete Oxford and Reneé Bish,
Quito, Ecuador 2005

Sleeping sea lion, Española Island.

Index

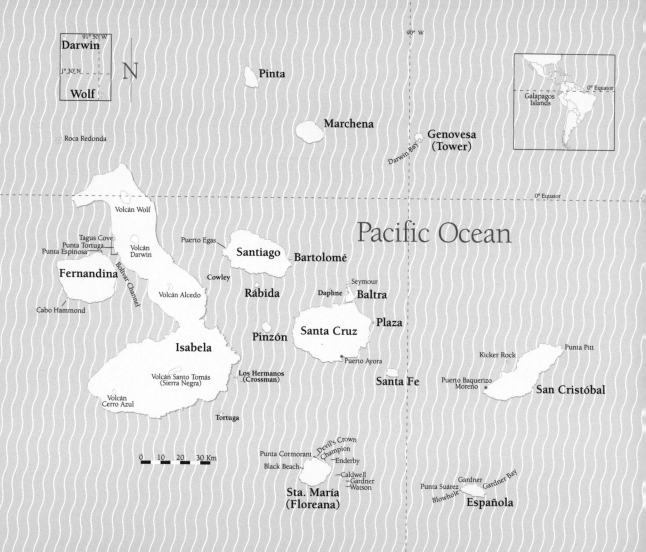

Darwin

91° 30' W

1° 30' N

Wolf

N

Pinta

Marchena

Galapagos
Islands

0° Equator

Roca Redonda

Genovesa
(Tower)

Darwin Bay

90° W

0° Equator

Volcán Wolf

Pacific Ocean

Tagus Cove
Punta Tortuga
Punta Espinosa

Puerto Egas

Santiago

Bartolomé

Volcán
Darwin

Cowley

Fernandina

Bolívar Channel

Volcán Alcedo

Rábida

Seymour

Daphne

Baltra

Cabo Hammond

Plaza

Pinzón

Santa Cruz

Kicker Rock

Punta Pitt

Isabela

Puerto Ayora

Volcán Santo Tomás
(Sierra Negra)

Los Hermanos
(Crossman)

Santa Fe

Puerto Baquerizo
Moreno

San Cristóbal

Volcán
Cerro Azul

Tortuga

0   10   20   30 Km

Devil's Crown

Punta Cormorant

Champion

Enderby

Black Beach

Caldwell
Gardner
Watson

Gardner

Punta Suárez

Gardner Bay

**Sta. María
(Floreana)**

Blowhole

Española

The Human Body in Health and Disease

Ruth Lundeen Memmler, M.D.

Professor Emeritus, Life Sciences;
formerly Coordinator, Health, Life Sciences, and Nursing,
East Los Angeles College, Los Angeles, California

Dena Lin Wood, R.N., B.S., P.H.N.

Staff Nurse, Memorial Hospital of Glendale,
Glendale, California

Illustrated by Anthony Ravielli

The Human Body in Health and Disease

Sixth Edition

J.B. Lippincott Company Philadelphia

London Mexico City New York St. Louis São Paulo Sydney

Sponsoring Editor: Patricia L. Cleary
Developmental Editor: Joyce Mkitarian
Manuscript Editor: Martha Hicks-Courant
Indexer: Angela Holt
Design Director: Tracy Baldwin
Cover Photo & Illustration: Eric Pervukhin and Kathy Ziegler
Cover Designer: Anthony Frizano
Production Manager: J. Corey Gray
Production Coordinator: Rosanne Hallowell
Compositor: Circle Graphics
Text Printer/Binder: Kingsport Press
Cover Printer: The Lehigh Press, Inc.

6th Edition

6

Library of Congress Cataloging-in-Publication Data

Memmler, Ruth Lundeen.
  The human body in health and disease.

  Bibliography: p.
  Includes index.
  1. Human physiology.   2. Physiology, Pathological.
3. Anatomy, Human.   I. Wood, Dena Lin.   II. Title.
[DNLM: 1. Anatomy.   2. Pathology.   3. Physiology.
QT 200 M533h]
QP34.5.M48   1987   612   86-20848
ISBN 0-397-54637-8
ISBN 0-397-54604-1 (soft)

A Note to Students

The Human Body in Health and Disease, Sixth Edition, traces the organization of the body from the single cell to the coordinated whole. A main theme is the interaction of all body systems for the maintenance of an internal state of balance or homeostasis. Each chapter, except the two introductory chapters, also contains a discussion of conditions that may upset this balance to produce disease.

This edition of the book contains many aids to learning:

1. Each chapter begins with a list of objectives which are the learning goals for that chapter. The knowledge that should be gained by careful study of the chapter is clearly stated.

2. The new and important terms in each chapter are listed at the start of the chapter. These terms and other important terms in the text are defined in the glossary at the back of the book.

3. New terms are emphasized in the text with boldface type, and each is followed by a phonetic pronunciation. In these pronunciations, a single accent mark (′) shows the strongest accent in a word; a double mark (″) shows a secondary, lesser accent.

4. New charts have been added to summarize information in the text.

5. New illustrations have been added to the excellent illustrations found in previous editions.

6. A summary outline of each chapter is provided for review and reference.

7. Charts on the metric system and temperature conversions have been added to the appendix for fast reference.

8. A revised workbook based directly on the text is available. This can be used to review, to measure what information has been learned, and to study for tests.

The study of the human body has fascinated people for thousands of years. Even at a beginning level, the amount of information to be learned about the structure and function of the human body can be staggering. At times a beginning course may seem to be a course in a foreign language—there are so many new terms to learn! To make the student's job even more difficult, there may be two or even more terms that mean the same thing. In this text, these terms may be included in parentheses along with the term used most commonly.

A good approach to study is to say each new word aloud according to the phonetic pronunciation so that you get to know how it sounds and can pronounce it yourself. This practice will also help with spelling, because most scientific words are spelled exactly as they sound. A list of each important term and its definition should be kept. These definitions can be taken from the text or from the glossary at the end of the book. If the terms are kept on 3 × 5 cards with the word on one side and the definition on the other, the cards can be used for self-testing and study.

Because most scientific words are taken from Latin and Greek, word parts keep the same meaning even when they are used in different combinations. Frequent reference to the Medical Terminology section at the end of the book will help you to learn the meaning of the prefixes, roots, and suffixes used to build scientific words. These words may seem long and complicated at first, but they are meant to describe what the word means in a sort of "shorthand." With time, your vocabulary will build, and you will find yourself able to recognize the various word parts and able to figure out the meaning of new words.

The study of the human body is challenging and ever-changing. Hopefully, this book will be the start of a continuing learning process for each student.

Contents

1

Introduction to the Human Body

Behavioral Objectives

After careful study of this chapter, you should be able to:

Define the terms anatomy, physiology, *and* pathology

Describe the organization of the body from cells to the whole organism

List ten body systems and give the general function of each

Define metabolism *and name the two phases of metabolism*

Differentiate between extracellular and intracellular fluids

Briefly explain the role of ATP in the body

Define homeostasis *and* negative feedback

List and define the main directional terms for the body

List and define the three planes of division of the body

Name the subdivisions of the dorsal and ventral cavities

Name the basic metric units of length, weight, and volume

Define the metric prefixes kilo-, centi-, *and* milli-

Selected Key Terms

The following terms are defined in the glossary:

anabolism
anatomy
ATP
catabolism
cell
feedback
gram
homeostasis
liter
metabolism
meter
organ
pathology
physiology
system
tissue

☰ Studies of the Human Body

With this book you begin a serious study of the human body and how it is affected by disease. The scientific term for the study of body structure is **anatomy** (ah-nat'o-me). Part of this word means "to cut," because one of the many ways to learn about the human body is to cut it apart, or **dissect** it. **Physiology** (fiz-e-ol'o-je) is the term for the study of how the body functions, and the two sciences are closely related. Anything that upsets the normal structure or working of the body is considered a **disease** and is studied as the science of **pathology** (pah-thol'o-je). It is hoped that from these studies you will gain an appreciation for the design and balance of the human body and for living organisms in general.

All living things are organized from very simple levels to more complex levels. Living matter begins with simple chemicals. These chemicals are formed into the complex substances that make living **cells—** the basic units of all life. Specialized groups of cells form **tissues**, and tissues may function together as **organs**. Organs functioning together for the same general purpose make up organ **systems**, which maintain the whole body.

☰ Body Systems

The body systems have been variously stated to be nine, ten, or eleven in number, depending on how much detail one wishes to include. Here is one list of systems:

1 The **skeletal system**. The basic framework of the body is a system of over 200 bones with their joints, collectively known as the **skeleton**.
2 The **muscular system**. Body movements result from the action of the muscles, which are attached to the bones. Other types of muscles are present in the walls of such organs as the intestine and the heart.
3 The **circulatory system**. The heart and blood vessels make up the system whereby blood is pumped to all the body tissues, bringing with it food, oxygen, and other substances and carrying away waste materials. Lymph vessels and nodes play an important supporting role.
4 The **digestive system**. This system comprises all organs that have to do with taking in food and

converting the useful parts of it into substances that the body cells can use. Examples of these organs are the mouth, esophagus, stomach, intestine, liver, and pancreas.
5 The **respiratory system**. This includes the lungs and the passages leading to them. The purpose of this system is to take in air and from it extract oxygen, which is then dissolved into the blood and conveyed to all the tissues. A waste product of the cells, carbon dioxide, is taken by the blood to the lungs, where it is expelled to the outside air.
6 The **integumentary** (in-teg"u-men'tar-e) **system**. The word **integument** (in-teg'u-ment) means skin. The skin is considered by some authorities to be a separate body system. It includes the skin and its appendages, the hair, the nails and the sweat and oil glands.
7 The **urinary system**. This is also called the **excretory system**. Its main components are the kidneys, the ureters, the bladder, and the urethra. Its chief purpose is to rid the body of certain waste products and excess water. (Note that other waste products are removed by the digestive and the respiratory systems.)
8 The **nervous system**. The brain, the spinal cord, and the nerves make up this very complex system by which most parts of the body are controlled and coordinated. The organs of special sense (such as the eyes, ears, taste buds, and organs of smell), together with the sense of touch, receive stimuli from the outside world. These stimuli are converted into impulses that are transmitted to the brain. The brain directs the body's responses to these messages and also to messages coming from within the body. Such higher functions as memory and reasoning also occur in the brain.
9 The **endocrine system**. The scattered organs known as **endocrine glands** produce special substances called **hormones**, which regulate such body functions as growth, food utilization within the cells, and reproduction. Examples of endocrine glands are the thyroid and the pituitary glands.
10 The **reproductive system**. This system includes the external sex organs and all related inner structures that are concerned with the production of offspring.

Body Processes

All of the life-sustaining reactions that go on within the body systems together make up **metabolism** (me-tab'o-lizm). Metabolism can be divided into two types of activities:

Catabolism (kah-tab'o-lizm), in which the foods that we eat are broken down and used to supply simple compounds and energy to the cells

Anabolism (ah-nab'o-lizm), in which the products of digestion are used to manufacture new body materials needed for growth, structure, and function

All the energy that is obtained within the cells from food is converted to a compound described as the "energy currency" of the cells because it supplies the energy for all activities. This is a complex substance with the long name of **adenosine triphosphate** (ah-den'o-seen tri-fos'fate), commonly abbreviated **ATP**. Chapter 19 contains more information on metabolism and ATP.

It is important to recognize that our bodies are composed of large amounts of fluids. Certain kinds of fluids bathe the cells, carry nutrient substances to and from the cells, and transport the nutrients in and out of the cells. This group of fluids is called **extracellular fluid** because it includes all body fluids outside of the cells. A second type of fluid is that contained within the cells, called **intracellular fluid**. Extracellular and intracellular fluids account for approximately 60% of an adult's weight.

Homeostasis

The purpose of metabolism is to maintain a state of balance within the organism, an important characteristic of all living things. Such conditions as body temperature, the composition of body fluids, heart rate, respiration rate, and blood pressure must be kept within set limits in order to maintain health. This steady state within the organism is called **homeostasis** (ho"me-o-sta'sis), which literally means "staying (stasis) the same (homeo)."

Homeostasis is maintained primarily by what is called **negative feedback systems**. Feedback systems are easily understood but difficult to explain. The most familiar example is probably the household thermostat. The thermostat regulates the tempera-

ture of your house by starting the furnace when the temperature of the house falls below the temperature setting on the thermostat. When the household temperature is above the thermostat setting, the furnace remains off. Thus, the heat produced when the furnace is on "feeds back" to the thermostat to control the working of the furnace itself. The term *negative feedback* means that the information in the system is used to reverse changes in the system to bring it back to normal. Many examples of negative feedback systems will be given throughout this book.

Directions in the Body

Because it would be awkward and incorrect to speak of bandaging the "southwest part" of the chest, a number of terms have been devised to designate specific regions and directions in the body. Some of the more important of these are listed as follows. Note that they refer to the body in the **anatomic position**—upright with palms facing forward:

1. **Superior** is a relative term meaning above, or in a higher position. Its opposite, **inferior**, means below, or lower. The heart, for example, is superior to the intestine.
2. **Ventral** and **anterior** mean the same thing in humans: located near the belly surface or front of the body. Their corresponding opposites, **dorsal** and **posterior**, refer to locations nearer the back.
3. **Cranial** means near the head; **caudal**, near the sacral region of the spinal column (*i.e.,* where the tail is located in lower animals).
4. **Medial** means near an imaginary plane that passes through the midline of the body, dividing it into left and right portions. **Lateral**, its opposite, means farther away from the midline, toward the side.
5. **Proximal** means nearest the origin of a structure; **distal**, farthest from that point. For example, the part of your thumb where it joins your hand is its proximal region; the tip of the thumb is its distal region.

Planes of Division

For convenience in visualizing the spatial relationships of various body structures to each other, anato-

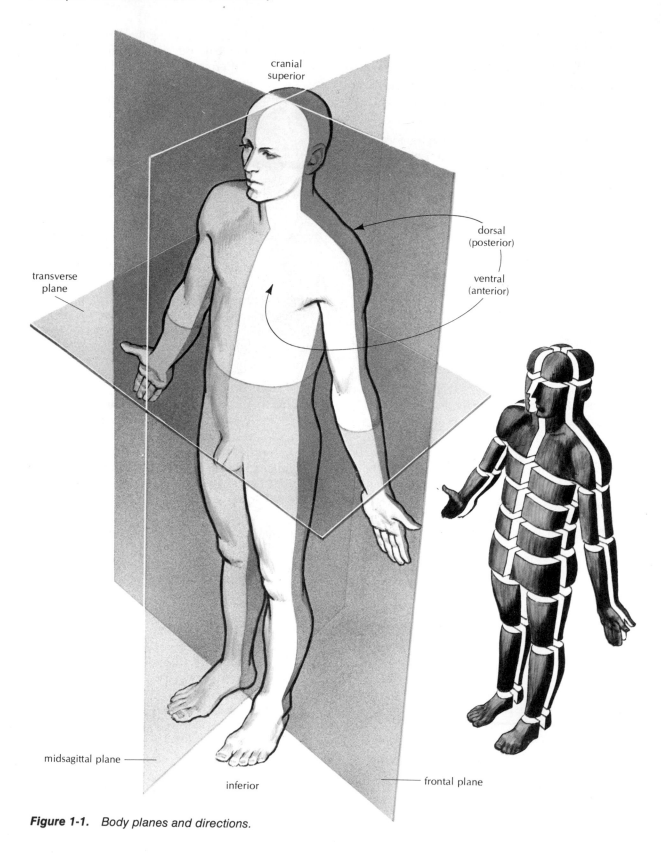

cranial
superior

transverse
plane

dorsal
(posterior)

ventral
(anterior)

midsagittal plane

inferior

frontal plane

Figure 1-1. *Body planes and directions.*

mists have divided the body by means of three imaginary planes, each of which is a cut through the body in a different direction (Fig. 1-1).

1 The **sagittal** (saj′i-tal) **plane**. If you were to cut the body in two from front to back, separating it into right and left portions, the sections you would see would be sagittal sections. A cut exactly down the midline of the body, separating it into equal right and left halves, is a **midsagittal** section.

2 The **frontal plane**. If the cut were made in line with the ears and then down the middle of the body, creating a front and a rear portion, you would see a front (anterior or ventral) section and a rear (posterior or dorsal) section.

3 The **transverse plane**. If the cut were made horizontally, across the other two planes, it would divide the body into an upper (superior) part and a lower (inferior) part. There could be many such cross sections, each of which would be on a transverse plane.

Body Cavities

The body contains a few large internal spaces, or **cavities**, within which various organs are located. There are two groups of cavities: **dorsal** and **ventral** (Fig. 1-2).

Dorsal Cavities

There are two dorsal cavities: the **cranial cavity**, containing the brain, and the **spinal canal**, enclosing the spinal cord. Both of these cavities join to form a continuous space.

Ventral Cavities

The ventral cavities are much larger than the dorsal ones. There are two ventral cavities: the **thoracic** (tho-ras′ik) **cavity**, containing mainly the heart, the lungs, and the large blood vessels, and the **abdominal cavity**. This latter space is subdivided into two portions, one containing the stomach, most of the intestine, the kidneys, the liver, the gallbladder, the pancreas, and the spleen, and a lower one called the **pelvic cavity**, in which are located the urinary bladder, the rectum, and the internal parts of the reproductive system.

Unlike the dorsal cavities, the ventral cavities are

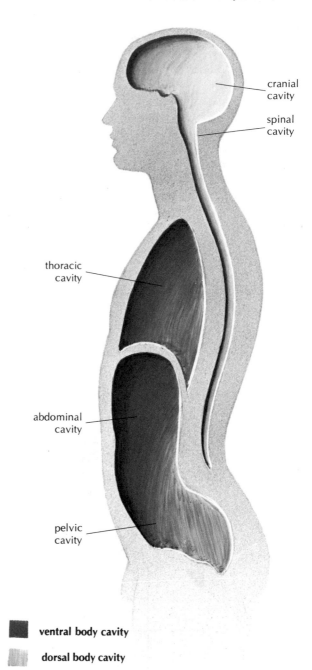

■ **ventral body cavity**

▨ **dorsal body cavity**

Figure 1-2. *Side view of body cavities.*

not continuous. They are separated by a muscular partition, the **diaphragm** (di′ah-fram), the function of which is discussed in Chapter 17.

Regions in the Abdominal Cavity

Because the abdominal cavity is so large, it is helpful to divide it into nine regions. These are shown in

Fig. 1-3. The three central regions are the **epigastric** (ep-i-gas′trik) **region**, located just below the breastbone; the **umbilical** (um-bil′i-kal) **region** around the umbilicus (um-bil′i-kus), commonly called the *navel;* and the **hypogastric** (hi-po-gas′trik) **region**, the lowest of all of the midline regions. At each side are the right and left **hypochondriac** (hi-po-kon′dre-ak) **regions**, just below the ribs; then the right and left **lumbar regions**; and finally the right and left **iliac**, or **inguinal** (in′gwi-nal), **regions**. A much simpler division into four quadrants (right upper, left upper, right lower, left lower) is now less frequently used.

☰ The Metric System

Now that we have set the stage for further study of the body and its structure and processes, a look at the metric system is in order, since this is the system used for all scientific measurements. The drug industry and the health care industry already have converted to the metric system, so anyone who plans a career in health should be acquainted with metrics.

To use the metric system easily and correctly may require a bit of effort, as is often the case with any new idea. Actually, you already know something about the metric system because our monetary system is similar to it in that both are decimal systems. One hundred cents equal one dollar; one hundred centimeters equal one meter. The decimal system is based on multiples of the number 10, which are indicated by prefixes:

kilo = 1000
centi = 1/100
milli = 1/1000

The basic unit of length in the metric system is the

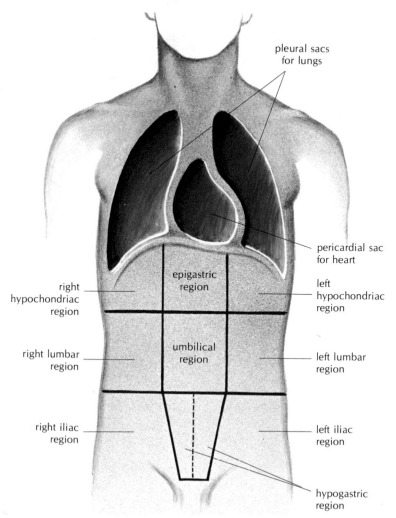

pleural sacs
for lungs

pericardial sac
for heart

Figure 1-3. *Front view of body cavities and the regions of the abdomen.*

right
hypochondriac
region

epigastric
region

left
hypochondriac
region

right lumbar
region

umbilical
region

left lumbar
region

right iliac
region

left iliac
region

hypogastric
region

meter. Thus, 1 kilometer is equal to 1000 meters. A centimeter is 1/100 of a meter; stated another way, there are 100 centimeters in 1 meter. A changeover to the metric system has been slow in coming to the United States. Often measurements on packages, bottles, and yard goods are now given according to both scales. In this text, equivalents in the more familiar units of inches, feet, and so on are included along with the metric units for comparison. There are 2.5 centimeters (cm) and 25 millimeters (mm) in 1 inch, as shown in Figure 1-4. Some equivalents that may help you to appreciate the size of various body parts are as follows:

1 mm = 0.04 inch, or 1 inch = 25 mm
1 cm = 0.4 inch, or 1 inch = 2.5 cm
1 m = 3.3 feet, or 1 foot = 30 cm

The same prefixes are used for weights and volumes as for linear measurements. The **gram** is the standard unit of weight. Thirty grams are approximately equal to 1 ounce, and 1 kilogram to 2.2 pounds. Drug dosages are usually stated in grams or milligrams. One thousand milligrams equal 1 gram; a 500-milligram (mg) dose would be the equivalent of 0.5 gram (g), and 250 mg are equal to 0.25 g.

The dosages of liquid medications are given in units of volume. The standard metric measurement for volume is the **liter** (le′ter). There are 1000 milliliters (ml) in a liter. A liter is slightly greater than a quart, a liter being equal to 1.06 quarts. For smaller quantities, the milliliter is used most of the time. There are 5 ml in a teaspoon and 15 ml in a tablespoon. A fluid ounce contains 30 ml.

The Celsius (centigrade) temperature scale, now in use by most other countries as well as by scientists in this country, is discussed in Chapter 19. A chart of all the common metric measurements and their equivalents as well as a Celsius–Fahrenheit temperature conversion scale are shown in the Appendix.

Figure 1-4. *Comparison of centimeters and inches.*

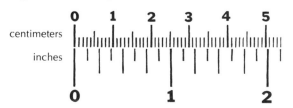

Summary

I Studies of the human body
  A Anatomy—study of structure
  B Physiology—study of function
  C Pathology—study of disease

II Organization
  A Levels—cell, tissue, organ, organ system
  B Body systems
    1 Skeletal system—support
    2 Muscular system—movement
    3 Circulatory system (includes lymphatic system)—transport
    4 Digestive system—intake and breakdown of food
    5 Respiratory system—intake of oxygen and release of carbon dioxide
    6 Integumentary system—skin and associated structures
    7 Urinary system—elimination of waste and water
    8 Nervous system—receipt of stimuli and control of responses
    9 Endocrine system—production of hormones for regulation of growth, metabolism, reproduction
    10 Reproductive system—production of offspring

III Body processes
  A Metabolism—all the chemical reactions needed to sustain life
    1 Catabolism—breakdown of food for energy and simple compounds
    2 Anabolism—building of body materials
  B ATP (adenosine triphosphate)—energy compound of cells
  C Body fluids
    1 Extracellular—outside the cells
    2 Intracellular—inside the cells
  D Homeostasis—steady state of body conditions maintained mostly by negative feedback

IV Body positions, directions, planes
  A Anatomic position—upright, palms forward
  B Directions
    1 Superior—above or higher; inferior—below or lower
    2 Ventral (anterior)—near belly or front surface; dorsal (posterior)—near back surface

    3 Cranial—near head; caudal—near sacrum
    4 Medial—toward midline;
       lateral—toward side
    5 Proximal—near point of origin;
       distal—away from point of origin
  B Planes of division
    1 Sagittal—from front to back, dividing the
       body into left and right parts
      a Midsagittal—exactly down the midline
    2 Frontal—from left to right, dividing the
       body into anterior and posterior parts
    3 Transverse—horizontally, dividing the body
       into superior and inferior parts
V **Body cavities**
  A Dorsal—contains cranial and spinal cavities
    for brain and spinal cord
  B Ventral
    1 Thoracic—chest cavity containing heart and
       lungs and divided from abdominal cavity by
       diaphragm
    2 Abdominal
      a Upper region contains stomach, most of
        intestine, kidneys, liver, spleen, etc.
      b Lower region (pelvic cavity) contains re-
        productive organs, urinary bladder, rec-
        tum
      c Abdomen divided for reference into nine
        regions: epigastric, umbilical, hypogastric,
        right and left hypochondriac, right and
        left lumbar, right and left iliac (inguinal)
VI **Metric system**—based on multiples of ten
  A Basic units
    1 Meter—length
    2 Liter—volume
    3 Gram—weight
  B Prefixes—indicate multiples of ten
    1 Kilo—1000 times
    2 Centi—1/100th (0.01)
    3 Milli—1/1000th (0.001)

  C Temperature—measured in Celsius (centi-
    grade) scale

Questions for Study and Review

1 List three types of study of the human body and define each.
2 Define *cell, tissue, organ, system.*
3 List ten body systems and briefly describe the function of each.
4 Name and define the two phases of metabolism.
5 What is ATP?
6 Define homeostasis and give two examples. How is homeostasis maintained?
7 Stand in the anatomic position.
8 List the opposite term for each of the following body directions: superior, ventral, anterior, cranial, medial, proximal. Define each term and its opposite.
9 Describe the location of the elbow with regard to the wrist; with regard to the shoulder.
10 Describe the location of the stomach with regard to the urinary bladder; with regard to the lungs.
11 Describe the location of the ears with regard to the nose.
12 What are the three main body planes? Explain the division each makes.
13 Name the cavities within the dorsal and ventral cavities. Name one organ found in each.
14 Make a rough sketch of the abdomen and label the nine divisions.
15 Why should you learn the metric system? What are its advantages?

2

Chemistry, Matter, and Life

Behavioral Objectives

After careful study of this chapter, you should be able to:

Describe the structure of an atom

Differentiate between atoms and molecules

Define the atomic number of an atom

Differentiate among elements, compounds, and mixtures and give several examples of each

Explain why water is so important to the body

Define mixture; list the three types of mixtures and give two examples of each

Differentiate between ionic and covalent bonds

Define the terms acid, base, and salt

Explain how the numbers on the pH scale relate to acidity and alkalinity

Define buffer and explain why buffers are important in the body

Define radioactivity and cite several examples of how radioactive substances are used in medicine

List three characteristics of organic compounds

Name the three main types of organic compounds and the building blocks of each

Selected Key Terms

The following terms are defined in the glossary:

acid
atom
base
buffer
carbohydrate
compound
covalent bond
electrolyte
electron
element
enzyme
ion
lipid
mixture
molecule
neutron
organic
pH
protein
proton
solute
solution
solvent
suspension

☰ What Is Chemistry?

Great strides toward an understanding of living organisms, including the human being, have come to us through **chemistry**, the science that deals with the composition of matter. Knowledge of chemistry and chemical changes helps us understand the normal and abnormal functioning of the body and its parts. The digestion of food in the intestinal tract, the production of urine by the kidneys, the regularity of breathing—all body processes—are based on chemical principles. Chemistry also is important in **microbiology** (the study of microscopic plants and animals) and **pharmacology** (the study of drugs). The various solutions that are used to cleanse the skin before a surgical operation are chemicals, as are aspirin, penicillin, and all other drugs used in treating disease. In order to provide some understanding of the importance of chemistry in the health field, this chapter briefly describes **atoms** and **molecules**, **elements**, **compounds**, and **mixtures**, which are the fundamental units of matter.

☰ A Look at Atoms

Atoms are small particles that form the building blocks of matter, the smallest complete units of which all matter is made. To visualize the size of an atom, one can think of placing millions of them on the sharpened end of a pencil and still have room for many more. Everything about us, everything we can see and touch, is made of atoms—the food we eat, the atmosphere, the water in the ocean, the smoke coming out of a chimney.

Despite the fact that the atom is such a tiny particle, it has been carefully studied and has been found to have a definite structure. At the center of the atom is a nucleus, which contains positively charged electric particles called **protons** and noncharged particles called **neutrons** (Outside the nucleus, in regions called **orbitals**, are negatively charged particles called **electrons** (Fig. 2-1).

The protons and electrons always are equal in number in any atom. Collectively, they are responsible for all of the atom's characteristics. The neutrons and protons are tightly bound in the nucleus, contributing nearly all of the atom's weight. The positively charged protons keep the negatively charged electrons in the orbital area around the nucleus because of the opposite charge the particles possess. Positively (+) charged protons attract negatively (−) charged electrons. The electrons contribute important chemical characteristics to the atom.

Most atoms have several orbitals of electrons. However, each orbital can hold only two electrons. The orbitals are arranged into energy levels. Energy levels are identified by their distance from the nucleus of the atom. The first energy level, the one closest to the nucleus, is composed of one orbital. The second energy level, the next in distance away from the nucleus, can have four orbitals. Since each orbital contains two electrons, the second energy level has the capacity to hold eight electrons. The electrons farthest away from the nucleus are the particles that give the atom its chemical characteristics.

If the outermost energy level has more than four electrons but fewer than its capacity of eight, the atom normally completes this level by gaining electrons. Such an atom is called a **nonmetal**. The oxygen atom illustrated in Figure 2-1 has six electrons in its second, or outermost, level. When oxygen enters into chemical reactions, its chemical behavior is to gain two electrons. The oxygen atom then has two more electrons than protons. If the outermost shell has fewer than four electrons, the atom normally loses those electrons to attain a complete outer energy level. Such an atom is called a **metal**.

☰ Elements, Molecules, and Compounds

Atoms are the fundamental units that make up the chemical **elements** from which all matter is made. An element is a substance that cannot be decomposed—that is, changed into something else—by physical means (*e.g.,* by the use of heat, pressure, or electricity). Examples of elements include various gases, such as hydrogen, oxygen, and nitrogen; liquids, such as the mercury used in thermometers and blood pressure instruments; and many solids, such as iron, aluminum, gold, silver, and carbon. Graphite (the so-called lead in a pencil), coal, charcoal, and diamonds are examples of the element carbon. The entire universe is made up of about 105 elements.

Elements can be identified by their names, their symbols, or their atomic numbers. Chemists use sym-

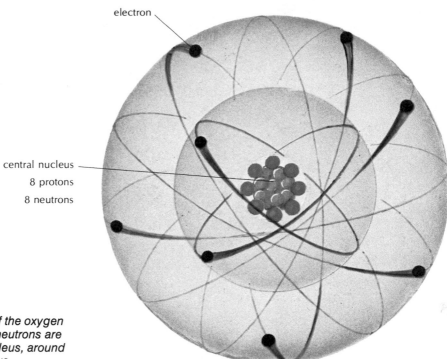

electron

central nucleus
8 protons
8 neutrons

Figure 2-1. *Representation of the oxygen atom. Eight protons and eight neutrons are tightly bound in the central nucleus, around which the eight electrons revolve.*

bols as a shorthand method to name elements. The atomic number of an element is equal to the number of protons that are present in the nucleus. Since the number of protons is equal to the number of electrons in an atom, the atomic number also identifies the number of electrons whirling about the nucleus. Table 2-1 lists some elements found in the human body.

When, on the basis of electron structure, two or more atoms unite, a **molecule** is formed. A molecule can be made of like atoms—the oxygen molecule is made of two identical atoms—but more often it is made of two or more different atoms. For example, a molecule of water (H_2O) contains 1 atom of oxygen (O) and 2 atoms of hydrogen (H) (Fig. 2-2). Substances that contain molecules formed by the union of two or more different atoms are called **compounds**. Compounds may be made of a few elements in a simple combination; for example, the gas carbon monoxide (CO) contains 1 atom of carbon (C) and 1 atom of oxygen (O). Alternatively, compounds may be very complex; some proteins, for example, have thousands of atoms.

It is interesting to observe how different a com-

pound is from any of its constituents. For example, a molecule of liquid water is formed from oxygen and hydrogen, both of which are gases. Another example is a crystal sugar, glucose ($C_6H_{12}O_6$). Its constituents include 12 atoms of the gas hydrogen, 6 atoms of the

Table 2-1	Common Chemical Elements	
Name	**Symbol**	**Atomic Number**
Hydrogen	H	1
Carbon	C	6
Nitrogen	N	7
Oxygen	O	8
Sodium	Na	11
Phosphorus	P	15
Sulfur	S	16
Chlorine	Cl	17
Potassium	K	19
Iron	Fe	26

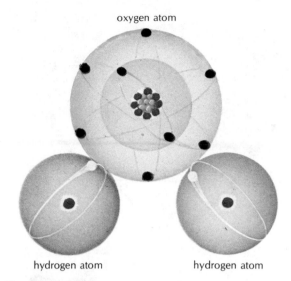

oxygen atom

hydrogen atom   hydrogen atom

Figure 2-2. *Molecule of water.*

gas oxygen, and 6 atoms of the solid element carbon. In this case, the component gases and the solid carbon do not in any way resemble the glucose.

More about Water

Water is the most abundant compound in the body. No plant or animal, including the human, can live very long without it. Water is of critical importance in all physiologic processes in body tissues. Water carries substances to and from the cells and makes possible the essential processes of absorption, exchange, secretion, and excretion. What are some of the properties of water that make it such an ideal medium for living cells?

1 Water can dissolve many different substances in large amounts. For this reason it is called the **universal solvent**. All the materials needed by the body, such as gases, minerals, and nutrients, dissolve in water to be carried from place to place in the body.

2 Water is very stable as a liquid at ordinary temperatures. Water does not freeze until the temperature drops to 0°C (32°F) and does not boil until the temperature reaches 100°C (212°F). This stability provides a constant environment for body cells. Water can also be used to distribute heat throughout the body and to cool the body by evaporation of sweat from the body surface.

3 Water participates in chemical reactions in the body. It is needed directly in the process of digestion and in many of the metabolic reactions that occur in the cells.

Mixtures, Solutions, and Suspensions

It is fortunate that not all elements or compounds combine chemically when brought together. If such were the case, we would be unable to keep intact the hundred or so different compounds in blood plasma while it is dried or frozen. Dried (powdered) plasma may be sent long distances easily and inexpensively. It may then be reconstituted by the addition of sterile water as it is needed in a war zone or at the scene of a major disaster. The many valuable compounds in the plasma remain separate entities with their own properties. Such combinations are called **mixtures**— blends of two or more substances. A mixture, such as salt water, in which the component substances remain evenly distributed is called a **solution**. The dissolving substance, in this case water, is the **solvent**; the substance dissolved, in this case salt, is the **solute**.

In some mixtures, the material distributed in the solvent settles out unless it is constantly shaken; this type of mixture is called a **suspension**. Settling occurs in a suspension because the particles in the mixture are large and heavy. Examples of suspensions are milk of magnesia, india ink, and, in the body, red blood cells suspended in blood plasma.

One other type of mixture is of importance in the body. In a **colloidal suspension**, the particles do not dissolve but remain distributed in the solvent because they are so small. The fluid that fills the cells (cytoplasm) is a colloidal suspension, as is blood plasma.

≡ Chemical Bonds

Ionic Bonds and Electrolytes

When discussing the structure of the atom, we mentioned the positively charged (+) protons that are located in the nucleus, with the corresponding number of negatively charged (−) electrons found in the surrounding space and neutralizing the protons. If a single electron were removed from the sodium atom, it would leave one proton not neutralized, and the atom would have a positive charge (Na^+). This actually happens during a chemical change. Similarly, atoms can gain electrons so that there are more electrons than protons. Chlorine, which has seven electrons in its outermost energy level, tends to gain one electron to fill the level to its capacity. Such an atom of chlorine is negatively charged (Cl⁻) (Fig. 2-3). An atom with a positive or negative charge is called an ion. An ion that is positively charged is a **cation**, while a negatively charged ion is an **anion**.

Let us imagine a sodium atom coming in contact with a chlorine atom. The chlorine atom gains an electron from the sodium atom, and the two newly formed ions (Na⁺ and Cl⁻), because of their opposite charges, which attract each other, cling together and produce the compound sodium chloride, ordinary table salt. A bond formed by this method of electron transfer is called an **ionic bond** (Fig. 2-4).

In the fluids and cells of the body, ions make it possible for materials to be altered, broken down, and recombined to form new substances. Calcium ions (Ca⁺⁺) are necessary for the clotting of blood, the normal relaxation of muscle, and the health of bone tissue. Bicarbonate ions (HCO₃⁻) are required

for the regulation of acidity and alkalinity of the tissues. The stable condition of the normal organism, homeostasis, is influenced by ions (see Chap. 1).

Compounds that form ions whenever they are in solution are called **electrolytes** (e-lek′tro-lites). Electrolytes are responsible for the acidity and the alkalinity of solutions. They also include a variety of mineral salts, such as sodium and potassium chloride. Electrolytes must be present in exactly the right quantities in the fluid within the cell (intracellular) and outside the cell (extracellular), or there will be very damaging effects, preventing the cells in the body from functioning properly.

Because ions are charged particles, electrolytes can conduct an electric current. Records of electric currents in tissues are valuable indications of the functioning or malfunctioning of tissues and organs. The **electrocardiogram** (e-lek″tro-kar′de-o-gram) and the **electroencephalogram** (e-lek″tro-en-sef′ah-lo-gram) are graphic tracings of the electric currents generated by the heart muscle and the brain, respectively (see Chaps. 9 and 13).

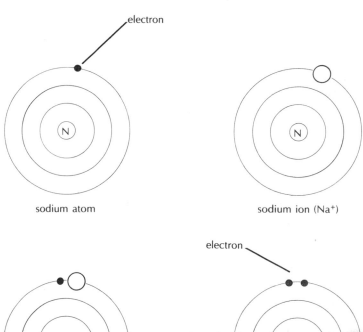

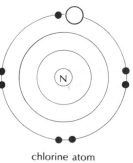

Figure 2-3. *Formation of Na⁺ cation and Cl⁻ anion.*

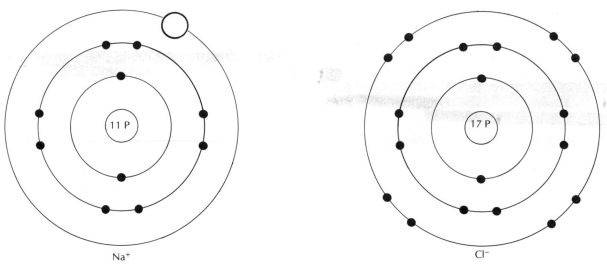

Figure 2-4. *A sodium ion with 11 protons in the nucleus and 10 electrons in orbitals is attracted to a chlorine ion with 17 protons in the nucleus and 18 electrons in orbitals to form the compound sodium chloride.*

Covalent Bonds

Although many chemical compounds are formed by ionic bonds, a much larger number are formed by another type of chemical bond. This type of bond involves not the exchange of electrons but a sharing of electrons between the atoms in the molecule. The electrons orbit around both of the atoms in the bond to make both of them stable. The electrons may be equally shared, as in the case of a hydrogen molecule (H_2), or they may be held closer to one atom than the other, as in the case of water (H_2O), shown in Figure 2-2. These bonds are called **covalent bonds**. Covalently bonded compounds do not conduct an electric current in solution. Carbon, the element that is the basis of organic chemistry, forms covalent bonds. Thus, the compounds that are characteristic of living things are covalently bonded compounds. Covalent bonds may involve the sharing of one, two, or three pairs of electrons between atoms.

≡ Acids, Bases, and Buffers

An **acid** is a chemical substance capable of donating a proton as a hydrogen ion (H^+) to another substance. A common example is hydrochloric acid, the acid found in stomach juices:

$$HCl \longrightarrow H^+ + Cl^-$$
hydrochloric   hydrogen   chlorine
acid   ion   ion

A **base** is a chemical substance, usually a hydroxide ion (OH^-), that can accept a proton. Sodium hydroxide, which releases hydroxide ion in solution, is an example of a base:

$$NaOH \longrightarrow Na^+ + OH^-$$
sodium   sodium   hydroxide
hydroxide   ion   ion

A reaction between an acid and a base produces a **salt**, such as sodium chloride:

$$HCl + NaOH \longrightarrow NaCl + H_2O$$

The greater the concentration of hydrogen ions in a solution, the greater is the acidity of that solution. As the concentration of hydrogen ions becomes less than it is in pure water, the more alkaline (basic) the solution becomes. Acidity is indicated by pH units, which represent the concentration of hydrogen ions in a solution. These units are listed on a scale from 0 to 14, with 0 being the most acidic and 14 being the most basic (Fig. 2-5).

A pH of 7.0 is neutral, having an equal number of hydrogen and hydroxide ions. Each pH unit on the scale represents a tenfold change in the number of hydrogen and hydroxide ions present. A solution registering 5.0 on the scale has 10 times the number of hydrogen ions as a solution that registers 6.0. A solution registering 9.0 has one tenth the number of hydrogen ions and 10 times the number of hydroxide ions as one registering 8.0. Thus, the lower the pH

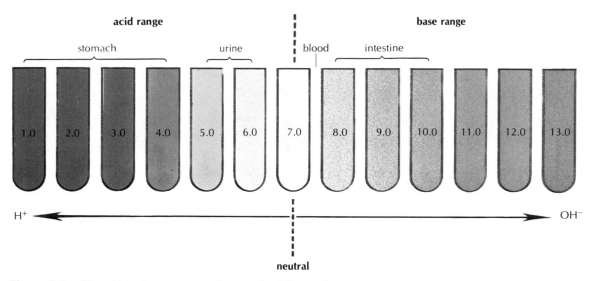

Figure 2-5. *The pH scale measures degree of acidity or alkalinity.*

rating, the greater is the acidity, and the higher the *p*H, the greater is the alkalinity. Blood is only slightly alkaline, with a *p*H range of 7.35 to 7.45, or nearly neutral.

A delicate balance exists in the acidity or alkalinity of body fluids. If a person is to remain healthy, these chemical characteristics must remain within narrow limits. The substances responsible for the balanced chemical state are the acids, bases, and buffers. **Buffers** form a chemical system that prevents sharp changes in hydrogen ion concentration and thus maintains a relatively constant *p*H. Buffers are very important in maintaining the stability of body fluids.

Radioactivity

No discussion of atoms is complete without reference to the part some play in the diagnosis and treatment of disease. Atoms of an element may exist in several forms, called **isotopes**. These forms are alike in their chemical reactions but different in weight, like heavy oxygen and regular oxygen. The greater weight of the heavier isotopes is due to the presence of one or more extra neutrons in the nucleus. Some isotopes are stable and maintain a constant character. Others disintegrate (fall apart) as they give off small particles and rays; these are said to be **radioactive**. Radioactive elements may occur naturally, as is the case with such very heavy isotopes as radium and uranium. Others may be produced artificially from nonradioactive elements such as iodine and gold by

bombardment (smashing) of the atoms in special machines.

The rays given off by some radioactive elements have the ability to penetrate and destroy tissues and so are used in the treatment of cancer. Radiation therapy is often given by means of special machines (such as linear accelerators) that are able to release particles to destroy tumors. The sensitivity of the younger and the dividing cells in a growing cancer allows selective destruction of the abnormal cells with a minimum of damage to normal tissues. Modern radiation instruments produce tremendous amounts of energy (in the multimillion electron-volt range) and yet can destroy deep-seated cancers without causing serious skin reactions.

Radioactive isotopes, such as cobalt 60, in the form of pellets, may be sealed in stainless steel cylinders. These cylinders are mounted on arms or cranes that permit the proper alignment for directing the beams through a porthole to the area to be treated.

In the form of needles, seeds, or tubes, implants containing radioactive isotopes are widely used in the treatment of many types of cancer.

In addition to its therapeutic values, irradiation is extensively used in diagnosis. X rays penetrate tissues and produce an impression of their interior on a photographic plate. Radioactive iodine and other "tracers" taken orally or injected into the bloodstream are used to diagnose abnormalities of several body organs. Rigid precautions must be followed by hospital personnel to protect themselves and the patient when using irradiation in diagnosis or therapy because the rays can destroy healthy as well as diseased tissues.

The Chemistry of Living Matter

Of the 100 or more elements that have been found in nature, only a relatively small number, and those the lighter ones, are important components of living cells. Hydrogen, oxygen, carbon, and nitrogen are the elements that make up about 99% of the cells. Calcium, sodium, potassium, phosphorus, sulfur, chlorine, and magnesium are the seven elements that make up most of the remaining 1% of tissue elements. A number of others are present in trace amounts, such as iron, copper, iodine, and fluorine.

The chemical compounds that characterize living things are called **organic compounds.** All of these contain the element **carbon.** Since carbon can combine with a variety of different elements and can even bond to other carbon atoms to form long chains, most organic compounds are composed of large, complex molecules. The starch found in potatoes, the fat in the tissue under the skin, and many drugs are examples of organic compounds. These large molecules are often formed from simpler molecules called *building blocks,* which bond together in long chains. The main types of organic compounds are carbohydrates, fats, and proteins. All three contain carbon, hydrogen, and oxygen as their main ingredients.

Organic Compounds

Carbohydrates are the simple sugars, called **monosaccharides** (mon″o-sak′ah-rides), or molecules made from simple sugars linked together. Carbohydrates in the form of sugars and starches are important sources of energy in the diet. Examples of carbohydrates in the body are the glucose that circulates in the blood as food for the cells and a storage form of glucose called **glycogen.**

Fats, or **lipids,** are also stored for energy in the body. In addition, they provide insulation and protection for the body organs. Fats are made from a substance called **glycerol** (glycerine) in combination with fatty acids. A group of complex lipids containing phosphorus, called **phospholipids** (fos′fo-lip″ids), is important in the body. Among other things, phospholipids make up a major part of the membrane around living cells.

All proteins contain, in addition to carbon, hydrogen, and oxygen, the element **nitrogen.** They may also contain sulfur and phosphorus. Proteins are composed of building blocks called **amino** (ah-me′no) **acids.** Although there are only about twenty different amino acids found in the body, a vast number of proteins can be made by linking them together in different combinations. Proteins are the structural materials of the body, found in muscle, bone, and connective tissue. They also make up the pigments that give hair, eyes, and skin their color. It is the proteins in each individual that makes him or her physically distinct from others. All three categories of organic compounds, in addition to minerals and vitamins, must be taken in as part of a normal diet. These will be discussed further in Chapters 18 and 19.

Enzymes

An important group of proteins are the **enzymes.** Enzymes function as **catalysts** in the hundreds of reactions that occur in metabolism. A catalyst is a substance that speeds up the rate of a reaction but is not changed or used up in that reaction. Each chemical reaction in the body requires a specific enzyme to occur, so enzymes really control the metabolism of the cells. Some of the vitamins and minerals needed in the diet are important because they make up parts of enzymes.

Summary

I **Atoms**—basic units of matter that make up the various elements on earth
  A Structure
    1 Protons—positively charged particles in the nucleus
    2 Neutrons—neutral particles in the nucleus
    3 Electrons—negatively charged particles in energy levels around the nucleus
II **Molecules**—combinations of two or more atoms
  A Compounds—combinations of different atoms (*e.g.,* water)
III **Mixtures**—blends of two or more substances
  A Solution—substance (solute) remains evenly distributed in solvent (*e.g.,* salt in water)
  B Suspension—material settles out of mixture on standing (*e.g.,* red cells in blood plasma)
  C Colloidal suspension—particles do not dissolve but remain suspended (*e.g.,* cytoplasm)

IV **Chemical bonds**
  A Ionic bonds—atoms exchange electrons to become stable
  B Covalent bonds—atoms share electrons to become stable
V **pH scale**—goes from 0 to 14
  A Acid—donates protons (hydrogen ions)
  B Base—accepts protons (usually is a hydroxide ion)
  C Salt—formed by reaction between acid and base
  D Buffer—maintains constant pH of a solution
VI **Radioactive elements** (isotopes)
  A Diagnosis
  B Cancer therapy
  C X-ray films
VII **Organic compounds**—contain carbon, hydrogen, and oxygen
  A Carbohydrates
  B Lipids (*e.g.,* fats)
  C Proteins
    1 Enzymes

Questions for Study and Review

1 Define *chemistry* and tell something about what is included in this study.

2 What are atoms and what is known of their structure?

3 Define *molecule, element, compound,* and *mixture.*

4 What is an element and what are some examples of elements?

5 Why is water so important to life?

6 How does a mixture differ from a compound? Give two examples of each.

7 You dissolve a teaspoon of sugar in a cup of tea. Which is the solute? the solvent?

8 What are ions and how are they related to electrolytes? What are some examples of ions and of what importance are they in the body?

9 Explain how covalent bonds are formed. Give two examples of covalently bonded compounds.

10 What would a pH reading of 6.5 indicate about a solution? 8.5? 7.0?

11 What is meant by *radioactivity* and what are some of its practical uses?

12 What are organic compounds and what element is found in all of them?

13 What elements are found in the largest amounts in living cells?

14 What are the building blocks of carbohydrates? fats? proteins?

15 What are enzymes? What type of organic compound are they?

3

Cells and Their Functions

Behavioral Objectives

After careful study of this chapter, you should be able to:

List three types of microscopes used to study cells

Describe the function and composition of cytoplasm

Name and describe the main organelles in the cell

Give the composition, location, and function of DNA in the cell

Give the location and function of RNA in the cell

Explain briefly how cells make proteins

Describe briefly the steps in cell division

List four methods by which substances enter and leave cells

Explain what will happen if cells are placed in solutions with the same or different concentrations than the cell

Define cancer

List several causes of cancer

Selected Key Terms

The following terms are defined in the glossary:

active transport
cancer
cell membrane
centriole
chromosome
cytoplasm
diffusion
DNA
isotonic
micrometer
mitochondria
mitosis
mutation
nucleus
organelle
osmosis
phagocytosis
ribosome
RNA

As noted in Chapter 1, the cell is the basic unit of all life. It is the simplest structure that shows all the characteristics of life: growth, metabolism, responsiveness, reproduction, and homeostasis. In fact, it is possible for a single cell to live independently of other cells. Examples of such independent cells are some of the organisms that produce disease (to be studied in Chap. 5) and other microscopic organisms. All the activities of the human body, composed of millions of cells, result from the activities of individual cells. Any materials produced within the body are produced by cells.

The scientific study of cells began some 350 years ago with the invention by Anton van Leeuwenhoek of the microscope. In time, this single-lens microscope was replaced by the modern compound light microscope, which has two sets of lenses. This is the type in use in most laboratories. In recent years, a great boon to cell biologists has been the development of the **transmission electron microscope**, which by a combination of magnification and enlargement of the resulting image affords magnification to 1 million times or more (Fig. 3-1). Another type, the **scanning electron microscope**, does not magnify as much ($\times 250,000$) but gives a three-dimensional picture of an object.

Before they are examined under the microscope, cells and tissues are usually colored with special dyes called **stains** to aid in viewing. These stains produce the variety of colors you see when looking at pictures of cells and tissues taken under a microscope. The metric unit used for microscopic measurements is the **micrometer** (mi′kro-mee-ter). This unit is 1/1000 of a millimeter and is symbolized with a Greek letter as μm.

☰ The Organelles

Just as the body has different organs to carry out special functions, the cell contains specialized subdivisions within it that perform different functions. These structures are called **organelles**, which means "little organs." Each of these will be examined in turn (Fig. 3-2).

The outer covering of the cell is the **cell membrane**. This membrane is composed of two layers of lipid molecules in which float a variety of different proteins and a small amount of carbohydrates. The proteins may act as receptors, that is, points of attachment for materials coming to the cell in the blood; they may also act as carriers, shuttling materials into or out of the cell. The cell membrane is very important in regulating what can enter and leave the cell.

The main substance that fills the cell and holds the organelles is the **cytoplasm** (si′to-plazm). This is a colloidal suspension of water, food, minerals, enzymes, and other specialized materials. Although the composition of the cytoplasm has been analyzed, no one has been able to produce it in a laboratory; there must be something about the organization of these substances that has not yet been discovered.

The largest organelle is the **nucleus** (nu′kle-us). This is often called the *control center* of the cell because it contains the genetic material, which governs all of the activities of the cell, including cell reproduction. Within the nucleus is a smaller globule called the **nucleolus** (nu-kle′o-lus), which means "little nucleus." Its functions are not entirely understood, but it is believed to act in the manufacture of proteins within the cell. The actual formation of proteins occurs in small bodies called **ribosomes** (ri′bo-somes). These may be loose in the cytoplasm or attached to a network of membranes throughout the cell called the **endoplasmic reticulum** (en-do-plas′mik re-tik′u-lum). The name literally means "network" (reticulum) "within the cytoplasm" (endoplasmic), but for ease it is almost always called simply the *ER*. The areas of the ER to which ribosomes are attached are described as "rough" ER because they have an uneven, granular appearance; where no ribosomes are attached, the ER is described as "smooth."

Fairly large and important organelles are the **mitochondria** (mi-to-kon′dre-ah). These are round or bean-shaped structures with folded membranes on the inside. Within the mitochondria food is converted to energy for the cell in the form of ATP. These are the "power plants" of the cell. Active cells have large numbers of mitochondria. Other organelles in a typical cell include the **centrioles**, rod-shaped bodies near the nucleus that function in cell division, **lysosomes** (li′so-somes), which contain digestive enzymes, and the **Golgi** (gol′jee) **Apparatus**, which formulates special substances, such as mucus, released from cells. All of these cell structures are summarized in Table 3-1 for easy study.

Although the basic structure of all body cells is the same, individual cells may vary widely in size, shape, and composition according to the function of

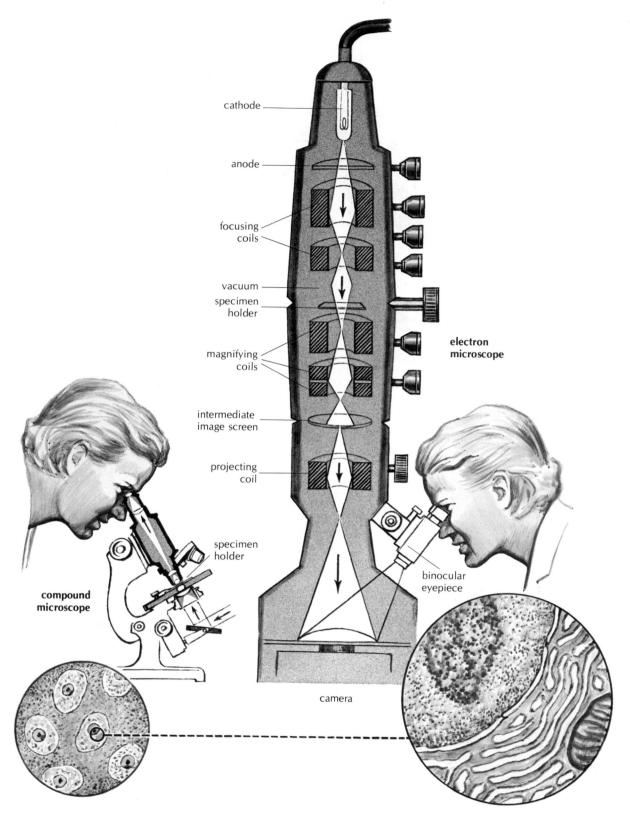

cathode

anode

focusing
coils

vacuum

specimen
holder

magnifying
coils

intermediate
image screen

projecting
coil

electron
microscope

specimen
holder

binocular
eyepiece

compound
microscope

camera

Figure 3-1. *A simplified comparison of an optical (compound) microscope and an electron microscope.*

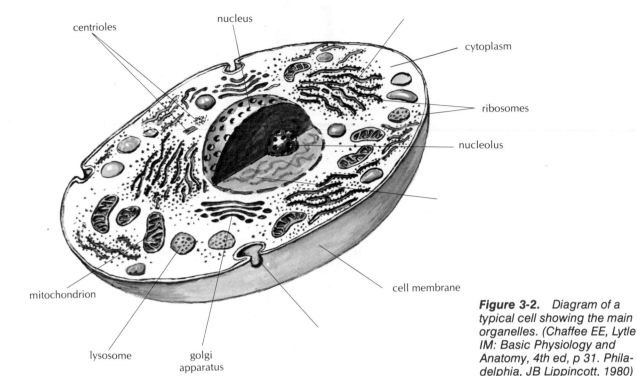

centrioles

nucleus

cytoplasm

ribosomes

nucleolus

cell membrane

mitochondrion

lysosome

golgi apparatus

Figure 3-2. *Diagram of a typical cell showing the main organelles. (Chaffee EE, Lytle IM: Basic Physiology and Anatomy, 4th ed, p 31. Philadelphia, JB Lippincott, 1980)*

each. In size they may range from the 7 μm of a red blood cell to the 200 μm or more of a muscle cell. A neuron with its long fibers is much different in appearance from a muscle cell or from a transparent cell in the clear lens of the eye. Most human cells have all of the organelles described, but these may vary in number. Some cells have small, hairlike projections from the surface called **cilia** (si′le-ah), which wave to create movement around the cell. The cells that line the passageways of the respiratory and reproductive tracts are examples. A long, whiplike projection from the cell is a **flagellum** (fla-jel′lum). Each human sperm cell has a flagellum that is used for locomotion. Thus, each cell is specialized for its own particular function.

≡ Cell Functions

Protein Synthesis

Since protein molecules play an indispensable part in the body's activities, we need to identify the cellular substances that direct the production of protein. In the cytoplasm and in the nucleus are chemicals called

nucleic (nu-kle′-ik) **acids.** The two nucleic acids important in protein production are **ribonucleic** (ri′bo-nu-kle″ik) **acid,** abbreviated **RNA,** and **deoxyribonucleic** (de-ok′se-ri′bo-nu-kle″ik) **acid,** or **DNA.** Both of these are large, complex molecules composed of subunits called **nucleotides** (nu′kle-o-tides).

DNA molecules are found mostly in the nucleus of the cell, where they make up the **chromosomes** (kro′mo-somes), dark-staining threadlike bodies. These threads of DNA are arranged in double spirals (Fig. 3-3). The two strands of each double spiral are held by hydrogen bonds, weak bonds formed by the sharing of a hydrogen atom between two other atoms. Specific regions of the DNA in the chromosomes make up the **genes,** the hereditary factors of each cell. It is the genes that carry the messages for the development of particular inherited characteristics, such as brown eyes or curly hair. For this reason, the nucleus is considered the cell's control center and DNA is considered the master blueprint.

A blueprint is only a map. The directions it illustrates must be translated into appropriate actions. RNA is the substance needed for this step. RNA is much like DNA except that it is a single strand and

Table 3-1 Organelles

Organelle	Description	Function
Cell membrane	Outer layer of the cell; composed mainly of lipids and proteins	Limits the cell; holds cell contents; regulates what enters and leaves the cell
Nucleus	Large, dark-staining body near the center of the cell; composed of DNA and proteins	Contains the chromosomes with the genes (the hereditary material that directs all cell activities)
Nucleolus	Small body in the nucleus; composed of RNA, DNA, and protein	Needed for protein manufacture
Endoplasmic reticulum (ER)	Network of membranes in the cytoplasm	Used for storage and transport; holds ribosomes
Ribosomes	Small bodies in the cytoplasm or attached to the ER; composed of RNA and protein	Manufacture proteins
Mitochondria	Large organelles with folded membranes inside	Manufacture energy as ATP from food
Golgi apparatus	Layers of membranes	Put together special substances such as mucus
Lysosomes	Small sacs of digestive enzymes	Digest substances within the cell
Centrioles	Rod-shaped bodies (usually 2) near the nucleus	Help separate the chromosomes in cell division
Cilia	Short, hairlike projections from the cell	Create movement around the cell
Flagella	Long, whiplike projections from the cell	Move the cell

differs by one type of nucleotide in its chemical makeup. RNA carries the DNA message and transmits it to the organelles responsible for protein synthesis, the ribosomes in the cytoplasm and on the ER. The ribosomes are so named because they are composed mainly of RNA. DNA sends the code by breaking its hydrogen bonds and uncoiling into single strands. The sequence of nucleotides on the single strand of DNA contains the map for the production of a particular protein. When the DNA uncoils and reveals its sequence of nucleotides, RNA copies the message and carries it to the ribosomes. Here the message is decoded to produce chains of amino acids, the building blocks of protein.

Cell Division

To ensure that every cell in the body has similar genetic information, cell reproduction occurs by a dividing process called **mitosis** (my-to′sis). The original parent cell divides to form two identical daughter cells.

Before every cell division, changes must occur in the nucleus. DNA uncoils from its double-stranded spiral form and each strand duplicates itself according to the pattern of the nucleotides. As mitosis begins, the strands return to their spiral organization and become visible under the microscope as the dark, threadlike chromosomes. Because each chromosome has doubled itself, there are now two sets of chromosomes. These soon separate to supply identical information to each of the future daughter cells.

Meanwhile, in the cytoplasm, the two centrioles move to opposite ends of the cell, trailing very thin threadlike substances that form a structure resembling a spindle stretched across the cell. Then the chromosomes line up in the nuclear area across the threadlike spindle, and the duplicated chromosomes begin to move toward opposite ends of the cell. As mitosis continues, the nuclear area becomes pinched in the middle until two nuclear regions have formed. A similar change occurs in the cell membrane, making the cell resemble a dumbbell. The midsection between the two halves of the dumbbell becomes progressively smaller until, finally, the cell splits in two. There are now two identical daughter cells, which are themselves identical to, but smaller than, the parent cell (Fig. 3-4). The two new cells will grow and mature and continue to carry out life functions.

During mitosis, all of the organelles, except those needed for the division process, temporarily disap-pear. After the cell splits, these organelles reappear in each daughter cell. Also at this time, the centrioles usually duplicate in preparation for the next cell divi-sion.

Some body cells reproduce more readily than others. Some, such as nerve cells and muscle cells, stop dividing at some point in development and are

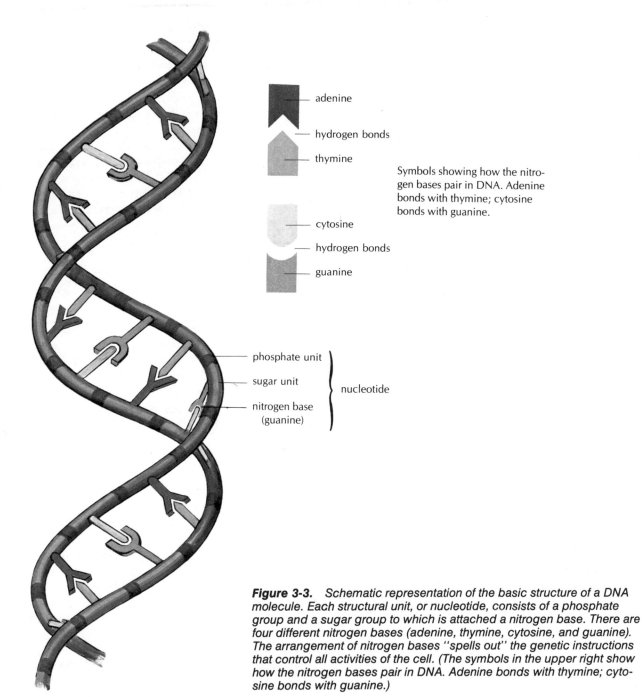

adenine

hydrogen bonds

thymine

Symbols showing how the nitro-gen bases pair in DNA. Adenine bonds with thymine; cytosine bonds with guanine.

cytosine

hydrogen bonds

guanine

phosphate unit

sugar unit

nitrogen base (guanine)

nucleotide

Figure 3-3. *Schematic representation of the basic structure of a DNA molecule. Each structural unit, or nucleotide, consists of a phosphate group and a sugar group to which is attached a nitrogen base. There are four different nitrogen bases (adenine, thymine, cytosine, and guanine). The arrangement of nitrogen bases "spells out" the genetic instructions that control all activities of the cell. (The symbols in the upper right show how the nitrogen bases pair in DNA. Adenine bonds with thymine; cyto-sine bonds with guanine.)*

not replaced if they die. On the other hand, many thousands of new cells are formed daily in the skin and other tissues to replace those destroyed by injury, disease, or certain natural processes. As a person ages, characteristic changes in the overall activity of his or her body cells take place. One example of these is the slowing down of repair processes. The fracture of a bone, for example, takes considerably longer to heal in an aged person than in a young one.

Movement of Substances Across the Cell Membrane

In order to function, cells require food. How to receive this nourishment would seem to be a problem, since most cells are surrounded by a protective membrane. However, if a cell is bathed in a liquid containing dissolved food materials, an interesting thing happens: the liquid with the dissolved food particles passes through the cell membrane. Not only do the dissolved nutrient molecules pass in, but waste products pass out of the cell in the opposite direction, enabling the cell to perform the function of elimination. The membrane also keeps valuable proteins and other substances from leaving the cell and prevents the admission of undesirable substances. For this reason, the cell membrane is classified as a **semipermeable** (sem″e-per′me-ah-b'l) membrane. It is permeable or passable to some molecules but impassable to others.

Water, a tiny molecule, is always able to penetrate the membrane. In contrast, certain sugars, such as sucrose, cannot pass through because their molecules are too large, even though readily soluble; so, by the process of digestion, sucrose is converted to glucose, which is a smaller molecule and therefore can diffuse through the membrane.

Various physical processes are responsible for exchanges through cell membranes or through tissue membranes, which are made up of many cells. Some of these processes are listed here:

1 **Diffusion,** the constant movement of molecules from a region of relatively higher concentration to one of lower concentration. Molecules, especially those in solution, tend to spread throughout an area until they are equally concentrated in all parts of the container (Figs. 3-5 and 3-6).

2 **Osmosis,** the diffusion of water through a semipermeable membrane, with the water molecules going from the less concentrated solution to the more concentrated solution. The dissolved molecules in the more concentrated solution "pull" the water molecules from the less concentrated solution across the semipermeable membrane. The tendency of a solution to pull water into it is called the **osmotic pressure** of the solution. It is directly related to the concentration of solutes in the solution. The higher the concentration of the solution, the greater is its tendency to pull water into it.

As already stated, water moves easily through

Figure 3-4. *Mitosis. The two centrioles migrate, the chromatin material of the nucleus changes into threadlike chromosomes, and two daughter cells form within the cell membrane. (The cell shown is for illustration only. It is not a human cell, which has 46 chromosomes.)*

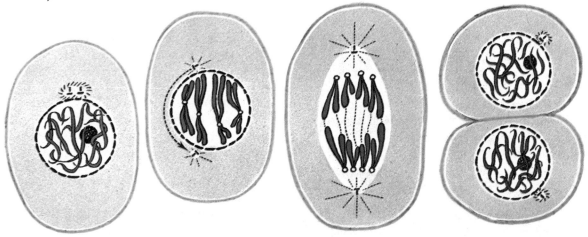

Figure 3-5. *Diffusion of gaseous molecules throughout a given space. Regardless of whether a bottle contains perfume, a spray of some kind, or a chlorine bleach, there is a tendency for the molecules to spread throughout the area.*

the cell membrane. Therefore, for a normal balance to be maintained, all cells must be kept in solutions that have the same concentration of molecules as the fluids on the inside of the cell—the intracellular fluids. Such solutions are described as **isotonic**. An isotonic solution for body cells contains approximately 0.9% salt. Tissue fluids, blood plasma, and physiologic (normal) saline are isotonic for body cells.

A solution that is less concentrated than the intracellular fluid is described as **hypotonic**. A cell placed in a hypotonic solution draws water in, swells, and may burst. When this occurs to a red blood cell, the cell is said to **hemolyze** (he'mo-lize). If a cell is placed in a **hypertonic** solution, which is more concentrated than the cell fluids, it loses water to the surrounding fluids and shrinks. One consequence of this ionic distribution is described by the saying, "Where salt is, water follows" (Fig. 3-7). When the body retains salt, large amounts of water may also be retained. The largest amount of this water re-

mains in the extracellular fluid spaces, producing a condition called **edema** (e-dee'mah). If the body excretes large amounts of salt, water will also be lost. This process may lead to a condition called **dehydration**. Body fluids are discussed in more detail in Chapter 20.

3 **Filtration,** the passage of water containing dissolved materials through a membrane as a result of a mechanical ("pushing") force on one side (Fig. 3-8). Normally, large particles cannot pass through an intact membrane (Fig. 3-9). An example of filtration in the human body is the formation of urine in the microscopic functional units of the kidney as described in Chapter 20.

4 **Active transport.** Often molecules move into or out of a living cell in an opposite direction from the way in which they would normally flow by diffusion. That is, they move from an area where they are in relatively lower concentration to an area where they are in higher concentration. This movement, because it is against the natural flow, requires energy in the form of ATP. It also

Figure 3-6. *Diffusion of a solid and a liquid. The solid diffuses into the water; the water diffuses into the solid; the molecules of the solid tend to spread throughout the water.*

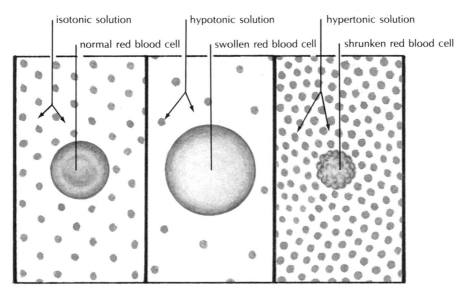

Figure 3-7. *Osmosis. Water molecules moving through a red blood cell membrane in three different concentrations of fluid. (Left) The normal saline solution has a concentration nearly the same as that inside the cell, and water molecules move into and out of the cell at the same rate. (Center) The dilute solution causes the cell to swell and eventually hemolyze (burst) because of the large number of water molecules moving into the cell. (Right) The concentrated solution causes the water molecules to move out of the cell, leaving it shrunken.*

requires proteins in the cell membrane that act as **carriers** for the molecules. This process, called **active transport**, is a function of the living cell membrane. It allows the cell to take in what it needs from the surrounding fluids and to release materials from the cell. Because the cell membrane can carry on active transport, it is most accurately described as **selectively permeable**. It regulates what can enter and leave the cell based on the needs of the cell.

5 **Phagocytosis and pinocytosis.** The cell membrane can also surround fairly large particles or droplets and move them into the cell. The engulfing of large particles is called **phagocytosis**

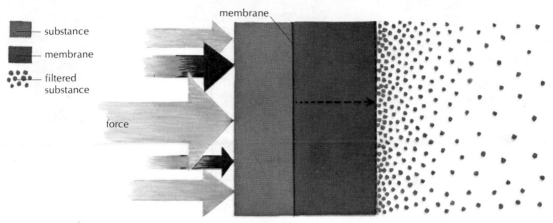

Figure 3-8.   *Filtration. A mechanical force pushes a substance through a membrane.*

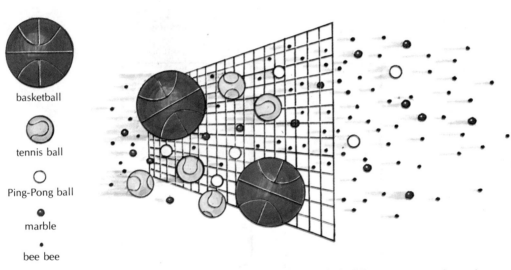

Figure 3-9.   *Filtration. Large objects (basketballs and tennis balls) cannot pass through the net. In the human body, large particles (proteins and blood cells) do not pass through intact membranes.*

(fag″o-si-to′sis). Certain white blood cells carry out phagocytosis to rid the body of foreign material and dead cells. The intake of smaller particles and droplets is called **pinocytosis** (pi″no-si-to′sis).

☰ Cells and Cancer

In the study of cells we gain some insight into the laws of growth. For reasons that remain obscure, cells develop various forms, and those that are of the same kind congregate to form one of the basic tissues. These tissues, in turn, become the specialized or-

gans. In the early stages of the body's development the cells multiply rapidly, and hence the body grows until a point of maximum growth has been reached. From here on, cell division is not so rapid. It continues, however, at a rate sufficient to replace cells that for one reason or another have become used up and discarded. In this manner, the tissues are maintained, and every cell and formation of cells has its purpose.

Occasionally, some change, a **mutation,** occurs in the genetic material of a cell. If such a cell does not die naturally or get destroyed by the immune system, it may begin to multiply out of control and spread to other tissues, producing **cancer**. Cancer cells form tumors, which interfere with normal functions, crowding out normal cells and robbing them of nutrients. There is more information on the various types of tumors in Chapter 4.

The causes of cancer are very complex, involving both the cell and factors in the environment. Much progress has been made in identifying possible causes of cancer, which include the following:

1 **Chemicals.** Certain industrial and environmental chemicals are known to increase the risk of cancer. Any chemical that causes cancer is called a **carcinogen** (car-sin'o-jen). The most common carcinogens in our society are those present in cigarette smoke.

2 **Ionizing radiation.** Certain types of radiation can produce damage to the DNA of cells that may lead to cancer. These include x rays, rays from radioactive substances, and ultraviolet rays. For example, the ultraviolet rays received from exposure to the sun are very harmful to the skin.

3 **Physical irritation.** Continued irritation, such as the intake of hot foods or the contact of a hot pipestem on the lip, increases cell division and thus increases the chance of mutation.

In addition, heredity is a factor. Certain types of cancer occur more frequently in some families than in others indicating that there is some inherited predisposition to the development of cancer. Even in these cases, however, environment plays a part. Because cancer may take a very long time to develop, it is often difficult to identify its cause or causes.

At this point, we are ready to proceed from discussion of the individual cell to the subject of the specialized groups of cells of which our bodies are made. Such groups are known as tissues.

Summary

I Microscopes
  A Types
    1 Compound light microscope
    2 Transmission electron microscope—magnifies up to 1 million times
    3 Scanning electron microscope—gives three-dimensional image
  B Stains—dyes used to aid in viewing cells under the microscope
  C Micrometer—metric unit commonly used for microscopic measurements

II **Organelles**—subdivisions within the cell that carry out special functions
  A Cell membrane
  B Nucleus
  C Nucleolus
  D Ribosomes
  E Endoplasmic reticulum (ER)
  F Mitochondria
  G Centrioles
  H Lysosomes
  I Golgi apparatus
  J Cilia
  K Flagella

III **Cell functions**
  A Protein synthesis—carried out by nucleic acids
    1 DNA—double stranded; located in the nucleus
    2 RNA—single stranded; located in the cytoplasm
  B Cell division—mitosis
    1 Duplication of chromosomes
    2 Movement of centrioles to opposite ends of cell
    3 Formation of spindle (protein threads)
    4 Arrangement of chromosomes across center of spindle
    5 Separation of duplicated chromosomes
    6 Movement of chromosomes to opposite ends of cell
    7 Division of cell
    8 Reappearance of all organelles
  C Movement of substances across cell membrane
    1 Diffusion—molecules move from area of higher concentration to area of lower concentration
    2 Osmosis—diffusion of water through semipermeable membrane
      a Isotonic solution—same concentration as cell
      b Hypotonic solution—lower concentration than cell
      c Hypertonic solution—higher concentration than cell
    3 Filtration—movement of materials through cell membrane under mechanical force
    4 Active transport—movement of molecules from area of lower concentration to area of higher concentration

5 Phagocytosis—engulfing of large particles by cell membrane

6 Pinocytosis—intake of smaller particles and droplets of fluid

IV Cells and cancer

  A Causes

    1 Chemicals

    2 Ionizing radiation

    3 Physical irritation

    4 Heredity

Questions for Study and Review

1 Why is the study of cells so important in the study of the body?

2 Define the term *organelle*. List ten organelles found in cells and give the function of each.

3 Compare DNA and RNA with respect to location in the cell and function.

4 What are chromosomes? Where are they located in the cell and what is their function?

5 Name the process of cell division. What happens to the chromosomes during cell division? to the organelles?

6 List four methods by which materials cross the cell membrane. Which of these requires cellular energy?

7 What substance moves most easily through the cell membrane?

8 What will happen to a red blood cell placed in a 5.0% salt solution? in distilled water?

9 Why is the cell membrane described as selectively permeable?

10 Name three causes of cancer.

4

Tissues, Glands, and Membranes

Behavioral Objectives

After careful study of this chapter, you should be able to:

Name the four main groups of tissues and give the location and general characteristics of each

Describe the difference between exocrine and endocrine glands and give examples of each

Give examples of soft, hard, and liquid connective tissues

Name four types of membranes and give the location and functions of each

Describe two types of epithelial membranes

Explain the difference between benign and malignant tumors and give several examples of each type

List four methods of diagnosing cancer

List four methods of treating cancer

Selected Key Terms

The following terms are defined in the glossary:

adipose
areolar
benign
cartilage
collagen
endocrine
epithelium
exocrine
fascia
histology
malignant
membrane
metastasis
mucosa
myelin
neoplasm
neurilemma
neuroglia
neuron
serosa

Tissues are groups of cells similar in structure and substance, arranged in a characteristic pattern, and specialized for the performance of specific tasks. The study of tissues is known as **histology** (his-to'lo-je). The tissues in our bodies might be compared with the different materials used to construct a building. Think for a moment of the great variety of materials used according to need—wood, stone, steel, plaster, insulation, and so forth. Each of these has different properties, but together they contribute to the building as a whole. The same may be said of tissues in the body.

Tissue Classification

The four main groups of tissue are the following:

1 **Epithelial** (ep-i-the'le-al) **tissue** forms glands, covers surfaces, and lines cavities.
2 **Connective tissue** supports and forms the framework of all parts of the body.
3 **Nerve tissue** conducts nerve impulses.
4 **Muscle tissue** is designed to contract and produce movement.

This chapter concentrates mainly on epithelial and connective tissues; the other types of tissues receive more attention in later chapters.

Epithelial Tissue

Epithelial tissue, or **epithelium** (ep-e-the'le-um), forms a protective covering for the body and all the organs. It is the main tissue of the outer layer of the skin. It forms the lining of the intestinal tract, the respiratory and urinary passages, the blood vessels, the uterus, and other body cavities.

Epithelium has many forms and many purposes, and the cells of which it is composed vary accordingly. Epithelial tissue is classified according to the shape and the arrangement of its cells.

The cells may be

1 **Squamous** (skwa'mus)—flat and irregular
2 **Cuboidal**—square
3 **Columnar**—long and narrow

They may be arranged in a single layer, described as **simple,** or in many layers, termed **stratified.** Thus, a single layer of flat, irregular cells would be described as *simple squamous epithelium,* whereas tissue with many layers of these same cells would be described

as *stratified squamous epithelium.* Examples of these cells are shown in Figure 4-1.

The cells of some kinds of epithelium produce secretions, such as **mucus** (mu'kus) (a clear, sticky fluid), digestive juices, sweat, and other substances. The digestive tract is lined with a special kind of epithelium, the cells of which not only produce secretions but also are designed to absorb digested foods. The air that we breathe passes over yet another form of epithelium that lines the respiratory tract. This lining secretes mucus and is also provided with tiny hairlike projections called **cilia.** Together, the mucus and the cilia help trap bits of dust and other foreign particles that could otherwise reach the lungs and damage them.

Some organs, such as the urinary bladder, must vary a great deal in size during the course of their work; for this purpose there is a special wrinkled, crepelike type of tissue, called **transitional epithelium,** which is capable of great expansion yet will return to its original form once the tension is relaxed—as when, in this case, the bladder is emptied. Certain areas of the epithelium that forms the outer layer of the skin are capable of modifying themselves for greater strength whenever they are subjected to unusual wear and tear; the growth of calluses is a good example of this.

Epithelium repairs itself very quickly if it is injured. If, for example, there is a cut, the cells near and around the wound immediately form daughter cells, which grow until the cut is closed. Epithelial tissue reproduces frequently in areas of the body subject to normal wear and tear, such as the skin, the inside of the mouth, and the lining of the intestinal tract.

Glands

Because epithelial cells are the secreting cells of many glands, a discussion of glands is appropriate. All glands in the body fall into two categories:

1 **Endocrine** (en'do-krin) **glands** are the so-called ductless glands because they release their secretions directly into the bloodstream. These are the glands that secrete hormones; they are discussed more fully in Chapter 11.
2 **Exocrine** (ek'so-krin) **glands** release their secretions into organs, into body cavities, or to the outside through ducts. These glands may be simple, tubelike structures, as found in the stomach wall and the lining of the intestine, or complex,

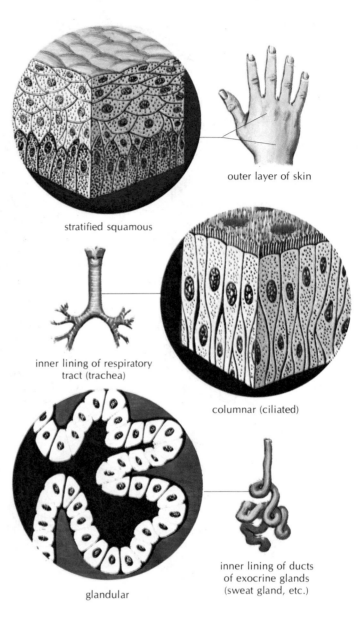

outer layer of skin

stratified squamous

Figure 4-1. *Three types of epithelium.*

inner lining of respiratory
tract (trachea)

columnar (ciliated)

glandular

inner lining of ducts
of exocrine glands
(sweat gland, etc.)

treelike systems of ducts, as found in the liver, pancreas, and salivary glands. They produce a variety of secretions along with varying amounts of cellular material. Examples of exocrine secretions are mucus, sweat, saliva, and other digestive juices.

≡ Connective Tissue

The supporting fabric of the organs and other parts of the body is connective tissue (Fig 4-2). If we were able to dissolve all the tissues except connective tis-

sue, we would still be able to recognize the contour of the parts and the organs of the entire body.

Connective tissue has large amounts of nonliving material, called **intercellular material**, between the cells. This material contains varying amounts of water, fibers, and hard minerals. Connective tissue may be classified simply according to its degree of hardness:

1 Soft connective tissue—adipose tissue and fibrous connective tissue

2 Hard connective tissue—cartilage and bone

3 Liquid connective tissue—blood and lymph

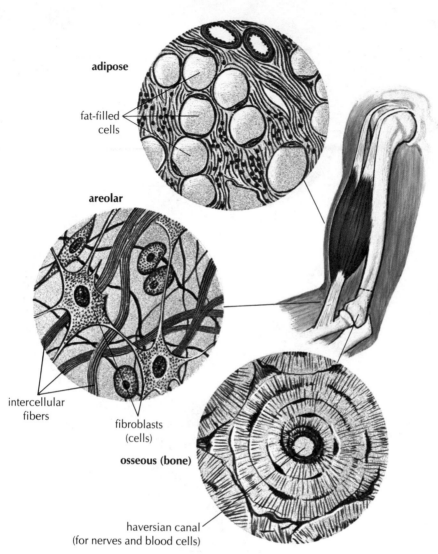

adipose

fat-filled
cells

areolar

intercellular
fibers

fibroblasts
(cells)

osseous (bone)

haversian canal
(for nerves and blood cells)

Figure 4-2. *Connective tissue.*

Soft Connective Tissue

Adipose (ad'e-pose) **tissue** stores up fat for the body as reserve food. Fat also serves as a heat insulator, and as padding for various structures.

Fibrous connective tissue may be very loosely held together or densely packed with fibers. The loose, or **areolar** (ah-re'o-lar), form is found in membranes around vessels and organs, between muscles, and under the skin. It is the most common type of connective tissue in the body. The dense type of connective tissue has large numbers of fibers that give it strength. The main fibers in soft and hard connective tissue are made of a flexible white protein called **collagen** (kol'ah-jen). There are also elastic fibers. This type of connective tissue serves as a binding between organs and also as a framework for some

organs. Particularly strong forms make up the tough **capsules** around certain organs, such as the kidneys, liver, and glands, the deep fascia around muscles, and the **periosteum** (per-e-os'te-um) around bones. These covering tissues are sometimes referred to as **fibrous membranes**. If the fibers in the connective tissue are all arranged in the same direction like the strands of a cable, the tissue can pull in that direction. Examples are the cordlike **tendons**, which connect muscles to bones, and the **ligaments**, which connect bones to other bones.

Fascia
The word *fascia* (fa'she-ah) means "band"; hence, fascial membranes are bands or sheets that support the organs and hold them in place. An example of a fascia is the continuous sheet of tissue that underlies

the skin. This contains fat (adipose tissue or "padding") and is called the **superficial fascia**. *Superficial* refers to a surface; the superficial fascia is closer than any other kind of fascia to the surface of the body.

As we penetrate more deeply into the body, we find examples of the **deep fascia**, which contains no fat and has many different purposes. Deep fascia covers and protects the muscle tissue with coverings known as **muscle sheaths**. The blood vessels and the nerves also are sheathed with fascia; the brain and the spinal cord are encased in a multilayered covering called the **meninges** (me-nin′jez). In addition, fascia serves to anchor muscle tissue to structures such as the bones.

Tissue Repair

Another interesting function of fibrous connective tissue is the repair of muscle and nerve tissue as well as the repair of connective tissue itself. Like epithelial tissue, fibrous connective tissue can repair itself easily. A large, gaping wound requires a correspondingly large growth of this new connective tissue; such new growth is called *scar tissue*. Excess production of collagen in the formation of a scar may result in the development of **keloids** (kee′loids), sharply raised areas on the surface of the skin. These are not dangerous but may be removed for the sake of appearance. The process of repair includes stages in which new blood vessels are formed in the wound, followed by the growth of the scar tissue. Overdevelopment of the blood vessels in the early stages of repair may lead to the formation of excess tissue, or "proud flesh." Normally, however, the blood vessels are gradually replaced by white fibrous connective tissue, which forms the scar. Suturing (sewing) the edges of a clean wound together, as is done in the case of operative wounds, decreases the amount of scar tissue needed and hence reduces the size of the resulting scar. Such scar tissue may be stronger than the original tissue.

Hard Connective Tissues

The hard connective tissues, which as the name suggests are more solid than the other groups, include cartilage and bone. A common form of cartilage is the tough, elastic, translucent material popularly called *gristle*. This and other forms of cartilage are found in such places as between the segments of the spine and at the ends of the long bones. In these positions, cartilage acts as a shock absorber as well as a bearing surface that reduces friction between moving parts. Cartilage is found in other structures also, such as the nose, the ear, and parts of the larynx, or "voice box." Except in joint cavities, cartilage is covered by a layer of fibrous connective tissue called **perichondrium** (per-e-kon′dre-um).

The tissue of which bones are made, called **osseous** (os′e-us) **tissue** (see Fig. 4-2), is very much like cartilage in its cellular structure. In fact, the bones of the unborn baby, in the early stages of development, are (except for some of the skull bones) made of cartilage; however, gradually this tissue becomes impregnated with calcium salts, which makes the bones characteristically hard and stony. Within the bones are nerves, blood vessels, bone-forming cells, and a special form of tissue, bone marrow, in which blood cells are manufactured.

The liquid connective tissues, blood and lymph, are discussed in Chapters 12 and 15, respectively.

≡ Nerve Tissue

The human body is made up of countless structures, both large and small, each of which contributes something to the action of the whole organism. This aggregation of structures might be compared to an army. For all the members of the army to work together, there must be a central coordinating and order-giving agency somewhere; otherwise chaos would ensue. In the body this central agency is the **brain**. Each structure of the body is in direct communication with the brain by means of its own set of telephone wires, called **nerves**. The nerves from even the most remote parts of the body all come together and form a great trunk cable called the **spinal cord**, which in turns leads directly into the central switchboard of the brain. Here, messages come in and orders go out 24 hours a day. This entire communication system, brain and all, is made of nerve tissue.

The basic structural unit of nerve tissue is the **neuron** (nu′-ron) (Fig. 4-3). A neuron consists of a nerve cell body plus small branches, like those of a tree, called *fibers*. One type of fiber, the **dendrite**, carries nerve impulses, or messages, to the nerve cell body. A single fiber, the **axon**, carries impulses away from the nerve cell body. Neurons may be quite long; their fibers can extend for several feet.

Nerve tissue (clusters of neurons) is supported by ordinary connective tissue everywhere except in the

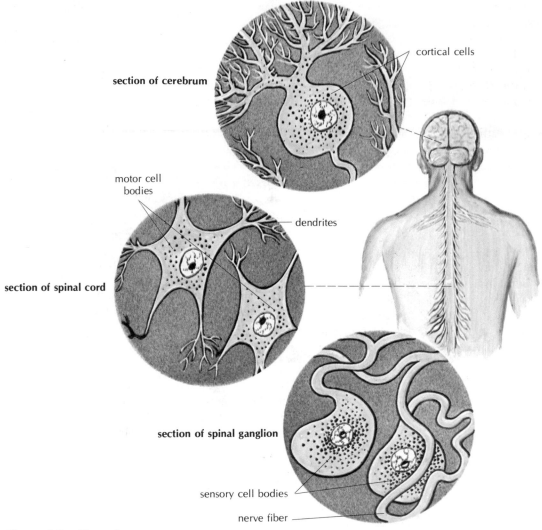

section of cerebrum

cortical cells

motor cell bodies

dendrites

section of spinal cord

section of spinal ganglion

sensory cell bodies

nerve fiber

Figure 4-3. *Nerve tissue.*

brain and spinal cord. Here, the supporting tissue is **neuroglia** (nu-rog′li-ah), which has a protective function as well.

All the nerves outside the brain and the spinal cord are called **peripheral** (peh-rif′er-al) **nerves**. The axons of these cells may have a thin coating known as a **neurilemma** (nu-re-lem′mah). The neurilemma is a part of the mechanism by which some peripheral nerves repair themselves when damaged. The brain and the spinal cord, on the other hand, have no neurilemma; if they are injured, the injury is permanent. However, even in the peripheral nerves, repair is a slow and uncertain process.

Telephone wires are insulated to keep them from being short-circuited, and so are some nerve fibers, which actually do transmit something very much like an electric current. The insulating material of nerve fibers is called **myelin** (mi′-el-in), and groups of these fibers form "white matter," so-called because of the color of the myelin, which is very much like fat in appearance and consistency. Not all neurons have myelin, however; some axons are unmyelinated, as are all dendrites and all cell bodies. These areas appear gray in color. Since the outer layer of the brain has large collections of cell bodies and unmyelinated fibers, the brain is popularly termed *gray matter*. A more detailed discussion of nerve tissue is taken up in Chapter 9.

☰ *Muscle Tissue*

Muscle tissue is designed to produce movement by a forcible contraction. The cells of muscle tissue are threadlike and so are called **muscle fibers**. If a piece of well-cooked meat is pulled apart, small groups of these muscle fibers may be seen. Muscle tissue is usually classified as follows (Fig. 4-4):

1 **Skeletal muscle**, which combines with connective tissue structures such as tendons (discussed later along with the skeleton) to provide for movement of the body. This type of tissue is also known as **voluntary muscle**, since it can be made to contract by an act of will. In other words, in theory at least, any of your skeletal muscles can be made to contract as you want them to.

The next two groups of muscle tissue are known as **involuntary muscle**, since they typically contract independently of the will. In fact, most of the time we do not think of their actions at all. These are

2 **Cardiac muscle**, which forms the bulk of the heart wall and is known also as **myocardium** (mi-o-kar′de-um). This is the muscle that produces the regular contractions known as *heartbeats*.

3 **Smooth muscle**, known also as **visceral muscle**, which forms the walls of the **viscera** (vis′er-ah), or organs of the ventral body cavities (with the exception of the heart). Some examples of vis-

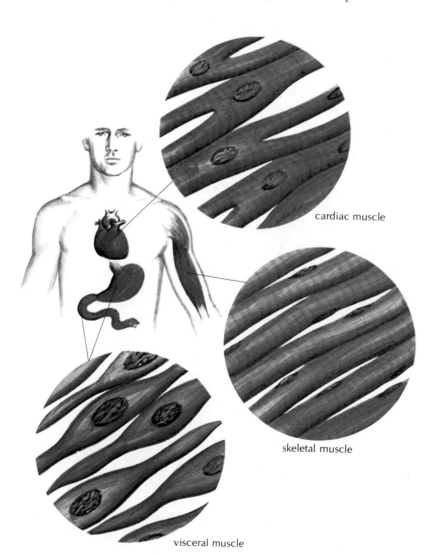

Figure 4-4. *Muscle tissue.*

cardiac muscle

skeletal muscle

visceral muscle

ceral muscles are those that move the food and waste materials along the digestive tract. Visceral muscles are found in other kinds of structures as well. Many tubular structures contain them, such as the blood vessels and the tubes that carry urine from the kidneys. Even certain structures at the base of body hair have this type of muscle. When these muscles contract, there results the skin condition we call *gooseflesh.* Other types of visceral muscles are taken up under discussions of the various body systems.

A general disorder of the muscles called a **spasm** is a sudden and involuntary muscular contraction. A spasm is always painful. A spasm of the visceral muscles is called **colic**, a good example of which is the spasm of the intestinal muscles often referred to as *bellyache.* Spasms may occur also in the skeletal muscles; if the spasms occur in a series, the condition may be called a **seizure** or **convulsion**. Specific diseases of which these abnormal muscle contractions are symptomatic are discussed later.

Muscle tissue, like nerve tissue, repairs itself only with difficulty or not at all once an injury has been sustained. When injured, muscle tissue is frequently replaced with connective tissue.

≡ Membranes

Membranes are thin sheets of tissue. Their properties vary: some are fragile, others tough; some are transparent, others opaque (*i.e.,* they cannot be seen through). Membranes may cover a surface, may serve as dividing partitions, may line hollow organs and body cavities, or may anchor various organs. They may contain cells that secrete lubricants to ease the movement of organs such as the heart and the movement of joints.

Epithelial Membranes

Epithelial membrane is so named because its outer surface is made of epithelium. Underneath, however, there is a layer of connective tissue that strengthens the membrane, and in some cases there is a thin layer of smooth muscle under that. Epithelial membranes may be divided into two subgroups:

1 **Mucous** (mu′kus) **membranes** line tubes and other spaces that open to the outside of the body.
2 **Serous** (se′rus) **membranes** line the external

walls of body cavities and are folded back onto the surface of exposed organs, forming the outermost layer of many of them.

Epithelial membranes are made of closely crowded active cells that manufacture lubricants and protect the deeper tissues from invasion by microorganisms. Mucous membranes produce a rather thick and sticky substance called **mucus**, while serous membranes secrete a much thinner lubricant. (Note that the adjective in each case contains an "o," while the nouns naming the secretion do not.)

In referring to the mucous membrane of a particular part, the noun **mucosa** (mu-ko′sah) may be used, while the special serous membrane lining a closed cavity or covering an organ is called the **serosa** (se-ro′sah).

Mucous Membranes

Mucous membranes form extensive continuous linings in the digestive, the respiratory, the urinary, and the reproductive systems, all of which are connected with the outside of the body. They vary somewhat in both structure and function. The cells that line the nasal cavities and most parts of the respiratory tract are supplied with tiny, hairlike extensions of the protoplasm, called *cilia,* which have already been mentioned. The microscopic cilia move in a wavelike manner that forces the secretions outward away from the deeper parts of the lungs. In this way foreign particles such as bacteria and dust become trapped in the sticky mucus and are prevented from causing harm. Ciliated epithelium is also found in certain tubes of both the male and the female reproductive systems.

The mucous membranes that line the digestive tract have their own special functions. For example, the mucous membrane of the stomach serves to protect the deeper tissues from the action of certain powerful digestive juices. If for some reason a portion of this membrane is injured, these juices begin to digest a part of the stomach itself—as in the case of peptic ulcers. Mucous membranes located farther along in this system are designed to absorb food materials, which are then transported to all the cells of the body. Other mucous membranes are discussed in more detail later.

Serous Membranes

Serous membranes, unlike mucous membranes, do not usually communicate with the outside of the body. This group lines the closed ventral body cavities. There are three serous membranes:

1 The **pleurae** (ploor′e) or **pleuras** (ploor′ahs) line the thoracic cavity and cover each lung.
2 The **pericardium** (per-e-kar′de-um) is a sac that encloses the heart. It fits into a space in the chest between the two lungs.
3 The **peritoneum** (per-i-to-ne′um) is the largest serous membrane. It lines the walls of the abdominal cavity, covers the organs of the abdomen, and forms supporting and protective structures within the abdomen. The abdominal cavity is closed in the male, but it is connected with the outside through the reproductive system in the female (see Figs. 18-2 and 21-6).

The epithelium covering serous membranes is of a special kind called **mesothelium** (mes-o-the′le-um). The mesothelium is smooth and glistening and is lubricated so that movements of the organs can take place with a minimum of friction.

Serous membranes are so arranged that one portion forms the lining of the closed sac while another part covers the surface of the organs. The serous membrane attached to the wall of a cavity or sac is known as the **parietal** (pah-ri′e-tal) **layer**; the word *parietal* refers to a wall. Parietal pleura lines the chest wall, and parietal pericardium lines the sac that encloses the heart. Because organs are called *viscera*, the membrane attached to the organs is the **visceral layer**. On the surface of the heart is visceral pericardium, and each lung surface is covered by visceral pleura.

Other Membranes

Other membranes in the body include the skin, or **cutaneous** (ku-ta′ne-us) **membrane**, which is also considered an epithelial membrane, and **synovial** (si-no′ve-al) **membranes**. The skin is described fully in Chapter 6. Synovial membranes are thin connective tissue membranes that line the joint cavities. They secrete a lubricating fluid that reduces friction between the ends of bones, thus permitting free movement of the joints.

With this we conclude our brief introduction to membranes. As we study each system in turn, other membranes will be encountered. They may have unfamiliar names, but they will be either epithelial or connective tissue membranes, and we will also become familiar with their general locations; in short, they will be easy to recognize and remember.

Membranes and Disease

We are all familiar with a number of diseases that directly affect membranes. These range all the way from the common cold, which is an inflammation of the mucosa of the nasal passages, to the sometimes fatal condition known as **peritonitis**, an infection of the peritoneum, which can follow rupture of the appendix. More of these diseases of membranes will be covered in due course.

Membranes can act as pathways along which disease may spread. In general, epithelial membranes seem to have more resistance to infections than do layers made of connective tissue. However, lowered resistance may allow the transmission of infection along any membrane. For example, infections may travel along the lining of the tubes of the reproductive system into the urinary system in males. In females, an infection may travel up the tubes and spaces of the reproductive system into the peritoneal cavity (see Figs. 21-1 and 21-6).

Sometimes fibrous membranes form planes of division extending in such a way that infection in one area is prevented from reaching another space. In other cases a vertical plane that separates two areas may seem to encourage the travel of bacteria either upward or downward. An infection of the tonsils, for example, may travel down to the chest along fibrous membranes.

The connective tissue or collagen diseases, such as **lupus erythematosus** (loo′pus er″i-them′ah-to-sus) and **rheumatoid arthritis**, may affect many parts of the body, since collagen is the major intercellular protein in soft and hard connective tissue. In lupus erythematosus, serous membranes such as the pleura, pericardium, and peritoneum are often involved. In rheumatoid arthritis, the synovial membrane becomes inflamed and swollen, and the cartilage in the joints is gradually replaced with fibrous connective tissue.

Benign and Malignant Tumors

As noted in Chapter 3, the normal pattern of cell and tissue growth may be broken by an upstart formation of cells having no purpose whatsoever in the body. Any abnormal growth of cells is called a **tumor**, or **neoplasm**. If the tumor is confined to a local area and does not spread, it is called a **benign** (be-nine′) tumor. If the tumor spreads to neighboring tissues or to distant parts of the body, it is called a **malignant** (mah-lig′-nant) tumor. The general term for any type of malignant tumor is **cancer**. The process of tumor cell spread is called **metastasis** (ma-tas′-ta-sis).

Tumors are found in all kinds of tissue, but they occur most frequently in those tissues that repair themselves most quickly; these tissues are epithelium and connective tissue, in that order.

Benign Tumors

Benign tumors, theoretically at least, are not dangerous in themselves; that is, they do not spread. Their cells adhere together, and often they are encapsulated, that is, surrounded by a containing membrane. Benign tumors grow as a single mass within a tissue, lending themselves neatly to complete surgical removal. Of course, some benign tumors can be quite harmful; they may grow within an organ, increase in size, and cause considerable mechanical damage. A benign tumor of the brain, for example, can kill a person just as a malignant one can, since it grows in an enclosed area and compresses vital brain tissue. Some examples of benign tumors are given below (note that most of the names end in *-oma,* which means "tumor").

1 **Papilloma** (pap-i-lo′mah). This grows in epithelium as a projecting mass. One example is a wart.
2 **Adenoma** (ad-e-no′mah). This is an epithelial tumor that grows in and about the glands (*aden-* means "gland").
3 **Lipoma** (lip-o′mah). This is a connective tissue tumor originating in fatty (adipose) tissue.
4 **Osteoma** (os-te-o′mah). This is a connective tissue tumor that originates in the bones.
5 **Myoma** (mi-o′mah). This is a tumor of muscle tissue. Rare in voluntary muscle, it is common in some types of involuntary muscle, particularly the uterus (womb). When found in this organ, however, it is ordinarily called a *fibroid.*
6 **Angioma** (an-je-o′mah). This tumor usually is composed of small blood or lymph vessels; an example is a birthmark.
7 **Nevus** (ne′vus). This is a small skin tumor of one of a variety of tissues. Some nevi are better known as moles; some are angiomas. Ordinarily, these tumors are harmless, but they can become malignant.
8 **Chondroma** (kon-dro′mah). This is a tumor of

cartilage cells that may remain within the cartilage or develop on the surface, as in the joints.

Malignant Tumors

Malignant tumors, unlike benign tumors, can cause death no matter where they occur. The word *cancer* means "crab," and this is descriptive: a cancer sends out clawlike extensions into neighboring tissue. A cancer also spreads "seeds," which plant themselves in other parts of the body. These seeds are, of course, cancer cells, and they are transported everywhere by either the blood or the lymph (a fluid related to the blood). When the cancer cells reach their destination, they immediately form new (secondary) growths, or **metastases** (me-ta′sta-seez). Malignant tumors, moreover, grow much more rapidly than benign ones.

Malignant tumors generally are classified in two categories according to the type of tissue in which they originate:

1 **Carcinomas** (kar-si-no′mahs). These cancers originate in epithelium and are by far the most common type of cancer. Common sites of carcinoma are the skin, mouth, lung, breast, stomach, colon, and uterus. Carcinomas are usually spread by the lymphatic system (see Chap. 15).
2 **Sarcomas** (sar-ko′mahs). These are cancers of connective tissue of all kinds and hence may be found anywhere in the body. Their cells are usually spread by the blood stream, and they often form secondary growths in the lungs.

There are other types of malignant tumors as well. Those that originate in birthmarks or in moles are called **melanomas** (mel″ah-no′mahs), those that originate in the connective tissue of the brain and spinal cord are called **gliomas** (gli-o′mahs), and those of the lymph tissue are called **lymphomas** (lim-fo′mahs).

Symptoms of Cancer

Everyone should be familiar with certain signs that may be indicative of early cancer, so that these signs can be reported immediately, before the condition spreads. It is unfortunate that early cancer is painless; otherwise, cancer would not be the problem that it is. Early symptoms may include unaccountable loss of weight, unusual bleeding or discharge, persistent indigestion, chronic hoarseness or cough, changes in the color or size of moles, a sore that does not heal in a reasonable time, the presence of an unusual lump, and the presence of white patches inside the mouth or white spots on the tongue.

Detection and Treatment of Cancer

Cancer diagnosis is becoming increasingly specific, leading to more precise methods of treatment. The diagnostic methods listed below include some exciting new techniques for showing the size and location of tumors and other abnormalities.

1 **Biopsy** is the removal of living tissue for the purpose of microscopic examination of the cells.
2 **Ultrasound** is the use of reflected high-frequency sound waves to differentiate various kinds of tissue.
3 **Computed-tomography (CT)** is the use of x-rays to produce a cross-sectional picture of body parts, such as the brain (see Fig. 9-8).
4 **Magnetic resonance imaging (MRI)** is the use of magnetic fields and radio waves to show changes in soft tissues without the use of x-rays.

These studies are used for a process called **staging**, which means the classification of a tumor based on size and extent of invasion. Staging helps the physician select appropriate treatment and predict the outcome of the disease.

Benign tumors can be removed completely by surgery; malignant tumors cannot be treated so easily, for a number of reasons. If cancerous tissue is removed surgically, there is always the probability that a few hidden cells will be left behind to grow anew. If the cells have spread to distant parts of the body, there is little that anyone can do. Sometimes surgery is preceded by or followed by radiation. Radiation therapy is administered by x-ray machines or by the placement of radiactive seeds within the involved organ. Radiation destroys the more rapidly dividing cancer cells while causing less damage to the more slowly dividing normal cells. Methods are being developed that will permit more accurate focusing of the beam of radiation and thus reduce the damage to normal body structures.

Drugs used for the treatment of cancer include those that act selectively on tumor cells. Known as **antineoplastic** (an″ti-ne″o-plas′-tik) **agents**, these drugs are most effective when used in combination.

The treatment of cancer with antineoplastic agents is one form of **chemotherapy** (keem-oh-ther′-a-py) (see Chap. 5). Certain types of leukemia and various cancers of the lymphatic system are often effectively treated by this means. Research continues to develop new drugs and more effective drug combinations.

A newer technique is **immunotherapy** (i-mu″-no-ther′-ah-pe). Immunotherapy involves giving the patient a special type of inoculation to strengthen his or her own body defenses and thus prevent the spread of the cancer cells.

The **laser** (la′zer), a device that produces a very highly concentrated and intense beam of light, may sometimes successfully destroy the tumor or may be employed as a cutting device for removing the growth. Important advantages of the laser are its ability to coagulate blood so that bleeding is largely prevented and the capacity to direct a narrow beam of light accurately to attack harmful cells and avoid normal ones.

Summary

I **Tissues**—groups of cells specialized for specific tasks
  A Epithelial tissue—covers surfaces, lines cavities
    1 Squamous, cuboidal, and columnar cells
    2 Simple or stratified cell layers
    3 Glands
      a Endocrine
      b Exocrine
  B Connective tissue—supports, binds, forms framework of body
    1 Soft
      a Adipose—stores fat
      b Fibrous—consists of collagen and elastic fibers between cells; may be loose (areolar) or dense (fascia, ligaments, tendons, capsules)
    2 Hard
      a Cartilage—found at ends of bones, nose, outer ear, trachea, etc.
      b Bone—contains calcium salts
    3 Liquid
      a Blood
      b Lymph

C Nerve tissue
  1 Organization
    a Central nervous system—brain and spinal cord
    b Peripheral nervous system—all other nerves
  2 Components
    a Neuron—nerve cell
      (1) Cell body—contains nucleus
      (2) Dendrite—fiber carrying impulses toward cell body
      (3) Axon—fiber carrying impulses away from cell body
      (4) Neurilemma—outer layer of some peripheral axons
    b Neuroglia—support and protect nerve tissue
    c Myelin—fatty material that insulates some axons
      (1) Myelinated fibers—make up white matter
      (2) Unmyelinated cells and fibers—make up gray matter
D Muscle tissue—contracts to produce movement
  1 Skeletal muscle—voluntary; moves skeleton
  2 Cardiac muscle—forms the heart
  3 Smooth muscle—involuntary; forms visceral organs
II **Membranes**—thin sheets of tissue
  A Main types
    1 Epithelial membranes—outer-layer epithelium
      a Mucous membranes—line tubes and spaces that open to the outside (*e.g.,* respiratory, digestive, reproductive tracts)
      b Serous membranes—line body cavities (parietal layer) and cover internal organs (visceral layer)
    2 Cutaneous membrane—skin
    3 Synovial membranes—line the joints
  B Membranes and disease
III **Tumors (neoplasms)**—uncontrolled growth of cells
  A Types
    1 Benign—localized
    2 Malignant—invades tissue and spreads to other parts of the body (metastasizes)
  B Symptoms—weight loss, bleeding, persistent

indigestion, hoarseness or cough, change in mole, lump, nonhealing sore
C Detection
  1 Biopsy (study of tissue), ultrasound, CT, MRI
  2 Staging—classification based on size of tumor and extent of invasion
D Treatment
  1 Surgical removal
  2 Radiation
  3 Chemotherapy—drugs
  4 Immune therapy

Questions for Study and Review

1 Define *tissue*. Give a few general characteristics of tissues.
2 Define *epithelium* and give two examples.
3 Describe the difference between endocrine and exocrine glands and give examples of each.
4 Define *connective tissue*. Name the main kinds of connective tissue and give an example of each.
5 What kinds of fibers are found in connective tissue?
6 What is the main purpose of nerve tissue? What is its basic structural unit called?
7 Define *neurilemma*. Where is it present or absent?
8 Define *myelin*. Where is it found?
9 Name three kinds of muscle tissue and give an example of each.
10 What is the difference between voluntary and involuntary muscle?
11 Compare how easily the four basic groups of tissues repair themselves.
12 What are some general characteristics of epithelial membranes?
13 Name two types of epithelial membrane. Give their general characteristics and two examples of each.
14 Name and describe the two layers of serous membranes.
15 Give two examples of fascia.
16 What is an infection of the peritoneum called? What is a possible cause of this condition?
17 Name two diseases of membranes.

18 What is the relationship between membranes and disease?

19 What is a tumor? In what kinds of tissue are tumors most commonly found?

20 What is the difference between a benign and a malignant tumor?

21 Name four examples of benign tumors and tell where each is found.

22 Name the two categories of malignant tumor. In what kinds of tissue are these tumors found? Which kind is the most common?

23 Name some early symptoms of cancer.

24 In what ways is cancer diagnosed?

25 In what ways is cancer treated?

26 What is staging and how is it used?

5

Disease and Disease-Producing Organisms

Behavioral Objectives

After careful study of this chapter, you should be able to:

Define disease and list seven causes of disease

List eight predisposing causes of disease

Differentiate between acute and chronic disease

List four types of organisms studied in microbiology and give the characteristics of each

List some diseases caused by each type of microorganism

Describe the three types of bacteria according to shape

List several diseases in humans caused by worms

Describe how infections may be spread

Describe several public health measures taken to prevent the spread of disease

Differentiate among sterilization, disinfection, and antisepsis

Define chemotherapy

Describe several methods used to identify microorganisms in the laboratory

Selected Key Terms

The following terms are defined in the glossary:

acute
asepsis
chemotherapy
chronic
diagnosis
disease
epidemic
etiology
microorganism
pathogen
pathophysiology
prognosis
sign
spore
sterilization
symptom
systemic
toxin

What Is Disease?

Disease may be defined as the abnormal state in which part or all of the body is not properly adjusted or is not capable of carrying on all its required functions. There are marked variations in the extent of disease and in its effect on the person. Disease can have a number of direct causes, such as the following:

1 **Disease-producing organisms.** Some of these are discussed in this chapter. These are believed to play a part in at least half of all human illnesses.
2 **Malnutrition.** This is a lack of essential vitamins, minerals, proteins, or other substances required for normal life processes.
3 **Physical agents.** These include excessive heat or cold, and injuries that cause cuts, fractures, or crushing damage to tissues.
4 **Chemicals.** Some chemicals that may be poisonous or otherwise injurious if present in excess, are lead compounds (in paints), carbolic acid (in certain antiseptic solutions), and certain laundry aids.
5 **Birth defects.** Abnormalities of structure and function that are present at birth are termed *congenital.* Such abnormalities may be inherited (passed on by the parents through their reproductive cells) or acquired during the process of development within the mother's uterus (womb) (see Chap. 22).
6 **Degenerative processes. Degeneration** (de-jen-er-a′shun) means "breaking down." With aging, tissue degenerates and thus becomes less active and less capable of performing its normal functions. Such deterioration may be caused by continuous infection, by repeated minor injuries to tissues by poisonous substances, or by the normal "wear and tear" of life. Thus, degeneration is an anticipated result of aging.
7 **Neoplasms.** The word *neoplasm* means "new growth" and refers to cancer and other types of tumors (see Chap. 4)

Other factors that enter into the production of a disease are known as **predisposing causes.** Although a predisposing cause may not in itself give rise to a disease, it increases the probability of a person's becoming ill. Examples of predisposing causes include the following:

1 **Age.** As we saw, the degenerative processes of aging can be a direct cause of disease. But a person's age also can be a predisposing factor. For instance, measles is more common in children than in adults.
2 **Sex.** Certain diseases are more characteristic of one sex than the other. Men are more susceptible to heart disease, while women are more likely to develop diabetes.
3 **Heredity.** Some individuals inherit a "tendency" to acquire certain diseases—particularly diabetes and many allergies.
4 **Living conditions and habits.** Persons who habitually drive themselves to exhaustion, do not get enough sleep, or pay little attention to diet are highly vulnerable to the onslaught of disease. Overcrowding invites epidemics, and lack of sunshine can cause rickets in children. The use of narcotics and the abuse of alcohol and tobacco also can lower vitality and predispose to disease.
5 **Occupation.** A number of conditions are classified as "occupational diseases." For instance, coal miners are susceptible to lung damage caused by the constant inhalation of coal dust.
6 **Physical exposure.** Undue chilling of all or part of the body, or prolonged exposure to heat, can lower the body's resistance to disease.
7 **Preexisting illness.** Any preexisting illness, even the common cold, increases one's chances of contracting another disease.
8 **Psychogenic influences.** *Psycho* refers to the mind, *genic* to origin. Some physical disturbances are due either directly or indirectly to emotional upsets caused by conditions of stress and anxiety in daily living. Peptic ulcers and so-called nervous indigestion are examples.

The Study of Disease

The modern approach to the study of disease emphasizes the close relationship of the pathologic and physiological aspects and the need to understand the fundamentals of each in treating any body disorder. The term used for this combined study in medical science is **pathophysiology.**

Underlying the basic medical sciences are the still more fundamental disciplines of physics and chemistry. A knowledge of both of these is essential to any real understanding of the life processes.

Disease Terminology

The study of the cause of any disease, or the theory of its origin, is **etiology** (e-te-ol′o-je). Any study of a disease usually includes some indication of **incidence**, which means its range of occurrence and its tendency to affect certain groups of individuals more than others. Information about its geographic distribution and its tendency to appear in one sex, age group, or race more or less frequently than another is usually included in a presentation on disease incidence.

Diseases are often classified on the basis of severity and duration as

1 **Acute.** These are relatively severe but usually last a short time.
2 **Chronic.** These are often less severe but likely to be continuous or recurring for long periods of time.
3 **Subacute.** These are intermediate between acute and chronic, not being quite so severe as acute infections nor as long lasting as chronic disorders.

Still another term used in describing certain diseases is **idiopathic** (id-e-o-path′ik), which means "self-originating" or "without known cause."

A **communicable** disease is one that can be transmitted from one person to another. If many people in a given region acquire a certain disease at the same time, that disease is said to be **epidemic**. If a given disease is found to a lesser extent but continuously in a particular region, the disease is **endemic** to that area. A disease that is prevalent throughout an entire country or continent, or the whole world, is said to be **pandemic**.

Diagnosis, Treatment, Prognosis, and Prevention

In order to treat a patient, the doctor obviously must first reach a conclusion as to the nature of the illness—that is, make a **diagnosis**. To do this the doctor must know the **symptoms**, which are the conditions of disease noted by the patient, and the **signs**, which are the objective manifestations the doctor or other health care professional can observe. Some-

times a characteristic group of symptoms and signs accompanies a given disease. Such a group is called a **syndrome** (sin′drome). Frequently, the physician uses laboratory tests to help establish the diagnosis. A **prognosis** (prog-no′sis) is a prediction of the probable outcome of a disease based on the condition of the patient and the physician's knowledge about the disease.

Although nurses do not diagnose, they play an extremely valuable role in this process by observing closely for signs, encouraging patients to talk about themselves and their symptoms, and then reporting this information to the doctor. Once a patient's disorder is known, the doctor prescribes a course of treatment, also referred to as **therapy**. Many measures in this course of treatment are carried out by the nurse under the physician's orders.

In recent years, physicians, nurses, and other health care workers have taken on increasing responsibilities in **prevention**. Throughout most of medical history, the physician's aim has been to cure patients of existing diseases. However, the modern concept of prevention seeks to stop disease before it actually happens—to keep people well through the promotion of health. A vast number of organizations exist for this purpose, ranging from the World Health Organization (WHO) on an international level down to local private and community health programs. A rapidly growing responsibility of the nursing professional and of other health occupations is educating individual patients toward the maintenance of total health, physical and mental.

Modes of Infection

The predominant cause of disease in humans is the invasion of the body by disease-producing **microorganisms** (mi″kro-or′gan-izms). The word *organism* means "anything having life"; *micro* means "small." Hence, a microorganism is a tiny living thing, too small to be seen by the naked eye. Other terms for microorganism are **microbe** and more popularly, *germ*. Parasitology (par-ah-si-tol′o-je) is the general study of parasites, a **parasite** being any organism that lives on or within another (called the **host**) at that other's expense.

Although the great majority of microorganisms are beneficial to man, or at least are harmless, a certain few types cause illness; that is, they are pathogenic (path-o-jen'ic). Any disease-causing organism is a **pathogen** (path'o-jen). If the body is invaded by pathogens, with adverse effects, the condition is called an **infection**. If the infection is restricted to a relatively small area of the body, it is **local**. A generalized, or **systemic** (sis-tem'ik), infection is one in which the whole body is affected. Systemic infections usually are spread by the blood.

Modes of Transmission

Microorganisms may be transmitted from an infected human, insect, or animal host to a susceptible human being; this transfer may be by direct or indirect contact. For example, infected human hosts may transfer their microorganisms to other individuals through direct personal contact such as shaking hands, kissing, or having sexual intercourse. Indirect contact involves touching objects that have been contaminated by an infected person. For example, microorganisms may be transferred indirectly through bedding, toys, food, and dishes. Also, insects may deposit infectious material on food, skin, or clothing. Pets may be the source of a number of infections.

Portal of Entry and Exit

There are several avenues through which microorganisms may enter the body: the skin, respiratory tract, and digestive system, as well as the urinary and reproductive systems. These portals of entry may also serve as exit routes. For example, discharges from the respiratory and intestinal tracts may spread infection through contamination of air, through contamination of hands, and through contamination of food and water supplies. (Microbial control is discussed later in this chapter.)

☰ The Microorganisms

Microorganisms are simple, usually single-celled forms of life (Fig. 5-1). The study of these microscopic organisms is **microbiology** (mi-kro-bi-ol'o-je). Other sciences have grown up within the science of microbiology, and each has become a specialty in itself. Some examples of these more specialized sciences include the following:

Figure 5-1. *Some examples of microorganisms.*

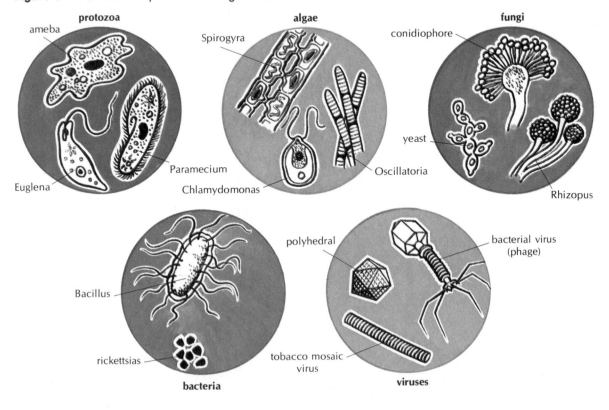

1 Bacteriology (bak-te-re-ol′o-je) is the study of bacteria, both beneficial and disease producing. It includes the study of rickettsias and chlamydias, which are extremely small bacteria that multiply within living cells.

2 Mycology (my-col′o-je) is the study of fungi, which include yeasts and molds.

3 Virology (vi-rol′o-je) is the study of viruses, extremely small infectious agents that can multiply only within living cells.

4 Protozoology (pro-to-zo-ol′o-je) is the study of single-celled animals, called *protozoa.*

Although this book is concerned with pathogenic forms, most microorganisms not only are harmless to humans but also are absolutely essential to the continuation of all life on earth. It is through the actions of microorganisms that dead animals and plants are decomposed and transformed into substances that enrich the soil. Sewage is rendered harmless by microorganisms. Several groups of bacteria transform the nitrogen of the air into a form usable by plants, a process called **nitrogen fixation**. Farmers take advantage of this by allowing a field to lie fallow (untilled) so that the nitrogen of its soil can be replenished. Certain bacteria and fungi produce the antibiotics that make our lives safer. Others produce the fermented products that make our lives more enjoyable, such as beer, wine, cheeses, and yoghurt.

We have a population (flora) of microorganisms that normally grows on and within our bodies. We live in balance with these organisms, and they prevent the growth of other harmful varieties. However, some microorganisms that are normally harmless may become pathogenic for persons who are in a weakened state as a result, for example, of disease, injury, or malnutrition.

Bacteria

Bacteria are one-celled organisms that are among the most primitive forms of life on earth. They can be seen only with a microscope; from 10 to 1000 bacteria (depending on the species) would, if lined up, span a pinhead. Staining of the cells with dyes helps make their structures more clearly visible and reveals information about their properties.

Bacteria are found everywhere: in soil, in hot springs, in polar ice, and on and within plants and animals. Their requirements for water, food, oxygen, temperature, and other factors vary widely according to species. Some are capable of carrying out photosynthesis, like green plants; others must take in organic food, as do animals. Some, described as **anaerobic** (an-air-o′bik), can grow only in the absence of oxygen; others, called **aerobic** (air-o′bik), require oxygen. Some bacteria can produce **spores**, resistant forms that can tolerate long periods of dryness or other adverse conditions. Because these spores are resistant to ordinary methods of disinfection, pathogenic organisms that form spores are particularly dangerous. Some bacteria are capable of swimming rapidly about by themselves by means of threadlike appendages called **flagella** (flah-jel′ah).

Bacteria compose the largest group of pathogens. Not surprisingly, these pathogenic bacteria are most at home within the "climate" of the human body. When living conditions are ideal, the organisms reproduce by binary fission (simple cell division) with unbelievable rapidity. If they succeed in overcoming the body's natural defenses, they can cause damage in two ways: by producing poisons, or **toxins**, and by entering the body tissues and growing within them. In Table 1 of Appendix 3 are listed some typical pathogenic bacteria and the diseases they cause.

There are so many different types of bacteria that their classification is complicated. For our purposes, a convenient and simple grouping is based on the shape and arrangement of these organisms as seen with a microscope (Figs. 5-2 and 5-3):

1 Rod-shaped cells—**bacilli** (bah-sil′i). These cells are straight and slender. Some are cigar-shaped, with tapering ends. Typical bacillary diseases include tetanus, diphtheria, tuberculosis, typhoid fever, and Legionnaire's (le′jun-nars) disease.

2 Spherical cells—**cocci** (kok′si). These cells are round and are seen in characteristic arrangements. Those that are in pairs are called **diplococci** (*diplo*—means "double"). Those that are arranged in chains, like a string of beads, are called **streptococci** (*strepto*—means "chain"). A third group, seen in large clusters, are known as **staphylococci** (staf-i-lo-kok′si) (*staphylo*—means "bunch of grapes"). Among the diseases caused by diplococci are gonorrhea and meningitis; streptococci and staphylococci are responsible for a wide variety of infections.

3 Curved rods. One type, which has only a slight curvature, like a comma, is called **vibrio**

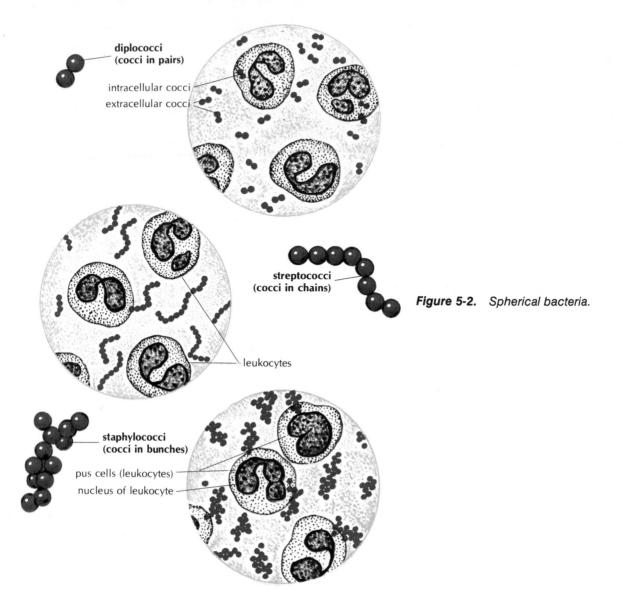

diplococci (cocci in pairs)

intracellular cocci

extracellular cocci

streptococci (cocci in chains)

Figure 5-2. *Spherical bacteria.*

leukocytes

staphylococci (cocci in bunches)

pus cells (leukocytes)

nucleus of leukocyte

(vib′re-o). Cholera is caused by a vibrio. Another form, which resembles a corkscrew, is known as **spirillum** (spi-ril′um). (The plural is **spirilla.**) Bacteria very similar to the spirilla, but capable of waving and twisting motions, are called **spirochetes** (spi′ro-ketes). The most serious and wide-spread spirochetal infection is syphilis. In syphilis, the spirochetes enter the body at the point of contact, usually through the genital skin or mucous membranes. They then travel to the bloodstream and thus set up a systemic infection. (See Table 1 in Appendix 3 for a summary of the three stages of syphilis.)

4 **Rickettsias** (ri-ket′se-ahs) and the **chlamydias** (klah-mid′e-ahs) (sometimes called *rickettsiae* and *chlamydiae*) are classified as bacteria, although they are considerably smaller. These microorganisms can exist only inside living cells. Because they exist at the expense of their hosts, they are parasites, and because they can grow only within living cells, they are referred to as **obligate parasites.**

The rickettsias are the cause of a number of serious diseases in humans, such as typhus and Rocky Mountain spotted fever. In almost every instance, these organisms are transmitted

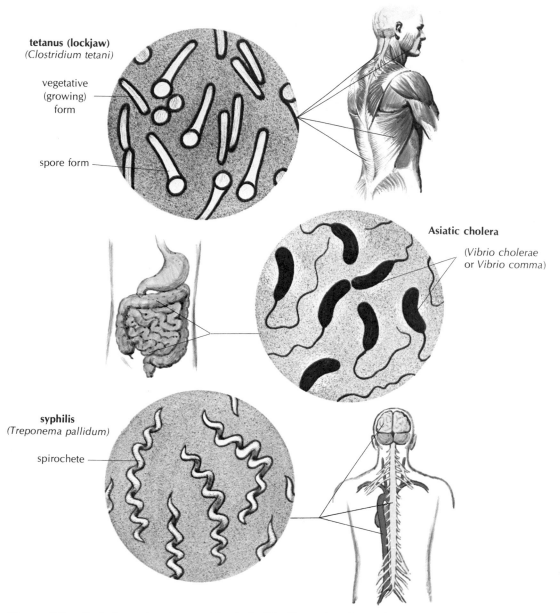

tetanus (lockjaw)
(Clostridium tetani)

vegetative
(growing)
form

spore form

Asiatic cholera

(Vibrio cholerae
or *Vibrio comma)*

syphilis
(Treponema pallidum)

spirochete

Figure 5-3. *Rod-shaped and curved bacteria. The illustration shows the areas of the body invaded by these pathogens.*

through the bites of insects, such as lice, ticks, and fleas. A few common rickettsial diseases are listed in Table 1 of Appendix 3.

The chlamydias are smaller than the rickettsias. They are the causative organisms in trachoma (a serious eye infection that ultimately causes blindness), parrot fever or psittacosis, the venereal disease lymphogranuloma venereum,

and some respiratory diseases (see Appendix, Table 1).

Fungi

The true **fungi** (fun'ji) are a large group of simple plantlike organisms. Only a very few types are pathogenic. Although fungi are much larger and more complicated than bacteria, they are still a low order of life. They differ from the higher plants in that they lack the green pigment chlorophyll, which enables most plants to use the energy of sunlight to manufacture food. Like bacteria, fungi grow best in dark, damp places. Fungi reproduce in several ways, including by simple cell division and by production of large numbers of reproductive spores. Single-celled forms of fungi are generally referred to as **yeasts**; the fuzzy, filamentous forms are called **molds**.

Familiar examples of fungi are mushrooms, puffballs, bread molds, and the yeasts used in baking and brewing. Diseases caused by fungi are called **mycotic** (mi-kot′ik) infections (*myco*—means "fungus"). Examples of these are athlete's foot and ringworm. Tinea capitis (tin′e-ah kap″i-tis), which involves the scalp, and tinea corporis (kor-po′ris), which may be found almost anywhere on the nonhairy parts of the body, are common types of ringworm. One yeastlike fungus that may infect a weakened host is *Candida.* This is a normal inhabitant of the mouth and digestive tract that may produce skin lesions, an oral infection called *thrush,* digestive upset, or inflammation of the vaginal tract (vaginitis) as a secondary infection. Although few systemic diseases are caused by fungi, some are very dangerous, and all are difficult to cure. Pneumonia can be caused by the inhalation of fungal spores contained in dust particles.

Table 2 in Appendix 3 is a list of typical fungal diseases.

Viruses

Although bacteria seem small, they are enormous in comparison with **viruses**. Viruses are comparable in size to large molecules, but unlike other molecules, they contain genetic material and are able to reproduce. Viruses are so tiny that they are invisible with a light microscope; they can be seen only with an electron microscope. Because of their very small size and the difficulties associated with growing them in the laboratory, viruses were not studied with much success until the middle of this century.

Viruses are the smallest known infectious agents. They have some of the fundamental properties of living matter, but they are not cellular and they have no enzyme system. Like the rickettsias and the chlamydias, they can grow only within living cells—they are obligate parasites; unlike these, however, the viruses are not usually susceptible to antibiotics.

There is no universally accepted classification of viruses. For our purposes it is appropriate to think of them in relation to the diseases they cause. There are a considerable number of them—measles, poliomyelitis, hepatitis, chickenpox, and the common cold, to name a few. **AIDS** (acquired immune deficiency syndrome) is a very serious viral disease discussed in Chapter 16. This and other representative viral diseases are listed in Table 3 in Appendix 3.

Protozoa

With the **protozoa** (pro-to-zo′ah), we come to the only group of microbes that can be described as animal-like. Although protozoa are one celled, like bacteria, they are much larger.

Protozoa are found all over the world in the soil and in almost any body of water from moist grass to mud puddles to the sea. There are four main divisions of protozoa:

1 **Amebas** (ah-me′bas). An ameba is an irregular blob of cytoplasm that propels itself by extending part of its cell (a "false foot") and then flowing into the extension. Amebic dysentery is caused by a pathogen of this group.
2 **Ciliates** (sil′e-ates). This type of protozoon is covered with tiny hairs called **cilia** that produce a wave motion to propel the organism.
3 **Flagellates** (flaj′e-lates). This organism is propelled by long, whiplike filaments called **flagella**. One of this group, a trypanosome (tri-pan′o-som), causes African sleeping sickness (see Fig. 5-4).
4 **Sporozoa** (spo-ro-zo′ah). Unlike other protozoa, sporozoa cannot propel themselves. They are parasites, unable to grow outside a host. Malaria is caused by members of this group called **plasmodia** (plaz-mo′de-ah). These protozoa, carried by a kind of mosquito that is especially prevalent in the tropics, cause serious illness and many deaths. Although it is being fought against, malaria still causes 2 million deaths each year, according to the latest estimates.

Figure 5-4 illustrates some of the pathogenic protozoa and their portals of entry. Table 4 in Appendix 3 presents a list of typical pathogenic protozoa with the diseases for which they are responsible.

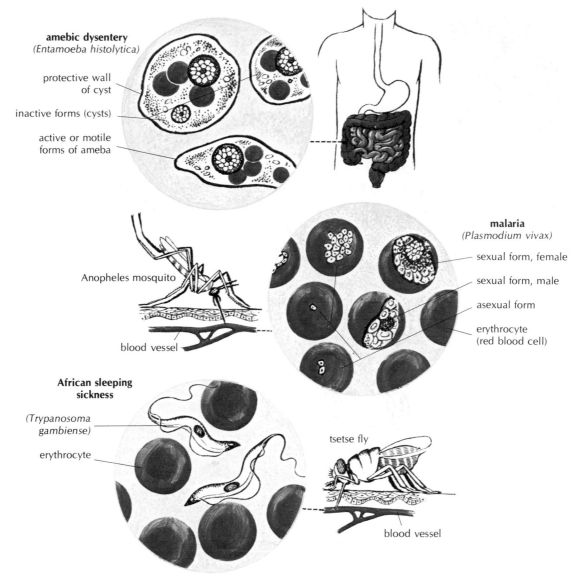

Figure 5-4. *Pathogenic protozoa.*

≡ Parasitic Worms

Many species of worm (also referred to as **helminths**) are parasitic by nature and select the human organism as their host. The study of worms, particularly parasitic ones, is called **helminthology** (hel-min-thol′o-je). Whereas invasion by any form of organism is usually called an *infection,* the presence of parasitic worms in the body also can be termed an **infestation** (Fig. 5-5). A microscope is required for one to see the eggs or larval forms of most worm infestations.

Roundworms

Intestinal Roundworms

Many human parasitic worms are classified as roundworms, one of the most common of which is the large worm **ascaris** (as′kah-ris). This worm is very prevalent in many parts of Asia, where it is found

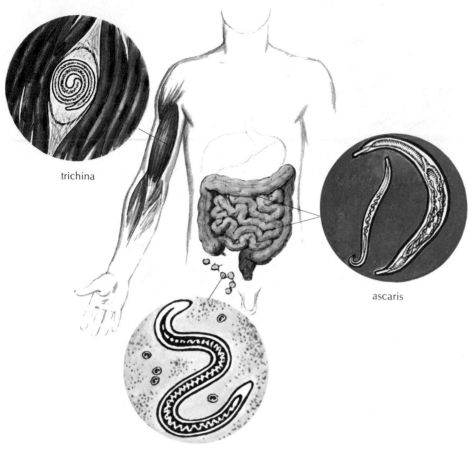

trichina

ascaris

filaria

Figure 5-5. *Common parasitic worms.*

mostly in larval form. In the United States, it is found especially frequently in children (ages 4–12 years) of the rural South. *Ascaris* is a long, whitish yellow worm pointed at both ends. It may infest the lungs or the intestines, producing intestinal obstruction if present in large numbers. The eggs produced by the adult worms are very resistant so that they can live in soil during either freezing or hot, dry weather and cannot be destroyed even by strong antiseptics. The embryo worms develop within the eggs deposited with excreta in the soil, and later reach the digestive system of a victim by means of contaminated food. Discovery of this condition may be made by a routine stool examination.

Pinworms

Another fairly common infestation, particularly in children, is the seat worm, or **pinworm** (*Enterobius vermicularis*), which is also very hard to control and eliminate. The worms average 12 mm (somewhat less

than ½ inch) in length and live in the large intestine. The adult female moves outside the vicinity of the anus to lay its thousands of eggs. These eggs are often transferred by a child's fingers from the itching anal area to the mouth. In the digestive system of the victim, the eggs develop to form new adult worms, and thus a new infestation is begun. The child also may infect others by this means. In addition, pinworm eggs that are expelled from the body also constitute a hazard, since they may live in the external environment for several months. Patience and every precaution, with careful attention to medical instructions, are necessary to rid the patient of the worms. Washing the hands, keeping the fingernails clean, and avoiding finger sucking are all essential.

Hookworms

Hookworms are parasites that live in the small intestine. They are dangerous because they suck blood from the host, causing such a severe anemia (blood deficiency) that the victim becomes sluggish, both physically and mentally. Most victims become susceptible to various chronic infections because of extremely reduced resistance following such a great and continuous blood loss. Hookworms lay thousands of eggs, which are distributed in the soil by contaminated excreta. The eggs develop into small larvae, which are able to penetrate the intact skin of bare feet. They enter the blood and, by way of the circulating fluids, the lungs, and the upper respiratory tract, finally reach the digestive system. Prevention of this infestation is best accomplished by the proper disposal of excreta, attention to sanitation, and the wearing of shoes in areas where the soil is contaminated.

Other Roundworms

Most roundworms are transmitted by excreta; however, the small **trichina** (trik-i″nah), found in pork and muscle foods, is an exception. These tiny, round worms become enclosed in cysts, or sacs, inside the muscles of rats, pigs, and humans. If undercooked pork is eaten, the cysts in it are dissolved by the host's digestive juices, and the tiny worms mature and travel to the host's muscles, where they again become encased. This disease is known as **trichinosis** (trik-i-no′sis).

The tiny, threadlike worm that causes **filariasis** (fil-ah-ri′ah-sis) is transmitted by such biting insects as flies and mosquitoes. The worms grow in large numbers, causing various body disturbances. If the lymph vessels become clogged by them, there results a condition called **elephantiasis** (el-e-fan-ti′ah-sis) in which the lower extremities and the scrotum may become tremendously enlarged. Filariasis is most common in tropical and subtropical lands, such as southern Asia and many of the South Pacific islands.

Flatworms

Some flatworms resemble long ribbons, whereas others have the shape of a leaf. Tapeworms may grow in the intestinal tract to a length of from 1.5 meters to 15 meters (5–50 feet) (Fig. 5-6). They are spread by infected, improperly cooked meats, including beef, pork, and fish. Like that of most intestinal worm parasites, the flatworm's reproductive system is very highly developed, so that each worm produces an almost unbelievable number of eggs, which then may contaminate food, water, and soil. Leaf-shaped flat-

worms, known as *flukes,* may invade various parts of the body, including the blood, lungs, liver, and intestine.

≡ Microbial Control

The Spread of Microorganisms

There is scarcely a place on earth that is naturally free of microorganisms. One exception is the interior of normal body tissue. However, body surfaces and passageways leading to the outside of the body—such as the mouth, throat, nasal cavities, and large intestine—harbor an abundance of both harmless and pathogenic microbes. As is explained in Chapter 16, the body has natural defenses against these organisms. If these natural defenses are sound, a person may harbor many microbes without ill effect. However, if that person's resistance becomes lowered, an infection can result.

Microbes are spread about through an almost infinite variety of means. The simplest way is by person-to-person contact. The more crowded the living conditions, the greater are the chances of epidemics. The atmosphere is a carrier of microorganisms. Although microbes cannot fly, the dust of the air is alive with them. In close quarters, the atmosphere is further contaminated by bacteria-laden droplets discharged by sneezing, coughing, and even normal conversation. Pathogens also are spread by such pests as rats, mice, fleas, lice, flies, and mosquitoes. Microbial growth is further abetted by a prevalence of dirt and lack of sunlight. In slum areas, there is often a combination of crowded conditions and poor sanitation, and many of a slum's inhabitants have lowered resistance because of poor nutrition and other undesirable health practices. As a result, epidemics are apt to begin in these districts.

Microbes and Public Health

All civilized societies establish and enforce measures designed to protect the health of their populations. Most of these practices are concerned with preventing the spread of infectious organisms. A few examples of fundamental public health considerations are listed below:

1 **Sewage and garbage disposal**. In times past, when people disposed of the household "slops"

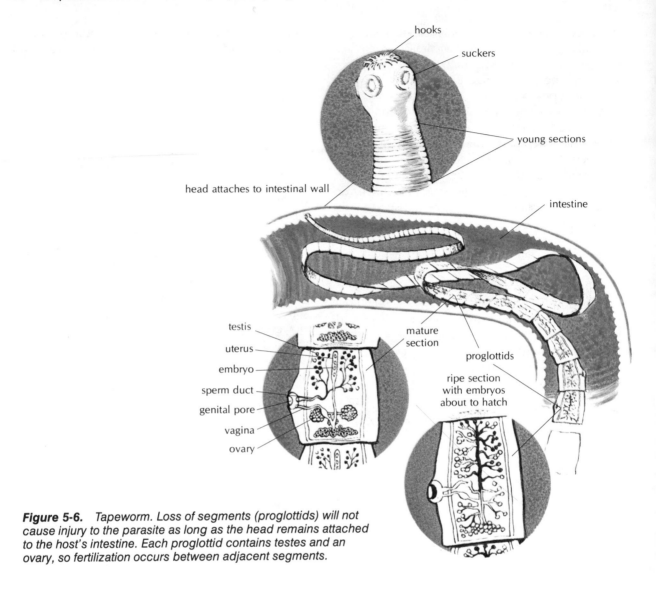

hooks
suckers
young sections
head attaches to intestinal wall
intestine
testis
uterus
embryo
sperm duct
genital pore
vagina
ovary
mature section
proglottids
ripe section with embryos about to hatch

Figure 5-6. *Tapeworm. Loss of segments (proglottids) will not cause injury to the parasite as long as the head remains attached to the host's intestine. Each proglottid contains testes and an ovary, so fertilization occurs between adjacent segments.*

by the simple expedient of throwing them out the window, great epidemics were inevitable. Modern practice is to divert sewage into a processing plant in which harmless microbes are put to work destroying the pathogens. The resulting non-infectious "sludge" makes excellent fertilizer.

2 **Purification of the water supply.** Drinking water that has become polluted with untreated sewage may be contaminated with such dangerous pathogens as typhoid bacilli, the viruses of polio and hepatitis, and dysentery amebas. The municipal water supply usually is purified by a filtering process, and a close and constant watch is kept on its microbial population. Industrial and chemical wastes, such as asbestos fibers, acids and detergents from homes as well as from industry, and pesticides used in agriculture, complicate the problems of obtaining pure drinking water.

3 **Prevention of food contamination.** Various national, state, and local laws seek to prevent outbreaks of disease through contaminated food. Not only can certain animal diseases (tuberculosis, tularemia) be passed on, but food is a natural breeding place for many dangerous pathogens. Two organisms that cause food poisoning are the rod-shaped botulism bacillus

(*Clostridium botulinum*) and the grapelike "staph" (*Staphylococcus aureus*). For further information, see Table 1 of Appendix 3.

Most cities have sanitary regulations requiring, among other things, compulsory periodic inspection of food-handling establishments.

4 Milk pasteurization. Milk is rendered free of pathogens by pasteurization, a process in which it is heated to 63°C (145°F) for 30 minutes and then allowed to cool rapidly before being bottled. The entire pasteurization process, including the cooling and bottling, is accomplished in a closed system, without any exposure to air. Pasteurized milk still contains microbes, but no harmful ones. Sometimes slightly higher temperatures are used for a much shorter time with satisfactory results. Pasteurization is also used to preserve other beverages and dairy products.

Aseptic Methods

In the practice of medicine, surgery, nursing, and other health fields, specialized procedures are performed for the purpose of reducing to a minimum the influence of pathogenic organisms. The word *sepsis* means "poisoning due to pathogens"; **asepsis** (a-sep′sis) is its opposite: a condition in which no pathogens are present. Procedures that are designed to kill, remove, or prevent the growth of microbes are called **aseptic methods.**

There are a number of terms designating aseptic practices, many of which are often confused with one another. Some of the more commonly used terms and their definitions are as follows (Fig. 5-7):

1 Sterilization. To sterilize an object means to kill *every* living microorganism on it. In operating rooms and delivery rooms especially, as much of the environment as possible is kept sterile, including the gowns worn by operating room personnel and the instruments used. The usual sterilization agent is live steam under pressure or dry heat. Most pathogens can be killed by exposure to boiling water for 4 minutes. However, a very few types of pathogenic bacteria are capable of developing a highly resistant form called a **spore.** The time and temperature required to ensure the destruction of all spore-forming organisms in sterilization are much greater than those required to kill most pathogens.

2 Disinfection. Disinfection refers to any measure

Figure 5-7. *Aseptic methods.* (A) *Sterilization.* (B) *Disinfection.* (C) *Antisepsis.*

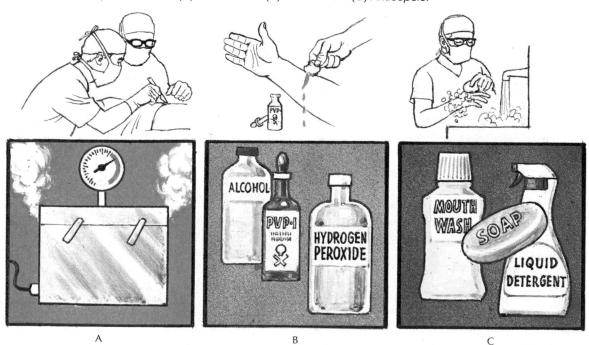

A   B   C

that kills all pathogens (except spores), but not necessarily all harmless microbes as well. Most disinfecting agents (**disinfectants**) are chemical; examples are iodine and phenol (carbolic acid). Two other terms for bacteria-killing agents, synonymous with *disinfectant,* are **bactericide** and **germicide.**

3 **Antisepsis.** This term refers to any process in which pathogens are not necessarily killed but are prevented from multiplying, a state called **bacteriostasis** (bak-te-re-os′tah-sis). **Antiseptics** are less powerful than disinfectants.

Chemotherapy

Chemotherapy (ke-mo-ther′ah-pe) means the treatment of a disease by the administration of a chemical agent. The definiton has come to include the treatment of disease by any natural or artificial (synthetic) substance.

Antibiotics

An antibiotic is a chemical substance produced by living cells. It has the power to kill or arrest the growth of pathogenic microorganisms by upsetting vital chemical processes within them. Antibiotics that are relatively nontoxic to the host are used for the treatment of infectious diseases. Most antibiotics are derived from molds and soil bacteria. Penicillin, the first widely used antibiotic, is made from a common blue mold, *Penicillium.* Another large group of antibiotics is produced by *Streptomyces,* a genus of soil bacteria; a well-known example of this group is streptomycin.

Although the development of antibiotics has been of incalculable benefit to mankind, it has also given rise to serious complications. One danger is that of secondary infection. It may well be that coexisting in the body with disease-causing bacteria is a second type of disease organism, such as a fungus. Up to the time of administration of antibiotics, the fungus is of no danger to the body because its growth is suppressed by the bacteria. However, if antibiotics eliminate the natural enemy of the fungus without affecting the fungus itself, there is nothing to prevent the fungus from growing unrestrainedly and setting up a new infection, which is very difficult to cure.

Another danger in the use of antibiotics is the development of allergies (immunologic reactions) to these substances. This complication can have very dangerous consequences.

Finally, the widespread use of antibiotics has resulted in the natural evolution of strains of pathogens that are resistant to such medications. One of the greatest problems in hospitals today is the prevalence of antibiotic-resistant pathogens, including certain streptococci, staphylococci, and bacilli. These pathogens may cause serious infections that are unresponsive to chemotherapy. About 5% of hospital patients contract one or more of these infections. Patients who are elderly or severely debilitated are most susceptible to these so-called **nosocomial** (nos″o-ko′me-al) diseases (hospital-acquired diseases).

Antineoplastic Agents

Antineoplastic agents are a group of chemotherapeutic drugs extensively employed to treat cancers. These agents are toxic to the host as well as to the tumor cells and should be administered by persons who understand the complications caused by these drugs (see Chap. 4).

Laboratory Identification of Pathogens

The nurse, physician, or laboratory worker may obtain specimens from patients in order to identify bacteria and other organisms. Specimens most frequently studied are blood, spinal fluid, feces, urine, and sputum, as well as swabbings from other areas. Swabs are used to collect specimens from the nose, throat, eyes, and cervix, as well as from ulcers or other infected areas.

There are so many different kinds of bacteria requiring identification that the laboratory must use a number of procedures for determining which organisms are present in the material obtained from a patient. One of the most frequently used methods for beginning the process of identification involves the application of colored dyes, known as *stains,* to a thin smear of the specimen on a glass slide. One stain used to identify organisms is the **acid-fast stain.** After being stained with a reddish dye (carbolfuchsin), the smear is treated with acid. Most bacteria quickly lose their stain upon application of the acid, but the organisms that cause tuberculosis and leprosy remain colored. Such organisms are said to be **acid fast.**

The most commonly used staining procedure is

known as the **Gram stain**. A bluish dye (such as methyl violet or gentian violet) is applied and then a weak solution of iodine added. This causes a color-fast combination within certain organisms so that the use of alcohol or other solvents does not remove the dye. These bacteria are said to be **gram positive**. Examples are the pathogenic staphylococci and streptococci, the cocci that cause certain types of pneumonia, and the bacilli that produce diphtheria, tetanus, and anthrax. Other organisms are said to be **gram negative** because the coloring can be removed from them by the use of a solvent such as acetone or alcohol. Examples of gram-negative organisms are the diplococci that cause gonorrhea and epidemic meningitis and the bacilli that produce typhoid fever, influenza, and one type of dysentery. The colon bacillus normally found in the bowel is also gram negative, as is the cholera vibrio. A few organisms, such as the spirochetes of syphilis and the rickettsias, do not stain with any of the commonly used dyes. Special staining techniques must be used to identify these organisms.

In addition to the various staining procedures, laboratory techniques for identifying bacteria include growing cells in cultures, a process using substances called **media** (such as nutrient broth or agar) that bacteria can use as food; studying the ability of bacteria to act on (ferment) various carbohydrates (sugars); observing reactions to various test chemicals; inoculating animals and analyzing their reactions to the injections; and studying bacteria by serologic (immunologic) tests based on the antigen–antibody reaction (see Chap. 16). These are but a few of the many laboratory procedures that play a vital part in the process of diagnosing disease.

Summary

I Causes of disease
   A Direct—disease-producing organisms, malnutrition, physical and chemical agents, congenital and inherited abnormalities, degeneration, neoplasms
   B Indirect—age, sex, heredity, living conditions and habits, occupation, physical exposure, preexisting illness, psychogenic influences

II Study of disease—pathophysiology
   A Terminology

     1 Etiology—study of causation
     2 Incidence—range of occurrence
     3 Disease description
       a Acute—severe, of short duration
       b Chronic—less severe, of long duration
       c Subacute—intermediate between acute and chronic
       d Idiopathic—of unknown cause
       e Communicable—transmissible
       f Epidemic—widespread in a given region
       g Endemic—characteristic of a given region
       h Pandemic—prevalent throughout an entire country
     4 Diagnosis—determination of the nature of the illness
       a Symptom—change in body function felt by the patient
       b Sign—change in body function observable by others
       c Syndrome—characteristic group of signs and symptoms
     5 Prognosis—prediction of probable outcome of disease
     6 Therapy—course of treatment
     7 Prevention—removal of potential causes of disease
   B Infection—invasion of body by microorganisms (pathogens)
     1 Modes of transmission—direct and indirect
     2 Portals of entry and exit—skin; respiratory, digestive, and reproductive systems

III Microorganisms—single-celled organisms visible only with a microscope
   A Microbiology—the study of microorganisms
     1 Bacteriology—study of bacteria
     4 Protozoology—study of protozoa
     2 Mycology—study of fungi
     3 Virology—study of viruses
   B Bacteria
     1 Bacilli—straight rods; may produce spores (resistant forms)
     2 Cocci—spheres
       a Diplococci—pairs
       b Streptococci—chains
       c Staphylococci—clusters
     3 Curved rods
       a Vibrios—comma shaped
       b Spirilla—corkscrew or wavy
       c Spirochetes—flexible spirals

     4 Modified bacteria—obligate parasites
       a Rickettsias
       b Chlamydias
  C Fungi—simple, plant-like organisms including yeasts and molds
  D Viruses—smallest infectious agents; obligate parasites
  E Protozoa—single-celled, animal-like organisms, including amebas, ciliates, flagellates, sporozoa

IV **Parasitic worms**—helminths
  A Roundworms—ascaris, pinworms, trichinas, filarias, hookworms
  B Flatworms—tapeworms, flukes

V **Microbial control**
  A Spread of microorganisms
  B Public health measures—sewage disposal, water purification, food inspection, milk pasteurization
  C Aseptic methods
    1 Sterilization—total removal of organisms
    2 Disinfection—destruction of all pathogens except spores
    3 Antisepsis—bacteriostasis

VI **Chemotherapy**—drug treatment
  A Antibiotics—used for nontoxic treatment of infection
  B Antineoplastics—used for treatment of cancer

VII **Laboratory identification of pathogens**
  A Cultivation of organisms
  B Staining of cells
    1 Acid-fast stain—identifies tuberculosis
    2 Gram stain—most commonly used stain
  C Other tests

Questions for Study and Review

1 What is disease? List five direct and five indirect causes.

2 Explain the difference between the terms in each of the following pairs:
  a *etiology* and *incidence*
  b *epidemic* and *endemic*
  c *diagnosis* and *prognosis*
  d *acute* and *chronic*
  e *idiopathic* and *nosocomial*
  f *symptom* and *sign*
  g *pathogen* and *parasite*

3 What are the three characteristic shapes of bacterial cells? Name a typical disease caused by each group.

4 Name the portals of entry for disease.

5 What are spores? Why are they important in the study of disease?

6 In what ways are microorganisms beneficial to humans?

7 How do the rickettsias and the chlamydias differ from other bacteria in size and living habits?

8 What is the typical mode of transmission of rickettsial infections?

9 What microbial group is described as animal-like? Name three diseases these microbes cause.

10 Name two types of pathogenic fungi and one common fungal infection.

11 Name two diseases caused by rickettsias and two due to chlamydias.

12 List four viral diseases. What does the acronym (abbreviation) *AIDS* mean?

13 What are the most common ways by which disease organisms are spread? What measures do communities take to prevent outbreaks of disease?

14 Define the terms *asepsis, sterilization, disinfection, antisepsis,* and *chemotherapy.*

15 What are some disadvantages of the use of antibiotics?

16 What are laboratory stains and why are they used? What are examples of acid-fast, gram-negative, and gram-positive organisms?

6

The Skin in Health and Disease

Behavioral Objectives

After careful study of this chapter, you should be able to:

Describe the layers of the skin

Identify the roles of keratin and melanin in the integumentary system

Describe the locations and functions of the two types of sweat glands

Describe the function of the sebaceous glands

List three functions of the skin

Summarize the information that can be gained by observation of the skin

List the main diseases of the skin

Selected Key Terms

The following terms are defined in the glossary:

dermatitis
dermis
eczema
epidermis
erythema
integument
keratin
lesion
melanin
sebaceous
sebum
sudoriferous

Is the skin merely a body covering, is it an organ, or is it a composite of parts that make it properly a system? Actually, it has some properties of each of these and so may be classified in three different ways:

1 It may be called an **enveloping membrane** because it is a layer of tissue covering the entire body. The term **cutaneous** (ku-ta′ne-us) refers to the skin

2 It may be referred to as an **organ** (the largest one, in fact) because it contains several kinds of tissue, including epithelial, connective, and nerve tissues

3 It is also known as the **integumentary system**, *integument* (integ′u-ment) meaning "covering," because it includes sweat and oil glands as well as other parts that work together as a body system

≡ Structure of the Skin

The skin covers the entire surface of the body. It consists of two main layers, different from each other in structure and function (Fig. 6-1). These are

1 The **epidermis** (ep-i-der′mis), or outermost layer, which is subdivided into **strata** (stra′tah), or layers, and is made entirely of epithelial cells with no blood vessels

2 The **dermis**, or true skin, which has a framework of connective tissue and contains many blood vessels, nerve endings, and glands

Epidermis

The epidermis is the surface layer of the skin, the outermost cells of which are constantly lost through

Figure 6-1. *Cross section of the skin.*

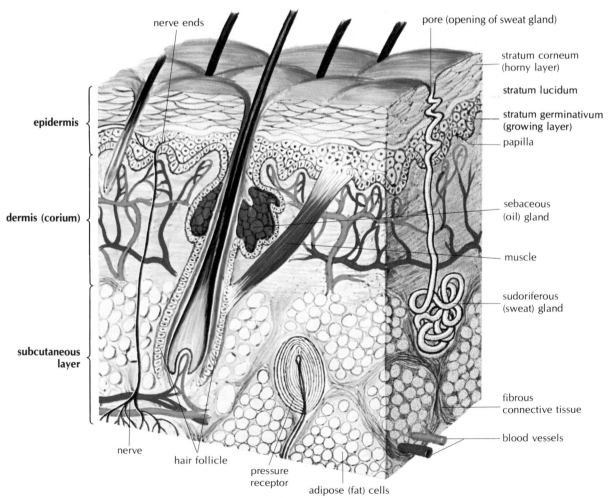

nerve ends

pore (opening of sweat gland)

stratum corneum (horny layer)

stratum lucidum

stratum germinativum (growing layer)

papilla

epidermis

dermis (corium)

sebaceous (oil) gland

muscle

sudoriferous (sweat) gland

subcutaneous layer

fibrous connective tissue

blood vessels

nerve

hair follicle

pressure receptor

adipose (fat) cells

wear and tear. Since there are no blood vessels in the epidermis, the only living cells are in its deepest layer, the **stratum germinativum** (jer-min-a-tee'vum), where nourishment is provided by capillaries in the underlying dermis. The cells in this layer are constantly dividing and producing daughter cells, which are pushed upward toward the surface. As the surface cells die from the gradual loss of nourishment, they undergo changes. Mainly, they develop large amounts of a protein called **keratin** (ker'ah-tin), which serves to thicken and protect the skin.

By the time epidermal cells reach the surface, they have become flat and horny, forming the uppermost layer of the epidermis, the **stratum corneum** (kor'nee-um). Depending on thickness, skin may have additional layers between the stratum germinativum and the stratum corneum. Cells in the deepest layer of the epidermis also produce **melanin** (mel'ah-nin), the pigment that gives skin its color; irregular patches of melanin are called *freckles*. Ridges and grooves in the skin of the fingers, palms, toes, and soles form unchanging patterns determined by heredity. These ridges actually serve to prevent slipping, but because they are unique to each individual, fingerprints and footprints are excellent means of identification. The ridges are due to elevations and depressions in the epidermis and the dermis. The deep surface of the epidermis is accurately molded upon the outer part of the dermis, which has raised and depressed areas.

Dermis

The **dermis**, or **corium** (ko're-um), the so-called true skin, has a framework of elastic connective tissue and is well supplied with blood vessels and nerves. The thickness of the dermis as well as that of the epidermis varies, so that some areas, such as the soles of the feet and the palms of the hands, are covered with very thick layers of skin while others, such as the eyelids, are covered with very thin and delicate layers. Most of the appendages of the skin, including the sweat glands, the oil glands, and the hair, are located in the dermis and may extend into the subcutaneous layer.

Subcutaneous Layer

The dermis rests on the **subcutaneous** (sub ku-ta'ne-us) **layer** or under-the-skin layer. Subcutaneous tissue is a combination of elastic and fibrous tissue as well as adipose tissue (fat). This layer, sometimes referred to as the **superficial fascia** (see Chap. 4), is the means of connecting the skin proper to the surface muscles. The fat in this sheet of tissue serves as insulation as well as a reserve store for energy.

≡ Appendages of the Skin

Sweat Glands

The **sudoriferous** (su″dō-rif'er-us) **glands,** or sweat glands, are coiled, tubelike structures located in the dermis and the subcutaneous tissue. The most common and most widely distributed of these glands are the ones that function primarily to regulate body temperature by the evaporation of sweat from the surface of the body. These glands secrete a mixture of water, mineral salts, and waste. Their excretory ducts spiral upward and open as pores on the surface of the skin.

The other type of sweat gland is located mainly in the armpits and the groin area. These glands release their secretions through the hair follicles in response to emotional stress and sexual stimulation. These secretions contain cellular material that is broken down by bacteria, producing body odor.

The **ceruminous** (se-roo'mi-nus), or wax, **glands** in the ear canal and the **ciliary** (sil'e-er″e) **glands** at the edges of the eyelids are modifications of sweat glands, as are the **mammary glands.**

Sebaceous Glands

The **sebaceous** (se-ba'shus) **glands** are saclike in structure, and their oily secretion, **sebum** (see'bum), helps lubricate the skin and hair and prevent drying. The ducts of the sebaceous glands open into the hair follicles.

Babies are born with a covering produced by these glands that resembles cream cheese; this secretion is called the **vernix caseosa** (ver'niks kā-se-o'sah).

Blackheads consist of a mixture of dirt and sebum that may collect at the openings of the sebaceous glands. If these glands become infected, pimples result. If sebaceous glands become blocked by accumulated sebum, a sac of this secretion may form and gradually increase in size. These sacs are referred to as **sebaceous cysts.** Usually it is not difficult to remove such tumor-like cysts by surgery.

Hair and Nails

Almost all of the body is covered with hair, which in most areas is very soft and fine. Hair is composed mainly of keratin and is not living. Each hair develops within a sheath called a **follicle**, and new hairs are formed from cells at the bottoms of follicles (Fig. 6-1). Attached to most hair follicles is a thin band of involuntary muscle. When this muscle contracts, the hair is raised, forming "goose bumps" on the skin. As it contracts, the muscle presses on the sebaceous gland associated with the hair follicle, causing the release of sebum to lubricate the skin. Hair is a useful tool for diagnosis. Analysis of hair may reveal metal poisoning, malnutrition, and certain diseases such as cystic fibrosis.

Nails are protective structures made of hard keratin produced by cells that originate in the outer layer of the epidermis (stratum corneum). New cells form continuously at the proximal end of the nail in an area called the **nail root**. Nails of both the toes and the fingers are affected by general health. They may become discolored, dry and cracked in chronic diseases of the nervous system and of the skin, as well as in conditions accompanied by prolonged fever.

≡ Functions of the Skin

Although the skin has several functions, the three that are by far the most important are the following:

1 Protection of deeper tissues against drying and against invasion by pathogenic organisms or their toxins through a mechanical barrier

2 Regulation of body temperature by dissipation of heat to the surrounding air

3 Receipt of information about the environment by means of the nerve endings, which are profusely distributed in the skin. Some sensory information has a protective function in that it enables one to withdraw from harmful stimuli, such as a hot stove.

The intact skin is incapable of defense against sharp objects, but it can defend against pathogens, toxins, and water loss. A break in the skin by **trauma** (traw′mah), that is, a wound or injury of any kind, may be followed by serious infection. The care of wounds involves, to a large extent, prevention of the entrance of pathogens and toxins into deeper tissues and body fluids.

The regulation of body temperature is also a very important function of the skin. Normal temperature may vary slightly, but we think of 37°C (98.6°F) as the standard when a thermometer is placed in the mouth for 3 to 5 minutes. The body temperature reading may be expected to be somewhat less if taken in the axilla (armpit) and somewhat more if taken in the rectum. The skin forms a large surface for radiating body heat to the air. When the blood vessels dilate (enlarge), more blood is brought to the surface so that heat can be dissipated into the air. The evaporation of sweat from the surface of the body also helps cool the body. As is the case with so many body functions, the matter of temperature regulation is complex and involves several parts of the body, including certain centers in the brain.

A child loses heat faster than does an adult, since a higher proportion of a child's body is skin surface and thus relatively more area is exposed. Therefore, it is important to prevent undue exposure to the elements in infants and small children. The elderly do not produce heat in the body so easily or to so great an extent as do younger adults; therefore, they also should be protected against cold.

Another important function of the skin is obtaining information from the environment. Because of the many nerve endings and other special receptors for pain, touch, pressure, and temperature, which are located mostly in the dermis, the skin may be regarded as one of the chief sensory organs of the body. Many of the reflexes that make it possible for humans to adjust themselves to the environment begin as sensory impulses from the skin. Here, too, the skin works with the brain and the spinal cord to make these important functions possible.

The functions of absorption and excretion are minimal in the skin. Most medicated ointments used on the skin are for the treatment of local conditions only, and the injection of medication into the subcutaneous tissues is limited by the slow absorption that occurs here. The skin excretes a mixture of water and mineral salts in perspiration. Some nitrogen-containing wastes are also eliminated through the skin, but even in disease the amount of waste products excreted by the skin is small.

The human skin does not "breathe." The pores of the epidermis serve only as outlets for perspiration and oil from the sweat glands and sebaceous glands. Misinformation about the skin abounds, its sole purpose often being to sell lotions, potions, and all sorts of supposedly magical preparations. Beware of cosmetics that purportedly aid the skin in breathing.

≡ Observation of the Skin

What can the skin tell you? What do its color, texture, and other attributes indicate? Much can be learned by the astute observer.

In fact, the first indication of a serious systemic disease (such as syphilis) may be a skin disorder.

The color of the skin depends on a number of factors, including the following:

1 The amount of pigment in the epidermis
2 The quantity of blood circulating in the surface blood vessels
3 The composition of the circulating blood
   a Presence or absence of oxygen
   b Concentration of hemoglobin
   c Presence of bile, silver compounds, or other chemicals

Pigment

The pigment of the skin, as we have noted, is called **melanin**. This pigment is found also in the hair, the middle coat of the eyeball, the iris of the eye, and certain tumors. Melanin is common to all races, but the darker peoples have a much larger quantity of it distributed in these tissues. A normal increase in this skin pigment occurs as a result of exposure to the sun. Abnormal increases in the quantity of melanin may occure either in localized areas or over the entire body surface. Diffuse spots of pigmentation may be characteristics of some endocrine disorders.

Discoloration

A yellowish discoloration of the skin may be due to the presence of excessive quantities of bilirubin (bile pigment) in the blood. This condition, called **jaundice** (jawn'dis), may be a symptom of a number of disorders, such as the following:

1 A tumor pressing on the common bile duct or a stone within the duct, either of which would obstruct the flow of bile into the small intestine
2 Inflammation of the liver (hepatitis)
3 Certain diseases of the blood in which red blood cells are rapidly destroyed

Another cause of a yellowish discoloration of the skin is the excessive intake of carrots and other deeply colored vegetables. This condition is known as **carotinemia** (kar″o-tin-e′me-ah).

Chronic poisoning may cause grayish or brown discoloration of the skin. A peculiar bronze cast is present in Addison's disease (malfunction of the adrenal gland). Many other disorders also cause discoloration of the skin, but their discussion is beyond the scope of this chapter.

Injuries

A wound or local injury is called a **lesion** (le′zhun). Lesions of the skin that should be noted by those who care for the sick include the following:

1 **Excoriations** (eks-ko-re-a′shuns), which may be evidence of scratching
2 **Lacerations** (las″er-a′shuns), which are rough, jagged wounds made by tearing of the skin
3 **Ulcers** (ul′sers), which are sores associated with disintegration and death of tissue
4 Areas of redness, called **erythema** (er-e-the′mah), as well as other discoloration
5 Spots of any kind

Eruptions

A skin rash (eruption) may be localized, as in diaper rash, or generalized, as in measles and other systemic infections. Some terms often used to describe skin eruptions are the following (Fig. 6-2):

1 **Macules** (mak′ules), or macular (mak′u-lar) rash. These spots are neither raised nor depressed. They are typical of measles and descriptive of freckles.
2 **Papules** (pap′ules), or papular (pap′u-lar) rash. These are firm, raised areas, as in some stages of chickenpox and in the second stage of syphilis. Pimples are papules.
3 **Vesicles** (ves′e-kals), or vesicular (ve-sik′u-lar) eruptions. These blisters or small sacs are full of fluid, such as may be found in some of the eruptions of chickenpox.
4 **Pustules** (pus′tules), or pustular (pus′tu-lar) lesions. These may follow the vesicular stage of chickenpox.
5 **Crusts**. These are made of dried pus and blood and are commonly referred to by laymen as *scabs*.

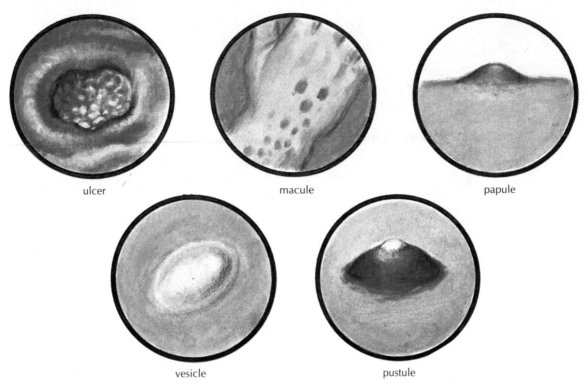

ulcer   macule   papule

vesicle   pustule

Figure 6-2. *Some common skin eruptions.*

Effects of Aging on Skin, Hair, and Nails

As persons age, wrinkles, or crow's feet, develop around the eyes and mouth owing to the loss of fat and collagen in the underlying tissues. The dermis becomes thinner, and the skin may become quite transparent and lose its elasticity, the effect of which is so-called parchment skin. The hair does not replace itself as rapidly as before and thus becomes thinner. The formation of pigment also decreases with age, causing hair to become gray or white. However, there may be localized areas of extra pigmentation in the skin with the formation of brown spots, especially on areas exposed to the sun (*e.g.,* the hands). The sweat glands decrease in number, so there is less output of perspiration. The fingernails may flake, become brittle, or develop ridges. Toenails may become discolored or abnormally thickened.

☰ Skin Diseases

Dermatosis and Dermatitis

Dermatosis (der-mah-to′sis) is a general term referring to any skin disease.

Inflammation of the skin is called **dermatitis** (der-mah-ti′tis). It may be due to many kinds of irritants, such as the oil of poison oak or poison ivy plants, detergents, and strong acids or alkalies or other chemicals. Prompt removal of the irritant is the most effective method of prevention and treatment. A thorough soap-and-water bath as soon as possible after contact with plant oils may prevent the development of itching eruptions.

Sunburn

Sunlight may cause chemical and biologic changes in the skin. The skin first becomes reddened (erythematous) and then may become swollen and blistered. Some persons suffer from severe burns and become seriously ill. There is considerable evidence that continued excessive exposure to the sun is an important cause of skin cancer. The current fad for tanning requires the skin to protect itself by producing considerably more than usual amounts of melanin. This increase in pigmentation may have the effect of reducing the ability of the body to profit from the desirable smaller amounts of sun available during some parts of the year.

Eczema

Eczema (ek′ze-mah) is an unpleasant disease that may be found in all age groups and in both sexes; however, it is most common in the very young and in the elderly. Eczema may affect any and all parts of the skin surface. It is a noncontagious disease that may manifest itself by redness (erythema), blisters (vesicles), pimple-like (papular) lesions, and scaling and crusting of the skin surface. Eczema may be a manifestation of excessive sensitivity to detergents, soaps, and other chemicals. For example, if used frequently, even the mildest soap may cause irritation. The skin also may overreact to heat, dryness, rough fabrics (especially wool), and even perspiration.

Common Acne

Acne (ak′ne) is a disease of the sebaceous (oil) glands connected with the hair follicles. The common type, called **acne vulgaris** (vul-ga′ris), is found most often in individuals between the ages of 14 and 25. The infection of the oil glands takes the form of pimples, which generally surround blackheads. Acne is usually most severe at adolescence, when certain endocrine glands in the body that control the secretions of the sebaceous glands are particularly active. Frequent, thorough cleansing of the skin with mild soap and warm water may be effective treatment of the condition. Special diets are not usually necessary. Oral antibiotics may prove useful but should be taken only as prescribed by a physician. Picking at the lesions may result in scarring and should be avoided.

Impetigo

Impetigo (im-pe-ti′go) is an acute contagious disease of staphylococcal or streptococcal origin that may be serious enough to cause death in newborn infants. It takes the form of blister-like lesions that become filled with pus and contain millions of virulent bacteria. It is found most frequently among poor and undernourished children. Affected persons may reinfect themselves or infect others. Sometimes the infection is spread by contaminated linen or dishes. In a nursery, for example, utmost care in handling infants is extremely important to prevent spread of the condition from baby to baby. Despite ordinary precautions, fatalities from impetigo have occurred at various times in the United States. Impetigo is so contagious that children who develop the disease should not be permitted to return to school until a health professional certifies that the condition is cured.

Alopecia (Baldness)

Alopecia (al-o-pe′she-ah) may be due to infection as well as to a number of other factors. It may be inherited, particularly in males. Baldness may be an expression of aging, in which case it usually begins at the crown of the head and is associated with atrophy of the structures of the scalp. It may be a result of such a systemic disease as syphilis or myxedema. A severe infection such as scarlet fever may cause hair loss, but in such cases recovery from the disease usually is accompanied by regrowth of the hair. A chronic fungous infection that involves the oil glands and hair follicles may result in alopecia. In these cases, frequent shampooing and constant attention to skin hygiene may prevent balding. Dandruff is often due to fungous disease of the scalp, and the assistance of a physician should be sought if one is to prevent alopecia. Baldness also is a common temporary side-effect of chemotherapeutic drugs used in treating neoplasms.

Athlete's Foot

Fungi are the usual cause of athlete's foot, also known as **epidermophytosis** (ep-e-der-mo-fi-to′sis). The disease most commonly involves the toes and the soles but occasionally affects the fingers, the palms, and the groin region. In acute cases the lesions may include vesicles, fissures, and ulcers. Predisposition to fungous infection varies. Some individuals may be exposed to pathogenic fungi with no ill effects, whereas other persons develop severe skin infections with only mild exposure. Those who perspire a great deal are particularly susceptible to athlete's foot. Frequent changing of hose and of shoes, together with thorough drying of the feet, with particular attention to the spaces between the toes, discourages infection. Dusting powders in the shoes and on the feet also deter fungous growth. Patent medicines may or may not be effective. It is better to see a physician and follow his or her instructions.

Other Disorders of the Skin

In addition to the disorders discussed above, other skin diseases include the following:

1 **Furuncles** (fu′rung-kls), or boils, which are localized collections of pus in cavities formed by the disintegration of tissue. They are caused by bacteria that enter hair follicles or sebaceous glands.

2 **Carbuncles** (kar'bung-kls), which are pus-producing lesions that result from the extension of infectious processes, such as boils. They involve both the skin and subcutaneous tissues and have numerous drainage channels that extend to the skin surface.

3 **Psoriasis** (so-ri'ah-sis), which is characterized by sharply outlined, red, flat areas (plaques) covered with silvery scales. The cause of this chronic, recurrent skin disease is unknown.

4 **Herpes** (her'pez) **simplex**, which is characterized by the formation of watery vesicles (cold sores, fever blisters) on the skin and mucous membranes, including the genital area (see Appendix 3, Table 3)

5 **Cancer** of the skin, which in the United States is most common among persons who have fair skin and who live in the Southwest, where exposure to the sun is consistent and may be intense. Early treatment in most cases means cure. Neglect can result in death.

6 **Urticaria** (ur"ti-ka're-ah), which is an allergic reaction characterized by the transient appearance of elevated red patches (hives) often accompanied by severe **pruritus** (proo-ri'tus), or itching

7 **Scleroderma** (skle"ro-der'mah), which together with some of the metabolic diseases, such as certain forms of lupus erythematosus, causes thickening of the dermis.

≡ Care of the Skin and Its Appendages

It is ironic that more money is spent on skin, hair, and nail care than on the combination of all types of medical and health services. Yet authorities agree that the one most important factor in keeping the skin and the hair attractive is good general health. A person with even a slightly underactive thyroid gland (see Chap. 11) will have dry skin and hair, and no amount of cream can take the place of thyroid extract tablets. The pallor of the anemia victim could be remedied much more effectively by appropriate health care than by any amount of cosmetics.

Normal skin secretions are slightly acid. Quacks have taken advantage of this by applying testing material (such as litmus paper) to the skin and then calling attention to the acid reaction with the warning that this "condition" should be corrected; naturally they sell the pills or potions for that purpose at a handsome profit. Actually, this acid secretion is produced as a protection against pathogens. As the acid stomach juice kills bacteria in the food we eat, so the skin secretions tend to destroy or at least inhibit bacterial growth. Dirt and dead skin cells, however, dilute this acid; hence, cleanliness is important too. Careful handwashing with soap and water, with attention to the undernail areas, is a simple measure to reduce the spread of disease.

The cleansing soap-and-water bath or shower is an important part of good grooming and health. Here individuals should know themselves and their peculiar personal needs. Those who have dry skin need to replace some of the oil that is removed by bathing if general health measures fail to remedy the dryness. For those who have very active sweat and oil glands, soap and water twice a day or more may be advisable, and creams and oily applications should be avoided. For most persons, so-called cleansing cream is not a proper substitute for soap and water.

Exposure to the elements, particularly to wind and sun, may call for applications of zinc ointment or some other fatty protective substance. Many sunburn lotions are of dubious value. A layer of an opaque ointment on the nose and other exposed surfaces helps prevent overexposure to ultraviolet rays and may help prevent undue drying of the skin.

Some of the newer sunscreening lotions have proved fairly effective. These contain a chemical known as **PABA** (para-aminobenzoic acid) or derivatives of this compound. They are clear liquids or creams, so they are not as visible as the zinc oxide ointments. All of these preparations wash off during swimming and should be reapplied as may be indicated by conditions.

Even though a sun tan is regarded as a symbol of health, continued exposure to sunlight can cause premature aging and other undesirable changes in the skin.

≡ Summary

I **Classification of the skin**
   A Membrane (cutaneous)
   B Organ
   C System (integumentary)

II **Structure of the skin**
 A Epidermis—outermost portion
  1 Stratified epithelial cells
  2 No blood vessels
  3 Several layers (strata)
   a Stratum germinativum—innermost layer
   b Stratum corneum—outermost layer
  4 Melanin—pigment that gives color to skin
 B Dermis—contains glands, hair follicles, sensory receptors
 C Subcutaneous layer

III **Appendages of the skin**
 A Sweat (sudoriferous) glands
 B Sebaceous glands
 C Hair
 D Nails

IV **Functions of the skin**
 A Protection
 B Regulation of body temperature
  1 Dilation of surface blood vessels
  2 Evaporation of sweat
 C Sensory perception

V **Observation of the skin**
 A Discoloration
  1 Endocrine disorders
  2 Jaundice (bile pigment)
  3 Destruction of red blood cells
  4 Poisoning
 B Injuries (lesions)—ulcers, erythema (redness), spots, lacerations, etc.
 C Skin eruptions
  1 Macules—flat spots
  2 Papules—raised areas
  3 Vesicles—blisters
  4 Pustules
  5 Crusts—scabs

VI **Skin diseases—dermatoses**
 A Dermatitis—inflammation
 B Sunburn—may lead to skin cancer
 C Eczema—redness, blisters, lesions
 D Acne—disease of sebaceous glands related to increased endocrine secretions
 E Impetigo—infectious disease of infants and children
 F Alopecia—baldness
 G Athletes' foot—fungous infection
 H Other disorders

VII **Care of the skin**

Questions for Study and Review

1 What characteristics of the skin classify it as a membrane? as an organ? as a system?
2 Of what type of cells is the epidermis composed?
3 Explain how the outermost cells of the epidermis are replaced.
4 What kind of tissue forms the framework of the dermis?
5 What glands extend down into the dermis and into the subcutaneous layer, and what are their functions?
6 Describe the distribution and functions of the two types of sweat glands.
7 What is the subcutaneous layer made of and what is the importance of this layer?
8 How can hair and nails be used in diagnosis?
9 Explain the three most important functions of the skin.
10 What are the facts about the skin as an organ of respiration and excretion?
11 What are the most important contributors to the color of the skin, normally?
12 What changes may occur in the skin with age?
13 What is the difference between a laceration and an ulcer?
14 Define *acne*. When is it usually most severe? Why?
15 What are some examples of irritants that frequently cause dermatitis?
16 What are the dangers of overexposure to the sun, and what precautions against it need to be considered?
17 What is eczema? Name its most important causes.
18 At what ages are patients with impetigo in the most danger, and what are some of the precautions that need to be taken against the disorder?
19 What are the most common causes of baldness?
20 What are the best measures to take to prevent and control athlete's foot?
21 Define *furuncles, herpes simplex,* and *carbuncles.*
22 Name some instances in which cosmetics are ineffective in remedying a basic defect. Why are they ineffective?
23 What is the value of the acid secretion of the skin?

7

The Skeleton—Bones and Joints

Behavioral Objectives

After careful study of this chapter, you should be able to:

Name the three different types of bone cells and describe the functions of each

Differentiate between compact bone and spongy bone with respect to structure and location

Describe the structure of a long bone

Explain how a long bone grows

Differentiate between red and yellow marrow with respect to function and location

List the bones in the axial skeleton

List the bones in the appendicular skeleton

Describe five bone disorders

Describe three abnormal curves of the spine

List and define six types of fractures

Define the three types of joints based on type of movement

Describe the structure of a synovial joint and give six examples of synovial joints

Define six types of movement that occur at synovial joints

Describe four types of arthritis

Selected Key Terms

The following terms are defined in the glossary:

amphiarthrosis
arthritis
bursa
circumduction
diaphysis
diarthrosis
endosteum
epiphysis
fontanel
joint
osteoblast
osteoclast
osteocyte
periosteum
resorption
synarthrosis
synovial

The bones are the framework of the body. They are a combination of several kinds of tissue and contain blood vessels and nerves. Bones are attached to each other at joints. The combination of bones and joints together with related connective tissues forms the skeletal system.

The Bones

Bone Structure

In Chapter 4 we saw that the bones are composed chiefly of bone tissue, called **osseous** (os′e-us) **tissue**. Bones are not lifeless. Even though the spaces between the cells of bone tissue are permeated with stony deposits of calcium, these cells themselves are very much alive. Bones are organs, with their own system of blood, lymphatic vessels, and nerves.

In the embryo (the early developmental stage of a baby) most of the bones-to-be are composed of cartilage. Bone formation begins during the second and third months of embryonic life. At this time, bone-building cells, called **osteoblasts** (os′te-o-blasts″), become very active. First, they manufacture a substance, the **intercellular** (in″ter-sel′u-lar) **material**, which is located between the cells and contains large quantities of a protein called **collagen**. Then, with the help of enzymes, calcium compounds are deposited within the intercellular material. Once the intercellular material has hardened around these cells, they are called **osteocytes**. They are still living and continue to maintain the bone, but they do not produce new bone tissue. Other cells, called **osteoclasts** (os′te-o-klasts″), are responsible for the process of **resorption**, or the breakdown of bone. Enzymes also implement this process.

The complete bony framework of the body, known as the **skeleton** (Fig. 7-1), consists of bones of many different shapes. They may be flat (rib, skull), cube shaped (wrist, ankle), or irregular (vertebra). However, typical bones, which make up most of the arms and legs, are described as *long bones*. This type of bone has a long shaft, called the **diaphysis** (di-af′i-sis), which has a central marrow cavity and two irregular ends, each called an **epiphysis** (e-pif′i-sis) (Fig. 7-2).

There are two types of bone tissue. One type is **compact bone**, which is hard and dense. This makes up the main shaft of a long bone and the outer layer of other bones. The osteocytes in this type of bone are located in rings of bone tissue around a central canal containing nerves and blood vessels (Fig. 7-2). The second type, called **spongy bone**, has more spaces than compact bone. It is made of a meshwork of small, bony plates filled with red marrow and is found at the ends of the long bones and at the center of other bones.

Bones contain two kinds of marrow: **red marrow**, found at the end of the long bones and at the center of other bones, which manufactures blood cells; and **yellow marrow** of the "soup bone" type, found chiefly in the central cavities of the long bones. Yellow marrow is largely fat.

Bones are covered on the outside (except at the joint region) by a membrane called the **periosteum** (per″e-os′te-um). The inner layer of this membrane contains osteoblasts, which are essential in bone formation, not only during growth but also in the repair of fractures. Blood and lymph vessels in the periosteum play an important role in the nourishment of bone tissue. Nerve fibers in the periosteum make their presence known when one suffers a fracture, or when one receives a blow, such as on the shinbone. A thinner membrane, the **endosteum** (en-dos′te-um), lines the marrow cavities of bone; it too contains cells that aid in the growth and repair of bone tissue.

Bone Growth and Repair

In a long bone, the transformation of cartilage into bone begins at the center of the shaft. Later, secondary bone-forming centers develop across the ends of the bones. The long bones continue to grow in length at these centers through childhood and into the late teens. Finally, by the late teens or early 20s, the bones stop growing in length. The bone-forming regions harden and can be seen in x-ray films as thin lines across the ends of the bones. Physicians can judge the future growth of a bone by the appearance of these lines on x-ray films.

As a bone grows in length, the shaft is remodeled so that it grows wider as the central marrow cavity increases in size. Thus, alterations in the shape of the bone are a result of bone's being added to some surfaces and resorbed from others. The processes of bone formation and bone resorption continue throughout life, more rapidly at some times than at others. The bones of small children are relatively

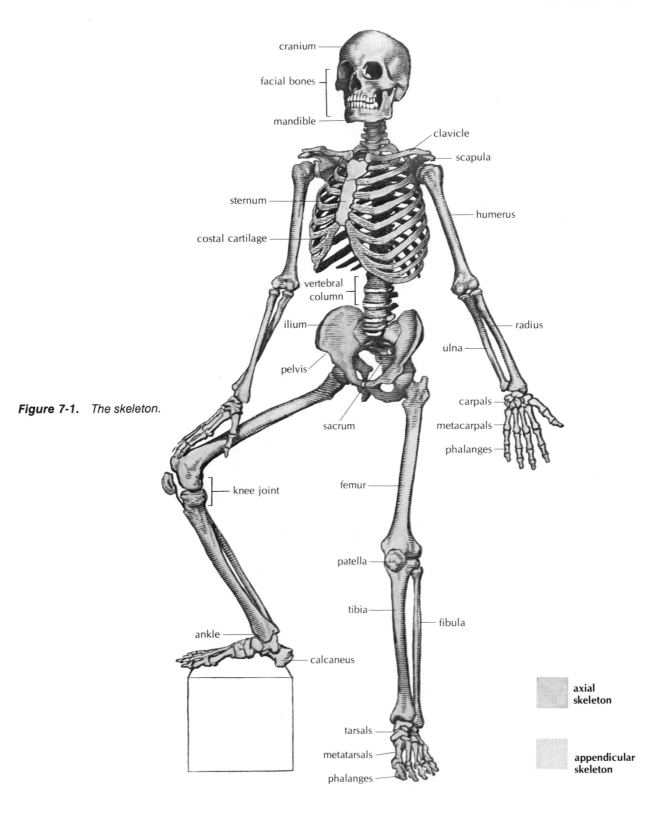

Figure 7-1. The skeleton.

cranium

facial bones

mandible

clavicle

scapula

sternum

humerus

costal cartilage

vertebral column

ilium

radius

ulna

pelvis

sacrum

carpals

metacarpals

phalanges

femur

knee joint

patella

tibia

fibula

ankle

calcaneus

tarsals

metatarsals

phalanges

axial skeleton

appendicular skeleton

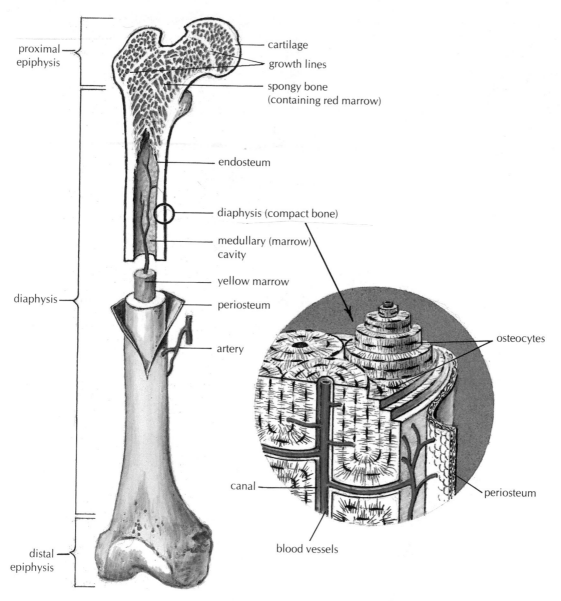

proximal epiphysis

cartilage

growth lines

spongy bone (containing red marrow)

endosteum

diaphysis (compact bone)

medullary (marrow) cavity

yellow marrow

periosteum

diaphysis

artery

osteocytes

canal

periosteum

distal epiphysis

blood vessels

Figure 7-2. *The structure of a long bone; the composition of compact bone.*

pliable because they contain a larger proportion of cartilage and a smaller amount of the firm calcium salts than those of adults. In elderly persons there is much less of the softer tissues such as cartilage and a high proportion of calcium salts; therefore, the bones of the elderly are brittle. Fractures of bones in old people heal with difficulty mainly because of this relatively high proportion of inert material and the small amount of the more vascular softer tissues.

Main Functions of Bones

Bones have a number of functions, many of which are not at all obvious. Some of these are listed below:

1 To serve as a firm framework for the entire body
2 To protect such delicate structures as the brain and the spinal cord
3 To serve as levers, which are actuated by the muscles that are attached to them

4 To serve as a storehouse for calcium, which may be resorbed into the blood if there is not enough calcium in the diet
5 To produce blood cells (in the red marrow)

Divisions of the Skeleton

The skeleton may be divided into two main groups of bones (see Fig. 7-1):

1 The **axial** (ak′se-al) **skeleton**, which includes the bony framework of the head and the trunk

2 The **appendicular** (ap-en-dik′u-lar) **skeleton**, which forms the framework for the arms and legs, or the **extremities**, as well as for the shoulders and hips.

Framework of the Head

The bony framework of the head, called the **skull**, is subdivided into two parts: the cranium and the facial portion. Refer to Figures 7-3 to 7-6, which show different views of the skull, as you study the following descriptions. The numbers in brackets refer to the numbers in Figure 7-3.

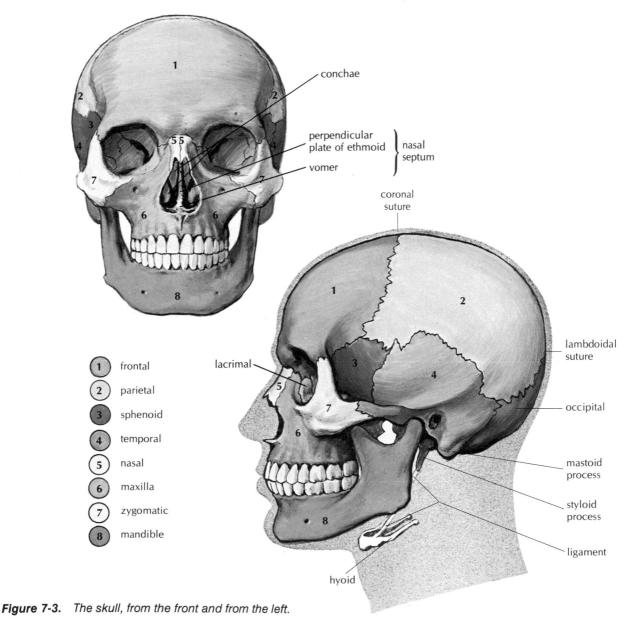

Figure 7-3. *The skull, from the front and from the left.*

1. frontal
2. parietal
3. sphenoid
4. temporal
5. nasal
6. maxilla
7. zygomatic
8. mandible

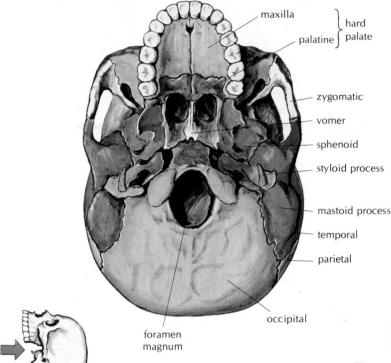

maxilla

palatine } hard palate

zygomatic

vomer

sphenoid

styloid process

mastoid process

temporal

parietal

occipital

foramen magnum

Figure 7-4. *The skull from below, lower jaw removed.*

A The **cranium** is a rounded box that encloses the brain; it is composed of eight distinct cranial bones.

1 The **frontal bone** [1] forms the forehead, the front of the skull's roof, and helps form the roof over the eyes and the nasal cavities. The **frontal sinuses** (air spaces) communicate with the nasal cavities.

2 The two **parietal** (pah-ri′e-tal) **bones** [2] form most of the top and the side walls of the cranium.

3 The two **temporal bones** [4] form part of the sides and some of the base of the skull. Each one contains **mastoid sinuses** as well as the ear canal, the eardrum, and the entire middle and internal ears.

4 The **ethmoid** (eth′moid) **bone** is located between the eyes, in the orbital cavities. Its upper surface forms the roof of the nasal cavities and part of the base of the cranium. A thin plate of bone extends downward to form the upper part of the nasal septum (medial partition).

5 The **sphenoid** (sfe′noid) **bone** [3], when seen from above, resembles a bat with its wings extended. It lies at the base of the skull in front of the temporal bones.

6 The **occipital** (ok-sip′i-tal) **bone** forms the back and a part of the base of the skull.

B The **facial portion** of the skull is composed of 14 bones.

1 The **mandible** (man′di-b-l) [8], or lower jaw bone, is the only movable bone of the skull.

2 The **two maxillae** (mak-sil′e) [6] fuse in the mid-line to form the upper jaw bone, including the front part of the hard palate (roof of the mouth). Each maxilla contains a large air space, called the **maxillary sinus**, that communicates with the nasal cavity.

3 The two **zygomatic** (zi-go-mat′ik) **bones** [7], one on each side, form the prominences of the cheeks.

4 Two slender **nasal bones** [5] lie side by side, forming the bridge of the nose.

5 The two **lacrimal** (lak′ri-mal) **bones**, each about the size of a fingernail, lie near the in-

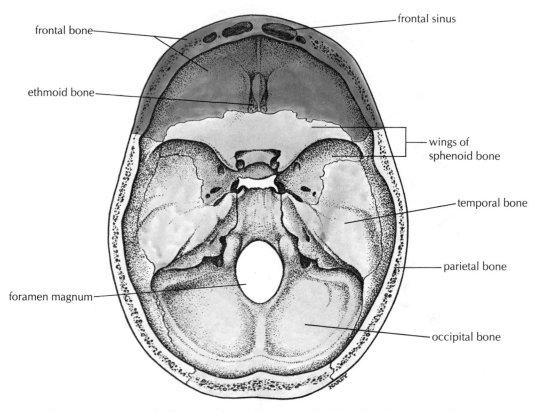

frontal bone

frontal sinus

ethmoid bone

wings of
sphenoid bone

temporal bone

parietal bone

foramen magnum

occipital bone

Figure 7-5. *Base of the skull as seen from above, showing the internal surfaces of some of the cranial bones. (Chaffee EE, Lytle IM: Basic Physiology and Anatomy, 4th ed, p 95. Philadelphia, JB Lippincott, 1980)*

side corner of the eye in the front part of the medial wall of the orbital cavity.

6 The **vomer** (vo′mer), shaped like the blade of a plow, forms the lower part of the nasal septum.

7 The paired **palatine bones** form the back part of the hard palate.

8 The two **inferior nasal conchae** (kon′ke) extend horizontally along the lateral wall (sides) of the nasal cavities. The paired superior and middle conchae are part of the ethmoid bone.

In addition to the bones of the cranium and the facial bones, there are three tiny bones, or **ossicles** (os′sik-ls), in each middle ear (see Chap. 10) and a single horseshoe, or U-shaped, bone just below the skull proper, called the **hyoid** (hi′oid) **bone**, to which the tongue is attached.

Openings in the base of the skull provide spaces for the entrance and exit of many blood vessels,

nerves, and other structures. Projections and slightly elevated portions of the bones provide for the attachment of muscles. Some portions contain delicate structures, such as the part of the temporal bone that encloses the middle and internal sections of the ear. The air sinuses provide lightness and serve as resonating chambers for the voice.

Framework of the Trunk

The bones of the trunk include the **vertebral** (ver′te-bral) **column** and the bones of the chest, or **thorax** (tho′raks). The vertebral column is made of a series of irregularly shaped bones. These number 33 or 34 in the child, but because of fusions that occur later in the lower part of the spine, there usually are just 26 separate bones in the adult spinal column (Figs. 7-7 and 7-8). Each of these vertebrae (ver′te-bre), except the first two cervical vertebrae, has a drum-shaped body located toward the front (anteriorly) that serves as the weight-bearing part;

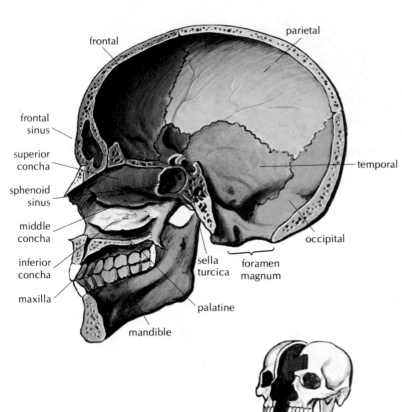

Figure 7-6. *The skull, internal view.*

disks of cartilage between the vertebral bodies act as shock absorbers and provide flexibility. In the center of each vertebra is a large hole, or **foramen** (for-a′men), for the spinal cord. Projecting backward from the bony arch that encircles the spinal cord is the spinous process, which usually can be felt just under the skin of the back. When all the vertebrae are linked in series by strong connective tissue bands (ligaments), the result is a bony cylinder that protects the spinal cord.

The bones of the vertebral column are named and numbered from above downward, on the basis of location:

1   The **cervical** (ser′vi-kal) **vertebrae**, seven in number, are located in the neck. The first vertebra, called the **atlas**, supports the head; when one nods the head, the skull (occipital bone) rocks on the atlas. The second cervical vertebra, called the **axis**, serves as a pivot when the head is turned from side to side.
2   The **thoracic vertebrae**, 12 in number, are lo-cated in the thorax. The posterior ends of the ribs (12 pairs) are attached to these vertebrae.
3   The **lumbar vertebrae**, five in number, are located in the small of the back. They are larger and heavier than the other vertebrae to support more weight.
4   The **sacral** (sa′kral) **vertebrae** are five separate bones in the child. However, they eventually fuse to form a single bone, called the **sacrum** (sa′krum), in the adult. Wedged between the two hip bones, the sacrum completes the posterior part of the bony pelvis.
5   The **coccyx** (kok′siks), or tailbone, consists of four or five tiny bones in the child. These fuse to form a single bone in the adult.

When viewed from the side, the vertebral column can be seen to have four curves, corresponding to the four groups of vertebrae. In the newborn infant the entire column is concave forward (curves away from a viewer facing the infant). This is the primary curve. When the infant begins to assume an erect posture,

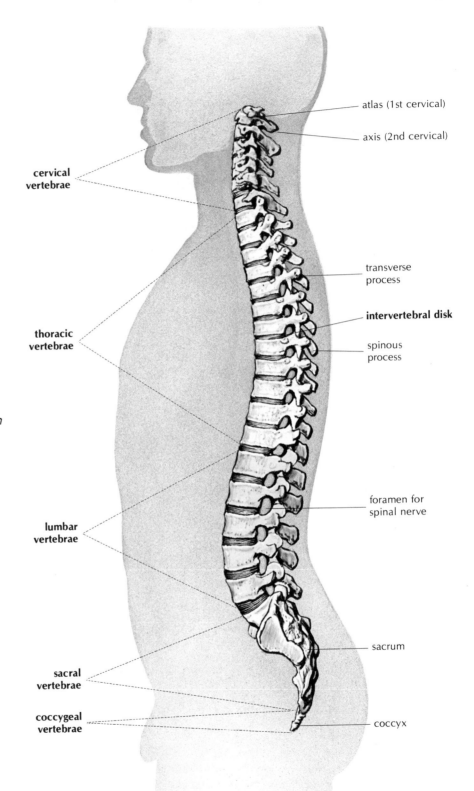

atlas (1st cervical)

axis (2nd cervical)

**cervical
vertebrae**

transverse
process

intervertebral disk

spinous
process

**thoracic
vertebrae**

Figure 7-7. *Vertebral column
from the side.*

**lumbar
vertebrae**

foramen for
spinal nerve

sacrum

**sacral
vertebrae**

**coccygeal
vertebrae**

coccyx

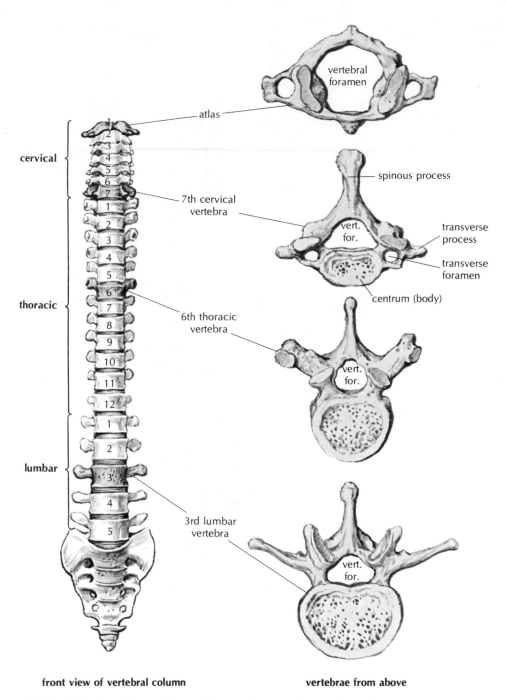

front view of vertebral column   vertebrae from above

Figure 7-8. *Front view of the vertebral column; vertebrae from above.*

secondary curves, which are convex (curve toward the viewer) may be noted (see Fig. 7-7). For example, the cervical curve appears when the infant begins to hold up the head at about 3 months of age; the lumbar curve appears when he or she begins to walk. The

curves of the vertebral column provide some of the resilience and spring so essential in walking and running.

The bones of the **thorax** form a cone-shaped cage. Twelve pairs of **ribs** form the bars of this cage, completed by the **sternum** (ster′num), or breast-bone, anteriorly. The thorax protects the heart, the lungs, and other organs.

All 24 of the ribs are attached to the vertebral column posteriorly. However, variations in the *anterior* attachment of these slender, curved bones have led to the following classification:

1 **True ribs**, the first seven pairs are those that attach directly to the sternum by means of individual extensions called **costal** (kos′tal) **cartilages**.

2 **False ribs** are the remaining five pairs. Of these, the eighth, ninth, and tenth pairs attach to the cartilage of the rib above. The last two pairs have no anterior attachment at all and are known as **floating ribs**.

The spaces between the ribs, called **intercostal spaces**, contain muscles, blood vessels, and nerves.

Bones of the Appendicular Skeleton

The appendicular skeleton may be considered in two divisions: upper and lower. The upper division includes the shoulders, the arms (between the shoulders and the elbows), the forearms (between the elbows and the wrists), the wrists, the hands, and the fingers. The lower division includes the hips (pelvic girdle), the thighs (between the hips and the knees), the legs (between the knees and the ankles), the ankles, the feet, and the toes.

The bones of the upper division may be divided into two groups for ease of study.

A The **shoulder girdle** consists of two bones:
   1 The **clavicle** (klav′i-kle), or collar bone
   2 The **scapula** (skap′u-lah), or shoulder blade
B Each **upper extremity** (arm) consists of the following bones:
   1 The arm bone called the **humerus** (hu′mer-us), forms a joint with the scapula above and with the two forearm bones at the elbow.
   2 The forearm bones are the **ulna** (ul′nah), which lies on the medial, or little finger, side, and the **radius** (ra′de-us), on the lateral, or thumb, side. When the palm is up, or forward, the two bones are parallel; when the palm is turned down, or back, the lower end of the radius moves around the ulna so that the shafts of the two bones are crossed.
   3 The wrist contains eight small **carpal** (kar′pal) **bones** arranged in two rows of four each. Each

is different from the others, and has a name of its own (Fig. 7-9).

4 Five **metacarpal bones** are the framework for the body of each hand. Their rounded distal ends form the knuckles.

5 There are 14 **phalanges** (fa-lan′jez), or finger bones, in each hand, two for the thumb and three for each finger. Each of these bones is called a **phalanx** (fa′lanx). They are identified as the first, or proximal, which is attached to a metacarpal; the second, or middle; and the third, or distal. Note that the thumb has only a proximal and a distal phalanx.

The bones of the lower division are grouped together in a simlar fashion.

A The bony pelvis supports the trunk and the organs in the lower abdomen, or pelvic cavity, including the urinary bladder, the internal reproductive organs, and parts of the intestine. The female pelvis is adapted for pregnancy and childbirth; it is broader and lighter than the male pelvis (Fig. 7-10).

The **pelvic girdle** is a strong bony ring that forms the walls of the pelvis. It is composed of two hip bones, which form the front and the sides of the ring, and the sacrum, which articulates (joins) with the hip bones to complete the ring at the back (posteriorly). Each hip bone (os coxa) begins its development as three separate parts:
   1 The **ilium** (il′e-um), which forms the upper, flared portion
   2 The **ischium** (is′ke-um), which is the lowest and strongest part
   3 The **pubis** (pu′bis), which forms the anterior part. The joint formed by the union of the two hip bones anteriorly is called the **symphysis** (sim′fi-sis) **pubis**.
B Each **lower extremity** (leg) consists of the following bones:
   1 The thigh bone, called the **femur** (fe′mer), is the longest and strongest bone in the body.
   2 The **patella** (pah-tel′lah), or kneecap, is embedded in the tendon of the large anterior thigh muscle, the quadriceps femoris, where it crosses the knee joint. It is an example of a **sesamoid** (ses′ah-moid) **bone**, a type that develops within a tendon or a joint capsule.
   3 There are two bones in the leg. Medially (on

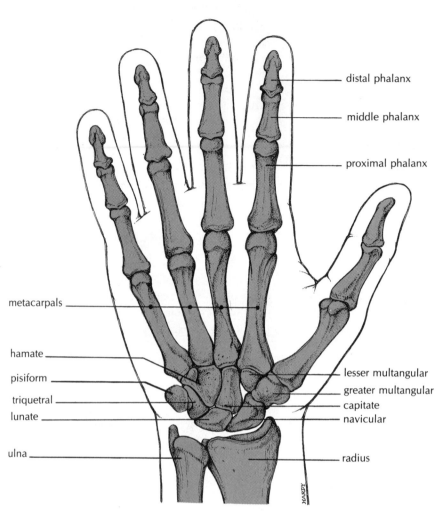

distal phalanx

middle phalanx

proximal phalanx

metacarpals

hamate

pisiform

triquetral

lunate

ulna

lesser multangular

greater multangular

capitate

navicular

radius

Figure 7-9. *Bones of right hand, anterior view. (Chaffee EE, Lytle IM: Basic Physiology and Anatomy, 4th ed, p 110. Philadelphia, JB Lippincott, 1980)*

the big toe side), the **tibia**, or shin bone, is the longer, weight-bearing bone. Laterally, the slender **fibula** (fib′u-lah) does not reach the knee joint; thus, it is not a weight-bearing bone.

4 The structure of the foot is similar to that of the hand. However, the foot supports the weight of the body, so it is stronger and less mobile than the hand. There are seven **tarsal bones** associated with the ankle and foot; the largest of these is the **calcaneus** (kal-ka′ne-us), or heel bone. Five **metatarsal bones** form the framework of the instep, and the heads of these bones form the ball of the foot.

5 The **phalanges** of the toes are counterparts of those in the fingers. There are three of these in each toe except for the great toe, which has only two.

Landmarks of Bones

The contour of bones resembles the topography of an interesting, varied landscape with hills and valleys. The projections often serve as regions for muscle attachments. There are hundreds of these prominences, or **processes**, with different names. A few of the most important points of reference are identified below (the landmarks described in numbers 4 to 7 can be seen in Fig. 7-10):

1 The **mastoid process** of the temporal bone projects downward immediately behind the external part of the ear. It contains the mastoid air cells and serves as a place for muscle attachment.

2 The **acromion** (ah-kro′me-on) **process** of the scapula forms the highest point of the shoulder. It overhangs the **glenoid cavity**, a smooth, shal-

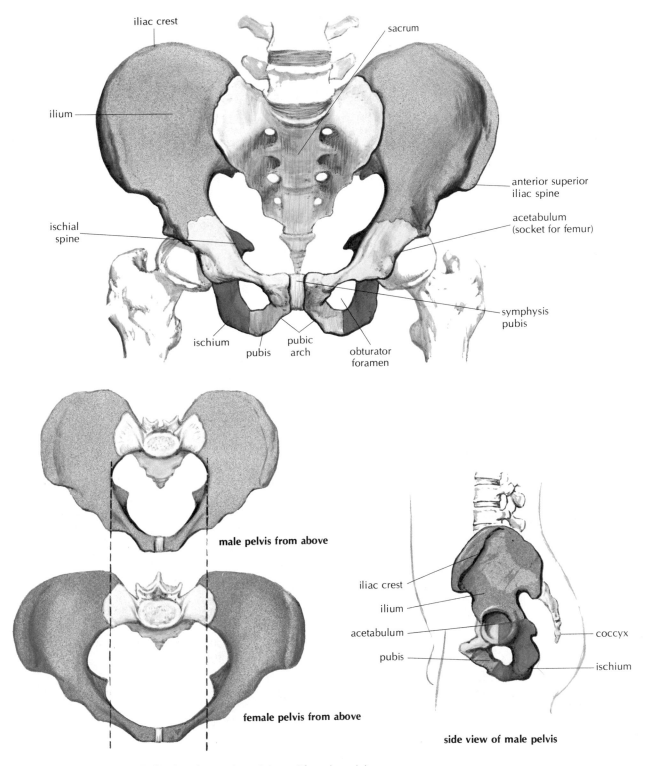

iliac crest

sacrum

ilium

anterior superior
iliac spine

acetabulum
(socket for femur)

ischial
spine

symphysis
pubis

ischium

pubis

pubic
arch

obturator
foramen

male pelvis from above

female pelvis from above

iliac crest

ilium

acetabulum

coccyx

pubis

ischium

side view of male pelvis

Figure 7-10. *Pelvic girdle showing male pelvis and female pelvis.*

low socket that articulates with the humerus to form the shoulder joint.

3 The **olecranon** (o-lek′rah-non) **process** at the upper end of the ulna forms the point of the elbow.

4 The **iliac** (il′e-ak) **crest** is the curved rim along the upper border of the ilium. It can be felt near the level of the waist. At either end of the crest are two bony projections, the most prominent of which is the **anterior superior iliac spine**. The anterior superior spine is often used as a landmark, or reference point, in diagnosis and treatment.

5 The **ischial** (is′ke-al) **spine** at the back of the pelvic outlet is used as a point of reference during childbirth to indicate the progress of the presenting part (usually the baby's head) down the birth canal. Just below this spine is the large **ischial tuberosity**, which helps support the weight of the trunk when one sits down.

6 The **acetabulum** (as″e-tab′u-lum) is a deep socket in the hip bone; it receives the head of the femur to form the hip joint.

7 The **greater trochanter** (tro-kan′ter) of the femur is a large protuberance located at the top of the shaft, on the lateral side. The **lesser trochanter**, a smaller elevation, is located on the medial side.

8 The **medial malleolus** (mal-le′o-lus) is a downward projection at the lower end of the tibia; it forms the prominence on the inner aspect of the ankle. The **lateral malleolus**, at the lower end of the fibula, forms the prominence on the outer aspect of the ankle.

Holes that extend into or through bones are called **foramina** (fo-ram′i-nah). Numerous foramina permit the passage of blood vessels to and from the bone tissue and the marrow cavities. Larger foramina in the base of the skull and in other locations allow for the passage of cranial nerves, blood vessels, and other structures that connect with the brain. For example, the **foramen magnum**, located at the base of the occipital bone, is a large opening through which the spinal cord communicates with the brain. When viewed from the side, the vertebral column can be seen to have a series of **intervertebral foramina** through which spinal nerves emerge as they leave the spinal cord. The largest foramina in the entire body are found in the pelvic girdle, near the front of each

hip bone, one on each side of the symphysis pubis. Called the **obturator** (ob′tu-ra-tor) **foramina**, these are partially covered by a membrane.

Valley-like depressions on a bone surface are called **fossae** (fos′se), the singular form being **fossa** (fos′sah). Some of these, such as the large fossae of the two scapulae, are filled with muscle tissue. Other depressions are narrow, elongated areas called **grooves**, which may allow for the passage of blood vessels or nerves. In the ribs, for example, grooves contain intercostal nerves and vessels.

The Infant Skull

The skull of the infant has areas in which the bone formation is incomplete, leaving so-called soft spots. Although there are a number of these, the largest and best known is near the front at the junction of the two parietal bones with the frontal bone. It is called the **anterior fontanel** (fon-tah-nel′), and it does not usually close until the child is about 18 months old (Fig. 7-11).

Disorders of Bone

Cleft palate is a congenital deformity in which there is an opening in the roof of the mouth owing to faulty union of the maxillary bones. Infants born with this defect have difficulty nursing, since their mouths communicate with the nasal cavities above and they therefore suck in air rather than milk. Surgery is usually performed to correct the condition.

Osteoporosis (os″te-o-po-ro′sis) is a disorder of bone formation in which there is a lack of normal calcium deposits and a decrease in bone protein. Usually there is also a reduction in the number of osteoblasts (bone-forming cells), so that bone does not repair itself continuously as it normally does. The bones thus become fragile and break easily. The condition is fairly common in postmenopausal women as a result of a decrease in hormone levels; most often it involves the spine and pelvis. Possible causes include poor nutrition, particularly a lack of protein, and vitamins, as well as inactivity. Treatment has included adminstration of hormones (estrogens, calcitonin), an increase in exercise, and an increase in dietary calcium ingestion. It is recommended that all women take 1000 mg to 1500 mg calcium daily throughout their adult life.

Osteomyelitis (os-te-o-mi-e-li′tis) is an inflammation of bone caused by **pyogenic** (py′o-jen′ik) (pus-

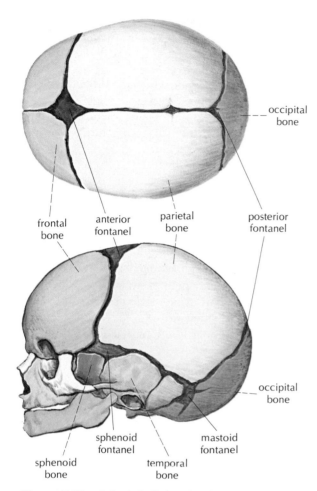

frontal bone
anterior fontanel
parietal bone
posterior fontanel
occipital bone

sphenoid bone
sphenoid fontanel
temporal bone
mastoid fontanel
occipital bone

Figure 7-11. *Infant skull showing fontanels.*

producing) bacteria. It may remain localized or it may spread through the bone to involve the marrow and the periosteum. The bacteria may reach the bone through the bloodstream or by way of an injury in which the skin has been broken. Before the advent of antibiotic drugs, bone infections were very resistant to treatment, and the prognosis for persons with such infections was poor. Now there are fewer cases because many bloodstream infections are prevented or treated early enough so they do not progress to affect the bones. If those bone infections that do appear are treated promptly, the chance of a cure is usually excellent.

Tumors that develop in bone tissue may be benign, as is the case with certain cysts, or they may be malignant, as are osteosarcomas. In the latter case, the tumor originates most often in the bone tissue of a femur or a tibia, usually in a young person. In older persons, metastases from epithelial tumors or carcinomas of various organs may spread to many bones.

Abnormal body chemistry involving calcium may cause various bone disorders. In one of these, called Paget's disease, or **osteitis deformans** (os-te-i'tis de-for'mans), the bones undergo periods of calcium loss followed by periods of excessive deposition of calcium salts. As a result the bones become deformed. Cause and cure are not known at the present time. The bones also can become decalcified owing to the effect of a tumor of the parathyroid gland (see Chap. 11).

Rickets is primarily a disease of children characterized by a hampering of growth and the failure of the bones to calcify sufficiently. The main cause of rickets is a deficiency of calcium and phosphorus, which can result directly from not having enough of these minerals in the diet. It can also result indirectly from a deficiency of vitamin D, a fat-soluble vitamin that is necessary for calcium and phosphorus to be absorbed by the body. Consequently, unless foods containing vitamin D are provided, the body will not be able to use these minerals, no matter how great the quantities of them taken in with food. Insufficient sunlight can be another predisposing factor in rickets, since the ultraviolet rays of the sun act on the skin to manufacture vitamin D. Rickets is most prevalent among children who grow up in polluted city slums and among children with heavy pigmentation.

The failure of the bones to calcify keeps them soft and easily bent. Certain deformities, notably bowlegs, may result.

There are also abnormalities of the spinal curves, including an exaggeration of the thoracic curve, or **kyphosis** (ki-fo'sis) (hunchback), and an excessive lumbar curve called **lordosis** (lor-do'sis). The most common distorder is **scoliosis** (sko-le-o'sis), a lateral curvature of the vertebral column; in extreme cases there may be compression of some of the internal organs. Scoliosis occurs in the rapid growth period of teens, more often in girls than in boys. Early discovery and treatment produce good results.

Skeletal Changes in the Aging

Various changes occur in the skeleton as one ages. Changes in the vertebral column lead to a loss in height. Approximately 1.2 cm (about 0.5 inches) are lost each 20 years beginning at age 40, owing primarily to a thinning of the intervertebral disks (between the bodies of the vertebrae). Even the vertebral bodies themselves may lose height in later years. The costal (rib) cartilages become calcified and less flexible, and the chest may decrease in diameter by 2 cm to 3 cm (about 1 inch), mostly in the lower part. As previously noted, the bony (osseous) tissues contain a higher proportion of calcium, become more brittle, break more easily, and heal more slowly in the elderly than in younger persons.

Fractures

Severe force is capable of causing a **fracture** in almost any bone (Fig. 7-12). The word *fracture* means "a break or rupture in a bone." Such injuries may be classified as follows:

1 **Compound fractures**, in which the skin and other soft tissues are torn and the bone protrudes through the skin
2 **Simple fractures**, in which the break in the bone is not accompanied by a break in the skin

3 **Greenstick fractures**, which are incomplete breaks in which the bone splits in much the same way as a piece of green wood might. These are most common in children.
4 **Impacted fractures**, in which the broken ends of the bone are jammed into each other
5 **Comminuted** (kom′i-noot-ed) **fractures**, in which there is more than one fracture line with several fragments resulting
6 **Spiral fractures**, in which the bone has been twisted apart. These are relatively common in skiing accidents.

The most important step in first aid care of fractures is to prevent movement of the affected parts. Protection by simple splinting after careful evaluation of the situation, leaving as much as possible "as is," and a call for expert help is usually safest. Persons who have back injuries may be spared serious spinal cord damage if they are carefully and correctly moved on a firm board or door. If a doctor or ambu-

Figure 7-12. *Types of fractures.*

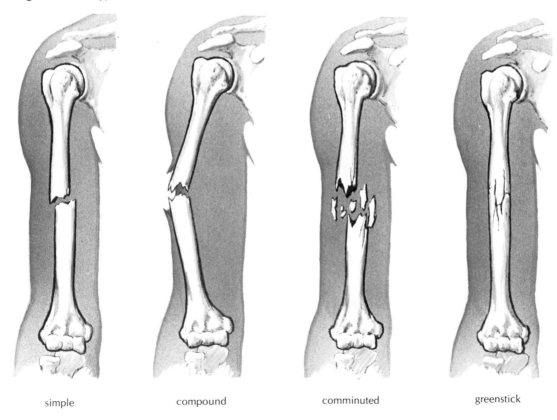

simple   compound   comminuted   greenstick

lance can reach the scene, a "hands off" rule for the untrained is strongly recommended. If there is no external bleeding, covering the victim with blankets may help combat shock. First aid should always be immediately directed toward the control of hemorrhage.

The Joints

An **articulation**, or **joint**, is an area of junction or union between two or more bones.

Kinds of Joints

Joints are classified into three main groups on the basis of the degree of movement permitted:

1 **Synarthrosis** (sin-ar-thro′sis), an immovable joint. The bones in this type of joint are usually held together by fibrous connective tissue. An example is a suture between the bones of the skull.
2 **Amphiarthrosis** (am-fe-ar-thro′sis), a slightly movable joint. The bones in this type of joint are usually connected by cartilage. Examples are the joint between the pubic bones of the pelvis and the joints between the bodies of the vertebrae of the spine.
3 **Diarthrosis** (di-ar-thro′sis), a freely movable joint. The bones in this type of joint have a space between them, the **joint cavity**. This is filled with a fluid called **synovial** (si-no′ve-al) **fluid**, so these joints are called **synovial joints**. Most joints of the skeleton are synovial joints; they are described in more detail below. A summary is given in Table 7-1.

Structure of Synovial Joints

The bones in a freely movable joint are held together by bands of fibrous connective tissue called **ligaments**. In some cases these completely enclose the joint, making up the **joint capsule**. Additional ligaments reinforce and help stabilize the joints at various points (Fig. 7-13). The contacting surfaces of each freely movable joint are covered by a smooth layer of gristle called the **articular** (ar-tik′u-lar) **cartilage**. Inside the joint space is the rather thick, colorless synovial fluid, which resembles uncooked egg white.

Near some joints are small sacs called **bursae** (ber′see), which are filled with synovial fluid. These lie in areas subject to stress and help ease movement over and around the joints. Inflammation of a bursa, as a result of injury or irritation, is called **bursitis**.

Types of Synovial Joints

Synovial joints may be classified according to the types of movement they allow as follows:

1 **Gliding** joint, in which the bone surfaces slide over one another. Examples are joints in the wrist and ankle.
2 **Hinge** joint, which allows movement in one direction, changing the angle of the bones at the joint. Examples are the elbow and knee joints.
3 **Pivot** joint, which allows rotation around the length of the bone. Examples are the joint between the first and second cervical vertebrae and the joint at the proximal ends of the radius and ulna.
4 **Condyloid** joint, which allows movement in two

Table 7-1 Types of Joints

Name	Movement	Material between the Bones	Examples
Synarthrosis	Immovable	No joint cavity; usually fibrous connective tissue between bones	Sutures between bones of skull
Amphiarthrosis	Slightly movable	No joint cavity; usually cartilage between bones	Pubic symphysis; joints between vertebrae
Diarthrosis	Freely movable	Joint cavity filled with synovial fluid	Gliding, hinge, pivot, condyloid, saddle, ball-and-socket joints

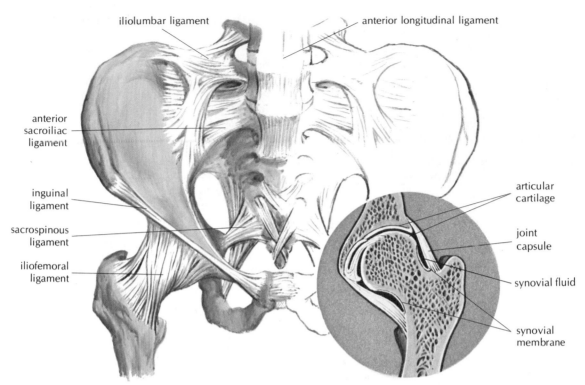

cross section of movable joint of hip

Figure 7-13. Ligaments of hip and pelvis.

directions. An example is the joint between the wrist and the bones of the forearm.

5 **Saddle** joint, which is like a condyloid joint, but with deeper articulating surfaces. An example is the joint between the wrist and the metacarpal bone of the thumb.

6 **Ball-and-socket** joint, which allows movement in many directions around a central point. This type of joint gives the greatest freedom of movement, but it is also the most easily dislocated. Examples are the hip and shoulder joints.

Function of Synovial Joints

The chief function of the freely movable joints is to allow for changes of position and so provide for motion. These movements are given names to describe the nature of the changes in the positions of the body parts. For example, there are four kinds of angular movement, or movement that changes the angles between bones, as listed below:

1 **Flexion** (flek'shun) is a bending motion that decreases the angle between bones, as in bending the fingers to close the hand.

2 **Extension** is a straightening motion that increases the angle between bones, as in straightening the fingers to open the hand.

3 **Abduction** (ab-duk'shun) is movement away from the midline of the body, as in moving the arms straight out to the sides.

4 **Adduction** is movement toward the midline of the body, as in bringing the arms back to their original position beside the body.

A combination of these angular movements enables one to execute a movement referred to as **circumduction** (ser"kum-duk'shun). To perform this movement, stand with your arm outstretched and draw a large imaginary circle in the air. Note the smooth combination of flexion, abduction, extension, and adduction that makes circumduction possible.

Rotation refers to a twisting or turning of a bone

on its own axis, as in turning the head from side to side to say "no".

There are special movements that are characteristic of the forearm and the ankle:

1 **Supination** (su"pi-na'shun) is the act of turning the palm up or forward; **pronation** (pro-na'shun) turns the palm down or backward.

2 **Inversion** (in-ver'zhun) is the act of turning the sole inward, so that it faces the opposite foot; **eversion** (e-ver'zhun) turns the sole outward, away from the body.

Disorders of Joints

Joints are subject to certain disorders of a mechanical nature, examples of which are **dislocations** and **sprains**. A dislocation is a derangement of the parts of the joint. A sprain is the name for the wrenching of a joint with rupture or tearing of the ligaments.

Arthritis

The most common type of joint disorder is termed **arthritis**, which means "inflammation of the joints." There are different kinds of arthritis, including the following:

1 **Osteoarthritis** (os"te-o-arth-ri'tis) is a degenerative joint disease (DJD) that usually occurs in elderly persons as a result of normal wear and tear. Although it appears to be a natural result of aging, such factors as obesity and repeated trauma can help bring it about. Osteoarthritis occurs mostly in joints used in weight bearing, such as the hips, knees, and spinal column. It involves degeneration of the joint cartilage with growth of new bone at the edges of the joints. Degenerative changes include the formation of spurs at the edges of the articular surfaces, thickening of the synovial membrane, atrophy of the cartilage, and calcification of the ligaments.

2 **Rheumatoid arthritis** is a crippling condition characterized by swelling of the joints of the hands, the feet, and other parts of the body as a result of inflammation and overgrowth of the synovial membranes and other joint tissues. The articular cartilage is gradually destroyed, and the joint cavity develops adhesions—that is, the surfaces tend to stick together—so that the joints stiffen and ultimately become useless. The cause of rheumatoid arthritis is uncertain, but it is now considered to be an autoimmune disease (see Chap. 16). The administration of steroids and gold salts may provide some relief.

3 **Infectious arthritis** can be brought on by such infections as rheumatic fever and gonorrhea. Gonorrheal arthritis is becoming widespread as a result of the tremendous increase in the number of cases of gonorrhea.

The joints as well as the bones proper are subject to attack by the tuberculosis organism, and the result may be gradual destruction of parts of the bone near the joint. The organism is carried by the blood stream, usually from a focus in the lungs or lymph nodes, and may cause considerable damage before it is discovered. The bodies of several vertebrae sometimes are affected, or one hip or other single joint may be diseased. Tuberculosis of the spine is called **Pott's disease**. The patient may complain only of difficulty in walking, and diagnosis is difficult unless an accompanying lung tuberculosis has been found. This disorder is most common in children.

4 **Gout** is a kind of arthritis caused by a disturbance of metabolism. One of the products of metabolism is uric acid, which normally is excreted in the urine. If there happens to be an overproduction of uric acid, or for some reason not enough is excreted, the accumulated uric acid forms crystals, which are deposited as masses about the joints and other parts of the body. As a result, the joints become inflamed and extremely painful. Any joint can be involved, but the one most commonly affected is the big toe. Most victims of gout are men past middle life.

Backache

Backache is another common complaint Some of its causes are listed below:

1 Diseases of the vertebrae, such as infections or tumors, and in older persons, osteoarthritis, or atrophy (wasting away) of the bone, following long illnesses

2 Disorders of the intervertebral disks, especially those in the lower lumbar region. Pain may be very severe, with muscle spasms and the exten-

sion of symptoms along the course of the sciatic nerve (back of the thigh to the toes)

3 Abnormalities of the lower vertebrae or of the ligaments and other supporting structures

4 Disorders involving organs of the pelvis or those in the retroperitoneal space (such as the pancreas). Variations in the position of the uterus are seldom a cause.

5 Strains on the **lumbosacral** joint (where the lumbar region joins the sacrum) or strains on the **sacroiliac** joint (where the sacrum joins the ilium of the pelvis)

Summary

I Bone structure
  A Cells
    1 Osteoblasts—bone-forming cells
    2 Osteocytes—mature bone cells that maintain bone
    3 Osteoclasts—bone cells that break down (resorb) bone
  B Tissue
    1 Compact—shaft (diaphysis) of long bones; outside of other bones
    2 Spongy—end (epiphysis) of long bones; center of other bones
  C Marrow
    1 Red—ends of long bones, center of other bones
    2 Yellow—center of long bones
  D Membranes—contain bone-forming cells
    1 Periosteum—covers bones
    2 Endosteum—lines marrow cavities
II Long bone growth—begins in center of shaft and continues at ends of bone; growing area forms line across epiphysis
III Bone functions—serve as body framework; protect organs; serve as levers; store calcium; form blood cells
IV Divisions of the skeleton
  A Axial
    1 Head
      a Cranial—frontal, parietal, temporal, ethmoid, sphenoid, occipital
      b Facial—mandible, maxillae, zygomatic bones, nasal bones, lacrimal bones, vomer, palatine bones, inferior nasal conchae
      c Other—ossicles (of ear), hyoid bone
    2 Trunk
      a Vertebral column—cervical, thoracic, lumbar, sacral, coccygeal
      b Thorax
        (1) Sternum
        (2) Ribs
          (a) True—first seven pairs
          (b) False—remaining five pairs, including two floating ribs
  B Appendicular
    1 Shoulder girdle—clavicle, scapula
    2 Upper extremity (arm)—humerus, ulna, radius, carpals, metacarpals, phalanges
    3 Pelvic girdle—ilium, ischium, pubis
    4 Lower extremity (leg)—femur, patella, tibia, fibula, tarsal bones, metatarsal bones, phalanges
V Landmark of bones
  A Processes—mastoid process, acromion process, olecranon process, iliac crest, iliac spines, ischial spine and tuberosity, trochanters, malleoli
  B Foramina—foramen magnum, intervertebral foramina, obturator foramina
  C Fossae and grooves
  D Fontanels—anterior and others in infant skull
VI Disorders of bone
  A Miscellaneous disorders—cleft palate, osteoporosis, osteomyelitis, tumors
  B Metabolic disorders—osteitis deformans, rickets
  C Curvatures of the spine–kyphosis (thoracic), lordosis (lumbar), scoliosis (lateral)
  D Changes in aging—thinning of intervertebral disks, calcification
  E Fractures—compound, simple, greenstick, impacted, comminuted, spiral
VII Joint classification
  A Synarthrosis—immovable
  B Amphiarthrosis—slightly movable
  C Diarthrosis (synovial joints)—freely movable
VIII Structure of synovial joints
  A Joint capsule (ligaments)—holds joint together
  B Cartilage—covers ends of bones
  C Joint cavity—filled with synovial fluid

D Bursae—fluid-filled sacs near joints; cushion and protect joints and surrounding tissue

IX **Types of synovial joints**—gliding, hinge, pivot, condyloid, saddle, ball-and-socket

X **Movement at synovial joints**—flexion, extension, abduction, adduction, circumduction, rotation, supination, pronation, inversion, eversion

XI **Disorders of joints**
  A Dislocations and sprains
  B Arthritis—osteoarthritis, rheumatoid arthritis, arthritis due to infection, gout
  C Backache

Questions for Study and Review

1 Explain the difference between the terms in each of the following pairs:
  a *osteoblast* and *osteoclast*
  b *red marrow* and *yellow marrow*
  c *periosteum* and *endosteum*
  d *compact bone* and *spongy bone*
  e *epiphysis* and *diaphysis*
2 Define *resorption* as it applies to bone.
3 Name five general functions of bones.
4 Name the main cranial and facial bones.

5 What are the main divisions of the vertebral column? the ribs?
6 Name the bones of the upper and lower appendicular skeleton.
7 Name the bones on which you would find the following processes: mastoid, acromion, olecranon, iliac crest, trochanter, medial malleolus.
8 Define *fontanel* and name the largest fontanel.
9 What is a foramen? Give at least two examples of foramina.
10 Describe cleft palate, osteoporosis, osteomyelitis, and rickets.
11 Describe five types of fractures.
12 Name and describe three abnormal curvatures of the spine.
13 Name three effects of aging on the skeletal system.
14 List three types of joints.
15 Describe where each of the following is found in a synovial joint: joint capsule, articular cartilage, and synovial fluid.
16 Name six types of synovial joints and give one example of the location of each.
17 Differentiate between the terms in each of the following pairs:
  a *flexion* and *extension*
  b *abduction* and *adduction*
  c *supination* and *pronation*
  d *inversion* and *eversion*
  e *circumduction* and *rotation*
18 Describe four joint diseases.

8

The Muscular System

Behavioral Objectives

After careful study of this chapter, you should be able to:

List the characteristics of skeletal muscle

Briefly describe how muscles contract

List the substances needed in muscle contraction and describe the function of each

Define oxygen debt

Differentiate between isotonic and isometric contractions

Explain how muscles work in pairs to produce movement

Name some of the major muscles in each muscle group and describe the main function of each

Describe how muscles change with age

List the major muscular disorders

Selected Key Terms

The following terms are defined in the glossary:

actin
antagonist
aponeurosis
bursitis
epimysium
glycogen
insertion
lactic acid
myalgia
myoglobin
myosin
neuromuscular junction
origin
oxygen debt
prime mover
tendinitis
tendon
tone

The muscular system is composed of more than 600 individual muscles, which together make up about 40% of total body weight. Each muscle is a distinct structure; however, muscles usually act in groups to execute body movements. Muscles produce movement by shortening in length. Thus, the ability to contract is an important property of muscle cells.

☰ Characteristics of Skeletal Muscle

As noted in Chapter 4, there are three basic kinds of muscle tissue: skeletal, smooth, and cardiac muscle. This chapter is concerned only with the skeletal muscles, which are attached to the bones. These constitute the majority of the muscles in the body (Figs. 8-1 and 8-2). Skeletal muscle also is known as *voluntary muscle* because it is normally under conscious control.

Skeletal muscles are regarded as organs because they each have, in addition to the specialized muscle cells, a connective tissue framework and a supply of blood vessels and nerves. When seen through a microscope, individual muscle cells are long and threadlike; therefore, they are usually referred to as **muscle fibers**. These fibers are arranged in bundles that are held together by connective tissue. Groups of these bundles are held together by additional connective tissue, and the entire muscle is encased in a tough connective tissue sheath called the **epimysium** (ep-i-mis′e-um). The epimysium is part of the **deep fascia.**

Excitability, or **irritability**, is the capacity to respond to a stimulus; it is an important property of muscle tissue. Muscle cells can be excited by chemical, electric, or mechanical means. Skeletal muscles usually are excited by nerve impulses that travel from the brain and the spinal cord (see Chap. 9). Nerve fibers carry impulses to the muscles, each fiber supplying from a few up to more than 100 individual muscle cells. The point at which a nerve fiber contacts a muscle cell is called the **neuromuscular** (sometimes **myoneural**) **junction**. The stimulus received by way of the nerve ending results in an electric change, called an **action potential**, that is transmitted along the cell membrane.

Contractility is the capacity of a muscle fiber to undergo shortening and to change its shape, becoming thicker. Studies with the electron microscope

reveal that the cytoplasm of each skeletal muscle fiber contains special protein threads, or filaments, called **actin** (ak′tin) and **myosin** (mi′o-sin). These filaments slide over each other in such a way that the muscle fiber contracts, becoming shorter and thicker. Calcium ions are needed for this contraction. Calcium allows cross bridges to form between the actin and myosin filaments so that the sliding action can begin. The calcium needed for contraction is stored within the membranes (ER) of the muscle cell and is released into the cytoplasm when the cell is stimulated by a nerve fiber.

Muscle contraction also requires energy. The direct source of energy for contraction is ATP, which stores energy that is released by the oxidation, or burning, of food within the cells. The energy stored in ATP is then available for the cells as needed. Chapter 19 has more on the subject of energy metabolism.

In order to produce ATP, muscle cells must have an adequate supply of oxygen and glucose (food). These substances are brought to the cells by the circulation, but muscle cells also store a reserve supply of each. Additional oxygen is stored in the form of a compound similar to hemoglobin but located specifically in muscle cells, as indicated by its name, **myoglobin**. Additional glucose is stored as a compound that is built from glucose molecules and called **glycogen**. Glycogen can be broken down into glucose when needed by the muscle cells.

Oxygen plays an important role in preventing the accumulation of **lactic acid**, a waste product that can cause muscle fatigue. During strenuous activity, a person may not be able to breathe in oxygen rapidly enough to meet the needs of the hard-working muscles. If lactic acid accumulates, the person is said to develop an **oxygen debt**. After he has stopped his exercise, he must continue to take in more oxygen until the debt is paid in full; that is, enough oxygen must be taken in to convert the lactic acid to other substances that can be used in metabolism. Additional information on the effects of exercise is presented later in this chapter.

Muscle **tone** refers to a partially contracted state of the muscles that is normal even when the muscles are not in use. The maintenance of this tone, or **tonus** (to′nus), is due to the action of the nervous system, and its effect is to keep the muscles in a constant state of readiness for action. Muscles that are little used soon become flabby, weak, and lacking in tone.

In addition to the partial contractions that are

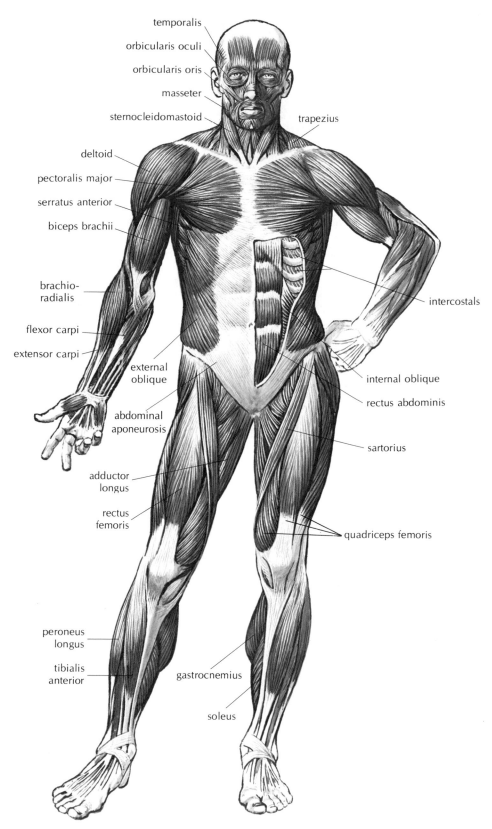

Figure 8-1. *Muscles of the body, anterior (front) view.*

95

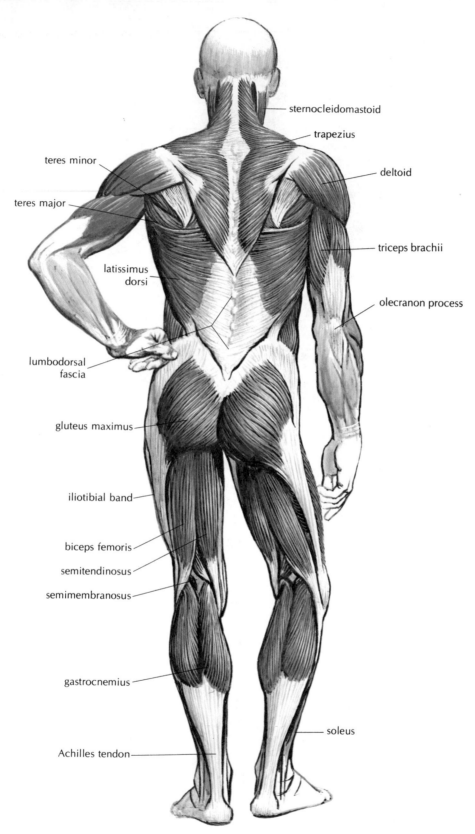

Figure 8-2. *Muscles of the body, posterior (back) view.*

responsible for muscle tone, there are two other types of contractions on which the body depends:

1 **Isotonic** (i″so-ton′ic) **contractions** are those in which the tone or tension within the muscle remains the same but the muscle as a whole shortens, producing movement. Lifting weights, walking, running, or any other activity in which the muscles become shorter and thicker (forming bulges) are isotonic contractions.
2 **Isometric** (i″so-met′rik) **contractions** are those in which there is no change in muscle length but there is a great increase in muscle tension. For example, if you push against a brick wall, there is no movement, but you can feel the increased tension in your arm muscles.

Most muscles contract either isotonically or isometrically, but most movements of the body involve a combination of the two types of contraction.

Attachments of Skeletal Muscles

Most muscles have two or more attachments to the skeleton. The method of attachment varies. In some instances the connective tissue within the muscle ties directly to the periosteum of the bone. In other cases the connective tissue sheath and partitions within the muscle extend to form specialized structures that aid in attaching the muscle to the bone. Such an extension may take the form of a cord, called a **tendon** (Fig. 8-3); alternatively, a broad sheet called an **aponeurosis** (ap″o-nu-ro′sis) may attach muscles to bones or to other muscles, as in the abdomen (see Fig. 8-1) or across the top of the skull (Fig. 8-4).

Whatever the nature of the muscle attachment, the principle remains the same: to furnish a means of harnessing the power of the muscle contractions. A muscle has two (or more) attachments, one of which

Figure 8-3. *Diagram of a muscle showing three attachments to bones—two by tendons of origin and one by a tendon of insertion.*

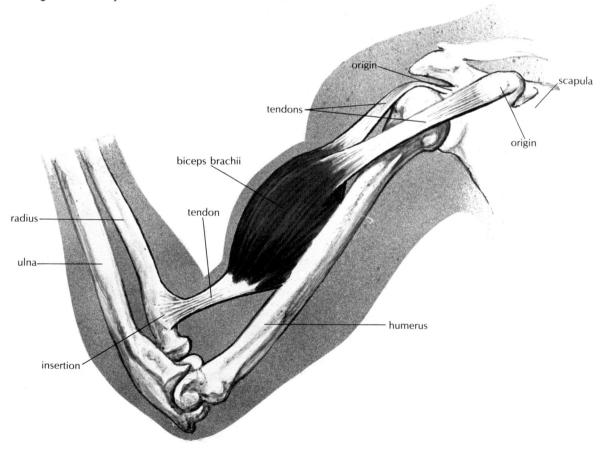

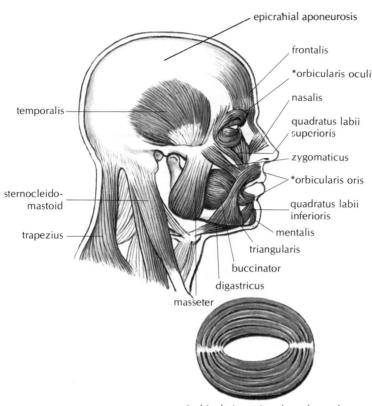

epicranial aponeurosis

frontalis

*orbicularis oculi

nasalis

quadratus labii superioris

zygomaticus

*orbicularis oris

quadratus labii inferioris

temporalis

mentalis

triangularis

buccinator

sternocleido-mastoid

trapezius

digastricus

masseter

Figure 8-4. *Muscles of the head.*

*orbicularis or ring-shaped muscle

is connected to a more freely movable part than the other. The less movable (more fixed) attachment is called the **origin**; the attachment to the part of the body that the muscle puts into action is called the **insertion**. When a muscle contracts, it pulls on both points of attachment, bringing the more movable insertion closer to the origin and thereby causing movement of the body part (see Fig. 8-3).

☰ Muscle Movement

Many of the skeletal muscles function in pairs. A movement is performed by one muscle or set of muscles called the **prime mover**; the muscle or set of muscles that produce an opposite movement is known as the **antagonist**. Clearly, for any given movement, the antagonist must relax when the prime mover contracts. For example, when the biceps brachii contracts to flex the arm, the triceps brachii must relax, and when the triceps brachii contracts to extend the arm, the biceps brachii must relax. In addition to prime movers and antagonists, there are also muscles that serve to steady body parts or to assist prime movers.

In this way, body movements are coordinated, and a large number of complicated movements can be carried out. At first, however, any new, complicated movement must be learned. Think of a child learning to walk or to write, and consider the number of muscles he uses unnecessarily or forgets to use when the situation calls for them.

Exercise

The rate of muscle metabolism increases during exercise, resulting in a relative deficiency of oxygen and muscle nutrients. In turn, this deficiency causes **vasodilation** (vas-o-di-la′shun)—an increase in the caliber of blood vessels—thereby allowing blood to flow easily back to the heart. The temporarily increased load on the heart acts to strengthen the heart muscle and to improve the circulation within the heart muscle. Regular exercise also improves respiratory efficiency; circulation in the capillaries surrounding the alveoli, or air sacs, is increased, and this brings about enhanced gas exchange and deeper breathing.

At first the increased demands during muscular exercise are met by the energy-rich compounds that are stored in the tissues. Continual exercise depletes these stores. For a short period of time, glucose may be used without the benefit of oxygen, in which case lactic acid is formed. This anaerobic (without oxygen) process permits greater magnitude of activity than would otherwise be possible, as, for example, allowing sprinting instead of jogging. After a period of great exertion, extra oxygen is consumed to remove the lactic acid and replenish the energy-carrying compounds. As noted earlier in this chapter, the body has accumulated an oxygen debt, which must be repaid by continued rapid breathing for some time after the activity has been completed. Training permits the more efficient distribution and utilization of oxygen so that less lactic acid is produced and the oxygen debt is smaller. The untrained person who has an excessive accumulation of lactic acid will suffer from such symptoms as muscle soreness and cramps.

Levers and Body Mechanics

Proper body mechanics help conserve energy and ensure freedom from strain and fatigue; conversely, such ailments as lower back pain—a common complaint—can be traced to poor body mechanics. Body mechanics have special significance to health workers, who are frequently called upon to move patients, handle cumbersome equipment, and so on. Maintaining the body segments in correct relation to one another has a direct effect on the working capacity of the vital organs that are supported by the skeletal structure.

If you have had a course in physics, recall your study of levers. A lever is simply a machine consisting of a rigid bar that moves about a fixed point, the fulcrum. There are three classes of levers, which differ only in the location of the fulcrum, the effort (force), and the resistance (weight). In a first-class lever, the fulcrum is located between the resistance and the effort; scissors, which you probably use every day, are an example of this class. The second-class lever has the resistance located between the fulcrum and the effort; a mattress lifted at one end is an illustration of this class. In the third-class lever, the effort is between the resistance and the fulcrum; your arm supporting an object held in your hand is an example of this class of lever. The musculoskeletal system can be considered a system of levers. By understanding and applying knowledge of levers to body mechanics, the health worker can improve his or her

skill in carrying out numerous clinical maneuvers and procedures.

≡ Skeletal Muscle Groups

Refer to Figures 8-1 and 8-2 as you study the locations and functions of some of the skeletal muscles, and try to figure out why each has the name that it does. Although they are described in the singular, most of the muscles are present on both sides of the body. The information is summarized in Table 8-1.

Muscles of the Head

The principal muscles of the head are those of facial expression and of mastication (chewing) (see Fig. 8-4).

The muscles of facial expression include ring-shaped ones around the eyes and the lips, called the **orbicularis** (or-bik-u-la′ris) **muscles** because of their shape (think of "orbit"). The muscle surrounding each eye is called the **orbicularis oculi** (ok′u-li), while the muscle of the lips is the **orbicularis oris**. These muscles, of course, all have antagonists. For example, the **levator palpebrae** (pal′pe-brae) **superioris**, or lifter of the upper eyelid, is the antagonist for the orbicularis oculi.

One of the largest muscles of expression forms the fleshy part of the cheek and is called the **buccinator** (buk′se-na-tor). Used in whistling or blowing, it is sometimes referred to as the *trumpeter's muscle*. You can readily think of other muscles of facial expression: for instance, the antagonists of the orbicularis oris can produce a smile, a sneer, or a grimace. There are a number of scalp muscles by means of which the eyebrows are lifted or drawn together into a frown.

There are four pairs of muscles of mastication, all of which insert on the mandible and move it. The largest are the **temporal** (tem′po-ral), located above and near the ear, and the **masseter** (mas-se′ter) at the angle of the jaw.

The tongue has two groups of muscles. The first group, called the **intrinsic muscles**, are located entirely within the tongue. The second group, the **extrinsic muscles**, originate outside the tongue. It is because of these many muscles that the tongue has such remarkable flexibility and can perform so many different functions. Consider the intricate tongue motions involved in speaking, chewing, and swallowing.

Table 8-1   Review of Muscles

Name	Location	Function
Muscles of the Head and Neck		
Orbicularis oculi	Encircles eyelid	Closes eye
Levator palpebrae superioris	Back of orbit to upper eyelid	Opens eye
Orbicularis oris	Encircles mouth	Closes lips
Buccinator	Fleshy part of cheek	Flattens cheek; helps in eating, whistling, and blowing wind instruments
Temporal	Above and near ear	Closes jaw
Masseter	At angle of jaw	Closes jaw
Sternocleidomastoid	Along side of neck, to mastoid process	Flexes head; rotates head toward opposite side from muscle
Muscles of the Upper Extremities		
Trapezius	Back of neck and upper back, to clavicle and scapula	Raises shoulder and pulls it back; extends head
Latissimus dorsi	Middle and lower back, to humerus	Extends and adducts arm behind back
Pectoralis major	Upper, anterior chest, to humerus	Flexes and adducts arm across chest; pulls shoulder forward and downward
Serratus anterior	Below axilla on side of chest to scapula	Moves scapula forward; aids in raising arm
Deltoid	Covers shoulder joint, to lateral humerus	Abducts arm
Biceps brachii	Anterior arm, to radius	Flexes forearm and supinates hand
Triceps brachii	Posterior arm, to ulna	Extends forearm
Flexor and extensor carpi groups	Anterior and posterior forearm, to hand	Flex and extend hand
Flexor and extensor digitorum groups	Anterior and posterior forearm, to fingers	Flex and extend fingers

(Continued)

Muscles of the Neck

The neck muscles tend to be ribbon-like and extend up and down or obliquely in several layers and in a complex manner. The one you will hear of most frequently is the **sternocleidomastoid** (ster″no-kli-do-mas′toid), sometimes referred to simply as the *sternomastoid*. There are two of these strong muscles, which extend from the sternum upward, across either side of the neck, to the mastoid process. Working together, they bring the head forward on the chest (flexion). Working alone, each muscle tilts and rotates the head so as to orient the face toward the side opposite that muscle. If the head is abnormally fixed in this position, the person is said to have **torticollis** (tor″ti-kol′is), or *wryneck;* this condition may be due to injury or spasm of the muscle. A portion of the trapezius muscle (described later) is located in the back of the neck where it helps hold the head up (extension). Other larger deep muscles are the chief extensors of the head and neck.

Muscles of the Upper Extremities

Movement of the Shoulder and Arm

The position of the shoulder depends to a large extent on the degree of contraction of the **trapezius** (trah-pe′ze-us), a triangular muscle that covers the back of the neck and extends across the back of the shoulder to insert on the clavicle and scapula. The trapezius muscles enable one to raise the shoulders and

Table 8-1   Review of Muscles (Continued)

Name	Location	Function
Muscles of the Trunk		
Diaphragm	Dome-shaped partition between thoracic and abdominal cavities	Dome descends to enlarge thoracic cavity from top to bottom
External intercostals	Between ribs	Elevate ribs and enlarge thoracic cavity
External and internal oblique; transversus and rectus abdominis	Anterolateral abdominal wall	Compress abdominal cavity and expel substances from body; flex spinal column
Levator ani	Pelvic floor	Aids defecation
Sacrospinalis	Deep in back, vertical mass	Extends vertebral column to produce erect posture
Muscles of the Lower Extremities		
Gluteus maximus	Superficial buttock, to femur	Extends thigh
Gluteus medius	Deep buttock, to femur	Abducts thigh
Iliopsoas	Crosses front of hip joint, to femur	Flexes thigh
Adductor group	Medial thigh, to femur	Adduct thigh
Sartorius	Winds down thigh, ilium to tibia	Flexes thigh and leg (sit cross-legged)
Quadriceps femoris	Anterior thigh, to tibia	Extends leg
Hamstring group	Posterior thigh, to tibia and fibula	Flex leg
Gastrocnemius	Calf of leg, to calcaneus	Extends foot (as in tiptoeing)
Tibialis anterior	Anterior and lateral shin, to foot	Dorsiflexes foot (as in walking on heels); inverts foot (sole inward)
Peroneus longus	Lateral leg, to foot	Everts foot (sole outward)
Flexor and extensor digitorum groups	Posterior and anterior leg, to toes	Flex and extend toes

pull them back. The upper portion of each trapezius can also extend the head and turn it from side to side.

The **latissimus** (lah-tis′i-mus) **dorsi** originates from the vertebral spine in the middle and lower back and covers the lower half of the thoracic region. The fibers of each muscle converge to a tendon that inserts on the humerus. The latissimus dorsi powerfully extends the arm, bringing it down forcibly as, for example, in swimming.

A large **pectoralis** (pek-to-ra′lis) **major** is located on either side of the upper part of the chest at the front of the body. This muscle arises from the sternum, the upper ribs, and the clavicle and forms the anterior "wall"of the arm pit or axilla; it inserts on the upper part of the humerus. The pectoralis major flexes and adducts the arm, pulling it across the chest.

Below the axilla, on the side of the chest, is the **serratus** (ser-ra′tus) **anterior.** It originates on the upper eight or nine ribs on the side and the front of the thorax and inserts in the scapula on the side toward the vertebrae. The serratus anterior moves the scapula forward when, for example, one is pushing something. It also aids in raising the arm above the horizontal level.

The **deltoid** covers the shoulder joint and is responsible for the roundness of the upper part of the arm just below the shoulder. This area is often used as an injection site. Arising from the shoulder girdle (clavicle and scapula), the deltoid fibers converge to insert on the lateral side of the humerus. Contraction of this muscle abducts the arm, raising it laterally to the horizontal position.

Movement of the Forearm and Hand

The **biceps brachii** (bra′ke-i), located on the front of the arm, is often displayed by children as proof of their strength. It inserts on the radius and serves to flex the forearm. It is a supinator of the hand (see Fig. 8-3).

The **triceps brachii**, located on the back of the arm, inserts on the olecranon of the ulna. The triceps has been called the *boxer's muscle,* since it straightens the elbow when a blow is delivered. It is also important in pushing, since it converts the arm and forearm into a sturdy rod.

Most of the muscles that move the hand and fingers originate from the radius and the ulna; some of them insert on the carpal bones of the wrist, whereas others have long tendons that cross the wrist and insert on bones of the hand and the fingers. The **flexor carpi** and the **extensor carpi muscles** are responsible for many movements of the hand. Muscles that produce finger movements are the several **flexor digitorum** (dij″e-to′rum) and the **extensor digi-** torum muscles. Special groups of muscles in the fleshy parts of the hand are responsible for the intricate movements that can be performed with the thumb and the fingers. The position and freedom of movement of the thumb have been one of the most useful endowments of humans.

Muscles of the Trunk

Muscles of Respiration

The most important muscle involved in the act of breathing is the **diaphragm**. This dome-shaped muscle forms the partition between the thoracic cavity above and the abdominal cavity below (Fig. 8-5). When the diaphragm contracts, the central dome-shaped portion is pulled downward, thus enlarging the thoracic cavity from top to bottom. The **intercostal muscles** are attached to and fill the spaces between the ribs. The external and internal intercostals run at angles in opposite directions. Contraction of the external intercostal muscles serves to elevate the

Figure 8-5. *The diaphragm forms the partition between the thoracic cavity and the abdominal cavity.*

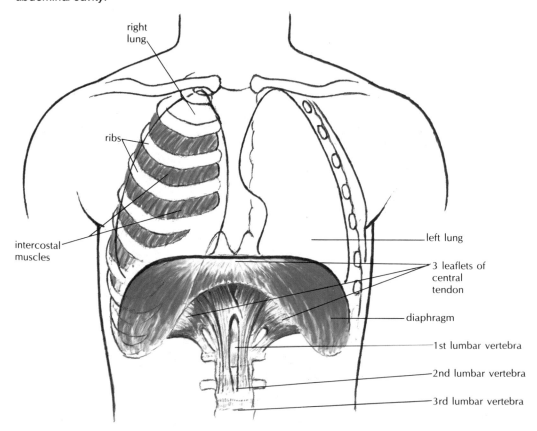

right lung

ribs

intercostal muscles

left lung

3 leaflets of central tendon

diaphragm

1st lumbar vertebra

2nd lumbar vertebra

3rd lumbar vertebra

ribs, thus enlarging the thoracic cavity from side to side and from front to back. The mechanics of breathing are described in Chapter 17.

Muscles of the Abdomen and Pelvis

The front and side (anterolateral) walls of the abdomen have three main muscles arranged in layers: the **external oblique** on the outside, the **internal oblique** in the middle, and the **transversus abdominis**, which is the innermost layer. The fibers of these three muscles all run in different directions. With these layers acting together, the total effect is like that of a piece of plywood; the result is a very strong abdominal wall. The front of the abdomen is closed in by the long, narrow **rectus abdominis**, which originates at the pubis and ends at the ribs. It is surrounded by connective tissue layers from the other three muscles.

The abdominal muscles have a number of functions in addition to protecting the underlying organs. They assist indirectly with the process of respiration, relaxing when the diaphragm contracts and vice versa. They also help expel substances from the body by compressing the abdominal cavity and increasing pressure within that cavity (*e.g.,* coughing, vomiting, childbirth). Another function of the abdominal muscles is to help bend the trunk forward and sideways.

The pelvic floor, or **perineum** (per-i-ne′um), has its own form of diaphragm, shaped somewhat like a shallow dish. One of the principal muscles of this pelvic diaphragm is the **levator ani** (le-va′tor a′ni), which acts on the rectum and thus aids in defecation.

Deep Muscles of the Back

The deep muscles of the back, which act on the vertebral column itself, are thick vertical masses that lie under the trapezius and latissimus dorsi. The longest muscle is the **sacrospinalis** (sa″kro-spin-a′lis), which helps maintain the vertebral column in an erect posture.

Muscles of the Lower Extremities

The muscles in the lower extremities, among the longest and strongest muscles in the body, are specialized for locomotion and balance.

Movement of the Thigh and Leg

The **gluteus maximus** (gloo′te-us mak′si-mus), which forms much of the fleshy part of the buttock, is relatively large in humans because of its support function when a person is standing in the erect position. This muscle extends the thigh and is very important in walking and running. The **gluteus medius,** which is partially covered by the gluteus maximus, serves to abduct the thigh.

The **iliopsoas** (il-e-o-so′as) arises from the ilium and the bodies of the lumbar vertebrae; it crosses the front of the hip joint to insert on the femur. It is a powerful flexor of the thigh and helps keep the trunk from falling backward when one is standing erect.

The **adductor muscles** are located on the medial part of the thigh. They arise from the pubis and ischium and insert on the femur. These strong muscles press the thighs together, as in grasping a saddle between the knees when riding a horse.

The **sartorius** is a long, narrow muscle that begins at the iliac spine, winds downward and inward across the entire thigh, and ends on the upper medial surface of the tibia. It is called the *tailor's muscle* because it is used in crossing the legs in the manner of tailors, who in days gone by sat cross-legged on the floor.

The front and sides of the femur are covered by the **quadriceps femoris** (kwod′re-seps fem′or-is), a large muscle that has four heads of origin. One of these heads is from the ilium and three are from the femur, but all four have a common tendon of insertion on the tibia. You may remember that this is the tendon that encloses the knee cap, or patella. This muscle extends the leg, as in kicking a ball.

The **hamstring muscles** are located in the posterior part of the thigh. Their tendons can be felt behind the knee as they descend to insert on the tibia and fibula. The hamstrings flex the leg on the thigh, as in kneeling.

Movement of the Foot

The **gastrocnemius** (gas-trok-ne′me-us) is the chief muscle of the calf of the leg. It has been called the *toe dancer's muscle* because it is used in standing on tiptoe. It ends near the heel in a prominent cord called the **Achilles tendon,** which attaches to the calcaneus (heel bone). The Achilles tendon is the largest tendon in the body.

Another leg muscle that acts on the foot is the **tibialis** (tib-e-a′lis) **anterior,** located on the front of the leg. This muscle performs the opposite function of the gastrocnemius. Anyone who feels inclined to walk on the heels will use the tibialis anterior to raise the rest of the foot off the ground (dorsiflexion). This muscle is also responsible for inversion of the foot. The muscle for eversion of the foot is the **peroneus** (per-o-ne'us) **longus,** located on the lateral side of the leg. The long tendon of this muscle crosses under the foot, forming a sling that supports the transverse (metatarsal) arch.

The toes, like the fingers, are provided with flexor and extensor muscles. The tendons of the extensor muscles are located in the top of the foot and insert on the superior surface of the toe bones (phalanges). The flexor digitorum tendons cross the sole of the foot and insert on the undersurface of the toe bones.

Effects of Aging on Muscles

Beginning about the age of 40, there is a gradual loss of muscle cells with a resulting decrease in the size of each individual muscle. There is also a loss of power, notably in the extensor muscles, such as the large sacrospinalis near the vertebral column. This causes the "bent over" appearance of a hunchback (kyphosis), which in women is often referred to as the *dowager's hump.* Sometimes there is a tendency to bend (flex) the hips and knees. In addition to causing the previously noted changes in the vertebral column (see Chap. 7), these effects on the extensor muscles result in a further decrease in the elderly person's height. Activity and exercise throughout life delay and decrease these undesirable effects of aging.

Muscular Disorders

Atrophy (at'ro-fe) is a wasting or decrease in the size of a muscle when it cannot be used, such as when an extremity must be placed in a cast following a fracture. **Strains** and **sprains** are typical injuries that often affect muscles. Severe and excessive exertion can cause detachment of muscles from bones or tearing of some of the muscle cells. Sprains can involve damage to other structures besides the ligaments, specifically blood vessels, nerves, and muscles. Much of the pain and swelling accompanying a sprain can be prevented by the immediate application of ice packs, which constrict some of the smaller blood vessels and reduce internal bleeding.

Muscular dystrophy (dis'tro-fe) is really a group of disorders, most of which are hereditary. These disorders all progress at different rates. The most common type, which is found most frequently in male children, leads to complete helplessness and ends in death within 10 to 15 years of onset. The cure for any muscular dystrophy is not yet known. **Myasthenia gravis** (mi"as-the'ne-ah gra'vis) is characterized by chronic muscular fatigue brought on by the slightest exertion. If affects adults and begins with the muscles of the head. Drooping of the eyelids (ptosis) is a common early symptom.

Myalgia (mi-al'je-ah) means "muscular pain"; **myositis** (mi-o-si'tis) is a term that indicates actual inflammation of muscle tissue. **Fibrositis** (fi-bro-si'tis) means "inflammation of connective tissues" and refers particularly to those tissues connected with muscles and joints. Usually it appears as a combination disorder that is properly called **fibromyositis** but is commonly referred to as *rheumatism, lumbago,* or *charleyhorse.* The disorder may be acute, with severe pain on motion, or it may be chronic. Sometimes the application of heat, together with massage and rest, relieves the symptoms.

Bursitis is inflammation of a **bursa,** a fluid-filled sac that minimizes friction between tissues and bone. Some bursae communicate with joints; others are closely related to muscles. Sometimes bursae develop spontaneously in response to prolonged friction.

Bursitis can be very painful, with swelling and limitation of motion. Some examples of bursitis are listed below:

1 **Students' elbow,** in which the bursa over the point of the elbow (olecranon) is inflamed owing to long hours of leaning on the elbow while studying
2 **Ischial bursitis,** which is said to be common among persons who must sit a great deal, such as taxicab drivers and truckers
3 **Housemaid's knee,** in which the bursa in front of the patella is inflamed. This form of bursitis is found in persons who must often be on their knees.
4 **Subdeltoid bursitis** in the shoulder region, a fairly common form. In some cases a local anesthetic and/or corticosteroids may be injected to relieve the pain.

Bunions are enlargements commonly found at the base and medial side of the great toe. Usually, prolonged pressure has caused the development of a bursa, which has then become inflamed. Special shoes may be necessary if surgery is not performed.

Tendinitis (ten″di-ni′tis), an inflammation of muscle tendons and their attachments, occurs most often in athletes who overexert themselves. It frequently involves the shoulder, the hamstring muscle tendons at the knee, and the Achilles tendon near the heel. **Tenosynovitis** (ten″o-sin″o-vi′tis), which involves the synovial sheath that encloses tendons, is found most often in women in their 40s following an injury or surgery. It may involve swelling and severe pain with activity. **Carpal tunnel syndrome** involves the tendons of the flexor muscles of the fingers as well as the nerves supplying the hand and fingers. It is found in certain factory workers and in persons who use their hands and fingers strenuously. Constant pressure by tools may cause the damage.

Muscle **cramps** include strong, painful contractions of leg and foot muscles during the night (recumbancy cramps). They are most likely to occur following unusually strenuous activity.

Flatfoot is a common disorder in which the arch of the foot, the normally raised portion of the sole, breaks down so that the entire sole rests on the ground. This condition may be congenital, in which case it usually gives little trouble. However, flatfoot can result from a progressive weakening of the muscles that support the arch, in which case it is usually accompanied by a great deal of pain. Incorrect use of the muscles that support the arch (such as toeing out when walking) or lack of exercise is thought to bring about flatfoot. Wearing properly fitted shoes and walking with the toes pointed straight forward may help prevent flatfoot and other painful foot disorders. Exercises performed under medical supervision can be helpful in strengthening the muscles that help maintain the foot arches.

Summary

I **Structure of skeletal muscles**
  A Bundles of muscle fibers (cells)
  B Connective tissue
  C Epimysium (deep fascia)—forms sheath enclosing entire muscle

II **Characteristics of skeletal muscles**
  A Excitability (irritability)—capacity to respond to nerve impulses transmitted at neuromuscular junction

  B Contractility—ability to shorten based on sliding together of actin and myosin
    1 Isotonic contractions—muscle shortens to produce movement
    2 Isometric contractions—tension increases but muscle does not shorten

III **Attachments of skeletal muscles**
  A Types
    1 Tendon—cord of connective tissue that attaches muscle to bone
    2 Aponeurosis—broad band of connective tissue that attaches muscle to bone or other muscle
  B Functions
    1 Origin—attached to less movable part
    2 Insertion—attached to movable part

IV **Muscle movement**
  A Types of muscles
    1 Prime movers—initiate movement
    2 Antagonists—produce opposite movement
    3 Others—steady body parts and assist prime mover
  B Exercise—improves circulation, strengthens heart, improves respiration and gas exchange
  C Body mechanics—muscles function with skeleton as levers

V **Skeletal muscle groups**
  A Muscles of the head and neck
  B Muscles of the upper extremities
  C Muscles of the trunk
  D Muscles of the lower extremities

VI **Effects of aging on muscles**
  A Decrease in size of muscles
  B Weakening of muscles, especially extensors

VII **Muscular disorders**
  A Strains, sprains
  B Muscular dystrophy—group of disorders
  C Myasthenia gravis
  D Bursitis, tendinitis
  E Flatfoot

Questions for Study and Review

1 Describe the structure of muscles from fiber to epimysium.

2 Differentiate between the terms in each of the following pairs:

a *tendon* and *aponeurosis*

b *muscle origin* and *muscle insertion*

c *prime mover* and *antagonist*

d *isometric contraction* and *isotonic contraction*

e *bursitis* and *tendinitis*

3 Explain the role of each of the following in muscle contraction: actin and myosin, calcium, ATP, myoglobin, glycogen.

4 When does oxygen debt occur? What is the role of lactic acid in oxygen debt? How is oxygen debt eliminated?

5 Name and describe the functions of the principal muscles of the head and neck, upper extremities, trunk, and lower extremities.

6 List several characteristics according to which muscles are named.

7 What are some valuable effects of exercise?

8 What are levers and how do they work? The forceps is an example of which class of lever? When muscles and bones act as lever systems, what part of the body is the fulcrum?

9 What effect does aging have on muscles?

10 Define *atrophy* and give one cause.

11 What are muscular dystrophies, and what are some of their effects?

12 What is bursitis? Describe several forms.

9

The Nervous System

Behavioral Objectives

After careful study of this chapter, you should be able to:

Describe the organization of the nervous system according to structure and function

Briefly describe the transmission of a nerve impulse

Define synapse

Explain the role of neurotransmitters at the synapse

Identify three different types of nerves

Give the locations and functions of three main divisions of the brain

Cite one function of the cerebral cortex in each lobe of the brain

List several functions of the spinal cord

Name the three meninges

Cite the function of cerebrospinal fluid and describe where and how this fluid is formed

Cite the names and functions of the 12 cranial nerves

Compare the sympathetic and parasympathetic nervous systems with respect to location and function

Selected Key Terms

The following terms are defined in the glossary:

action potential
afferent
autonomic nervous system
axon
brain stem
cerebellum
cerebral cortex
cerebrospinal fluid
cerebrum
dendrite
effector
efferent
ganglion
medulla oblongata
meninges
midbrain
nerve
nerve impulse
neurotransmitter
plexus
pons
receptor
reflex
synapse
ventricle

None of the body systems is capable of functioning alone. All are interdependent and work together as one unit so that normal conditions (homeostasis) within the body may prevail. The nervous system serves as the chief coordinating agency. Conditions both within and outside the body are constantly changing; one purpose of the nervous system is to respond to these internal and external changes (known as *stimuli*) and so cause the body to adapt itself to new conditions. It is through the instructions and directions sent to the various organs by the nervous system that a person's internal harmony and the balance between that person and the environment are maintained. The nervous system has been compared to a telephone exchange, in that the brain and the spinal cord act as switching centers and the nerve trunks act as cables for carrying messages to and from these centers.

The Nervous System as a Whole

The parts of the nervous system may be grouped according to structure or function. The anatomic, or structural, divisions of the nervous system are as follows:

1 The **central nervous system (CNS)** includes the brain and spinal cord.
2 The **peripheral nervous system** is made up of all the nerves outside the CNS. It includes all of the **cranial** and **spinal nerves**. Cranial nerves are those that carry impulses to and from the brain. Spinal nerves are those that carry messages to and from the spinal cord.

From the standpoint of structure, the CNS and peripheral nervous system together include most of the nerve tissue in the body. However, certain peripheral nerves have a special function, and for this reason they are grouped together under the designation **autonomic** (aw″to-nom′ik) **nervous system**. The reason for this separate classification is that the autonomic nervous system largely has to do with activities that go on more or less automatically. This system carries impulses from the CNS to the glands, the involuntary (smooth) muscles found in the walls of tubes and hollow organs, and the heart. Both cranial and spinal nerves carry autonomic nervous system impulses. The system is subdivided into the **sympathetic** and **parasympathetic nervous systems**, both of which are explained later in this chapter.

The autonomic nervous system makes up a part of the **involuntary**, or **visceral**, **nervous system**, which controls smooth muscle, cardiac muscle, and glands. The **voluntary**, or **somatic** (so-ma′tik), **nervous system** consists of all of the nerves that control the action of the skeletal muscles (described in Chap. 8), which are under conscious control.

Nerve Cells and Their Functions

As stated in Chapter 4, the nerve cell is called a *neuron*. Each neuron is composed of a cell body, containing the nucleus, and of nerve fibers, which are thread-like projections of the cytoplasm.

Nerve fibers are of two kinds: **dendrites** (den′drites), which conduct impulses *to* the cell body; and **axons**, which conduct impulses *away from* the cell body (Fig 9-1). The dendrites of sensory neurons (which carry impulses toward the CNS) are different from those of other neurons: they may be long (as long as 1 meter) or short, but they are usually single and they do not have the treelike appearance so typical of other dendrites. Each dendrite has a special structure, called the **receptor**, where a stimulus is received and the sensory impulse begins. Sensations that involve these sensory neurons, such as pain, touch, hearing, and sight, are discussed in Chapter 10.

Some axons in the central and peripheral nervous systems are covered with a fatty insulating material called **myelin**. This covering is produced by special cells that wrap around the axon, forming a sheath. Small spaces that remain between the cells, called **nodes**, are important in the conduction of nerve impulses (see Fig. 9-1).

Axons covered with myelin are called *white fibers* and are found in the **white matter** of the brain and spinal cord as well as in the nerve trunks in all parts of the body. The fibers and cell bodies of the **gray matter** are not covered with myelin. Myelinated axons of the peripheral nervous system are covered by a thin outer sheath, the **neurilemma**. The neurilemma aids in the repair of damaged nerve fibers.

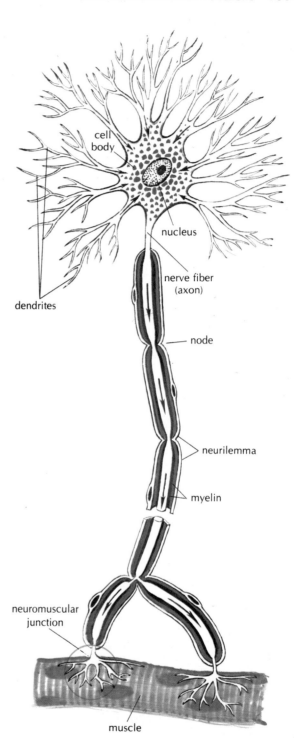

Figure 9-1. *Diagram of a motor neuron. The break in the axon denotes length. The arrows show the direction of the nerve impulse.*

The Nerve Impulse

The cell membrane of an unstimulated (resting) neuron carries an electric charge. Because of positive and negative ions concentrated on either side of the membrane, the inside of the membrane at rest is negative as compared with the outside. A **nerve impulse** is a local reversal in the charge on the nerve cell membrane that then spreads along the membrane like an electric current. This sudden electric change in the membrane is called an **action potential**. A stimulus, then, is any force that can initiate an action potential. This electric change results from rapid shifts in sodium and potassium ions across the cell membrane. The reversal occurs very rapidly (in less than one thousandth of a second) and is followed by a rapid return of the membrane to its original state so that it can be stimulated again.

A myelinated nerve fiber conducts impulses more rapidly than an unmyelinated fiber of the same size because the electric impulse "jumps" from space (node) to space in the myelin sheath instead of traveling continuously along the fiber.

The Synapse

Each neuron is a separate unit, and there is no anatomic connection between neurons. Therefore, how is it possible for neurons to communicate? In other words, how does the axon of one neuron make functional contact with the dendrite of another neuron? This is accomplished by the **synapse** (si′naps), from a Greek word meaning "to clasp." Synapses are points of junction for the transmission of nerve impulses. Certain chemicals, called **neurotransmitters** or *transmitter substances,* are released from the nerve fiber endings to enable impulses to leap the synaptic junction. Although there are many known neurotransmitters, the main ones are **epinephrine** (ep-i-nef′rin), also called *adrenalin;* a related compound, **norepinephrine** (nor″ep-i-nef′rin), or *noradrenalin;* and **acetylcholine** (as-e-til-ko′len). Acetylcholine is the neurotransmitter released at the neuromuscular junction; all three are released by fibers of the autonomic nervous system.

With the aid of chemical transmitters, impulses can be conducted between neurons and from a neuron or group of neurons to another type of cell. Like switches that open an electric current to permit the passage of electricity, the neurotransmitters allow the conduction of nerve impulses from cell to cell across the synapse.

Nerves

A **nerve** is a bundle of nerve fibers located *outside* the CNS. Bundles of nerve fibers *within* the CNS are **tracts**. These are located within the brain and also within the spinal cord to conduct impulses to and from the brain. A nerve or tract can be compared to an electric cable made up of many wires. In the case of nerves, the "wires," or nerve fibers, are bound together with connective tissue.

Neurons that are connected with receptors (for receiving stimuli) and that conduct impulses *to* the brain and spinal cord are described as **sensory**, or **afferent, neurons.** Those fibers that carry impulses *from* the CNS out to the muscles and glands form the **motor**, or **efferent, neurons** (see Fig. 9-1). Although some nerves contain only one type of fiber and are classified as sensory (afferent) or motor (efferent) nerves, most nerves contain both types of fibers and are referred to as **mixed nerves**.

≡ The Central Nervous System

The Brain

Main Parts of the Brain

The brain occupies the cranial cavity and is covered by membranes, fluid, and the bones of the skull. Although the various regions of the brain are in communication and may function together, the brain may be divided into distinct areas for ease of study (Fig. 9-2):

1 The **cerebrum** (ser′e-brum) is the largest part of the brain. It is divided into right and left **cerebral** (ser′e-bral) **hemispheres** by a deep groove called the **longitudinal fissure**. The area between the cerebral hemispheres and the brain stem is the **diencephalon** (di-en-sef′ah-lon).

2 The **brain stem** connects the cerebrum with the spinal cord. The upper portion of the brain stem is the **midbrain**. Below it and plainly visible from the underview of the brain are the **pons** (ponz) and the **medulla oblongata** (me-dul′lah ob-long-ga′tah). The pons connects the midbrain with the medulla, while the medulla connects the

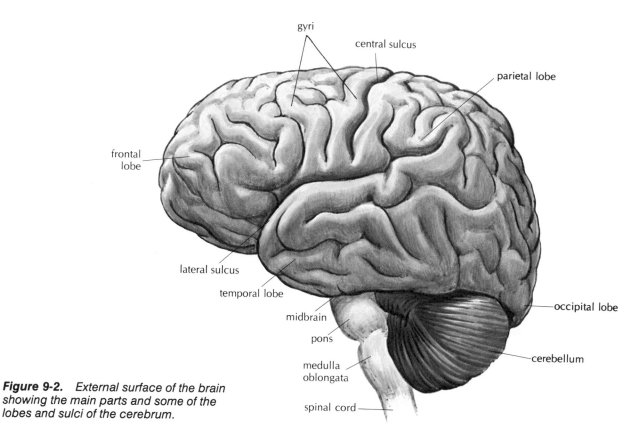

Figure 9-2. *External surface of the brain showing the main parts and some of the lobes and sulci of the cerebrum.*

brain with the spinal cord through a large opening in the base of the skull (foramen magnum).

3 The **cerebellum** (ser-e-bel′um) is located immediately below the back part of the cerebral hemispheres and is connected with the cerebrum, brain stem, and spinal cord by means of the pons. The word *cerebellum* means "little brain."

Each of these divisions is described in greater detail below.

The Cerebral Hemispheres

The outer nerve tissue of the cerebral hemispheres is gray matter called the **cerebral cortex**. This gray cortex is arranged in folds forming elevated portions known as **gyri** (ji′ri), which are separated by shallow grooves called **sulci** (sul′si) (see Fig. 9-2). Internally, the cerebral hemispheres are made largely of white matter and a few islands of gray matter. Inside the hemispheres are two spaces extending in a somewhat irregular fashion. These are the **lateral ventri-** cles, which are filled with a watery fluid, common to both the brain and the spinal cord, called **cerebrospinal** (ser-e-bro-spi′nal) **fluid (CSF)**, to be discussed later.

Although there are many sulci, a few are especially important landmarks, such as

1 The **central sulcus**, which lies between the frontal and parietal lobes of each hemisphere at right angles to the longitudinal fissure

2 The **lateral sulcus**, which curves along the side of each hemisphere and separates the temporal lobe from the frontal and parietal lobes (see Fig. 9-2)

The cerebral cortex is the layer of gray matter that forms the surface of each cerebral hemisphere. It is within the cerebral cortex that impulses are received and analyzed. These form the basis of knowledge; the brain "stores" information, much of which can be recalled on demand by means of the phenomenon called *memory*. It is in the cerebral cortex that thought processes such as association, judgment, and discrimination take place. It is also from the cerebral cortex that conscious deliberation and voluntary actions emanate.

Functions of the Cerebral Cortex. Each cerebral hemisphere is divided into four visible lobes named from the overlying cranial bones. Although the various areas of the brain act in coordination to produce behavior, certain portions of the cortex influence particular categories of function. The four lobes are described below:

1 The **frontal lobe**, relatively larger in the human being than in any other organism, lies in front of the central sulcus. This lobe contains the motor cortex, which directs actions (Fig. 9-3). The left side of the brain governs the right side of the

Figure 9-3. *Controlling areas of the brain. The parts of the body are shown drawn in proportion to the area of control.*

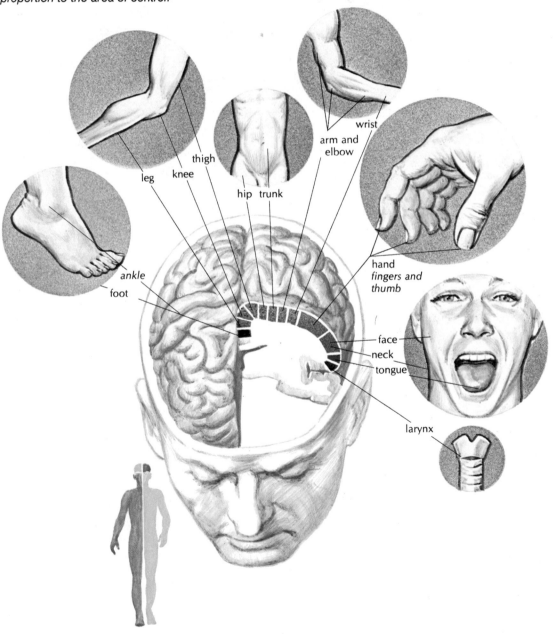

body, and the right side of the brain governs the left side of the body (Fig. 9-4). The frontal lobe also contains two areas important in speech (the speech centers are discussed later).

2 The **parietal lobe** occupies the upper part of each hemisphere and lies just behind the central sulcus. This lobe contains the **sensory area**, in which impulses from the skin, such as touch, pain, and temperature, are interpreted. The determination of distances, sizes, and shapes also take place here.

3 The **temporal lobe** lies below the lateral sulcus and folds under the hemisphere on each side. This lobe contains the **auditory area** for receiving and interpreting impulses from the ear. The **olfactory area**, concerned with the sense of smell, is located in the medial part of the temporal lobe; it is stimulated by impulses arising from receptors in the nose.

4 The **occipital lobe** lies behind the parietal lobe and extends over the cerebellum. This lobe contains the **visual area** for interpreting impulses arising from the retina of the eye.

In addition to the above, there is a small fifth lobe in each hemisphere that cannot be seen from the surface because it lies deep within the lateral sulcus. Not much is known about this lobe, which is called the **insula.**

Beneath the gray matter of the cerebral cortex is the white matter, consisting of myelinated nerve fibers that connect the cortical areas with each other and with other parts of the nervous system. An important band of white matter is the **corpus callosum** located at the bottom of the longitudinal fissure. This band acts as a bridge between the right and left hemispheres, permitting impulses to cross from one side of the brain to the other. The **internal capsule** is a crowded strip of white matter composed of many myelinated nerve fibers (forming tracts). **Basal nuclei** are masses of gray matter located deep within each cerebral hemisphere. These groups of neurons help regulate body movement and facial expressions communicated from the cerebral cortex. The neurotransmitter **dopamine** (do′pah-men) is secreted by the neurons of the basal nuclei.

Communication Areas. The ability to communicate by written and verbal means is an interesting example of the way in which areas of the cerebral cortex are interrelated (Fig. 9-5). The development

and use of these areas are closely connected with the process of learning.

1 The **auditory areas** are located in the temporal lobe. In one of these areas sound impulses transmitted from the environment are detected, while in the surrounding area (auditory speech center) the sounds are interpreted and understood. The beginnings of language are learned by auditory means, so the auditory area for understanding sounds is very near the auditory receiving area of the cortex. Babies often seem to understand what is being said long before they do any talking themselves. It is usually several years before children learn to read or write words.

2 The **motor areas** for communication (for talking and writing) are located in front of the lowest part of the motor cortex in the frontal lobe. Since the lower part of the motor cortex controls the muscles of the head and neck, it seems logical to think of the motor speech center as an extension forward in this area. Control of the muscles of speech (in the tongue, the soft palate, and the larynx) is carried out here. Similarly, the written speech center is located in front of the cortical area that controls the muscles of the arm and hand. The ability to write words is usually one of the last phases in the development of learning words and their meanings.

3 The **visual areas** of the cortex are involved in communication by receiving visual impulses in the occipital lobe. These images are interpreted as words in the visual area that lies in front of the receiving location. The ability to read with understanding is also developed in this area. You might *see* writing in the Japanese language, for example, but this would involve only the visual receiving area in the occipital lobe unless you could also *read* the words.

There is a functional relationship among areas of the brain. Many neurons must work together to enable a person to receive, interpret, and respond to verbal and written messages as well as to touch (tactile) and other sensory stimuli.

Memory and the Learning Process. Memory is the mental faculty for recalling ideas. In the initial stage of the memory process, sensory signals (*e.g.,* visual, auditory) are retained for a very short time, perhaps only fractions of a second. Nevertheless, they can be used for further processing. **Short-term**

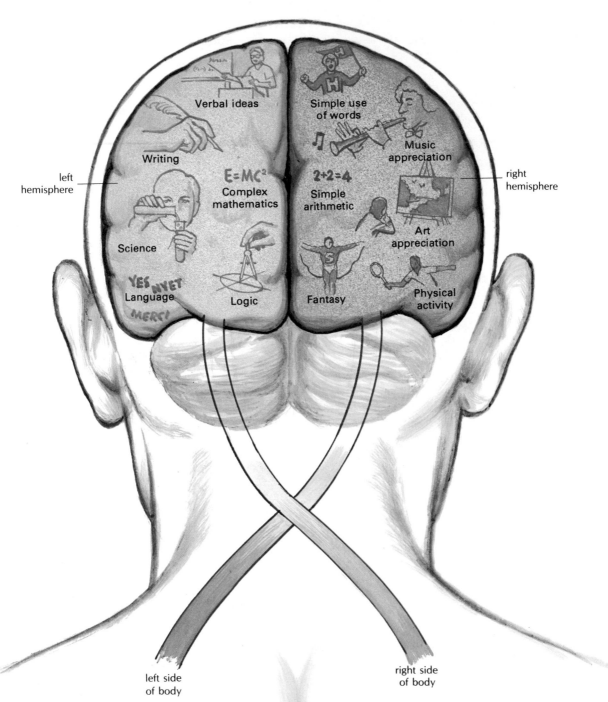

Figure 9-4. *Schematic representation of cerebral dominance showing that the two sides of the cerebrum send impulses to, and receive impulses from, opposite sides of the body. (Chaffee EE, Lytle IM: Basic Physiology and Anatomy, 4th ed, p 210. Philadelphia, JB Lippincott, 1980)*

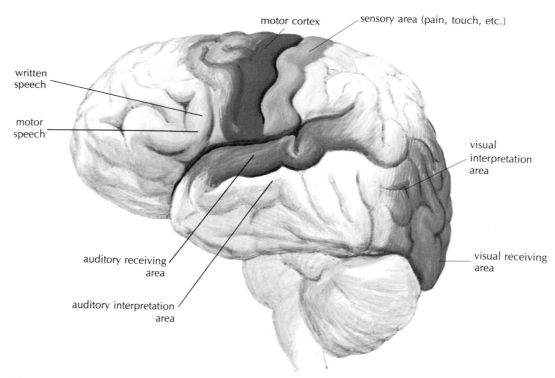

motor cortex

sensory area (pain, touch, etc.)

written speech

motor speech

visual interpretation area

auditory receiving area

visual receiving area

auditory interpretation area

Figure 9-5. *Functional areas of the cerebrum.*

memory refers to the retention of bits of information for a few seconds or maybe a few minutes, after which the information is lost unless reinforced. **Long-term memory** refers to the storage of information that can be recalled at a later time. It has been noted that there is a tendency for a memory to become more fixed the more often a person repeats the remembered experience; thus, short-term memory signals can lead to long-term memories. Furthermore, the more often a memory is recalled, the more indelible it becomes; such a memory can be so deeply fixed in the brain that it can be recalled immediately.

Careful anatomic studies have shown that tiny extensions called **fibrils** form at the synapses in the cerebral cortex so impulses can travel more easily from one neuron to another. The number of these fibrils increases with age. Physiological studies show that rehearsal (repetition) of the same information again and again accelerates and potentiates the degree of transfer of short-term memory into long-term memory. It has been found that a person who is wide awake memorizes far better than a person who is in a state of mental fatigue. It has also been noted that the brain is able to organize information so that new ideas are stored in the same areas in which similar ones have been stored before.

The Diencephalon

The **diencephalon**, or interbrain, can be seen by cutting into the central section of the brain. It includes the **thalamus** (thal'ah-mus) and the **hypothalamus** (Fig 9-6). Nearly all sensory impulses travel through the masses of gray matter that form the thalamus. The action of the thalamus is to sort out the impulses and direct them to particular areas of the cerebral cortex. The hypothalamus, located in the midline area below the thalamus, contains cells that help control body temperature, water balance, sleep, appetite, and some emotions, such as fear and pleasure. Both the sympathetic and parasympathetic divisions of the autonomic nervous system are under the control of the hypothalamus, as is the pituitary gland. Thus, the hypothalamus influences the heart beat, the contraction and relaxation of the walls of blood vessels, hormone secretion, and other vital body functions.

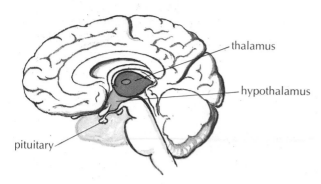

Figure 9-6. *Diagram showing the relationship among the thalamus, hypothalamus, and pituitary (hypophysis). (Chaffee EE, Lytle IM: Basic Physiology and Anatomy, 4th ed, p 211. Philadelphia, JB Lippincott, 1980)*

Division and Functions of the Brain Stem

The brain stem is composed of the midbrain, the pons, and the medulla oblongata. These structures connect the cerebrum with the spinal cord.

The **midbrain**, located just below the center of the cerebrum, forms the forward part of the brain stem. Four rounded masses of gray matter that are hidden by the cerebral hemispheres form the upper part of the midbrain; these four bodies act as relay centers for certain eye and ear reflexes. The white matter at the front of the midbrain conducts impulses between the higher centers of the cerebrum and the lower centers of the pons, medulla, cerebellum, and spinal cord. Cranial nerves III and IV originate from the midbrain.

The **pons** lies between the midbrain and the medulla, in front of the cerebellum. It is composed largely of myelinated nerve fibers, which serve to connect the two halves of the cerebellum with the brain stem as well as with the cerebrum above and the spinal cord below. The pons is an important connecting link between the cerebellum and the rest of the nervous system, and it contains nerve fibers that carry impulses to and from the centers located above and below it. Certain reflex (involuntary) actions, such as some of those regulating respiration, are integrated in the pons. Cranial nerves V through VIII originate from the pons.

The **medulla oblongata** of the brain is located between the pons and the spinal cord. It appears white externally because, like the pons, it contains many myelinated nerve fibers. Internally, it contains collections of cell bodies (gray matter) called **nuclei**,

or *centers.* Among these are vital centers such as the following:

1 The **respiratory center** controls the muscles of respiration in response to chemical and other stimuli.
2 The **cardiac center** helps regulate the rate and force of the heart beat.
3 The **vasomotor** (vas-o-mo′tor) **center** regulates the contraction of smooth muscle in the blood vessel walls and thus helps determine blood pressure.

The last four pairs of cranial nerves are connected with the medulla. The sensory nerve fibers that carry messages through the spinal cord up to the brain travel through the medulla, as do descending motor fibers. These groups of nerve fibers form tracts (bundles) and are grouped together according to function. The motor fibers from the motor cortex of the cerebral hemispheres extend down through the medulla, and most of them cross from one side to the other (decussate) while going through this part of the brain. It is in the medulla that the shifting of nerve fibers occurs that causes the right cerebral hemisphere to control muscles in the left side of the body and the upper portion of the cortex to control muscles in the lower portions of the person. The medulla is an important reflex center; here, certain neurons end and impulses are relayed to other neurons. Cranial nerves IX through XII arise from the medulla.

The Cerebellum

The **cerebellum** is made up of three parts: the middle portion and two lateral hemispheres. Like the cerebral hemispheres, the cerebellum has an outer area of gray matter and an inner portion that is largely white matter. The functions of the cerebellum are

1 To aid in the **coordination of voluntary muscles** so that they will function smoothly and in an orderly fashion. Disease of the cerebellum causes muscular jerkiness and tremors.
2 To aid in the **maintenance of balance** in standing, walking, and sitting, as well as during more strenuous activities. Messages from the internal ear and from the tendon and muscle sensory receptors aid the cerebellum.
3 To aid in the **maintenance of muscle tone** so that all muscle fibers are slightly tensed and ready to produce necessary changes in position as quickly as may be necessary.

Ventricles of the Brain

Within the brain are four fluid-filled spaces, called **ventricles**, which extend into the various parts of the brain in a somewhat irregular fashion. We have already mentioned the largest, the lateral ventricles in the two cerebral hemispheres. Their extensions into the lobes of the cerebrum are called **horns** (Fig. 9-7). These paired ventricles communicate with a midline space, the third ventricle, by means of openings called **foramina** (fo-ram′i-nah). The third ventricle is bounded on each side by the two parts of the thalamus, while the floor is occupied by the hypothalamus. Continuing down from the third ventricle, a small canal, called the **cerebral aqueduct**, extends through the midbrain into the fourth ventricle. The latter is continuous with the neural, or central, canal of the spinal cord. In the roof of the fourth ventricle are three openings that allow the escape of CSF to the area that surrounds the brain and spinal cord.

Brain Studies

Diagnostic tests can be performed on the brain and related structures. One such test involves the removal of cerebrospinal fluid. Air or another substance may then be injected, after which x-ray films, called **encephalograms** (en-sef′ah-lo-grams) or **ventriculograms** (ven-trik′u-lo-grams), are taken.

This procedure has been largely replaced by the CT scan (mentioned in Chap. 4). The CT (computed tomographic) scan provides multiple x-ray pictures taken from different angles simultaneously. By means of a computer, the information is organized and dis-

Figure 9-7. *Ventricles of the brain.*

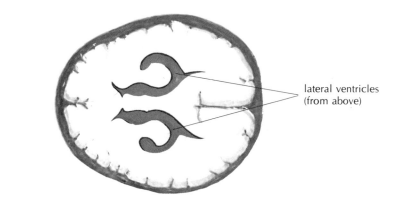

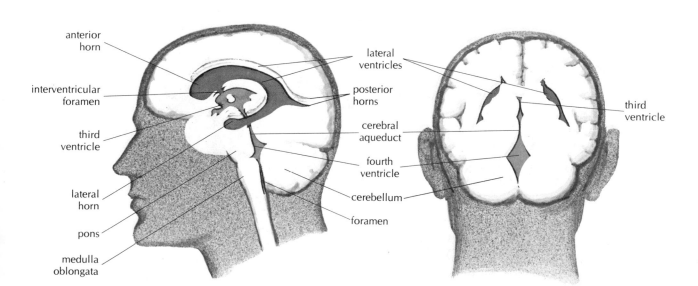

played as photographs of the bone, soft tissue, and cavities of the brain (Fig 9-8). Anatomic lesions such as tumors or scar tissue accumulations are readily seen.

The interactions of the billions of nerve cells in the brain give rise to measurable electric currents. These may be recorded by an instrument called the **electroencephalograph** (e-lek″tro-ensef′ah-lo-graf″). The recorded tracings or brain waves produce an electroencephalogram (EEG).

Disorders of the Brain

The scientific name for the brain is encephalon; therefore, inflammation of the brain is known as **encephalitis** (en-sef″ah-li′tis). There are many causes of such disease, but the two chief pathogens are described below:

1 **Viruses** carried by insects cause some of the epidemic types of encephalitis sometimes found in the United States and other parts of the world.

Figure 9-8. *CT scanner.*

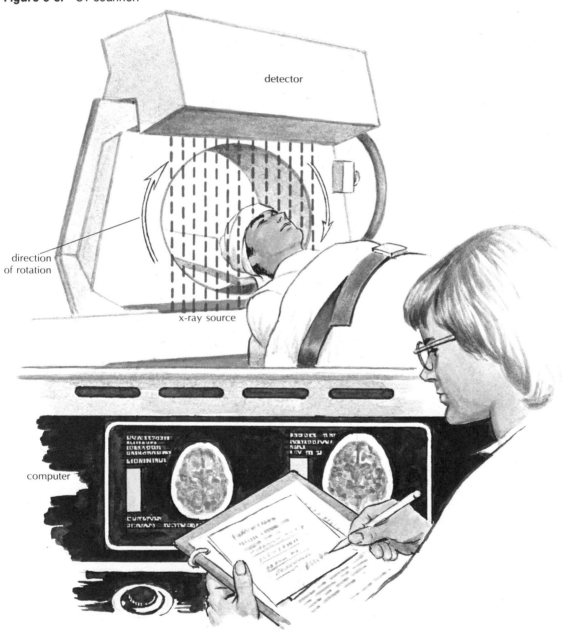

2 Certain **protozoa**, called *trypanosomes* (tri″pan′o-somes), cause the so-called African sleeping sickness. These protozoa, which are carried by a kind of fly (tsetse), are capable of invading the CSF of humans and infecting the surrounding tissue.

Stroke, or **cerebrovascular** (ser″e-bro-vas′ku-lar) **accident** (CVA), is by far the most common kind of brain disorder. Rupture of a blood vessel (with a consequent **cerebral hemorrhage**), thrombosis, or embolism may cause destruction of brain tissue. Such disorders are most frequent in persons with artery wall disease, and hence are most common in persons over the age of 40. The effect of a stroke depends on the location of the artery and the extent of the involvement. A hemorrhage into the white matter of the internal capsule in the lower part of the cerebrum may cause extensive paralysis of the side opposite the affected area. Such a paralysis is called **hemiplegia** (hem″e-ple′je-ah), and the paralyzed person is called a **hemiplegic** (hem″e-ple′jik).

Alzheimer's (alz′hi-merz) **disease** is another disorder of the brain. Although it may occur in persons under 60, it is more common among the elderly. The disorder develops gradually and eventually causes severe intellectual impairment. Memory loss, especially for recent events, is a common early symptom. Some studies indicate that a lack of the neurotransmitted acetylcholine, rather than destruction of brain cells, is the cause. Efforts at treatment have centered on methods to increase the amount of this neurotransmitter present in brain tissue, but at present there is no cure. Persons with Alzheimer's disease require help and understanding, as do those who must care for them.

Parkinson's disease also appears most commonly in individuals over 60 years of age. It is characterized by tremors, slowness of movement, body rigidity, and inability to maintain posture. The disease originates in areas of the brain that make up the basal nuclei and is related to a deficiency of the neurotransmitter dopamine. The most successful treatment so far has been with a form of the neurotransmitter called *levodopa* (L-dopa).

Cerebral palsy (pawl′ze) is a disorder caused by brain damage occurring before or during the birth process. It is characterized by diverse muscular disorders varying in degree: it may consist of only slight weakness of the lower extremity muscles or, at the other extreme, of paralysis of all four extremities as well as the speech muscles. With muscle and speech training and other therapeutic approaches, children with cerebral palsy can be helped.

Epilepsy is a chronic disorder involving an abnormality of the electric activity of the brain with or without apparent changes in the nerve tissues. One manifestation of epilepsy is seizure activity, which may be so mild as to be hardly noticeable or so severe as to result in loss of consciousness. In most cases the cause is not known. The study of brain waves obtained with the EEG usually shows abnormalities and is helpful in both diagnosis and treatment. Many persons with epilepsy can lead normal, active lives if they use appropriate medication as outlined by a physician. Newer techniques of laser surgery may prove to be beneficial in controlling seizure activity.

Tumors of the brain may develop in persons of any age but are somewhat more common in young and middle-aged adults than in other groups. The majority of brain tumors originate from the neuroglia and are called **gliomas** (see Chap 4). The symptoms produced depend on the type of tumor, its location, its destructiveness, and the degree to which it compresses the brain tissue. Involvement of the frontal portion of the cerebrum often causes mental symptoms, such as changes in personality and in levels of consciousness. Early surgery, chemotherapy, and radiation therapy offer hope of cure in some cases.

Aphasia (ah-fa′ze-ah) is a term that refers to loss of the ability to speak or write or to loss of understanding of written or spoken language. There are several different kinds of aphasia, depending on what part of the brain is affected. The lesion that causes aphasia in the right-handed person is likely to be in the left cerebral hemisphere. Often much can be done for affected persons by patient retraining and much understanding. The brain is an organ that has a marvelous capacity for adapting itself to different conditions, and its resources are tremendous. Often some means of communication can be found even though speech areas are damaged.

The Spinal Cord

Location of the Spinal Cord

In the embryo, the spinal cord occupies the entire spinal canal and so extends down into the tail portion of the vertebral column. However, the column of bone grows much more rapidly than the nerve tissue of the cord, so that eventually the end of the cord no longer reaches the lower part of the spinal canal. This disparity in growth continues to increase; in the adult the cord ends in the region just below the area to which the last rib attaches (between the first and second lumbar vertebrae).

Structure of the Spinal Cord

The spinal cord has a small, irregularly shaped internal section that consists of gray matter (nerve cell bodies) and a larger area surrounding this gray part that consists of white matter (nerve fibers). A cross section of the cord shows that the gray matter is so arranged that a column of cells extends up and down dorsally, one on each side; another column is found in the ventral region. These two pairs of columns of gray matter give this cross section an H-shaped appearance (Fig. 9-9). The white matter consists of thousands of nerve fibers arranged in three areas external to the gray matter on each side.

Functions of the Spinal Cord

The functions of the cord may be divided into three categories:

1 **Reflex activities,** which involve the transfer and integration of messages that enter the cord, so that sensory (afferent) impulses may enter and motor (efferent) messages may leave the cord without involving the brain

2 **Conduction of sensory impulses** from afferent nerves upward through ascending tracts to the brain

3 **Conduction of motor (efferent) impulses** from the brain down through descending tracts to the nerves that supply muscles or glands

The reflex pathway through the spinal cord usually involves three or more neurons, as illustrated in Figure 9-9 and listed here:

1 The **sensory neuron,** which has its beginning in a receptor and its nerve fiber in a nerve that leads to the cord

2 One or more **central neurons,** which are entirely within the cord

3 The **motor neuron,** which receives the impulse from a central neuron and then carries it by way of its long axon through a nerve to a muscle or a gland, described as the **effector**

The knee jerk is an example of a spinal reflex. The nerve pathway for this reflex includes a sensory neu-

ron that has its receptor in the tendon just below the knee, its sensory nerve fibers in the nerves that extend to the spinal cord, central neurons inside the lower part of the cord, and motor neurons that send impulses through nerves from the cord to the effector, the quadriceps femoris (the thigh's kicking muscle).

Medical Procedures Involving the Spinal Cord

Lumbar Puncture. Since the cord is only about 18 inches long and ends some distance above the level of the hip line, a lumbar puncture or spinal tap is usually done between the third and fourth lumbar vertebrae, at about the level of the top of the hipbone. During this procedure, a small amount of CSF may be removed from the space below the spinal cord. The fluid can then be studied in the laboratory for evidence of disease or injury.

Administration of Drugs. Anesthetics or medications are sometimes injected into the space below the cord. The anesthetic agent temporarily blocks all sensation from the lower part of the body. This method of giving anesthesia has an advantage for certain types of procedures or surgery; the patient is awake but feels nothing in his or her lower body.

Disorders Involving the Spinal Cord

An acute viral disease affecting both the spinal cord and the brain is **poliomyelitis** (po″li-o-my-e-li′tis) ("polio"), which occurs most commonly in children. The polio virus enters the body through the nose and the throat; it multiplies in the gastrointestinal tract and then travels to the CNS, possibly by way of the blood. The virus may destroy the motor nerve cells in the spinal cord, in which case paralysis of one or more limbs results. The virus can also attack some of the cells of the brain and cause death. Prevention of poliomyelitis by means of the oral Sabin vaccine is one of many significant advances in preventive medicine.

Injuries to the spinal cord occur in instances in which bones of the spinal column are broken or dislocated, such as in swimming and diving accidents. Gunshot or shrapnel wounds may damage the cord to varying degrees. Because the nerve tissue of the brain and cord cannot repair itself, severing of the cord causes paralysis of all the muscles supplied by

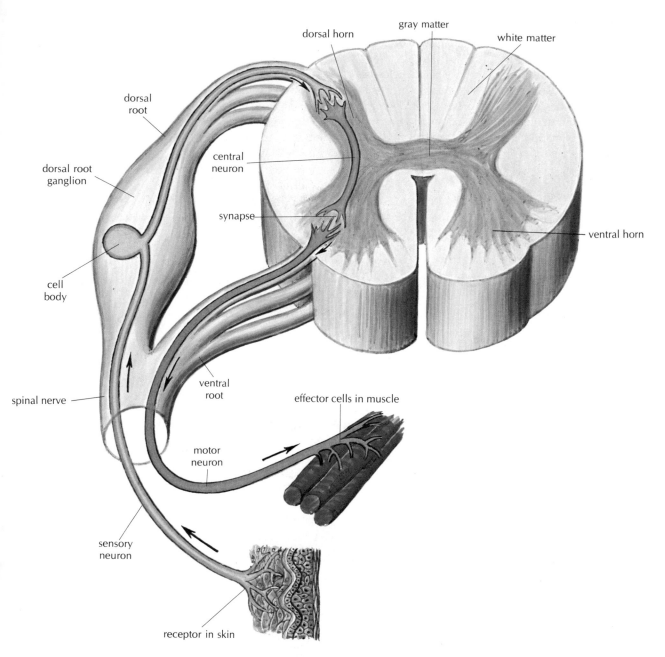

Figure 9-9. *Reflex arc showing the pathway of impulses and cross section of the spinal cord.*

nerves below the level of the injury. Loss of sensation and motion in the lower part of the body is called **paraplegia** (par″ah-ple′je-ah).

Other disorders of the spinal cord include tumors that grow from within the cord or that compress the cord from outside.

Multiple sclerosis (*sclerosis* means "hardening") involves the entire spinal cord as well as the brain. In this disease the myelin, a fatlike substance that forms a sheath around certain nerve fibers, disappears and the nerve axons themselves degenerate. Multiple sclerosis is an extremely disabling disease; however, it usually progresses very slowly, so that affected persons may have many years of relatively comfortable life.

Amyotrophic (ah-mi″o-trof′ik) **lateral sclerosis** is a disorder of the nervous system in which motor neurons are destroyed. The progressive destruction causes muscle atrophy and loss of motor control until finally the affected person is unable to swallow or talk.

Coverings of the Brain and Spinal Cord

The **meninges** (me-nin′jez) are three layers of connective tissue that surround the brain and spinal cord to form a complete enclosure. The outermost of these membranes, the **dura mater** (du′rah ma′ter), is the thickest and toughest of the meninges. Inside the skull, the dura mater splits in certain places to provide venous channels (dural sinuses) for the blood coming from the brain tissue. The middle layer of the meninges is the **arachnoid** (ah-rak′-noid). This membrane is loosely attached to the deepest of the meninges by weblike fibers allowing a space for the movement of CSF between the two membranes. The innermost layer around the brain, the **pia mater** (pi′ah ma′ter), is attached to the nerve tissue of the brain and spinal cord and dips into all the depressions (Fig. 9-10). It is made of a delicate connective

Figure 9-10. *Frontal (coronal) section of the top of the head showing meninges and related parts.*

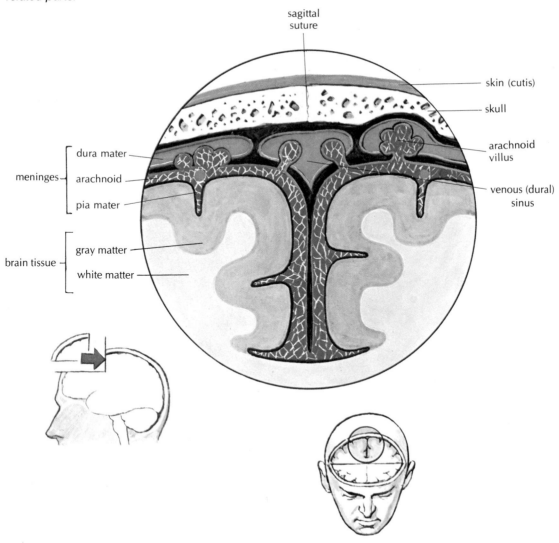

tissue in which there are many blood vessels. The blood supply to the brain is carried, to a large extent, by the pia mater.

Inflammation of the Meninges

Meningitis (men-in-ji′tis) is an inflammation of the brain and spinal cord coverings caused by pathogenic bacteria, notably a diplococcus called the *meningococcus* (me-ning″o-kok′us). If this organism attacks only the membranes around the spinal cord, the condition is called *spinal meningitis;* if it attacks the entire membranous enclosure, it is called *cerebrospinal meningitis.* Occasionally, other bacteria or viruses cause inflammation of the meninges. Sometimes the inflammatory process is so severe as to cause permanent brain damage or even death.

Trauma to the Meninges

Trauma to the head may cause bleeding between the skull and the brain. Arterial bleeding outside the dura causes **epidural hematomas,** with rapidly progressing symptoms (such as coma and dilated pupils). Tears in the dural walls of the venous sinuses cause **subdural hematomas,** with a slow leak and less dramatic symptoms. Frequent observation of level of consciousness, pupil response, and extremity reflexes is important in the patient with a head injury.

Cerebrospinal Fluid

CSF is a clear liquid formed inside the ventricles of the brain, mostly by vascular networks called **choroid plexuses.** The fluid is formed by filtration of the blood and by cellular secretions. The function of CSF is to cushion shocks that would otherwise injure the delicate structures of the CNS. This fluid also carries nutrients to the cells and transports waste products from the cells. The CSF normally flows freely from ventricle to ventricle and finally out into the subarachnoid space, which surrounds the brain and spinal cord. Much of the fluid is returned to the blood in the venous sinuses through projections called *arachnoid villi* (Fig. 9-11).

Any obstruction to the flow of CSF, as for example in injury to the membranes around the three exit openings, may cause the condition called **hydrocephalus** (hi-dro-sef′ah-lus). As the fluid accumulates, the mounting pressure can squeeze the brain against the skull and destroy brain tissue.

Hydrocephalus is more common in infants than in adults. Because the fontanels of the skull have not closed in the infant, the cranium itself can become greatly enlarged; in contrast, in the adult cranial enlargement cannot occur, so that even a slight increase in fluid results in symptoms of increased pressure within the skull and damage of brain tissue. A treatment for hydrocephalus involves the creation of a shunt to drain excess CSF from the brain.

≣ The Peripheral Nervous System

Cranial Nerves

Location of the Cranial Nerves

There are 12 pairs of cranial nerves (henceforth, when a cranial nerve is identified, a pair is meant). They are numbered according to their connection with the brain, beginning at the front and proceeding back (Fig. 9-12). The first 9 pairs and the 12th pair supply structures in the head.

General Functions of the Cranial Nerves

From a functional point of view, we may think of the kinds of messages the cranial nerves handle as belonging to one of four categories.

1 **Special sensory impulses,** such as for smell, vision, and hearing
2 **General sensory impulses,** such as for pain, touch, temperature, deep muscle sense, pressure, and vibrations
3 **Somatic motor impulses** resulting in voluntary control of skeletal muscles
4 **Visceral motor impulses** producing involuntary control of glands and involuntary (cardiac and smooth) muscles

Names and Functions of the Cranial Nerves

The 12 cranial nerves are always numbered according to the traditional Roman style. A few of the cranial nerves—I, II, and VIII—contain only sensory fibers; some—III, IV, VI, XI, and XII—contain all or mostly motor fibers. The remainder—V, VII, IX, and X—contain both sensory and motor fibers; they are known as *mixed nerves.* All 12 nerves are listed below:

 I The **olfactory nerve** carries smell impulses from receptors in the nasal mucosa to the brain.
 II The **optic nerve** carries visual impulses from the eye to the brain.

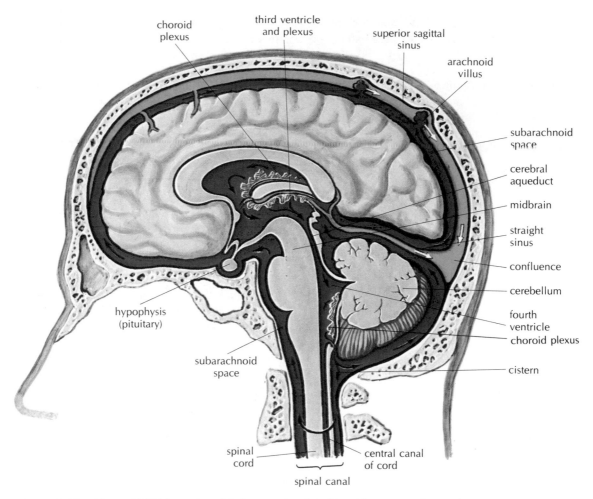

Figure 9-11. *Flow of CSF from choroid plexuses back to blood in venous sinuses is shown by the black arrows; flow of blood is shown by the white arrows.*

III The **oculomotor nerve** is concerned with the contraction of most of the eye muscles.

IV The **trochlear** (trok′le-ar) **nerve** supplies one eyeball muscle.

V The **trigeminal** (tri-jem′i-nal) **nerve** is the great sensory nerve of the face and head. It has three branches that carry general sense impulses, (*e.g.,* pain, touch, temperature) from the face to the brain. The third branch is joined by motor fibers to the muscles of mastication (chewing).

VI The **abducens** (ab-du′senz) **nerve** is another nerve sending controlling impulses to an eyeball muscle.

VII The **facial nerve** is largely motor. The muscles of facial expression are all supplied by branches from the facial nerve. This nerve also includes special sensory fibers for taste (anterior two

thirds of the tongue), and it contains secretory fibers to the smaller salivary glands (the submaxillary and sublingual) and to the lacrimal gland.

VIII The **vestibulocochlear** (ves-tib″u-lo-kok′le-ar) (**acoustic**) **nerve** contains special sensory fibers for hearing as well as those for balance from the semicircular canals of the internal ear.

IX The **glossopharyngeal** (glos″o-fah-rin′ge-al) **nerve** contains general sensory fibers from the back of the tongue and the pharynx (throat). This nerve also contains sensory fibers for taste from the posterior third of the tongue, secretory fibers that supply the largest salivary gland (parotid), and motor nerve fibers to control the swallowing muscles in the pharynx.

X The **vagus** (va′gus) **nerve** is the longest cranial

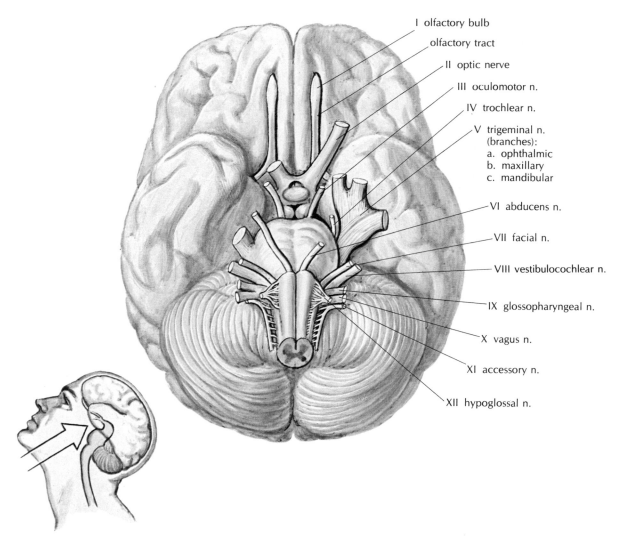

I olfactory bulb
olfactory tract
II optic nerve
III oculomotor n.
IV trochlear n.
V trigeminal n.
(branches):
  a. ophthalmic
  b. maxillary
  c. mandibular
VI abducens n.
VII facial n.
VIII vestibulocochlear n.
IX glossopharyngeal n.
X vagus n.
XI accessory n.
XII hypoglossal n.

Figure 9-12. *Base of the brain showing cranial nerves.*

nerve. It supplies most of the organs in the thoracic and abdominal cavities. This nerve also contains motor fibers to glands that produce digestive juices and other secretions.

XI The **accessory nerve** (formerly called the *spinal accessory nerve)* is made up of motor nerve fibers controlling two muscles of the neck, the trapezius and sternocleidomastoid.

XII The **hypoglossal nerve**, the last of the 12 cranial nerves, carries impulses controlling the muscles of the tongue.

Disorders Involving the Cranial Nerves

Destruction of optic nerve (II) fibers may result from increased pressure of the eye fluid on the nerves, as occurs in glaucoma, from the influence of poisons, and from some infections. Certain medications, when used in high doses for a long period of time, can damage the branch of the vestibulocochlear nerve responsible for hearing.

Injury to a nerve that contains motor fibers causes paralysis of the muscles supplied by these fibers. The oculomotor nerve (III) may be damaged by certain infections or various poisonous substances. Since this nerve supplies so many muscles connected with the eye, including the levator, which raises the eyelid, injury to it causes a paralysis that usually interferes with eye function. **Bell's palsy** is a facial paralysis due to damage to the facial (VII) nerve, usually on one side of the face. This injury results in distortion of the face because of one-sided paralysis of the muscles of facial expression.

Neuralgia (nu-ral′je-ah) means "nerve pain" and is used particularly to refer to a severe spasmodic pain affecting the fifth cranial nerve. The condition goes by various names, including **trigeminal neuralgia**, **trifacial neuralgia**, and **tic douloureux** (tik doo-loo-roo′). At first the pain comes at relatively long intervals, but as time goes on, it is likely to appear at shorter intervals and to be of longer duration. Treatments include microsurgery and high-frequency current.

Spinal Nerves

Location and Structure of the Spinal Nerves

There are 31 pairs of spinal nerves, each pair numbered according to the level of the spinal cord from which it arises. Each nerve is attached to the spinal cord by two roots, the **dorsal root** and the **ventral root**. On each dorsal root is a marked swelling of gray matter called the **dorsal root ganglion**, which contains the cell bodies of the sensory neurons. A **ganglion** (plural, **ganglia**) is a collection of nerve cell bodies located outside the central nervous system.

Nerve fibers from the sensory receptors of various areas of the body lead to these ganglia. A sensory receptor is a nerve ending that responds to a stimulus. There are two categories of receptors. Those for general sensation are located in the skin and the body wall. They respond to stimuli that give rise to sensations of pain, touch, and temperature and of the location and position of body parts. The second category includes receptors for the special senses: taste, smell, vision, and hearing. Impulses from these receptors are carried by cranial nerves from the special sense organ to the brain. These organs are discussed in the next chapter.

Whereas sensory fibers form the dorsal roots, the ventral roots of the spinal nerves are a combination of motor (efferent) nerve fibers supplying voluntary muscles, involuntary muscles, and glands. The cell bodies for the voluntary fibers are located in the ventral part of the cord gray matter (anterior, or ventral, gray horns) (see Fig. 9-9). The cell bodies for the involuntary fibers are found in small, lateral, gray horns. The dorsal (sensory) and ventral (motor) roots are combined in the spinal nerve, making all spinal nerves mixed nerves.

Branches of the Spinal Nerves

Each spinal nerve continues only a very short distance away from the spinal cord and then branches into small posterior divisions and rather large anterior divisions. The larger anterior branches interlace to form networks called **plexuses** (plex′sus-es), which then distribute branches to the body parts. The three main plexuses are described as follows:

1 The **cervical plexus** supplies motor impulses to the muscles of the neck and receives sensory impulses from the neck and the back of the head. The phrenic nerve, which activates the diaphragm, arises from this plexus.
2 The **brachial** (bra′ke-al) **plexus** sends numerous branches to the shoulder, arm, forearm, wrist, and hand. The radial nerve emerges from the brachial plexus.
3 The **lumbosacral** (lum-bo-sa′kral) **plexus** supplies nerves to the lower extremities. The largest of these branches is the **sciatic** (si-at′ik) **nerve**, which leaves the dorsal part of the pelvis, passes beneath the gluteus maximus muscle, and extends down the back of the thigh. At its beginning it is nearly 1 inch thick, but it soon branches to the thigh muscles; near the knee it forms two subdivisions that supply the leg and the foot.

Disorders of the Spinal Nerves

Neuritis (nu-ri′tis) means "inflammation of a nerve." The term is also used to refer to degenerative and other disorders that may involve nerves. It may affect a single nerve or many nerves throughout the body, as a result of blows, bone fractures, or other mechanical injuries. Neuritis may be caused by nutritional deficiency, as well as by various poisons such as alcohol, carbon monoxide, and barbitals.

Neuritis is fairly common in chronic alcoholics and is thought to be related to the severe malnourished state of these persons. B vitamin deficiencies, especially of thiamin (thi′ah-min), are related to both the malnourished state and chronic alcoholism. Neuritis is really a symptom rather than a disease, so that thorough physical and laboratory studies may be needed to establish the cause.

Sciatica (si-at′e-kah) is a form of neuritis characterized by severe pain along the sciatic nerve and its branches. There are many causes of this disorder, but probably the most common are rupture of a disk between the lower lumbar vertebrae and arthritis of the lower part of the spinal column.

Herpes zoster, commonly known as *shingles,* is characterized by numerous blisters along the course of certain nerves, most commonly the intercostal nerves, which are branches of the thoracic spinal nerves in the waist area. The cause is the chicken pox virus, which attacks the sensory cell bodies inside the spinal ganglia. Recovery in a few days is usual, but neuralgic pains may persist for years and be very distressing. This infection may also involve the first branch of the fifth cranial nerve and cause pain in the eyeball and surrounding tissues.

The Autonomic Nervous System

Parts of the Autonomic Nervous System

Although the internal organs such as the heart, lungs, and stomach contain nerve endings and nerve fibers for conducting sensory messages to the brain and cord, most of these impulses do not reach consciousness. These *afferent* impulses from the viscera are translated into reflex responses without reaching the higher centers of the brain; the sensory neurons from the organs are grouped with those that come from the skin and voluntary muscles. In contrast, the *efferent* neurons, which supply the glands and the involuntary muscles, are arranged very differently from those that supply the voluntary muscles. This variation in the location and arrangement of the *visceral efferent* neurons has led to their classification as part of a separate division called the **autonomic nervous system** (Fig. 9-13).

The autonomic nervous system has many ganglia that serve as relay stations. In these ganglia each message is transferred at a synapse from the first neuron to a second one and from there to the muscle or gland cell. This differs from the voluntary (somatic) nervous system, in which each motor nerve fiber extends all the way from the spinal cord to the skeletal muscle with no intervening synapse. The locations of parts of the autonomic nervous system are roughly as follows:

1. The sympathetic pathway begins in the spinal cord with cell bodies in the thoracic and lumbar regions, the **thoracolumbar** (tho-rah-ko-lum′

bar) area. The sympathetic fibers arise from the spinal cord at the level of the first thoracic nerve down to the level of the second lumbar spinal nerve. From this part of the cord, nerve fibers extend to the ganglia of the **sympathetic chains** (trunks), two cordlike strands of ganglia that extend along either side of the spinal column from the lower neck to the upper abdominal region. The beadlike ganglia of this trunk, called the **lateral ganglia**, contain the cell bodies of the second set of neurons, the fibers of which extend to the glands and involuntary muscle tissues. These second neurons release mainly the neurotransmitter norepinephrine (noradrenalin) to the effector tissue.

2. The parasympathetic pathway begins in the **craniosacral** areas, with fibers arising from cell bodies of the midbrain, medulla, and lower (sacral) part of the spinal cord. From these centers the first set of fibers extends to autonomic ganglia that are usually located near or within the walls of the effector organs. The pathways then continue along a second set of neurons that stimulate the visceral tissues. These neurons release the neurotransmitter acetylcholine.

Functions of the Autonomic Nervous System

The autonomic nervous system regulates the action of the glands, the smooth muscles of hollow organs, and the heart. These actions are all carried on automatically; whenever any changes occur that call for a regulatory adjustment, the adjustment is made without the person's being conscious of it. The sympathetic part of the autonomic nervous system tends to act as an accelerator for those organs needed to meet a stressful situation. It promotes what is called the **fight-or-flight response.** If you think of what happens to a person who is frightened or angry, you can easily remember the effects of impulses from the sympathetic nervous system:

1. Stimulation of the adrenal gland. This produces hormones, including epinephrine, that prepare the body to meet emergency situations in many ways (see Chap. 11). The sympathetic nerves and hormones from the adrenal reinforce each other.

2. Dilation of the pupil and decrease in focusing ability (for near objects)

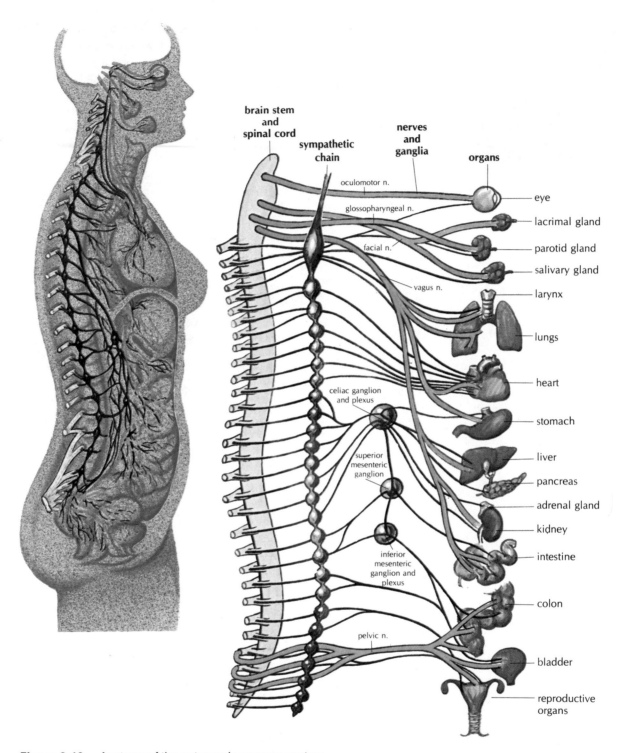

Figure 9-13. *Anatomy of the autonomic nervous system.*

3 Increase in the rate and forcefulness of heart contractions

4 Increase in blood pressure due partly to the more effective heartbeat and partly to constriction of small arteries in the skin and the internal organs

5 Dilation of the bronchial tubes to allow more oxygen to enter

6 Increase in metabolism

The sympathetic system also acts as a brake on those systems not directly involved in the response to stress, such as the urinary and digestive systems. If you try to eat while you are angry, you may note that your saliva is thick and so small in amount that you can swallow only with difficulty. Under these circumstances, when food does reach the stomach, it seems to stay there longer than usual.

The parasympathetic part of the autonomic nervous system normally acts as a balance for the sympathetic system once a crisis has passed. The parasympathetic system brings about constriction of the pupils, slowing of the heart rate, and constriction of the bronchial tubes. It also stimulates the formation and release of urine and activity of the digestive tract. Saliva, for example, flows more easily and profusely and its quantity and fluidity increase.

Thus, most organs of the body receive both sympathetic and parasympathetic stimulation, the effects of the two systems on a given organ generally being opposite. Table 9-1 shows some of the actions of these two systems.

Disorders of the Autonomic Nervous System

Injuries due to wounds by penetrating objects or to tumors, hemorrhage, or spinal column dislocations or fractures may cause damage to the sympathetic chain. In addition to these rather obvious kinds of disorders, there are a great number of conditions in which symptoms such as heart palpitations, increased blood pressure, and stomachaches suggest autonomic malfunctions but in which the cause is not well understood. These disorders are related to psychologic factors involved in the functioning of the viscera owing to the close interrelationships of the brain, brain stem, and spinal cord and the autonomic nervous system.

The autonomic nervous system, together with the endocrine system, regulates our responses to stress. This interrelationship and the effects of prolonged stress are discussed in more detail in Chapter 11.

Table 9-1 Effects of the Sympathetic and Parasympathetic Systems on Selected Organs

Effector	Sympathetic system	Parasympathetic system
Pupils of eye	Dilation	Constriction
Sweat glands	Stimulation	None
Digestive glands	Inhibition	Stimulation
Heart	Increased rate and strength of beat	Decreased rate and strength of beat
Bronchi of lungs	Dilation	Constriction
Muscles of digestive system	Decreased contraction (peristalsis)	Increased contraction
Kidneys	Decreased activity	None
Urinary bladder	Relaxation	Contraction and emptying
Liver	Increased release of glucose	None
Penis	Ejaculation	Erection
Adrenal medulla	Stimulation	None
Blood vessels to		
Skeletal muscles	Dilation	Constriction
Skin	Constriction	None
Respiratory system	Dilation	Constriction
Digestive organs	Constriction	Dilation

Summary

I **Organization of the nervous system**
  A Structural divisions
    1 Central nervous system (CNS)—brain and spinal cord
    2 Peripheral nervous system—all nerves outside the CNS (cranial and spinal nerves)
  B Functional divisions
    1 Somatic (voluntary) nervous system—supplies skeletal muscles
    2 Visceral (involuntary) nervous system—supplies smooth muscle, cardiac muscle, glands
      a Autonomic nervous system—involuntary motor nerves

II **Nerves**
  A Neuron—nerve cell
    1 Cell body
    2 Nerve fibers
      a Dendrite—carries impulses to cell body
      b Axon—carries impulses away from cell body
        (1) White fiber—axon covered with myelin
  B Nerve impulse—electric current that spreads along nerve fiber
  C Synapse—junction between neurons where a nerve impulse is transmitted from one neuron to the next
  D Nerve—bundle of nerve fibers outside the CNS
    1 Sensory (afferent) nerve—contains only fibers that carry impulses toward the CNS (from the receptor)
    2 Motor (efferent) nerve—contains only fibers that carry impulses away from the CNS (to the effector)
    3 Mixed nerve—contains both motor and sensory fibers

III **Central nervous system**
  A Brain
    1 Divisions
      a Cerebrum—largest part of brain
        (1) Right and left hemispheres
          (a) Lobes—frontal, parietal, temporal, occipital, insula
          (b) Cortex—outer layer of gray matter
      b Diencephalon—area between cerebral hemispheres and brain stem
        (1) Thalamus—directs sensory impulses to cortex
        (2) Hypothalamus—maintains homeostasis, controls pituitary
      c Brain stem
        (1) Midbrain—involved in eye and ear reflexes
        (2) Pons—connecting link for other divisions
        (3) Medulla oblongata—connects with spinal cord; contains vital centers for respiration, heart rate, vasomotor activity
      d Cerebellum—regulates coordination, balance, muscle tone
    2 Ventricles—chambers in which cerebrospinal fluid (CSF) is produced by vascular networks (choroid plexuses)
    3 Brain studies—encephalogram (ventriculogram), computed tomographic (CT) scan, electroencephalogram (EEG)
    4 Disorders—encephalitis, cerebrovascular accident (CVA), Alzheimer's disease, Parkinson's disease, cerebral palsy, epilepsy, tumors, aphasia
  B Spinal cord
    1 Structure—H-shaped area of gray matter surrounded by white matter
    2 Function—reflex activities, conduction of sensory and motor impulses to and from brain
    3 Disorders—poliomyelitis, multiple sclerosis, amyotropic lateral sclerosis
    4 Meninges—coverings of brain and spinal cord
      a Layers
        (1) Dura mater—outermost
        (2) Arachnoid—middle
        (3) Pia mater—innermost
      b Disorders—meningitis, hematoma
    5 Cerebrospinal fluid

IV **Peripheral nervous system**
  A Cranial nerves—12 pairs
    1 Types
      a Sensory
      b Motor
      c Mixed
    2 Disorders—Bell's palsy, neuralgia

B Spinal nerves—31 pairs
   1 Anterior branches
      a Cervical plexus
      b Brachial plexus
      c Lumbosacral plexus
   2 Disorders—neuritis, sciatica, herpes zoster
V **Autonomic nervous system**—motor (efferent) division of the visceral (involuntary) nervous system
  A Sympathetic system
  B Parasympathetic system

Questions for Study and Review

1 What is the main function of the nervous system?
2 Name the two structural divisions of the nervous system.
3 Name the organs or structures controlled by the somatic nervous system; by the visceral nervous system.
4 Define *neurotransmitter* and give several examples.
5 Differentiate between the terms in each of the following pairs:
  a *axon* and *dendrite*
  b *gray matter* and *white matter*
  c *receptor* and *effector*
  d *afferent* and *efferent*
  e *sensory* and *motor*
  f *nerve* and *tract*

6 Without the label, how would you know that the neuron in Figure 9-1 is a motor neuron? Is this neuron a part of the somatic or visceral nervous system?

7 Name and locate the main parts of the brain and briefly describe the main functions of each.
8 Name four divisions of the cerebral cortex and state what each does.
9 Name and describe the speech centers.
10 What are the differences between short-term and long-term memory, and how is each attained?
11 Describe the thalamus; where is it located? What are its functions?
12 What activities does the hypothalamus regulate?
13 Name and describe six typical brain disorders.
14 Locate and describe the spinal cord. Name three of its functions.
15 Describe a typical reflex action.
16 Name and describe two spinal cord disorders.
17 Name the covering of the brain and the spinal cord and its divisions. What is an infection of this covering called?
18 What is the purpose of the cerebrospinal fluid? Describe hydrocephalus.
19 Name four general functions of the cranial nerves.
20 Name and describe the functions of the 12 cranial nerves.
21 Name the three main plexuses of the spinal nerves.
22 Differentiate between the dorsal and ventral roots of a spinal nerve.
23 Name two disorders of the spinal nerves.
24 Describe the function of the autonomic nervous system.
25 Name the two parts of the autonomic nervous system, and show how they work during and following a moment of extreme fear.

10

The Sensory System

Behavioral Objectives

After careful study of this chapter, you should be able to:

Describe the function of the sensory system

List the major senses

Describe the structure of the eye

Define refraction and list the refractive media of the eye

Differentiate between the rods and the cones of the eye

List several disorders of the eye

Describe the three divisions of the ear

Describe the receptors for hearing and for equilibrium with respect to location and function

Define general sense and give five examples of such senses

Selected Key Terms

The following terms are defined in the glossary:

accommodation
cataract
choroid
cochlea
conjunctiva
cornea
crystalline lens
glaucoma
lacrimal
ossicle
proprioceptor
refraction
retina
sclera
semicircular canal
stimulus
tympanic membrane
vestibule

Senses and Sensory Mechanisms

The sensory system serves fundamentally to protect the individual by detecting changes in the environment. Recall from Chapter 9 that such an environmental change becomes a stimulus when it initiates a nerve impulse, which then travels to the CNS by way of a sensory (afferent) neuron. Many stimuli arrive from the external environment and are detected at or near the surface of the body. Others, such as the stimuli from the viscera, which help maintain homeostasis, originate internally. The receptors for these stimuli may be widely distributed throughout the body, as are those for pain, touch, and temperature, or they may be localized as special sense organs, as are those for light, sound, and chemicals. A receptor itself is either a specialized ending on the dendrite of an afferent neuron, called an **end-organ**, or a cell associated with an afferent neuron. Regardless of the type of stimulus or the type of receptor involved, a stimulus becomes a sensation—something we experience—only when the nerve impulse it generates is interpreted by a specialized area of the cerebral cortex to which it travels.

There is no completely satisfactory classification of the senses. A partial list includes the following:

1 **Vision** from receptors in the eye
2 **Hearing** from receptors in the ear
3 **Taste** from the tongue receptors
4 **Smell** from receptors in the upper nasal cavities
5 **Pressure, heat, cold, pain,** and **touch** from the skin
6 **Position** and **balance** from the muscles, joints, and semicircular canals in the ear

The Eye

Protection of the Eyeball and Its Parts

In the embryo, the eye develops as an outpocketing of the brain. The eye is a delicate organ, and nature has carefully protected it by means of the following structures:

1 The skull bones form the eye orbit (cavity) and serve to protect more than half of the dorsal part of the eyeball.

2 The lids and eyelashes aid in protecting the eye anteriorly.
3 Tears wash away small foreign objects that enter the eye.
4 A sac lined with an epithelial membrane separates the front of the eye from the eyeball proper and aids in the destruction of some of the pathogenic bacteria that may enter from the outside.

Coats of the Eyeball

The eyeball has three separate coats, or tunics (Fig. 10-1). The outermost layer, called the **sclera** (skle′rah), is made of tough connective tissue. It is commonly referred to as the *white of the eye*. The second tunic of the eyeball is the **choroid** (ko′roid). Composed of a delicate network of connective tissue interlaced with many blood vessels, this layer contains much dark brown pigment. The choroid may be compared to the dull black lining of a camera in that it prevents incoming light rays from scattering and reflecting off the inner surface of the eye. The innermost coat, called the **retina** (ret′i-nah), includes ten layers of nerve cells, including the cells commonly called **rods** and **cones** (Fig. 10–2). These are the receptors for the sense of vision. The rods are highly sensitive to light and thus function in dim light but do not provide a very sharp image. The cones function in bright light and are sensitive to color. When you enter a darkened room, such as a movie theater, you cannot see for a short period of time. It is during this time that the rods are beginning to function, a change described as **dark adaptation.**

As far as is known, there are three types of cones, each sensitive to red, green, or blue light. Persons who completely lack cones are totally color blind; those who lack one type of cone are partially color blind. Color blindness is an inherited condition that occurs almost exclusively in males.

The rods and cones function by means of pigments that are sensitive to light. Manufacture of these pigments requires vitamin A, so a person who lacks vitamin A in the diet may have difficulty seeing in dim light, that is, may have **night blindness.**

Pathway of Light Rays

Light rays pass through a series of transparent, colorless eye parts. On the way they undergo a process of bending known as **refraction**. This refraction of the

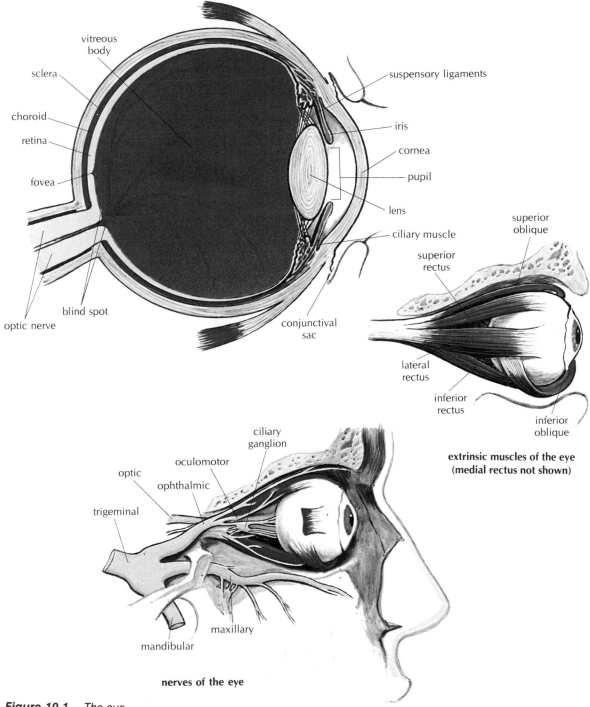

Figure 10-1. *The eye.*

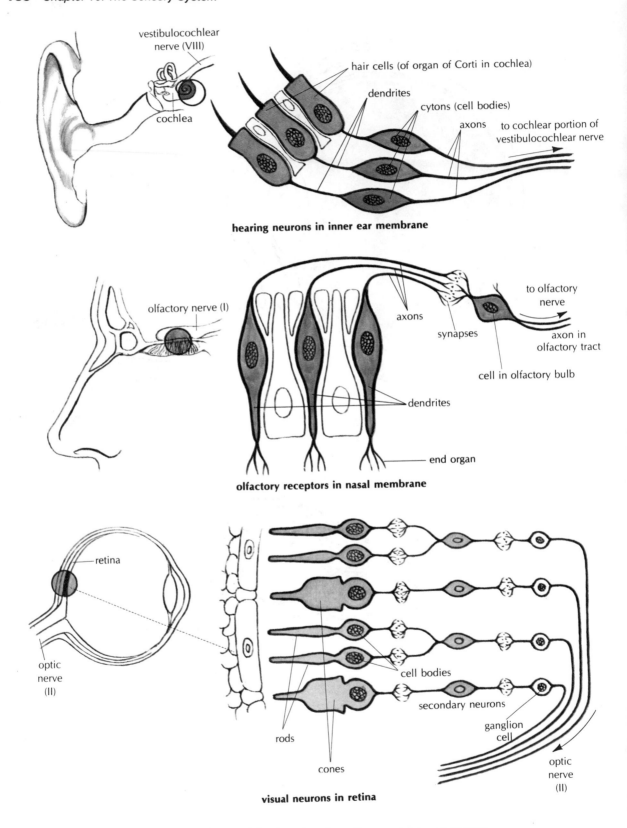

Figure 10-2. *Diagram of neurons for receiving impulses from the special sense organs.*

light rays makes it possible for light from a very large area to be focused on a very small surface, the retina, where the receptors are located. The following are, in order from outside in, the transparent refracting parts, or **media**, of the eye:

1 The **cornea** (kor′ne-ah) is a forward continuation of the sclera, but it is transparent and colorless, whereas the rest of the sclera is opaque and white.
2 The **aqueous humor**, a watery fluid that fills much of the eyeball in front of the lens, helps maintain the slight forward curve of the cornea.
3 The **crystalline lens** is a circular structure made of a jelly-like material.
4 The **vitreous body** is a jelly-like substance that fills the entire space behind the lens and keeps the eyeball in its spherical shape.

The cornea is referred to frequently as the *window* of the eye. It bulges forward slightly and is the most important refracting structure. Injuries caused by foreign objects or by infection may result in scar formation in the cornea, leaving an area of opacity through which light rays cannot pass. If such an injury involves the central area in front of the pupil (the hole in the center of the colored part of the eye), blindness may result. Eye banks store corneas obtained from donors, and corneal transplantation is a fairly common procedure.

The next light-bending medium is the aqueous humor, followed by the crystalline lens. The lens has two bulging surfaces, so it may be best described as biconvex. Because this lens is elastic, its thickness can be adjusted to focus light for near or distance vision.

The last of these transparent refracting parts of the eye is the vitreous body. Like the aqueous humor, it is important in maintaining the ball-like shape of the eyeball as well as in aiding in refraction. The vitreous body is not replaceable; an injury that causes loss of an appreciable amount of the jelly-like vitreous material will cause collapse of the eyeball. This requires removal of the eyeball, an operation called **enucleation** (e-nu-kle-a′shun).

Muscles of the Eye

The muscles inside the eyeball are **intrinsic** (in-trin′sik) **muscles**; those attached to bones of the eye orbit as well as to the sclera are **extrinsic** (eks-trin′sik) **muscles**.

The intrinsic muscles are found in two circular structures, as follows:

1 The **iris**, the colored or pigmented part of the eye, is composed of two types of muscles. The size of the central opening of the iris, called the **pupil**, is governed by the action of these two sets of muscles, one of which is arranged in a circular fashion, while the other extends in a radial manner resembling the spokes of a wheel.
2 The **ciliary body** is shaped somewhat like a flattened ring with a hole the size of the outer edge of the iris. This muscle alters the shape of the lens during the process of accommodation (described below).

The purpose of the iris is to regulate the amount of light entering the eye. If a strong light is flashed in the eye, the circular muscle fibers of the iris, which form a sphincter, contract and thus reduce the size of the pupil. In contrast, if the light is very dim, the radial involuntary iris muscles, which are attached at the outer edge, contract; the opening is thereby pulled outward and thus enlarged. This pupillary enlargement is known as **dilation** (di-la′shun).

The pupil changes size, too, according to whether one is looking at a near object or a distant one. Viewing a near object causes the pupil to become smaller; viewing a distant object causes it to enlarge.

The muscle of the ciliary body is similar in direction and method of action to the radial muscle of the iris. When the ciliary muscle contracts, it draws forward and removes the tension on the **suspensory ligaments**, which hold the lens in place (see Fig. 10-1). The elastic lens then recoils and becomes thicker in much the same way that a rubber band thickens when the pull on it is released. When the ciliary body relaxes, the lens becomes flattened. These actions change the refractive ability of the lens.

The process of **accommodation** involves coordinated eye changes to enable one to focus on near objects. The ciliary body contracts, thereby thickening the lens, and the circular muscle fibers of the iris contract to decrease the size of the pupillary opening. In young persons the lens is elastic, and therefore its thickness can be readily adjusted according to the need for near or distance vision. With aging, the lens loses its elasticity and therefore its ability to adjust to near vision by thickening, making it difficult to focus clearly on close objects. This condition is called **presbyopia** (pres″be-o′pe-ah), which literally means "old eye".

The six extrinsic muscles connected with each eye are ribbon-like and extend forward from the apex of the orbit behind the eyeball (see Fig. 10-1). One end of each muscle is attached to a bone of the skull, while the other end is attached to the sclera. These muscles pull on the eyeball in a coordinated fashion that causes the two eyes to move together to center on one visual field. Another muscle located within the orbit is attached to the upper eyelid. When this muscle contracts, it keeps the eye open; as the muscle becomes weaker with age, the eyelids may droop (a condition called **ptosis**) and interfere with vision.

Nerve Supply to the Eye

Two sensory nerves supply the eye (see Fig. 10-1):

1 The **optic nerve** (cranial nerve II) carries visual impulses initiated by the rods and cones in the retina to the brain.

2 The **ophthalmic** (of-thal′mic) **branch of the trigeminal** (tri-jem′i-nal) **nerve** (cranial nerve V) carries impulses of pain, touch, and temperature from the eye and surrounding parts to the brain.

The optic nerve arises from the retina a little toward the medial or nasal side of the eye. Visual impulses are transmitted from the retina, ultimately to the cortex of the occipital lobe. There are no rods and cones in the retina near the area of the optic nerve fibers, so this circular white area is a blind spot, known as the **optic disk**. There is a tiny depressed

area in the retina, called the **fovea centralis** (fo′ve-ah sen-tra′lis), which contains a high concentration of cones and is the point of most acute vision.

There are three nerves that carry motor impulses to the muscles of the eyeball. The largest is the oculomotor nerve (cranial nerve III), which supplies voluntary and involuntary motor impulses to all the muscles but two. The other two nerves, the trochlear (cranial nerve IV) and the abducens (cranial nerve VI), each supply one voluntary muscle.

The Conjunctiva and the Lacrimal Apparatus

The **conjunctiva** (kon-junk-ti′vah) is a membrane that lines the eyelid and covers the anterior part of the sclera. As the conjunctiva extends from the eyelid to the front of the eyeball, recesses, or sacs, are formed. Tears, produced by the **lacrimal** (lak′ri-mal) **gland**, serve to keep the conjunctiva moist. As tears flow across the eye from the lacrimal gland, located in the upper lateral part of the orbit, the fluid carries away small particles that have entered the conjunctival sacs. The tears are then carried into ducts near the nasal corner of the eye where they drain into the nose by way of the **nasolacrimal** (na″zo-lak′ri-mal) **duct** (Fig. 10-3). Any excess of tears causes a "runny nose"; a greater overproduction of them results in the spilling of tears onto the cheeks.

With age there is often a thinning and drying of

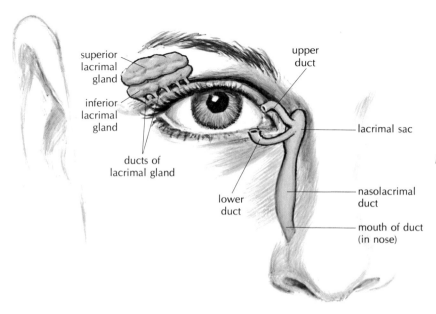

Figure 10-3. *Lacrimal apparatus.*

the conjunctiva, resulting in inflammation and enlarged blood vessels. The lacrimal gland produces less secretion, but those tears that are produced may overflow to the cheek because of plugging of the nasolacrimal ducts, which would normally carry the tears away from the eye.

Eye Infections

Inflammation of the membrane that lines the eyelid and covers the front of the eyeball is called **conjunctivitis** (kon-junk″te-vi′tis). It may be acute or chronic, and may be caused by a variety of irritants and pathogens. "Pinkeye" is a highly contagious acute conjunctivitis that is usually caused by cocci or bacilli. Sometimes irritants such as wind and excessive glare cause an inflammation, which may in turn lead to susceptibility to bacterial infection.

Trachoma (trah-ko′mah), sometimes referred to as **granular conjunctivitis,** is caused by the bacterium *Chlamydia trachomatis* (klah-mid′e-ah trah-ko′mahtes). This disease was formerly quite common in the mountains of the southern United States and among native Americans, and it is still prevalent in the Far East, Egypt, and southern Europe. Trachoma is characterized by the formation of granules on the lids, which may cause such serious irritation of the cornea as to result in blindness. Better hygiene and the use of antibiotic drugs have reduced the prevalence and seriousness of this infection.

If a pregnant woman has a gonococcal infection, an eye infection in her newborn infant may result; this infection is called **ophthalmia neonatorum** (of-thal′me-ah ne-o-na-to′rum). The bacterium enters the conjunctival sac of the fetus as it proceeds through the birth canal during the process of delivery. Prevention in babies at risk for the development of ophthalmia neonatorum is achieved by the instillation of an appropriate antiseptic or antibiotic solution into the conjunctiva just after birth.

The iris, choroid coat, ciliary body, and other parts of the eyeball may become infected by various organisms. Such disorders are likely to be very serious; fortunately, they are not very common. Syphilis spirochetes, tubercle bacilli, and a variety of cocci may cause these painful infections. They may follow a sinus infection, tonsillitis, conjunctivitis, or other disorder in which the infecting agent can spread from nearby structures. The care of these conditions usually should be in the hands of an **ophthalmologist** (of″thal-mol′o-jist), a physician who specializes in the diagnosis and treatment of disorders of the eye.

Eyestrain and Eye Defects

Eyestrain, or fatigue of the eye, may result from overuse of the eyes; improper conditions for reading, such as poor lighting or very small print; or disturbances in the focusing ability of the eye.

Some of the symptoms of eyestrain include the following:

1 Inflammation and infection of structures in the eyelids, such as sty formation, in which oil glands on the lid edges become infected

2 Excessive tear formation and pain in the eyes

3 Pain in the orbit and forehead

Eyestrain is very common but can easily be avoided with attention to proper eye care. Some points to remember are listed below:

1 Books read by children should have larger than customary type and letters spaced relatively far apart to make them easy to differentiate.

2 There should be enough light without glare.

3 The table or desk at which reading is being done should be of the proper height.

4 The eyes should be properly examined and the appropriate corrective lenses used. The notion that glasses will weaken the eyes has absolutely no basis in fact.

Several disorders of the eye can lead to eyestrain. **Hyperopia** (hi″per-o′pe-ah), or farsightedness, is usually due to the eyeball's being too short (Fig. 10-4). In this situation, the focal point is behind the retina because light rays cannot bend sharply enough to focus on the retina. Objects must be moved away from the eye to be seen clearly. Farsightedness is normal in the infant but usually corrects itself by the time the child uses the eyes more for near vision. To a certain extent, the ciliary muscle can thicken the lens (accommodate) and thereby enable a person to focus objects on the too-near retina. However, this effort causes eyestrain and its symptoms of pain in the eye and forehead. Visual tests may not show that the condition exists unless drops that temporarily paralyze the ciliary muscle are instilled before the examination. Glasses that aid in refracting light rays—convex lenses—alleviate the symptoms of eyestrain by de-

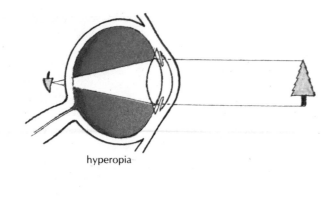

hyperopia

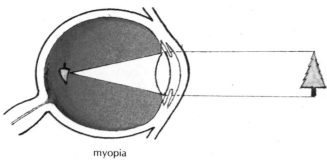

myopia

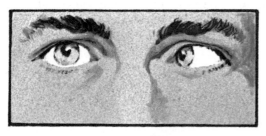

convergent strabismus

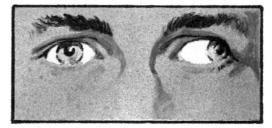

divergent strabismus

Figure 10-4. *Disorders of the eye.*

creasing the amount of work the ciliary muscle must do.

Myopia (mi-o'pe-ah), or nearsightedness, is another defect of the eye also related to development. In this case the eyeball is too long or the bending of the light rays too sharp, so that the focal point is in front of the retina (see Fig. 10-4). Distant objects appear blurred and may appear clear only if brought very near the eye. Only by use of concave lenses that alter the angle of refraction so that the focal point is moved backward can myopia be corrected. Nearsightedness in a young person becomes worse each year until the person reaches the 20s. By wearing appropriate eyeglasses, the nearsighted person can avoid development of eyestrain.

Another rather common visual defect, **astigmatism** (ah-stig'mah-tism), is due to irregularity in the curvature of the cornea or the lens. As a result, light rays are incorrectly bent, causing blurred vision and severe eyestrain. Astigmatism is often found in combination with hyperopia or myopia, so a careful eye examination and use of properly fitted glasses should reduce or prevent eyestrain.

Strabismus (strah-biz'mus) means that the muscles of the eyeballs do not coordinate, so that the two eyes do not work together (see Fig. 10-4). There are several types of strabismus. One common type is **convergent strabismus,** in which the eye deviates toward the nasal side, or medially. This disorder gives an appearance of cross-eyedness. A second type of strabismus is **divergent strabismus,** in which the affected eye deviates laterally. If correction of these disorders is not accomplished early, the transmission and interpretation of visual impulses from the affected eye to the brain will be decreased. The brain will not develop ways to "see" images from the eye. Care by an ophthalmologist as soon as the condition is detected may result in restoration of muscle balance. In some cases, glasses and exercises correct the defect, while in others surgery may be required.

Blindness and Its Causes

The most frequent cause of blindness is formation of **cataracts,** opacities of the lens or its capsule. Sometimes the areas of opacity can be seen through the pupil, which may become greatly enlarged to increase the amount of light that reaches the retina. In other cases there is very gradual loss of vision, and frequent changes in glasses may aid in maintaining useful vision for some time. Removal of the lens may restore some vision, but the addition of eyeglasses or a contact lens is required to achieve satisfactory visual acuity as well as binocular vision, which is needed for driving a car, for example. Most affected persons need reading glasses for close work. Surgical techniques are now available to implant an artificial lens, and this procedure has been successful in restoring normal vision. Although the cause of cataracts is not known, there is some evidence that excess exposure to ultraviolet radiation is a factor. Some eye doctors recommend that persons over the age of 40 wear good sunglasses that filter out ultraviolet rays when the eyes are exposed to the sun.

A second important cause of blindness is **glaucoma,** a condition characterized by excess pressure of the aqueous humor. This fluid is produced constantly by the blood, and after circulation it is reabsorbed into the bloodstream. Interference with the normal reentry of this fluid to the bloodstream leads to an increase in pressure inside the eyeball. Like cataracts, glaucoma usually progresses rather slowly, with vague visual disturbances and gradual impairment of vision. Halos around lights, headaches, and the need for frequent changes of glasses (particularly by persons over 40) are symptoms that should be

investigated by an ophthalmologist. There are different forms of glaucoma, some occurring in the very young, and each type requires a different management. Since continued high pressure of the aqueous humor may cause destruction of the optic nerve fibers, it is important to obtain continuous treatment, beginning early in the disease, to avoid blindness.

Diabetes as a cause of blindness is increasing in the United States. Disorders of the eye directly related to diabetes include optic atrophy, in which the optic nerve fibers die; cataracts, which occur earlier and with greater frequency among diabetics than among nondiabetics; and diabetic **retinopathy** (ret″i-nop′ah-the), in which the retina can be damaged by blood vessel hemorrhages and other causes.

Another cause of blindness is retinal detachment. This disorder may develop slowly or may occur suddenly. In this condition, the retina becomes detached from the underlying layer as a result of trauma or an accumulation of fluid or tissue between the layers. If it is left untreated, complete detachment can occur, resulting in blindness. Surgical treatment includes a sort of "spot welding" with an electric current or a weak laser beam. A series of pinpoint scars (connective tissue) develop to reattach the retina.

There are many other causes of blindness, many of which are preventable. Injuries by pieces of glass and other sharp objects are a frequent cause of eye damage. The incidence of industrial accidents involving the eye has been greatly reduced by the use of protective goggles. If an injury occurs, it is very important to prevent infection. Even a tiny scratch can become so seriously infected that blindness may result.

☰ The Ear

The ear is a sense organ related to both hearing and equilibrium (Fig. 10-5). It may be divided into three main sections:

1 The **external ear** includes the outer projection and a canal.
2 The **middle ear** is an air space containing three small bones.
3 The **internal ear** is the most important part, since it contains the sensory receptors for hearing and equilibrium.

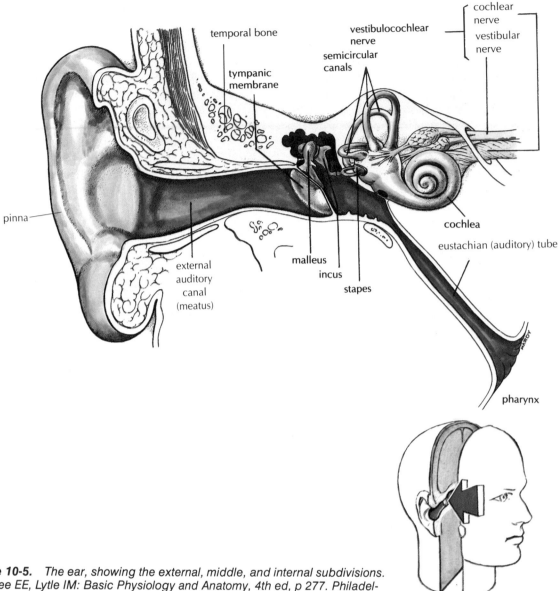

Figure 10-5. *The ear, showing the external, middle, and internal subdivisions. (Chaffee EE, Lytle IM: Basic Physiology and Anatomy, 4th ed, p 277. Philadelphia, JB Lippincott, 1980)*

The External Ear

The projecting part of the ear is known as the **pinna** (pin′nah), or the **auricle** (aw′re-kl). From a functional point of view, it is probably of little importance in the human. Then follows the opening itself, the **external auditory canal**, or **meatus** (me-a′tus), which extends medially for about 2.5 cm or more, depending on which wall of the canal is measured. The skin lining this tube is very thin, and in the first part of the canal contains many **ceruminous** (se-roo′me-nus) **glands**. The **cerumen** (se-roo′men), or wax, may become dried and impacted in the canal and must then be removed. The same kinds of disorders that involve the skin elsewhere—eczema, boils, and other infections—may affect the skin of the external auditory canal as well.

At the end of the auditory canal is the **tympanic** (tim-pan′ik) **membrane**, or eardrum, which serves as a boundary between the external auditory canal and the middle ear cavity. It may be injured by bobby pins or toothpicks inserted into the ear. A good rule for children is "Never put anything into your ear except your elbow!" Normally the air pressure on the two sides of the tympanic membrane is equalized by means of the **eustachian** (u-sta′ke-an) **tube** (auditory tube) which connects the middle ear cavity and the throat, or pharynx (far-inks), allowing the eardrum to vibrate freely with the incoming sound waves.

The Middle Ear

The middle ear cavity is a small, flattened space that contains air and three small bones, or **ossicles** (os′e-kles). Air enters the cavity from the pharynx through the eustachian tube. The mucous membrane of the pharynx is continuous through the eustachian tube into the middle ear cavity, and infection may travel along the membrane, causing middle ear disease. At the back of the middle ear cavity is an opening into the mastoid air cells, which are spaces inside the mastoid process of the temporal bone.

The three ossicles are joined in such a way that they amplify the sound waves received by the tympanic membrane and then transmit the sounds to the fluid in the internal ear. The handle-like part of the first bone, or **malleus** (mal′e-us), is attached to the tympanic membrane, while the headlike portion is connected with the second bone, called the **incus** (ing′kus). The innermost of the ossicles is shaped somewhat like a stirrup and is called the **stapes** (sta′pez). It is connected with the membrane of the **oval window**, which in turn vibrates and transmits these waves to the fluid of the internal ear.

The Internal Ear

The most complicated and important part of the ear is the internal portion, which consists of three separate spaces hollowed out inside the temporal bone (Fig. 10-6). This part of the ear, called the **bony labyrinth** (lab′i-rinth), consists of three divisions. One is the **vestibule**, next to the oval window. The second and third divisions are the **cochlea** (kok′le-ah) and the **semicircular canals**. All three divisions contain a fluid called **perilymph** (per′i-limf). The cochlea is a bony tube, shaped like a snail shell toward the front, and the semicircular canals are bony processes toward the back. In the fluid of the bony semicircular canals are the **membranous** (mem′brah-nus) **canals**, which contain another fluid called **endolymph** (en′do-limf). A **membranous cochlea**, situated in the perilymph of the bony cochlea, also is filled with endolymph.

The organ of hearing consists of receptors connected with nerve fibers in the **cochlear nerve** (a part of the eighth cranial nerve); it is located inside the membranous cochlea, or **cochlear duct**. The sound waves enter the external auditory canal and cause the tympanic membrane to vibrate. These vibrations are amplified by the ossicles and transmitted by them to the perilymph. They then are conducted by the perilymph through the membrane to the endolymph. The waves of the endolymph stimulate the tiny hairlike receptors, which then initiate nerve impulses that are conducted to the brain.

Other sensory receptors in the internal ear include those related to equilibrium, some of which are located at the base of the semicircular canals. These canals are connected with two small sacs in the vestibule, one of which contains sensory cells for obtaining information on the position of the head. The sense of equilibrium also depends on the movement of ciliated cells. As the head moves, a shift in the position of the cilia generates a nerve impulse. Nerve fibers from these sacs and from the canals form the **vestibular** (ves-tib′u-lar) **nerve**, which joins the cochlear nerve to form the vestibulocochlear nerve, the eighth cranial nerve (see Chap. 9).

Disorders of the Ear

Sudden great changes in the pressure on either side of the tympanic membrane may cause excessive stretching and inflammation of the membrane. There may even be perforation of the tympanic membrane to relieve the pressure.

Infection of the middle ear cavity, called **otitis media** (o-ti′tis me′de-ah), is rather common. A variety of bacteria as well as viruses may cause otitis media. It is also a frequent complication of measles, influenza, and other infections, especially those of the pharynx. Transmission of pathogens from the pharynx to the middle ear happens most often in children, partly because the eustachian tube is relatively short and horizontal in the child; in the adult the tube is longer and tends to slant down toward the pharynx. Antibiotic drugs have reduced complications and have caused a marked reduction in the amount of surgery done to drain middle ear infections. However, in some cases pressure from pus or exudate in the middle ear can be relieved only by

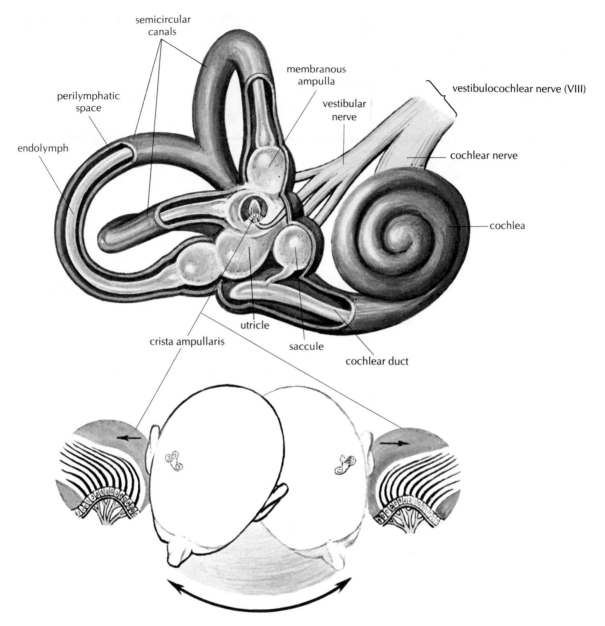

Figure 10-6. *The internal ear, including a section showing the crista ampullaris, where sensory receptors for balance are located.*

cutting the tympanic membrane, a procedure called a **myringotomy** (mir″in-got′o-me).

Another disorder of the ear is hearing loss, which may be partial or complete. When the loss is complete, the condition is called **deafness**. The two main types of hearing loss are **conduction deafness** and **nerve deafness**. Conduction deafness is due to interference with the passage of sound waves from the outside to the inner ear. In this condition there may be obstruction of the external canal by wax or a foreign body. Blockage of the eustachian tube prevents the equalization of air pressure on both sides of the tympanic membrane, thereby decreasing the ability of the membrane to vibrate. Another cause of conduction deafness is damage to the tympanic membrane and ossicles resulting from chronic otitis media or from **otosclerosis** (o″to-skle-ro′sis), a hereditary disease that causes bone changes in the stapes that prevent its normal vibration. Surgical removal of the diseased stapes and its replacement with an artificial device allow conduction of sound from the ossicles to the oval window and the cochlea. Nerve deafness is due to a disorder of the sensory mechanism affecting the cochlea, the vestibulocochlear nerve, or the brain areas concerned with hearing. It may result from prolonged exposure to loud noises, to the use of certain drugs for long periods of time, or to exposure to various infections and toxins.

Presbycusis (pres″be-ku′sis) is a slowly progressive hearing loss that often accompanies aging. The condition involves gradual atrophy of the sensory receptors and the nerve fibers in the cochlear nerves. As a result, the affected person may experience a sense of isolation and depression, so that psychologic help may be desirable. Since the ability to hear high-pitched sounds is usually lost first, it is important to address elderly persons in clear, low-pitched tones.

Other Special Sense Organs

Sense of Taste

The sense of taste involves receptors in the tongue and two different nerves that carry taste impulses to the brain. The taste receptors, known as **taste buds**, are located along the edges of small depressed areas called **fissures**. Taste buds are stimulated only if the substance to be tasted is in solution. Tastes have been described as essentially of four kinds:

1 **Sweet** tastes are most acutely experienced at the tip of the tongue.
2 **Sour** tastes are most effectively detected by the taste buds located at the sides of the tongue.
3 **Salty** tastes, like sweet tastes, are most acute at the tip of the tongue.
4 **Bitter** tastes are detected at the back part of the tongue.

The nerves of taste include the facial and the glossopharyngeal cranial nerves (VII and IX). The interpretation of taste impulses probably is accomplished by the lower front portion of the brain, although

there may be no sharply separate taste, or **gustatory** (gus′tah-to-re), **center** (Fig. 10-7).

Sense of Smell

The receptors for smell are located in the **olfactory epithelium** of the upper part of the nasal cavity. Because these receptors are high in the nasal cavity, one must "sniff" to bring the gases responsible for an odor upward in the nose. The impulses from the receptors for smell are carried by the olfactory nerve (I), which leads to the olfactory center in the brain. The interpretation of smell is closely related to the sense of taste, but a greater variety of chemicals can be detected by smell than by taste. The smell of foods is just as important in stimulating appetite and the flow of digestive juices as is the sense of taste.

The olfactory receptors deteriorate with age, the result being that food becomes less appealing. It is important when feeding elderly persons to present them with food that looks appetizing so as to stimulate their appetites.

General Senses

Unlike the *special* sensory receptors, which are limited to a relatively small area, the *general* sensory receptors are scattered throughout the body. These include receptors for pressure, heat, cold, pain, touch, position, and balance (Fig. 10-8).

Sense of Pressure

It has been found that even when the skin is anesthetized, there is still consciousness of pressure. These sensory end-organs for deep sensibility are located in the subcutaneous and deeper tissues. They are sometimes referred to as *receptors for deep touch*.

Sense of Temperature

Heat and cold receptors have separate nerve fiber connections. Each has a type of end-organ structure peculiar to it, the distribution of which varies considerably from that of the other. A warm object stimulates only the heat receptors, and a cool object affects only the cold receptors. As in the case of other sensory receptors, continued stimulation results in **adaptation**; that is, the receptors adjust themselves in such

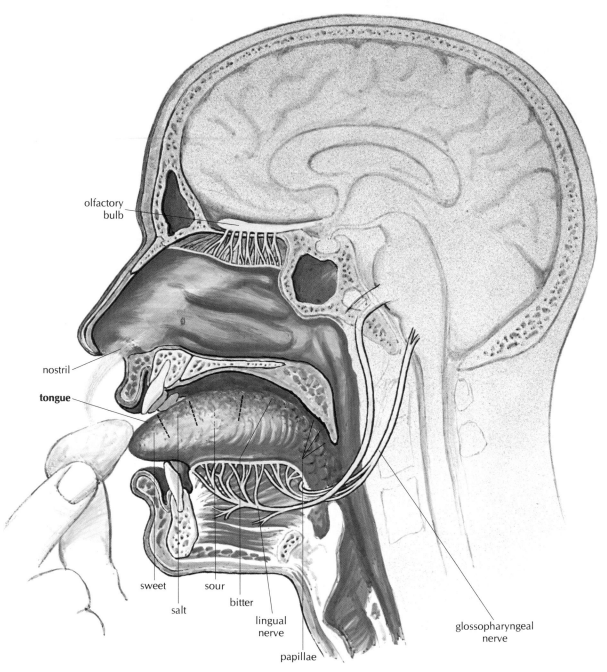

Figure 10-7. *Organs of taste and smell.*

a way that the sensation becomes less acute if the original stimulus is continued. For example, if you immerse your hand in hot water, it may be uncomfortable; however, if you leave your hand there, very soon the water will feel less hot (even if it has not cooled appreciably). Receptors for warmth, cold, and light pressure adapt rapidly. In contrast, those for pain adapt slowly; this is nature's way of being certain that the warnings of the pain sense are heeded.

Sense of Touch

The touch receptors are small, rounded bodies called **tactile** (tak′til) **corpuscles**. They are found mostly in the dermis and are especially numerous

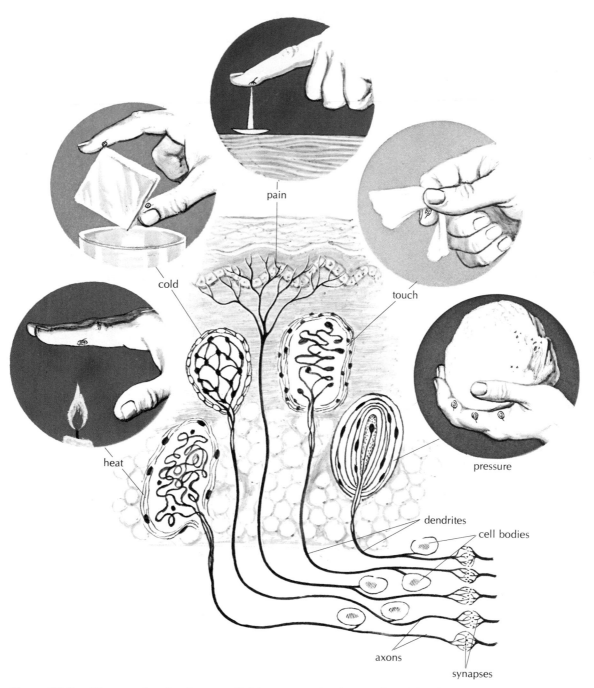

Figure 10-8. *Diagram showing the superficial receptors (end-organs) and the deeper cell bodies and synapses, suggesting the continuity of sensory pathways into the CNS.*

and close together in the tips of the fingers and the toes. The tip of the tongue also contains many of these receptors and so is very sensitive to touch, whereas the back of the neck is relatively insensitive.

Sense of Pain

Pain is the most important protective sense. The receptors for pain are very widely distributed. They are found in the skin, muscles, and joints, and to a lesser extent in most internal organs (including the blood vessels and viscera). Pain receptors are not enclosed in capsules as are the sensory end-organs; rather, they are merely branchings of the nerve fiber, called **free nerve endings**. **Referred pain** is a term used in cases in which pain that seems to be in an outer part of the body, particularly the skin, actually originates in an internal organ located near that particular area of skin. These areas of referred pain have been mapped out on the basis of much experience and many experiments. It has been found, for example, that liver and gallbladder disease often cause referred pain in the skin over the right shoulder. Spasm of the coronary arteries that supply the heart may cause pain in the left shoulder and the left arm. One reason for this is that some neurons have the twofold duty of conducting impulses both from visceral pain receptors and from pain receptors in neighboring areas of the skin. The brain cannot differentiate between these two possible sources, but since most pain sensations originate in the skin, the brain automatically assigns the pain to this more likely place of origin.

Sometimes the cause of pain cannot be remedied quickly, and occasionally it cannot be remedied at all. In the latter case it is desirable to relieve the pain. Some pain relief methods that have been found to be effective include the following:

1   **Application of cold**, especially crushed ice in ice caps, for headaches; in bags for localized areas of injury or inflammation; or in cold compresses made from a towel (or gauze) dipped in cold water and then wrung out.
2   **Pressure** applied to the site of pain or to certain other locations in the body.
3   **Analgesic** (an-al-je′zik) **drugs**, which are mild pain relievers. Examples are **acetaminophen** (as″et-am′i-no-fen) and **aspirin.**
4   **Narcotic drugs**, which produce stupor and sleep. These are often very effective pain re-

lievers. An example of a narcotic drug is **morphine.**
5   **Anesthetics**, which may be either local, rendering only a certain area insensitive, or general, producing total unconsciousness. These are used largely to prevent pain during surgery.
6   **Endorphins** (en-dor′fins) and **enkephalins** (en-kef′ah-lins), which are released naturally from certain regions of the brain and are associated with the control of pain. These substances are under intensive study, and several theories have been proposed about the circumstances that can cause them to be released from the hypothalamus, the pituitary, and other areas of the brain.

Sense of Position

Receptors located in muscles, tendons, and joints relay impulses that aid in judging one's position and changes in the locations of body parts with respect to each other. They also inform the brain of the amount of muscle contraction and tendon tension. These rather widespread end-organs, known as **proprioceptors** (pro″pre-o-sep′tors), are aided in this function by the semicircular canals and related internal ear structures. Information received by these receptors is needed for the coordination of muscles and is important in such activities as walking, running, and many more complicated skills, such as playing a musical instrument. These muscle receptors also play an important part in maintaining muscle tone and good posture, as well as allowing for the adjustment of the muscles for the particular kind of work to be done. The nerve fibers that carry impulses from these receptors enter the spinal cord and ascend to the brain in the posterior part of the cord. The cerebellum is a main coordinating center for these impulses.

Summary

I   **Sensory System**—protects by detecting changes (stimuli) in the environment
    A General senses—pain, touch, temperature, pressure, position
    B Special senses—vision, hearing, equilibrium, taste, smell

II Eye

  A Protective structures—eyelids, bony orbit, eyelashes, tears (lacrimal apparatus), conjunctiva

  B Layers (tunics)

    1 Sclera—white of the eye

      a Cornea

    2 Choroid—pigmented; contains blood vessels

    3 Retina—nerve tissue

      a Rods—detect white and black; function in dim light

      b Cones—detect color; function in bright light

  C Refracting parts (media)—cornea, aqueous humor, crystalline lens, vitreous body

  D Muscles

    1 Extrinsic muscles—six move each eyeball

    2 Intrinsic muscles

      a Iris—opening is the pupil; regulates the amount of light entering the eye

      b Ciliary body—regulates the thickness of the lens

  E Nerve supply

    1 Optic nerve (II)—carries impulses from retina to brain

    2 Ophthalmic branch of trigeminal (V)—sensory nerve

    3 Oculomotor (III), trochlear (IV), abducens (VI) nerves—move eyeball

  F Disorders

    1 Infections—conjunctivitis, gonorrhea (newborn), trachoma

    2 Eyestrain

    3 Structural defects—hyperopia (farsightedness), myopia (nearsightedness), astigmatism

    4 Strabismus

    5 Blindness—cataracts, glaucoma, diabetes

III Ear

  A Divisions

    1 External ear—pinna, auditory canal (meatus), tympanic membrane (eardrum)

    2 Middle ear—ossicles (malleus, incus, stapes)

      a Eustachian tube—connects middle ear with pharynx to equalize pressure

    3 Internal ear—bony labyrinth

      a Vestibule—contains receptors for equilibrium

      b Cochlea—contains receptors for hearing

      c Semicircular canals—contain receptors for equilibrium

  B Nerve—vestibulocochlear (auditory) nerve (VIII)

  C Disorders—otitis media, deafness, otosclerosis

IV Other special sense organs

  A Taste—gustatory sense

    1 Receptors—taste buds

    2 Tastes—sweet, sour, salty, bitter

    3 Nerves—facial (VII) and glossopharyngeal (IX)

  B Smell—olfactory sense

    1 Receptors—in upper part of nasal cavity

    2 Nerve—olfactory nerve (I)

V General Senses

  A Pressure

  B Temperature

  C Touch

  D Pain—receptors are free nerve endings

    1 Relief—cold, pressure, analgesics, narcotics, anesthetics, endorphins and enkephalins

  E Position

Questions for Study and Review

1 Give a general definition of *sense* and name six of the senses.

2 Name the main parts of the eye.

3 Trace the path of a light ray from the outside of the eye to the retina.

4 List the extrinsic muscles of the eye. What is their function?

5 List the intrinsic muscles of the eye. What is their function?

6 What is near accommodation? What structures of the eye are necessary for near accommodation?

7 List five protective devices for the eye.

8 List five cranial nerves associated with the eye and give the function of each.

9 Describe three changes that occur in the eye with age.

10 Describe three eye infections and four eye defects. What are the main causes of blindness?

11 Describe the structures that sound waves pass through in traveling through the ear to the receptors for hearing.

12 Where are the receptors for the senses of position and balance (equilibrium) located?

13 What cranial nerve carries impulses from the ear? Name the two branches.

14 Name and describe two ear disorders and list some causes of deafness.

15 Name the four kinds of taste. Where are the taste receptors?

16 Describe the olfactory apparatus.

17 What is the difference between a general and a special sense? Give three examples of each.

18 What does *adaptation* mean with respect to the senses? Does this occur in the case of every sense?

19 Explain the term *referred pain* and give an example of the occurrence of such pain.

20 Name three categories of pain-relieving drugs.

21 Differentiate between the terms in each of the following pairs:

a. *hyperopia* and *myopia*

b. *presbyopia* and *presbycusis*

c. *rods* and *cones*

d. *endolymph* and *perilymph*

e. *gustatory* and *olfactory*

11

The Endocrine System and Hormones

Behavioral Objectives

After careful study of this chapter, you should be able to:

Compare the effects of the nervous system and the endocrine system in controlling the body

Compare protein and steroid hormones with respect to position and method of action and give several examples of each type

Describe three methods for regulating the release of hormones

Identify the glands of the endocrine system on a diagram

List the hormones produced by each endocrine gland and describe the effects of each on the body

Describe how the hypothalamus controls the anterior and posterior pituitary

Explain why the anterior pituitary is called the master gland

Explain how the endocrine system responds to stress

Selected Key Terms

The following terms are defined in the glossary:

endocrine
hormone
hypothalamus
pituitary (hypophysis)
prostaglandin
receptor
steroid
target tissue

The nervous system and the endocrine system are the two main coordinating and controlling systems of the body. There are several differences between these two systems. For example, the nervous system acts by means of electric impulses and chemical stimuli, whereas the endocrine system acts by means of chemical stimuli only. Also, the nervous system has an immediate and short-term effect on muscles and glands, whereas the endocrine system has more widespread, slower, and longer lasting effects. The endocrine system also has more generalized effects on such activities as growth, metabolism, and reproduction. Despite these differences, however, the two systems are closely interrelated.

☰ Hormones

The chemical messengers released by the glands of the endocrine system are called **hormones**. Hormones are released directly into the bloodstream and carried to the tissues they affect. These tissues may be far from where the hormone is produced.

The blood reaches all cells of the body, but only certain cells respond to specific hormones; these responding cells are unique in that they have **receptors** to which the hormones attach. Only cells that have receptors for a given hormone will respond to that hormone; these cells make up what is called the **target tissue.**

Chemistry

Hormones fall chemically into two categories:

1 **Proteins.** Most hormones are proteins or related compounds composed of amino acids. All hormones except those of the adrenal cortex and the sex glands are proteins.
2 **Steroids** are hormones derived from lipids and produced by the adrenal cortex and the sex glands.

All hormones are extremely potent, that is, they are effective in very small amounts.

Action

Steroid hormones can pass through the cell membrane and enter the target cell. Once inside the cell, they combine with receptors and enter the nucleus. Here they have a direct effect on the DNA, thus altering the activity of the cell.

Most protein hormones do not enter the target cell. Instead, they attach to the surface and activate another substance within the cell that alters the cell activity. This substance within the cell is called a **second messenger**. In general, the effect of hormones is to change the rate of protein manufacture in the cytoplasm. As a result, hormones can have a profound effect on growth, metabolism, reproduction, and behavior.

Regulation

The release of most hormones is controlled by a mechanism called a *negative feedback system.* As you may recall from Chapter 1, in a negative feedback system the result of an action in the body regulates that action and keeps it in a steady state, or homeostasis. A simple example of how negative feedback works to control the release of hormones may be seen in the regulation of insulin from pancreatic cells. When the level of glucose in the blood is high, the islet cells of the pancreas release insulin. This hormone stimulates body cells to take up more glucose, thus lowering glucose levels in the blood. When blood glucose levels are lowered, the islet cells release less insulin and the blood glucose level increases. Thus, negative feedback mechanisms reverse increases or decreases in body conditions to maintain a state of balance.

In addition to being regulated by negative feedback, the release of hormones may also be regulated by other hormones, such as those from the anterior pituitary, or by nervous stimulation, such as the sympathetic stimulation that causes the release of epinephrine from the adrenal medulla.

☰ The Endocrine System

The endocrine system consists of the glands that secrete hormones. These glands are also called the *ductless glands* because they secrete directly into the bloodstream, in contrast to the exocrine glands, described in Chapter 4, which secrete into body cavities or to the outside by means of ducts.

Most endocrine glands, like exocrine glands, are made of epithelial tissue. Although they have no ducts, they have an extensive blood vessel network. Operations on endocrine glands, for example on the thyroid, require care in the control of bleeding. The organs believed to have the very richest blood supply of any in the body are the tiny adrenal, or suprarenal, glands, which are located near the upper part of the kidneys.

Some of the glands included in this system, such as the pancreas and the sex glands, have other non-endocrine functions as well, but hormone secretion is one of their main functions. In addition, some body organs, such as the stomach, small intestine, and kidney, produce hormones, but since their main function is not hormone production, they are not discussed in detail in this chapter.

The remainder of this chapter deals with the en-docrine glands. Refer to Figure 11-1 to locate each of the glands as you study it. See also Table 11-1 for a summary of these glands and their hormones.

≡ The Endocrine Glands and Their Hormones

The Pituitary

The **pituitary** (pi-tu′i-tar-e), or **hypophysis** (hi-pof′i-sis), is a small gland about the size of a cherry. It is located in a saddle-like depression of the sphenoid

Figure 11-1. *Glands of the endocrine system.*

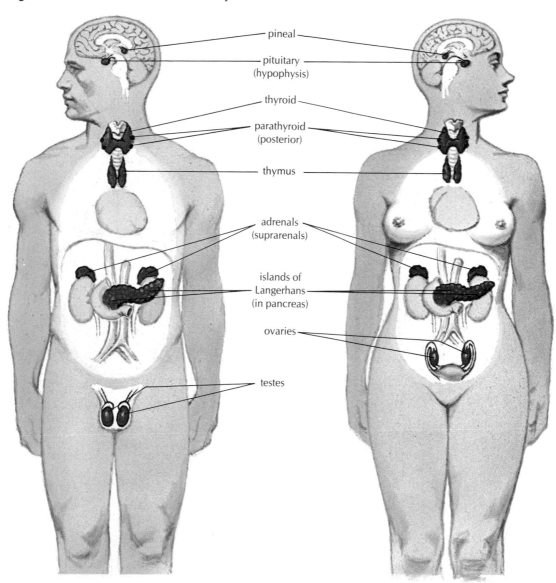

pineal

pituitary
(hypophysis)

thyroid

parathyroid
(posterior)

thymus

adrenals
(suprarenals)

islands of
Langerhans
(in pancreas)

ovaries

testes

Table 11-1 The Endocrine Glands and their Hormones

Gland	Hormone	Principal Functions
Anterior pituitary	GH (growth hormone)	Promotes growth of all body tissues
	TSH (thyroid-stimulating hormone)	Stimulates thyroid gland to produce thyroid hormones
	ACTH (adrenocorticotropic hormone)	Stimulates adrenal cortex to produce cortical hormones; aids in protecting body in stress situations (injury, pain)
	FSH (follicle-stimulating hormone)	Stimulates growth and hormone activity of ovarian follicles; stimulates growth of testes; promotes development of sperm cells
	LH (luteinizing hormone); ICSH (interstitial cell–stimulating hormone) in males	Causes development of corpus luteum at site of ruptured ovarian follicle in female; stimulates secretion of testosterone in male
	PRL (prolactin)	Stimulates secretion of milk by mammary glands
Posterior pituitary	ADH (antidiuretic hormone; vasopressin)	Promotes reabsorption of water in kidney tubules; stimulates smooth muscle tissue of blood vessels to constrict
	Oxytocin	Causes contraction of muscle of uterus; causes ejection of milk from mammary glands
Thyroid	Thyroid hormone (thyroxin and triiodothyronine)	Increases metabolic rate, influencing both physical and mental activities; required for normal growth
	Calcitonin	Decreases calcium level in blood
Parathyroids	Parathyroid hormone	Regulates exchange of calcium between blood and bones; increases calcium level in blood
Adrenal medulla	Epinephrine and norephinephrine	Increases blood pressure and heart rate; activates cells influenced by sympathetic nervous system plus many not affected by sympathetic nerves
Adrenal cortex	Cortisol (95% of glucocorticoids)	Aids in metabolism of carbohydrates, proteins, and fats; active during stress
	Aldosterone (95% of mineralocorticoids)	Aids in regulating electrolytes and water balance
	Sex hormones	May influence secondary sexual characteristics in male
Pancreatic islets	Insulin	Aids transport of glucose into cells; required for cellular metabolism of foods, especially glucose; decreases blood sugar levels
	Glucagon	Stimulates liver to release glucose, thereby increasing blood sugar levels
Testes	Testosterone	Stimulates growth and development of sexual organs (testes, penis, others) plus development of secondary sexual characteristics such as hair growth on body and face and deepening of voice; stimulates maturation of sperm cells
Ovary	Estrogens (*e.g.,* estradiol)	Stimulate growth of primary sexual organs (uterus, tubes, etc.) and development of secondary sexual organs such as breasts, plus changes in pelvis to ovoid, broader shape
	Progesterone	Stimulates development of secretory parts of mammary glands; prepares uterine lining for implantation of fertilized ovum; aids in maintaining pregnancy
Thymus	Thymosin	Important in development of T-lymphocytes needed for immunity and early development of lymphoid tissue
Pineal	Melatonin	May regulate activity of gonads in response to light

bone just behind the point at which the optic nerves cross. It is surrounded by bone except where it connects with the brain by a stalk called the **infundibulum** (in″fun-dib′u-lum). The gland is divided into two parts, the **anterior lobe** and the **posterior lobe**. The hormones released from each lobe are shown in Figure 11-2.

The pituitary is often called the *master gland* because it releases hormones that affect the working of other glands, such as the thyroid, gonads, and adrenal glands. (Hormones that affect other glands may be recognized by the ending *-tropic,* as in *gonadotropic hormone.*) However, the pituitary itself is controlled by the region of the brain called the **hypothalamus** (hi″po-thal′ah-mus) under which it is located (see Fig. 11-2).

The hormones produced in the anterior pituitary are not released from the gland until chemical messengers called **releasing hormones** arrive from the hypothalamus. These releasing hormones are sent by way of a special circulatory pathway called a **portal system**, described in Chapter 14; that is, some of the blood that leaves the hypothalamus travels into capillaries in the anterior pituitary before returning to the heart, delivering releasing hormones to the gland.

The two hormones of the posterior pituitary are actually produced in the hypothalamus and stored in the posterior pituitary. Their release is controlled by nerve impulses that travel over pathways between the hypothalamus and the posterior pituitary.

The effects produced by these hormones in turn feed back to the hypothalamus to control its working. This key relationship between the nervous system and the endocrine system explains some of the interactions between these two systems and how a person's mental and emotional states can affect that person's hormone levels and vice versa.

Hormones of the Anterior Lobe

1 **Growth hormone (GH)** or **somatotropic** (so″mah-to-trop′ik) **hormone,** stimulates the growth of bones, muscles, and other organs. Varying amounts of this hormone are produced throughout life. A person born with a deficiency of this hormone will remain a small, though well-proportioned, individual unless treated with adequate hormones.

2 **Thyroid-stimulating hormone (TSH),** or **thyro-** tropic (thi″ro-trop′ik) **hormone,** stimulates the thyroid gland to produce thyroid hormones.

3 **Adrenocorticotropic** (ad-re″no-kor′te-ko-trop′ik) **hormone (ACTH)** stimulates the cortex of the adrenal glands.

4 **Gonadotropic** (gon″ah-do-trop′ik) **hormones** regulate the growth, development, and functioning of the reproductive systems in both males and females. **Follicle-stimulating hormone (FSH)** stimulates the development of eggs in the ovaries and sperm cells in the testes. **Luteinizing hormone (LH)** causes ovulation in females and sex hormone secretion in both males and females; in males the hormone is called interstitial cell–stimulating hormone (ICSH).

5 **Prolactin** (pro-lak′tin) **(PRL)** or **lactogenic** (lak″to-jen′ik) **hormone** stimulates the production of milk in the female.

Hormones of the Posterior Lobe

1 **Antidiuretic** (an″ti-di″u-ret′ik) **hormone (ADH)** promotes the reabsorption of water from the kidney tubules and thus decreases the excretion of water. Large amounts of this hormone cause contraction of the smooth muscle of blood vessels and raise blood pressure. Inadequate amounts of ADH cause excessive loss of water and result in a disorder called **diabetes insipidus.** This type of diabetes should not be confused with diabetes mellitus, which is due to inadequate amounts of insulin.

2 **Oxytocin** (ox″se-tō′sin) causes contraction of the muscle of the uterus and milk ejection from the breasts. Under certain circumstances, commercial preparations of this hormone are administered during or after childbirth to cause the uterus to contract.

Tumors of the Pituitary

The effects of pituitary tumors depend on the types of cells the new or excess tissue contains. Some of these tumors contain an excessive number of the cells that produce GH. A person who develops such a tumor in childhood will grow to an abnormally tall stature, a condition called **gigantism** (ji-gan′tizm). Although persons with this condition are large, they are usually very weak.

If the growth-producing cells become overactive

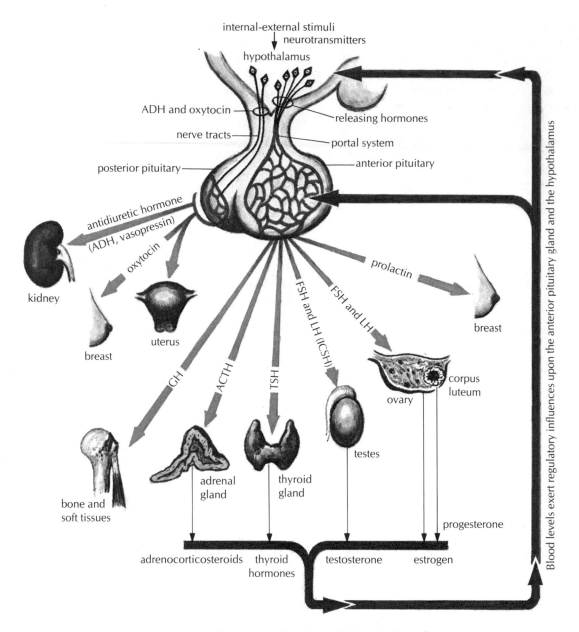

Figure 11-2. *The pituitary gland and its interrelationships with the brain and target tissues. Hypothalamic releasing hormones influence the anterior pituitary gland by way of a portal system. Anterior pituitary gland tropic hormones affect the working of various other glands. The secretions of these glands influence the metabolism of specific tissues and exert feedback effects on the anterior pituitary and hypothalamus. The posterior pituitary communicates with the hypothalamus through nerve tracts. It stores and releases other hypothalamic hormones that affect the functioning of specific target tissues.*

in the adult, a disorder known as **acromegaly** (ak″ro-meg′ah-le) develops. In acromegaly the bones of the face, hands, and feet widen. The fingers resemble a spatula, and the face takes on a grotesque appearance: the nose widens, the lower jaw protrudes, and the forehead bones may bulge. Often these pituitary tumors involve the optic nerves and cause blindness.

Tumors or disease may destroy the secreting tissues of the gland so that signs of underactivity develop. Patients with this condition often become obese and sluggish and may exhibit signs of underactivity of other endocrine glands such as the ovaries, testes, or thyroid. Evidence of tumor formation in the pituitary gland may be obtained by x-ray examinations of the skull; the saddle-like space for the pituitary is distorted by the pressure of the tumor.

The Thyroid Gland

The largest of the endocrine glands is the **thyroid**, which is located in the neck. It has two oval parts called the *lateral lobes,* one on either side of the voice box. A narrow band called the **isthmus** (is′mus) connects these two lobes. The entire gland is enclosed by a connective tissue capsule. This gland produces hormones, the principal one being **thyroxin** (thi-rok′sin). A hormone called **calcitonin** (kal″si-tō′nin), produced in the thyroid but active in calcium metabolism, will be discussed later in connection with the parathyroid gland. The main function of thyroid hormones is to regulate metabolism for the production of heat and energy in the body tissues. In order for these hormones to be manufactured, there must be an adequate supply of iodine in the blood. The iodine content may be maintained by ingestion of vegetables grown in iodine-containing soils or of seafood. In some parts of the United States, as well as in certain regions of Italy and Switzerland, the soil is so deficient in iodine that serious disorders may develop in the inhabitants. The use of iodized salt may prevent such difficulties.

One result of an iodine deficiency in the blood is the formation of a **goiter**, a swelling of the neck due to an enlarged thyroid. As will be seen, there are other causes of goiter as well but in this case, known as **simple**, or **endemic**, **goiter**, the thyroid becomes enlarged as the size and number of glandular cells increase in an attempt to produce enough thyroid hormones.

Another form of goiter is **adenomatous** (ad-e-no′mah-tus), or **nodular**, **goiter**; as the name indicates, this type of goiter is accompanied by tumor formation, which is due to the overgrowth of the cells of the thyroid tissue. The tumors may be single or multiple; they are more likely to become malignant if they are single.

For various reasons, the thyroid gland may become either underactive or overactive. Underactivity of the thyroid, known as **hypothyroidism** (hi-po-thi′roi-dizm), shows up as two characteristic states:

1 **Cretinism** (kre′tin-izm), a condition in which there is a serious lack of thyroid activity from the beginning of the individual's life. A blood test of newborns for thyroid hormone is now mandatory in most states. Sometimes this condition is due to the complete absence of thyroid tissue. The infant becomes dwarfed and mentally deficient because of a lack of physical growth and mental development. Only if continuous thyroid replacement is begun early is there any hope of altering the prognosis. This disorder is fortunately rather rare in the United States, though endemic in certain regions where iodine is lacking.

2 **Myxedema** (mik″se-de′mah), the result of atrophy of the thyroid in the adult. The patient becomes sluggish both mentally and physically. The skin and the hair become dry, and a peculiar swelling of the tissues of the face develops. Since thyroid extract or the hormone itself may be administered by mouth, the patient with myxedema can be restored to health very easily, though treatment must be maintained throughout the remainder of his or her life.

Hyperthyroidism is the opposite of hypothyroidism: overactivity of the thyroid gland. The development of a simple goiter might suggest hyperthyroidism, but there is a difference. In a simple goiter the thyroid is usually normal but enlarges because it has more work to do than normal, just as the heart will enlarge if something causes its work load to increase. Hyperthyroidism, however, is abnormal activity of the thyroid with production of excess hormone.

A common form of hyperthyroidism is **exophthalmic** (ek-sof-thal′mik) **goiter**, or **Graves' disease**, which is characterized by a goiter, bulging of the eyes, a strained appearance of the face, intense nervousness, weight loss, a rapid pulse, sweating, tremors, and an abnormally quick metabolism. In many cases the administration of drugs or surgical removal of a part of the thyroid gland remedies the condition.

An exaggerated form of hyperthyroidism with a sudden onset is called a **thyroid storm**. Untreated, it is usually fatal, but with appropriate care, the majority of affected persons can be saved.

Tests for Thyroid Function

The most frequently used tests for thyroid function are blood tests in which the uptake of radioactive iodine added to the blood sample is measured. These tests are named after the type of radioactive iodine used. If the results of such an up-take test are abnormal, the person may have further testing in which radioactive iodine is taken orally and the radioactivity of the thyroid gland measured.

Other tests that are used for determining the activity of the thyroid gland include the following:

1 **Measurement of thyroid hormones** in the blood plasma
2 The **protein-bound iodine test**, which measures the amount of iodine that is combined with protein in the blood
3 The **basal metabolism test**, which measures the amount of oxygen a person uses while at rest

The Parathyroid Glands

Behind the thyroid gland, and embedded in its capsule, are four tiny epithelial bodies called the **parathyroid glands**. The secretion of these glands, **parathyroid hormone (PTH)**, is one of three substances that regulate calcium metabolism. The other two are **calcitonin** and **hydroxycholecalciferol** (hi-drok″se-ko″le-kal-sif′e-rol). PTH promotes the release of calcium from bone tissue, thus increasing the amount of calcium circulating in the bloodstream. Calcitonin, which is produced in the thyroid gland, acts to lower the amount of calcium circulating in the blood. Hydroxycholecalciferol is produced from vitamin D after first being modified by the liver and then the kidney. It increases absorption of calcium by the intestine to raise blood calcium levels.

If the parathyroid glands are removed, there follows a series of muscle contractions involving particularly the hand and the face muscles. These spasms are due to a low concentration of blood calcium, and the condition is called tetany (tet′ah-ne),

which should not be confused with the infection called *tetanus* (lockjaw). In contrast, if there is excess production of PTH, as may happen in tumors of the parathyroids, calcium is removed from its normal storage place in the bones and released into the bloodstream. Since this calcium is finally excreted by the kidneys, the formation of kidney stones is common in such cases. The loss of calcium from the bones leads to bone weakness and easy fractures.

The Adrenal Glands

The **adrenals**, or **suprarenals**, are two small glands, each one situated above a kidney. An adrenal gland has two separate parts, each of which acts as an entire gland. The inner area is called the **medulla**, while the outer portion is the **cortex**.

Hormones from the Adrenal Medulla

The hormones of the adrenal medulla are released in response to stimulation by the sympathetic nervous system. The principal hormone produced by the medulla is one we already have learned something about because it acts as a neurotransmitter. It is **epinephrine**, also called **adrenalin** (ad-ren′al-in). Another hormone, **norepinephrine** (nor″ep-i-nef′rin), is closely related chemically and is similar but not identical in its actions. These are referred to as the *fight-or-flight hormones* because of their effects during emergency situations. Some of these effects are as follows:

1 Stimulation of the involuntary muscle in the walls of the arterioles, causing these muscles to contract and blood pressure to rise accordingly
2 Conversion of the glycogen stored in the liver into glucose, which is poured into the blood and brought to the voluntary muscles, permitting them to do an extraordinary amount of work
3 Increase in the heart rate
4 Increase in the metabolic rate of body cells
5 Dilation of the bronchioles, through relaxation of the smooth muscle of their walls

Hormones from the Adrenal Cortex

There are three main groups of hormones secreted by the adrenal cortex:

1 **Glucocorticoids** (gloo″ko-kor′ti-koids) maintain the carbohydrate reserve of the body by controlling the conversion of amino acids into sugar in-

stead of protein. These hormones are produced in larger than normal amounts in times of stress and so aid the body in responding to unfavorable conditions. They have the ability to suppress the inflammatory response and are often administered as medication for this purpose. A major hormone of this group is cortisol.

2 **Mineralocorticoids** (min″er-al-o-kor′ti-koids) are important in the regulation of electrolyte balance by controlling the reabsorption of sodium and the secretion of potassium by the kidney tubules. The major hormone of this group is aldosterone.

3 **Sex hormones** are normally secreted, but in small amounts; their effects in the body are slight.

The adrenal cortex is essential to life; it is largely by means of this part of the adrenal glands that the body succeeds in adapting itself to the constant changes in the environment. Hypofunction of the adrenal cortex gives rise to a condition known as **Addison's disease**, a disease characterized chiefly by atrophy (loss of muscle tissue), weakness, skin pigmentation, and disturbances in salt and water balance. Hyperfunction of the adrenal cortex results in a condition known as **Cushing's syndrome**, the symptoms of which include obesity with a round face, thin skin that bruises easily, muscle weakness, bone loss, and elevated blood sugar. Use of steroid drugs may also produce these symptoms.

Adrenal gland tumors give rise to a wide range of symptoms resulting from an excess or a deficiency of the hormones secreted.

The Pancreas, Insulin, and Diabetes

Scattered throughout the **pancreas** are small groups of specialized cells called **islets** (i′lets), also known as the **islets of Langerhans** (lahng′er-hanz). These cells make up the endocrine portion of the pancreas and function independently from the exocrine part of the pancreas, which produces digestive juices and releases them through ducts. The most important hormone secreted by these islets is **insulin.**

Insulin is active in the transport of glucose across the cell membrane. Once inside the cell, the glucose can be used for energy metabolism or stored. In the presence of insulin, excessive amounts of carbohydrates enter fat cells, to be converted and stored as fat. Insulin also increases the transport of amino acids

into the cells and improves their use in the manufacture of proteins. When insulin is lacking, there is not enough glucose for cell metabolism, and this causes an abnormal breakdown of proteins and fats.

A second hormone produced by the islet cells is **glucagon** (gloo′kah-gon), which works with insulin to regulate blood sugar levels. Glucagon causes the liver to release stored glucose into the bloodstream, thus raising blood sugar levels. Its effect is the exact opposite of that of insulin.

If for some reason the pancreatic islets fail to produce enough insulin, sugar is not oxidized ("burned") in the tissues for transformation into energy; instead, the sugar remains in the blood and is simply excreted along with the urine. This condition is called **diabetes mellitus** (di-ah-be′teez mel-li′tus). In order that the diabetic patient may lead a normal life, proper utilization of the body's fuel must be restored and maintained. In mild cases of diabetes this can be achieved by a modification of diet, sometimes with the addition of oral medications to increase the output of insulin by the pancreas. In severe cases, however, the patient must also receive insulin from an outside source in daily periodic doses. Insulin must be given by injection because it is destroyed by the action of digestive juices.

As a rule it is considered desirable for diabetic patients to learn to give themselves their injections. They should learn to adjust their diets, exercise, and other activities in order to maintain the proper balance between intake of insulin and sugar needs. They should also each carry a special identification card to let people know that they are diabetics taking insulin, and that a dazed condition might indicate a need for some sugar.

Special pumps that provide a round-the-clock supply of insulin are now available. The insulin is placed in a device that then injects it into the subcutaneous tissues of the abdomen. The consistent blood sugar level thus achieved results in a more nearly normal metabolism.

Insulin has been and still is obtained from animal pancreases, but human insulin produced by bacteria through genetic engineering is also available.

Long-term complications of diabetes are many. Resistance to infection is lessened. The arteries, including those of the retina, the kidney, and heart, may be seriously damaged. The peripheral nerves are affected also, with accompanying pain and loss of sensation.

The Sex Glands

The sex glands, the ovaries of the female and the testes of the male, not only produce the sex cells but are also important endocrine organs. The hormones produced by these organs are needed in the development of the sexual characteristics, which usually appear in the early teens, and for the maintenance of the reproductive apparatus once full development has been attained. The main androgen (an'dro-jen) produced by the male sex glands, **testosterone** (tes-tos'ter-one), is responsible for the growth and functioning of the male reproductive tract. Those structures directly concerned with reproduction are considered **primary sex characteristics**. Testosterone is also responsible for male **secondary sex characteristics** such as a deep voice and facial hair.

In the female, the hormones that most nearly parallel testosterone in their actions are the **estrogens** (es'tro-jens). Estrogens contribute to the development of the female secondary sex characteristcs and stimulate the development of the mammary glands, the onset of menstruation, and the development and functioning of the reproductive organs.

The other hormone produced by the female sex glands, called **progesterone** (pro-jes'ter-one), assists in the normal development of pregnancy. All of the sex hormones are discussed in more detail in Chapter 21.

The Thymus Gland

The thymus gland lies in the upper part of the chest above the heart. This gland is important in the immune system, as will be discussed more fully in Chapters 15 and 16. Through the production of a hormone called **thymosin** (thi'mo-sin), it helps in the development of certain white blood cells, called *T-lymphocytes,* that help protect the body against foreign organisms. Because this gland is most active before birth and early in life, it is large during childhood but gradually shrinks in size as one reaches adulthood.

The Pineal Gland

The **pineal** (pin'-e-al) **gland**, a small, flattened, cone-shaped structure located between the two parts of the thalamus, produces a hormone called **melatonin** (mel-ah-tō'nin) in a number of animals and also in humans. Melatonin, or some other hormone from the pineal, is thought to regulate the release of certain substances from the hypothalamus, which may in turn regulate the secretion of gonadotropins from the pituitary. There is evidence from animal studies that the production of melatonin is regulated by the amount of light in the environment. The human pineal gland may be invaded by tumor tissue, which can either increase the production of pineal hormone or destroy the gland. The symptoms of these conditions indicate that the pineal gland may play a role in gonadal activity.

≡ Other Hormone-Producing Structures

Cells in the lining of the stomach and small intestine secrete hormones that stimulate the production of digestive juices and help regulate the process of digestion.

The kidneys produce a hormone called **renin**, which acts on the blood vessels to produce constriction (narrowing) and stimulates the adrenal cortex to release aldosterone; both of these actions result in increased blood pressure. The second hormone produced in the kidneys is **erythropoietin** (e-rith"ro-poi'e-tin), which stimulates red blood cell production in the bone marrow.

The placenta (plah-sen'tah) produces several hormones during pregnancy. These cause changes in the uterine lining and later in pregnancy help prepare the breasts for lactation. Pregnancy tests are based on the presence of placental hormones.

All of the hormones described above are discussed more fully in later chapters.

Prostaglandins

Hormone-like substances called **prostaglandins** (pros-tah-glan'dins) have been found widely dis tributed in cells throughout the body. Organs that have been named as manufacturers of prostaglandins include the seminal vesicles (male reproductive system), thymus, brain, and kidney medulla. A bewildering array of functions has been ascribed to these substances. Some prostaglandins cause constriction of blood vessels, of bronchial tubes, and of the intestine, while others cause dilation of these same structures. Prostaglandins are active in promoting inflammation; certain anti-inflammatory drugs, such as aspirin, may act by blocking the production of prostaglandins. Some of the prostaglandins have been used to induce labor or abortion and have been recommended as possible contraceptive agents. Overproduction of prostaglandins by the uterine lining (endometrium) can cause painful cramps of the muscle of the uterus. Treatment with drugs that are prostaglandin inhibitors has been successful in some cases. Much has been written about these substances, and extensive research on them continues.

Hormones and Treatment

Many hormones may be extracted from animal tissues for use as medication. However, some hormone and hormone-like substances are available in synthetic form, meaning that they are manufactured in commercial laboratories.

A few examples of the use of natural and synthetic hormones in treatment are noted here:

1 **Insulin** is used in the treatment of diabetes mellitus.
2 **Adrenal steroids**, primarily the glucocorticoids, are used for the relief of inflammation in such diseases as rheumatoid arthritis, lupus erythematosus, and nephritis; for immunosuppression after organ transplants; and for the relief of the stress symptoms of shock.
3 **Epinephrine** (adrenalin) has many uses, including stimulation of the heart muscle when rapid response is required; treatment of asthmatic attacks by relaxation of the muscles of the small bronchial tubes; and treatment of the acute allergic reaction called **anaphylaxis** (an″ah-fi-lak′sis).
4 **Thyroid extracts**, either mixtures or purified derivatives of thyroid hormones, are used in the treatment of hypothyroid conditions (cretinism and myxedema) and as replacement therapy following surgical removal of the thyroid gland.
5 **Oxytocin** is used to contract the uterine muscle.
6 **Androgens**, including testosterone and androsterone, are used in severe chronic illness to promote healing. They may be used to stimulate red blood cell production in chronic kidney failure.
7 **Oral contraceptives** (birth control pills; "the pill") contain estrogen and progesterone. They are highly effective in preventing pregnancy. Oc-

casionally they give rise to unpleasant side-effects, such as nausea. More rarely, they cause serious complications such as thrombophlebitis, embolism, and hypertension. Any woman taking birth control pills should have a medical examination every six months.

Hormones and Stress

Stress in the form of physical injury, disease, emotional anxiety, and even pleasure calls forth a specific response from the body that involves both the nervous system and the endocrine system. The nervous system response, the "fight-or-flight" response, is mediated by parts of the brain, especially the hypothalamus, and by the autonomic nervous system. The hypothalamus also triggers the release of ACTH from the anterior pituitary. The hormones released from the adrenal cortex as a result of stimulation by ACTH raise the blood sugar level, inhibit inflammation, decrease the immune response, and limit the release of histamine. GH, thyroid hormones, sex hormones, and insulin may also be released. These substances help the body meet stressful situations, but unchecked they are harmful to the body and may lead to such stress-related disorders as high blood pressure, heart disease, ulcers, back pain, and headaches.

Although no one would enjoy a life totally free of stress in the form of stimulation and challenge, unmanaged stress, or "distress," has negative effects on the body. For this reason, techniques such as biofeedback and meditation to control stress are useful. Simply setting priorities, getting adequate periods of relaxation, and getting regular physical exercise are important in maintaining total health.

Summary

I Hormones—chemical messengers carried in the blood
 A Categories
  1 Proteins and related compounds—usually act at cell surface
  2 Steroids—sex hormones and hormones of adrenal cortex; enter cell and affect DNA
 B Regulation

1 Negative feedback

2 Other hormones

3 Nervous stimulation

II Endocrine glands

A Pituitary

1 Anterior lobe hormones—growth hormone (GH), thyroid-stimulating hormone (TSH), adrenocorticotropic hormone (ACTH), follicle-stimulating hormone (FSH), luteinizing hormone (LH), prolactin (PRL)

2 Posterior lobe hormones—antidiuretic hormones (ADH), oxytocin

3 Pituitary tumors—may cause underactivity or overactivity of pituitary

B Thyroid

1 Hormones

a Thyroxin—influences cell metabolism

b Calcitonin—decreases blood calcium levels

2 Abnormalities

a Goiter—enlarged thyroid

b Hypothyroidism—causes cretinism or myxedema

c Hyperthyroidism—produces exophthalmic goiter

C Parathyroids—secrete parathyroid hormone (PTH), which increases blood calcium levels

D Adrenals

1 Structure

a Medulla—inner region

b Cortex—outer region

2 Hormones

a Medulla

(1) Epinephrine and norepinephrine—act as neurotransmitters

b Cortex

(1) Glucocorticoids—released during stress; example, cortisol

(2) Mineralocorticoids—regulate water and electrolyte balance; example, aldosterone

(3) Sex hormones—produced in small amounts

E Islet cells of pancreas—secrete insulin, which lowers blood glucose, and glucagon, which raises blood glucose

F Sex glands—needed for reproduction and development of secondary sex characteristics

1 Testes—secrete testosterone

2 Ovaries—secrete estrogen and progesterone

G Thymus—secretes thymosin, which aids in development of T-lymphocytes

H Pineal—secretes melatonin, which may regulate sexual development

III Other hormone–producing structures

A Stomach and small intestine—secrete hormones that regulate digestion

B Kidneys

1 Renin—raises blood pressure

2 Erythropoietin—increases production of red blood cells

C Placenta—secretes hormones that maintain pregnancy and prepare breasts for lactation

D Other—cells throughout body produce prostaglandins, which have varied effects

IV Hormones and treatment

A Insulin—treatment of diabetes mellitus

B Steroids—reduction of inflammation, suppression of immunity

C Epinephrine—treatment of asthma, anaphylaxis, shock

D Thyroid hormone—treatment of hypothyroidism

E Estrogen and progesterone—contraception

V Hormones and stress

Questions for Study and Review

1 Name some general functions of hormones.

2 Give three examples of protein hormones; of steroid hormones.

3 Why are certain cells the target tissue for a given hormone?

4 Name the two divisions of the pituitary and describe the effects of the hormones from each.

5 What type of system connects the anterior pituitary with the hypothalamus? What is carried to the pituitary by this system?

6 Where is the thyroid gland located? What is its main hormone, and what does it do?

7 What is the cause of simple goiter?

8 Describe the effects of hypothyroidism and hyperthyroidism.

9 Name and describe briefly four tests for thyroid function.

10 What is the main purpose of PTH? What are the effects of removal of the parathyroid glands? of excess secretion?

11 Name the two divisions of the adrenal glands and describe the effects of the hormones from each.

12 What are the results of hypofunction of the adrenal cortex?

13 What are the results of hyperfunction of the adrenal cortex? What common therapy produces similar symptoms?

14 What are the main purposes of insulin in the body? Name and describe the condition characterized by insufficient production of insulin.

15 Name the male and female sex hormones and briefly describe what each does.

16 What is the present status in research on the thymus and the pineal body?

17 What are some of the various functions that have been ascribed to prostaglandins?

18 Name three organs other than the endocrine glands that secrete hormones.

19 List several hormones that are released during stress.

12

The Blood

Behavioral Objectives

After careful study of this chapter, you should be able to:

List the functions of the blood

List the main ingredients in plasma

Name the three types of formed elements in the blood

Describe five types of leukocytes

Describe the formation of the blood cells and give the approximate lifespan of each type

Briefly describe the steps in blood clotting

Cite three steps in hemostasis

Define blood type and explain the effect of blood type on transfusions

List the reasons for transfusions of whole blood and blood components

Define anemia and list the causes of anemia

Define leukemia and name the two types of leukemia

Describe the tests used to study blood

Selected Key Terms

The following terms are defined in the glossary:

anemia
centrifuge
coagulation
erythrocyte
fibrin
hematocrit
hemogloblin
hemolysis
leukemia
leukocyte
plasma
platelet
serum
thrombocytopenia

Blood is classified as a connective tissue, since nearly half of it is made up of cells. However, it differs from other connective tissues in that its cells are not fixed in position; instead, they move freely in the liquid portion of the blood, the **plasma.**

Blood is a viscous (thick) fluid that varies in color from bright scarlet to dark red, depending on how much oxygen it is carrying. The quantity of circulating blood differs with the size of the person; the average adult male, weighing 70 kg (154 pounds) has about 5 liters (5.2 quarts) of blood. This volume accounts for about 8% of total body weight.

The blood is carried through a closed system of vessels pumped by the heart. The circulating blood is of fundamental importance in maintaining the internal environment in a constant state (homeostasis).

≡ Functions of the Blood

The circulating blood serves the body in three ways: transportation, regulation, and protection.

Transportation

1 Oxygen from inhaled air diffuses into the blood through the thin lung membranes and is carried to all the tissues of the body. Carbon dioxide, a waste product of cell metabolism, is carried from the tissues to the lungs, where it is breathed out.
2 The blood transports food and other needed substances, such as minerals and vitamins, to the cells. These materials may enter the blood from the digestive system or may be released into the blood from body stores.
3 The blood transports the waste products from the cells to the sites from which they are released. The kidney removes excess water, minerals, and urea from protein metabolism and maintains the acid–base balance of the blood. The liver removes bile pigments and drugs.
4 The blood carries hormones from their sites of origin to the organs they affect.

Regulation

1 Buffers in the blood help keep the pH of body fluids at about 7.4.
2 The blood serves to regulate the amount of fluid in the tissues by means of substances (mainly

proteins) that maintain the proper osmotic pressure.
3 The blood transports heat that is generated in the muscles to other parts of the body, thus aiding in the regulation of body temperature.

Protection

1 The blood carries the cells that are among the body's defenders against pathogens. It also contains substances (antibodies) that are concerned with immunity to disease.
2 The blood contains factors that protect against blood loss from the site of an injury.

≡ Blood Constituents

The blood is composed of two prime elements: as already mentioned, the liquid element is called *plasma*; the cells and fragments of cells are called **formed elements** or **corpuscles** (kor'pus-ls) (Fig. 12-1). The formed elements are classified as follows:

1 **Erythrocytes** (e-rith'ro-sites), from *erythro,* meaning "red," are the red blood cells, which transport oxygen.
2 **Leukocytes** (loo'ko-sites), from *leuko,* meaning "white," are the several types of white blood cells, which protect against infection.
3 **Platelets**, also called **thromboyctes** (throm'bo-sites), are cell fragments that participate in blood clotting.

Blood Plasma

Over half of the total volume of blood is plasma. The plasma itself is 90% water. Many different substances, dissolved or suspended in the water, make up the other 10%. The plasma content varies somewhat, since the substances carried by the blood to and from the organs get used and added to. However, the body tends to maintain a fairly constant level of these substances. For example, the level of glucose, a simple sugar, is maintained at a remarkably constant level of about one tenth of a 1% solution.

After water, the next largest percentage of material in the plasma is **protein.** Proteins are the principal constituents of cytoplasm and are essential to the growth and the rebuilding of body tissues. The plasma proteins include the following:

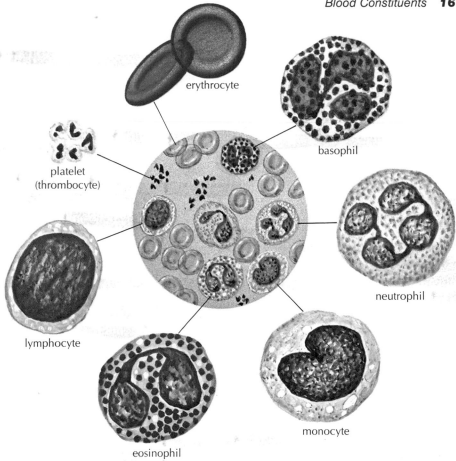

erythrocyte

basophil

platelet
(thrombocyte)

neutrophil

lymphocyte

monocyte

eosinophil

Figure 12-1. *Blood cells.*

1 **Albumin**, the most abundant protein in plasma, is important for maintaining the osmotic pressure of the blood. This protein is manufactured in the liver.
2 The **antibodies** combat infection.
3 The blood **clotting factors** are also manufactured in the liver.
4 A system of enzymes made of several proteins, collectively known as **complement**, helps antibodies in their fight against pathogens (see Chap. 16).

Nutrients are also found in the plasma. One group of nutrients is the **carbohydrates** (kar″bo-hi′drates). The principal form of carbohydrate found in the plasma is glucose, which is absorbed by the capillaries of the intestine following digestion. Glucose is stored mainly in the liver as glycogen and is released as needed to supply energy.

Amino acids, the products of protein digestion, are also found in the plasma. These are also absorbed into the blood through the intestinal capillaries.

Lipids constitute a small percentage of blood plasma. Lipids include fats. They may be stored as fat for reserve energy or carried to the cells as a source of energy.

The **mineral salts** in the plasma appear primarily as chloride, carbonate, or phosphate salts of sodium, potassium, calcium, and magnesium. These salts have a variety of functions, including the formation of bone (calcium and phosphorus), the production of hormones by certain glands (iodine for the production of thyroid hormone), the transportation of the gases oxygen and carbon dioxide (iron), and the maintenance of the acid–base balance (sodium and potassium carbonates and phosphates). Small amounts of other elements also help maintain homeostasis.

Many other materials, such as waste products and hormones, are also transported in the plasma.

The Formed Elements

Erythrocytes

Erythrocytes, the red cells, are tiny, disk-shaped bodies with a central area that is thinner than the edges. They are different from other cells in that the mature form found in the circulating blood does not have a nucleus. These cells, like almost all the blood cells, live a much shorter time than most other cells in the body, some of which last a lifetime. One purpose of the red cells is to carry oxygen from the lungs to the tissues. The oxygen is bound in the red cells to hemoglobin (he″mo-glo′bin), a protein that contains iron. Hemoglobin combined with oxygen gives the blood its characteristic red color. The more oxygen carried by the hemoglobin, the brighter is the red color of the blood. Therefore, the blood that goes from the lungs to the tissues is a bright red because it carries a great supply of oxygen; in contrast, the blood that returns to the lungs is a much darker red, since it has given up much of its oxygen to the tissues. Hemoglobin that has given up its oxygen is able to carry hydrogen ions; in this way, hemoglobin acts as a buffer and plays an important role in acid–base balance (see Chaps. 2 and 20). The red cells also carry a small amount of carbon dioxide from the tissues to the lungs for elimination in exhalation.

Carbon monoxide is a harmful gas that combines with hemoglobin to form a stable compound. It displaces the oxygen that is normally carried by the hemoglobin and reduces the oxygen-carrying ability of the blood. Carbon monoxide may be produced by incomplete burning of various fuels, such as gasoline, coal, wood, and other carbon-containing materials. It occurs also in automobile exhaust fumes and in cigarette smoke.

The erythrocytes are by far the most numerous of the corpuscles, averaging from 4.5 to 5 million per cubic millimeter of blood.

Leukocytes

The leukocytes, or white blood cells, are very different from the erythrocytes in appearance, quantity, and function. They contain nuclei of varying shapes and sizes; the cells themselves are round. Leukocytes are outnumbered by red cells by 700 to 1, numbering but 5,000 to 10,000 per cubic millimeter of blood.

Whereas the red cells have a definite color, the leukocytes tend to be colorless.

The different types of white cells are identified by their size, the shape of the nucleus, and the appearance of granules in the cytoplasm when the cells are stained, usually with Wright's blood stain. Granulocytes (gran′u-lo-sites″) include neutrophils (nu′trofils), which show lavender granules; eosinophils (e″o-sin′o-fils), which have beadlike, bright pink granules; and basophils (ba′so-fils), which have large, dark blue granules that often obscure the nucleus. The neutrophils are the most numerous of the white cells, constituting up to 60% of all leukocytes.

Because the nuclei of the neutrophils are of various shapes, they are also called polymorphs (meaning "many forms") or simply *polys*.

The agranulocytes, so named because they lack easily visible granules, are the lymphocytes and monocytes. The ratio of the different types of leukocytes is often a valuable clue in arriving at a diagnosis (see Fig. 12-1).

The most important function of leukocytes is to destroy pathogens. Whenever pathogens enter the tissues, as through a wound, certain white blood cells (neutrophils and monocytes) are attracted to that area. They leave the blood vessels and proceed by ameboid (ah-me′boid) or ameba-like motion to the area of infection. There they engulf the invaders by a process called phagocytosis (Fig. 12-2). If the pathogens are extremely virulent or numerous, they may destroy the leukocytes. A collection of dead and living bacteria, together with dead and living leukocytes, forms pus. A collection of pus localized in one area is known as an abscess.

The lymphocytes destroy foreign invaders by attacking the cells directly or by producing antibodies that circulate in the blood and help destroy the cells. They are part of the immune system described in Chapter 16.

Platelets

Of all the formed elements, the blood platelets (thrombocytes) are the smallest (see Fig. 12-1). These tiny structures are not cells in themselves, but fragments of cells. The number of platelets in the circulating blood has been estimated at 200,000 to 400,000 per cubic millimeter. Platelets are essential to blood coagulation (clotting). When, as a result of injury, blood comes in contact with any tissue other than the lining of the blood vessels, the platelets stick together

leukocyte   capillary   bacteria

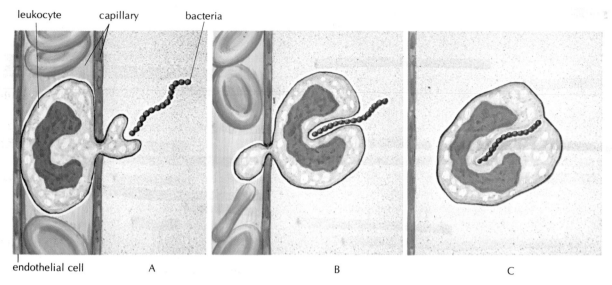

endothelial cell   A   B   C

Figure 12-2. (A) *A white blood cell squeezes through a capillary wall in the region of an infection.* (B and C) *The white cell engulfs the bacteria. This process, called* phagocytosis, *is a part of the body's mechanism for fighting infection.*

and form a plug that seals the wound. They then release chemicals that take part in a series of reactions that eventually results in the formation of a clot. The last step in these reactions is the conversion of a plasma protein called **fibrinogen** (fi-brin'o-jen) into solid threads of **fibrin**, which form the clot.

Origin of the Formed Elements

The erythrocytes, the platelets, and most of the leukocytes are formed in red bone marrow. In adults red marrow is found only in the ends of the long bones and in the flat bones: the ribs, sternum, vertebrae, and cranial and hip bones. In children the shafts of the long bones also contain active red marrow; however, by age 20 most of the marrow in the shafts has become inactive and is infiltrated with fat. This replacement of red marrow with fatty (yellow) marrow continues with age.

The ancestors of blood cells, called **stem cells**, are all formed in the red marrow. Each stem cell develops into one of the blood cell types within the red marrow. One group of white cells, the lymphocytes, develops to maturity in lymphoid tissue and can multiply in this tissue as well (see Chap. 15).

As already mentioned, when an invader enters the tissues, the leukocytes in the blood are attracted to the area. In addition, the bone marrow goes into emergency production, with the result that the number of leukocytes in the blood is enormously increased. Detection in a blood examination of an abnormally large number of white cells may thus be an indication of an infection.

The platelets are believed to originate in the red marrow as fragments of certain giant cells called **megakaryocytes** (meg"ah-kar'e-o-sites), which are formed in the red marrow. Platelets do not have nuclei or DNA, but they do contain active enzymes and mitochondria.

As has been noted, red cells as they normally appear in the bloodstream have no nuclei. However, when these cells are being formed in the red marrow, they do have nuclei. Each red cell must lose its nucleus before it is considered to be mature and ready for release into the bloodstream. Therefore, the finding of nucleated erythrocytes in a routine blood examination is a sign that the cells are being released too soon and is thus an indication of disease.

The life spans of the different types of blood cells vary considerably. For example, after leaving the bone marrow, erythrocytes circulate in the bloodstream for approximately 120 days. Leukocytes may appear in the circulating blood for only 6 to 8 hours. However, they may then enter the tissues, where they survive for longer periods of time—days, months, or even years. Blood platelets have a life span of about

10 days. In comparison with other tissue cells, those in the blood are very short lived. Thus, the need for constant replacement of blood cells means that normal activity of the red bone marrow is absolutely essential to life.

☰ Blood Clotting

Blood clotting, or coagulation, is a protective device that prevents blood loss when a blood vessel is ruptured by an injury. The many substances necessary for clotting are normally inactive in the blood stream. A balance is maintained between compounds that promote clotting, known as **procoagulants**, and those that prevent clotting, known as **anticoagulants**. In addition, there are also chemicals in the circulation that act to dissolve clots. Under normal conditions the substances that prevent clotting prevail. However, when an injury occurs, the procoagulants are activated and a clot is formed.

Basically, the clotting process consists of the following essential steps (Fig. 12-3):

1 The injured tissues release **thromboplastin** (throm-bo-plas′tin), a substance that triggers the clotting mechanism.
2 Thromboplastin reacts with certain protein factors and calcium ions to form **prothrombin** activator, which in turn reacts with calcium ions to convert the prothrombin to **thrombin**.
3 Thrombin, in turn, converts soluble fibrinogen into insoluble fibrin. **Fibrin** forms a network of threads that entraps red blood cells and platelets to form a clot.

Several methods are in use to measure the body's ability to coagulate blood. These are described later in this chapter.

Figure 12-3. *Formation of a clot.*

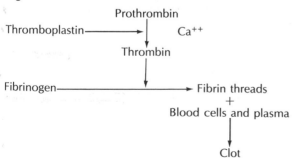

Hemostasis

Blood clotting is but one step in a series of events that serves to prevent blood loss. **Hemostasis** (he″mo-sta′sis) is the process that prevents the loss of blood from the circulation. Events in hemostasis include the following:

1 **Contraction** of the muscles in the wall of the blood vessel. This reduces the flow of blood and loss from the defect in the vessel wall.
2 Formation of a **platelet plug**. Activated platelets become sticky and adhere to the defect to form a temporary plug.
3 Formation of a **blood clot**.

☰ Blood Typing and Transfusions

Blood Groups

If for some reason the amount of blood in the body is severely reduced, through **hemorrhage** (hem′or-ij) (excessive bleeding) or disease, the body cells suffer from lack of oxygen and food. The obvious measure to take in such an emergency is to inject blood from another person into the veins of the patient, a procedure called **transfusion**.

The patient's plasma may contain substances, called **antibodies**, that can cause the red cells of the donor's blood to become clumped, a process called **agglutination** (ah-gloo-ti-na′shun). Alternatively, the donor's red blood cells may rupture and release their hemoglobin; such cells are said to be **hemolyzed** (he′mo-lized), and the resulting condition can be very dangerous.

These reactions are determined largely by certain proteins, called **antigens** (an′ti-gens), on the red cell membranes. There are many types of these proteins, but only two groups are particularly likely to cause a transfusion reaction, the so-called A and B antigens and the Rh factor. Four blood types involving the A and B antigens have been recognized: A, B, AB, and O. These letters indicate the type of antigen present on the red cells, with O indicating that neither A nor B antigen is present. It is these antigens on the donor's red cells that react with the antibodies in the patient's plasma and cause a transfusion reaction.

Blood serum containing antibodies that can agglutinate and destroy red cells that have A antigen on the surface is called **anti-A serum**; blood serum containing antibodies that can destroy red cells with B antigen on the surface is called **anti-B serum**. These sera are used to test for blood type (Fig. 12-4).

An individual's blood type is determined by heredity. The percentage of persons with each of the different blood types varies in different populations. About 45% of the white population of the United States is type O. Persons with type O blood are said to be **universal donors** because they lack the AB red cell antigens and in an emergency their blood can be given to anyone. Type AB individuals are called uni-

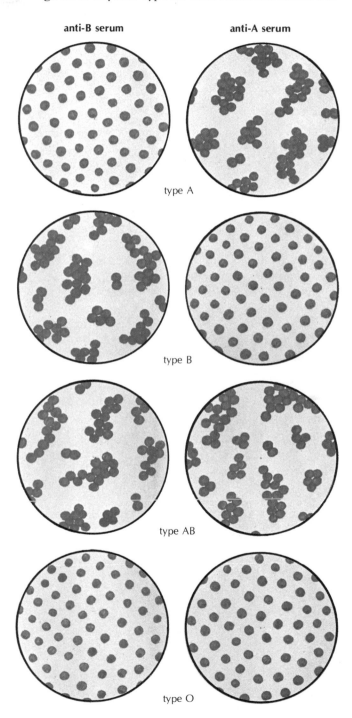

Figure 12-4. *Blood typing. Red cells in type A blood are agglutinated (clumped) by anti-A serum; those in type B blood are agglutinated by anti-B serum. Type AB blood cells are agglutinated by both sera, and type O blood is not agglutinated by either serum.*

versal recipients, since their blood contains no antibodies to agglutinate red cells and they can therefore receive blood from most donors (Table 12-1).

Usually a person can safely give blood to any person with the same blood type. However, because of other factors that may be present in the blood, determination of blood type must be accompanied by additional tests (cross matching) for compatibility before a transfusion is given.

The Rh Factor

About 85% of the white population of the United States has another red cell antigen group called the **Rh factor**. Such individuals are said to be **Rh positive**. About 15% lack this protein and are said to be **Rh negative**. If Rh-positive blood is given to an Rh-negative person, he or she may become sensitized to the protein in the Rh-positive blood. The sensitized person's blood cells may then produce antibodies to the "foreign" Rh antigens and destroy the transfused red cells.

A pregnant woman who is Rh negative may become sensitized by proteins from her Rh-positive fetus (this factor having been inherited from the father) if these proteins enter the mother's circulation before or during childbirth. During a subsequent pregnancy with an Rh-positive fetus, some of the anti-Rh antibodies may pass from the mother's blood into the blood of her fetus and cause destruction of the fetus's red cells. This condition is called **erythroblastosis fetalis** (e-rith″ro-blas-to′sis fe-ta′lis), or **hemolytic disease of the newborn**.

Erythroblastosis fetalis may be prevented by administration of immune globulin Rho (D), or Rho-GAM, to the mother shortly after delivery. This destroys the Rh-positive fetal cells in the mother's blood and prevents her sensitization.

Blood Banks

Blood can be packaged and kept in blood banks for emergencies. In order to keep the blood from clotting, a solution such as citrate–phosphate–dextrose–adenine (CPDA-1) is added. The blood may then be stored for up to 35 days. The supplies of blood in the bank are dated with an expiration date so that blood in which red cells may have disintegrated is not used. Blood banks usually have all types of blood available. However, it is important that there be a particularly large supply of type O, Rh-negative blood, since in an emergency this type can be used for any patient. As already mentioned, a patient's blood must be tested for compatibility with the donor's blood before any transfusion is begun.

☰ Uses of Blood and Blood Components

The transfer of whole human blood from a healthy person to a patient is often a lifesaving process. Blood transfusions may be used for any condition in which there is loss of a large volume of blood, for example

1 In the treatment of massive hemorrhage from serious mechanical injuries

2 For blood loss during internal bleeding, as from bleeding ulcers

3 For blood replacement in the treatment of erythroblastosis fetalis

4 During or after an operation that causes considerable blood loss.

Most often, when some ingredient of the blood is needed, it is not whole blood but a blood component that is given. Blood can be broken down into its various components, and the substances derived

Table 12-1   The ABO Blood Group System

Blood Type	Red Blood Cell Antigen	Reacts with Antiserum	Plasma Antibodies	Can Take From	Can Donate To
A	A	Anti-A	Anti-B	A, O	A, AB
B	B	Anti-B	Anti-A	B, O	B, AB
AB	A, B	Anti-A, anti-B	None	AB, A, B, O	AB
O	None	None	Anti-A, anti-B	O	O, A, B, AB

from it may be used for a number of purposes. One of the more common of these processes is separation of the blood plasma from the formed elements. This is accomplished by means of a **centrifuge** (sen'tre-fuge), a machine that spins in a circle at high speed to separate components of a mixture according to density. When a container of blood is spun rapidly, all the formed elements of the blood are pulled into a clump at the bottom of the container. They are thus separated from the plasma, which is less dense. The formed elements may be further separated and used for specific purposes. Blood losses to the donor can be minimized by removal of the blood, separation of the desired components, and return of the remainder to the donor. The general term for this procedure is **hemapheresis** (hem'ah-fer"e-sis). If the plasma is removed and the formed elements returned to the donor, the procedure is called **plasmapheresis** (plas"ma-fer'e-sis).

Blood plasma is a very useful substance; it may be given as an emergency measure to combat shock and replace blood volume. For storage, the water can be removed, leaving the solids, which keep in a dry state for a considerable length of time. Later, sterile distilled water may be added to reconstitute the plasma so it can be given to an injured person. Plasma is especially useful in situations in which blood typing and the use of whole blood are not possible, such as on battlefields or in mass disasters. Since the red cells have been removed from plasma, there are no incompatibility problems; plasma can be given to anyone. Plasma separated from the cellular elements can be further separated by chemical means into various components such as plasma protein fraction, serum albumin, and gamma globulin.

Fresh plasma may be frozen and saved. When frozen plasma is thawed, a white precipitate called **cryoprecipitate** (kri'o-pre-sip'i-tate) forms in the bottom of the container. Plasma frozen when it is less than 6 hours old and cryoprecipitate contain most of the factors needed for clotting and may be given when there is a special need for these factors.

Gamma globulin is a group of plasma proteins (antibodies) produced by lymphocytes when they come in contact with foreign agents such as pathogenic bacteria and viruses. They play an important role in the immune system (see Chap. 16). Gamma globulin is prepared commercially from pooled human serum and used to prevent or reduce the severity of measles, hepatitis, and pertussis, especially in infants and in persons who have been exposed to the disease and are in a debilitated (weakened) condition.

☰ Blood Disorders

Abnormalities involving the blood may be divided into three groups:

1 The **anemias** (ah-ne'me-ahs), a group of disorders in which there is an abnormally low level of hemoglobin, or red cells, in the blood and thus impaired delivery of oxygen to the tissues. Anemia may result from the following:

  a **Excessive loss or destruction of red blood cells.** This may occur with hemorrhage or with conditions that cause hemolysis, the rupture of red cells.

  b **Impaired production of red cells or hemoglobin.** Both nutritional deficiencies and suppression of bone marrow may cause anemia.

2 **Neoplastic diseases** of the blood and blood-forming organs. A neoplasm is a new growth of abnormal cells or tissues. Neoplastic diseases, which may be cancerous, include the **leukemias** (lu-ke'me-ahs), a group of disorders characterized by an increase in the number of white blood cells.

3 **Clotting disorders.** These disorders are characterized by an abnormal tendency of the body to bleed due to a breakdown in the body's clotting mechanism.

The Anemias

Anemia Due to Excessive Loss or Destruction of Red Cells

Excessive loss of red cells occurs with hemorrhage, which may be sudden and acute or gradual and chronic.

As we know, the average adult has about 5 liters of blood. If a person loses as much as 2 liters suddenly, death usually results. However, if the loss is gradual, over a period of weeks, or months, the body can compensate and withstand the loss of as much as 4 or 5 liters. If the cause of the chronic blood loss, such as bleeding ulcers, excessive menstrual flow, and bleeding hemorrhoids (piles), can be corrected, the body is usually able to restore the blood to normal. However, this process can take as long as 6 months, and until the blood returns to normal, the affected person may have anemia.

Anemia caused by the excessive destruction of red cells is called **hemolytic** (he-mo-li′tik) **anemia.** The spleen normally destroys old red blood cells. Occasionally, an overactive spleen destroys the cells too rapidly, causing anemia. Infections may also cause the loss of red blood cells. For example, the malarial parasite multiplies in red cells and destroys them, and certain bacteria, particularly streptococci, produce a toxin that causes hemolysis.

Certain inherited diseases that involve the production of abnormal hemoglobin may also result in hemolytic anemia. The hemoglobin in normal adult cells is of the A type and is designated *HbA*. In the inherited disease, **sickle cell anemia,** the hemoglobin in many of the red cells is abnormal. When these cells give up their oxygen to the tissues, they are transformed from the normal disk shape into a sickle shape (Fig. 12-5). These sickle cells are fragile and tend to break easily. Because of their odd shape, they also tend to become tangled in masses that can block smaller blood vessels. When obstruction occurs,

there may be severe joint swelling and pain, especially in the fingers and toes, as well as abdominal pain. This development is referred to as *sickle cell crisis.*

Sickle cell anemia is seen almost exclusively in black persons. About 8% of American blacks have one of the genes for the abnormal hemoglobin and are said to have the **sickle cell trait**. It is only when the involved gene is transmitted from both parents that the clinical disease appears. About 1% of American blacks have two of these genes and thus have **sickle cell disease**.

Anemia Due to Impaired Production of Red Cells or Hemoglobin

Many factors can interfere with normal red cell production. Some result from the deficiency of some nutrient; they are referred to as *nutritional anemias.* These conditions may arise from a deficiency of the specific nutrient in the diet, from an inability to absorb the nutrient, or from drugs that interfere with the body's use of the nutrient.

Figure 12-5. *Sickling of red blood cells in sickle cell anemia.*

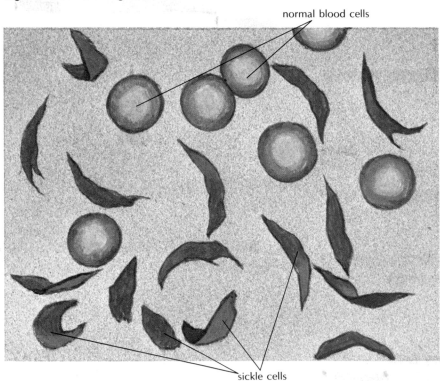

normal blood cells

sickle cells

Deficiency Anemias. The most common nutritional anemia is **iron deficiency anemia.** Iron is an essential constituent of hemoglobin. The average diet usually provides enough iron to meet the needs of the adult male, but this diet often is inadequate to meet the needs of growing children and women of childbearing age.

A diet deficient in proteins or vitamins can also result in anemia. Folic acid, one of the B complex vitamins, is necessary for the production of blood cells. Folic acid deficiency anemia occurs in alcoholics, in elderly person on poor diets, and in infants or others suffering from intestinal disorders that interfere with the absorption of this water-soluble vitamin.

Pernicious (per-nish′us) **anemia** is characterized by a deficiency of vitamin B_{12} a substance essential for the proper formation of red blood cells. The initial cause is a permanent deficiency of a factor in the gastric juice that is responsible for the absorption of vitamin B_{12} from the intestine. Neglected pernicious anemia can bring about deterioration in the nervous system, causing difficulty in walking, weakness and stiffness in the extremities, mental changes, and permanent damage to the spinal cord. Early treatment, including the intramuscular injection of vitamin B_{12} and attention to a prescribed diet, assures an excellent outlook. This treatment must be kept up for the rest of the patient's life if good health is to be maintained.

Bone Marrow Suppression. The decreased production of red blood cells may also be brought about by **bone marrow suppression** or failure. One type of bone marrow failure, **aplastic** (ay-plas′tick) **anemia,** may be caused by a variety of physical and chemical agents. Chemical substances that injure the bone marrow include benzene, arsenic, nitrogen mustard, gold compounds, and in some persons, prescribed drugs. Physical agents that may injure the marrow include x-rays, atomic radiation, radium, and radioactive phosphorus. The damaged bone marrow fails to produce either red or white cells, so that the anemia is accompanied by **leukopenia** (loo″ko-pe′ne-ah), a drop in the number of white cells. Removal of the toxic agent followed by blood transfusions until the marrow is able to resume its activity may result in recovery. Bone marrow transplants have also been successful.

A less severe depression of the bone marrow may develop in persons with certain chronic diseases, such as cancer, kidney or liver disorders, and rheumatoid arthritis.

Neoplastic Blood Disease

Neoplastic blood diseases are characterized by an enormous increase in the number of white cells owing to a cancer of the tissues that produce these cells. As noted, the white cells have two main sources: red marrow, also called *myeloid tissue,* and lymphoid tissue. If this wild proliferation of white cells stems from a tumor of the marrow, the condition is called **myelogenous** (mi-e-loj′e-nus) **leukemia.** When the cancer arises in the lymphoid tissue, so that the majority of abnormal cells are lymphocytes, the condition is called **lymphocytic leukemia.**

At present the cause of leukemia is unknown. Both inherent factors and various environmental agents have been implicated. Among the latter are chemicals such as benzene, x-rays, radioactive substances, and viruses.

Patients with leukemia exhibit the general symptoms of anemia. In addition, they have a tendency to bleed easily owing to a lack of platelets. The spleen is greatly enlarged, and several other organs may be increased in size because of the accumulation of white cells within them. Treatment consists of x-ray therapy along with drugs, but the disease is malignant and may thus be fatal. With new methods of chemotherapy, the outlook is improving, and many patients survive for years.

Clotting Disorders

A characteristic common to all clotting disorders is a disruption of the coagulation process bringing about abnormal bleeding. A rare but interesting example of a bleeding disorder is **hemophilia** (he-mo-fil′e-ah), an inherited disorder made famous by its occurrence in some of the royal families of Russia and Western Europe. Hemophilias are all characterized by a deficiency of certain clotting factors, so that any cut or bruise may cause serious abnormal bleeding. The deficient clotting factors are now available in concentrated form for treatment in case of injury, preparation for surgery, and painful bleeding into the joints, a frequent occurrence in hemophilia.

The most common cause of clotting disorders is a deficient number of circulating platelets (thrombocytes). The condition, called **thrombocytopenia** (throm"bo-si"to-pe'ne-ah), results in hemorrhages in the skin or mucous membranes. The decrease in the number of platelets may be due to decreased production or to increased destruction of the platelets. A number of causes have been suggested, including diseases of the red bone marrow, liver disorders, and various drug toxicities. When a drug is the cause of the disorder, its withdrawal leads to immediate recovery.

A serious disorder of clotting involving excessive coagulation is **disseminated intravascular coagulation (DIC)**. This disease occurs in cases of tissue damage due to massive burns, trauma, certain acute infections, cancer, and some disorders of childbirth. During the progress of DIC, platelets and various clotting factors are used up faster than they can be produced, and serious hemorrhaging may result.

Blood Studies

Many kinds of studies may be made of the blood, and some of these have become a standard part of a routine physical examination. Machines that are able to perform several tests at the same time have largely replaced manual procedures, particularly in large institutions.

The Hematocrit

The **hematocrit** (he-mat'o-krit), the volume percentage of red blood cells in whole blood, is determined by spinning of a blood sample in a high-speed centrifuge for 3 to 5 minutes. In this way the cellular elements are separated out from the plasma.

The hematocrit is expressed as the volume of red cells per unit volume (100 ml) of whole blood. For example, if a laboratory report states "hematocrit, 38%," that means that there are 38 ml red cells per 100 ml whole blood. In other words, 38% of the whole blood is red cells. For males, the normal range is 42 ml to 54 ml per 100 ml blood, whereas for females the range is slightly lower, 36 ml to 46 ml per 100 ml blood. These normal ranges, like all normal ranges for humans, may vary depending on the method used and the interpretation of the results by an individual laboratory. Hematocrit values much below or much above these figures point to an abnormality requiring further study.

Hemoglobin Tests

A sufficient amount of hemoglobin in red cells is required for adequate delivery of oxygen to the tissues. To measure this level, the hemoglobin is released from the red cells and a comparison made between the color of the blood and a known color scale. Hemoglobin is expressed in grams per 100 ml whole blood. Normal hemoglobin concentrations for adult males range from 14 g to 17 g per 100 ml blood. Values for adult females are in a somewhat lower range, at 12 g to 15 g per 100 ml blood. A decrease in hemoglobin indicates anemia.

Normal and abnormal types of hemoglobin can be separated and measured by the process of **electrophoresis** (e-lek"tro-fo-re'sis). In this procedure an electric current is passed through the liquid that contains the hemoglobin. This test is useful in the diagnosis of sickle cell anemia as well as of other disorders due to abnormal types of hemoglobin.

Blood Cell Counts

In most laboratories today, automatic counters such as the Coulter counter are used to count blood cells. In very small laboratories, a **hemocytometer** may be used (Fig. 12-6). The normal count for red blood cells varies from 4.5 to 5.5 million cells per cubic millimeter of blood. The leukocyte count varies from 5,000 to 10,000 cells per cubic millimeter of blood.

An increase in the red blood cell count is called **polycythemia** (pol"e-si-the'me-ah). This condition may be found in persons who live at high altitudes as well as persons with the disease polycythemia (pol"e-si-the'me-ah) **vera**.

In **leukopenia** the white count is below 5000 cells per cubic millimeter. This condition is indicative of depressed bone marrow or a neoplasm of the bone marrow. In **leukocytosis** (loo"ko-si-to'sis) the white blood count is in excess of 10,000 cells per cubic millimeter. This condition is characteristic of most bacterial infections. It may also occur after hemorrhage and in gout and uremia, a result of kidney disease.

It is difficult to count platelets directly because they are so small. More accurate counts can be obtained with automated methods. These counts are necessary for the evaluation of platelet loss (thrombocytopenia) such as occurs following radiation

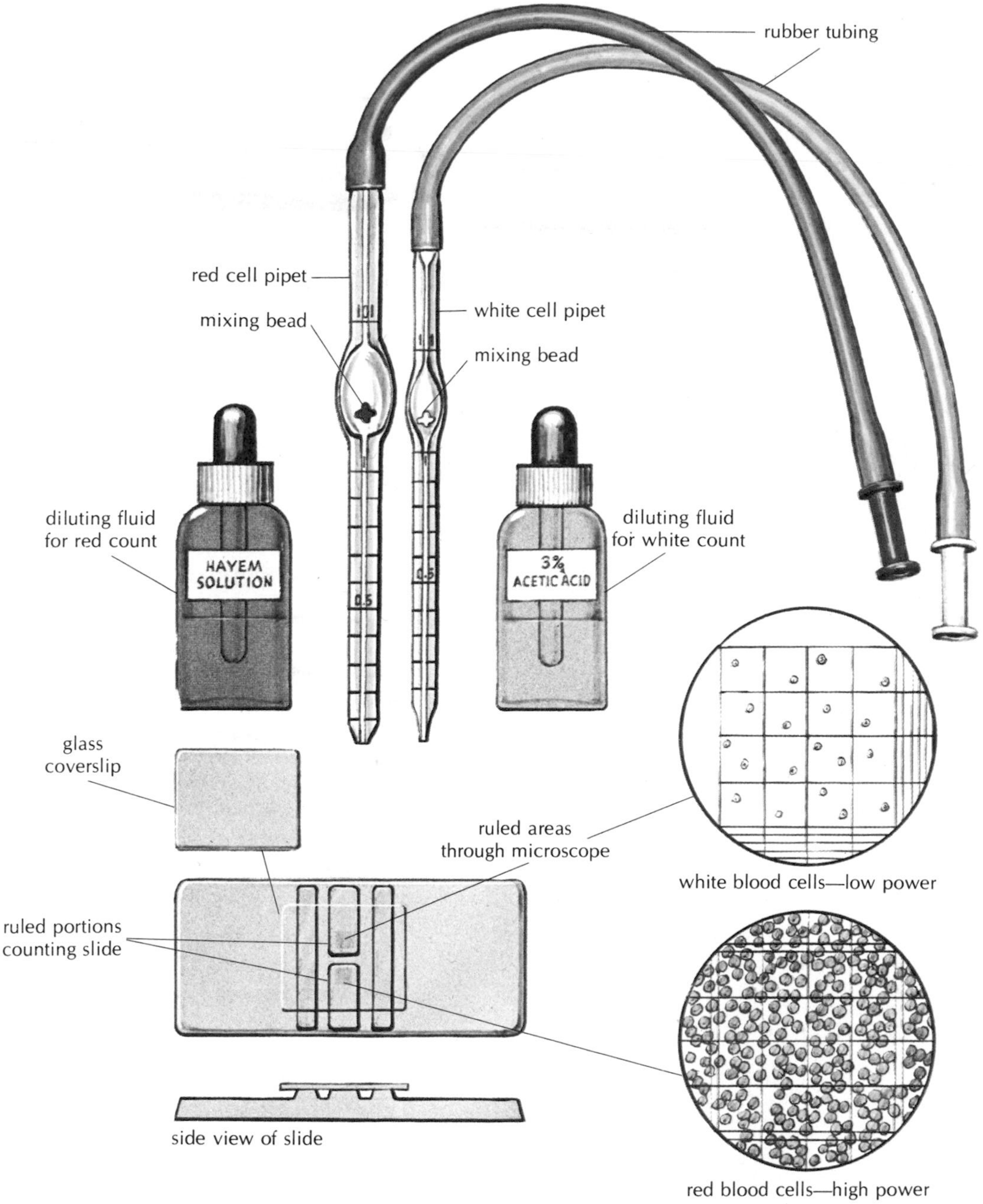

Figure 12-6. *Parts of a hemocytometer.*

therapy or cancer chemotherapy. The normal platelet count varies from 130,000 to 370,000 per cubic millimeter of blood, but counts may fall to half these values without causing serious bleeding problems. If a count is very low, a platelet transfusion may be given.

The Blood Slide (Smear)

In addition to the above tests, the **complete blood count (CBC)** includes the examination of a stained blood slide. In this procedure a drop of blood is spread very thinly and evenly over a glass slide and a special stain (Wright's) is applied to differentiate the otherwise colorless white cells. The slide is then studied under the microscope. Abnormalities in the cells may be observed and the number of platelets estimated. Parasites such as the malarial organism and others may be found. In addition, a **differential white count** is done. This is an estimation of the percentage of every type of white blood cell in the smear. Since each type of white blood cell has a specific function, changes in their proportions can be a valuable diagnostic aid.

Blood Chemistry Tests

Batteries of tests on blood serum are often done by machine. One, the Sequential Multiple Analyzer (SMA), provides for the running of some 12 or more tests per minute. Tests for electrolytes, such as sodium, potassium, chloride, and bicarbonate, as well as for blood glucose, blood urea nitrogen (BUN), and **creatinine** (kre-at′i-nin), another nitrogen waste product, may all be performed together.

Other tests check for enzymes. **Transaminase** (trans-am′i-nase) is an enzyme that may indicate tissue damage, such as that which may occur in heart disease. An excess of **alkaline phosphatase** (fos′fahtase) could indicate a liver disorder or metastatic cancer involving bone.

Blood can be tested for amounts of lipids (fats) such as cholesterol and triglycerides or for amounts of plasma proteins. Many of these tests help in evaluating disorders that may involve various vital organs. For example, the presence of more than the normal amount of glucose (sugar) dissolved in the blood, a condition called **hyperglycemia** (hi″per-gli″se′me-ah), is found most frequently in unregulated diabetic persons. Sometimes several evaluations of sugar content are done following the administration of a known amount of glucose. This procedure is called the **glucose tolerance test** and usually is given along with another test that determines the amount of sugar in the urine. This combination of tests can indicate faulty cell metabolism. The list of blood chemistry tests is extensive and is constantly increasing. We may now obtain values for various hormones, vitamins, the immune response, and toxic or therapeutic drug levels.

Coagulation Studies

Nature prevents the excessive loss of blood from small vessels by the formation of a clot. Preceding surgery and under some other circumstances, it is important to know that the time required for coagulation to take place is not long. Since clotting is a rather complex process involving many elements, a delay may be due to a number of different factors, including lack of certain hormone-like substances, calcium salts, and vitamin K.

The various clotting factors have each been designated by a Roman numeral, I through XIII. Factor I is fibrinogen, factor II is prothrombin, factor III is thromboplastin, and factor IV is assigned to calcium ions. The amounts of all 13 factors may be determined and evaluated on a percentage basis, aiding in the diagnosis and treatment of some bleeding disorders.

Additional tests for coagulation include tests for bleeding time, clotting time, capillary strength, and platelet function.

Bone Marrow Biopsy

A special needle is used to obtain a small sample of red marrow from the sternum, sacrum, or iliac crest in a procedure called a **bone marrow biopsy**. If marrow is taken from the sternum, the procedure may referred to as a **sternal puncture**. Examination of the cells by a trained person gives valuable information that can aid in the diagnosis of bone marrow disorders, including leukemia and certain kinds of anemia.

Summary

I Functions of blood

   A Transportation—of oxygen, carbon dioxide, food, minerals, vitamins, waste, hormones

   B Regulation—of *p*H, fluid balance, body temperature

   C Protection—against foreign organisms, blood loss

II Blood constituents

   A Plasma—liquid component

      1 Water—main ingredient

      2 Proteins—albumin, clotting factors, antibodies, complement

      3 Food—carbohydrates, lipids, amino acids

      4 Minerals

5 Waste products
6 Hormones and other materials

B Formed elements

  1 Erythrocytes—red blood cells

  2 Leukocytes—white blood cells

    a Granulocytes—neutrophils (polymorphs), eosinophils, basophils

    b Agranulocytes—lymphocytes, monocytes

  3 Platelets (thrombocytes)

III **Blood clotting**

  A Factors

    1 Procoagulants—promote clotting

    2 Anticoagulants—prevent clotting

  B Process—thromboplastin converts prothrombin to thrombin; thrombin converts fibrinogen to solid threads of fibrin; threads form clot

  C Hemostasis—prevention of blood loss

    1 Contraction of blood vessels

    2 Formation of platelet plug

    3 Formation of blood clot

IV **Blood typing**

  A AB antigens—result in A, B, AB, and O blood types

  B Rh antigens—positive or negative

V **Uses of blood and blood components**

  A Whole blood—used only to replace large blood losses

  B Formed elements—separated by centrifugation

  C Plasma

    1 Protein fractions

    2 Cryoprecipitate—obtained by freezing; contains clotting factors

    3 Gamma globulin—contains antibodies

VI **Blood disorders**

  A Anemia—lack of hemoglobin

    1 Loss of cells

    2 Destruction of cells

    3 Impaired production of cells

      a Deficiency anemia

      b Pernicious anemia

      c Bone marrow suppression

  B Leukemia—excess production of white cells

    1 Myelogenous leukemia—cancer of bone marrow

    2 Lymphocytic leukemia—cancer of lymphoid tissue

  C Clotting disorders

    1 Hemophilia—lack of clotting factors

    2 Thrombocytopenia—lack of platelets

    3 Disseminated intravascular coagulation (DIC)

VII **Blood studies**

  A Hematocrit—measures percentage of packed red cells in whole blood

  B Hemoglobin tests—color test, electrophoresis

  C Blood cell counts

  D Blood slide (smear)

  E Blood chemistry tests—electrolytes, waste products, enzymes, glucose, hormones

  F Coagulation studies—clotting factor assays, bleeding time, clotting time, capillary strength, platelet function

  G Bone marrow biopsy

Questions for Study and Review

1 How does the color of blood vary with the amount of oxygenation?

2 Name the three main purposes of blood.

3 Name the two prime components of blood.

4 Name and describe the three main groups of cellular structures in blood.

5 Name four main ingredients of blood plasma. What are their purposes?

6 What is the main function of erythrocytes? leukocytes? platelets? Where do they originate?

7 What are the names usually given to the four main blood groups? What determines the different groupings?

8 What is the Rh factor? What proportion of the white population of the United States possesses this factor? In what situations is this factor of medical importance? Why?

9 Describe the three basic steps involved in the clotting process.

10 Define *hemostasis*. Describe the three main steps in hemostasis.

11 What are the advantages of blood banks? Are there any disadvantages? If so, what are they, and how might they be counteracted?

12 What are some of the conditions for which blood transfusions are useful?

13 What precautions should always be taken before a transfusion is given?

14 What blood components may be useful in the treatment of the sick, and in what way is each of these blood derivatives used?

15 Name the three general categories of blood disorders.

16 Differentiate among the types of anemia and give an example of each.

17 Name two kinds of leukemia. What is the chief symptom of leukemia, and what is the reason for it?

18 Name the main characteristics of clotting disorders and give an example of these.

19 What is the value of the hematocrit?

20 Differentiate between leukopenia and leukocytosis. What are some of the conditions that are due to abnormal white counts?

21 What can be learned by studying the blood smear? What is determined by a differential white count?

22 What are some evaluations made by blood chemistry tests?

23 What can be determined by a bone marrow biopsy?

13

The Heart and Heart Disease

Behavioral Objectives

After careful study of this chapter, you should be able to:

Describe the three layers of the heart

Name the four chambers of the heart

Name the valves at the entrance and exit of each ventricle

Briefly describe blood circulation through the myocardium

Name the components of the heart's conduction system

Briefly describe the cardiac cycle

Explain what produces the two main heart sounds

List and define several terms that describe different heart rates

Describe several common types of heart disease

List six areas that might contribute to the prevention of heart disease

Briefly describe five instruments used in the study of the heart

Describe three aproaches to the treatment of heart disease

Selected Key Terms

The following terms are defined in the glossary:

arrhythmia
atrium
coronary
diastole
echocardiograph
electrocardiograph
endocardium
epicardium
infarct
ischemia
murmur
myocardium
pacemaker
pericardium
septum
stenosis
systole
thrombus
valve
ventricle

≡ Circulation and the Heart

The next two chapters investigate the manner in which the blood acquires its food and oxygen to be delivered to the cells and disposes of the waste products of cell metabolism. This continuous one-way movement of the blood is known as its **circulation**. The fact that blood circulates throughout the body means that there must be some sort of propelling mechanism, the prime mover in this case being the **heart**. We shall have a look at the heart before going into the subject of the circulatory vessels in any detail.

The heart is a muscular pump that drives the blood through the blood vessels. Slightly bigger than a fist, this organ is located between the lungs in the center and a bit to the left of the midline of the body. The strokes (contractions) of this pump average about 72 per minute and are carried on unceasingly for the whole of a lifetime.

The importance of the heart has been recognized for centuries. The fact that its rate of beating is affected by the emotions may be responsible for the very frequent references to the heart in song and poetry. However, the vital functions of the heart and its disorders are of more practical importance to us.

≡ Structure of the Heart

Layers of the Heart Wall

The heart is a hollow organ the walls of which are formed of three different layers. Just as a warm coat might have a smooth lining, a thick and bulky interlining, and an outer layer of a third fabric, so the heart wall has three tissue layers (Fig. 13-1).

1. The **endocardium** (en″do-kar′de-um) is a very thin smooth layer of cells that resembles squamous epithelium. This membrane lines the interior of the heart. The valves of the heart are formed by reinforced folds of this material.
2. The **myocardium** (mi″o-kar′de-um), the muscle of the heart, is the thickest layer.
3. The **epicardium** (ep″i-kar′de-um) forms the thin outermost layer of the heart wall and is continuous with the serous lining of the fibrous sac that encloses the heart. These membranes together make up the **pericardium** (per″i-kar′de-um). The serous lining of the pericardial sac is separated from the epicardium on the heart surface by a thin fluid-filled space.

Two Hearts and a Partition

Physicians often refer to the *right heart* and the *left heart*. This is because the human heart is really a double pump. The two sides are completely separated from each other by a partition called the **septum**. The upper part of this partition is called the **interatrial** (in″ter-a′tre-al) **septum**, while the larger lower portion is called the **interventricular** (in″ter-ven-trik′u-lar) **septum**. The septum, like the heart wall, consists largely of myocardium.

Four Chambers

On either side of the heart are two chambers, one a receiving chamber (atrium) and the other a pumping chamber (ventricle):

1. The **right atrium** is a thin-walled chamber that receives the blood returning from the body tissues. This blood, which is low in oxygen, is carried in the **veins**, the blood vessels leading *to* the heart from the body tissues.
2. The **right ventricle** pumps the venous blood received from the right atrium and sends it to the lungs.
3. The **left atrium** receives blood high in oxygen content as it returns from the lungs.
4. The **left ventricle**, which has the thickest walls of all, pumps oxygenated blood to all parts of the body. This blood goes through the **arteries**, the vessels that take blood *from* the heart to the tissues.

Four Valves

Since the ventricles are the pumping chambers, the valves, which are all one way, are located at the entrance and the exit of each ventricle. The entrance valves are the **atrioventricular** (a″tre-o-ven-trik′u-lar) **valves**, while the exit valves are the **semilunar** (sem″e-lu′nar) **valves**. *Semilunar* means "resembling a half-moon." Each valve has a specific name, as follows:

1. The **right atrioventricular valve** also is known as the **tricuspid** (tri-kus′pid) **valve**, since it has

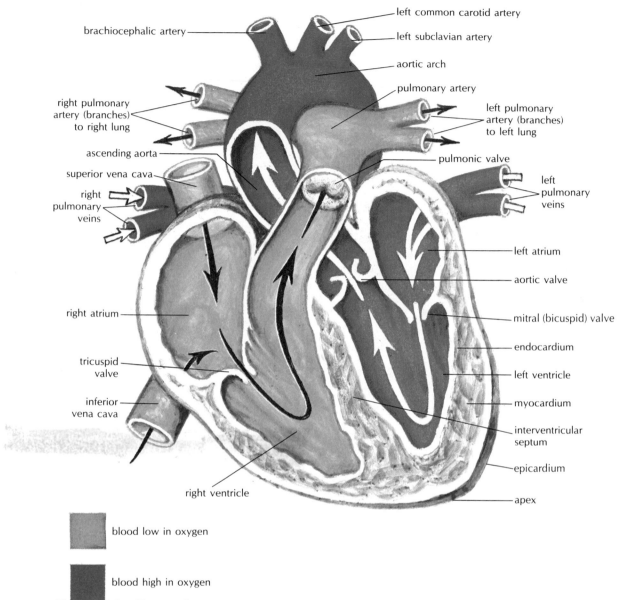

brachiocephalic artery

left common carotid artery

left subclavian artery

aortic arch

pulmonary artery

right pulmonary artery (branches) to right lung

left pulmonary artery (branches) to left lung

ascending aorta

superior vena cava

right pulmonary veins

pulmonic valve

left pulmonary veins

left atrium

aortic valve

right atrium

mitral (bicuspid) valve

endocardium

tricuspid valve

left ventricle

inferior vena cava

myocardium

interventricular septum

epicardium

right ventricle

apex

blood low in oxygen

blood high in oxygen

Figure 13-1. *Heart and great vessels.*

three cusps, or flaps, that open and close. When this valve is open, blood flows freely from the right atrium into the right ventricle. However, when the right ventricle begins to contract, the valve closes so that blood cannot return to the right atrium; this ensures forward flow into the pulmonary artery.

2 The **left atrioventricular valve** is the bicuspid valve, but it is usually referred to as the **mitral** (mi'tral) **valve**. It has two rather heavy cusps that permit blood to flow freely from the left atrium into the left ventricle. However, the cusps close when the left ventricle begins to contract; this prevents blood from returning to the left atrium and ensures the forward flow of blood into the **aorta** (a-or′tah). Both the tricuspid and mitral valves are attached by means of thin fibrous threads to the walls of the ventricles. The function of these threads, called the **chordae tendineae** (see Fig. 13-5), is to keep the valve flaps from flipping up into the atria when the ventricles contract and thus causing a backflow of blood.

3 The **pulmonic** (pul′mo-nik) (semilunar) **valve** is located between the right ventricle and the pulmonary artery that leads to the lungs. As soon as the right ventricle has finished emptying itself, the valve closes in order to prevent blood on its way to the lungs from returning to the ventricle.

4 The **aortic** (a-or′-tik) (semilunar) **valve** is located between the left ventricle and the aorta. Following contraction of the left ventricle, the aortic valve closes to prevent the flow of blood back from the aorta to the ventricle.

The appearance of the heart valves in the closed position is illustrated in Figure 13-2.

Blood Supply to the Myocardium

Although blood flows through the heart chambers, only the endocardium comes into contact with it. Therefore, the myocardium must have its own blood vessels to provide oxygen and nourishment and to remove waste products. The arteries that supply blood to the muscle of the heart are called the **right** and **left coronary arteries** (Fig. 13-3). These arteries, which are the first branches of the aorta, arise just above the aortic semilunar valve (see Fig. 13-2). They

receive blood when the heart relaxes. After passing through capillaries in the myocardium, blood drains into the cardiac veins and finally into the coronary (venous) sinus for return to the right atrium.

≡ Physiology of the Heart

The Work of the Heart

Although the right and left sides of the heart are separated from each other, they work together. The blood is squeezed through the chambers by a contraction of heart muscle beginning in the thin-walled upper chambers, the atria, followed by a contraction of the thick muscle of the lower chambers, the ventricles. This active phase is called **systole** (sis′to-le), and in each case it is followed by a resting period known as **diastole** (di-as′to-le). The contraction of the walls of the atria is completed at the time the contraction of the ventricles begins. Thus, the resting phase (diastole) begins in the atria at the same time as the contraction (systole) begins in the ventricles. After the ventricles have emptied, both chambers are relaxed for a short period of time as they fill with blood. Then another beat begins with contraction of the atria followed by contraction of the ventricles. This sequence of heart relaxation and contraction is called the **cardiac cycle**. Each cycle takes an average of 0.8 seconds (Fig. 13-4).

Cardiac muscle tissue has several unique properties. One of these is the interconnection of the muscle fibers. (see Fig. 4-4). The fibers are interwoven so the stimulation that causes the contraction of one fiber results in the contraction of the whole group.

Figure 13-2. *Valves of the heart, seen from above, in the closed position.*

aortic (semilunar) valve

tricuspid valve

mitral valve

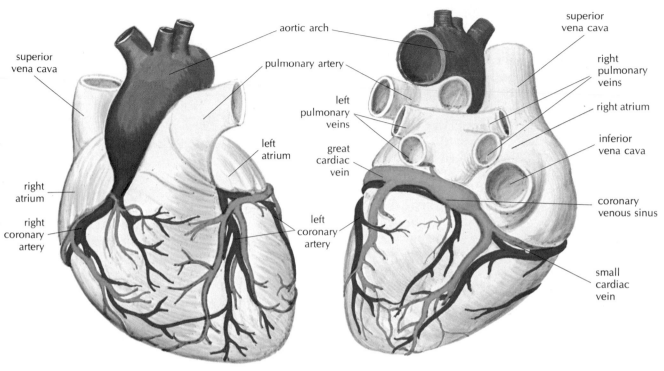

Figure 13-3.   *Coronary arteries and cardiac veins.* (Left) *Anterior view.* (Right) *Posterior view.*

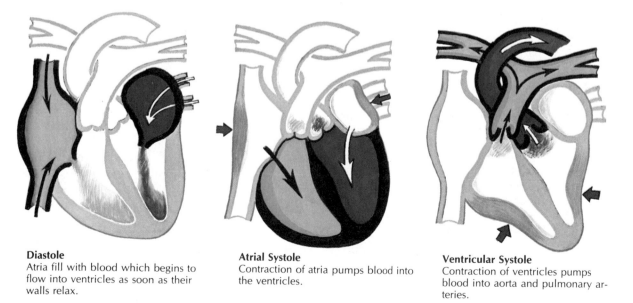

Diastole
Atria fill with blood which begins to flow into ventricles as soon as their walls relax.

Atrial Systole
Contraction of atria pumps blood into the ventricles.

Ventricular Systole
Contraction of ventricles pumps blood into aorta and pulmonary arteries.

Figure 13-4.   *Pumping cycle of the heart.*

This plays an important role in the process of conduction and the working of the heart muscle.

Another property of heart muscle is its ability to adjust contraction strength to the amount of blood received. When the heart chamber is filled and the wall stretched (within limits), the contraction is strong. As less blood enters the heart, the contraction becomes weaker. As more blood enters the heart, as occurs during exercise, the muscle contracts with greater strength to push the larger volume of blood out into the blood vessels.

The volume of blood pumped by each ventricle in 1 minute is termed the **cardiac output**. It is determined by the volume of blood ejected from the ventricle with each beat—the **stroke volume**—and the number of beats of the heart per minute—the **heart rate**. The cardiac output averages 5 liters/minute for an adult at rest.

The Conduction System of the Heart

The cardiac cycle is regulated by specialized areas in the heart wall that form the conduction system of the heart. Two of these areas are tissue masses called **nodes**; the third is a group of fibers called the **atrioventricular bundle**. The **sinoatrial node**, which is located in the upper wall of the right atrium and initiates the heartbeat, is called the **pacemaker**. The second node, located in the interatrial septum at the bottom of the right atrium, is called the **atrioventricular node**. The **atrioventricular bundle**, also known as the **bundle of His**, is located at the top of the interventricular septum; it has branches that extend to all parts of the ventricle walls. Fibers travel first down both sides of the interventricular septum in groups called the **right** and **left bundle branches**. Smaller **Purkinje** (pur-kin′jee) **fibers** then travel in a branching network throughout the myocardium of the ventricles (Fig. 13-5). The order in which the impulses travel is as follows:

1   The sinoatrial node generates the electric impulse that begins the heartbeat.
2   The excitation wave travels throughout the muscle of each atrium, causing it to contract.
3   The atrioventricular node is stimulated. The relatively slower conduction through this node allows time for the atria to contract and complete the filling of the ventricles.
4   The excitation wave travels rapidly through the bundle of His and then throughout the ventricular walls by means of the bundle branches and Purkinje fibers. The entire musculature of the ventricles contracts practically at once.

As a safety measure, a region of the conduction system other than the sinoatrial node can generate a heartbeat if the sinoatrial node fails, but it does so at a slower rate.

Control of the Heart Rate

Although the fundamental beat of the heart originates within the heart itself, the heart rate can be influenced by the nervous system and by other factors in the internal environment. Recall from Chapter 9 that stimulation from the sympathetic nervous system increases the heart rate and that stimulation from the parasympathetic nervous system decreases the heart rate. These influences allow the heart to meet changing needs rapidly. The heart rate is also affected by such factors as hormones, ions, and drugs in the blood.

Heart Rates

1   **Bradycardia** (brad″e-kar′de-ah) is a relatively slow heart rate of less than 60 beats/minute. During rest and sleep, the heart may beat less than 60 beats/minute but usually does not fall below 50 beats/minute.
2   **Tachycardia** (tak″e-kar′de-ah) refers to a heart rate over 100 beats/minute.
3   **Sinus arrhythmia** (ah-rith′me-ah) is a regular variation in heart rate due to changes in the rate and depth of breathing. It is a normal phenomenon.
4   **Premature beats**, also called *extrasystoles* are beats that come in before the expected normal beats. They may occur in normal persons initiated by caffeine, nicotine, or psychologic stresses. They are also common in persons with heart disease.

Heart Sounds and Murmurs

The normal heart sounds are usually described by the syllables "lubb" and "dupp." The first is a longer, lower-pitched sound that occurs at the start of ventricular systole. It is probably caused by a combination of things, including closure of the atrioventricular valves. The second, or "dupp," sound is

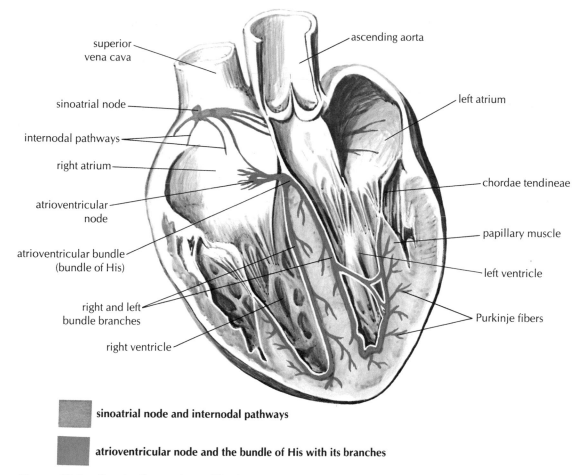

superior vena cava

ascending aorta

sinoatrial node

left atrium

internodal pathways

right atrium

chordae tendineae

atrioventricular node

papillary muscle

atrioventricular bundle (bundle of His)

left ventricle

right and left bundle branches

Purkinje fibers

right ventricle

■ sinoatrial node and internodal pathways

■ atrioventricular node and the bundle of His with its branches

Figure 13-5. *Conduction system of the heart.*

shorter and sharper. It occurs at the beginning of ventricular relaxation and is due in large part to sudden closure of the semilunar valves. Some abnormal sounds called **murmurs**, are usually due to faulty action of the valves. For example, if the valves fail to close tightly and blood leaks back, a murmur is heard. Another condition giving rise to an abnormal sound is the narrowing (stenosis) of a valve opening. The many conditions that can cause abnormal heart sounds include congenital defects, disease, and physiological variations. A murmur due to rapid filling of the ventricles is called a **functional**, or **flow, murmur**; such a murmur is not abnormal. An abnormal sound caused by any structural change in the heart or the vessels connected with the heart is called an **organic murmur**.

☰ Heart Disease

Classification of Heart Disease

There are many ways of classifying heart disease. The anatomy of the heart forms the basis for one grouping of heart pathology:

1 **Endocarditis** (en″do-kar-di′tis) means "inflammation of the lining of the heart cavities," but it most commonly refers to valvular disease.
2 **Myocarditis** (mi″o-kar-di′tis) is inflammation of heart muscle.
3 **Pericarditis** (per″i-kar-di′tis) refers to disease of the serous membrane on the heart surface, as well as that lining the pericardial sac.

These inflammatory diseases are often due to infection. They may also occur secondary to respiratory or other systemic diseases.

Another classification of heart disease is based on causative factors:

1 **Congenital** heart disease is present at birth.
2 **Rheumatic** heart disease begins with an attack of rheumatic fever in childhood or in youth.
3 **Coronary** (kor′o-na-re) heart disease involves the walls of the blood vessels that supply the muscle of the heart.
4 **Heart failure** is due to deterioration of the heart tissues and is frequently the result of disorders of long duration such as high blood pressure.

Congenital Heart Disease

Congenital heart diseases include certain abnormalities that have been present since birth; they usually represent a failure of normal development.

The most common congenital heart defects are holes in the septum between the left and right sides of the heart. Blood flow from one side of the heart to the other results in a mixture of deoxygenated and oxygenated blood being pumped to the tissues. This defect may be in the interatrial or interventricular septum.

The circulation of the fetus differs in several respects from that of the child after birth, one difference being that the lungs are not used until the child is born. Before birth the nonfunctional lungs are bypassed by a blood vessel (ductus arteriosus) that normally closes of its own accord once the lungs are in use. Sometimes, however, the vessel fails to close, with the result that much blood is detoured around the lungs instead of through them and therefore does not receive enough oxygen.

Coarctation (ko″ark-ta′shun) of the aorta, a localized narrowing of the arch of the aorta, is often accompanied by other congenital defects. The aortic and pulmonary valves may be hardened and narrowed, a condition called **stenosis** (ste-no′sis).

Another congenital heart defect is an obstruction or narrowing of the pulmonary artery that prevents the blood from passing in sufficient quantity from the right ventricle to the lungs.

The so-called blue baby is often suffering from congenital heart disease. The blueness, or **cyanosis** (si″ah-no′sis), of the skin and mucous membranes is caused by a relative lack of oxygen. (See Chap. 17 for other causes.)

In recent years many congenital defects have been remedied by heart surgery, one of the more spectacular advances in modern medicine.

Rheumatic Fever and the Heart

Streptococcal infections are indirectly responsible for rheumatic fever and rheumatic heart disease. The toxin produced by the streptococci causes an immune reaction that may be followed some 2 to 4 weeks later by rheumatic fever with marked swelling of the joints. Then the antibodies formed to combat the toxin attack the heart valves, producing a condition known as *rheumatic endocarditis*. The heart valves, particularly the mitral valve, become inflamed, and the normally flexible valve cusps thicken and harden so they do not open sufficiently (mitral stenosis) or close effectively (mitral regurgitation). Either condition interferes with the flow of blood from the left atrium into the left ventricle, causing pulmonary congestion, an important characteristic of mitral heart disease. The incidence of rheumatic fever and hence of rheumatic heart disease is being drastically reduced owing to increasingly prompt and effective antibiotic and other medical treatment of streptococcal infections.

Coronary Heart Disease

The heart muscle receives its own blood supply through the coronary arteries. A common cause of sudden death, or at least disability, from heart disease is **coronary occlusion** (o-kloo′shun), that is, closure of one or more branches of the coronary arteries. The result is **ischemia** (is-kee′me-ah), a lack of blood supply to the areas fed by those arteries. Such interference with the blood supply results in damage to the myocardium. The degree of injury sustained depends on a number of factors, including the size of the involved artery and whether the occlusion is gradual or sudden.

Arteries of the heart as well as the rest of the body can undergo degenerative changes. It may happen that the lumen (space) inside the vessel narrows gradually owing to progressive thickening and hardening of the arteries. As a consequence of this, the volume of blood supplied to the heart muscle is reduced and the action of the heart weakened. Degenerative changes of the artery wall may cause the inside surface to become roughened as well. This roughened artery wall is highly conducive to the formation of a **thrombus** (throm'bus), or blood clot. The thrombus may cause sudden closure of the vessel with complete obstruction of the blood flow, a life-threatening condition known as **coronary thrombosis**. The area that has been cut off from its blood supply is called an **infarct** (in'farkt). The outcome of a myocardial infarction depends on the extent of the damage and whether other branches of the artery can supply enough blood to maintain the heart's action. Death may occur swiftly if a large area of heart muscle is suddenly deprived of blood supply. If a smaller area is involved, the heart may continue to function. However, complete and prolonged lack of blood to any part of the myocardium results in death of tissue and weakening of the heart wall. In some cases the weakened area ruptures but in most cases a scar forms in the area of the infarct.

The person who suffers an acute coronary occlusion must be put on complete bed rest for a variable period of time, depending on the severity of the attack and on the time required for the damaged heart muscle to be replaced by scar tissue. During this period the most meticulous medical and nursing care is required.

Although myocardial infarction is one of the leading causes of death in the United States, prompt and effective treatment enables many individuals to survive a "heart attack," or "coronary." Despite heart damage, a person can usually lead a fairly normal life so long as he or she exercises moderately, gets sufficient rest, follows a prescribed diet, and tries to minimize stressful situations.

Inadequate blood flow to the heart muscle results in a characteristic discomfort, felt in the region of the heart and in the left arm and the shoulder, called **angina pectoris** (an-ji'nah pek'to-ris). Severe angina pectoris may be accompanied by a feeling of suffocation and a general sensation of forthcoming doom. Coronary artery disease is a common cause of angina pectoris, although the condition has other causes as well.

Abnormalities of Heart Rhythm

Myocardial infarction commonly results in an abnormality in the rhythm of the heartbeat, or **arrhythmia** (ah-rith'mē-ah). Extremely rapid but coordinated contractions, numbering up to 300 per minute, are described as a **flutter**. Rapid, wild, and uncoordinated contractions of the heart muscle are called **fibrillations**. Fibrillations begin as small, local contractions of a few cells followed by multiple areas of contraction of cells within the muscle wall. They usually affect only the atria but may also involve the ventricles. Fibrillations are a very serious cardiac disorder requiring first aid procedures, including cardiopulmonary resuscitation (CPR) and transfer by a paramedical unit to a hospital.

An interruption of electric impulses in the conduction system of the heart is called **heart block**. The seriousness of this condition depends on how completely the impulses are blocked. It may result in independent beating of the chambers if the ventricles respond to a second pacemaker.

Heart Failure

During a person's lifetime many toxins, infections, and other kinds of injuries may cause weakening of the heart muscle. Over a period of years high blood pressure, known as **hypertension** (hi″per-ten'shun), may cause an enlargement of the heart and finally heart failure (see Chap. 14). Malnutrition, chronic infections, and severe anemias may cause degeneration of the heart muscle. Hyperthyroidism, with its tendency to cause overactivity of all parts of the body, including the heart, is another cause of heart failure. Although heredity may be responsible for undue susceptibility to degenerative heart disease, poor health habits and various illnesses may cause damage to the heart.

The Heart in the Elderly

As a result of accumulated damage, the heart may become less efficient with age. On the average, by the age of 70 there has been a decrease in cardiac output of about 35%. Because of a decrease in the reserve strength of the heart, elderly persons are often limited in their ability to respond to emergencies, infections, blood loss, or stress. A disorder known as **Adams–Stokes syndrome**, which is characterized by periodic loss of consciousness because of heart block, is most common in the elderly.

☰ Prevention of Heart Ailments

Although there may not be complete agreement on any set of rules for preventing or delaying the onset of heart disease, many authorities concur on the following:

1 Proper nutrition, including all the basic food elements, will help maintain all tissues in optimum condition. Amounts of fats, especially animal fats, and sugar in the diet should be limited. Foods high in fiber, such as whole grains, fruits, and vegetables, should be included in the diet. Total food intake should be reduced if necessary to prevent obesity.

2 Infections should be avoided as much as possible. Mild infections should be treated to prevent serious complications from developing. Dental care should include the treatment of abscesses and the cleaning and filling of decayed teeth.

3 Temperate habits and adequate rest are desirable. Persons who wish to avoid heart disease need to avoid the use of tobacco, as well as excesses of alcohol and food. On the basis of numerous studies, it appears that smokers are 10 times more likely to die of coronary heart disease than are nonsmokers. Emotional upsets and psychologic upheavals may not be conducive to maintaining a healthy heart. Playing too hard is just as damaging as working too hard.

4 Regular physical examinations are important, particularly for elderly persons and persons who have had symptoms that suggest the presence of disease.

5 About 20% of adults in the United States suffer from hypertension. One of the serious problems of hypertension is that it usually produces no symptoms until damage to vital structures has already occurred. Blood pressure should be checked regularly, and treatment should be given if the readings are abnormal. If modification of diet, weight control, and exercise programs are unsuccessful, treatment with medication may be needed.

6 Appropriate exercise programs are an important part of prevention as well as of the treatment of heart disease. Regular exercise programs, with gradual increases in the length and difficulty of activity, have been found to be very helpful. To begin with, simple walking may be most effective, followed by such activities as swimming, bicycling, and jogging. Aerobic dancing or other vigorous exercises, in which the person increases the heart rate and oxygen demand as well as getting recreation, are now used in some physical therapy programs.

Instruments Used in Heart Studies

The **stethoscope** (steth′o-skope) is a relatively simple instrument used for conveying sounds from within the patient's body to the ear of the examiner. Experienced listeners can gain much information using this device.

The **electrocardiograph** (**ECG** or **EKG**) is used for making records of the changes in electric currents produced by the contracting heart muscle. It may thus reveal certain myocardial injuries. Electric activity is picked up by electrodes placed on the surface of the skin and appears as **waves** on the ECG tracing. The P wave represents the activity of the atria; the QRS and T waves represent the activity of the ventricles (Fig. 13-6). Changes in the waves and the intervals between them are used to diagnose heart damage and arrhythmias.

The **fluoroscope** (floor′o-scope), an instrument for examining deep structures with x-rays, may be used to reveal heart action as well as to establish the sizes and relationships of some of the thoracic organs. It may be used in conjunction with **catheterization** (kath″e-ter-i-za′shun) of the heart. In right heart catheterization, an extremely thin tube (catheter) is passed through the veins of the right arm or right groin and then into the right side of heart. During the procedure, the fluoroscope is used for observation of the route taken by the catheter. The tube is passed all the way through the pulmonary valve into the large lung arteries. Samples of blood are obtained along the way and removed for testing, pressure readings being taken meanwhile.

In left heart catheterization, a catheter is passed through an artery in the left groin or arm to the heart. Dye can then be injected into the coronary arteries. The tube may also be passed through the aortic valve into the left ventricle for further studies.

Ultrasound consists of sound waves generated at a frequency above the range of sensitivity of the human ear. In **echocardiography** (ek″o-kar″de-og′rah-fe), also known as *ultrasound cardiography,* high-frequency sound waves are sent to the heart from a small instrument on the surface of the chest. The ultrasound waves bounce off the heart and are recorded as they return, showing the heart in action. Movement of the echoes is traced on an electronic instrument called an *oscilloscope* and recorded on

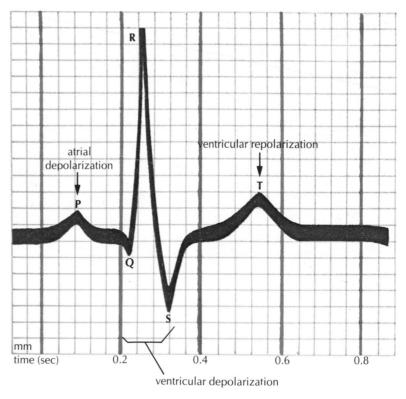

Figure 13-6. *Normal ECG showing one cardiac cycle.*

film. (The same principle is employed by submarines to detect ships.) The method is totally safe and painless, and it does not use x-rays. It provides information on the sizes and shapes of heart structures, on cardiac function, and on possible heart defects.

≡ Treatment of Heart Disease

Medications

One of the oldest and still the most important drug for many heart patients is **digitalis** (dij″i-tal′is). This agent, which slows and strengthens contractions of the heart muscle, is obtained from the leaf of the foxglove, a plant originally found growing wild in many parts of Europe. Foxglove is now cultivated to ensure a steady supply of digitalis for medical purposes.

Several forms of **nitroglycerin** are used to relieve angina pectoris. This drug dilates (widens) the vessels in the coronary circulation and improves the blood supply to the heart.

Beta-adrenergic blocking agents (*i.e.,* propranolol) control sympathetic stimulation of the heart. They reduce the rate and strength of heart contractions, thus reducing the heart's oxygen demand.

Antiarrhythmic agents (*i.e.,* quinidine) are used to regulate the rate and rhythm of the heartbeat.

Slow channel calcium blockers function by dilating vessels, controlling the force of heart contractions, or regulating conduction through the atrioventricular node to aid in the treatment of coronary heart disease and hypertension. Their actions are based on the fact that calcium ions must enter muscle cells before contraction can occur.

Anticoagulants (an″ti-ko-ag′u-lants) also are valuable drugs for heart patients. They may be used to prevent clot formation in persons with damage to heart valves or blood vessels or in persons who have had a myocardial infarction.

Artificial Pacemakers

Electric, battery-operated pacemakers that supply impulses to regulate the heartbeat have been implanted under the skin of many thousands of individuals. The site of implantation is usually in the left chest area. Electrode catheters attached to the pacemaker are then passed into the heart and anchored to the chest wall. The frequency of battery pack replacement varies with the type of pacemaker. Many people whose hearts cannot beat effectively alone have been saved by this rather simple device. In an emergency, a similar stimulus can be supplied to the heart muscle through electrodes placed externally on the chest wall.

Heart Surgery

The heart–lung machine has made possible many operations on the heart and other thoracic organs that otherwise could not have been done. There are several types of machines in use, all of which serve as temporary substitutes for the patient's heart and lungs.

The machine siphons off the blood from the large vessels entering the heart on the right side so that no blood passes through the heart and lungs. While passing through the machine, the blood is oxygenated by means of an oxygen inlet, and carbon dioxide is removed by various chemical means. These are the processes that normally take place between the blood and the air in the lung tissue. While in the machine, the blood is also "defoamed," or rid of air bubbles, since such bubbles could be fatal to the patient by obstructing blood vessels. An electric motor in the machine serves as a pump during the surgical procedure to return the processed blood to the general circulation by way of a large artery.

Coronary bypass surgery to relieve obstruction in the coronary arteries is a common and often successful treatment. While the damaged coronary arteries remain in place, healthy segments of blood vessels from other parts of the patient's body are inserted in such a way that blood bypasses whatever obstruction exists in the coronary arteries. Usually parts of the saphenous vein (a superficial vein in the leg) are used. Sometimes as many as six or seven segments are required to provide an adequate blood supply if the coronary vessels are seriously damaged. The mortality associated with this operation is low. Most patients are able to return to a nearly normal life-style following recovery from the surgery.

Diseased valves may become so deformed and scarred from endocarditis that they are ineffective and often obstructive. In most cases there is so much damage that valve replacement is the best treatment. Substitute valves made of plastic materials have proved to be a lifesaving measure for many patients. Very thin butterfly valves made of Dacron or other synthetic material have been successfully used, as have animal valves, such as pig valves.

Recently, the various news media have given considerable attention to the surgical transplantation of human hearts and sometimes of lungs and hearts together. Tissues of the recently deceased donor and of the recipient should be as closely matched as possible to avoid rejection (see Chap. 16). Even more attention has been given to the implantation of artificial hearts. These efforts at replacing defective human hearts are still in an experimental stage.

Summary

I Structure of the heart
  A Layers
    1 Endocardium—thin inner layer
    2 Myocardium—thick muscle layer
    3 Epicardium—thin outer layer
  B Pericardium—membrane that encloses the heart
  C Chambers
    1 Atria—left and right receiving chambers
    2 Ventricles—left and right pumping chambers
    3 Septa—partitions between chambers
  D Valves—prevent backflow of blood
    1 Tricuspid—right atrioventricular valve
    2 Mitral (bicuspid)—left atrioventricular valve
    3 Pulmonic (semilunar) valve—at entrance to pulmonary artery
    4 Aortic (semilunar) valve—at entrance to aorta
  E Blood supply to myocardium
    1 Coronary arteries—first branches of aorta; fill when heart relaxes
    2 Coronary sinus—collects venous blood from heart and empties into right atrium

II Physiology of the heart
  A Cardiac cycle
    1 Diastole—relaxation phase
    2 Systole—contraction phase

B Cardiac output—volume pumped by each ventricle per minute
  1 Stroke volume—amount pumped with each beat
  2 Heart rate—number of beats per minute
C Conduction system
  1 Sinoatrial node—pacemaker—at top of right atrium
  2 Atrioventricular node—between atria and ventricles
  3 Atrioventricular bundle (bundle of His)—branches into right and left bundle branches on either side of septum
D Heart rates—controlled by internal and external factors
  1 Bradycardia—slower rate than normal; less than 60 beats/minute
  2 Tachycardia—faster rate than normal; more than 100 beats/minute
  3 Extrasystole—premature beat
E Heart sounds
  1 Normal
    a "Lubb"—occurs at closing of atrioventricular valves
    b "Dupp"—occurs at closing of semilunar valves
  2 Abnormal—murmur

III Heart disease
A Anatomic classification
  1 Endocarditis
  2 Myocarditis
  3 Pericarditis
B Causal classification
  1 Congenital heart diseases—present at birth
    a Holes in septum
    b Failure of fetal lung bypasses to close
    c Coarctation of aorta
    d Pulmonary artery obstruction
  2 Rheumatic heart disease
    a Mitral stenosis—valve cusps don't open
    b Mitral regurgitation—valve cusps don't close
  3 Coronary heart disease
    a Coronary occlusion—closure of coronary arteries, as by a thrombus
    b Ischemia results—lack of blood to area fed by occluded arteries
    c Infarct—area of damaged tissue
    d Arrhythmia—abnormal rhythm
      (1) Flutter—rapid, coordinated beats
      (2) Fibrillation—rapid, uncoordinated contractions of heart muscle
      (3) Heart block—interruption of electric conduction
    e Angina pectoris—pain caused by lack of blood to heart muscle
  4 Heart failure—due to hypertension, disease, malnutrition, anemia, age

IV **Prevention of heart ailments**—proper diet, avoidance of infections, temperate habits, physical examinations, control of hypertension, exercise

V **Instruments used in heart studies**
A Stethoscope—used to listen to heart sounds
B Electrocardiograph (ECG)—records electric activity as waves
C Fluoroscope—examines deep tissue with x-rays
D Catheter—thin tube inserted into heart for blood samples, pressure readings, etc.
E Echocardiograph—uses ultrasound to record picture of heart in action

VI **Treatment of heart disease**
A Medications—digitalis, nitroglycerin, beta-adrenergic blocking agents, antiarrhythmic agents, slow channel calcium blockers, anticoagulants
B Artificial pacemakers—electronic devices implanted under skin to regulate heartbeat
C Surgery
  1 Bypass—other vessels inserted to augment blood supply for damaged vessels
  2 Valve replacement
  3 Heart transplants, artificial hearts—experimental

Questions for Study and Review

1 What are the three layers of the heart wall?
2 Name the sac around the heart.
3 What is a partition in the heart called? Name two.
4 Name the chambers of the heart and tell what each does.
5 Name the valves of the heart and explain the purpose of each valve.

6 Why does the myocardium need its own blood supply? Name the arteries that supply blood to the heart.

7 Explain *systole* and *diastole* and tell how these phases are related to each other in the four chambers of the heart.

8 How does the heart's ability to contract differ from that of other muscles? What is required to maintain an effective rate of heartbeat?

9 What are the parts of the heart's conduction system called and where are these structures located? Outline the order in which the excitation waves travel.

10 What two syllables are used to indicate normal heart sounds, and at what time in the heart cycle can they be heard?

11 Distinguish between *tachycardia* and *bradycardia*.

12 Define *cardiac output*. What determines cardiac output?

13 Inflammation of the heart structures is the basis for a classification of heart pathology. List the three terms in this classification and explain each.

14 What is meant by *congenital heart disease*? Give an example.

15 What part does infection play in rheumatic heart disease?

16 What type of heart disease is the most frequent cause of sudden death?

17 What is the effect of a thrombus in an artery supplying the heart wall? What are some of the precautions that need to be taken by a person recovering from thrombosis?

18 What are some of the factors that contribute to heart failure?

19 What are some rules that may delay or avoid the onset of heart ailments?

20 What is a fluoroscope and what is its purpose in heart studies?

21 Of what value is heart catheterization and how is it carried out?

22 What is an electrocardiograph and what is its purpose?

23 How does echocardiography differ from electrocardiography?

24 How does digitalis help a person who has heart muscle damage?

25 What are artificial heart valves made of and how valuable are they?

26 What is the purpose of coronary bypass surgery?

27 Why are artificial pacemakers used?

14

Blood Vessels and Blood Circulation

Behavioral Objectives

After careful study of this chapter, you should be able to:

Differentiate among the three main types of vessels in the body with regard to structure and function

Compare the locations and functions of the pulmonary and systemic circuits

Describe the three coats of the blood vessels

Name the four sections of the aorta

Name the main branches of the aorta

Define venous sinus and give four examples

Name the main vessels that drain into the superior and inferior venae cavae

Describe the structure and function of the hepatic portal system

Explain how materials are exchanged across the capillary wall

Describe the effects of vasodilation and vasoconstriction on blood distribution

Define pulse and list factors that affect the pulse rate

Explain how blood pressure is commonly measured

List some disorders that involve the blood vessels

List four types of shock

Selected Key Terms

The following terms are defined in the glossary:

anastomosis
aorta
arteriole
arteriosclerosis
artery
atherosclerosis
capillary
embolus
endothelium
hypertension
hypotension
phlebitis
pulse
shock
sinusoid
sphygmomanometer
vasoconstriction
vasodilation
vein
vena cava
venous sinus
venule

The vascular system will be easier to understand if you refer to the appropriate illustrations in this chapter as the vessels are described. If this information is added to what you already know about the blood and the heart, a picture of the circulatory system as a whole will emerge.

Blood Vessels

Functional Classification

The blood vessels, together with the four chambers of the heart, form a closed system for the flow of blood; only if there is an injury to some part of the wall of this system does any blood excape. On the basis of function, blood vessels may be divided into three groups:

1 **Arteries** carry blood from the ventricles (pumping chambers) of the heart out to the capillaries in organs and tissues. The smallest arteries are called **arterioles** (ar-te′re-olz).
2 **Veins** drain capillaries in the tissues and organs and return the blood to the heart. The smallest veins are the **venules** (ven′ulz).
3 **Capillaries** allow for exchanges between the blood and body cells, or between the blood and air in the lung tissues. The capillaries connect the arterioles and venules.

All the vessels together may be subdivided into two groups or circuits: pulmonary and systemic.

1 **Pulmonary vessels** carry blood to and from the lungs. They include the pulmonary artery and its branches to the capillaries in the lungs, as well as the veins that drain those capillaries. The pulmonary arteries carry blood low in oxygen from the right ventricle, while the pulmonary veins carry blood high in oxygen from the lungs into the left atrium (Fig. 14-1). This circuit functions to eliminate carbon dioxide from the blood and replenish its supply of oxygen.
2 **Systemic** (sis-tem′ik) arteries and veins serve the rest of the body. This circuit supplies food and oxygen to all the tissues and carries away waste materials from the tissues for disposal.

Structure

Artery Walls

The arteries have thick walls because they must receive blood pumped under pressure from the ventri-cles of the heart. The three coats (tunics) of the arteries resemble the three tissue layers of the heart:

1 The innermost membrane of simple, flat epithelial cells making up the **endothelium** forms a smooth surface over which the blood may easily move.
2 The second, more bulky layer is made of smooth (involuntary) muscle combined with elastic connective tissue.
3 An outer tunic is made of a supporting connective tissue.

The largest artery, the **aorta**, is about 2.5 cm (1 inch) in diameter and has the thickest wall because it receives blood under the highest pressure from the left ventricle. The smallest subdivisions of arteries, the arterioles, have thinner walls in which there is very little elastic connective tissue but relatively more smooth muscle.

Capillary Walls

The microscopic branches of these tiny connecting vessels have the thinnest walls of any vessels: one cell layer. The capillary walls are transparent and are made of smooth, platelike cells that continue from the lining of the arteries. Because of the thinness of these walls, exchanges between the blood and the body cells are possible. The capillary boundaries are the most important center of activity for the entire circulatory system. Their function is explained later in this chapter.

Vein Walls

The smallest veins, the *venules,* are formed by the union of capillaries, and their walls are only slightly thicker than those of the capillaries. As veins become larger, their walls become thicker. However, the walls of veins are much thinner than the walls of arteries of a comparable size, and the blood within them is carried under much lower pressure. Although there are three layers of tissue in the walls of the larger veins, as in the artery walls, the middle tunic is relatively thin in vein walls. Therefore, veins are easily collapsed, and only slight pressure on a vein by a tumor or other mass may interfere with return blood flow. Most veins are equipped with one-way valves that permit blood to flow in only one direction, toward the heart. Such valves are most numerous in the veins of the extremities (Fig. 14-2).

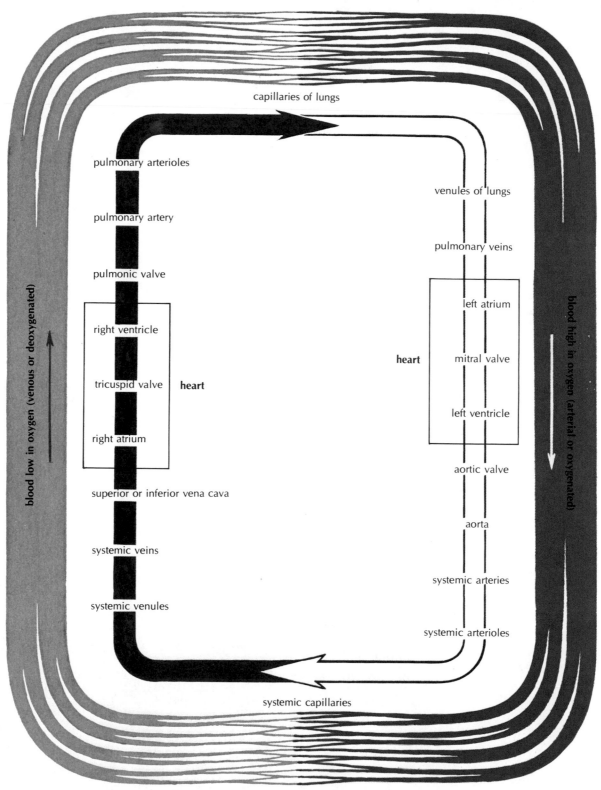

Figure 14-1. *Blood vessels constitute a closed system for the flow of blood. Note that changes in oxygen content occur as blood flows through the capillaries.*

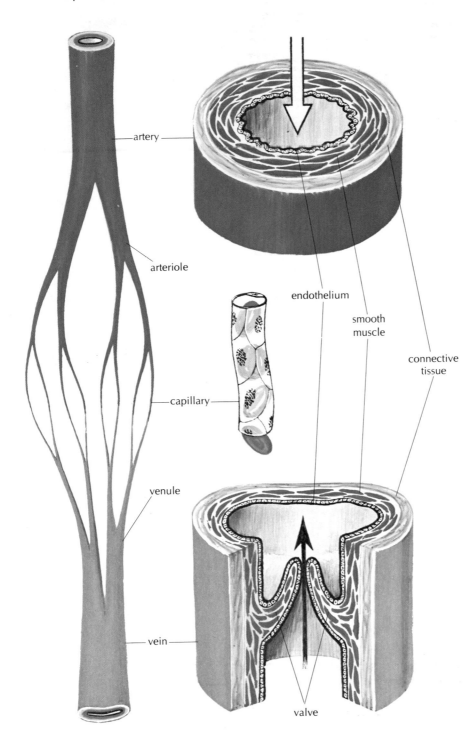

artery

arteriole

endothelium

smooth
muscle

connective
tissue

capillary

venule

vein

valve

Figure 14-2. *Sections of small blood vessels showing the thick arterial walls and the thin walls of veins and capillaries. Venous valves also are shown. The arrows indicate the direction of blood flow.*

☰ Names of Systemic Arteries

The Aorta and Its Parts

The aorta extends upward and to the right from the left ventricle. Then it curves backward and to the left. It continues down behind the heart just in front of the vertebral column, through the diaphragm, and into the abdomen (Figs. 14-3 and 14-4). The aorta is one continuous artery, but it may be divided into sections:

1 The **ascending aorta** is near the heart and inside the pericardial sac.
2 The **aortic arch** curves from the right to the left and also extends backward.
3 The **thoracic** (tho-ras′ik) **aorta** lies just in front of the vertebral column behind the heart and in the space behind the pleura.
4 The **abdominal aorta** is the longest section of the aorta, spanning the abdominal cavity.

The thoracic and abdominal aorta together make up the descending aorta.

Branches of the Ascending Aorta

The first, or ascending, part of the aorta has two branches near the heart, called the **left** and **right coronary arteries**, that supply the heart muscle. These form a crown around the base of the heart and give off branches to all parts of the myocardium.

Branches of the Aortic Arch

The arch of the aorta, located immediately beyond the ascending aorta, gives off three large branches.

1 The **brachiocephalic** (brak″e-o-se-fal′ik) **trunk** is a short artery formerly called the *innominate*. Its name means that it supplies the head and the arm. After extending upward somewhat less than 5 cm (2 inches), it divides into the **right subclavian** (sub-kla′ve-an) **artery**, which supplies the right upper extremity (arm), and the **right common carotid** (kah-rot′id) **artery**, which supplies the right side of the head and the neck.
2 The **left common carotid artery** extends upward from the highest part of the aortic arch. It supplies the left side of the neck and the head.
3 The **left subclavian artery** extends under the left collar bone (clavicle) and supplies the left upper extremity. This is the last branch of the aortic arch.

Branches of the Thoracic Aorta

The third part of the aorta supplies branches to the chest wall, to the esophagus (e-sof′ah-gus), and to the bronchi (the subdivisions of the trachea) and their treelike subdivisions in the lungs. There are usually nine to ten pairs of **intercostal** (in-ter-kos′tal) **arteries** that extend between the ribs, sending branches to the muscles and other structures of the chest wall.

Branches of the Abdominal Aorta

As in the case of the thoracic aorta, there are unpaired branches extending forward and paired arteries extending toward the side. The unpaired vessels are large arteries that supply the abdominal viscera. The most important of these visceral branches are listed below:

1 The **celiac** (se′le-ak) **trunk** is a short artery about 1.25 cm (½ inch) long that subdivides into three branches: the **left gastric artery** goes to the stomach, the **splenic** (splen′ik) **artery** goes to the spleen, and the **hepatic** (he-pat′ik) **artery** carries oxygenated blood to the liver.
2 The **superior mesenteric** (mes′en-ter′ik) **artery**, the largest of these branches, carries blood to most of the small intestine as well as to the first half of the large intestine.
3 The much smaller **inferior mesenteric artery**, located below the superior mesenteric and near the end of the abdominal aorta, supplies the second half of the large intestine.

The lateral (paired) branches of the abdominal aorta include the following right and left divisions:

1 The **phrenic** (fren′ik) **arteries** supply the diaphragm.
2 The **suprarenal** (su-prah-re′nal) **arteries** supply the adrenal (suprarenal) glands.
3 The **renal** (re′nal) **arteries**, the largest in this group, carry blood to the kidneys.
4 The **ovarian arteries** in the female and **testicular** (tes-tik′u-lar) **arteries** in the male (formerly called the *spermatic arteries*), supply the sex glands.
5 Four pairs of **lumbar** (lum′bar) **arteries** extend into the musculature of the abdominal wall.

(*Text continues on page 202*)

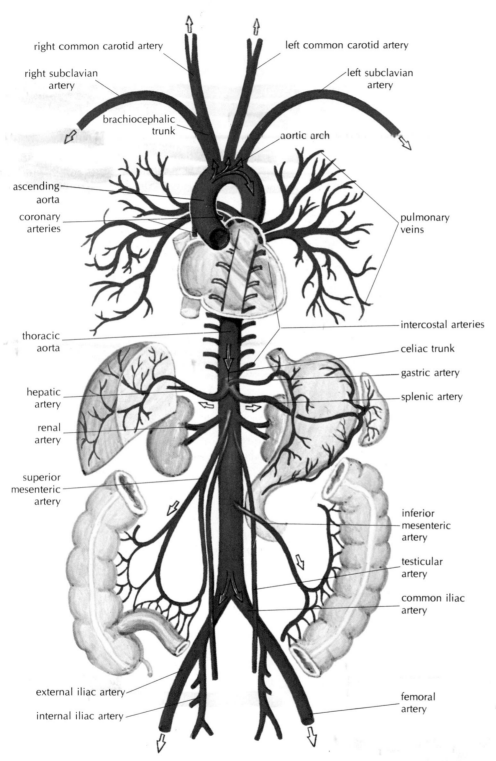

right common carotid artery

left common carotid artery

right subclavian artery

left subclavian artery

brachiocephalic trunk

aortic arch

ascending aorta

coronary arteries

pulmonary veins

thoracic aorta

intercostal arteries

celiac trunk

gastric artery

splenic artery

hepatic artery

renal artery

superior mesenteric artery

inferior mesenteric artery

testicular artery

common iliac artery

external iliac artery

internal iliac artery

femoral artery

Figure 14-3. *Aorta and its branches. The arrows indicate the flow of blood. The pulmonary veins carry oxygenated blood from the lungs to the left atrium of the heart.*

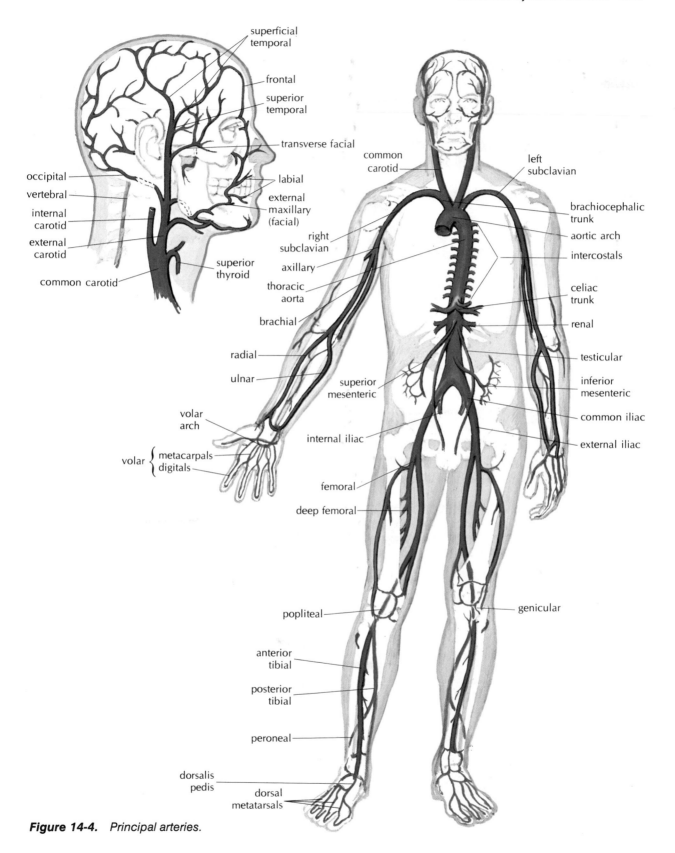

Figure 14-4. *Principal arteries.*

Iliac Arteries and Their Subdivisions

The abdominal aorta finally divides into two **common iliac arteries**. Both of these vessels, about 5 cm (2 inches) long, extend into the pelvis, where each one subdivides into an **internal** and an **external iliac artery**. The internal iliac vessels then send branches to the pelvic organs, including the urinary bladder, the rectum, and some of the reproductive organs. The external iliac arteries continue into the thigh as the **femoral** (fem′or-al) **arteries**. These vessels give off branches in the thigh and then become the **popliteal** (pop-lit′e-al) **arteries**, which subdivide below the knee. The subdivisions include the **tibial arteries** and the **dorsalis pedis** (dor-sa′lis pc′dis), which supply the leg and the foot.

Other Subdivisions of Systemic Arteries

Just as the larger branches of a tree give off limbs of varying sizes, so the arterial tree has a multitude of subdivisions. Hundreds of names might be included, but we shall mention only a few. For example, each common carotid artery gives off branches to the thyroid gland and other structures in the neck before dividing into the **external** and **internal carotid arteries**, which supply parts of the head. The hand receives blood from the subclavian artery, which becomes the **axillary** (ak′si-lar-e) in the axilla (armpit). The longest part of this vessel, the **brachial artery**, is in the arm proper. It subdivides into two branches near the elbow: the **radial artery**, which continues down the thumb side of the forearm and wrist, and the **ulnar artery**, which extends along the medial or little finger side into the hand.

Anastomoses

A communication between two arteries is called an **anastomosis** (ah-nas-to-mo′sis). By this means, blood reaches vital organs by more than one route. Some examples of such unions of end arteries are described below:

1   The **circle of Willis** receives blood from the two internal carotid arteries as well as from the **basilar** (bas′i-lar) **artery**, which is formed by the union of two vertebral arteries. This arterial circle lies just under the center of the brain and sends branches to the cerebrum and other parts of the brain.

2   The **volar** (vo′lar) **arch** is formed by the union of the radial and ulnar arteries in the hand. It sends branches to the hand and the fingers.
3   The **mesenteric arches** are made of communications between branches of the vessels that supply blood to the intestinal tract.
4   **Arterial arches** are formed by the union of branches of the tibial arteries in the foot, and similar anastomoses are found in various parts of the body.

Arteriovenous anastomoses are found in a few parts of the body, including the external ears, the hands, and the feet. Vessels that have muscular walls connect arteries directly with veins and thus bypass the capillaries. This provides a more rapid flow and a greater volume of blood to these areas than elsewhere, thus protecting these exposed parts from freezing in cold weather.

≡ Names of Systemic Veins

Superficial Veins

Whereas most arteries are located in protected and rather deep areas of the body, many veins are found near the surface. The most important of these superficial veins are in the extremities. These include the following:

1   The veins on the back of the hand and at the front of the elbow. Those at the elbow are often used for removing blood samples for test purposes, as well as for intravenous injections. The largest of this group of veins are the **cephalic** (se-fal′ik), the **basilic** (bah-sil′ik), and the **median cubital** (ku′be-tal) **veins.**
2   The **saphenous** (sah-fe′nus) **veins** of the lower extremities, which are the longest veins of the body. The great saphenous vein begins in the foot and extends up the medial side of the leg, the knee, and the thigh. It finally empties into the femoral vein near the groin.

Deep Veins

The deep veins tend to parallel arteries and usually have the same names as the corresponding arteries. Examples of these include the **femoral** and the **iliac** vessels of the lower part of the body and the **brachial, axillary,** and **subclavian** vessels of the upper extremities. However, exceptions are found in the veins of the head and the neck. The **jugular** (jug′u-lar) **veins** drain the areas supplied by the carotid arteries. Two **brachiocephalic** (innominate) **veins** are formed, one on each side, by the union of the subclavian and the jugular veins. (Remember, there is only one brachiocephalic artery).

Superior Vena Cava

The veins of the head, neck, upper extremities, and chest all drain into the **superior vena cava** (ve′nah ka′vah), which goes to the heart. It is formed by the union of the right and left brachiocephalic veins, which drain the head, neck, and upper extremities. The **azygos** (az′i-gos) **vein** drains the veins of the chest wall and empties into the superior vena cava just before the latter empties into the heart (Fig 14-5).

Inferior Vena Cava

The **inferior vena cava**, which is much longer than the superior vena cava, returns the blood from the parts of the body below the diaphragm. It begins in the lower abdomen with the union of the two common iliac veins. It then ascends along the back wall of the abdomen, through a groove in the posterior part of the liver, through the diaphragm, and finally through the lower thorax to empty into the right atrium of the heart.

Drainage into the inferior vena cava is more complicated than drainage into the superior vena cava. The large veins below the diaphragm may be divided into two groups:

1. The right and left veins that drain paired parts and organs. They include the **iliac veins** from near the groin, four pairs of **lumbar veins** from the dorsal part of the trunk and from the spinal cord, the **testicular veins** from the testes of the male and the **ovarian veins** from the ovaries of the female, the **renal** and **suprarenal veins** from the kidneys and adrenal glands near the kidneys, and finally the large **hepatic veins** from the liver. For the most part, these vessels empty directly into the inferior vena cava. The left testicular in the male and the left ovarian in the female empty into the left renal vein, which then takes this blood to the inferior vena cava; these veins thus constitute exceptions to the rule that the paired veins empty directly into the vena cava.

2. Unpaired veins that come from the spleen and from parts of the digestive tract (stomach and intestine) and empty into a vein called the *portal vein*. Unlike other veins, which empty into the inferior vena cava, the hepatic portal vein is part of a special system that enables blood to circulate through the liver before returning to the heart.

Venous Sinuses

The word *sinus* means "space" or "hollow." A **venous sinus** is a large channel that drains deoxygenated blood but does not have the usual tubular structure of the veins. An important example of a venous sinus is the **coronary sinus**, which receives most of the blood from the veins of the heart wall (see Fig. 13-3). It lies between the left atrium and left ventricle on the under (inferior) surface of the heart, and it empties directly into the right atrium along with the two venae cavae.

Other important venous sinuses are the **cranial venous sinuses**, which are located inside the skull and which drain the veins that come from all over the brain (Fig. 14-6). The largest of the cranial venous sinuses are described below.

1. The two **cavernous sinuses**, situated behind the eyeballs, serve to drain the **ophthalmic veins** of the eyes.

2. The **superior sagittal** (saj′i-tal) **sinus** is a single long space located in the midline above the brain and in the fissure between the two hemispheres of the cerebrum. It ends in an enlargement called the **confluence** (kon′floo-ens) **of sinuses**.

3. The two **transverse sinuses**, also called the **lateral sinuses**, are large spaces between the layers of the dura mater (the outermost membrane around the brain). They begin posteriorly, in the region of the confluence of sinuses, and then extend toward either side. As each sinus extends around the inside of the skull, it receives blood draining those parts not already drained by the superior sagittal and other sinuses that join the back portions of the transverse sinuses. This means that nearly all the blood that comes from the veins of the brain eventually empties into one or the other of the transverse sinuses. On either side the sinus extends far enough forward to empty into an internal jugular vein, which then passes through a hole in the skull to continue downward in the neck.

(*Text continues on page 206*)

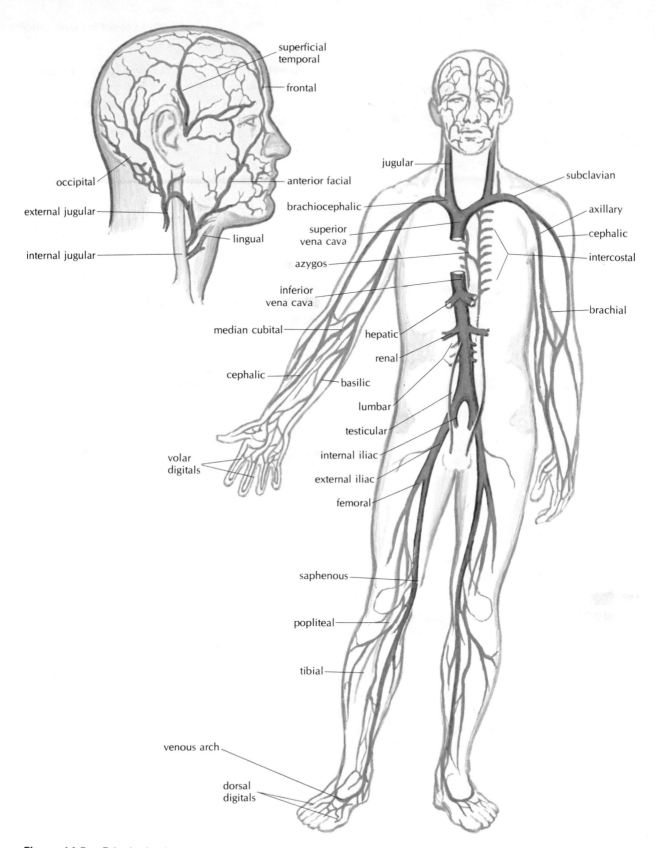

Figure 14-5. *Principal veins.*

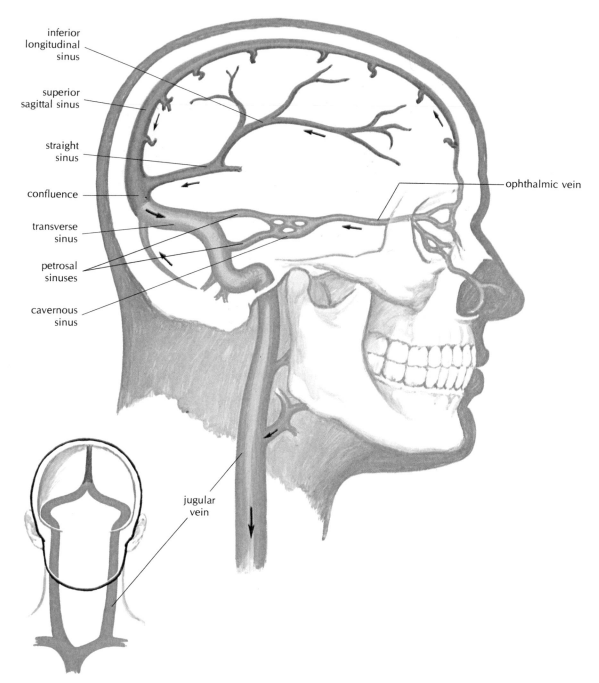

Figure 14-6. *Cranial venous sinuses. The paired transverse sinuses, which carry blood from the brain into the jugular veins, are shown in light blue in the inset.*

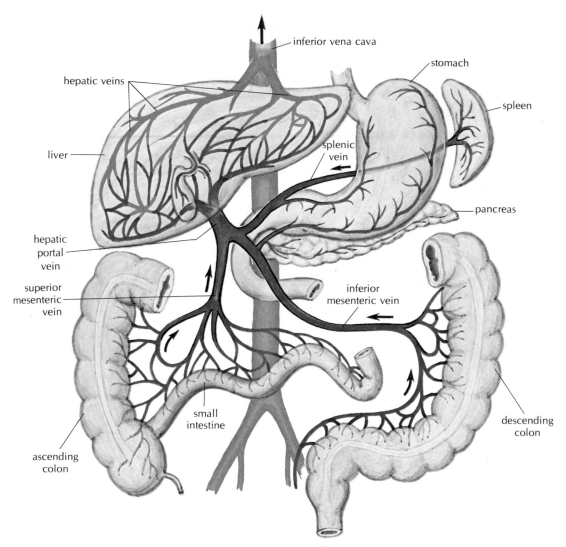

Figure 14-7. *Hepatic portal circulation.*

Hepatic Portal System

Almost always, when blood leaves a capillary bed it returns directly to the heart. In a portal system, however, blood circulates through a second capillary bed, usually in a second organ, before returning to the heart. Thus, a portal system is a kind of detour in the pathway of venous return that can transport materials directly from one organ to another. The portal system between the hypothalamus and the anterior pituitary has already been described (see Chap. 11). The largest portal system in the body is the **hepatic portal system,** which carries blood from the abdominal organs to the liver.

The hepatic portal system includes the veins that drain blood from capillaries in the spleen, stomach, pancreas, and intestine. Instead of emptying their blood directly into the inferior vena cava, they deliver it by way of the **hepatic portal vein** to the liver. The largest tributary of the portal vein is the **superior mesenteric vein.** It is joined by the **splenic vein** just under the liver. Other tributaries of the portal circulation are the **gastric, pancreatic,** and **inferior mesenteric veins.**

Upon entering the liver, the portal vein divides and subdivides into ever smaller branches. Eventually, the portal blood flows into a vast network of sinuslike vessels called **sinusoids** (si′nu-soids). These are enlarged capillaries that serve as blood channels within the tissues of the liver. (Similar channels are found in the spleen, certain glands, and red bone marrow.) After leaving the sinusoids, blood is finally collected by the hepatic veins, which empty into the inferior vena cava (Fig. 14-7).

The purpose of the portal system of veins is to transport blood from the digestive organs and the spleen to the liver sinusoids so the liver cells can carry out their functions. For example, when food is digested, most of the end products are absorbed from the small intestine into the bloodstream and transported to the liver by the portal system. In the liver, these nutrients are processed, stored, and released as needed into the general circulation (see Chap. 18).

≡ The Physiology of Circulation
How Capillaries Work

In a general way, the circulating blood might be compared to a train that travels around the country, loading and unloading freight in each of the cities it serves. For example, as blood flows through capillaries surrounding the air sacs in the lungs, it picks up oxygen and unloads carbon dioxide. Later, when this oxygenated blood is pumped to capillaries in other parts of the body, it unloads the oxygen and picks up carbon dioxide (Fig. 14-8) as well as other substances resulting from cellular activities in the areas being served. The microscopic capillaries are of fundamental importance in these activities. It is only through and between the cells of these thin-walled vessels that the aforementioned exchanges can take place.

All living cells are immersed in a slightly salty liquid called *tissue fluid*. Looking again at Figure 14-8, one can see how this fluid serves as "middleman" between the capillary membrane and the neighboring cells. As water, oxygen, and other materials necessary for cellular activity pass through the capillary walls, they enter the tissue fluid. Then these substances make their way by diffusion to the cells. At the same time, carbon dioxide and other end products of cell metabolism come from the cells and move in the opposite direction. These substances enter the capillary and are carried away in the bloodstream, to reach other organs or to be eliminated from the body.

Figure 14-8. *Diagram showing the connection between the small blood vessels through capillaries. Note the lymph capillary, a part of tissue drainage.*

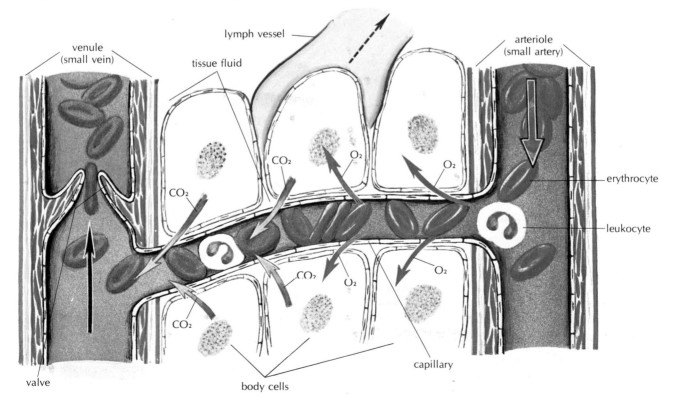

The movement of blood through the capillaries is relatively slow owing to the much larger size of the cross-sectional area of the capillaries compared with that of the larger vessels from which capillaries branch. This slow progress through the capillaries allows time for exchanges to occur.

Vasoconstriction and Vasodilation

Vasoconstriction refers to a decrease in the diameter of a blood vessel; **vasodilation** refers to an increase in the diameter of a blood vessel. These changes in vessel diameter, together called *vasomotor activities,* serve in part to regulate blood pressure. (Other factors include total blood volume, cardiac output, and blood viscosity.) When vessels constrict, blood pressure increases, and when vessels dilate, blood pressure decreases. Vasomotor changes result from the contraction or relaxation of the smooth muscle in the vessel wall. These activities are controlled by a **vasomotor center** in the medulla of the brain stem that functions by means of the autonomic nervous system.

Blood Distribution

Vasomotor changes are also important in regulating the amount of blood that flows to various parts of the body. Some organs, such as the brain, liver, and kidneys, even at rest require large quantities of blood. Other organs, such as the skeletal muscles and digestive organs, need an increased supply of blood during increased activity. (The blood flow in muscle can increase 20 times during exercise.) The changing needs of body tissues are met by vasomotor changes, particularly in the arterioles. Vasodilation of the arterioles allows delivery of more blood to the tissues, whereas vasoconstriction decreases the amount of blood flowing into the tissues. As noted, the vasomotor center of the medulla controls these activities, but hormones and local changes in the tissues are also involved.

Return of Blood to the Heart

As blood flows through the system, it gets farther and farther from the pumping action of the heart. It also begins to flow in vessels (veins), which tend to give way under pressure and hold the blood. What is it that brings blood back to the heart, even against the pull of gravity in the lower part of the body?

One force that promotes venous return is the pressure of the skeletal muscles against the veins. As the muscles contract, they squeeze the blood forward in the veins, and the valves prevent it from flowing backward. Lack of movement, as in standing at attention, results in poor blood return to the heart.

Breathing is another factor in venous return. When the chest expands in breathing, pressure in the chest cavity drops (see Chap. 17), causing the large veins in the chest to expand and draw blood back toward the heart.

☰ Pulse and Blood Pressure

Meaning of the Pulse

The ventricles pump blood into the arteries regularly about 70 to 80 times a minute. The force of ventricular contraction starts a wave of increased pressure that begins at the heart and travels along the arteries. This wave, called the **pulse**, can be felt in any artery that is relatively close to the surface, particularly if the vessel can be pressed down against a bone. At the wrist the radial artery passes over the bone on the thumb side of the forearm, and the pulse is most commonly obtained here. Other vessels sometimes used for obtaining the pulse are the carotid artery in the neck and the dorsalis pedis on the top of the foot.

Normally, the pulse rate is the same as the heart rate. Only if a heartbeat is abnormally weak, or if the artery is obstructed, may the beat not be detected as a pulse. In checking the pulse of another person, it is important to use your second or third finger. If you use your thumb, you may find that you are getting your own pulse. When taking a pulse, it is important to gauge the strength as well as the regularity and the rate.

Various factors may influence the pulse rate. We will enumerate just a few:

1 The pulse is somewhat faster in small persons than in large persons and usually slightly faster in women than in men.
2 In a newborn infant the rate may be from 120 to 140 beats/minute. As the child grows, the rate tends to become slower.
3 Muscular activity influences the pulse rate. During sleep the pulse may slow down to 60 a

minute, while during strenuous exercise the rate may go up to well over 100 a minute. In a person in good condition, the pulse does not remain rapid despite continued exercise.

4 Emotional disturbances may increase the pulse rate.

5 In many infections, the pulse rate increases with the increase in temperature.

6 An excessive amount of secretion from the thyroid gland may cause a rapid pulse. The pulse rate may serve as a partial guide for persons who must take thyroid extract.

Blood Pressure and Its Determination

Since the pressure inside the blood vessels varies with the condition of the heart, the blood, and the vessels, as well as with other factors, the measurement and careful interpretation of blood pressure may prove a valuable guide in the care and evaluation of a person's health. Because blood pressure decreases as the blood flows from arteries into capillaries and finally into veins, measurements ordinarily are made of arterial pressure only. The instrument used is called a **sphygmomanometer** (sfig″mo-mah-nom′e-ter), and two variables are measured:

1 **Systolic pressure**, which occurs during heart muscle contraction, averages around 120 and is expressed in millimeters of mercury (mm Hg).

2 **Diastolic pressure**, which occurs during relaxation of the heart muscle, averages around 80 mm Hg.

The sphygmomanometer is essentially a graduated column of mercury connected to an inflatable cuff. The cuff is wrapped around the patient's upper arm and inflated with air until the brachial artery is compressed and the blood flow cut off. Then, listening with a stethoscope, the doctor or nurse slowly lets air out of the cuff until the first pulsations are heard. At this point the pressure in the cuff is equal to the systolic pressure, and this pressure is read off the mercury column. Then, more air is let out until a characteristic muffled sound indicates the point at which the diastolic pressure is to be read. Considerable practice is required to ensure an accurate reading.

Abnormal Blood Pressure

Lower-than-normal blood pressure is called **hypotension** (hi″po-ten′shun). However, because of individual variations in normal pressure levels, what would be a low pressure for one person might be a normal or even a high pressure for someone else. For this reason, hypotension is best evaluated in terms of how well the body tissues are being supplied with blood. For example, a person whose systolic pressure is consistently below his normal range may experience episodes of fainting because of inadequate blood flow to the brain. The sudden lowering of blood pressure below a person's normal level is one symptom of shock; it may also occur in certain chronic diseases as well as in heart block.

Hypertension, or high blood pressure, has received a great deal of attention. Often it occurs temporarily as a result of excitement or exertion. It may be persistent in a number of conditions, including the following:

1 Kidney disease and uremia or other toxic conditions

2 Endocrine disorders such as hyperthyroidism and acromegaly

3 Artery disease, including the so-called hardening of the artery walls

4 Tumors of the central portion of the adrenal (suprarenal) gland

Hypertension that has no apparent medical cause is called **essential hypertension**. This condition, which is fairly common, may cause strokes, heart failure, or kidney damage. Treatment should be begun while the patient is young when the diastolic pressure is over 90 mm Hg. An excess of a hormone produced in the kidney, called **renin** (re′nin), seems to play a role in the severity of this kind of hypertension. Drugs may be given to block excessive renin production and to prevent fluid retention. General health measures, such as weight control, avoidance of excessive alcohol and cigarette consumption, proper diet, and adequate exercise, are all beneficial.

Although stress has been placed on the systolic blood pressure, in many cases the diastolic pressure is even more important, since the condition of small arteries may have more of an effect on diastolic pressure. At any rate, the determination of what really constitutes hypertension depends on each person's normal range. As previously noted, a pressure that is normal for one individual may be abnormal for another.

☰ Disorders Involving the Blood Vessels

Aneurysm of the Aorta

An **aneurysm** (an'u-rizm) is a bulging sac in the wall of an artery or a vein due to a localized weakness in that part of the vessel. The aorta is the vessel most commonly involved. The damage to the wall may be congenital, due to infections, or due to degenerative changes referred to as *hardening of the arteries*. Whatever the cause, the aneurysm may continue to grow in size. As it swells it may cause some derangement of other structures, in which case definite symptoms are manifested. Eventually, however, the walls of the weakened area yield to the pressure, and the aneurysm bursts like a balloon, usually causing immediate death. Surgical replacement of the damaged segment with a synthetic graft may be lifesaving.

Arterial Degeneration

Changes in the walls of arteries frequently lead to loss of elasticity, which is accompanied by irregular thickening of the artery wall at the expense of the lumen (space inside the vessel). Areas of yellow, fat-like material may replace the muscle and elastic connective tissue, leading to a disorder called **athero-sclerosis** (ath"er-o"skle-ro'sis). Sometimes the lining of the artery is damaged, and a blood clot (thrombus) may form at this point. Such a thrombus may more or less completely obstruct the vessel, as it sometimes does in coronary thrombosis (Fig. 14-9). In other cases calcium salts and scar tissue (fibrous connective tissue) may cause hardening of the arteries, known as **arteriosclerosis** (ar-te"re-o-skle-ro'sis).

Artery damage may be present for years without causing any noticeable symptoms. As the thickening of the wall continues and the diameter of the passage for blood flow is decreased, a variety of symptoms appears. The nature of these disturbances will vary with the parts of the body affected and with the extent of the changes in the artery walls. Some examples are listed below:

1   Leg cramps, pain, and sudden lameness while walking may be due to insufficient blood supply

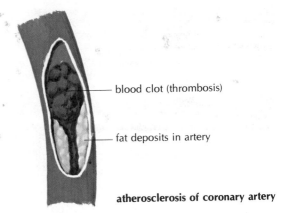

blood clot (thrombosis)

fat deposits in artery

atherosclerosis of coronary artery

Figure 14-9.   *Development of coronary thrombosis.*

to the lower extremities as a result of artery wall damage.

2   Headaches, dizziness, and mental disorders may be the result of cerebral artery sclerosis.

3   Hypertension may be due to a decrease in size of the lumina within many arteries all over the body. Although hypertension may be present in many young persons with no apparent artery damage, and arteriosclerosis may be present without causing hypertension, the two are often found together in elderly people.

4   Palpitation, dyspnea, paleness, weakness, and other symptoms may be the result of arteriosclerosis of the coronary arteries. The severe pain of angina pectoris may follow the lack of oxygen and myocardial damage associated with sclerosis of the vessels that supply the heart.

5   An increase in the amount of urine with the appearance of **albumin** (al-bu'min). Albumin is a normal body protein usually found in the urine only if there is kidney damage. Other symptoms referable to the kidneys may be due to damage to the renal arteries.

Gradual narrowing of the interior of the arteries, with a consequent reduction in the volume of blood that passes through them, gives rise to **ischemia** (is-kee'me-ah) (lack of blood). Those parts that are supplied by the damaged artery suffer from an inadequate blood supply, the result being that vital cells in these organs gradually die. The death of cells, for whatever cause, is called **necrosis** (ne-kro'sis).

Once these vital cells die, the organ loses its effectiveness. One example of necrosis due to ischemia is the death of certain cells of the brain, with mental disorders as a possible result. Another example is the chain of complications resulting from gradual closure of the arteries of the leg or (rarely) of the arm. The circulation of blood in the toes or the fingers, never too brisk even at the best of times, may cease altogether. Necrosis occurs; the dead tissue is invaded by bacteria, and putrefaction sets in. This condition, called **gangrene** (gang'grene), can result from a number of disorders that may injure the arteries, such as diabetes. Diabetic gangrene is a fairly common occurrence in elderly diabetic patients.

Hemorrhage and First Aid

A profuse escape of blood from the vessels is known as **hemorrhage**, a word that means "a bursting forth of blood." Such bleeding may be external or internal, may be from vessels of any size, and may involve any part of the body. Capillary oozing usually is stopped by the normal process of clot formation. Flow from larger vessels can be stopped by appropriate first aid measures carried out at the scene. In most cases, pressure with a clean bandage directly on the wound stops the bleeding effectively.

The loss of blood from a cut artery may be rapid. Often it is quickly fatal, but immediate appropriate action can be lifesaving. The Red Cross and other organizations that give instructions in first aid agree that excessive loss of blood can and should be prevented in all circumstances. Since hemorrhage is the most frequent problem in case of an accident, everyone should know that certain arteries can be pressed against a bone to stop hemorrhage. The most important of these "pressure points" are as follows:

1 The **facial artery**, which may be pressed against the lower jaw as the vessel extends along the side of the face, for hemorrhage around the nose, mouth, and cheek
2 The **temporal artery**, which may be pressed against the side of the skull just in front of the ear to stop hemorrhage on the side of the face and around the ear
3 The **common carotid artery** in the neck, which may be pressed back against the spinal column for bleeding in the neck and the head. Avoid prolonged compression, which can result in lack of oxygen to the brain.
4 The **subclavian artery**, which may be pressed against the first rib by a downward push with the thumb to stop bleeding from the shoulder or arm
5 The **brachial artery**, which may be pressed against the humerus (arm bone) by a push inward along the natural groove between the two large muscles of the arm. This stops hand, wrist, and forearm hemorrhage.
6 The **femoral artery** (in the groin), which may be pressed to avoid serious hemorrhage of the lower extremity

It is important not to leave the pressure on too long, since it may cause damage to tissues past the pressure point.

Shock

The word *shock* has a number of meanings. However, in terms of the circulating blood, it refers to a life-threatening condition in which there is inadequate blood flow to the tissues of the body. The factor common to all cases of shock is inadequate output by the heart. Shock can be instigated by a wide range of conditions that reduce the effective circulation. The exact cause of shock is often not known; however, a widely used classification is based on causative factors, the most important of which include the following:

1 **Cardiogenic** (kar″de-o-jen′ik) **shock**, sometimes called *pump failure,* is often a complication of heart muscle damage as is found in myocardial infarction. It is the leading cause of shock death.
2 **Septic shock** is second only to cardiogenic shock as a cause of shock death. It is usually due to an overwhelming bacterial infection.
3 **Hypovolemic** (hi″po-vo-le′mik) **shock** is due to a decrease in the volume of circulating blood and may follow severe hemorrhage or burns.
4 **Anaphylactic** (an″ah-fi-lak′tik) **shock** is a severe allergic reaction to foreign substances to which the person has been sensitized.

When the cause is not known, shock is classified according to its severity.

In **mild shock** regulatory mechanisms act to relieve the circulatory deficit. Symptoms are often subtle changes in heart rate and blood pressure. Constriction of small blood vessels and the detouring of blood away from certain organs increase the effective circulation. Mild shock may develop into a severe, life-threatening circulatory failure.

Severe shock is characterized by poor circulation, which causes further damage and deepening of the shock. Symptons of late shock include clammy skin, anxiety, very low blood pressure, rapid pulse, and rapid, shallow breathing. Contractions of the heart are weakened owing to the decrease in blood supply to the heart muscle. The muscles in the blood vessel walls are also weakened so that they dilate. The capillaries become more permeable and lose fluid owing to the accumulation of metabolic wastes.

The victim of shock should first be placed in a horizontal position and covered with a blanket. If there is bleeding, it should be stopped. The patient's head should be kept turned to the side to prevent aspiration (breathing in) of vomitus, an important cause of death in shock cases. Further treatment of shock depends largely on treatment of the causative factors. For example, shock due to fluid loss such as hemorrhage or burns is best treated with blood products or plasma expanders. Shock due to heart failure should be treated with drugs that improve the contractions of the heart muscle. In any case, all measures are aimed at supporting the circulation and improving the output of the heart. Oxygen is frequently administered to improve the delivery of oxygen to the tissues.

Varicose Veins

Varicose veins are a condition in which superficial veins have become swollen, tortuous, and ineffective. It may be a problem in the esophagus or in the rectum, but the veins most commonly involved are the saphenous veins of the lower extremities (Fig. 14-10). This condition is found frequently in persons who spend a great deal of time standing, such as salespeople. Pregnancy, with its accompanying pressure on the veins in the pelvis, may also be a predisposing cause. Varicose veins in the rectum are called **hemorrhoids** (hem'o-roids), or *piles.* The general term for varicose veins is **varices** (var'i-sez), the singular form being **varix** (var'iks).

Phlebitis

Inflammation of a vein, called **phlebitis** (fle-bi'tis), causes marked pain and often considerable swelling. The entire vein wall is involved. A blood clot may form, causing a dangerous condition called **throm-**

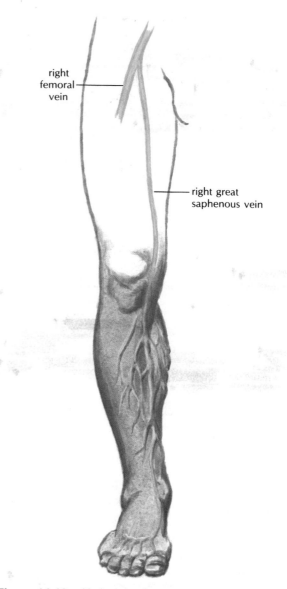

right femoral vein

right great saphenous vein

Figure 14-10.   *Varicose veins.*

bophlebitis (throm-bo-fle-bi'tis), in which a piece of the clot may become loose and float in the blood as an **embolus** (em'bo-lus). An embolus is carried through the circulatory system until it lodges in a vessel. If it reaches the lungs, sudden death from **pulmonary embolism** (em'bo-lizm) may result. Prevention of infection, early activity to ensure circulation following an injury or an operation, and the use of anticoagulant drugs when appropriate have greatly reduced the incidence of this condition.

Stasis Dermatitis and Ulcers

Stasis means a standing still or stoppage in normal blood flow. Often the valves in the veins of the lower extremity become incompetent and blood is not returned from the legs. The skin becomes inflamed and undergoes scaling; fissures (cracks) form, followed by ulcers. Treatment of the causes as well as attention to the local lesions should be in the hands of a physician, and patient cooperation is most important.

Arterial Obstruction

When the lumen of an artery is completely blocked by arteriosclerosis, the condition is known as **arteriosclerosis obliterans** (o-blit′er-ans). The complete obstruction to blood flow causes intense pain; if the disease is allowed to progress and is not treated, the affected part or parts may become ulcerated or gangrenous.

In some cases the obstruction can be removed surgically. First clamps are placed above and below the plug; then an incision is made into the artery and the plug removed by a special instrument.

In other instances, circulation can be restored by the use of vascular grafts. This is done by cutting out the diseased segment and suturing (sewing) a graft in its place. More often, however, grafts are implanted to bypass the obstructed segment. A vein from the patient's own body, usually the saphenous vein, or a synthetic vessel made of Dacron or Teflon may be used. Sometimes a patch graft is used to increase the lumen of small, narrowed areas of arteries. To accomplish this, the artery is clamped above and below the narrowed area and then incised in the long axis of the vessel. A patch of Teflon is then sewn to the edges of the incision, thereby increasing the diameter of the artery.

Summary

I **Blood vessels**
   A Functional classification
      1 Arteries—carry blood away from heart
         a Arterioles—small arteries
      2 Veins—carry blood toward heart
         a Venules—small veins
      3 Capillaries—allow for exchanges between blood and tissues, or blood and air in lungs; connect arterioles and venules
   B Circuits
      1 Pulmonary circuit—carries blood to and from lungs
      2 Systemic circuit—carries blood to and from rest of body
   C Structure
      1 Tissue layers
         a Innermost—single layer of flat epithelial cells (endothelium)
         b Middle—thicker layer of smooth muscle and elastic connective tissue
         c Outer—connective tissue
      2 Arteries—all three layers
      3 Arterioles—thinner walls, less elastic tissue, more smooth muscle
      4 Capillaries—only endothelium; single layer of cells
      5 Veins—all three layers, but thinner than arteries

II **Aorta**—largest artery
   1 Divisions
      a Ascending aorta
         (1) Left and right coronary arteries
      b Aortic arch
         (1) Brachiocephalic trunk
         (2) Left common carotid artery
         (3) Left subclavian artery
      c Descending aorta
         (1) Thoracic aorta
         (2) Abdominal aorta
   2 Anastomoses—communications between arteries

III **Systemic veins**
   A Location
      1 Superficial—near surface
      2 Deep—usually parallel to arteries with same names as corresponding arteries
   B Superior vena cava—drains upper part of body
   C Inferior vena cava—drains lower part of body
   D Venous sinuses—enlarged venous channels
   E Hepatic portal system—carries blood from abdominal organs to liver, where it is processed before returning to heart

IV **Physiology of circulation**
   A Capillary exchange
      1 Primary method—diffusion
      2 Medium—tissue fluid

B Vasomotor activities
   1 Vasoconstriction—decrease in diameter of blood vessel
   2 Vasodilation—increase in diameter of blood vessel
   3 Vasomotor center—controls contraction and relaxation of smooth muscle in vessel wall
   4 Effects
     a Regulation of blood pressure
     b Control of blood distribution
C Control of blood distribution
   1 Vasomotor changes,
   2 Vasomotor center
   3 Hormones and local tissue changes
D Return of blood to heart
   1 Pumping action of heart
   2 Pressure of skeletal muscles on veins
   3 Breathing—enlargement of veins in chest
V **Pulse**—wave of pressure that travels along arteries as ventricles contract
VI **Blood pressure**—varies with condition of heart, blood, vessels
A Measurement
   1 Stethoscope
   2 Sphygmomanometer—usually in brachial artery of upper arm
     (a) Systolic pressure—averages 120 mm Hg
     (b) Diastolic pressure—averages 80 mm Hg
B Abnormal blood pressure
   1 Hypotension—low blood pressure
   2 Hypertension—high blood pressure
     a Essential hypertension—has no apparent medical cause
VII **Disorders involving the blood vessels**
A Aneurysm—weakness and bulging of a vessel; may burst
B Arterial degeneration
   1 Atherosclerosis—fatty deposits in vessel; may result in thrombus
   2 Arteriosclerosis—hardening of arteries with scar tissue or calcium salts; may result in ischemia and cell necrosis
C Hemorrhage—massive loss of blood; pressure applied at pressure points will stop blood loss
D Shock—inadequate output of blood from heart

E Varicose veins—swelling and loss of function in superficial veins, usually in legs and rectum (hemorrhoids)
F Phlebitis—inflammation of a vein
   1 Embolus—piece of clot traveling in circulation
   2 Pulmonary embolism—clot lodged in lungs
G Other—stasis dermatitis, ulcers, arterial obstruction

Questions for Study and Review

1 Name the three main groups of blood vessels and describe their functions. How has function affected structure?

2 Trace a drop of blood through the shortest possible route from the capillaries of the foot to the capillaries of the head.

3 What are the names and functions of some cranial venous sinuses? Where is the coronary venous sinus and what does it do?

4 What large vessels drain the blood low in oxygen from most of the body into the right atrium? What vessels carry blood high in oxygen into the left atrium?

5 Trace a drop of blood from capillaries in the wall of the small intestine to the right atrium. What is the purpose of going through the liver on this trip?

6 What substances diffuse into the tissues from the capillaries? into the capillaries from the tissues?

7 What factors regulate blood flow to the various tissues?

8 What actions help force blood back to the heart?

9 What is meant by *pulse?* Where is the pulse usually determined? If a large part of the body were burned, leaving only the lower extremities accessible for obtaining the pulse, what vessel would you try to use?

10 What are some factors that cause an increase in the pulse rate?

11 What instrument is used for obtaining blood pressure? What are the two values usually obtained called, and what is the significance of each?

12 What are some examples of disorders that cause hypertension of a persistent kind? Of what importance is diastolic blood pressure?

13 What are some symptoms of arteriosclerosis and how are these produced?

14 What is the meaning of *hemorrhage?* What vessels cause the most serious bleeding if they are cut? What are some of the most effective ways of stopping hemorrhage?

15 What is shock, and why is it so dangerous? Name some symptoms of shock and identify four types of shock.

16 In what organs are varicose veins most commonly found? In what situations are they given special names? Give examples.

17 What is the serious complication of phlebitis of lower extremity veins?

18 Explain the difference between the terms in the following pairs:

   a *pulmonary circuit* and *systemic circuit*

   b *arteriole* and *venule*

   c *vasodilation* and *vasoconstriction*

   d *atherosclerosis* and *arteriosclerosis*

   e *hypotension* and *hypertension*

15

The Lymphatic System and Lymphoid Tissue

Behavioral Objectives

After careful study of this chapter, you should be able to:

List the three major functions of the lymphatic system

Explain how lymphatic capillaries differ from blood capillaries

Name the two main lymphatic ducts and describe the area drained by each

List the major structures of the lymphatic system and give the locations and functions of each

Describe the composition and function of the mononuclear phagocyte system

Selected Key Terms

The following terms are defined in the glossary:

chyle
duct
lacteal
lymph
lymphadenitis
lymphangitis
node
spleen
thymus
tonsil

The Lymphatic System

It may be recalled from the preceding chapter that body cells live in tissue fluid, a liquid derived from the bloodstream. Water and dissolved substances, such as oxygen and nutrients, are constantly filtering through capillary walls into the spaces between cells and constantly adding to the volume of tissue fluid. However, under normal conditions, fluid is also constantly removed so that it does not accumulate in the tissues. Part of this fluid simply returns (by diffusion) to the capillary bloodstream, taking with it some of the end products of cellular metabolism, including carbon dioxide and other substances. A second pathway for the drainage of tissue fluid involves the **lymphatic system**. In addition to the blood-carrying capillaries, there are miscroscopic vessels called **lymphatic capillaries**, which drain away excess tissue fluid that does not return to the blood capillaries (see Fig. 14-8). As soon as tissue fluid enters the lymphatic capillary, it is called **lymph**. The lymphatic capillaries join to form the larger lymphatic vessels, and these vessels (which we shall have a closer look at in a moment) eventually empty into the veins. However, before the lymph reaches the veins, it flows through a series of filters called **lymph nodes**, where bacteria and other foreign particles are trapped and destroyed. Thus, the lymph nodes may be compared in one way with the oil filter in an automobile.

Lymphatic Capillaries

The lymphatic capillaries resemble the blood capillaries in that they are made of one layer of flattened (squamous) epithelial cells, also called *endothelium,* which allows for easy passage of soluble materials and water. Unlike the capillaries of the blood stream, the lymphatic capillaries begin blindly; that is, they do not serve to bridge two larger vessels. Instead, one end simply lies within a lake of tissue fluid, while the other communicates with the larger lymphatic vessel.

In the small intestine are some specialized lymphatic capillaries, called **lacteals** (lak'te-als), which act as one pathway for the transfer of fats from digested food to the bloodstream. This process is covered in the chapter dealing with the digestive system.

Lymphatic Vessels

The lymphatic vessels are thin walled and delicate and have a beaded appearance because of indentations where valves are located. These valves prevent backflow in the same way as those found in some veins. Although there is no pumping mechanism comparable to the heart, compression of the lymphatic vessels by contraction of the skeletal muscles during movement and expansion of the chest in breathing help maintain the forward flow of lymph.

Lymphatic vessels include **superficial** and **deep** sets. The surface lymphatics are immediately below the skin, often continuing near the superficial veins. The deep vessels are usually larger and accompany the deep veins.

Lymphatic vessels are named according to location. For example, those in the breast are called **mammary** lymphatic vessels, those in the thigh **femoral** lymphatic vessels, and those in the leg **tibial** lymphatic vessels. All the lymphatic vessels form networks, and at certain points they carry lymph into the regional nodes (the nodes that "service" a particular area). For example, nearly all of the lymph from the upper extremity and the breast passes through the **axillary lymph nodes**, while that from the lower extremity passes through the **inguinal nodes**. Lymphatic vessels carrying lymph away from the regional nodes eventually drain into one of the two terminal vessels, the right lymphatic duct or the thoracic duct, which empty into the bloodstream.

The **right lymphatic duct** is a short vessel about 1.25 cm (½ inch) long that receives the lymph that comes from only the right side of the head, neck, and thorax, as well as from the right upper extremity. It empties into the right subclavian vein. Its opening into this vein is guarded by two pocket-like semilunar valves to prevent blood from entering the duct. The rest of the body is drained by the thoracic duct.

The Thoracic Duct

The **thoracic duct** is much the larger of the two terminal vessels; it is about 40 cm (16 inches) in length. As shown in Figure 15-1, the thoracic duct receives lymph from all parts of the body except those above the diaphragm on the right side. This duct begins in the posterior part of the abdominal cavity, below the attachment of the diaphragm. The first part of this duct is enlarged to form a cistern, or temporary storage pouch, called the **cisterna chyli** (sis-ter'nah ki'li). **Chyle** (kile) is the milky fluid, formed by the combination of fat globules and lymph, that comes from the intestinal lacteals. Chyle passes through the intestinal lymphatic vessels and the lymph nodes of the mesentery, finally entering

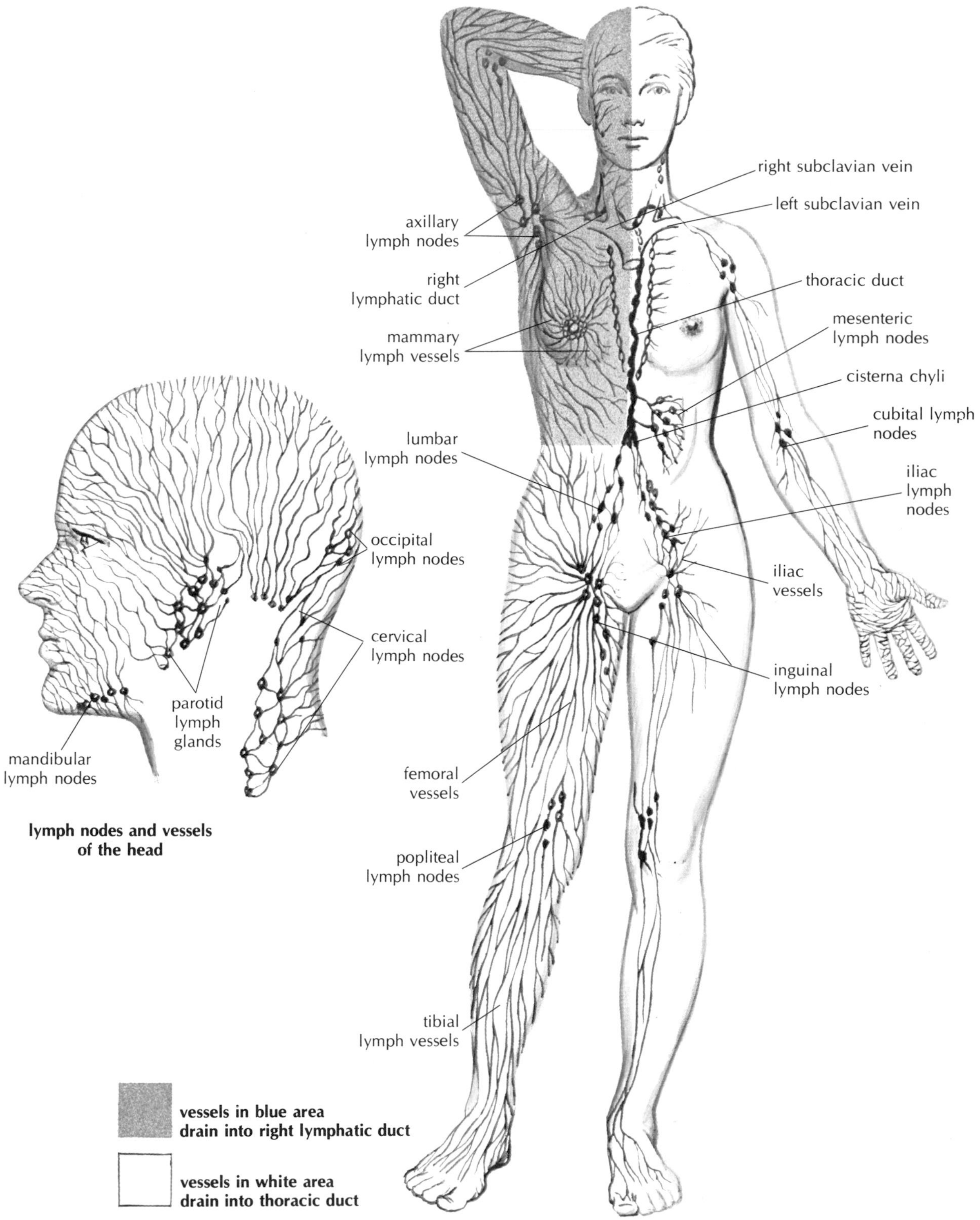

right subclavian vein

left subclavian vein

axillary
lymph nodes

right
lymphatic duct

thoracic duct

mesenteric
lymph nodes

mammary
lymph vessels

cisterna chyli

cubital lymph
nodes

lumbar
lymph nodes

iliac
lymph
nodes

occipital
lymph nodes

iliac
vessels

cervical
lymph nodes

inguinal
lymph nodes

parotid
lymph
glands

mandibular
lymph nodes

femoral
vessels

**lymph nodes and vessels
of the head**

popliteal
lymph nodes

tibial
lymph vessels

**vessels in blue area
drain into right lymphatic duct**

**vessels in white area
drain into thoracic duct**

Figure 15-1. *Lymphatic system.*

the cisterna chyli. In addition to chyle, all the lymph from below the diaphragm empties into the cisterna chyli by way of the various clusters of lymph nodes and then is carried by the thoracic duct into the bloodstream.

The thoracic duct extends upward through the diaphragm and along the back wall of the thorax up into the root of the neck on the left side. Here it receives the left jugular lymphatic vessels from the head and neck, the left subclavian vessels from the left upper extremity, and other lymphatic vessels from the thorax and its parts. In addition to the valves along the duct, there are two valves at its opening into the left subclavian vein to prevent the passage of blood into the duct.

≡ Lymphoid Tissue

The above section was just a brief survey of the system of lymph vessels and lymph transport. The lymph nodes, or filters, were mentioned repeatedly, but detailed discussion of them has been postponed until now. There has been a reason for this. The lymph nodes are made of a specialized tissue called **lymphoid** (lim′foid) **tissue.** A number of other organs are also made of lymphoid tissue, but some of them have nothing directly to do with the system of lymph transport itself.

Although lymphoid tissue is distributed throughout the body, some organs are specialized structures of the lymphatic system. We will look at some of these typical organs of lymphoid tissue, but first let us consider some properties of this kind of tissue and see what characteristics these organs have in common.

Functions

Some of the general functions of lymphoid tissue include the following:

1 Removal of impurities such as carbon particles, cancer cells, pathogenic organisms, and dead blood cells through filtration and phagocytosis
2 Processing of lymphocytes. Some of these lymphocytes produce antibodies, substances in the blood that aid in combating infection; others attack foreign invaders directly. These cells are discussed further in Chapter 16.

Lymph Nodes

The lymph nodes, as we have seen, are designed to filter the lymph once it is drained from the tissues. The lymph nodes are small, rounded masses varying from pinhead size to as long as 2.5 cm (1 inch). Each node has a fibrous connective tissue capsule from which partitions extend into the substance of the organ. Inside the node are masses of lymphatic tissue, with spaces set aside for the production of lymphocytes. At various points in the surface of the node, lymphatic vessels pierce the capsule to carry lymph into the spaces inside the pulplike nodal tissue. An indented area called the **hilus** (hi′lus) serves as the exit for lymph vessels carrying lymph out of the node. At this region other structures, including blood vessels and nerves, connect with the organ.

Lymph nodes are seldom isolated. As a rule, they are massed together in groups, the number in each group varying from 2 or 3 up to well over 100. Some of these groups are placed deeply, while others are superficial. Those of the most practical importance include the following:

1 **Cervical nodes,** located in the neck, are divided into deep and superficial groups, which drain various parts of the head and neck. They often become enlarged during upper respiratory infections as well as in certain chronic disorders.
2 **Axillary nodes,** located in the axillae (armpits), may become enlarged following infections of the upper extremities and the breasts. Cancer cells from the breasts often metastasize (spread) to the axillary nodes.
3 **Tracheobronchial** (tra″-ke-o-brong′ke-al) **nodes** are found near the trachea and around the larger bronchial tubes. In persons living in highly polluted areas, these nodes become so filled with carbon particles that they are solid black masses resembling pieces of coal.
4 **Mesenteric** (mes-en-ter′ik) **nodes** are found between the two layers of peritoneum that form the mesentery. There are some 100 to 150 of these nodes.
5 **Inguinal nodes,** located in the groin region, receive lymph drainage from the lower extremities and from the external genital organs. When they become enlarged, they are often referred to as **buboes** (bu′boes) (hence the name **bubonic plague**).

The Tonsils

There are masses of lymphoid tissue that are designed to filter not lymph, but tissue fluid. Found beneath certain areas of moist epithelium that are exposed to the outside, and hence to contamination, these masses include parts of the digestive, urinary, and respiratory tracts. Associated with the latter system are those well-known masses of lymphoid tissue called the **tonsils**, which include

1 The **palatine** (pal′ah-tin) **tonsils**, oval bodies located at each side of the soft palate. These are most commonly known as the *tonsils*.
2 The **pharyngeal** (fah-rin′je-al) **tonsil**, commonly referred to as **adenoids**. It is located behind the nose on the back wall of the upper pharynx.
3 The **lingual** (ling′gwal) **tonsils**, little mounds of lymphoid tissue at the back of the tongue

Any or all of these tonsils may become so loaded with bacteria that the pathogens gain the upper hand; removal then is advisable. A slight enlargement of any of them is not an indication for surgery. All lymphoid tissue masses tend to be larger in childhood, so that the physician must consider the patient's age in determining whether these masses are enlarged abnormally. Since the tonsils appear to function in immunity during early childhood, efforts are made *not* to remove them unless absolutely necessary.

The Thymus

Because of its appearance under the microscope, the **thymus** (thi′mus), located in the upper thorax beneath the sternum, has been considered part of the lymphoid system. However, recent studies suggest that this structure has a much more basic function than was originally thought. It now seems apparent that the thymus plays a key role in the development of the immune system before birth and during the first few months of infancy. Certain lymphocytes must mature in the thymus gland before they can perform their functions in the immune system (see Chap. 16). These **T-lymphocytes** develop under the effects of the hormone from the thymus gland called **thymosin**, which also promotes the growth and activity of lymphocytes in lymphoid tissue throughout the body. Removal causes a decrease in the production of T-lymphocytes, as well as a decrease in the size of the spleen and of lymph nodes throughout the body. The thymus is most active during early life. After puberty, the tissue undergoes changes and is replaced by connective tissue.

The Spleen

The spleen is an organ that contains lymphoid tissue designed to filter blood. It is located in the upper left hypochondriac region of the abdomen and normally is protected by the lower part of the rib cage because it is high up under the dome of the diaphragm. The spleen is rather soft and of a purplish color. It is a somewhat flattened organ about 12.5 cm to 16 cm (5–6 inches) long and 5 cm to 7.5 cm (2–3 inches) wide. The capsule of the spleen, as well as its framework, is more elastic than that of the lymph nodes. It contains involuntary muscle, which enables the splenic capsule to contract as well as to withstand some swelling.

The spleen has an unusually large blood supply, considering its size. The organ is filled with a soft pulp, one of the functions of which is to filter out the worn-out red blood cells. The spleen also harbors phagocytes, which engulf bacteria and other foreign particles. Round masses of lymphoid tissue are prominent structures inside the spleen, and it is because of these that the spleen is often classified with the other organs made of lymphoid tissue, although some other category might be better because of the other specialized functions of the spleen. Some of these functions are listed below:

1 Destroying old, worn-out red blood cells. As hemoglobin from the red cells is broken down, iron is salvaged and liberated into the bloodstream for reuse by the body.
2 Cleansing the blood by filtration and phagocytosis
3 Producing red blood cells before birth
4 Serving as a reservoir for blood, which can be returned to the bloodstream in case of hemorrhage or other emergency

Splenectomy (splen-nek′to-me), or surgical removal of the spleen, is usually tolerated quite well; although the spleen is the largest unit of lymphoid tissue in the body, other lymphoid tissues can take over its functions. The human body has thousands of lymphoid units, and the loss of any one unit or group ordinarily is not a threat to life.

The Mononuclear Phagocyte System

The **mononuclear phagocyte system** consists of related cells concerned with the destruction of worn-out blood cells, bacteria, cancer cells, and other foreign substances that are potentially harmful to the body. They include monocytes, relatively large white blood cells (see Fig. 12-1) that are formed in the bone marrow and then circulate in the bloodstream to various parts of the body. Upon entering the tissues, monocytes develop into **macrophages** (mak″ro-faj-es), a term that means "big eaters." Some of them are given special names; the **Kupffer's** (koop′ferz) **cells**, for example, are located in the lining of the liver blood channels (sinusoids). Other parts of the mononuclear phagocyte system are found in the spleen, bone marrow, and lymph nodes. Some macrophages are located in the lungs, where they are called *dust cells* because they ingest solid particles that enter the lungs; others are found in soft connective tissues all over the body.

An older name for this protective system is the **reticuloendothelial** (re-tik″u-lo-en″do-the′le-al) **system**. This term is still found in many books.

Disorders of the Lymphatic System and Lymphoid Tissue

Lymphangitis

In inflammation of the lymphatic vessels, called **lymphangitis** (lim-fan-ji′tis), red streaks can be seen extending along an extremity, usually beginning in the region of an infected and neglected injury. Such inflamed vessels are a danger signal, since the lymph nodes may not be able to stop a serious infection. The next step would be entrance of the pathogens into the bloodstream, causing **septicemia** (sep-ti-se′me-ah), or blood poisoning. Streptococci often are the invading organisms in such cases.

Elephantiasis

As mentioned in Chapter 5, **elephantiasis** is a great enlargement of the lower extremities resulting from blockage of lymphatic vessels by small worms called **filariae** (fi-la′re-e). These tiny parasites, carried by insects such as flies and mosquitoes, invade the tissues as embryos or immature forms. They then grow in the lymph channels and thus obstruct the flow of lymph. The swelling of the legs or, as sometimes happens in men, the scrotum, may be so great that the victim becomes incapacitated. This disease is especially common in certain parts of Asia and in some of the Pacific islands. No cure is known.

Lymphadenitis

In **lymphadenitis** (lim-fad′e-ni-tis), or inflammation of the lymph nodes, the nodes become enlarged and tender. This condition reflects the body's attempt to combat an infection. Cervical lymphadenitis occurs during measles, scarlet fever, septic sore throat, diphtheria, and frequently, the common cold. Chronic lymphadenitis may be due to the tubercle bacillus. Infections of the upper extremities cause enlarged axillary nodes, as does cancer of the mammary glands. Infections of the external genitals or the lower extremities may cause enlargement of the inguinal lymph nodes.

Lymphadenopathy

Lymphadenopathy (lim-fad″e-nop′ah-the) is a term meaning "disease of the lymph nodes." The condition may be caused by a variety of infections as well as by tumors. **Infectious mononucleosis** (mon″o-nu″kle-o′sis) is an acute viral infection the hallmark of which is enlargement of the cervical lymph nodes, a marked lymphadenopathy. Mononucleosis is fairly common among college students.

Splenomegaly

Enlargement of the spleen, known as **splenomegaly** (sple″no-meg′ah-le), accompanies certain acute infectious diseases, including scarlet fever, typhus fever, typhoid fever, and syphilis. Many tropical parasitic diseases cause splenomegaly. A certain blood fluke (flatworm) that is fairly common among workers in Japan and other parts of Asia causes marked splenic enlargement.

Splenic anemia is characterized by enlargement of the spleen, hemorrhages from the stomach, and accumulation of fluid in the abdomen. In this disease and others of the same nature, splenectomy appears to constitute a cure.

Hodgkin's Disease

Hodgkin's disease is a chronic malignant disorder, most common in young men, that is characterized by enlargement of the lymph nodes. The nodes in the neck particularly, and often those in the armpit, thorax, and groin, enlarge. The spleen may become enlarged as well. Chemotherapy and radiotherapy, either separately or in combination, have been used with good results, affording patients many years of life.

Lymphosarcoma

Lymphosarcoma (lim-fo-sar-ko'mah) is a malignant tumor of lymphoid tissue that is likely to be rapidly fatal. Fortunately, it is not a common disease. Early surgery in combination with appropriate radiotherapy offers the only possible cure at this time. (Note: A **lymphoma** is any tumor, benign or malignant, that occurs in lymphoid tissue.)

Summary

1 **Lymphatic system**
  A Functions
    1 Drainage of excess fluid from tissues
    2 Absorption of fats from small intestine
    3 Protection from foreign invaders
  B Structures
    1 Capillaries—made of endothelium (simple squamous epithelium)
    2 Lymphatic vessels
      a Superficial
      b Deep
    3 Right lymphatic duct—drains upper right part of body and empties into right subclavian vein
    4 Thoracic duct—drains remainder of body and empties into left subclavian vein
II **Lymphoid tissue**—distributed throughout body
  A General functions
    1 Removal of impurities by filtration and phagocytosis
    2 Processing of lymphocytes of immune system

  B Specialized functions
    1 Nodes—filtration of lymph
    2 Tonsils—filtration of tissue fluid
    3 Thymus
      a Processing of T-lymphocytes
      b Secretion of thymosin
      c Hormonal stimulation of T-lymphocytes in other lymphoid tissue
    4 Spleen
      a Filtration of blood
      b Destruction of old red cells
      c Production of red cells before birth
      d Storage of blood
III **Mononuclear phagocyte system**
IV **Disorders of the lymphatic system and lymphoid tissue**
  A Lymphangitis—inflammation of lymphatic vessels
  B Elephantiasis—blockage of lymphatic vessels by parasitic worms
  C Lymphadenitis—inflammation of lymph nodes that occurs during infection
  D Lymphadenopathy—disease of lymph nodes
  E Splenomegaly—enlargement of the spleen
  F Hodgkin's disease—malignant disease with enlargement of lymph nodes
  G Lymphosarcoma—malignant tumor of lymphoid tissue

Questions for Study and Review

1 What is lymph? How is it formed?
2 Briefly describe the system of lymph circulation.
3 Describe the lymphatic vessels with respect to design, appearance, and location.
4 Name the two main lymphatic ducts. What part of the body does each drain, and into what blood vessel does each empty?
5 What is the cisterna chyli and what are its purposes?
6 Name two functions of lymphoid tissue.
7 Describe the structure of a typical lymph node.
8 What are the neck nodes called and what are some of the causes of enlargement of these lymph nodes?

9 What parts of the body are drained by vessels entering the axillary nodes and what conditions cause enlargement of these nodes?

10 What parts of the body are drained by lymphatics that pass through the inguinal lymph nodes?

11 What are the different tonsils called and where are they located? What is the purpose of these and related structures?

12 What is the function of the thymus?

13 Give the location of the spleen and name several of its functions.

14 What is lymphangitis? lymphadenitis?

15 Describe elephantiasis and its cause.

16 Describe Hodgkin's disease and lymphosarcoma.

17 What is splenomegaly and what can cause it?

18 Describe the mononuclear phagocyte system.

16

Body Defenses, Immunity, and Vaccines

Behavioral Objectives

After careful study of this chapter, you should be able to:

List the factors that determine the occurrence of infection

Differentiate between nonspecific and specific body defenses and give examples of each

Briefly describe the inflammatory reaction

List several types of inborn immunity

Differentiate between natural and artificial acquired immunity

Differentiate between active and passive immunity

Define antigen and antibody

Compare T- and B-lymphocytes with respect to development and type of activity

Define the term vaccine and give several examples of vaccines

Define the term immune serum and give several examples of immune sera

List several disorders of the immune system

Selected Key Terms

The following terms are defined in the glossary:

allergy
antibody
antigen
antiserum
attenuated
autoimmunity
complement
gamma globulin
immunity
immunization
inflammation
lymphocyte
plasma cell
toxin
toxoid
transplant
vaccine

The Body's Defenses Against Disease

Chapter 5 presents a rather frightening list of harmful organisms that surround us in our environment. Fortunately, most of us survive contact with these invaders and even become more resistant to disease in the process. The job of protecting us from these harmful agents belongs in part to certain blood cells and the lymphatic system, which together make up our **immune system.**

The immune system is part of our general body defenses against disease. Some of these defenses are **nonspecific**; that is, they are effective against any harmful agent that enters the body. Other defenses are referred to as **specific**; that is, they act only against a certain agent and no other.

The Occurrence of Infection

Although the body is constantly exposed to pathogenic invasion, a large number of conditions determine whether an infection will actually occur. Many pathogens have a decided preference for certain body tissues. Some viruses attack only nerve tissue. The poliomyelitis pathogen, for example, may be inhaled or swallowed in large numbers and therefore may be in direct contact with the mucous membrane, yet it causes no apparent disorder of these respiratory or digestive system linings. In contrast, such pathogens as the influenza and cold viruses do attack these mucous membranes.

The respiratory tract is a common **portal of entry** for many pathogens. Other important avenues of entry include the digestive system and the tubes that open into the urinary and reproductive systems. Any break in the skin or in a mucous membrane allows organisms such as staphylococci easy access to the deeper tissues and nearly always leads to infection, whereas unbroken skin or membrane usually is not affected at all. The portal of entry, then, is an important condition influencing the occurrence of infection.

The **virulence** (vir′u-lens) of an organism, or the power of the organism to overcome the defenses of its host, must also be considered. Virulence has two aspects: one may be thought of as "aggressiveness," or invasive power; the other is the ability of the or-

ganism to produce **toxins**, which damage the body. The virulence of different organisms varies. The virulence of a specific organism can also change; in other words, an organism can be more dangerous at some times than at others. As a rule, organisms that come from an already infected host are more "vicious" than the same type of organism grown under laboratory conditions.

The **dose** (number) of pathogens that invade the body also has much to do with whether an infection develops. Even if the virulence of a particular organism happens to be low, infection has a better chance of occurring if the number of them that enters the body is large than if the number is small.

Finally, as noted in Chapter 5, the condition, or **predisposition**, of the individual to infection is also important. Disease organisms are around us all the time. Why does a person occasionally get colds, flus, or other infections? Part of the answer lies in the person's condition, as influenced by general physical and emotional health, nutrition, living habits, and age.

Nonspecific Defenses

The devices that protect the body against disease are usually considered successive "lines of defense," beginning with the relatively simple first, or outer, line and proceeding through progressively more complicated lines until the ultimate defense mechanism—immunity—is reached.

Chemical and Mechanical Barriers

The first line of defense against invaders includes the skin, which serves as a mechanical barrier as long as it remains intact. A serious danger to burn victims is the risk of infection due to destruction of the skin. The mucous membranes that line the passageways leading into the body also act as barriers, trapping foreign material in their sticky secretions. The cilia of the mucous membranes in the upper respiratory tract sweep impurities out of the body.

Body secretions such as tears, mucus, and digestive juices may contain acids, enzymes, or other chemicals that destroy invading organisms. Finally, certain reflexes aid in the removal of pathogens. Sneezing and coughing, for instance, tend to remove foreign matter, including microorganisms, from the upper respiratory tract. Vomiting and diarrhea are ways in which toxins (poisons) and bacteria may be expelled.

Phagocytosis

As previously noted, some white blood cells, particularly neutrophils and macrophages, have the ability to take in and destroy waste and foreign material by the process called **phagocytosis** (see Fig. 12-2). These white cells circulate in the blood or remain in the tissues. Organs such as the liver, spleen, and lungs, as well as the lymph nodes, contain large numbers of these phagocytic cells. Phagocytosis and the process of inflammation make up the second line of defense against invaders.

Inflammation

Inflammation is the body's effort to get rid of anything that irritates it (or, if this proves impossible, to limit the harmful effects of the irritant). Inflammation can occur as a result of any irritant, not only bacteria. Friction, fire, chemicals, x-rays, and cuts or blows all can be classed as irritants. If the irritant is due to pathogenic invasion, the resulting inflammation is termed an **infection**. With the entrance of pathogens and their subsequent multiplication, a whole series of defensive processes begins. Called an **inflammatory reaction**, this defense is accompanied by four classic symptoms: heat, redness, swelling, and pain.

What takes place in the course of an inflammatory reaction is briefly as follows: When tissues are injured, **histamine** (his'tah-meen) and other substances are released from the damaged cells and cause the small blood vessels to dilate. More blood then flows into the area, resulting in heat, redness, and swelling.

With the increased blood flow come a vast number of leukocytes. Now a new phenomenon occurs: the walls of the tiny blood vessels become "coarsened" in their texture (as does a piece of cloth when it is stretched), the blood flow slows down, and the leukocytes move through these altered walls and into the tissue, where they can get at the irritant directly. Fluid from the blood plasma also leaks out of the vessels into the tissues and begins to clot. When this response occurs in a local area, it helps prevent the spread of the foreign agent. The mixture of leukocytes and fluid, or the **inflammatory exudate**, causes pressure on the nerve endings; this, combined with

the increased amount of blood in the vessels, causes the pain of inflammation. As the phagocytes do their work, large numbers of them are destroyed, so that eventually the area becomes filled with dead leukocytes. The mixture of exudate, living and dead white blood cells, pathogens, and destroyed tissue cells is **pus**.

Meanwhile, the lymphatic vessels begin to drain fluid from the inflamed area and carry it toward the lymph nodes for filtration. The regional lymph nodes become enlarged and tender, a sign that they are performing their own protective function in working overtime to produce phagocytic cells that "clean" the lymph flowing through them.

Interferon

Cells infected with viruses and certain other agents produce a substance that prevents the infection of other cells. This substance was first found in cells infected with influenza virus, and it was called **interferon** because it "interferes" with multiplication of the virus. Interferon is also of interest because it has a nonspecific stimulatory effect on the immune system, to which the remainder of this chapter is devoted.

≡ Kinds of Immunity

Immunity is the final line of defense against disease. The term can be defined as "the power of an individual to resist or overcome the effects of a particular disease or other harmful agent." Immunity is a selective process; that is, immunity to one disease does not necessarily cause immunity to another. This selective characteristic is called **specificity** (spes-i-fis'i-te).

There are two main categories of immunity: **inborn** (or inherited) **immunity** and **acquired immunity**. Acquired immunity may be obtained by **natural** or **artifical** means; in addition, acquired immunity may be either **active** or **passive**. Let us investigate each category in turn.

Inborn Immunity

Although certain diseases found in animals may be transmitted to humans, many infections, such as chicken cholera, hog cholera, distemper, and various other animal diseases, do not affect human beings. However, the constitutional differences that make human beings immune to these disorders also make them susceptible to others that do not affect the lower animals. Such infections as measles, scarlet fever, diphtheria, and influenza do not seem to affect animals in contact with humans experiencing these illnesses. Thus, both humans and animals have what is called a **species immunity** to many of each other's diseases.

Another form of inborn immunity is **racial immunity**. Some racial groups appear to have a greater inborn immunity to certain diseases than other racial groups. For instance, in the United States, blacks are apparently more immune to poliomyelitis, malaria, and yellow fever than are whites. Of course, it is often difficult to tell how much of this variation in resistance to infection is due to environment and how much is due to inborn traits of the various racial groups.

Some members of a given group have a more highly developed **individual immunity** than other members. Newspapers and magazines sometimes feature the advice of an elderly person who is asked to give his secret for living to a ripe old age. One oldster may say that he practiced temperance and lived a carefully regulated life with the right amount of rest, exercise, and work, whereas the next may boast of his use of alcoholic beverages, constant smoking, lack of exercise, and other kinds of reputedly unhygienic behavior. However, it is possible that the latter person has lived through the onslaughts of toxins and disease organisms, resisted infection, and maintained health in spite of his habits, rather than because of them, thanks to the resistance factors and immunity to disease he inherited.

Acquired Immunity

Unlike inborn immunity, which is due to inherited factors, acquired immunity develops during an individual's lifetime as that individual encounters various specific harmful agents. The immune response is partially based on a reaction between substances called **antigens** (an'te-jenz) and substances called **antibodies**.

Antigens

An antigen is any foreign substance that enters the body and produces an immune response. Most antigens are large protein molecules, but carbohydrates and some lipids may also act as antigens. Antigens may be found on the surface of pathogenic organisms, on the surface of red blood cells and tissue cells, on pollens, in toxins, and in foods. The critical feature of any substance described as an antigen is that it stimulates the activity of certain white blood cells called **lymphocytes**.

Lymphocytes

Reaction to foreign substances is mediated by two different types of lymphocytes found in lymphoid tissue and in the circulating blood (see Fig. 12-1). These lymphocytes differ in their development and method of response, although both types arise from stem cells in bone marrow. Some of these immature stem cells migrate to the thymus gland and become T-cells, which constitute about 80% of the lymphocytes in the circulating blood. While in the thymus, these T-lymphocytes multiply and become capable of combining with specific foreign antigens, at which time they are described as **sensitized**. These thymus-derived cells produce an immunity that is said to be **cell mediated**.

How lymphocytes act in immunity has yet to be completely established; however, it is known that there are several types of T-lymphocytes with different functions. Some of these functions are as follows:

1 To destroy foreign cells directly
2 To help B-cells act
3 To suppress the immune response in order to regulate it
4 To release substances that stimulate other lymphocytes and macrophages and thereby assist in the destruction of foreign cells

This part of the immune system is responsible for defense against cancer cells, certain viruses, and some bacteria, as well as for the rejection of tissue transplanted from another person.

It is believed that, before entering the blood, the B-lymphocytes mature in the fetal liver, the lymphoid tissue associated with the small intestine, the tonsils, and the appendix. Exposure to an antigen stimulates B-lymphocytes to multiply rapidly and produce large numbers (clones) of **plasma cells** in the blood. These plasma cells produce specific antibodies that circulate in the blood, providing the form of immunity described as **humoral immunity**. All antibodies are contained in a portion of the blood plasma called the **gamma globulin** fraction.

The Antigen–Antibody Reaction

The antibody that is produced in response to a specific antigen, such as a bacterial cell or a toxin, has a shape that matches some part of that antigen, much in the same way that the shape of a key matches the shape of its lock. For this reason the antibody can bind specifically to the antigen that caused its production and thereby destroy or inactivate it. In the laboratory this can be seen as a settling (precipitation) or a clumping (agglutination) of the antigen–antibody combination, as is seen in the typing of red blood cells. The destruction of foreign cells sometimes requires the enzymatic activity of a group of nonspecific proteins in the blood called **complement**.

Naturally Acquired Immunity

Immunity may be acquired naturally through contraction of a specific disease. In this case, antibodies manufactured by the infected person's cells act against the infecting agent or its toxins. Each time a person is invaded by the organisms of a disease, his or her cells may manufacture antibodies that provide immunity against the infection. Such immunity may last for years and in some cases lasts for life. Because the host is actively involved in the production of antibodies, this type of immunity is called **active immunity**.

The infection that calls forth the immunity may be a subclinical or inapparent infection that is so mild as to cause no symptoms. Nevertheless, it may stimulate the host's cells to produce an active immunity.

Immunity may also be naturally acquired by a fetus through the passage of antibodies from the mother through the placenta. Because these antibodies come from an outside source, this type of immunity is called **passive immunity**. The antibodies obtained in this way do not last as long as actively produced antibodies, but they do help protect the infant for about 6 months, at which time the child's own immune system begins to function. Nursing an infant can lengthen this period of protection owing to the presence of specific antibodies in breast milk and colostrum. These are the only known examples of naturally acquired passive immunity.

Artificially Acquired Immunity

A person who is not exposed to repeated small doses of a particular organism has no antibodies against that organism and is therefore defenseless against a heavy onslaught of the pathogen. Therefore, artificial measures are usually taken to cause persons' tissues to actively manufacture antibodies. One could inject virulent pathogens into the tissues, but obviously this would be dangerous. Instead, the harmful agent is treated to reduce its virulence and then administered. In this way the tissues are made to produce antibodies without causing a serious illness. This process is known as **vaccination** (vak″sin-a′shun), or **immunization**, and the solution used is called a **vaccine** (vak-seen′). Ordinarily, the administration of a vaccine is a preventive measure designed to provide protection in anticipation of invasion by a certain disease organism.

Vaccines

Vaccines can be made with organisms killed by heat or chemicals or with live organisms. If live organisms are used, they must be nonvirulent for humans, such as the cowpox virus used for smallpox immunization, or they must be treated in the laboratory to weaken them as human pathogens. An organism weakened for use in vaccines is described as **attenuated**. A third type of vaccine is made from a form of the toxin produced by a disease organism. The toxin is altered with heat or chemicals to reduce its harmfulness, but it can still function as an antigen to induce immunity. Such an altered toxin is called a **toxoid**.

Examples of Vaccines

To nearly everyone, the word *vaccination* means inoculation against smallpox. According to the World Health Organization, however, smallpox is now virtually an extinct disease as a result of widespread immunization programs. Mandatory vaccination has been discontinued because the side-effects of the vaccine are thought to be more hazardous than the probability of contraction of the disease. The appearance of a few isolated cases may lead to rethinking about the need for vaccination against smallpox.

Because of the seriousness of whooping cough in young infants, early inoculation with whooping cough, or **pertussis** (per-tus′is), vaccine, made from heat-killed whooping cough bacteria, is recommended. The pertussis vaccine usually is given in conjunction with diphtheria toxoid and tetanus toxoid, all in one mixture. This combination, usually referred to as *DPT,* may be given as early as the second month of life and should be followed by additional injections at 4 and 6 months and again when the child enters a nursery, a school, or any other environment in which he or she might be exposed to one of these contagions.

Vaccines are now available against many common contagious diseases, exceptions being the common cold and chicken pox. The decrease in the incidences of smallpox and typhoid fever is so great that immunizations for these diseases in the United States no longer are recommended.

A great deal of intensive research in viruses has lead to the development of vaccines for an increasing number of viral diseases. Spectacular results in preventing poliomyelitis have been obtained by the use of a variety of vaccines. The first of these was the Salk vaccine made with killed poliovirus. Now the more convenient live attenuated oral vaccines, such as the Sabin, are used most. A number of vaccines have been developed against influenza, which is caused by several different strains of virus. The measles (rubeola), mumps, and rubella (German measles) vaccine, MMR, made with live attenuated viruses, is proving to be effective. The use of a rubella vaccine should lower the number of birth defects; rubella itself is very mild but has serious effects on the developing fetus (see Appendix, Table 3).

The rabies vaccine is an exception to the rule that a vaccine should be given before the invasion of the disease organism. Rabies is a viral disease transmitted by the bite of such animals as dogs, cats, wolves, coyotes, foxes, and bats. There is no cure for rabies; it is fatal in nearly all cases. However, the disease develops so slowly that affected persons vaccinated after transmission of the organism still have time to develop an active immunity. The vaccine now in use for humans is a killed virus vaccine. It may be given prophylactically to persons who are in routine contact with animals and to anyone bitten by an animal suspected of having rabies. An important factor in controlling rabies is the immunization of all pet dogs and cats.

A final word about the long-term efficacy of vaccines: in many cases an active immunity acquired by artificial (or even natural) means does not last a lifetime. Repeated inoculations, called *booster shots,* administered at intervals help maintain a high titer (level) of antibodies in the blood. The reason for this response has to do with the lymphocytes previously described. After contacting an antigen, some lympho-

cytes become **memory cells**. These memory cells survive for a long time in the body and are ready to respond immediately when they encounter that same antigen again. The number of booster injections recommended varies with the disease and with the environment or range of exposure of the individual.

Passive Immunization

It takes several weeks to produce a naturally acquired active immunity and even longer to produce an artificial active immunity through the administration of a vaccine. Therefore, a person who receives a large dose of virulent organisms and has no established immunity to them stands in great danger. To prevent catastrophe, then, the victim must quickly receive a counteracting dose of borrowed antibodies. This is accomplished through the administration of an **immune serum**, the nature and origin of which will be explained shortly. The immune serum gives short-lived but effective protection against the invaders in the form of an artificially acquired passive immunity. A serum that is given for the purpose of providing an immunity may also be called an **antiserum**.

There are a number of differences between vaccines and antisera. Administration of a vaccine causes antibody formation by the body tissues. In the administration of an antiserum, in contrast, the antibodies are supplied "ready made." However, the passive immunity produced by an antiserum does not last as long as that actively produced by the body tissues.

Sera prepared for immune purposes are often derived from animals, mainly horses. It has been found that the tissues of the horse produce large quantities of antibodies in response to the injection of organisms or their toxins. After repeated injections, the horse is bled according to careful sterile technique; because of the size of the animal it is possible to remove large quantities of blood without causing injury. The blood is allowed to clot, and the serum is removed and packaged in sterile glass vials or other appropriate containers. It is then sent to the hospital, clinic, or doctor's office for use. Immune sera are usually used in emergencies, that is, in situations in which there is no time to wait until an active immunity has developed. Injecting humans with serum derived from animals is not without its problems. The foreign proteins in animal sera may cause an often serious sensitivity reaction, called **serum sickness** (see Chap. 12). To avoid this problem, human antibody in the form of gamma globulin may be used.

Examples of Antisera

Some immune sera contain antibodies, known as **antitoxins**, that neutralize toxins but have no effect on the toxic organisms themselves. Certain antibodies act directly on pathogens, engulfing and destroying them or preventing their continued reproduction. Some antisera are obtained from animal sources, others from human sources. Some immune sera are listed below:

1 Diphtheria antitoxin, obtained from immunized horses

2 Tetanus immune globulin, effective in preventing lockjaw (tetanus), which is often a complication of neglected wounds. Because tetanus immune globulin is of human origin, there is less chance of untoward reactions with it than with sera obtained from horses.

3 Measles immune globulin, from human serum, used for susceptible infants or debilitated children who have been exposed to measles. Active immunization with the live vaccine should be done 8 to 10 weeks after the immune serum has been given.

4 Immune serum globulin, from pooled normal human plasma, which may be effective in the prevention of infectious hepatitis

5 The immune globulin Rho (D), a concentrated human antibody, given to prevent the formation of antibodies against the Rh factor in an Rh-negative mother following the birth of an Rh-positive infant (or even in a miscarriage of a presumably Rh-positive fetus) (see Chap. 12). It is also given when Rh transfusion incompatibilities occur.

6 Anti–snake bite sera, or **antivenins** (an-te-ven′ins), used to combat the effects of bites of certain poisonous snakes

7 Botulism antitoxin, from horses, an antiserum that offers the best hope for botulism victims, although only if given early

8 Rabies antiserum, from humans or horses, used with vaccine to treat victims of bites of rabid animals

Figure 16-1 gives a summary of the different types of immunity.

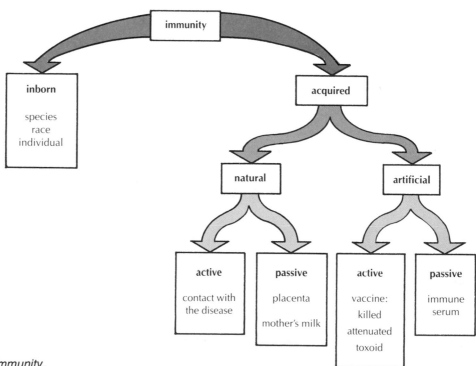

Figure 16-1. *Types of immunity.*

≡ Disorders of the Immune System

Allergy

Allergy involves antigens and antibodies, and its chemical processes are much like those of immunity. Allergy—a broader term for which is *hypersensitivity*—can be defined informally as a tendency to react unfavorably to the presence of certain substances that are normally harmless to most people.

These substances are called **allergens** (a'ler-jens) and, like most antigens, are often of a protein nature. Examples of typical allergens are pollens, house dust, horse dander (*dander* is the term for the minute scales that are found on hairs and feathers), and certain food proteins. When the tissues of a susceptible person are repeatedly exposed to an allergen—for example, the nasal mucosa to pollens—these tissues become **sensitized**; that is, antibodies are produced in them. When the next invasion of the allergen occurs, there is an antigen–antibody reaction. Normally this type of reaction takes place in the blood without harm, as in immunity. In allergy, however, the antigen–antibody reaction takes place within the cells of the sensitized tissues, with results that are disagreeable and sometimes dangerous. In the case of the nasal mucosa that has become sensitized to pollen, the allergic manifestation is **hay fever**, with symptoms much like those of the common cold.

As mentioned, an important allergic manifestation that may occur in connection with sera is serum sickness. Persons who are allergic to the proteins in serum derived from the horse or some other animal show such symptoms as fever, vomiting, joint pain, enlargement of the regional lymph nodes, and hives, or **urticaria** (ur-ti-ka're-ah). This type of allergic reaction can be severe but is rarely fatal.

Many drugs can bring about the allergic state, particularly aspirin, barbiturates, and the antibiotics (especially penicillin). In some cases of allergy, it is possible to desensitize a person by means of repeated injections of the offending allergen at short intervals. Unfortunately, this form of protection does not last long.

The antigen–antibody reaction in sensitive individuals may cause the release of excessive amounts of histamine. The histamine causes dilation and leaking from capillaries as well as contraction of involuntary muscles (*e.g.,* in the bronchi). Sometimes a group of drugs called *antihistamines* is effective in treating certain cases of allergy.

Some allergic disorders are strongly associated with emotional disturbances. Asthma and **migraine** (mi'grane), or sick headache, are two examples of this type. In such disorders the interaction of body and mind is not fully understood.

Autoimmunity

The term **autoimmunity** refers to an abnormal reactivity to one's own tissues. The body's immune system reacts to its own cells, described as "self," as if they were foreign substances, described as "nonself." Normally, the immune system learns to ignore (tolerate) the body's own tissues early in life. The loss of this immune tolerance may be a cause of such disorders as rheumatoid arthritis, lupus erythematosus, myasthenia gravis, glomerulonephritis, and some forms of diabetes.

Immune Deficiency Diseases

Occasionally, an individual is born with some failure in the immune system. This failure may involve any part of the immune system and may vary in severity. An infant in whom immune system failure is complete will not survive for more than one year unless extraordinary medical efforts are made to preserve his or her life. The rare but well-publicized cases of children kept alive in germ-free "bubbles" are examples.

Although most immune deficiencies are inherited, they may also be acquired as a result of disease. A tragic illustration of immune deficiency acquired as a result of infection is the disease **AIDS** (acquired immune deficiency syndrome), which has primarily affected a few limited population groups, including male homosexuals and intravenous drug users. The disease is caused by a virus called **HIV** that destroys T-lymphocytes. Because of the resulting weakness in the immune system, affected persons are subject to some uncommon diseases, including a parasitic pneumonia and a highly malignant sarcoma. Identification of the HIV virus has raised hopes for the development of a vaccine against AIDS.

Cancer

Cancer cells differ slightly from normal body cells and therefore should be recognized by the immune system. The fact that persons with AIDS and other immune deficiencies develop cancer at a higher than normal rate suggests that this is so. Cancer cells probably form continuously in the body but normally are destroyed by the immune system, a process called **immune surveillance** (sur-vay'lans). As a person ages, cell-mediated immunity declines and cancer is more likely to develop.

Some efforts are being made to treat cancer by stimulating the patient's immune system, a practice called **immunotherapy** (i-mu″no-ther′ah-pe). A vaccine originally used for the prevention of tuberculosis, BCG, has been used for this purpose. In combination with other standard cancer therapies, this method has helped in treating childhood leukemias, melanomas, and bronchial cancers, among others.

≡ Transplants and the Rejection Syndrome

The hope that organs and tissues might be obtained from animals or other human beings to replace injured or incompetent parts of the body has long been under discussion. Much experimental work with **transplantation** (grafting) of organs and tissues in animals has preceded transplant operations in humans. Transplants by grafting of bone marrow, lymphoid tissue, skin, eye corneas, parathyroid glands, ovaries, kidneys, lungs, heart, liver, and uterus are among those that have been attempted. The natural tendency of every organism to destroy foreign substances, including tissues from another person or any other animal, has been the most formidable obstruction to complete success. This normal antigen–antibody reaction has, in this case, been called the **rejection syndrome.**

In all cases of transplanting or grafting, the tissues of the donor, the person donating the part, should be typed in much the same way that blood is typed when a transfusion is given. Blood types are much fewer in number than tissue substances; thus, the process of obtaining matching blood is much less involved than is the process of obtaining matching tissues. Tissue typing is being done in a number of laboratories, and an effort is being made to obtain donors whose tissues contain relatively few antigens that might cause transplant rejection in a recipient (the person receiving the part).

Because it has been impossible to completely match all the antigens of a donor with those of the recipient, drugs that suppress the immune reaction to the transplanted organ are given to the recipient. As you must now realize, these drugs also leave the patient unprotected from infection. Since much of the reaction against the foreign material in transplants is believed to be generated by the T-lymphocytes, efforts are being made, using drugs and antilymphocyte antibodies, to suppress the action of these cells without damaging the B-lymphocytes. The B-cells produce humoral antibodies—those that circulate in the blood and lymph—and are thought to be most important in preventing infections. Success with transplants will increase when methods are found to suppress the immune response to transplants without destroying the recipient's ability to combat disease.

Summary

I Factors that influence occurrence of infection
  A Portal of entry of pathogen
  B Virulence of pathogen
    1 Invasive power
    2 Production of toxins (poisons)
  C Dose (number) of pathogens
  D Predisposition of host
II Nonspecific defenses against disease
  A Chemical and mechanical barriers
    1 Skin
    2 Mucous membranes
    3 Body secretions—acid pH, enzymes
    4 Reflexes—coughing, sneezing
  B Phagocytosis—mainly by neutrophils and macrophages
  C Inflammation
  D Interferon—substance released from virus-

infected cells that prevents infection of other cells and stimulates the immune response

III Immunity—specific defenses against disease

  A Inborn immunity (inherited)—species, racial, individual

  B Acquired immunity—obtained during life

    1 Immune response

      a Antigens—stimulate lymphocyte activity

      b Antibodies—destroy pathogens or neutralize toxins

      c Lymphocytes

        (1) T-lymphocytes—processed in thymus; produce cell-mediated immunity

        (2) B-lymphocytes—mature in lymphoid tissue and develop into plasma cells that produce circulating antibodies; produce humoral immunity

    2 Naturally acquired immunity

      a Active—acquired through contact with the disease

      b Passive—acquired from antibodies obtained through placenta and mother's milk

    3 Artificially acquired immunity

      a Active—immunization with vaccines

      b Passive—administration of immune serum (antiserum)

IV Disorders of the immune system

  A Allergy—hypersensitivity to normally harmless substances (allergens)

  B Autoimmunity—abnormal response to body's own tissues

  C Immune deficiency disease—failure in the immune system

    1 Hereditary

    2 Acquired through disease

  D Cancer—may be partly due to failure of immune system to destroy abnormal cells (surveillance)

V Transplantation

Questions for Study and Review

1 Name four conditions that determine whether an infection will occur in the body.

2 What are the body's "lines of defense" against disease?

3 Describe the process of inflammation.

4 Define *immunity* and describe the basic immune process.

5 Give three examples of inborn immunity.

6 What is the basic difference between inborn and acquired immunity?

7 How do T- and B-lymphocytes differ? In what ways are they the same?

8 Why is the reaction between an antigen and an antibody described as specific?

9 Outline the various categories of acquired immunity and give an example of each.

10 What is a vaccine? a toxoid? Give examples of each. What is a booster shot?

11 What is an immune serum? Give examples. Define *antitoxin*.

12 Name two sources of antisera. Why is one sometimes used in preference to another?

13 Define *allergy*. How is the process of allergy like that of immunity, and how do they differ?

14 What is an allergen? Give some examples.

15 Name and describe some typical allergic disorders. Why would the diagnosis of some of these be especially difficult?

16 What does *autoimmunity* mean? Name four disorders caused by autoimmunity.

17 Why are bone marrow transplants sometimes used to treat cases of immune deficiency disease?

18 What does *AIDS* stand for?

19 What is meant by *rejection syndrome* and what is being done to offset this syndrome?

17

Respiration

Behavioral Objectives

After careful study of this chapter, you should be able to:

Describe the purpose of the respiratory system

Differentiate between external and internal respiration

Name all of the structures of the respiratory system

Explain how food and foreign materials are kept out of the respiratory tract

Explain the mechanism for pulmonary ventilation

List and define five breathing volumes

List the ways in which oxygen and carbon dioxide are transported in the blood

Explain how carbon dioxide serves to regulate the pH of the blood

Describe the ways in which respiration is regulated

List and define five abnormal respiration rates

List and define five conditions resulting from abnormal respiration

Describe several types of respiratory infection

Name the diseases involved in chronic obstructive pulmonary disease (COPD)

Selected Key Terms

The following terms are defined in the glossary:

alveolus (pl., alveoli)
bronchiole
bronchus (pl., bronchi)
chemoreceptor
diaphragm
emphysema
epiglottis
hemoglobin
hilus (hilum)
hypoxia
larynx
lung
mediastinum
pharynx
pleura
pneumothorax
respiration
surfactant
trachea
ventilation

A primary requirement for all body cell activities and growth is oxygen, which is needed to obtain energy from food. The fundamental purpose of the respiratory system is to supply oxygen to the individual tissue cells and to remove their gaseous waste product, carbon dioxide. **Breathing**, or **ventilation**, refers to the inhalation and exhalation of air. Air is a mixture of oxygen, nitrogen, carbon dioxide, and other gases; the pressure of these gases varies, depending on the elevation above sea level. Respiration has two components. The first, called **external respiration**, takes place only in the lungs, where oxygen from the outside air enters the blood and carbon dioxide leaves the blood to be breathed into the outside air (Fig. 17-1). In the second, called **internal respiration**, gas exchanges take place between the blood and the body cells, with oxygen leaving the blood and entering the cells at the same time that carbon dioxide leaves the cells and enters the blood (see Fig. 14-8).

The respiratory system is an intricate arrangement of spaces and passageways that conduct air into the lungs. These spaces include the **nasal cavities**; the **pharynx** (far'inks), which is common to the digestive and respiratory systems; the voice box, or **larynx** (lar'inks); the windpipe, or **trachea** (tra'ke-ah); and the **lungs** themselves, with their conducting tubes

Figure 17-1. *Diagram of external respiration showing the diffusion of gas molecules through the cell membranes and throughout the capillary blood and air in the alveolus.*

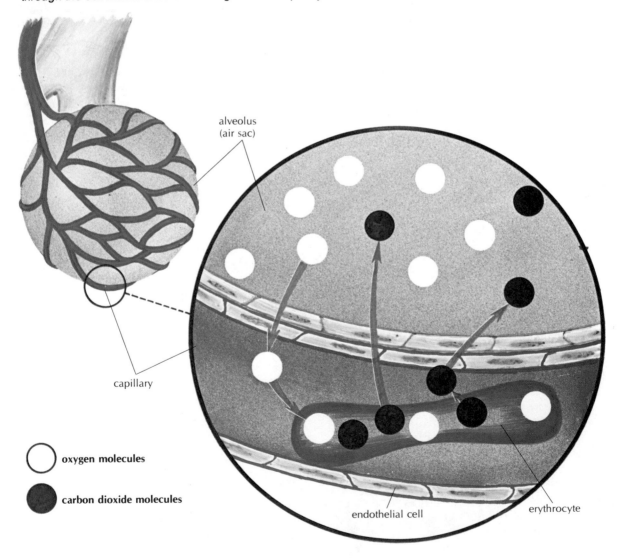

alveolus
(air sac)

capillary

○ **oxygen molecules**

● **carbon dioxide molecules**

endothelial cell

erythrocyte

and air sacs. The entire system might be thought of as a pathway for air between the atmosphere and the blood (Fig. 17-2).

The Respiratory System

The Nasal Cavities

Air makes its initial entrance into the body through the openings in the nose called the **nostrils**. Immediately inside the nostrils, located between the roof of the mouth and the cranium, are the two spaces known as the **nasal cavities**. These two spaces are separated from each other by a partition, the **nasal septum**. The septum and the walls of the nasal cavities are constructed of bone covered with mucous membrane. From the lateral (side) walls of each nasal cavity are three projections called the **conchae** (kong′ke). The conchae greatly increase the surface over which air must travel on its way through the nasal cavities.

The lining of the nasal cavities is a mucous membrane, which contains many blood vessels that bring heat and moisture to it. The cells of this membrane secrete a large amount of fluid—up to 1 quart each day. It is better to breathe through the nose than through the mouth because of changes produced in the air as it comes in contact with the lining of the nose:

1 Foreign bodies, such as dust particles and pathogens, are filtered out by the hairs of the nostrils or caught in the surface mucus.
2 Air is warmed by the blood in the vascular membrane.
3 Air is moistened by the liquid secretion.

The **sinuses** are small cavities lined with mucous membrane in the bones of the skull. The sinuses communicate with the nasal cavities, and they are highly susceptible to infection (see Chap. 5).

The Pharynx

The muscular **pharynx**, or throat, carries air into the respiratory tract and foods and liquids into the digestive system. The upper portion located immediately behind the nasal cavity is called the **nasopharynx** (na″zo-far′inks), the middle section located behind the mouth is called the **oropharynx** (o″ro-far′inks),

and the lowest portion is called the **laryngeal** (lah-rin′je-al) **pharynx**. This last section opens into the larynx toward the front and into the esophagus toward the back.

The Larynx

The **larynx**, or voice box, is located between the pharynx and the trachea. It has a framework of cartilage that protrudes in the front of the neck and sometimes is referred to as the *Adam's apple*. The larynx is considerably larger in the male than in the female; hence, the Adam's apple is much more prominent in the male. At the upper end of the larynx are the **vocal cords**, which serve in the production of speech. They are set into vibration by the flow of air from the lungs. A difference in the size of the larynx is what accounts for the difference between male and female voices; because a man's larynx is larger than a woman's, his voice is lower in pitch. The nasal cavities, the sinuses, and the pharynx all serve as resonating chambers for speech, just as the cabinet does for a stereo speaker.

The space between these two vocal cords is called the **glottis** (glot′is), and the little leaf-shaped cartilage that covers the larynx during swallowing is called the **epiglottis** (ep-e-glot′is). The epiglottis helps keep food out of the remainder of the respiratory tract. As the larynx moves upward and forward during swallowing, the epiglottis moves downward, covering the opening into the larynx. You can feel the larynx move upward toward the epiglottis during this process by placing the flat ends of your fingers on your larynx as you swallow.

The larynx is lined with ciliated mucous membrane. The cilia trap dust and other particles, moving them upward to the pharynx to be expelled by coughing, sneezing, or blowing the nose.

The Trachea, or Windpipe

The **trachea** is a tube that extends from the lower edge of the larynx to the upper part of the chest above the heart. It has a framework of cartilages to keep it open. These cartilages, shaped somewhat like a tiny horseshoe or the letter C, are found along the entire length of the trachea. All the open sections of these cartilages are at the back so that the esophagus can bulge into this region during swallowing. The purpose of the trachea is to conduct air between the larynx and the lungs.

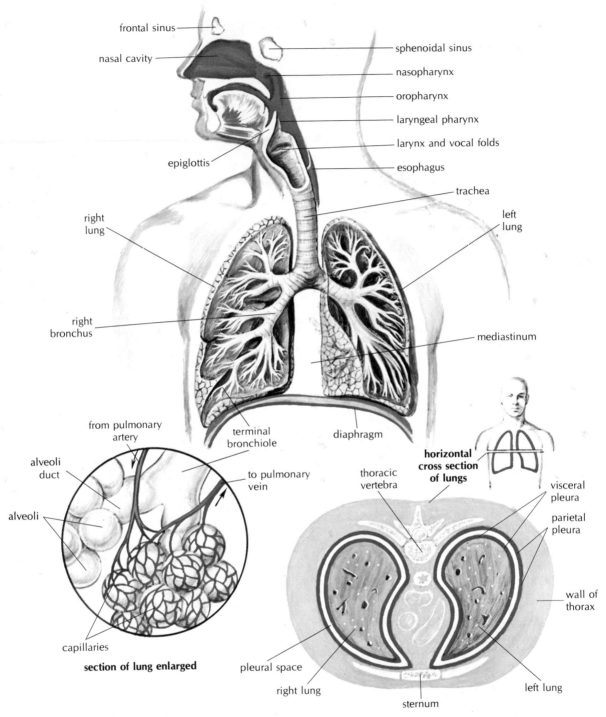

frontal sinus

nasal cavity

sphenoidal sinus

nasopharynx

oropharynx

laryngeal pharynx

larynx and vocal folds

esophagus

epiglottis

trachea

right lung

left lung

right bronchus

mediastinum

from pulmonary artery

terminal bronchiole

diaphragm

alveoli duct

to pulmonary vein

horizontal cross section of lungs

thoracic vertebra

visceral pleura

alveoli

parietal pleura

wall of thorax

capillaries

section of lung enlarged

pleural space

right lung

left lung

sternum

Figure 17-2. *Respiratory system.*

The Bronchi and Bronchioles

The trachea divides into two **bronchi** (brong'ki) which enter the lungs. The right bronchus is considerably larger in diameter than the left and extends downward in a more vertical direction. Therefore, if a foreign body is inhaled, it is likely to enter the right lung. Each bronchus enters the lung at a notch or depression called the **hilus** (hi'lus) or **hilum** (hi'lum). The blood vessels and nerves also connect with the lung in this region.

The Lungs

The **lungs** are the organs in which external respiration takes place through the extremely thin and delicate lung tissues. The two lungs, set side by side in the thoracic cavity, are constructed in the following manner:

Each bronchus enters the lung at the hilus and immediately subdivides. Because the subdivisions of the bronchi resemble the branches of a tree, they have been given the common name *bronchial tree*. The bronchi subdivide again and again, forming progressively smaller divisions, the smallest of which are called **bronchioles** (brong'ke-oles). The bronchi contain small bits of cartilage, which give firmness to the walls and serve to hold the passageways open so that air can pass in and out easily. However, as the bronchi become smaller, the cartilage decreases in amount. In the bronchioles there is no cartilage at all; what remains is mostly smooth muscle, which is under the control of the autonomic nervous system.

At the end of each of the smallest subdivisions of the bronchial tree, called **terminal bronchioles**, is a cluster of air sacs, resembling a bunch of grapes. These sacs are known as **alveoli** (al-ve'o-li). Each alveolus is a single-cell layer of squamous (flat) epithelium. This very thin wall provides easy passage for the gases entering and leaving the blood as it circulates through the millions of tiny capillaries of the alveoli. Certain cells in the alveolar wall produce **surfactant** (sur-fak'tant), a substance that prevents the alveoli from collapsing by reducing the surface tension ("pull") of the fluids that line them. There are millions of alveoli in the human lung. The resulting surface in contact with gases approximates 60 square meters, about three times as much lung tissue as is necessary for life. Because of the many air spaces, the lung is light in weight; normally a piece of lung tissue dropped into a glass of water will float.

As mentioned, the pulmonary circuit brings blood to and from the lungs. In the lungs the blood passes through the capillaries around the alveoli, where the gas exchange takes place.

The Lung Cavities

The lungs occupy a considerable portion of the thoracic cavity, which is separated from the abdominal cavity by the muscular partition known as the **diaphragm**. Each lung is enveloped in a double sac of serous membrane called the **pleura**. As noted in Chapter 4, the portion of the pleura that is attached to the chest wall is called **parietal pleura**, while the portion that is reflected onto the surface of the lung is called **visceral pleura**.

The pleural cavity around the lungs is an air-tight space with a partial vacuum, which causes the pressure in this space to be less than atmospheric pressure. Because the pressure inside the lungs is higher than that in the surrounding pleural cavity, the lungs tend to remain inflated. The entire thoracic cavity is flexible, capable of expanding and contracting along with the lungs.

The region between the lungs, the **mediastinum** (me"de-as-ti'num), contains the heart, great blood vessels, esophagus, trachea, and lymph nodes.

Physiology of Respiration

Pulmonary Ventilation

Ventilation is the movement of air into and out of the lungs, as in breathing. There are two phases of ventilation (Fig. 17-3):

1 **Inhalation** is the drawing of air into the lungs.
2 **Exhalation** is the expulsion of air from the lungs.

In **inhalation**, the active phase of breathing, the respiratory muscles contract to enlarge the thoracic cavity. The diaphragm is a strong dome-shaped muscle attached around the base of the rib cage. The contraction and flattening of the diaphragm cause a piston-like downward motion that results in an increase in the vertical dimension of the chest. The rib cage is also moved upward and outward by contraction of the external intercostal muscles and, during

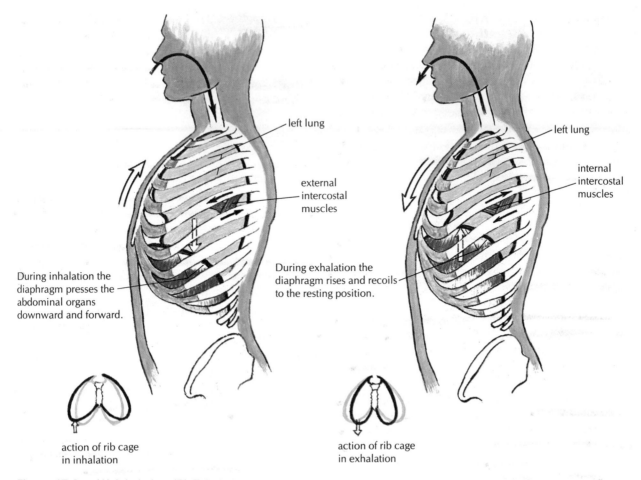

left lung

external
intercostal
muscles

During inhalation the
diaphragm presses the
abdominal organs
downward and forward.

During exhalation the
diaphragm rises and recoils
to the resting position.

left lung

internal
intercostal
muscles

action of rib cage
in inhalation

action of rib cage
in exhalation

Figure 17-3. (A) *Inhalation.* (B) *Exhalation.*

exertion, by contraction of other muscles of the neck and chest. During quiet breathing, the movement of the diaphragm accounts for most of the increase in thoracic volume.

As the thoracic cavity increases in size, gas pressure within the cavity decreases. When the pressure drops to slightly below atmospheric pressure, air is drawn into the lungs.

In **exhalation**, the passive phase of breathing, the muscles of respiration relax, allowing the ribs and diaphragm to return to their original positions. The tissues of the lung are elastic and recoil during exhalation. During forced exhalation, the internal intercostal muscles and the muscles of the abdominal wall contract, pulling the bottom of the rib cage in and down. The abdominal viscera are also pushed upward against the diaphragm.

Air Movement

Air enters the respiratory passages and flows through the ever-dividing tubes of the bronchial tree. As the air traverses this passage, it moves more and more slowly through the great number of bronchial tubes until there is virtually no forward flow as it reaches the alveoli. Here the air moves by diffusion, which soon equalizes any differences in the amounts of gases present. Each breath causes relatively little change in the gas composition of the alveoli, but normal continuous breathing ensures the presence of adequate oxygen and the removal of carbon dioxide.

Table 17-1 gives the definitions of and average values for some of the breathing volumes that are important in any evaluation of respiratory function.

Table 17-1 Breathing Volumes

Volume	Definition	Average value
Tidal volume	The amount of air moved into or out of the lungs in quiet, relaxed breathing	500 cc
Vital capacity	The volume of air that can be expelled from the lungs by maximum exhalation following maximum inhalation	4800 cc
Residual volume	The volume of air that remains in the lungs after maximum exhalation	1200 cc
Total lung capacity	The total volume of air that can be contained in the lungs after maximum inhalation	6000 cc
Functional residual capacity	The amount of air remaining in the lungs after normal exhalation	2400 cc

Gas Exchanges

The barrier that separates the air in the alveolus from the blood in the capillary is very thin and moist, ideally suited for the exchange of gases by diffusion. Normally, inspired air contains about 21% oxygen, while expired air has only 16% oxygen and 3.5% carbon dioxide. A two-way diffusion takes place through the walls of the alveoli.

Recall that **diffusion** refers to the movement of molecules from an area in which they are in higher concentration to an area where they are in lower concentration. Blood entering the lung capillaries is relatively low in oxygen, which means that oxygen will diffuse from the alveolus, where its concentration is higher, into the blood. Carbon dioxide diffuses out of the blood into the air of the alveolus for the same reason (see Fig. 17-1).

Gas Transport

Almost all the oxygen that diffuses into the capillary blood in the lungs is bound to the **hemoglobin** of the red blood cells. A very small percentage is carried in the plasma. The hemoglobin molecule is a large protein with four small iron-containing "heme" regions. The oxygen is bound to these heme portions. Arterial blood (in systemic arteries and pulmonary veins) is 97% saturated with oxygen, while venous blood (in systemic veins and pulmonary arteries) is about 70% saturated with oxygen. This 27% difference represents the oxygen that has been taken up by the cells.

In order to supply the cells, oxygen must separate from hemoglobin. Normally the bond between oxygen and hemoglobin is easily broken, with oxygen being released as blood travels into areas in which the oxygen concentration is relatively low.

The carbon dioxide produced in the tissues is transported to the lungs in three ways:

1 About 10% is dissolved in the plasma and red blood cell fluid.
2 About 20% is combined with the protein portion of hemoglobin and plasma proteins.
3 About 70% is transported as an ion, known as a **bicarbonate ion**, which is formed when carbon dioxide dissolves in blood fluids.

The bicarbonate ion is formed slowly in the plasma but much more rapidly inside the red blood cells, where an enzyme called **carbonic anhydrase** increases the speed of the reaction. The bicarbonate formed in the red blood cells moves to the plasma and then is carried to the lungs. Here, the process is reversed as bicarbonate re-enters the red blood cells and releases carbon dioxide for diffusion into the alveoli and exhalation.

Carbon dioxide is important in regulating the pH (acid–base balance) of the blood. As a bicarbonate ion is formed from carbon dioxide in the plasma, a hydrogen ion (H^+) is also produced. Therefore, the blood becomes more acid as the amount of carbon dioxide in the blood increases. The exhalation of carbon dioxide shifts the pH of the blood more toward the alkaline (base) range. The bicarbonate ion is also an important buffer in the blood (see Chap. 20).

Regulation of Respiration

Regulation of respiration is a complex process that must keep pace with moment-to-moment changes in cellular oxygen requirements and carbon dioxide production. Regulation depends primarily on the respiratory control centers located in the medulla and pons of the brain stem. Nerve impulses from the medulla are modified by the centers in the pons. Respiration is regulated so that the levels of oxygen, carbon dioxide, and acid are kept within certain limits. The control centers regulate the rate, depth, and rhythm of respiration.

From the respiratory center in the medulla, motor nerve fibers extend into the spinal cord. From the cervical (neck) part of the cord, these nerve fibers continue through the **phrenic** (fren'ik) **nerve** to the diaphragm. The diaphragm and the other muscles of respiration are voluntary in the sense that they can be regulated by messages from the higher brain centers, notably the cortex. It is possible for a person to deliberately breathe more rapidly or more slowly or to hold his breath and not breathe at all for a time. Usually we breathe without thinking about it, while the respiratory centers in the medulla and pons do the controlling.

Of vital importance in the control of respiration are the **chemoreceptors** (ke"mo-re-sep'tors). These receptors are found in structures called the *carotid* and *aortic bodies,* as well as outside the medulla of the brain stem. The carotid bodies are located near the bifurcation of the common carotid arteries, while the aortic bodies are located in the aortic arch. These bodies contain many small blood vessels and sensory neurons, which are sensitive to decreases in oxygen supply as well as to increases in carbon dioxide and acidity (H^+). Impulses are sent to the brain from the receptors in the carotid and aortic bodies. The receptor cells outside the medulla are affected by the concentration of hydrogen ion in cerebrospinal fluid (CSF) as determined by the concentrations of carbon dioxide in the blood (see Fig. 9-11).

The Effects of Abnormal Ventilation

Hyperventilation is deep, rapid respiration that occurs commonly during anxiety attacks. It causes an increase in the oxygen level and a decrease in the carbon dioxide level of the blood. The loss of carbon dioxide increases the pH of the blood (alkalosis), resulting in dizziness and tingling sensations. Breathing may stop because the respiratory control centers are not stimulated. Gradually the carbon dioxide level returns to normal and a regular breathing pattern is resumed. Symptoms of hyperventilation may be relieved by breathing into a paper bag to increase the carbon dioxide level in the blood.

In **hypoventilation**, an insufficient amount of air enters the alveoli. The many possible causes of this condition include respiratory obstruction, lung disease, toxins, damage to the respiratory center, and chest deformity. Hypoventilation results in an increase in the concentration of carbon dioxide in the blood leading to a decrease in blood pH (acidosis). Unless the respiratory center itself is injured or depressed, respiration rate may increase, but breathing is shallow and difficult.

Respiratory Rates

Normal rates of breathing vary from 12 to 20 times per minute for adults. In children, rates may vary from 20 to 40 times a minute, depending on age and size. In infants, the respiratory rate may be more than 40 times per minute. To determine the respiratory rate, the health worker counts the client's breathing for at least 30 seconds, observing in such a way that the person is unaware that a count is being made. Changes in respiratory rates are important in various disorders and should be carefully recorded.

Terms Describing Abnormal Respiration

The following is a list of terms designating various abnormalities of respiration. They are symptoms, not diseases.

1 **Hyperpnea** (hi"perp-ne'ah) refers to an increase in the depth as well as the rate of respiration.
2 **Apnea** (ap'ne-ah) is a temporary cessation of breathing.
3 **Dyspnea** (disp'ne-ah) is a subjective feeling of difficult or labored breathing.
4 **Cheyne–Stokes** (chan'stoks) respiration is a type of rhythmical variation in the depth of respiratory movements found in certain critically ill persons.
5 **Orthopnea** refers to a difficulty in breathing that is relieved by sitting in an upright position, either against two pillows in bed or in a chair.

Situations that may occur in relation to changes in respiration include the following:

1 **Cyanosis** (si"ah-no'sis) is a bluish color of the skin and mucous membranes caused by an insufficient amount of oxygen in the blood.
2 **Hypoxia** (hi-pok'se-ah) and **anoxia** (ah-nok'se-ah) are often used interchangeably to mean reduced oxygen supply to the tissues.
3 **Suffocation** is the cessation of respiration, often the result of a mechanical blockage of the respiratory passages. Suffocation can cause **asphyxia** (as-fik'se-ah), which is a lack of oxygen in inspired air.

≡ Disorders of the Respiratory System

Disorders of the Nasal Cavities and Related Structures

Sinusitis and Nasal Polyps

The sinuses are located close to the nasal cavities and in one case near the ear. Infection may easily travel into these sinuses from the mouth, the nose, and the throat along the mucous membrane lining; the resulting inflammation is called **sinusitis**. Long-standing, or chronic, sinus infection may cause changes in the epithelial cells, resulting in tumor formation. Some of these growths have a grapelike appearance and cause obstruction of the air pathway; these tumors are called **polyps** (pol'ips).

Deviated Septum

The partition separating the two nasal spaces from each other is called the *nasal septum*. Since many of us have minor structural defects, it is not surprising that the nasal septum is rarely exactly in the midline. If it is markedly to one side, it is described as a **deviated septum**. In this condition one nasal space may be considerably smaller than the other. If an affected person has an attack of hay fever or develops a cold with accompanying swelling of the mucosa, the smaller nasal cavity may be completely closed. Sometimes the septum is curved in such a way that both nasal cavities are occluded, forcing the individual to breathe through the mouth. Such an occlusion may also prevent proper drainage from the sinuses and aggravate a case of sinusitis.

Nosebleed

The most common cause of nosebleed, also called **epistaxis** (ep-e-stak'sis), is an injury or blow to the nose. Other causes include inflammation and ulceration such as may occur following a persistent discharge from a sinusitis. Growths, including polyps, can also be a cause of epistaxis. Rarely, abnormally high blood pressure causes the vessels in the nasal lining to break, resulting in varying degrees of hemorrhage. To stop a nosebleed, the affected person should remain quiet with the head slightly elevated. Pressure applied to the nostril of the bleeding side, as well as cold compresses over the nose, is usually helpful. In some cases, it may be necessary to insert a plug into the bleeding side in order to encourage adequate clotting. If these methods fail, a physician should be consulted.

Infection

The Spread of Infection

The mucosa of the respiratory tract is one of the most important portals of entry for disease-producing organisms. The transfer of disease organisms from the respiratory system of one human being to that of another occurs most rapidly in crowded places such as schools, auditoriums, theaters, churches, and prisons. Droplets from one sneeze may be loaded with many billions of disease-producing organisms. To a certain extent the mucous membranes can protect themselves by producing larger quantities of mucus. The runny nose, an unpleasant symptom of the common cold, is an attempt on the part of nature to wash away the pathogens and so protect the deeper tissues from further invasion by the infection. If the resistance of the mucous membrane is reduced, however, the membrane may act as a pathway for the spread of disease. The infection may travel along the membrane into the nasal sinuses, into the middle ear, or into the lung.

Among the infections transmitted through the respiratory passageways are the common cold, diphtheria, chickenpox, measles, influenza, pneumonia, and tuberculosis. Any infection that is confined to the nose, throat, larynx, or trachea is called an **upper respiratory infection** (often called *URI*). Records from children's wards in hospitals show that a great majority of patients with infectious diseases first developed symptoms of an upper respiratory infection.

Very often, such an infection can precipitate the onset of such a serious disease as rheumatic fever.

The respiratory passageways may become infected one by one as the organisms travel along the lining membrane. The disorder is named according to the part involved, such as pharyngitis (commonly called a *sore throat*), laryngitis, bronchitis, and so on.

The Common Cold

The common cold is the most widespread of all respiratory diseases—of all communicable diseases, for that matter. More time is lost from school and from work because of the common cold than because of any other disorder. The causative agents include many different cold viruses as well as other infectious organisms. Because there are so many causative organisms, the production of an effective vaccine against colds seems unlikely. Medical science has yet to establish the effectiveness of any method of preventing the common cold, although many methods have been proposed, including the use of large doses of vitamins, notably vitamin C.

The symptoms of the common cold are familiar: first the swollen and inflamed mucosa of the nose and the throat, then the copious discharge of watery fluid from the nose, and finally the thick and ropy discharge that occurs when the cold is subsiding. The scientific name for the common cold is **acute coryza** (ko-ri′zah); the word *coryza* can also simply mean "a nasal discharge."

A discharge from the nasal cavities may not only be a symptom of the common cold; it may also stem from sinusitis or be an important forerunner of a more serious disease.

The notion that all nasal mucus is undesirable is wrong. Mucous secretions are required to keep the tissues moist as well as to help protect the cells against invasion by pathogens. The idea that excess secretion is caused by eggs, milk, or any other food in the diet has not been proved, except in the case of an allergy.

Influenza

Influenza, or "flu," is an acute contagious disease characterized by an inflammatory condition of the upper respiratory tract accompanied by generalized aches and pains. It is caused by a virus and may spread to the sinuses as well as downward to the lungs. Inflammation of the trachea and the bronchi causes the characteristic cough of influenza, and the general infection causes an extremely weakened condition. The great danger of influenza is its tendency to develop into a particularly severe form of pneumonia. At intervals in history, there have been tremendous epidemics of influenza in which millions of people have died. Vaccines have been effective, though the immunity is of short duration.

Pneumonia

Pneumonia is an inflammation of the lungs in which the air spaces become filled with fluid. A variety of organisms, including staphylococci, pneumococci, streptococci, *Legionella pneumophilla* (as in legionnaire's disease), chlamydias, and viruses, may be responsible. Many of these pathogens may be carried by a healthy person in the mucosa of the upper respiratory tract. If the person remains in good health, these pathogens may be carried for an indefinite period with no ill effect. However, if the individual's resistance to infection is lowered, the pathogens may invade the tissues and cause disease. Exposure to inclement weather for long periods of time, alcoholism, malnutrition, a severe injury, and other debilitating or weakening conditions may cause a susceptibility to pneumonia.

There are two main kinds of pneumonia as determined by the extent of lung involvement and other factors. These are

1 **Lobar pneumonia**, in which an entire lobe of the lung is infected at one time. The organism is usually a pneumococcus, although other pathogens also may cause this disease. The Legionella organism is the causative agent of a severe lobar pneumonia that occurs mostly in localized epidemics.

2 **Bronchopneumonia**, in which the disease process is scattered here and there throughout the lung. The cause may be a staphylococcus, a gram-negative proteus or colon bacillus (not normally pathogenic), or a virus. Bronchopneumonia most often is secondary to an infection or to some agent that has lowered the individual's resistance to disease. This is the most common form of pneumonia.

A characteristic of most types of pneumonia is the formation of a fluid, or **exudate**, in the infected alveoli; this fluid consists chiefly of serum and pus cells, products of infection. Some red blood cells may be present, as indicated by red streaks in the sputum. Sometimes so many air sacs become filled with fluid that the victim finds it hard to absorb enough oxygen to maintain life.

Tuberculosis

Tuberculosis is an inflammation caused by the bacillus **Mycobacterium tuberculosis**. Although the tubercle bacillus may invade any tissue in the body, the lung is the usual site. Tuberculosis remains a leading cause of death from communicable disease primarily because of the relatively large numbers of cases among recent immigrants and poor population groups in metropolitan areas.

The lungs, with the pleurae, are the organs affected most often by tuberculosis, but other organs may also be infected. The lymph nodes in the thorax, especially those surrounding the trachea and the bronchi, frequently are involved. In tuberculous pleurisy (inflammation of the pleura) with fluid formation, fluid may collect in the pleural cavity; such a collection is called an **effusion** (e-fu'zhun). The fluid presses against the pleura and compresses the lung. If it is not removed artificially to relieve pressure against the lung, it may eventually be absorbed. Other organs that may be infected by tubercle organisms include the kidneys, certain tubes of the reproductive system, and, particularly in children, the bones of the vertebral column. Occasionally, vast numbers of the organisms may enter the bloodstream and cause a rapidly fatal tuberculosis.

Drugs are used quite successfully in many cases of tuberculosis. The best results have been obtained by use of a combination of several drugs, with prompt, intensive, and uninterrupted treatment once such a program is begun. Such therapy is usually continued for a minimum of 12 to 18 months; therefore, close supervision by the healthcare practitioner is important. Adverse drug reactions are rather common, necessitating changes in the drug combinations.

Hay Fever and Asthma

Sensitivity to plant pollens, dust, certain foods, and other allergens may lead to **hay fever** or **asthma** or both. Hay fever is characterized by a watery discharge from the eyes and nose. The symptoms of asthma are usually due to a spasm of the involuntary muscula-

ture of the bronchial tube walls. This spasm constricts the tubes so that the victim cannot exhale easily. He or she experiences a sense of suffocation and has labored breathing (dyspnea). Much has been written about the role that psychologic factors play in the causation of asthma, but individuals vary considerably, and most cases of asthma involve a multiplicity of problems.

One great difficulty in the treatment of hay fever or asthma is isolation of the particular substance to which the patient is allergic. Usually a number of skin tests are given, but in most cases the results of these are far from conclusive.

Persons with asthma may benefit from treatment with a series of injections to reduce their sensitivity to specific substances.

Emphysema and Bronchitis

Chronic obstructive pulmonary disease (COPD) is the term used to describe several lung disorders, including chronic bronchitis and emphysema. Most affected persons have symptoms and lung damage characteristic of both diseases. In chronic bronchitis the linings of the airways are chronically inflamed and produce excessive secretions. Emphysema is characterized by dilation and finally destruction of the alveoli.

In COPD respiratory function is impaired by obstruction to normal air flow, by air trapping and overinflation of parts of the lungs, and by reduced exchange of oxygen and carbon dioxide. In the early stages of these diseases, the small airways are involved, and several years may pass before symptoms become evident. Later the affected person develops dyspnea owing to the difficulty of exhaling air through the obstructed air passages.

The progressive character of these diseases may be reversed when they are detected early in their course and irritants to the respiratory system are eliminated. The major culprit is cigarette smoke, although industrial wastes and air pollution also play a large role. In the popular press the word *emphysema* is used to mean *COPD*.

Atelectasis

Atelectasis (at"e-lek'tah-sis) is the incomplete expansion of a lung or portion of a lung. This disorder may affect scattered groups of alveoli or an entire lobe, causing its collapse. The affected person will have hypoxia and dyspnea. Obstruction by mucous plugs in COPD, by foreign bodies, or by lung cancer is a cause of this disorder. Another cause may be the insufficient production of surfactant, as in **hyaline membrane disease** (seen in premature newborns) and **adult respiratory distress syndrome**. Atelectasis is also seen in cases of external compression of the lung or interference with deep breathing, for example with pain from fractured ribs.

Lung Cancer

Cancer of the lungs is the most common cause of death due to cancer in males, and it has overtaken breast cancer as a cause of death in females. By far the most important cause of lung cancer is cigarette smoking. Smokers suffer from lung cancer ten times as often as nonsmokers. The risk of getting cancer of the lungs is increased in persons who started smoking early in life, who smoke large numbers of cigarettes daily, and who inhale deeply. Smokers who are exposed to toxic chemicals or particles in the air have an even higher rate of lung cancer. Smoking has also been linked with an increase in COPD and cancers of respiratory passages.

Early lung cancer has few symptoms. However, it may be discovered during a routine chest x-ray examination. Too often, emphasis on the danger of exposure to radiation from x-ray machines can frighten people away from routine chest x-ray examination and thus prevent early diagnosis of lung cancer. Early detection is absolutely essential if there is to be any possibility of a cure. Modern x-ray machines in competent hands pose such slight danger, at least to persons over 40 years of age, as to be more than offset by the advantages of discovering a tumor while it is still small enough to be completely removed.

A common form of lung cancer is **bronchogenic** (brong-ko-jen′ik) **carcinoma**, so-called because the malignancy originates in a bronchus. The tumor may grow until the bronchus is blocked, cutting off the supply of air to that lung. The lung then collapses, and the secretions trapped in the lung spaces become infected, with a resulting pneumonia or formation of a lung abscess. Such a lung cancer can also spread, causing secondary growths in the lymph nodes of the chest and neck as well as in the brain and other parts of the body. A treatment that offers a possibility of cure, before secondary growths have had time to form, is complete removal of the lung. This operation is called a **pneumonectomy** (nu″mo-nek′to-me).

Malignant tumors of the stomach, breast, prostate gland, and other organs may spread to the lungs, causing secondary growths (metastases).

Disorders Involving the Pleural Cavity

Pleurisy (ploor′i-se), or inflammation of the pleura, usually accompanies a lung infection—particularly pneumonia or tuberculosis. This condition can be quite painful, because the inflammation produces a sticky exudate that roughens the pleura of both the lung and the chest wall; when the two surfaces rub together during ventilation, the roughness causes acute irritation. The two surfaces' sticking together is called an **adhesion** (ad-he′zhun). Infection of the pleura also causes an increase in the amount of pleural fluid. This may accumulate in the pleural cavity in such large quantities as to compress the lung, making the patient unable to obtain enough air. Withdrawal of the fluid by chest tube or syringe may be necessary.

Pneumothorax is an accumulation of air in the pleural cavity. The lung on the affected side collapses, causing the affected person to have great difficulty breathing. Pneumothorax may be caused by a wound in the chest wall or by rupture of lung air spaces. In a pneumothorax caused by a penetrating wound in the chest wall, an airtight cover over the opening will prevent further air from entering. The remaining lung can then function to provide adequate amounts of oxygen.

Blood in the pleural cavity, a condition called **hemothorax**, is also caused by penetrating wounds of the chest. In such cases the first priority is to stop the bleeding.

☰ Some Practical Aspects of Room Ventilation

People usually devote a great deal of thought to the food they take into their bodies but very little to the air they breathe. Consideration of the latter will go a long way toward the maintenance of health. Many ideas concerning ventilation are erroneous. There are fresh-air fiends who open windows at night, allowing cold air to chill their bodies unduly. This habit may be a carryover from the days when wood stoves or gas heaters had no vent to the outside, and it was important to prevent an accumulation of deadly carbon monoxide and other gases in the room. Other persons seemingly are not happy outside of a stuffy, unventilated, overheated room. Scientific studies have shown that the factors that make air healthy and comfortable are the following:

1   Enough coolness to remove some body heat without chilling
2   Avoidance of drafts, which have been shown to create disturbances within the body that cause a predisposition to colds and other infections
3   Enough circulation of air to remove unpleasant odors or other pollutants

Various mechanisms for modifying or conditioning the air have been devised. Most of their emphasis has been on the alteration of temperature, the air being heated if the outside temperature is low and cooled if the outside air is too warm. Modern heaters are vented so that noxious gases do not enter living quarters, and in many areas laws have been passed prohibiting the installation of unvented heaters. Nevertheless, deaths from the escape of poisonous gases from heaters still are all too common. The general public should be better informed about ventilation and air conditioning.

Desirable modification of air includes more than mere heating or cooling. The humidity should be maintained at the proper level, and some effective means of filtering the air should be provided. Air filters should be cleaned regularly; otherwise, they are worse than useless. An acceptable air conditioner should maintain adequate air circulation without blowing a gale and chilling everyone within its range.

≡ Special Equipment for Respiratory Tract Treatments

The **bronchoscope** (brong'ko-skope) is a tubular instrument arranged in such a way that the doctor can inspect the bronchi and the larger bronchial tubes. The bronchoscope is passed into the respiratory tract by way of the mouth and the pharynx. It may be used to remove foreign bodies or to inspect the bronchi or bronchioles for tumors or other evidence of disease. Children inhale a variety of objects, such as pins, beans, pieces of nuts, and small coins, all of which may be removed with the aid of a bronchoscope. If

such things are left in the lung, an abscess or other serious complication may cause death.

Oxygen therapy is used to sustain life when some condition interferes with adequate oxygen supply to the tissues. The oxygen must first have moisture added by being bubbled through water that is at room temperature or heated. Oxygen may be delivered to the patient by mask, catheter, or nasal prongs. Since there is danger of fire when oxygen is being administered, no one in the room should smoke.

A **suction apparatus** is used for removing mucus or other substances from the respiratory tract. Usually, the device takes the form of a drainage bottle, with one tube from it leading to the area to be drained, and another tube from the bottle leading to a suction machine. When the suction is applied, the drainage flows from the patient's respiratory tract into the bottle.

A **tracheostomy** (tra″ke-os′to-me) **tube** is used if the pharynx or the larynx is obstructed. It is a small metal or plastic tube that is inserted through a cut made in the trachea, and it acts as an artificial airway for ventilation. The procedure for the insertion of such a tube is a *tracheostomy.* The word **tracheotomy** (tra″ke-ot′o-me) refers to the incision in the trachea. Very often, emergency tracheotomies are performed on children who have inhaled something large enough to block the respiratory passages; without this procedure, such children would die in a very short time.

Artificial respiration is resorted to when an individual has temporarily lost the capacity to perform the normal motions of respiration. Such emergencies include cases of smoke asphyxiation, electric shock, and drowning.

Classes are offered by many public agencies in the techniques of mouth-to-mouth respiration as well as cardiac massage to revive persons experiencing respiratory or cardiac arrest. This technique is known as *cardiopulmonary resuscitation,* or *CPR.*

Summary

I   **Respiration**—supply of oxygen to tissue cells and removal of carbon dioxide
   A   External respiration—exchange of gases between alveoli and blood
   B   Internal respiration—exchange of gases between blood and cells

II Respiratory system

A Nasal cavities—filter, warm, and moisten air

B Pharynx (throat)—carries air into respiratory tract and food into digestive tract

C Larynx (voice box)—contains vocal cords

   1 Epiglottis—covers larynx on swallowing to help prevent food from entering

D Trachea (windpipe)

E Bronchi—branches of trachea that enter lungs and then subdivide

   1 Bronchioles—smallest subdivisions

F Lungs

   1 Pleura—membrane that encloses lung and lines chest wall

   2 Mediastinum—space and organs between lungs

G Alveoli—tiny air sacs in lungs

III Physiology of respiration

A Pulmonary ventilation

   1 Inhalation—drawing of air into lungs

   2 Exhalation—expulsion of air from lungs

   3 Breathing volumes—tidal volume, vital capacity, total lung capacity, residual volume

B Gas exchange—

   1 Diffusion of gases from area of higher concentration to area of lower concentration

   2 In lungs—oxygen enters blood and carbon dioxide leaves

   3 In tissues—oxygen leaves blood and carbon dioxide enters

C Gas transport

   1 Oxygen—almost totally bound to heme portion of hemoglobin in red blood cells; separates from hemoglobin when oxygen concentration is low (in tissues)

   2 Carbon dioxide—most carried as bicarbonate ion; regulates pH of blood

D Regulation of respiration

   1 Normal ventilation—controlled by centers in medulla and pons

   2 Abnormal ventilation

      a Hyperventilation—rapid, deep respiration

      b Hypoventilation—inadequate air in alveoli

E Abnormal respiration

   1 Types

      a Hyperpnea—increase in depth and rate of breathing

      b Apnea—temporary cessation of breathing

      c Dyspnea—difficulty in breathing

      d Cheyne–Stokes—irregularity found in critically ill

      e Orthopnea—difficulty relieved by upright position

   2 Possible results—cyanosis, anoxia, hypoxia, suffocation, asphyxia

IV Disorders of respiratory system

A Nasal problems—sinusitis, polyps, deviated septum, nosebleed (epistaxis)

B Infection—colds, influenza, pneumonia, tuberculosis

C Allergy—hay fever, asthma

D Chronic obstructive pulmonary disease (COPD)—involves emphysema and bronchitis

E Atelectasis—collapse of lung or portion of lung; seen in respiratory distress syndrome due to lack of surfactant

F Lung cancer—smoking a major causative factor

G Disorders involving pleural cavity

   1 Pleurisy—inflammation of pleura

   2 Pneumothorax—air in pleural cavity

V Room ventilation

A Proper temperature and humidity

B Avoidance of drafts

C Adequate circulation

VI Special equipment for respiratory tract treatment

A Bronchoscope—tube used to examine air passageways and remove foreign bodies

B Oxygen therapy

C Suction apparatus—removes mucus and other substances

D Tracheostomy—artificial airway

   1 Tracheotomy—incision into trachea

E Artificial respiration—cardiopulmonary resuscitation (CPR)

Questions for Study and Review

1 What is the purpose of respiration and what are its two components?

2 Trace the pathway of air from the outside into the blood.

3 What are the advantages of breathing through the nose?

4 Describe the lung cavities.

5 What muscles are used for inhalation? forceful exhalation?

6 How is oxygen transported in the blood? What causes its release to the tissues?

7 How is carbon dioxide transported in the blood?

8 How does the *p*H of the blood change as the level of carbon dioxide increases? decreases?

9 Why does hyperventilation cause a cessation of breathing?

10 What are chemoreceptors and how do they function to regulate breathing?

11 Name and describe five types of abnormal respiration.

12 Define four volumes used to measure breathing.

13 Define four terms related to lack of oxygen.

14 What are sinusitis, polyps, and deviated septum? What is the effect of each?

15 What are some causes of nosebleed?

16 Describe some possible developments and complications of upper respiratory infections.

17 Describe the common cold and influenza.

18 What changes occur in the lungs in chronic obstructive lung disease?

19 What are the symptoms of atelectasis?

20 What do hay fever and asthma have in common?

21 What are some possible causes of lung cancer?

22 What is pleurisy? What are its complications?

23 Describe pneumothorax. What first aid measure can be used for it?

24 Name three characteristics of ideal ventilation.

25 Name and describe three devices used in treatment of the respiratory tract.

18

Digestion

Behavioral Objectives

After careful study of this chapter, you should be able to:

Name the two main functions of the digestive system

Describe the four layers of the digestive tract wall

Describe the layers of the peritoneum

Name and describe the organs of the digestive tract

Name and describe the accessory organs

List the functions of each organ involved in digestion

Explain the role of enzymes in digestion and give examples of enzymes

Name the digestion products of fats, proteins, and carbohydrates

Define absorption

Define villi and state how villi function in absorption

Describe how bile functions in digestion

Name the ducts that carry bile into the digestive tract

List the main functions of the liver

Explain the use of feedback in regulating digestion and give several examples

Selected Key Terms

The following terms are defined in the glossary:

absorption
bile
chyle
chyme
colon
defecation
deglutition
digestion
duodenum
emulsification
enzyme
esophagus
hydrolysis
lacteal
mastication
mesentery
peristalsis
peritoneum
saliva
sphincter
ulcer
villi (*sing.,* villus)

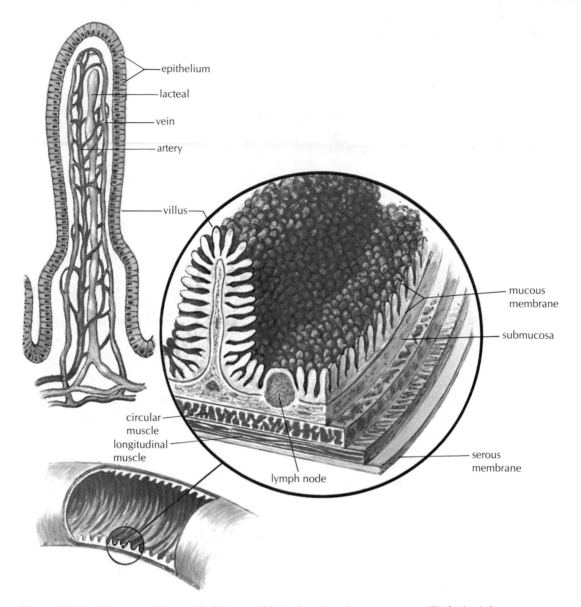

Figure 18-1. *Diagram of the wall of the small intestine showing numerous villi. At the left is an enlarged drawing of a single villus.*

≡ What the Digestive System Does

Every body cell needs a constant supply of food to provide energy and the building blocks needed to manufacture body substances. Food as we take it in, however, is too large to enter the cells. It must first be broken down into particles small enough to pass through the cell membrane. This process is known as

digestion. After digestion, food must be carried to the cells in every part of the body by the circulation. The transfer of food into the circulation is called **absorption**. Digestion and absorption are the two chief functions of the digestive system.

For our purposes the digestive system may be divided into two groups of organs:

1 The **digestive tract**, a continuous passageway beginning at the mouth, where food is taken in,

and terminating at the anus, where the solid waste products of digestion are expelled from the body

2 The **accessory organs**, which are necessary for the digestive process but are not a direct part of the digestive tract. They release substances into the digestive tract through ducts.

The Walls of the Digestive Tract

Although modified to perform specific functions in different organs, the walls of the digestive tract from the esophagus to the anus are similar in structure. Follow the diagram of the small intestine in Figure 18-1 as we describe the layers of this wall from the innermost to the outermost surface. First is the **mucous membrane**, so-called because its epithelial layer contains many mucus-secreting cells. The layer of connective tissue beneath this, the **submucosa**, contains blood vessels and some of the nerves that help regulate digestive activity. Next are layers of **smooth muscle**. The inner layer is circular and regulates the diameter of the lumen, or central opening; the outer layer has longitudinal fibers. The alternate contractions of these muscles create the wavelike movement that propels food through the digestive tract and mixes it with digestive juices. This movement is called **peristalsis** (per"i-stal'sis). The outermost layer of the wall consists of fibrous connective tissue, covered over most surfaces of the abdominal organs with a thin **serous membrane** that is part of the peritoneum.

The Peritoneum

The abdominal cavity is lined with a thin, shiny serous membrane that also folds over the abdominal viscera (Fig. 18-2). The layer of this membrane that lines the abdomen is called the **parietal peritoneum**; the portion that folds over the organs is called the **visceral peritoneum**. Around and between the organs are double layers of the peritoneum that insulate and support the organs, hold them in place, and carry blood vessels, lymph vessels, and nerves.

The sections of the peritoneum around the individual organs are given special names. The **mesentery** (mes'en-ter-e) is a double-layered peritoneal structure shaped somewhat like a fan. The handle portion is attached to the back wall, and the expanded long edge is attached to the small intestine.

Between the two layers of membrane that form the mesentery are the blood vessels, nerves, and other structures that supply the intestine. The section of the mesentery around the large intestine is called the **mesocolon**. A large double layer of the peritoneum containing much fat hangs like an apron over the front of the intestine. This **greater omentum** extends from the lower border of the stomach into the pelvic part of the abdomen and then loops back up to the transverse colon. There is also a smaller membrane, called the **lesser omentum**, that extends between the stomach and the liver.

Peritonitis is inflammation of the peritoneum. It may be a serious complication following infection of one of the organs covered by the peritoneum—often the appendix. The frequency and severity of peritonitis have been greatly reduced by the use of antibiotic drugs. However, the disorder still occurs and can be very dangerous. If the infection is kept in one area, it is said to be *localized peritonitis*. A *generalized peritonitis,* as caused by a ruptured appendix or perforated ulcer, may lead to absorption of so many disease organisms and their toxins as to be fatal. Immediate surgery to repair the rupture, together with meticulous medical care, will be needed to save the patient's life.

≡ The Digestive Tract

As we study the organs of the digestive system, locate each in Figure 18-3.

The digestive tract is a muscular tube extending through the body. It is composed of several parts: the **mouth, pharynx, esophagus, stomach, small intestine**, and **large intestine**. The digestive tract is sometimes called the **alimentary tract**, derived from a Latin word that means "food." It is more commonly referred to as the **gastrointestinal (GI) tract** because of the major importance of the stomach and intestine in the process of digestion.

The Mouth

The mouth, also called the **oral cavity** (Fig. 18-4), is where a substance begins its travels through the digestive tract. The mouth has three purposes:

1 To receive food, a process called **ingestion**
2 To prepare food for digestion
3 To aid in the production of speech

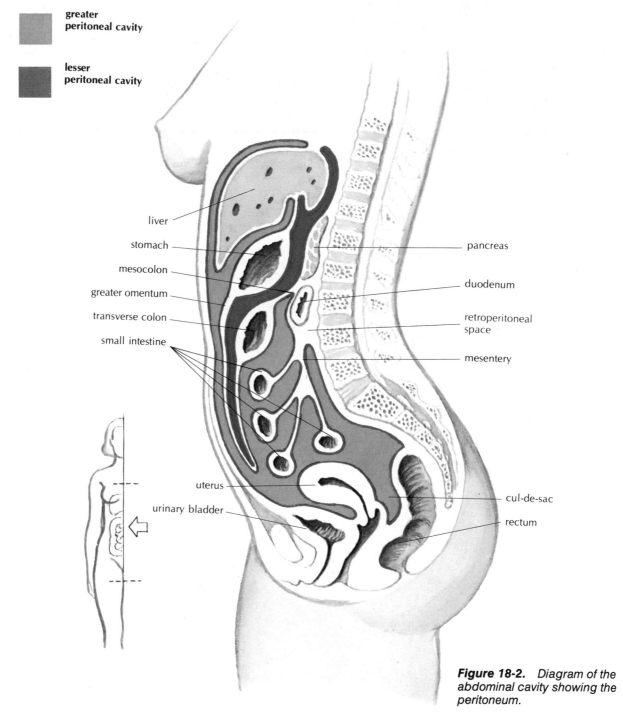

greater
peritoneal cavity

lesser
peritoneal cavity

liver

stomach

mesocolon

greater omentum

transverse colon

small intestine

uterus

urinary bladder

pancreas

duodenum

retroperitoneal
space

mesentery

cul-de-sac

rectum

Figure 18-2. *Diagram of the abdominal cavity showing the peritoneum.*

Into this space projects a muscular organ, the tongue, which is used for chewing and swallowing, and is one of the principal organs of speech. The tongue has in its surface a number of special organs, called *taste buds,* by means of which taste sensations (bitter, sweet, sour, or salty) can be differentiated.

The oral cavity also contains the teeth. A child between 2 and 6 years of age has 20 teeth; an adult with a complete set has 32. Among these, the cutting teeth, or **incisors**, occupy the front part of the oral cavity, while the larger grinding teeth, the **molars**, are in the back.

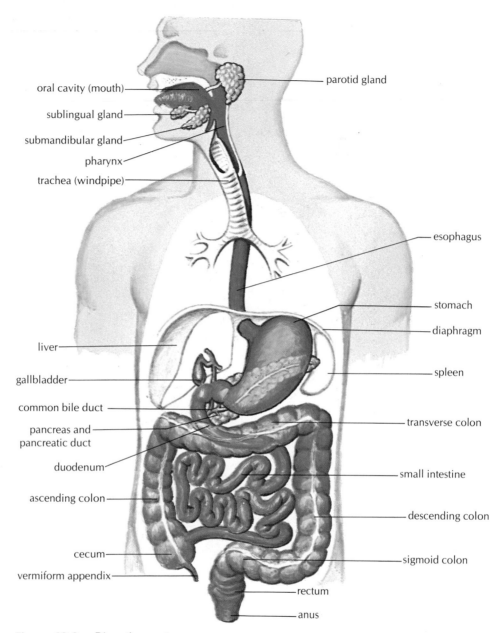

oral cavity (mouth)

sublingual gland

submandibular gland

pharynx

trachea (windpipe)

parotid gland

esophagus

stomach

diaphragm

liver

spleen

gallbladder

common bile duct

transverse colon

pancreas and
pancreatic duct

duodenum

small intestine

ascending colon

descending colon

cecum

sigmoid colon

vermiform appendix

rectum

anus

Figure 18-3. *Digestive system.*

Deciduous, or Baby, Teeth

The first eight **deciduous** (de-sid′u-us) teeth to appear through the gums are the incisors. Later the **canines** (eyeteeth) and molars appear. Usually, the 20 baby teeth have all appeared by the time a child has reached the age of 2 or 2½ years. During the first 2 years the permanent teeth develop within the jawbones from buds that are present at birth. The first permanent tooth to appear is the important 6-year

molar. This permanent tooth comes in before the baby incisors are lost. Because decay and infection of adjacent deciduous molars may spread to and involve new, permanent teeth, deciduous teeth need proper care.

Permanent Teeth

As a child grows, the jawbones grow, making space for additional teeth. After the 6-year molars have ap-

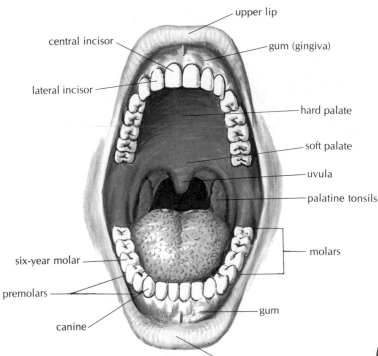

Figure 18-4. *The mouth, showing the teeth and the tonsils.*

Labels on figure:
upper lip
central incisor
gum (gingiva)
lateral incisor
hard palate
soft palate
uvula
palatine tonsils
molars
six-year molar
premolars
gum
canine
lower lip

peared, the baby incisors loosen and are replaced by permanent incisors. Next, the baby canines (cuspids) are replaced by permanent canines, and finally, the baby molars are replaced by the bicuspids (premolars) of the permanent teeth.

Now the larger jawbones are ready for the appearance of the 12-year, or second, permanent molar teeth. During or after the late teens, the third molars, or so-called wisdom teeth, may appear. In some cases the jaw is not large enough for these teeth or there are other abnormalities, so that the third molars may have to be removed.

Diseases of the Mouth and Teeth

Tooth decay is also termed dental **caries** (ka're-ez), which means "rottenness." It has a number of causes, including diet, heredity, mechanical problems, and endocrine disorders. Persons who ingest a lot of sugar are particularly prone to this disease. Since a baby's teeth begin to develop before birth, the diet of the mother during pregnancy is very important in ensuring the formation of healthy teeth in her baby.

Any infection of the gum is called **gingivitis** (jin-je-vi'tis). If such an infection continues and is untreated, it may lead to a more serious condition, pe-

riodontitis (per"e-o-don-ti'tis), which involves not only the gum tissue but also the supporting bone of the teeth. Loosening of the teeth and destruction of the supporting bone follow unless the process is halted by proper treatment and improved dental hygiene. Periodontitis is responsible for nearly 80% of loss of teeth in persons over the age of 35.

Vincent's disease, a kind of gingivitis caused by a spirochete, is most prevalent in teenagers and young adults. Characterized by inflammation, ulceration, and infection of the mucous membranes of the mouth and gums, this disorder is highly contagious, particularly by oral contact.

Patients on antibiotic therapy are more likely than normal to develop fungal infections of the mouth and tongue because these drugs may destroy the normal bacteria of the mouth and allow other organisms to grow.

Leukoplakia (loo"ko-pla'ke-ah) is characterized by thickened white patches on the mucous membranes of the mouth. It is common in smokers and may lead to cancer.

The Salivary Glands

While food is in the mouth, it is mixed with **saliva**, the purpose of which is to moisten the food and facilitate the processes of chewing, or **mastication** (mas″ti-ka′shun), and swallowing, or **deglutition** (deg″loo-tish′un). Saliva also helps keep the teeth and mouth clean and reduce bacterial growth.

This watery mixture contains mucus and an enzyme called **salivary amylase** (a′mi-laz), which begins the digestive process by converting starch to sugars. It is manufactured mainly by three pairs of glands that function as accessory organs:

1 The **parotid** (pah-rot′id) **glands**, the largest of the group, are located below and in front of the ear.

2 The **submandibular** (sub-man-dib′u-lar), or **submaxillary** (sub-mak′si-ler-e), **glands** are located near the body of the lower jaw.

3 The **sublingual** (sub-ling′gwal) **glands** are under the tongue.

All of these glands empty by means of ducts into the oral cavity.

The contagious disease commonly called *mumps* is a viral infection of the parotid salivary glands. **Parotitis** (par″o-ti′tis), or inflammation of the parotid glands, may lead to inflammation of the testicles by the same virus. Males affected after puberty are at risk for permanent damage to these sex organs, resulting in sterility. Another complication of mumps that occurs in about 10% of cases is meningitis. Like many contagious diseases, mumps is now preventable by use of a vaccine given to children early in life.

The Pharynx and Esophagus

The **pharynx** (far′inks) is often referred to as the *throat*. The oral part of the pharynx is visible when you look into an open mouth and depress the tongue. The palatine tonsils may be seen at either side of it. The pharynx also extends upward to the nasal cavity and downward to the level of the larynx. The **soft palate** is muscular tissue that forms the back of the roof of the oral cavity. From it hangs a soft, fleshy, V-shaped mass called the **uvula** (u′vu-lah).

In swallowing, a small portion of chewed food mixed with saliva, called a **bolus**, is pushed by the tongue into the pharynx. When the food reaches the pharynx, swallowing occurs rapidly by an involuntary reflex action. At the same time, the soft palate is raised to prevent food and liquid from entering the nasal cavity, and the tongue is raised to seal the back of the oral cavity. The entrance of the trachea is guarded during swallowing by a leaf-shaped cartilage, the **epiglottis**, which covers the opening of the larynx. The swallowed food is then moved by peristalsis into the **esophagus** (e-sof′ah-gus), a muscular tube about 25 cm. (10 inches) long that carries food into the stomach. No additional digestion occurs in the esophagus.

Before joining the stomach, the esophagus must pass through the diaphragm. It passes through a space in the diaphragm called the **esophageal hiatus** (e-sof″ah-je′al hi-ay′tus). If there is a weakness in the diaphragm at this point, a portion of the stomach or other abdominal organ may protrude through the space, a condition called **hiatal hernia**.

The Stomach

The stomach is an expanded J-shaped organ in the upper left region of the abdominal cavity (Fig. 18-5). In addition to having the two muscle layers already described, it has a third, inner oblique, layer that aids in grinding food and mixing it with digestive juices. Each end of the stomach is guarded by a muscular ring, or **sphincter** (sfink′ter), that permits the passage of substances in only one direction. Between the esophagus and the stomach is the **lower esophageal sphincter**, also called the cardiac sphincter because of its closeness to the heart. We are sometimes aware of the existence of this sphincter; sometimes it does not relax as it should, producing a feeling of being unable to swallow past that point. Between the distal, or far, end of the stomach and the small intestine is the **pyloric** (pi-lor′ik) **sphincter**. This valve is especially important in determing how long food remains in the stomach.

The stomach serves as a storage pouch, digestive organ, and churn. When the stomach is empty, the lining forms many folds called **rugae** (ru′ge). These folds disappear as the stomach expands. (It may be stretched to hold ½ gallon of food and liquid.) Special cells in the lining of the stomach secrete substances that mix together to form **gastric juice**, the two main components of which are

1 Hydrochloric acid (HCl), a strong acid that softens the connective tissue in meat and destroys foreign organisms

2 Pepsin, a protein-digesting enzyme. This enzyme is produced in an inactive form and is activated only when food enters the stomach and HCl is

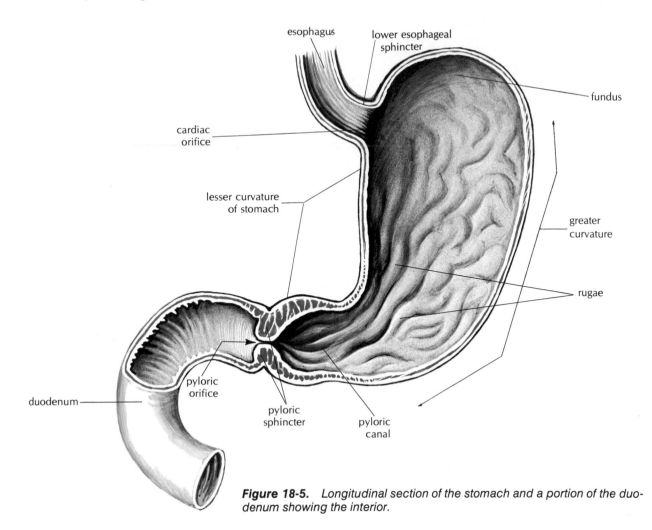

Figure 18-5. *Longitudinal section of the stomach and a portion of the duodenum showing the interior.*

produced. The semi-liquid mixture of gastric juice and food that leaves the stomach to enter the small intestine is called **chyme** (kime).

Disorders Involving the Stomach

A burning sensation in the region of the esophagus and stomach, popularly known as *heartburn,* is often caused by the sudden intake of a large amount of fluid or food resulting in excessive stretching of the lower esophagus. This interferes with the functioning of the lower esophageal sphincter, allowing gastric acid to enter the esophagus. Contrary to popular belief, heartburn is not due to hyperacidity of the stomach contents.

Nausea is an unpleasant sensation that may follow distention or irritation of the lower esophagus or of the stomach as a result of various nervous and mechanical factors. It may be a symptom of interference with the normal forward peristaltic motion of the stomach and intestine and thus may be followed by vomiting. **Vomiting** is the expulsion of gastric (and sometimes intestinal) contents through the mouth by reverse peristalsis. The contraction of the abdominal wall muscles forcibly empties the stomach. Vomiting is frequently caused by overeating or by inflammation of the stomach lining, a condition called **gastritis** (gas-tri'tis). Gastritis results from irritation of the mucosa by certain drugs, food, or drinks. For example, the long-term use of aspirin, highly spiced foods, or alcohol can lead to gastritis. The nicotine in cigarettes can also cause gastritis.

Flatus (fla'tus) usually refers to excessive

amounts of air (gas) in the stomach or intestine. The resulting condition is referred to as **flatulence** (flat′u-lens). In some cases, it may be necessary to insert a tube into the stomach or rectum to aid the patient in expelling flatus.

Stomach Cancer

Although stomach cancer has become rare in the United States, it is common in many parts of the world, and it is an important disorder owing to the high death rate associated with it. Males are more susceptible to stomach cancer than females. The tumor nearly always develops from the epithelial or mucosal lining of the stomach and is often of the type called *adenocarcinoma* (ad″e-no-kar″si-no′mah). Sometimes the victim has suffered from long-standing indigestion but has failed to consult a physician until the cancer has spread to other organs, such as the liver, in which there may be several metastases. Persistent indigestion is one of the important warning signs of cancer of the stomach.

Peptic Ulcer

An ulcer is an area of the skin or mucous membrane in which the tissues are gradually destroyed. An ulcer may be caused by the acid in gastric juice. Peptic ulcers (named for the enzyme pepsin) occur in the mucous membrane of the esophagus, stomach, or duodenum (the first part of the small intestine) and are most common in persons between the ages of 30 and 45. Peptic ulcers in the stomach are gastric ulcers; those in the duodenum are duodenal (du″o-de′nal) ulcers. Duodenal ulcers are much more common in males than in females. Emphasis is now being placed on mental and emotional factors as a contributing cause of ulcers. Persons suffering from peptic ulcers need the best possible medical and nursing care and most certainly should not depend on patent medicines such as antacids. Drugs that inhibit the secretion of stomach acids are often effective.

More about the Pyloric Sphincter

Normally, the stomach contents are moved through the pyloric sphincter within about 2 to 6 hours after eating. However, some infants, most often males, are born with an obstruction of the pyloric sphincter called **pyloric stenosis** (ste-no′sis). Usually, surgery is required in these cases to modify the muscle so food can pass from the stomach into the duodenum.

The Small Intestine

The small intestine is the longest part of the digestive tract. It is known as the small intestine because, although it is longer than the large intestine (3–4 m [10–13 feet], compared with 1.2–1.5 m [4–5 feet]), it is also smaller in diameter. The first 25 cm to 27 cm of the small intestine make up the **duodenum** (du″o-de′num). Beyond the duodenum are two more divisions: the **jejunum** (je-joo′num), which forms the next two fifths of the small intestine, and the **ileum** (il′e-um), which constitutes the remaining portion.

The wall of the duodenum contains glands that secrete large amounts of mucus to protect the small intestine from the strongly acid chyme entering from the stomach. Cells of the small intestine also secrete enzymes that digest proteins and carbohydrates. In addition, digestive juices from the liver and pancreas enter the small intestine through a small opening in the duodenum. Most of the digestive process takes place in the small intestine under the effects of these juices.

Most absorption of digested food also occurs through the walls of the small intestine. To increase the surface area of the organ for this purpose, the mucosa is formed into millions of tiny, finger-like projections, called **villi** (vil′li) (see Fig. 18-1), which give the inner surface a velvety appearance.

The Large Intestine

Any material that cannot be digested as it passes through the digestive tract must be eliminated from the body. In addition, most of the water secreted into the digestive tract for proper digestion must be reabsorbed into the body to prevent dehydration. The storage and elimination of undigested waste and the reabsorption of water are the functions of the large intestine.

At the beginning of the large intestine is a small pouch called the **cecum** (se′kum). Between the ileum of the small intestine and the cecum is a sphincter, called the **ileocecal** (il″e-o-se′kal) **valve**, that prevents food from traveling backward into the small intestine. Attached to the cecum is a small, blind tube containing lymphoid tissue; it is called the **vermiform** (ver′me-form) **appendix** (*vermiform* means "wormlike"). Inflammation of this tissue as a result of infection or obstruction is **appendicitis**. The outer longitudinal muscle fibers of the large intestine form three separate bands on the surface. These bands draw up the wall of the large intestine to give it its distinctive puckered appearance.

The large intestine begins in the lower right region of the abdomen. The second portion, the **ascending colon**, extends upward along the right side of the abdomen toward the liver. The large intestine then bends and extends across the abdomen, forming the **transverse colon**. At this point it bends sharply and extends downward on the left side of the abdomen into the pelvis, forming the **descending colon**. The lower part of the colon bends posteriorly in an S shape and continues downward as the **sigmoid colon**. The sigmoid colon empties into the **rectum**, which serves as a temporary storage area for indigestible or unabsorbable food residue (see Fig. 18-3). Enlargement of the veins in this area constitutes **hemorrhoids**. A narrow portion of the distal large intestine is called the **anal canal**. This leads to the outside of the body through an opening called the **anus** (a′nus).

Large quantities of mucus, but no enzymes, are secreted by the large intestine. At intervals, usually after meals, the involuntary muscles within the walls of the large intestine propel solid waste material, called **feces** or stool, toward the rectum. This material is then eliminated from the body by both voluntary and involuntary muscle actions, a process called **defecation**.

While the food residue is stored in the large intestine, bacteria that normally live in the colon act on it to produce vitamin K and some of the B-complex vitamins. As mentioned, systemic antibiotic therapy may destroy these bacteria and others living in the large intestine, causing side-effects.

Intestinal Disorders

Inflammation

Difficulties with digestion or absorption may be due to **enteritis** (en″ter-i′tis), an intestinal inflammation. When both the stomach and the small intestine are involved, the illness is called **gastroenteritis** (gas″tro-en-ter-i′tis). The symptoms of gastroenteritis include nausea, vomiting, and diarrhea, as well as acute abdominal pain or colic. The disorder may be caused by a variety of pathogenic organisms, including viruses, bacteria, and protozoa. Chemical irritants such as alcohol, sprays on fruits and vegetables, and other toxins have also been known to cause this disorder.

Diarrhea

Diarrhea is a symptom characterized by abnormally frequent watery bowel movements. The danger of diarrhea is dehydration and loss of salts, especially in infants. Diarrhea may result from excess activity of the colon, faulty absorption, or infection. Infections resulting in diarrhea include cholera, dysentery, and food poisoning; Tables 1 and 4 in the Appendix list some of the organisms causing these diseases. Such infections are often spread by poor sanitation and contaminated food, milk, or water. An examination of the stool may be required to establish the cause of diarrhea; such an examination may reveal the presence of pathogenic organisms, worm eggs, or blood.

Constipation

Millions of dollars are spent each year in an effort to remedy a condition called **constipation**. What is constipation? Many persons erroneously think they are constipated if they go a day or more without having a bowel movement. Actually, what is normal varies greatly; one person may normally have a bowel movement only once every 2 or 3 days, whereas another may normally have more than one movement daily. The term *constipation* is also used to refer to hard stools or difficulty with defecation.

On the basis of its onset, constipation may be classified as acute or chronic. Acute constipation occurs suddenly and may be due to an intestinal obstruction, such as a tumor associated with cancer or an inflammation of the saclike bulges (diverticula) of the intestinal wall as seen in **diverticulitis** (di″vertik″u-li′tis). Laxatives and enemas should be avoided, and a physician should be consulted at once. Chronic constipation, in contrast, has a more gradual onset and may be divided into two groups:

1 **Spastic** constipation, in which the intestinal musculature is overstimulated so that the canal becomes narrowed and the space (lumen) inside the intestine is not large enough to permit the passage of fecal material

2 **Flaccid** (flak′sid) constipation, which is characterized by a lazy, or **atonic** (ah-ton′ik), intestinal muscle. Elderly persons and persons on bed rest are particularly susceptible to this condition. Often it results from repeated denial of the urge to defecate.

Persons who have sluggish intestinal muscles may be helped by regular bowel habits, moderate exercise, an increase in the ingestion of vegetables and other bulky foods, and an increase in fluid intake.

The chronic use of laxatives and enemas should be avoided. The streams of hot water used in enemas may injure the lining of the intestine by removing the normal protective mucus. In addition, enemas aggravate piles (hemorrhoids). Enemas should be done only on the order of a physician, and sparingly.

Cancer of the Colon and Rectum

Tumors of the colon and rectum are among the most common types of cancer in the United States. These tumors are usually adenocarcinomas that arise from the mucosal lining. The occurrence of cancer of the colon is evenly divided between the sexes, but malignant tumors of the rectum are more common in men than in women. Tumors may be detected by examination of the rectum and lower colon with an instrument called a **sigmoidoscope** (sig-moi′do-scope) (named for the sigmoid colon). The presence of blood in the stool may also indicate cancer of the bowel or some other gastrointestinal disturbance. A simple chemical test can be used to detect extremely small quantities of blood in the stool, referred to as *occult* ("hidden") *blood*. Early detection and treatment are the key to increasing survival rates.

An instrument used for examining the interior of a tube or hollow organ is called an **endoscope** (en′do-skope), and the examination is known as **endoscopy** (en-dos′ko-pe). With a **fiberoptic** (fi″ber-op′tik) **endoscope**, which contains flexible bundles of glass or plastic that propagate light, transmitted images show the lining of internal organs. Such endoscopic examinations are used to detect structural abnormalities, bleeding, ulcers, inflammation, and tumors in such organs as the esophagus, stomach, and small and large intestine.

☰ The Accessory Structures

The Liver

The liver, often referred to by the Greek word root **hepat**, is the largest glandular organ of the body. It is located in the upper right portion of the abdominal cavity under the dome of the diaphragm. The lower edge of a normal-sized liver is level with the lower margin of the ribs. The human liver is the same reddish brown color as the animal liver seen in the supermarket. It has a large right lobe and a smaller left lobe; the right lobe includes two inferior smaller lobes. The liver has a double blood supply; the portal vein and the hepatic artery. These two vessels deliver about 1½ quarts of blood to the liver every minute. The hepatic artery carries oxygenated blood, while the portal system of veins carries blood that is rich in the end products of digestion. This most remarkable organ has so many functions that only some of its major activities can be listed here:

1 The storage of glucose (simple sugar) in the form of **glycogen**, an animal starch. When the blood sugar level falls below normal, liver cells convert glycogen to glucose and release it into the bloodstream; this serves to restore the normal concentration of blood sugar.

2 The formation of blood plasma proteins, such as albumin, globulins, and clotting factors

3 The synthesis of **urea** (u-re″ah), a waste product of protein metabolism. Urea is released into the blood for transport to the kidneys for elimination.

4 The modification of fats so they can be more efficiently used by cells all over the body

5 The manufacture of bile

6 The destruction of old red blood cells. The pigment released from these cells in both the liver and the spleen is eliminated in the bile. This pigment (bilirubin) gives the stool its characteristic dark color.

7 The **detoxification** (de-tok″si-fi-ka′shun) (removal of the poisonous properties) of harmful substances such as alcohol and certain drugs

8 The storage of some vitamins and iron

The main digestive function of the liver is the production of **bile**. The salts contained in bile act like a detergent to **emulsify** fat, that is, to break up fat into small droplets that can be acted upon more effectively by digestive enzymes. Bile also aids in the absorption of fat from the small intestine. Bile leaves the lobes of the liver by two ducts that merge to form the **common hepatic duct**. After collecting bile from the gallbladder, this duct, now called the **common bile duct**, delivers bile into the duodenum. These and the other accessory ducts are shown on Figure 18-6.

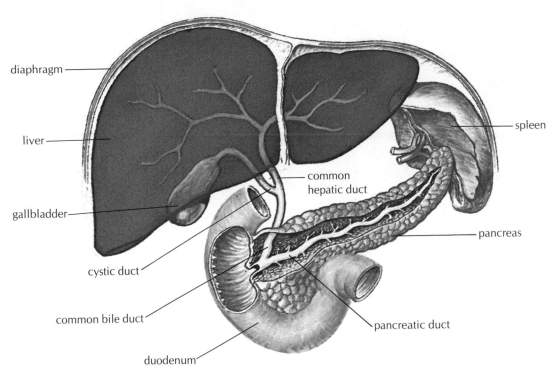

Figure 18-6. *The accessory organs of digestion.*

Diseases of the Liver

Hepatitis

Inflammation of the liver, called **hepatitis** (hep-ah-ti′tis), may be caused by drugs, alcohol, or infection. Hepatitis due to infection is caused by a virus that exists in several different forms. Type A hepatitis, often called *infectious hepatitis,* is most common in the fall and winter. Military camps and institutions are likely sites for epidemics of the disease. The Type A hepatitis varies in severity from cases that are so mild as to be scarcely recognizable to serious infections in which the liver becomes permanently damaged.

Type B hepatitis, a more prevalent type of infection, is often called *serum hepatitis.* The infection is usually transmitted by administration of infected blood, plasma, or blood products or by use of improperly sterilized needles and syringes (see Table 3 of the Appendix.) Because blood from the intestinal tract passes through the liver, any toxins or microorganisms that get into the intestinal (mesenteric) veins enter the liver. For example, the same organism that causes amebic dysentery may be carried into the liver and there cause the formation of an abscess. Type B hepatitis is very hard to treat.

Cirrhosis

Cirrhosis (si-ro′sis) of the liver is a chronic disease in which active liver cells are replaced by inactive connective (scar) tissue. The most common type of cirrhosis is alcoholic (portal) cirrhosis. Alcohol has a direct damaging effect on liver cells that is compounded by malnutrition. Destruction of the liver cells hampers the portal circulation, causing blood to accumulate in the spleen and gastrointestinal tract and causing fluid (ascites) to accumulate in the peritoneal cavity.

Jaundice

Damage to the liver or blockage in any of the bile ducts may cause bile pigment to accumulate in the blood. As a result, the stool may become pale in color while the skin and sclera of the eyes become yellowish; this symptom is called **jaundice**. Jaundice may also be caused by excess destruction of red blood cells. In addition, it is often seen in newborns, in whom the liver is immature and not yet functioning efficiently.

Cancer

Hepatic metastases are common in cases that begin as cancer in one of the organs of the abdominal cavity; the tumor cells are carried from the intestine or another organ through the veins that go to the liver.

The Gallbladder

The gallbladder is a muscular sac on the inferior surface of the liver that serves as a storage pouch for bile. Although the liver may manufacture bile continuously, the body is likely to need it only a few times a day. Consequently, bile from the liver flows into the hepatic ducts and then up through the **cystic** (si′stik) **duct** connected with the gallbladder. When chyme enters the duodenum, the gallbladder contracts, squeezing bile through the cystic duct and into the common bile duct leading to the duodenum.

The most common disease of the gallbladder is the formation of stones, or **cholelithiasis** (ko-le-le-thi′ah-sis). Stones are formed from the substances contained in bile, mainly cholesterol. They may remain in the gallbladder or may lodge in the bile ducts, causing extreme pain. Cholelithiasis is usually associated with inflammation of the gallbladder, or **cholecystitis** (ko-le-sis-ti′tis).

The Pancreas

The pancreas is a long gland that extends from the duodenum to the spleen. The pancreas produces enzymes that digest fats, proteins, carbohydrates, and nucleic acids. The protein-digesting enzymes are produced in inactive forms, which must be converted to active forms in the small intestine by the proper pH or the presence of other enzymes. The pancreas also produces large amounts of alkaline fluid, which neutralizes the chyme in the small intestine, thus protecting the digestive tract. These juices collect in a main duct that joins the common bile duct or empties into the duodenum near the common bile duct. Most persons also have an additional smaller duct that opens into the duodenum.

Since they are usually confined to proper channels, pancreatic enzymes do not damage body tissues. However, if the bile ducts become blocked, pancreatic enzymes back up into the pancreas. Also, in some cases of gallbladder disease, infection may extend to the pancreas and cause abnormal activation of the pancreatic enzymes. In either circumstance, the pancreas suffers destruction by its own juice, and the outcome can be fatal; this condition is known as **acute pancreatitis.**

The pancreas also produces hormones that regulate sugar metabolism. These, of course, are released directly into the blood.

☰ The Process of Digestion

Although the different organs of the digestive tract are specialized for digesting different types of food, the basic chemical process of digestion is the same for fats, proteins, and carbohydrates. This process requires enzymes. Enzymes, as you recall from Chapter 2, are proteins that speed the rate of chemical reactions but are not themselves changed or used up in these reactions. An enzyme is highly specific; that is, it acts only in a certain type of reaction involving a certain type of food molecule. For example, the carbohydrate-digesting enzyme amylase only splits starch into the disaccharide (double sugar) maltose. Another enzyme is required to split maltose into two molecules of the monosaccharide (simple sugar) glucose. Other enzymes split fats into their building blocks, glycerol and fatty acids, and still others split proteins into their building blocks, amino acids. Because water is added to these molecules as they are split by enzymes, the process is called **hydrolysis** (hi-drah′li-sis), which means "splitting by means of water." You can now understand why large amounts of water are needed in digestion. Water is not only needed to dilute food so that it can mix with digestive juices and move easily through the digestive tract, it is also needed in the chemical process of digestion itself.

Let us see what happens to a mass of food from the time it is taken into the mouth to the moment that it is ready to be absorbed.

In the mouth the food is chewed and mixed with saliva, softening it so that it can be swallowed easily. Salivary amylase initiates the process of digestion by changing some of the starches into sugars. When the food reaches the stomach, it is acted upon by gastric juice, which contains hydrochloric acid and enzymes.

The hydrochloric acid has the important function of liquefying the food. In addition, it activates the enzyme pepsin, which is secreted by the cells of the gastric lining in an inactive form. Once activated by hydrochloric acid, pepsin works to digest protein; nearly every type of protein in the diet is first digested by this enzyme. Two other enzymes are also secreted by the stomach, but they are of no importance in adults. The food, gastric juice, and mucus, the latter of which is also secreted by cells of the gastric lining, are mixed to form the semiliquid substance chyme. Chyme is moved from the stomach to the small intestine for further digestion.

In the duodenum the chyme is mixed with the greenish yellow bile delivered from the liver and the gallbladder through the common bile duct. Rather than containing enzymes, the bile contains salts that split (emulsify) fats into smaller particles to allow the powerful secretion from the pancreas to act on them most efficiently. The pancreatic juice contains a number of enzymes, including the following:

1 **Lipase**. Following the physical division of fats into tiny particles by the action of bile, the powerful pancreatic lipase does almost all the digesting of fats. In this process fats are usually broken down into two simpler compounds, glycerol and fatty acids, which are more readily absorbable. If pancreatic lipase is absent, fats are expelled with the feces in undigested form.
2 **Amylase** (am'i-lase). This changes starch to sugar.
3 **Trypsin** (trip'sin). This splits proteins into amino acids, which are the form in which proteins enter the blood stream.

The intestinal juice contains a number of enzymes, including three that act on complex sugars to transform them into the simpler form in which they are absorbed. These are **maltase, sucrase**, and **lactase**. It must be emphasized that most of the chemical changes in foods occur in the intestinal tract because of the pancreatic juice, which could probably adequately digest all foods even if no other digestive juice were produced. When pancreatic juice is absent, serious digestive disturbances always occur.

Table 18-1 contains a summary of the main substances used in digestion. Note that, except for HCl, sodium bicarbonate, and bile salts, all of the substances listed are enzymes.

Absorption

The means by which the digested food reaches the blood is known as **absorption**. Most absorption takes place through the mucosa of the small intestine by means of the villi (see Fig. 18-1). Within each villus are a small artery and a small vein bridged with capillaries. Simple sugars, amino acids, some simple fatty acids, and water are absorbed into the blood through the capillary walls in the villi. From here they pass by way of the portal system to the liver, to be stored or released and used as needed. Most fats have an alternative method of reaching the blood. Instead of entering the blood capillaries, they are absorbed by lymphatic capillaries in the villi that are called **lacteals** (the word *lacteal* means "like milk"). The mixture of lymph and fat globules that is drained from the small intestine after a quantity of fat has been digested is called **chyle** (kile). It circulates in the lymph and eventually enters the bloodstream near the heart.

Minerals and vitamins taken in with food are also absorbed from the small intestine. The minerals and some of the vitamins dissolve in water and are absorbed directly into the blood. Other vitamins are incorporated in fats and are absorbed along with the fats. Some other vitamins (such as vitamin K) are produced by the action of bacteria in the colon and are absorbed from the large intestine.

Control of Digestion

As food moves through the digestive tract, its rate of movement and the activity of each organ it passes through must be carefully regulated. If food moves too slowly or digestive secretions are inadequate, the body will not get enough nourishment. If food moves too rapidly or excess secretions are produced, digestion may be incomplete or the lining of the digestive tract may be damaged.

There are two types of control over digestion: nervous and hormonal. Both illustrate the principles of feedback control as described under the heading "Homeostasis" in Chapter 1. The nerves that control digestive activity are located in the submucosa and between the muscle layers of the organ walls. Stimulation comes from the autonomic (visceral) nervous system. In general, parasympathetic stimulation increases activity and sympathetic stimulation decreases activity. Excess sympathetic stimulation, as in

Table 18-1 *Digestive Juices Produced by the Organs of the Digestive Tract and the Accessory Organs*

Organ	Main Digestive Juices Secreted	Action
Salivary glands	Salivary amylase	Begins starch digestion
Stomach	Hydrochloric acid (HCl)	Breaks down proteins
	Pepsin	Begins protein digestion
Small intestine	Peptidases	Digest proteins to amino acids
	Lactase, maltase, sucrase	Digest disaccharides to monosaccharides
Pancreas	Sodium bicarbonate	Neutralizes HCl
	Amylase	Digests starch
	Trypsin	Digests protein to amino acids
	Lipases	Digest fats to fatty acids and glycerol
	Nucleases	Digest nucleic acids
Liver	Bile salts	Emulsify fats

stress, can block the movement of food through the digestive tract and inhibit secretion of the mucus that is so important in protecting the lining of the digestive tract.

The hormones involved in control are produced by the digestive organs. Let us look at some examples.

The sight, smell, thought, taste, or feel of food in the mouth stimulates the secretion of saliva and the release of gastric juice. Once in the stomach, food stimulates the release into the blood of the hormone **gastrin**, which promotes stomach secretions and movement. When chyme enters the duodenum, nerve impulses inhibit movement of the stomach so that food will not move too rapidly into the small intestine. This action is a good example of negative feedback. At the same time, hormones released from the duodenum feed back to the stomach to reduce its activity. Most of these hormones have the additional function of stimulating the liver, pancreas, or gallbladder to release their secretions. Table 18-2 lists some of the hormones that help regulate the digestive process.

Hunger and Appetite

Hunger is the desire for food and can be satisfied by the ingestion of a filling meal. Hunger is regulated by centers in the hypothalamus that can be modified by input from higher brain centers. Therefore, cultural factors and memories of past food intake can influence hunger. Strong, mildly painful contractions of the empty stomach may stimulate a feeling of hunger. Messages received by the hypothalamus reduce hunger as food is chewed and swallowed and begins to fill the stomach. The short-term regulation of food intake works to keep the amount of food taken in within the limits of what can be processed by the intestine. The long-term regulation of food intake maintains appropriate blood levels of certain nutrients.

Appetite differs from hunger in that, although it is basically a desire for food, it often has no relationship to the need for food. Even after an adequate meal that has relieved hunger, a person may still have an appetite for additional food. A chronic loss of appetite, called **anorexia** (an″o-rek′se-ah), may be due to a great variety of physical and mental disorders. Since the hypothalamus and the higher brain centers are involved in the regulation of hunger, it is possible that emotional and social factors contribute to the development of anorexia.

Anorexia nervosa is a psychologic disorder that mainly afflicts young women. In a desire to be excessively thin, affected persons literally starve themselves, sometimes to the point of death. A related disorder, **bulimia** (bu-lim′e-ah), is also called the

Table 18-2 Hormones Active in Digestion

Hormone	Source	Action
Gastrin	Stomach	Stimulates release of gastric juice
Gastric-inhibitory peptide (GIP)	Small intestine	Inhibits release of gastric juice
Secretin	Duodenum	Stimulates release of water and bicarbonate from pancreas; stimulates release of bile from liver
Cholecystokinin (CCK)	Duodenum	Stimulates release of digestive enzymes from pancreas; stimulates release of bile from gallbladder

binge–purge syndrome. Affected individuals take in huge quantities of food at one time and then induce vomiting or take large doses of laxatives to prevent absorption of the food.

Summary

I Digestive system

  A Functions—digestion and absorption

  B Structure of wall—mucosa, submucosa, smooth muscle, serosa

  C Peritoneum—serous membrane that lines abdominal cavity and folds over organs

    1 Peritonitis—peritoneal inflammation

II Digestive tract

  A Mouth

    1 Functions

      a Ingestion of food

      b Mastication of food

      c Lubrication of food

      d Digestion of starch with salivary amylase

    2 Structures

      a Tongue

      b Deciduous (baby) teeth—20 (incisors, canines, molars)

      c Permanent teeth—32 (incisors, canines, premolars, molars)

    3 Diseases of mouth and teeth—caries, gingivitis, periodontitis, Vincent's disease, leukoplakia, mumps

  B Pharynx (throat)—moves portion of food (bolus) into esophagus by reflex swallowing (deglutition)

  C Esophagus—long muscular tube that carries food to stomach by peristalsis

  D Stomach

    1 Functions

      a Storage of food

      b Breakdown of food by churning

      c Liquefaction of food with hydrochloric acid (HCl) to form chyme

      d Digestion of protein with enzyme pepsin

    2 Diseases—gastritis, ulcer, cancer

  E Small intestine

    1 Functions

      a Digestion of food

      b Absorption of food through villi (small projections of intestinal lining)

    2 Structures—duodenum, jejunum, ileum

  F Large intestine

    1 Functions

      a Storage and elimination of waste (defecation)

      b Reabsorption of water

    2 Structures—cecum, ascending, transverse, descending, sigmoid colons; rectum; anus

    3 Disorders—enteritis, diarrhea, constipation (spastic and flaccid), diverticulitis, appendicitis, cancer

III Accessory organs

  A Liver

    1 Functions

      a Storage of glucose

      b Formation of blood plasma proteins

      c Synthesis of urea

      d Modification of fats

      e Manufacture of bile

      f Destruction of old red blood cells

      g Detoxification of harmful substances

      h Storage of vitamins and iron

    2 Diseases—hepatitis, cirrhosis, jaundice, cancer

B Gallbladder

1 Function—storage of bile until needed for digestion

2 Diseases—gallstones (cholelithiasis), inflammation (cholecystitis)

C Pancreas—secretes powerful digestive juice; secretes neutralizing fluid

IV **Process of digestion**

A Products

1 Simple sugars (monosaccharides) from carbohydrates

2 Amino acids from proteins

3 Glycerol and fatty acids from fats

B Absorption—movement of digested food into the circulation

C Control

1 Nervous control

a Parasympathetic system—generally increases activity

b Sympathetic system—generally decreases activity

2 Hormonal control

a Stimulation of digestive activity

b Feedback to inhibit responses

Questions for Study and Review

1 Trace the path of a mouthful of food through the digestive tract.

2 What is the peritoneum? Name the two layers and describe their locations. Name four subdivisions of the peritoneum.

3 Differentiate between deciduous and permanent teeth with respect to kinds and numbers.

4 What is the pharynx? What is above and below it?

5 What is peristalsis? Name some structures in which it occurs.

6 Name two purposes of the acid in gastric juice.

7 Name the principal digestive enzymes. Where is each formed? What does each do?

8 Where does absorption occur and what structures are needed for absorption?

9 What types of digested materials are absorbed into the blood?

10 What types of digested materials are absorbed into the lymph?

11 Name the accessory organs of digestion and the functions of each.

12 Name five nondigestive functions of the liver.

13 Give examples of negative feedback in the control of digestion.

14 Name several hormones that regulate digestion.

15 Name several diseases that involve the organs of digestion.

16 Describe what happens in the formation of a peptic ulcer.

17 What is an important symptom of stomach cancer?

18 How is hunger regulated?

19

Metabolism, Nutrition, and Body Temperature

Behavioral Objectives

After careful study of this chapter, you should be able to:

Differentiate between catabolism and anabolism

Differentiate between the anaerobic and aerobic phases of catabolism and give the end products and the relative amount of energy released from each

Explain the role of glucose in metabolism

Compare the energy contents of fats, proteins, and carbohydrates

Define essential amino acid

Explain the roles of minerals and vitamins in nutrition and give examples of each

Define metabolic rate

Name several factors that affect the metabolic rate

Explain how heat is produced in the body

List the ways in which heat is lost from the body

Describe the role of the hypothalamus in regulating body temperature

Define fever

Describe some adverse effects of excessive heat and cold

Selected Key Terms

The following terms are defined in the glossary:

anabolism
catabolism
fever
glucose
hypothermia
malnutrition
metabolic rate
mineral
oxidation
pyrogen
vitamin

≡ Metabolism

The end products of digestion are used for all the cellular activities of the body which, taken all together, make up **metabolism**. These activities fall into two categories:

1 **Catabolism**, which is the breakdown of food into simple compounds and energy
2 **Anabolism**, which is the conversion of the building blocks of food into substances needed for cellular activities and the growth and repair of tissues

The Steps in Catabolism

Food is broken down for energy in a series of reactions, called **cellular respiration**, each step of which requires a specific enzyme, or organic catalyst. The first reactions in this process can occur without oxygen; that is, they are **anaerobic**. This phase of catabolism occurs in the cytoplasm. It yields a very small amount of energy and some organic end product, such as the lactic acid produced in muscles functioning without oxygen (see Chap. 8). Although some small and primitive organisms such as certain bacteria can survive using this process alone, humans would not survive long with so little energy. A more complete use of food is necessary, and this occurs in the second phase of catabolism, which is **aerobic** (requires oxygen).

The aerobic reactions of metabolism occur within the mitochondria of the cell and yield almost all the remaining energy of the food in the form of ATP (adenosine triphosphate). In the course of these reactions, carbon dioxide is released and oxygen is combined with hydrogen from the food molecules to form water. The carbon dioxide is eliminated by the lungs in breathing. Because of the type of chemical reactions involved, and because oxygen is used in the final steps, this process of cellular respiration is called **oxidation**. Although the oxidation of food is often compared to the burning of fuel, this comparison is inaccurate. Burning results in a sudden and often wasteful release of energy in the form of heat and light. In contrast, metabolic oxidation occurs in steps, and much of the energy released as a result is stored as ATP for later use by the cells; some of the energy is also released as heat, which is used to maintain body temperature, as discussed later in this chapter.

The Use of Foods for Energy

The main energy compound in the body is the simple sugar **glucose**. Other carbohydrates in the diet are converted to glucose for metabolism. Glucose circulates in the blood to provide energy for all the cells. Reserves of glucose are stored in liver and muscle cells in the form of **glycogen**, a compound built from glucose molecules. Glycogen is broken down to glucose when it is needed for energy. Glycerol and fatty acids (from fat digestion) and amino acids (from protein digestion) can also be used for energy, but they enter the metabolic pathway at different points. Food that is ingested in excess of need is converted to fat and stored in adipose tissue. Fat yields more than twice the amount of energy as protein or carbohydrate (it is more "fattening"); fat yields about 9 kilocalories (kcal) of energy per gram, whereas protein and carbohydrate each yields about 4 kcal per gram.

Before oxidation, the amino acids must have their nitrogen (amine) groups removed. This occurs in the liver, where the nitrogen groups are then formed into urea by combination with carbon dioxide. The urea is transported by the bloodstream to the kidneys to be eliminated. High-protein diets used for weight reduction make extra work for the kidneys. For this reason, an individual on such a diet should drink at least eight glasses of water each day and should not continue the diet for more than one to two weeks at a time.

Anabolism

Food molecules are built into body materials by other metabolic steps, all of which are catalyzed by enzymes. Ten of the 20 amino acids needed to build proteins can be manufactured by metabolic reactions. The remaining ten amino acids cannot be made by the body and therefore must be taken in with the diet; these are the **essential amino acids**. Most animal proteins supply all of the essential amino acids and are described as **complete proteins**. Vegetables may be lacking in one or more of the essential amino acids. Persons on strict vegetarian diets must learn to combine foods, such as beans with rice or wheat, in order to obtain all of the essential amino acids at the same time. The few essential fatty acids that are needed are easily obtained through a healthful, balanced diet.

Minerals and Vitamins

In addition to needing fats, proteins, and carbohydrates, the human body requires minerals and vitamins. **Minerals** are elements needed for body structure, fluid balance, and such activities as muscle contraction, nerve impulse conduction, and blood clotting. A list of the main minerals needed in a proper diet is given in Table 19-1. Some additional minerals not listed are also required for good health. Those needed in extremely small amounts are referred to as **trace elements**.

Vitamins are organic substances needed in very small quantities. Vitamins are parts of enzymes or other essential substances used in cell metabolism, and vitamin deficiencies lead to a variety of nutritional diseases. A list of vitamins is given in Table 19-2.

≡ Some Practical Aspects of Nutrition

As has been mentioned many times in this book, good nutrition is absolutely essential for the maintenance of health. If any vital food material is missing from the diet, the body will suffer from **malnutrition**. One commonly thinks of a malnourished person as

Table 19-1   Minerals

Mineral	Functions	Sources	Deficiencies
Potassium (K)	Nerve and muscle activity	Fruits, meats, seafood, milk	Muscular and neurologic disorders
Sodium (Na)	Body fluid balance; nerve impulse conduction	Most foods and table salt	Weakness, cramps, diarrhea, dehydration
Calcium (Ca)	Formation of bones and teeth, blood clotting, nerve conduction, muscle contraction	Dairy products, eggs, green vegetables, legumes (peas and beans)	Rickets, tetany, bone demineralization
Phosphorus (P)	Formation of bones and teeth; found in ATP, nucleic acids, cell membrane	Beef, egg yolk, dairy products	Bone demineralization, abnormal metabolism
Iron (Fe)	Oxygen carrier (hemoglobin)	Meat, eggs, spinach, prunes, cereals, legumes	Anemia, dry skin, indigestion
Iodine (I)	Thyroid hormones	Seafood, iodized salt	Hypothyroidism, goiter
Magnesium (Mg)	Catalyst for enzyme reactions, carbohydrate metabolism	Green vegetables, grains	Spasticity, arrhythmia, vasodilation
Manganese (Mn)	Catalyst in actions of calcium and phosphorus	Legumes, nuts, cereals, green leafy vegetables	Possible reproductive disorders
Copper (Cu)	Necessary for absorption and oxidation of vitamin C and iron and in formation of hemoglobin	Liver, fish, oysters, legumes, nuts	Anemia
Cobalt (Co)	Part of vitamin B_{12}, involved in blood cell production and in synthesis of insulin	Animal products	Pernicious anemia
Zinc (Zn)	Promotes carbon dioxide transport and energy metabolism; found in enzymes	Many foods	Alopecia (baldness) possibly related to diabetes
Fluorine (F)	Prevents tooth decay	Water and many foods	Dental caries

Table 19-2   Vitamins

Vitamins	Functions	Sources	Deficiencies
Retinol (A)	Required for healthy epithelial tissues and for eye pigments	Yellow vegetables, fish liver oils, dairy products	Night blindness; dry, scaly skin
Thiamin (B$_1$)	Required for enzymes involved in oxidation of food	Pork, cereal grains, meats, legumes	Beriberi, a disease of nerves (neuritis)
Riboflavin (B$_2$)	Needed for enzymes required for oxidation of food	Milk, eggs, kidney, liver, green leafy vegetables	Skin and tongue disorders
Niacin (nicotinic acid)	Involved in oxidation of food	Yeast, lean meat, liver, grains, legumes	Pellagra with dermatitis, diarrhea, mental disorders
Pyridoxine (B$_6$)	Involved in metabolism of various food substances and transport of amino acids	Liver, milk, cereals, eggs, yeast, vegetables	Irritability, convulsions, muscle twitching, skin disorders
Pantothenic acid	Essential for normal growth	Yeast, liver, eggs	Sleep disturbances, lack of coordination, skin lesions
Cyanocobalamin (B$_{12}$)	Production of blood cells (hemopoiesis)	Meat, liver, milk, eggs	Pernicious anemia
Biotin	Involved in fat and glycogen formation, amino acid metabolism	Peanuts, liver, tomatoes, eggs	Lack of coordination, dermatitis, fatigue
Folic acid and folates	Required for amino acid metabolism, maturation of red blood cells	Vegetables, liver	Anemia, digestive disorders
Ascorbic acid (C)	Maintains healthy skin and mucous membranes; involved in synthesis of collagen	Citrus fruits, green vegetables	Scurvy, poor bone and wound healing
Calciferol (D)	Aids in absorption of calcium from intestinal tract	Fish liver oils, dairy products	Rickets, bone deformities
Tocopherol (E)	Protects cell membranes	Seeds, green vegetables	In question

one who does not have enough to eat, but malnutrition can also occur from eating too much of the wrong foods. The simplest and perhaps best advice for maintaining a healthful diet is to eat a wide variety of fresh, whole foods daily, selected from the following four basic food groups:

1 High-protein foods, such as meats, fish, eggs, nuts, peas, and beans
2 Vegetables and fruits
3 Whole grains, including cereals and breads
4 Dairy products, such as milk, cheese, and yoghurt

Because proteins, unlike carbohydrates and fats, are not stored, protein foods should be taken in on a regular basis. The average U.S. diet, however, contains more than enough protein and too much fat, especially animal fat. It is currently recommended that calories from the three types of food be distributed as follows:

Fat	30%
Carbohydrate	58%
Protein	12%

The carbohydrates should be mainly complex, naturally occurring carbohydrates with a minimum of refined sugars. Less than half of the fats in the diet should be **saturated fats**. These are fats, mostly from animal sources, that are solid at room temperature, such as butter and lard. Also included in this group are fats that are artificially hardened (hydrogenated), such as vegetable shortening and margarine, which it is best to avoid. **Unsaturated fats** are mainly from plants. They are liquid at room temperature and are generally referred to as *oils*. Diets high in saturated fats are associated with a higher than normal incidence of cancer, heart disease, and cardiovascular problems, although the relationship between these factors is not clear.

A weight loss diet should follow the same guidelines as given above with a reduction in portion sizes. Exercise is also recommended.

The need for mineral and vitamin supplements to the diet is a subject of controversy. Some researchers maintain that adequate amounts of these substances can be obtained from a varied, healthful diet; others hold that pollution, depletion of the soils, and the storage, refining, and processing of foods make supplementation beneficial. Most agree, however, that children, elderly persons, pregnant and lactating women, and teenagers, who often do not get enough of the proper foods, would profit from additional minerals and vitamins.

When required, supplements should be selected by a physician or nutritionist to fit the particular needs of the individual. The so-called megavitamin dosages now fashionable in some places may cause unpleasant reactions and in some cases are hazardous. Vitamins A and D have both been found to cause serious toxic effects, and a relatively small excess of vitamin D may result in the appearance of dangerous symptoms.

The subject of allergies has received much attention recently, and it appears that food allergies may be much more common than suspected. Some persons develop clear allergic (hypersensitive) symptoms if they eat certain foods. The most common food allergens are wheat, yeast, milk, and eggs, but almost any food might cause an allergic reaction in a given individual. Although food allergies may be responsible for symptoms with no other known cause, most persons can probably eat all types of foods.

Metabolic Rate

Metabolic rate refers to the rate at which energy is released from food in the cells. It is affected by a person's size, body fat, sex, age, activity, and hormones, especially thyroid hormone (thyroxine). Metabolic rate is high in children and adolescents and decreases with age.

The **basal metabolic rate (BMR)** is a measure of the amount of energy needed to maintain life functions while the body is at rest. The BMR is generally determined by measurement of the amount of oxygen used in a given period while an individual is awake and at rest.

Because thyroid hormone is an important regulator of the metabolic rate, the BMR is an indirect measure of thyroid function. More accurate and direct methods for determining thyroid function are described in Chapter 11.

Body Temperature

Heat is an important byproduct of the many chemical activities constantly going on in tissues all over the body. Heat is always being lost through a variety of outlets. However, because of a number of regulatory devices, under normal conditions body temperature remains constant within quite narrow limits. Maintenance of a constant temperature in spite of both internal and external influences is one phase of homeostasis, the tendency of all body processes to maintain a normal state despite forces that tend to alter them.

Heat Production

Heat is produced when oxygen combines with food products in the cells. Thus, heat is a byproduct of the reactions in all cells as they produce energy. The amount of heat produced by a given organ varies with the kind of tissue and its activity. While at rest, muscles may produce as little as 25% of total body heat, but when a number of muscles contract, heat production may be multiplied hundreds of times owing to the increase in metabolic rate. Under basal conditions (rest), the abdominal organs, particularly the liver, produce about 50% of total body heat. While the body is at rest, the brain produces 15% of body heat, and an increase in nerve tissue activity produces very little increase in heat production. The largest amount of heat, therefore, is produced in the muscles and the glands. It would seem from this description that some parts of the body would tend to become much warmer than others. The circulating blood, however, distributes the heat fairly evenly.

The rate at which heat is produced is affected by a number of factors, which may include activity level, hormone production, food intake, and age. Hormones, such as thyroxine from the thyroid gland and epinephrine (adrenaline) from the medulla of the adrenal gland, may increase the rate of heat production. The intake of food is also accompanied by increased heat production. The reasons for this are not entirely clear, but a few causes are known. More fuel is poured into the blood with food intake and is therefore more readily available for cellular metabolism. The glandular structures and the muscles of the digestive system generate additional heat as they set to work. This does not account for all the increase, however, nor does it account for the much greater increase in metabolism following a meal containing a large amount of protein. Whatever the reasons, the intake of food definitely increases the chemical activities that go on in the body and thus adds to heat production.

Heat Loss

More than 80% of heat loss occurs through the skin. The remaining 15% to 20% is dissipated by the respiratory system and with the urine and feces. Networks of blood vessels in the deeper part (dermis) of the skin can bring considerable quantities of blood near the surface so that heat can be dissipated to the outside. This can occur in several ways. Heat can be transferred to the surrounding air (**conduction**). Heat also travels from its source in the form of heat waves or rays (**radiation**). If the air is moving so that the layer of heated air next to the body is constantly being carried away and replaced with cooler air (as by an electric fan), the process is known as **convection**. Finally, heat loss may be produced by **evaporation**, the process by which liquid changes to the vapor state. Rub some alcohol on your arm; it evaporates rapidly, and in so doing uses so much heat from the skin that your arm feels cold. Perspiration does the same thing, although not as quickly. The rate of heat loss through evaporation depends on the humidity of the surrounding air. When this exceeds 60% or so, perspiration does not evaporate so readily, making one feel generally miserable unless some other means of heat loss such as convection (by a fan) can be resorted to.

If the temperature of the surrounding air is lower than that of the body, excessive heat loss is prevented by both natural and artificial means. Clothing checks heat loss by trapping "dead air" both in its material and its layers. This noncirculating air is a good insulator. An effective natural insulation against cold is the layer of fat under the skin. Even when skin temperature is low, this fatty tissue prevents the deeper tissues from losing much heat. On the average, this layer is slightly thicker in females than in males. Naturally there are individual variations, but as a rule the degree of insulation depends on the thickness of this layer of subcutaneous fat.

Other factors that play a part in heat loss include the volume of tissue compared with the amount of skin surface. A child loses heat more rapidly than an adult. Such parts as fingers and toes are affected most by exposure to cold because they have a great amount of skin compared with total tissue volume.

Temperature Regulation

Given that body temperature remains almost constant in spite of wide variations in the rate of heat production or loss, there must be a temperature regulator. Many areas of the body take part in this process, but the most important heat-regulating center is the area inside the brain, located just above the pituitary gland, called the **hypothalamus**. Some of the cells in the hypothalamus control the production of heat in the body tissues, whereas another group of cells controls heat loss. This control comes about in response to the heat brought to the brain by the blood as well as to nerve impulses from temperature receptors in the skin. If these two factors indicate that too much heat is being lost, impulses are sent quickly from the hypothalamus to the autonomic (involuntary) nervous system, which in turn causes constriction of the skin blood vessels in order to reduce heat loss. Other impulses are sent to the muscles to cause shivering, a rhythmic contraction of many body muscles, which results in increased heat production. Furthermore, the output of epinephrine may be increased if conditions call for it. Epinephrine increases cell metabolism for a short period of time, and this in turn increases heat production. Also, the smooth muscle around the hair roots contracts, forming "gooseflesh," a reaction that conserves heat in many animals but only little heat in humans.

If there is danger of overheating, the hypothalamus will transmit impulses that stimulate the sweat glands to increase their activity and that dilate the blood vessels in the skin so that there is increased blood flow with a correspondingly greater loss of heat. The hypothalamus may also encourage the relaxation of muscles and thus minimize the production of heat in these organs.

Muscles are especially important in temperature regulation because variations in the amount of activity in these large masses of tissue can readily increase or decrease the total amount of heat produced. Since muscles form roughly one third of the bulk of the body, either an involuntary or a purposeful increase in the activity of this big group of organs can form enough heat to offset a considerable decrease in the temperature of the environment.

Very young and very old persons are limited in their ability to regulate body temperature when exposed to extremes in environment. The body temperature of a newborn infant will decrease if the infant is exposed to a cool environment for a long period of time. Elderly pesons also are not able to produce enough heat to maintain body temperature in a cool environment. Heat loss mechanisms are not fully developed in the newborn; the elderly do not lose as much heat from their skin. Both groups should be protected from extreme temperatures.

Normal Body Temperature

The normal temperature range obtained by either a glass or an electronic thermometer may extend from 36.2°C to 37.6°C (97°F to 100°F). Body temperature varies with the time of day. Usually it is lowest in the early morning, since the muscles have been relaxed and no food has been taken in for several hours. Temperature tends to be higher in the late afternoon and evening because of physical activity and consumption of food.

Normal temperature also varies with the part of the body. Skin temperature obtained in the **axilla** (armpit) is lower than mouth temperature, and mouth temperature is a degree or so lower than rectal temperature. It is believed that, if it were possible to place a thermometer inside the liver, it would register a degree or more higher than rectal temperature. The temperature within a muscle might be even higher during its activity.

Although the Fahrenheit scale is used in the United States, in most parts of the world temperature is measured with the **Celsius** (sel′se-us) thermometer. On this scale the ice point is at 0° and the normal boiling point of water is at 100°, the interval between these two points being divided into 100 equal units.

The Celsius scale is also called the **centigrade scale** (think of 100 cents). See the Appendix for a comparison of the Celsius and Fahrenheit scales and formulas for converting from one to the other.

Abnormal Body Temperature

Fever

Fever is a condition in which the body temperature is higher than normal. An individual with a fever is described as **febrile** (feb′ril). Usually the presence of fever is due to an infection, but there can be many other causes, such as malignancies, brain injuries, toxic reactions, reactions to vaccines, and diseases involving the CNS. Sometimes emotional upsets can bring on a fever. Whatever the cause, the effect is to reset the body's thermostat in the hypothalamus.

Curiously enough, fever usually is preceded by a chill—that is, a violent attack of shivering and a sensation of cold that such measures as blankets and hot water bottles seem unable to relieve. Owing to these reactions heat is being generated and stored in the body, and when the chill subsides, the body temperature is elevated.

The old adage that a fever should be starved is completely wrong. During a fever there is an increase in metabolism that is usually proportional to the amount of fever. In addition to the use of available sugar and fat, there is an increase in the use of protein, and during the first week or so of a fever there is definite evidence of destruction of body protein. A high-calorie diet with plenty of protein is therefore desirable.

When a fever ends, sometimes the drop in temperature to normal occurs very rapidly. This sudden fall in temperature is called the **crisis,** and it is usually accompanied by symptoms indicating rapid heat loss: profuse perspiration, muscular relaxation, and dilation of blood vessels in the skin. A gradual drop in temperature, in contrast, is known as **lysis.** A drug that reduces fever is described as **antipyretic** (an″ti-pi-ret′ik).

The mechanism of fever production is not completely understood, but we might think of the hypothalamus as a thermostat that is set higher during fever than normally. This change in the heat-regulating mechanism often follows the injection of a foreign protein or the entrance into the blood stream of bacteria or their toxins. Substances that produce fever are called **pyrogens** (pi′ro-jens). Up to a point, fever may be beneficial, because it steps up phagocytosis (the process by which white blood cells surround, engulf, and digest bacteria and other foreign bodies), inhibits the growth of certain organisms, and increases cellular metabolism, which may help recovery from disease.

Extreme Outside Temperatures

The body's heat-regulating devices are efficient, but there is a limit to what they can accomplish. High outside temperature may overcome the body's heat loss mechanisms, in which case body temperature will rise and cellular metabolism and accompanying heat production will increase. When body temperature goes up, the affected individual is apt to suffer from a series of disorders: heat cramps are followed by heat exhaustion, and then, if that is untreated, heat stroke.

In **heat cramps**, there is localized muscle cramping of the extremities and occasionally of the abdomen. The condition will abate with rest in a cool environment and adequate fluids.

With further heat retention and more fluid loss, **heat exhaustion** occurs. Symptoms of this disorder include headache, tiredness, vomiting, and a rapid pulse. There may be a decrease in circulating blood volume and lowered blood pressure. Heat exhaustion may also be treated by rest and fluid replacement.

Heat stroke (also called *sunstroke*) is a medical emergency. Heat stroke can be recognized by a body temperature of up to 41°C (105°F); hot, dry skin; and CNS symptoms, including confusion, dizziness, and loss of consciousness. The body has responded to the loss of fluid from the circulation by reducing blood flow to the skin and sweat glands. It is important to lower the sunstroke victim's body temperature immediately by removing the individual's clothing, placing him or her in a cool environment, and cooling him or her with cold water or ice. The patient should be treated with appropriate fluids containing the vital electrolytes, including sodium, potassium, calcium, and chloride. Supportive medical care is also necessary, since heat stroke can cause fatal complications.

The body is no more capable of coping with prolonged exposure to cold than it is to prolonged exposure to heat. If, for example, the body is immersed in cold water for a time, the water (a better heat conductor than air) removes more heat from the body than can be replaced, and body temperature falls. This can happen too, of course, in cold air, particularly when clothing is inadequate. The main effects of an excessively low body temperature, termed **hypothermia** (hi-po-ther′me-ah), are uncontrolled shivering, lack of coordination, and decreased heart and respiratory rates. Speech becomes slurred, and there is overpowering sleepiness, which may lead to coma and death. Outdoor activities in cool, not necessarily cold, weather cause many unrecognized cases of hypothermia. Wind, fatigue, and depletion of water and energy stores all play a part. Once the body is cooled below a certain point, cellular metabolism is slowed and heat production is inadequate for maintaining a normal body temperature. The person must then be warmed by heat from an outside source. The best first aid measure is to put the individual in a warmed sleeping bag with an unclothed companion until shivering stops. Administration of hot, sweetened fluids also helps.

Exposure to cold, particularly to moist cold, may result in **frostbite**, which can cause permanent local tissue damage. The areas most likely to be affected by frostbite are the face, ears, and extremities. The causes of damage include the formation of ice crystals and the reduction of blood supply to the area. Necrosis of the tissues with gangrene can result. The very young, the very old, and those who suffer from disease of the circulatory system are particularly susceptible to cold injuries.

A frostbitten area should *never* be rubbed; rather, it should be rapidly thawed by immersion in warm water or by contact with warm bare skin. The affected area should be treated very gently; a person with frostbitten feet should not be permitted to walk. Persons with cold-damaged extremities frequently have some lowering of body temperature. Warming of the whole person should not be neglected during warming of the affected part.

Hypothermia is employed in certain types of surgery. In such cases the hypothalamus is depressed by drugs and the body temperature reduced to as low as 25°C (77°F) before the operation is begun. In the case of heart surgery, further cooling to 20°C (68°F) is accomplished as the blood goes through the heart–lung machine. This has been successful even with tiny infants suffering from congenital heart abnormalities.

Summary

I Metabolism—life-sustaining reactions that occur in the living cell
  A Catabolism—breakdown of food into simple compounds and energy
    1 Cellular respiration—a series of reactions in which food is oxidized for energy
      a Anaerobic phase—does not require oxygen
        (1) Location—cytoplasm
        (2) Yield—small amount of energy
        (3) End product—organic (*i.e.,* lactic acid)
      b Aerobic phase—requires oxygen
        (1) Location—mitochondria
        (2) Yield—almost all remaining energy in food
        (3) End products—carbon dioxide and water
    2 Food energy
      a Glucose—main energy source
      b Fats and proteins—can also be used for energy
  B Anabolism—building of simple compounds into materials needed by the body
  C Minerals—elements needed for body structure and cell activities
    1 Trace elements—elements needed in extremely small amounts
  D Vitamins—organic substances needed in small amounts
II Practical aspects of nutrition
  A Malnutrition—too little food or inadequate amounts of specific foods
  B Components of healthy diet
    1 Four basic food groups
    2 Less than 10% of total daily calories in form of animal fats
III Metabolic rate—rate at which energy is released from food in the cells
  A Basal metabolic rate (BMR)—amount of energy needed to maintain life functions while at rest
IV Body temperature
  A Heat production—most heat produced in muscles and glands; distributed by the circulation

  B Heat loss
    1 Skin
    2 Urine
    3 Feces
    4 Breathing
  C Temperature regulation
    1 Hypothalamus—main temperature regulating center; responds to temperature of blood and temperature receptors in skin
    2 Results of decrease in body temperature
      a Constriction of blood vessels in skin
      b Shivering
      c Increased release of epinephrine
    3 Results of increase in body temperature
      a Dilation of skin vessels
      b Sweating
      c Relaxation of muscles
  D Normal body temperature—ranges from 36.2°C to 37.6°C; varies with time of day and location measured
  E Abnormal body temperature
    1 Fever—higher than normal body temperature resulting from infection, injury, toxin, damage to CNS, etc.
      a Pyrogen—substance that produces fever
      b Antipyretic—drug that reduces fever
    2 Extreme outside temperatures
      a Excessive heat—heat cramps, heat exhaustion, heat stroke
      b Excessive cold
        (1) Hypothermia—low body temperature
          (a) Results—coma and death
          (b) Uses—surgery
        (2) Frostbite—reduction of blood supply to areas such as face, ears, toes, fingers
          (a) Results—necrosis and gangrene

Questions for Study and Review

1 Define *cellular respiration*.
2 In what part of the cell does aerobic respiration occur? What are its end products?
3 Approximately how many kilocalories are released from a gram of butter as compared with a gram of egg white? with a gram of sugar?

4 Gelatin is not a complete protein. What are the dangers of eating flavored gelatin as a sole source of protein?

5 Name the foods in the four basic food groups.

6 Define *metabolic rate*. What factors affect the metabolic rate?

7 How is heat produced in the body? What structures produce the most heat during increased activity?

8 Name four factors that affect heat production.

9 How is heat lost from the body?

10 Name four ways in which heat escapes to the environment.

11 In what ways is heat kept in the body?

12 Name the main temperature regulator and describe what it does when the body is too hot and when it is too cold. What parts do muscles play?

13 What is the normal body temperature range? How does it vary with respect to the time of day and the part of the body?

14 Define *fever,* name some aspects of fever's course, and list some of fever's beneficial and detrimental effects.

15 Name and describe two consequences of excessive outside heat. Why do these conditions occur? What is the prime emergency measure for sunstroke?

16 What is hypothermia? Under what circumstances does it usually occur? List some of its effects. In what types of surgery is hypothermia induced?

17 Name and describe two common injuries resulting from cold. What happens in the body to bring these conditions about?

18 Differentiate between the terms in each of the following pairs:

   a *catabolism* and *anabolism*

   b *aerobic* and *anaerobic*

   c *mineral* and *vitamin*

   d *saturated fats* and *unsaturated fats*

   e *crisis* and *lysis*

20

The Urinary System and Body Fluids

Behavioral Objectives

After careful study of this chapter, you should be able to:

List the systems that eliminate waste and name the substances eliminated by each

Describe the parts of the urinary system and name the functions of each

Trace the path of a drop of blood as it flows through the kidney

Describe a nephron

Name the four processes involved in urine formation and describe the functions of each

Identify the role of ADH in urine formation

Name two hormones produced by the kidneys and describe the functions of each

List five signs of chronic renal failure

Explain the purpose of kidney dialysis

Name three normal and six abnormal constituents of urine

Compare intracellular and extracellular fluids

Name the systems that are involved in water balance

Describe three mechanisms for regulating the pH of body fluids

Describe five disorders involving body fluids

Selected Key Terms

The following terms are defined in the glossary:

acidosis
ADH
alkalosis
cortex
cystitis
dehydration
dialysis
edema
excretion
glomerular filtrate
glomerulonephritis
glomerulus
kidney
medulla
nephron
urea
ureter
urethra
urinary bladder
urine

The urinary system is also called the *excretory system* because one of its main functions is to remove waste products from the blood and eliminate them from the body. Other functions of the urinary system include regulation of the volume of body fluids and balance of the *p*H and electrolyte composition of these fluids. The last section of this chapter discusses body fluids and other mechanisms that help regulate body fluids.

The focus of this chapter is the urinary system; however, because body systems work interdependently to maintain the body's constant balance, or homeostasis, certain aspects of other systems will also be discussed. The chief excretory mechanisms of the body, and some of the substances that they eliminate, are listed below:

1   The **urinary system** excretes water, waste products containing nitrogen, and salts. These are all constituents of the urine.

2   The **digestive system** eliminates water, some salts, bile, and the residue of digestion, all of which are contained in the feces. The liver is important in eliminating the products of red blood cell destruction and in breaking down certain drugs and toxins.

3   The **respiratory system** eliminates carbon dioxide and water. The latter appears as vapor, as can be demonstrated by breathing on a window-pane. The lungs also eliminate certain cellular waste products and toxins.

4   The skin, or **integumentary system**, excretes water, salts, and very small quantities of nitrogenous wastes. These all appear in perspiration, though evaporation of water from the skin may go on most of the time without our being conscious of it.

≡ Organs of the Urinary System

The main parts of the urinary system, shown in Figure 20-1, are as follows:

1   Two **kidneys**. These organs extract wastes from the blood and balance body fluids. These are also the organs of excretion that form urine.

2   Two **ureters** (u-re′ters). These tubes conduct urine from the kidneys to the urinary bladder.

3   A single **urinary bladder**. This reservoir receives

and stores the urine brought to it by the two ureters.

4   A single **urethra** (u-re′thrah). This tube conducts urine from the bladder to the outside of the body for elimination.

≡ The Kidneys

Location of the Kidneys

The two kidneys lie against the muscles of the back in the upper abdomen. Since they are up under the dome of the diaphragm, they are protected by the lower ribs and the rib (costal) cartilages. Each kidney is enclosed in a membranous capsule that is made of fibrous connective tissue; it is loosely adherent to the kidney itself. In addition, there is a crescent of fat around the lateral perimeter of the organ, called the *adipose capsule*. This capsule is one of the chief supporting structures of the kidney. The kidneys, as well as the ureters, lie behind the peritoneum. Thus, they are not in the peritoneal cavity but rather in an area known as the **retroperitoneal** (re″tro-per″i-to-ne′al) **space**. The blood supply to the kidney is illustrated in Figure 20-2. Blood is brought to the kidney by a short branch of the abdominal aorta called the **renal artery**. After entering the kidney, the renal artery subdivides into smaller and smaller branches, which eventually make contact with the functional units of the kidney, the **nephrons** (nef′ronz) (see Figs. 20-3 and 20-4). Blood leaves the kidney by vessels that finally merge to form the **renal vein**. The renal vein carries blood into the inferior vena cava for return to the heart.

Structure of the Kidneys

The kidney is a somewhat flattened organ about 10 cm (4 inches) long, 5 cm (2 inches) wide, and 2.5 cm (1 inch) thick. On the inner, or medial, border there is a notch called the **hilus**, at which region the renal artery, the renal vein, and the ureter connect with the kidney. The outer, or lateral, border is convex (curved outward), giving the entire organ a bean-shaped appearance.

The kidney is divided into three regions: the renal cortex, the renal medulla, and the renal pelvis (Fig. 20-3). The renal **cortex** is the outer portion of the kidney. The renal **medulla** contains the tubes that collect urine. These tubes form a number of cone-

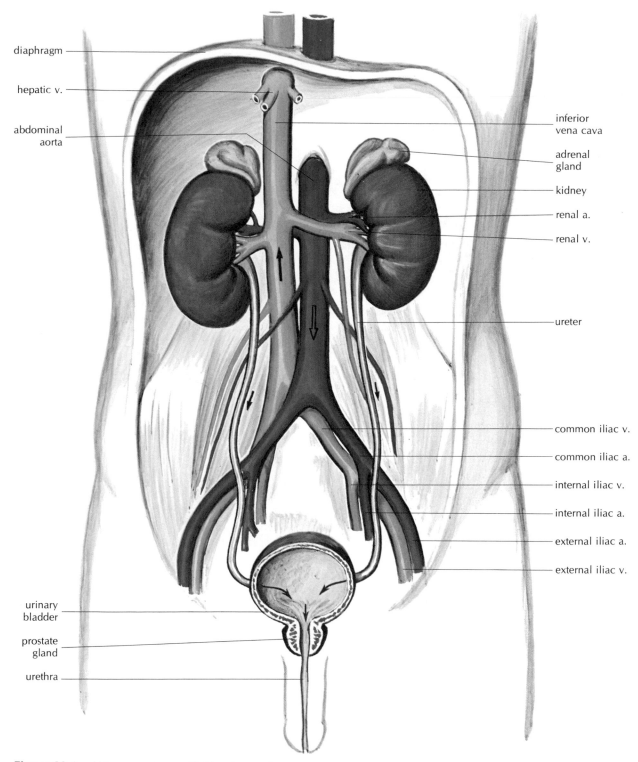

diaphragm

hepatic v.

abdominal
aorta

inferior
vena cava

adrenal
gland

kidney

renal a.

renal v.

ureter

common iliac v.

common iliac a.

internal iliac v.

internal iliac a.

external iliac a.

external iliac v.

urinary
bladder

prostate
gland

urethra

Figure 20-1. *Urinary system, with blood vessels.*

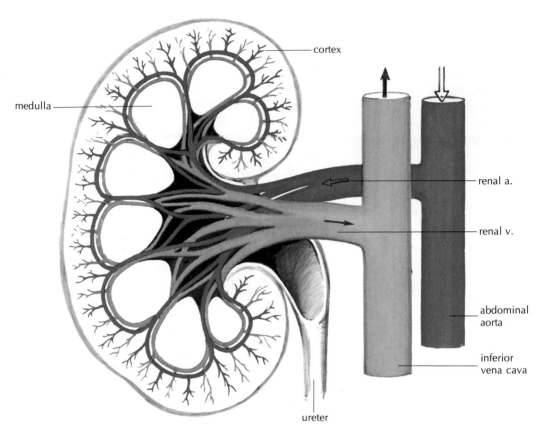

Figure 20-2. *Blood supply and circulation of the kidney.*

shaped structures called **pyramids**, the tip of each of which points toward the **renal pelvis**. The renal pelvis is a funnel-shaped basin that forms the upper end of the ureter. Cuplike extensions of the renal pelvis surround the tips of the pyramids and collect urine; these extensions are called **calyces** (kay′li-sez) (sing., **calyx** [kay′liks]). The urine that collects in the pelvis then passes down the ureters to the bladder.

The kidney is a glandular organ; that is, most of the tissue is epithelium with just enough connective tissue to serve as a framework. As is the case with most organs, the most fascinating aspect of the kidney is too small to be seen with the naked eye. This basic unit of the kidney, where the kidney's work is actually done, is the nephron (Fig. 20-4). The nephron is primarily a tiny coiled tube with a bulb at one end. This bulb, called **Bowman's capsule**, surrounds a cluster of capillaries called the **glomerulus** (glo-mer′u-lus). Each kidney contains about 1 million nephrons; if all these coiled tubes were separated,

straightened out, and laid end to end, they would span some 120 kilometers (75 miles)!

A small blood vessel, called the **afferent arteriole**, supplies the glomerulus with blood; another small vessel, called the **efferent arteriole**, carries blood from the glomerulus to the capillaries surrounding the coiled tube of the nephron. Since these capillaries surround the tube, they are called the **peritubular capillaries**.

The tubular part of the nephron consists of several portions. The coiled portion leading from Bowman's capsule is called the **proximal convoluted** (kon′vo-lut-ed) **tubule**, and the coiled portion at the other end is called the **distal convoluted tubule**. Between these two coiled portions is the **loop of Henle** (hen′lee).

The distal convoluted tubule curls back toward the glomerulus between the afferent and efferent arterioles. At the point at which the distal tubule contacts the arterioles, there are specialized glandular cells that form the **juxtaglomerular** (juks"tah-glo-mer′u-lar) **apparatus** (Fig. 20-5). The function of these specialized cells is discussed later in this chapter.

The glomerulus, Bowman's capsule, and the proximal and distal convoluted tubules of most nephrons are within the renal cortex. The loops of Henle extend varying distances into the medulla. The distal end of each tubule empties into a collecting tubule, which then continues through the medulla toward the renal pelvis.

Functions of the Kidneys

The kidneys are involved in the following processes:

1 Excretion of unwanted substances such as waste products from cell metabolism, excess salts, and toxins
2 Maintenance of water balance
3 Regulation of acid–base balance
4 Production of hormones, including renin (re′nin), which is important in the regulation of blood pressure

One product of amino acid metabolism is nitrogen-containing waste material, a chief form of which is **urea** (u-re′ah). The kidneys provide a specialized mechanism for the elimination of these nitrogenous (ni-troj′e-nus) wastes.

A second function of the kidneys is the maintenance of water balance. Although the amount of water consumed in a day can vary tremendously, the kidneys can adapt to these variations so that the volume of body water remains remarkably stable from day to day. Water is constantly lost in many ways; from the skin, from the respiratory system during exhalation, and from the intestinal tract. Normally, the amount of water taken in or produced (intake) is approximately equal to the amount lost (output).

Figure 20-3. *Longitudinal section through the kidney showing its internal structure and a much enlarged diagram of a nephron. There are more than 1 million nephrons in each kidney.*

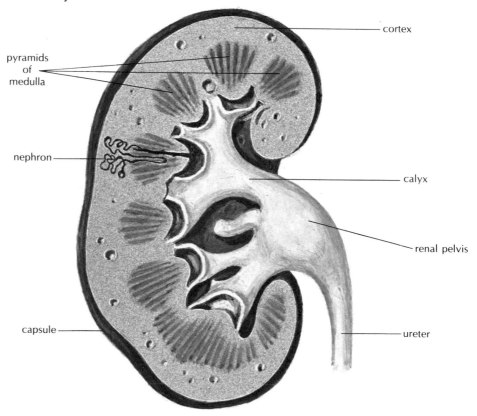

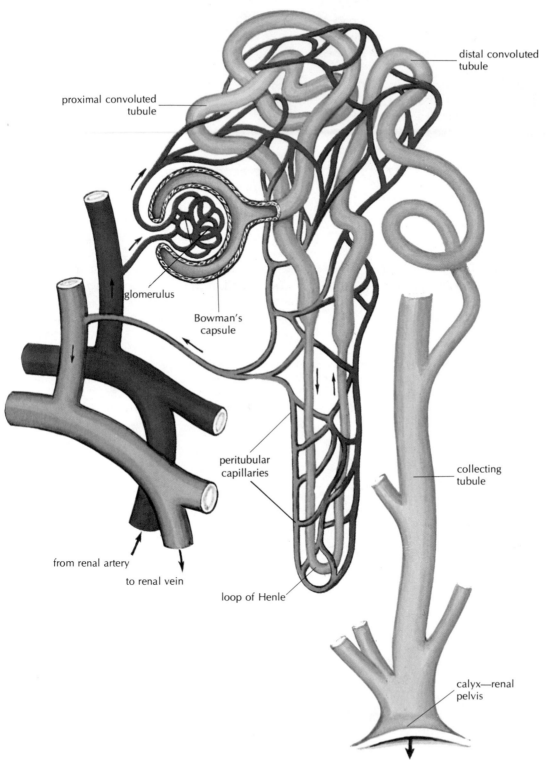

distal convoluted tubule

proximal convoluted tubule

glomerulus

Bowman's capsule

peritubular capillaries

from renal artery

to renal vein

loop of Henle

collecting tubule

calyx—renal pelvis

Figure 20-4. *Simplified nephron.*

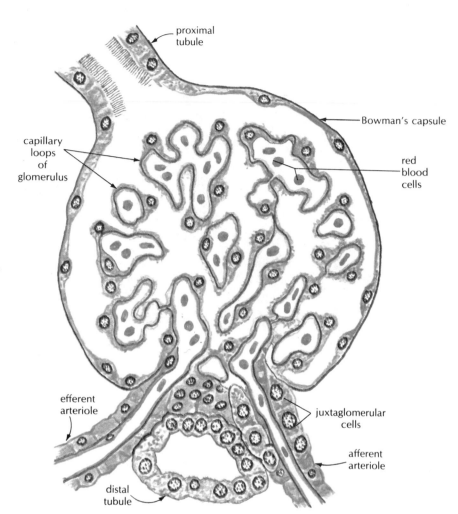

proximal
tubule

Bowman's capsule

capillary
loops
of
glomerulus

red
blood
cells

Figure 20-5. *Structure of the juxtaglomerular apparatus. Note how the distal tubule contacts the arterioles.*

efferent
arteriole

juxtaglomerular
cells

afferent
arteriole

distal
tubule

A third function of the kidneys is to aid in regulating the acid–base balance of the body fluids. Acids are constantly being produced by cell metabolism, and certain foods can also cause acids or bases to be formed in the body. Bases in the form of antacids, such as baking soda, may also be ingested. However, if the body is to function normally, a certain critical proportion of acids and bases must be maintained at all times (see Chaps. 2 and 12).

The fourth function of the kidneys involves the production of hormones, which is accomplished by the juxtaglomerular apparatus. If blood pressure is low, the cells of the juxtaglomerular apparatus release renin into the blood. There this hormone acts as an enzyme to activate a protein that causes blood vessels to constrict and thus to raise blood pressure. When the kidneys do not get enough oxygen, they

release another hormone-like substance that acts as an enzyme to produce **erythropoietin** (e-rith″ro-poi′e-tin). Erythropoietin stimulates the red bone marrow to produce red blood cells and thus prevents anemia.

Renal Physiology

Glomerular Filtration

The process of urine formation begins in the glomerulus and Bowman's capsule. The membranes that form the walls of the glomerular capillaries are sieve-like and permit the free flow of water and soluble materials through them. Like other capillary walls, these are impermeable (im-per′me-abl) to blood cells and large protein molecules, so these substances remain in the blood (Fig. 20-6).

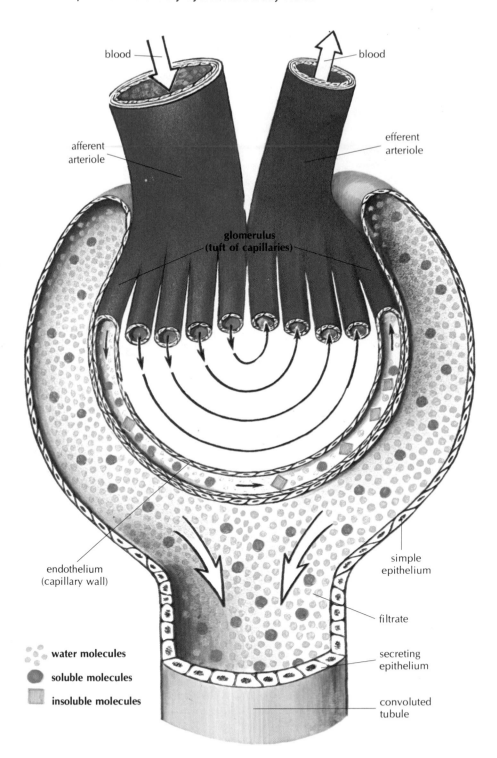

blood

blood

afferent
arteriole

efferent
arteriole

glomerulus
(tuft of capillaries)

endothelium
(capillary wall)

simple
epithelium

filtrate

water molecules

soluble molecules

insoluble molecules

secreting
epithelium

convoluted
tubule

Figure 20-6. *Diagram showing the process of filtration in the formation of urine. The high pressure inside the capillaries of the glomerulus forces the dissolved substances (but not plasma proteins) and much water into the space inside Bowman's capsule. The smaller caliber of the efferent vessel as compared with that of the larger afferent vessel causes this pressure.*

Because the diameter of the afferent arteriole is slightly larger than the diameter of the efferent arteriole, blood can enter the glomerulus more rapidly than it can leave. Thus, the pressure of the blood in the glomerulus is about three to four times as high as it is in other body capillaries. To understand this effect, think of placing your thumb over the end of a garden hose as water comes through. Because the diameter of the opening is made smaller, water is forced out under higher pressure. As a result of this increased pressure in the glomerulus, materials are constantly being "squeezed" out of the blood into Bowman's capsule. This process is known as **glomerular filtration**. The fluid that enters Bowman's capsule, called the **glomerular filtrate**, begins its journey along the tubular system of the nephron. In addition to water and the normal soluble substances in the blood, other substances, such as drugs, may also be filtered and become part of the glomerular filtrate.

Tubular Reabsorption and Secretion

About 160 to 180 liters of filtrate are formed each day in the kidneys. However, only 1 to 1.5 liters of urine are eliminated each day. Clearly, most of the water that enters the nephron is not excreted with the urine but rather is returned to the circulation. Moreover, in addition to waste materials, many substances that are needed by the body, such as nutrients and ions, also pass into the nephron as part of the filtrate. These must be returned to the body as well. Therefore, the process of filtration that occurs in the renal corpuscle is followed by a process of **reabsorption** in the tubular system of the nephron. As the filtrate travels through the nephron, water and other needed substances leave the tubule by diffusion and active transport and enter the tissue fluids surrounding the nephron. They then enter the blood in the peritubular capillaries and return to the circulation. Some nitrogen waste material, such as urea, also leaves, but most is kept within the tubule to be eliminated with the urine. As this modified filtrate continues its journey through the loop of Henle and the distal convoluted tubule, more waste materials and often drugs are removed from the blood by an active process called **tubular secretion**. Ions are also moved into the tubule by secretion, and this constitutes a method by which the *p*H of body fluids is regulated. The kidneys help regulate the *p*H of the blood by increasing or decreasing the number of hydrogen ions that are secreted into the tubules to be eliminated with the urine.

Concentration of the Urine

The amount of water that is eliminated with the urine is regulated by a complex mechanism within the nephron influenced by a hormone from the posterior pituitary gland called *antidiuretic hormone* (ADH). The mechanism is called the *counter-current mechanism* because it involves fluid traveling in opposite directions within the loop of Henle. The counter-current mechanism is illustrated in Figure 20-7. Its essentials are as described below.

As the filtrate passes through the loop of Henle, salts, especially sodium, are actively pumped out by the cells of the nephron, the result being that the interstitial fluid of the medulla becomes increasingly concentrated. Because the nephron is not very permeable to water at this point, the fluid within the nephron becomes increasingly dilute. As the fluid passes through the distal convoluted tubule, through the collecting tubule, and then out of the kidney, water is drawn out by the concentrated fluids around the nephron and returned to the blood, thus concentrating the urine. The role of ADH is to make the walls of the distal convoluted tubule and collecting tubule more permeable to water so that more water will be reabsorbed and the volume of water excreted with the urine will be reduced. The release of ADH is regulated by a feedback system. As the blood becomes more concentrated, the hypothalamus causes more ADH to be released from the posterior pituitary; as the blood becomes more dilute, less ADH is released. In diabetes insipidus there is inadequate secretion of ADH from the hypothalamus. This results in the elimination of large amounts of very dilute urine accompanied by excessive thirst.

≡ The Ureters

The two ureters are long, slender, muscular tubes that extend from the kidney basin down to and through the lower part of the urinary bladder. Their length naturally varies with the size of the individual and so may be anywhere from 25 cm to 32 cm (10–13 inches) long. Nearly 2.5 cm (1 inch) of its lower part enters the bladder by passing obliquely through the bladder wall. The ureters are entirely extraperitoneal, being located behind and, at the lower part, below the peritoneum.

The wall of the ureter includes a lining of epithelial cells, a relatively thick layer of involuntary muscle, and finally an outer coat of fibrous con-

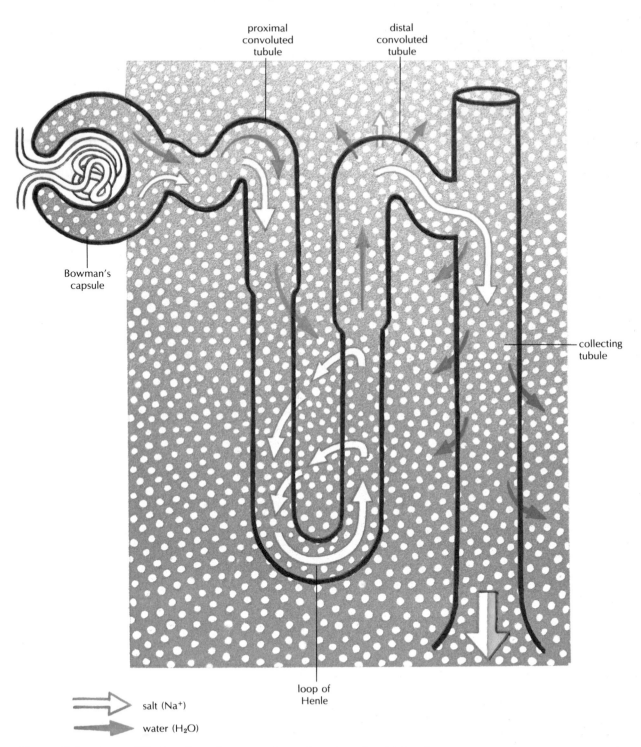

Figure 20-7. *Loop of Henle, where the proportions of waste and water in urine are regulated according to the body's constantly changing needs. The concentration of urine is determined by means of intricate exchanges of water and salt.*

nective tissue. The lining is continuous with that of the renal pelvis and the bladder. The muscles of the ureters are capable of the same rhythmic contraction (peristalsis) found in the digestive system. Urine is moved along the ureter from the kidneys to the bladder by peristalsis at frequent intervals. Because of the oblique direction of the last part of each ureter through the lower bladder wall, compression of the ureters by the full bladder prevents backflow of urine.

The Urinary Bladder

Characteristics of the Bladder

When it is empty, the urinary bladder is located below the parietal peritoneum and behind the pubic joint. When it is filled, it pushes the peritoneum upward and may extend well into the abdominal cavity proper. The urinary bladder is a temporary reservoir for urine, just as the gallbladder is a storage bag for bile.

The bladder wall has many layers. It is lined with mucous membrane; the lining of the bladder, like that of the stomach, is thrown into folds called *rugae* when the receptacle is empty. Beneath the mucosa is a layer of connective tissue. Then follows a three-layered coat of involuntary muscle tissue that is capable of great stretching. Finally, there is an incomplete coat of peritoneum that covers only the upper portion of the bladder. When the bladder is empty, the muscular wall becomes thick and the entire organ feels firm. As the organ fills, the muscular wall becomes thinner and the organ may increase from a length of 5 cm (2 inches) up to as much as 12.5 cm (5 inches) or even more. A moderately full bladder holds about 470 ml (1 pint) of urine.

Urination

The process of expelling urine from the bladder is called **urination** or **micturition** (mik"tu-rish'un). Near the outlet of the bladder, a circle of smooth muscle forms the **internal sphincter**, which contracts to prevent emptying of the bladder. As the bladder fills, stretch receptors send impulses to a center in the lower part of the spinal cord. From there, motor impulses are sent out to the bladder musculature and the organ is emptied. In the infant this emptying is automatic (a reflex action). As a child matures, higher

brain centers gain control over the reflex action and over a voluntary external sphincter that is located below the internal sphincter. The time of urination can then be voluntarily controlled unless the bladder becomes too full.

The Urethra

The **urethra**, the tube that extends from the bladder to the outside, is the means by which the bladder is emptied. The urethra differs in men and women; in men it is also a part of the reproductive system and is much longer than in women.

The female urethra is a thin-walled tube about 4 cm (1.5 inches) long. It is located behind the pubic joint and is embedded in the muscle of the front wall of the vagina. The external opening, called the **urethral meatus**, is located just in front of the vaginal opening or within the lower part of the front wall of the vagina.

The male urethra is about 20 cm (8 inches) long. Early in its course, it passes through the prostate gland, where the two ducts carrying the male sex cells join it. From here it leads through the **penis** (pe'nis), the male organ of copulation, to the outside. The male urethra, then, serves the dual purpose of conveying the sex cells and draining the bladder, while the female urethra performs only the latter function.

Disorders of the Urinary System

Kidney Disorders

Kidney disorders may be acute or chronic. Acute conditions usually arise suddenly, most frequently as the result of infection with inflammation of the nephrons. These diseases commonly run a course of a few weeks and are followed by complete recovery. Chronic conditions arise slowly and often are progressive with gradual loss of kidney function.

Acute glomerulonephritis (glo-mer"u-lo-ne-fri'tis) is the most common disease of the kidneys. This condition usually occurs in children about 1 to 4 weeks after a streptococcal infection of the throat. Antibodies formed in response to the streptococci attach to the glomerular membrane and injure it.

These damaged glomeruli allow protein, especially albumin, to filter into Bowman's capsule and ultimately to appear in the urine (albuminuria). They also allow red blood cells to filter into the urine (hematuria). Usually, the patient recovers without permanent kidney damage. Sometimes, however, particularly in adult patients, the disease becomes chronic with a gradual decrease in the number of functioning nephrons leading to chronic renal failure.

Pyelonephritis (py″el-o-ne-fri′tis), an inflammation of the kidney pelvis and the tissue of the kidney itself, may be either acute or chronic. In acute pyelonephritis, the inflammation results from a bacterial infection. Bacteria most commonly reach the kidney by ascending along the lining membrane from an infection in the lower part of the urinary tract (see Fig. 21-6). More rarely, bacteria are carried to the kidney by the blood. Acute pyelonephritis is often seen in persons with partial obstruction of urine flow with stagnation (urinary stasis). It is most likely to occur in pregnant women and in men with enlarged prostates. Usually, the disease responds to the administration of antibiotics, fluid replacement, rest, and fever control. Chronic pyelonephritis, a more serious disease, is frequently seen in patients with urinary tract blockage. It may be caused by persistent or repeated bacterial infections. Progressive damage of kidney tissue in this condition eventually leads to chronic renal failure.

Hydronephrosis (hi″dro-ne-fro′sis) is the distention of the renal pelvis and calyces caused by an accumulation of fluid due to an obstruction to normal urine flow. The obstruction may occur at any level in the urinary tract. The most common causes of obstruction, in addition to pregnancy and an enlarged prostate, are a kidney stone that has formed in the pelvis and dropped into the ureter, a tumor that presses on a ureter, and scars due to inflammation. Removal of the obstruction within a few weeks, before the kidney is damaged, may result in complete recovery. If the obstruction is not removed, the kidney will be permanently damaged.

Acute renal failure may result from a medical or surgical emergency or from toxins that damage the tubules. This condition is characterized by a sudden, serious decrease in kidney function and may be fatal without immediate medical treatment.

Chronic renal failure results from a gradual loss of nephrons. As more and more nephrons are destroyed, the kidneys gradually lose the ability to perform their normal functions. As the disease progresses, nitrogen waste products accumulate to high levels, causing a condition known as **uremia** (u-re′me-ah).

A few of the characteristic signs and symptoms of chronic renal failure are the following:

1 **Dehydration** (de″hi-dra′shun). Excessive loss of body fluid may occur early in renal failure when the kidneys cannot concentrate the urine and large amounts of water are eliminated.

2 **Edema** (e-de′mah). Accumulation of fluid in the tissue spaces may occur late in chronic renal disease when the kidneys cannot eliminate water in adequate amounts.

3 **Hypertension** may occur as the result of fluid overload and the increased production of renin.

4 **Anemia** occurs when the kidneys cannot produce the hormone to activate red bone marrow cell production.

5 **Uremia.** If levels of nitrogen waste products in the blood are very high, urea can be changed into ammonia in the stomach and intestine and cause ulcerations and bleeding.

Tumors of the kidneys usually grow rather slowly, but occasionally rapidly invading types are found. Blood in the urine and dull pain in the kidney region are warnings that should be heeded at once. Immediate surgery may be lifesaving. A **polycystic** (pol-e-sis′tik) **kidney** is one in which many fluid-containing sacs develop in the active tissue and gradually, by pressure, destroy the functioning parts. This disorder runs in families, and until now treatment has not proved very satisfactory, except for the use of dialysis machines or kidney transplants.

Kidney stones, or **calculi** (kal′ku-li), are made of certain substances, such as uric acid and calcium salts, that precipitate out of the urine instead of remaining in solution. They usually form in the renal pelvis, although the bladder can be another site of formation. The causes of this precipitation of stone-building materials include infection of the urinary tract and stagnation of the urine. These stones may vary in size from tiny grains resembling bits of gravel up to large masses that fill the kidney pelvis and extend into the calyces. The latter are described as **staghorn calculi.** There is no way of dissolving these stones, since substances that would be able to do so would also destroy the kidney tissue. Sometimes instruments can be used to crush small stones and thus allow them to be expelled with the urine, but more often surgical removal is required. A new device called a lithotriptor ("stone-cracker") uses external shock waves to shatter kidney stones.

Dialysis Machines and Kidney Transplants

Dialysis (di-al′e-sis) means "the diffusion of dissolved molecules through a semipermeable membrane." These molecules tend to pass from an area of greater concentration to one of less concentration. In patients who have defective kidney function, the accumulation of urea and other nitrogen waste products can be reduced by passage of the patient's blood through a dialysis machine. The principle of "molecules leaving the area of greater concentration" thus operates to remove the excess products from the blood.

There are two methods of dialysis in use: hemodialysis and peritoneal dialysis. Both are based on the principle of diffusion of dissolved molecules through a seimpermeable membrane. In hemodialysis the membrane is made of cellophane; in peritoneal dialysis the surface area of the peritoneum acts as the membrane. A 1973 amendment to the Social Security Act provides federal financial assistance for persons who have chronic renal disease and require dialysis. Recent technologic improvements have made home dialysis possible for many patients. Access to the bloodstream has been made safer and easier, and the size of the equipment has been reduced. Currently, researchers are developing a portable hemodialysis unit that patients can wear when they are away from home or the hospital. With improved methods of peritoneal dialysis, chronic as well as acute renal failure can be treated. Permanent catheters can be implanted into the abdomen, and machines can administer dialyzing fluid automatically.

Many hundreds of kidney transplants have been performed successfully during the last several years. Kidneys have so much extra functioning tissue that the loss of one kidney normally poses no problem. Records show that the likelihood that a transplant will be successful is greatest when a living donor who is closely related to the patient is used. However, organs from deceased donors have also proved satisfactory in many cases. The problem of tissue rejection (the rejection syndrome) is discussed in Chapter 16.

Disorders of the Ureters

Abnormalities in structure of the ureter include double portions at the kidney pelves and constricted or abnormally narrow parts, called **strictures** (strik′tures). Narrowing of the ureter may also be caused by abnormal pressure from tumors or other masses outside the tube. Obstruction of the ureters may be due to stones from the kidneys, or to kinking of the tube due to a dropping of the kidney, a condition known as **ptosis** (to′sis).

The passage of a small stone along the ureter causes excruciating pain. Relief of this pain, which is called *renal colic,* usually requires morphine or an equally powerful drug. The first "barber surgeons," operating without benefit of anesthesia, were permitted by their patients to cut through the skin and the muscles of the back to remove stones from the ureters. "Cutting for stone" in this way was relatively successful, despite the lack of sterile technique, because of the approach through the back and the avoidance of the peritoneal cavity, and thus of the risk of deadly peritonitis. Modern surgery employs a variety of instruments for removal of stones from the ureter, including endoscopes similar to those described in Chapter 18. The transurethral route through the urethra and urinary bladder and then into the ureters, as well as entrance through the skin and muscles of the back, may be used to remove calculi from the kidney pelvis or from the ureters.

Disorders Involving the Bladder

A full (distended) bladder lies in an unprotected position in the lower abdomen, and a blow may rupture it, necessitating immediate surgical repair. Blood in the urine is a rather common symptom of infection or tumors, which may involve the bladder. Inflammation of the bladder, called **cystitis** (sisti′tis), is ten times as frequent in women as in men. This may be due at least in part to the very short urethra in the female compared with that of the male. Usually, bacteria (*e.g.,* colon bacilli) ascend from the outside through the urethra into the bladder (see Fig. 21-6). Pain, urgency, and frequency are common symptoms. Another type of cystitis, called **interstitial cystitis**, may cause pelvic pain with discomfort before and after urination. The tissues below the mucosa are involved. The disease can be diagnosed only with the use of a cystoscope (a kind of endoscope). Since no bacteria are involved, antibiotics are not effective treatment and may even be harmful.

Obstruction by an enlarged prostate gland or from a pregnancy may lead to stagnation and cystitis. Reduction of a person's general resistance to infection, as in diabetes, may lead to cystitis. The danger is that the infection may ascend to other parts of the urinary tract.

Tumors of the bladder, which are most prevalent in males over 50, include benign papillomas and various kinds of cancer. About 90% of bladder tumors arise from the epithelial lining. Possible causes include toxins (particularly certain aniline dyes), chronic infestations (schistosomiasis), heavy cigarette smoking, and the presence of urinary stones, which may develop and increase in size within the bladder. Cystoscopic examinations and biopsies should be done as soon as blood is detected in the urine (hematuria). Removal before the tumor invades the muscle wall gives the best prognosis.

Disorders of the Urethra

Congenital anomalies (defects) present at birth involve the urethra as well as other parts of the urinary tract. The opening of the urethra to the outside may be too small, or the urethra itself may be narrowed. Occasionally it happens that an abnormal valvelike structure is located at the point at which the urethra enters the bladder. If they are not removed surgically, such valvelike folds of tissue can cause a back pressure of the urine with serious consequences. There is also a condition in the male in which the urethra opens on the undersurface of the penis instead of at the end. This is called **hypospadias** (hi-po-spa′de-as).

Urethritis, which is characterized by inflammation of the mucous membrane and the glands of the urethra, is much more common in the male than in the female and is often due to gonorrhea, although many other bacteria may also be responsible for the infection.

"Straddle" injuries to the urethra are common in men. This type of injury occurs when, for example, a man walking along a raised beam slips and lands with the beam between his legs. Such an accident may catch the urethra between the hard surfaces of the beam and the pubic arch and rupture the urethra. In accidents in which the bones of the pelvis are fractured, rupture of the urethra is fairly common.

The Effects of Aging

Even without kidney disease, aging causes the kidneys to lose some of their ability to concentrate urine. With aging, progressively more water is needed to excrete the same amount of waste. Old persons find it necessary to drink more water than young persons, and they eliminate larger amounts of urine (polyuria) even at night (nocturia). Beginning at about age 40 there is a decrease in the number and size of the nephrons. Often more than 50% of them are lost before age 80. There may be an increase in blood urea nitrogen (BUN) without serious symptoms. Elderly persons are more susceptible than young persons to infections of the urinary system. Childbearing may cause damage to the musculature of the pelvic floor, resulting in urinary tract problems in later years. Enlargement of the prostate, common in old men, may cause obstruction and a back pressure in the ureters and kidneys. If this condition is untreated, it will cause permanent damage to the kidneys. Age changes may predispose to but do not cause incontinence. Most elderly persons (60% in nursing homes and up to 90% living independently) have no incontinence.

≡ The Urine

Normal Constituents

Urine is a yellowish liquid that is about 95% water and 5% dissolved solids and gases. The amount of these dissolved substances is indicated by **specific gravity**. The specific gravity of pure water, used as a standard, is 1.000. Because of the dissolved materials it contains, urine has a specific gravity that normally varies from 1.002 (very dilute urine) to 1.040 (very concentrated urine). When the kidneys are diseased, they lose the ability to concentrate urine, and the specific gravity no longer varies as it does when the kidneys function normally.

Some of the dissolved substances normally found in the urine are the following:

1 **Nitrogenous waste products,** including urea, uric acid, and creatinine (kre-at′i-nin)
2 **Electrolytes,** including sodium chloride (as in common table salt) and different kinds of sulfates and phosphates. Electrolytes are excreted

in appropriate amounts to keep the blood concentration of them constant.

3 **Yellow pigment**, which is derived from certain bile compounds

Abnormal Constituents

Urine examination is one of the most important parts of an evaluation of a person's physical state. Among the most significant abnormal substances found in the urine are the following:

1 **Glucose** is usually an important indicator of a disease, known as **diabetes mellitus**, in which blood sugar is not adequately oxidized ("burned") in the body cells. The excess glucose, which cannot be reabsorbed, is excreted in the urine. The presence of glucose in the urine is known as **glycosuria** (gli″ko-su′re-ah).

2 **Albumin.** The presence of this protein, which is normally retained in the blood, may indicate a kidney disorder such as glomerulonephritis. Albumin in the urine is known as **albuminuria** (al″bu-mi-nu′re-ah).

3 **Blood** in the urine is usually an important indicator of urinary system disease, including nephritis. Blood in the urine is known as **hematuria** (hem″ah-tu-re′ah).

4 **Ketones** (kee′tones) are produced when fats are incompletely oxidized; ketones in the urine are seen in diabetes mellitus and starvation.

5 **White blood cells** (pus) are evidence of infection; they can be seen by microscopic examination of a centrifuged specimen. Pus in the urine is known as **pyuria** (pi-u′re-ah).

6 **Casts** are molds formed in the miscroscopic kidney tubules; they usually indicate disease of the nephrons.

≡ Body Fluids

The average adult is approximately 60% water. (An obese person has a lower percentage of water than a lean person because of a surfeit of adipose tissue, which has a very low water content.) The importance of water itself to living cells was described in Chapter 3. Dissolved or suspended in body water are various electrolytes, the building blocks of foods, gases, waste, and special substances such as enzymes and hormones. The composition of body fluids is very important for homeostasis. Whenever the volume or chemical makeup of these fluids deviates even slightly from normal, disease results. The ways in which the constancy of body fluids is maintained include the following:

1 The thirst mechanism, which maintains the volume of water at a constant level

2 Kidney activity, which regulates the volume and composition of body fluids

3 Hormones, which serve to regulate fluid volume and electrolytes

4 Regulators of pH, including buffers, respiration, and kidney function

Fluid Compartments

Although body fluids have much in common no matter where they are located, there are some important differences between fluid inside and fluid outside of cells. Accordingly, fluids are grouped into two main compartments:

1 **Intracellular fluid** is contained within the cells. About two thirds to three fourths of all body fluids are in this category.

2 **Extracellular fluid** includes all body fluids outside of cells. In this group are included the following:

a Blood plasma, which constitutes about 4% of an individual's body weight

b Interstitial (in″ter-stish′al), or more simply, tissue, fluid. This fluid is located in the spaces between the cells of tissues all over the body. It is estimated that tissue fluid constitutes about 15% of body weight.

c Lymph

Fluids are not locked into one compartment. There is a constant interchange between compartments as fluids are transferred across semipermeable cell membranes (Fig. 20-8).

Electrolytes and Their Functions

Most of the substances dissolved in body water are electrolytes. You may recall from Chapter 2 that electrolytes are compounds that separate in solution into positively and negatively charged ions. A few of the most important ions are reviewed below. The first three are positive ions (cations), and the last two are negative ions (anions).

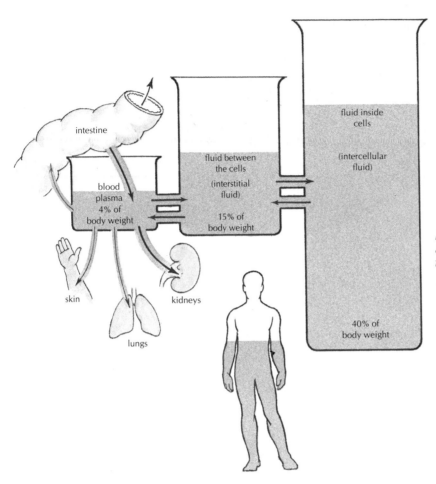

Figure 20-8. *Diagram showing absorption, circulation, and excretion of body fluids.*

1 **Sodium** is chiefly responsible for maintaining osmotic balance and body fluid volume. It is the main positive ion in extracellular fluids. Sodium is required for nerve impulse conduction and is important in maintaining acid–base balance.

2 **Potassium** is also important in the transmission of nerve impulses and is a major positive ion in intracellular fluids. Potassium is involved in cellular enzyme activities, and it helps regulate the chemical reactions by which carbohydrate is converted to energy and amino acids are converted to protein.

3 **Calcium** is required for bone formation, muscle contraction, nerve impulse transmission, and blood clotting.

4 **Phosphate** is essential in the metabolism of carbohydrates, bone formation, and acid–base balance. Phosphates are found in the cell membrane and in the nucleic acids (DNA and RNA).

5 **Chloride** is essential for formation of the hydrochloric acid of the gastric juice.

Electrolytes must be kept in the proper concentration in both intracellular and extracellular fluids. Although some electrolytes are lost in the feces and through the skin as sweat, the job of balancing electrolytes is left mainly to the kidneys, as previously described. Several hormones are also involved in this process. Aldosterone produced by the adrenal cortex promotes the reabsorption of sodium (and water) as well as the elimination of potassium. In **Addison's disease**, in which the adrenal cortex does not produce enough aldosterone, there is a loss of sodium and water and an excess of potassium. Calcium and phosphate levels are regulated by hormones from the parathyroid and thyroid glands (see Chap. 11). Parathyroid hormone increases blood calcium levels by causing the bones to release calcium, causing the kidneys to reabsorb calcium, and causing the intestine to absorb a greater than usual amount of calcium. The thyroid hormone calcitonin has the opposite effects and lowers blood calcium.

Intake and Output of Water

In a person whose health is normal, the quantity of water taken in (intake) is approximately equal to the quantity lost (output). Water is constantly being lost from the body by the following routes:

1 The **skin**. Although sebum and keratin help prevent dehydration, water is constantly evaporating from the surface of the skin. Larger amounts of water are lost from the skin in the form of sweat when it is necessary to cool the body.

2 The **lungs** expel water along with carbon dioxide.

3 The **intestinal tract** eliminates water along with the feces.

4 The **kidneys** excrete the largest quantity of water lost each day. About 1 to 1.5 liters of water are eliminated daily in the urine.

The quantity of water consumed in a day varies considerably. The average adult in a comfortable environment takes in about 2500 ml of water daily. About half of this quantity comes from drinking water and other beverages, and about half comes from foods—fruits, vegetables, soups. In many disorders it is important for the health care team to know whether a patient's intake and output are approximately equal; in such a case a 24-hour intake–output record is kept. The intake record includes *all* the liquid the patient has consumed, in the form of water, beverages, and food, as well as the quantity and kinds of foods that have been eaten in each 24-hour period. The output record includes the quantity of urine excreted in the same 24-hour period, as well as an estimation of fluid losses due to fever, vomiting, diarrhea, bleeding, wound discharge, or other causes.

Sense of Thirst

A major factor in the control of total fluid volume is the sense of thirst, which is located in the hypothalamus. A decrease in fluid volume or an increase in the concentration of body fluids stimulates the thirst center and thus causes an individual to drink water or other fluids containing large amounts of water. Dryness of the mouth also causes a sensation of thirst. When excessive thirst is due to excessive urine loss, as in diabetes, the condition is called **polydipsia** (pol-e-dip′se-ah).

The Acid–Base Balance

The pH of body fluids must be held within a narrow range at approximately 7.4; otherwise damage, even death, will result. Several systems act together to maintain acid–base balance. These are

1 Buffer systems
2 Kidney function
3 Respiration

Buffers, as noted in Chapter 2, are substances that help maintain a constant pH by accepting or releasing hydrogen ions (H^+). The main buffer systems in the body are bicarbonate buffers, phosphate buffers, and proteins, such as hemoglobin and plasma proteins.

The kidneys serve to regulate pH by reabsorbing or eliminating hydrogen ions as needed. Much of the hydrogen that is eliminated by the kidneys is transported into the nephron by tubular secretion.

The role of respiration in controlling pH was described in Chapter 17. Recall that the release of carbon dioxide from the lungs acts to increase the pH of the blood by reducing the amount of carbonic acid formed. In contrast, a reduction in the release of carbon dioxide will act to decrease the pH of the blood.

If shifts in pH cannot be controlled, the following conditions result:

A drop in the pH of body fluids produces a condition called **acidosis** (as″i-do′sis). Acidosis may result, for example, from respiratory obstruction, lung disease, kidney failure, or prolonged diarrhea, the latter of which drains the alkaline contents of the intestine. It may also result from inadequate carbohydrate metabolism, as occurs in diabetes mellitus, ingestion of a low-carbohydrate diet, or starvation. In these cases the body metabolizes too much fat and protein from food or body materials, leading to the production of excess acid.

Alkalosis (al″kah-lo′sis) results from an increase in pH. Its possible causes include hyperventilation (the release of too much carbon dioxide), ingestion of antacids, and prolonged vomiting with loss of stomach acids.

Disorders Involving Body Fluids

1 **Edema** is the accumulation of excessive fluid in the intercellular spaces. In some kinds of edema salt is retained, and "where salt is, water follows." Edema of the hands and feet causes these organs to swell and to have a boggy appearance. Among the underlying causes of edema are kidney failure, congestive heart failure, and too much dietary salt. Protein loss and ingestion of too little dietary protein over an extended period of time are also important causes of edema. The decrease in protein lowers the osmotic pressure of the blood, causing fluid to accumulate in the tissues. Some women experience premenstrual edema as a result of hormonal changes.

2 **Water intoxication** is a drastic dilution of body fluids in both the intracellular and the extracellular compartments. The resulting extreme imbalance can cause convulsions leading to death. Some underlying causes are the administration of very high quantities of intravenous fluids and secretion of excess ADH.

3 **Dehydration** (de″hi-dra′shun), a severe deficit of body fluids, will result in death if it is prolonged. The causes include vomiting, diarrhea, drainage from burns or wounds, excessive perspiration, and too little fluid intake. In such cases it may be necessary to administer intravenous fluids to correct fluid and electrolyte imbalances.

4 **Effusion** (e-fu′zhun) is the collection of fluid in a part or a space. An example is pleural effusion, fluid within the pleural sacs; in this condition fluid compresses the lung so that normal breathing is not possible. Tuberculosis, cancer, and some infections may give rise to effusion.

5 **Ascites** (ah-si′tez) is effusion with accumulation of fluid within the abdominal cavity. It may occur in disorders of the liver, kidneys, and heart, as well as in cancers and infection.

Summary

I **Urinary system**
  A Excretion—removal and elimination of waste materials from blood
  B Elimination of waste
    1 Digestive system—eliminates undigested food, water, salts, bile
    2 Respiratory system—eliminates carbon dioxide, water, cellular waste, toxins
    3 Skin—eliminates water, salts, nitrogen waste

II **Kidneys**—located in upper abdomen, against the back
  A Structure
    1 Cortex—outer portion
    2 Medulla—inner portion
    3 Pelvis
      a Upper end of ureter
      b Calyces—cuplike extensions that receive urine
    4 Nephron—functional unit of kidney
    5 Blood supply
      a Renal artery
        (1) Afferent arteriole—enters Bowman's capsule
        (2) Efferent arteriole—leaves Bowman's capsule
        (3) Glomerulus—coil of capillaries in Bowman's capsule
        (4) Peritubular capillaries—surround nephron
      b Renal vein
  B Physiology
    1 Filtration—pressure in glomerulus forces water and soluble substances out of blood and into Bowman's capsule
      a Glomerular filtrate—material that leaves blood and enters the nephron
    2 Reabsorption—most of filtrate leaves nephron by diffusion and active transport and returns to blood through peritubular capillaries
    3 Tubular secretion—materials moved from blood into nephron for excretion
    4 Counter-current mechanism—method for concentrating urine based on movement of ions out of nephron and influenced by ADH from hypothalamus (via pituitary)
  C Functions
    1 Excretion of waste, excess salts, toxins
    2 Water balance
    3 Regulation of pH
    4 Production of hormones
      a Renin
      b Erythropoietin

III **Ureters**—carry urine from the kidneys to the bladder

IV **Urinary bladder**—stores urine until it is eliminated

  A Micturition—urination

    1 Reflex control—impulses from central nervous system in response to stretching of bladder wall

    2 Voluntary control—external sphincter around urethra

V **Urethra**—carries urine out of body

  A Female urethra—4.0 cm long; opens in front of vagina

  B Male urethra—20 cm long; carries both urine and semen

VI **Disorders of urinary system**

  A Kidney disorders

    1 Acute glomerulonephritis—damages glomeruli

    2 Pyelonephritis—inflammation of kidney and renal pelvis

    3 Chronic renal failure

      a Signs—dehydration, edema, hypertension, anemia, uremia

    4 Calculi—kidney stones

  B Cystitis—inflammation of bladder; most common in females

  C Urethritis—inflammation of urethra

VII **Urine**

  A Normal constituents—water, nitrogenous waste, electrolytes, pigments

  B Abnormal constituents—glucose, albumin, blood, ketones, white blood cells, casts

VIII **Body fluids**

  A Regulating mechanisms

    1 Thirst mechanism—regulated by thirst center in hypothalamus

    2 Kidney function

    3 Hormones

    4 pH regulators—buffers, respiration, kidney function

  B Fluid compartments

    1 Intracellular water—⅔–¾ of body fluid

    2 Extracellular fluid

      a Blood plasma

      b Interstitial (tissue) fluid

      c Lymph

  C Electrolytes—regulated mainly by kidneys

    1 Kinds—sodium, potassium, calcium, phosphates, chloride

    2 Hormonal control

      a Aldosterone—reabsorption of sodium, excretion of potassium

      b Parathyroid hormone—increase in blood calcium level

      c Calcitonin—decrease in blood calcium level

  D Water balance

    1 Output—through skin, lungs, intestinal tract, kidneys

    2 Intake—through food and beverages

  E Acid–base balance—normal pH is 7.4

    1 Mechanisms to regulate pH

      a Buffers—maintain constant pH

      b Kidney—regulates amount of hydrogen ion excreted

      c Respiration—release of carbon dioxide increases pH (less acid); retention of carbon dioxide decreases pH (more acid)

    2 Abnormal pH

      a Acidosis—decrease in pH due to respiratory disorder, kidney failure, diarrhea, or diabetes mellitus

      b Alkalosis—increase in pH due to hyperventilation, prolonged vomiting, or ingestion of antacids

  F Disorders of body fluids

    1 Edema—accumulation of fluid in tissues

    2 Water intoxication—dilution of body fluids

    3 Dehydration—deficiency of fluid

    4 Effusion—collection of fluid

    5 Ascites—accumulation of fluid in abdominal cavity

Questions for Study and Review

1 Name the body systems that have excretory functions.

2 Where are the kidneys located?

3 Describe the external appearance of the kidneys and tell what tissues form most of the kidney structure.

4 Describe the structure of a nephron.

5 Name the blood vessels associated with the nephron.

6 What happens to the glomerular filtrate as it passes through the nephron?

7 What results from inadequate secretion of ADH? What disease is associated with this condition?

8 What is the function of the juxtaglomerular apparatus?

9 What structures empty into the kidney pelvis and what drains the pelvis?

10 What is micturition? How is it controlled?

11 Describe the female urethra and tell how it differs from the male urethra in structure and function.

12 What are some of the infections that involve the kidney and what parts are most often affected?

13 What are calculi and what are some of their causes?

14 What is meant by the word *dialysis* and how is this principle used for persons with kidney failure? What kinds of membranes are used for peritoneal dialysis? for hemodialysis?

15 What types of donors are best for kidney transplants?

16 What is inflammation of the bladder called? Why is it more common in women than in men?

17 What are some of the effects of aging on the urinary system?

18 What is urea? Where and how is it formed?

19 Tell the possible significance of six abnormal constituents of the urine.

20 List four ways in which body fluids are regulated.

21 Name five common ions in the body. How is each regulated?

22 In a healthy person, what is the ratio of fluid intake to output?

23 Name the three main buffer systems in the body.

24 How does the respiratory system help regulate *p*H?

25 Describe four or more disorders involving body fluids.

26 Compare the terms in each of the following pairs:

   a *afferent arteriole* and *efferent arteriole*
   b *intracellular fluid* and *extracellular fluid*
   c *acidosis* and *alkalosis*

21

Reproduction

Behavioral Objectives

After careful study of this chapter, you should be able to:

Name the male and female gonads and describe the function of each

State the purpose of meiosis

List the accessory organs of the male and female reproductive tracts and cite the function of each

Describe the composition and function of semen

Draw and label a spermatozoon

List in the correct order the hormones produced during the menstrual cycle and cite the source of each

Describe the functions of the main male and female sex hormones

Explain how negative feedback regulates reproductive function in both males and females

Briefly describe the major disorders of the male and female reproductive tracts

Describe fertilization and the early development of the fertilized egg

Describe the structure and function of the placenta

Briefly describe the four stages of labor

Cite the advantages of breastfeeding

Describe the changes that occur during and after menopause

Define contraception and cite the main methods of contraception currently in use

Selected Key Terms

The following terms are defined in the glossary:

abortion
contraception
corpus luteum
embryo
endometrium
estrogen
fertilization
fetus
follicle
menopause
ovary
ovulation
ovum (pl., ova)
placenta
progesterone
semen
spermatozoon (pl., spermatozoa)
testis (pl., testes)
testosterone
uterus
zygote

This chapter deals with what is certainly one of the most interesting and mysterious attributes of living matter: the ability to reproduce. The lowest forms of life, one-celled organisms, usually need no partner to reproduce; they simply divide by themselves. This form of reproduction is known as **asexual** (non-sexual) reproduction.

In most animals, however, reproduction is **sexual**, meaning that there are two kinds of individuals, males and females, each of which has specialized cells designed specifically for the perpetuation of the species. These specialized sex cells are known as **germ cells**, or **gametes** (gam′etes). In the male they are called **spermatozoa** (sper″mah-to-zo-′ah), and in the female they are called **ova** (o′vah). Germ cells are characterized by having half as many chromosomes as are found in any other cell in the body. During their formation they go through a special process of cell division, called **meiosis** (mi-o′sis), that reduces the chromosome number from 46 to 23.

Although the reproductive apparatuses of males and females are different, the organs of both sexes may be divided into two groups: primary and accessory.

1 The primary organs are the **gonads** (go′nads), or sex glands; they produce the germ cells and manufacture hormones. The male gonads are the **testes** (tes′teez), and the female gonads are the **ovaries** (o′vah-reez).

2 The **accessory organs** include a series of ducts that provide for the transport of germ cells, as well as various exocrine glands.

☰ The Male Reproductive System

The Testes

The male gonads (testes) are normally located outside the body proper, suspended between the thighs in a sac called the **scrotum** (skro′tum). The testes are egg-shaped organs measuring about 3.7 cm to 5 cm (1.5–2 inches) in length and approximately 2.5 cm (1 inch) in each of the other two dimensions. During embryonic life the testes develop from tissue near the kidney. A month or two before birth, the testes normally descend (move downward) through the **inguinal** (ing′gwi-nal) **canal** in the abdominal wall into the

scrotum. Each testis must descend completely if it is to function normally; in order to produce spermatozoa, the testes must be kept at the temperature of the scrotum, which is lower than that of the abdominal cavity.

The bulk of the specialized tissue of the testes consists of tiny coiled **seminiferous** (se″mi-nif′er-us) **tubules**. Cells in the walls of these tubules produce spermatozoa. Between the tubules are the specialized **interstitial** (in″ter-stish′al) **cells** that secrete the male sex hormone testosterone.

After being secreted by the testes, **testosterone** (tes-tos′te-rone) is absorbed directly into the bloodstream. This hormone has two functions. The first is maintenance of the reproductive structures, including development of the spermatozoa. A second involves the development of **secondary sex characteristics**, traits that characterize males and females but are not directly concerned with reproduction. In male humans they include a deeper voice, broader shoulders, narrower hips, a greater percentage of muscle tissue, and more body hair than are found in female humans.

The Duct System

The tubes that carry the spermatozoa begin with the tubules inside the testis itself. From these tubes the spermatozoa are collected by a greatly coiled tube 6 meters (20 feet) long, called the **epididymis** (ep″i-did′i-mis), which is located inside the scrotal sac (Fig. 21-1). While they are temporarily stored in the epididymis, the spermatozoa mature and become motile, that is, able to move, or "swim," by themselves. The epididymis finally extends upward as the **ductus deferens** (def′er-enz), also called the **vas deferens**. The ductus deferens continues through the inguinal canal in the abdominal wall and then curves behind the urinary bladder. There each ductus deferens joins with the duct of the **seminal vesicle** (ves′e-kal) on the same side to form the **ejaculatory** (e-jak′u-lah-to-re) **duct**. The two ejaculatory ducts enter the body of the prostate gland where they empty into the urethra.

As the ductus deferens travels upward through the abdominal wall, it is contained in a structure called the **spermatic cord**. This cord is composed of a combination of the ductus deferens, blood vessels, lymphatics, and nerves all wrapped in connective tissue.

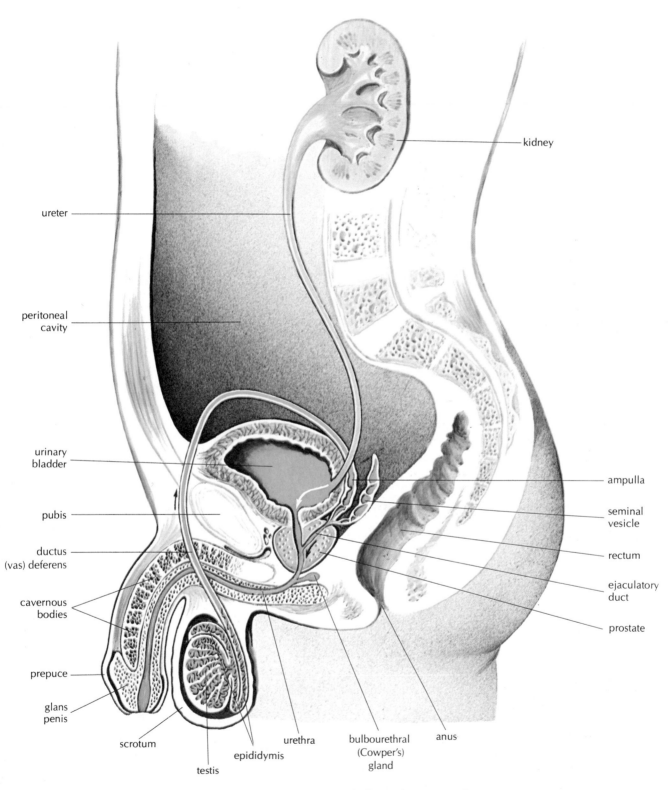

Figure 21-1. *Male genitourinary system. The black arrows indicate the course of spermatozoa through the duct system; the single white arrow indicates the course of urine.*

Formation of Semen

Semen (see'men) is a mixture of spermatozoa and various secretions that is expelled from the body. The secretions serve to nourish and transport the spermatozoa, neutralize the acidity of the vaginal tract, and lubricate the reproductive tract during sexual intercourse. The glands discussed below contribute secretions to the semen.

The Seminal Vesicles

The seminal vesicles are tortuous muscular tubes with small outpouchings. They are about 7.5 cm (3 inches) long and are attached to the connective tissue at the back of the urinary bladder. The glandular lining produces a thick, yellow, alkaline secretion containing large quantities of simple sugar and other substances that provide nourishment for the spermatozoa. The seminal fluid forms a large part of the volume of the semen.

The Prostate Gland

The prostate gland lies immediately below the urinary bladder, where it surrounds the first part of the urethra. Ducts from the prostate carry its secretions into the urethra. The thin, alkaline prostatic secretion helps neutralize the acidity of the vaginal tract and enhance the motility of the spermatozoa. The prostate gland is also supplied with muscular tissue, which upon signal from the nervous system contracts to aid in the expulsion of the semen from the body.

Mucus-Producing Glands

The largest of the mucus-producing glands in the male reproductive system are **Cowper's**, or **bulbourethral** (bul"bo-u-re'thral), **glands,** a pair of pea-sized organs located in the pelvic floor just below the prostate gland. The ducts of these glands extend about 2.5 cm (1 inch) from each side and empty into the urethra before it extends within the penis. Other very small glands secrete mucus into the urethra as it passes through the penis. The mucus from all of these glands serves mainly as a lubricant.

The Urethra and the Penis

The male urethra, as we saw earlier, serves the dual purpose of conveying urine from the bladder and carrying the reproductive cells and their accompanying secretions to the outside. The ejection of semen into the receiving canal (vagina) of the female is made possible by the **erection,** or stiffening and enlargement, of the penis, through which the longest part of the urethra extends. The penis is made of a spongelike tissue containing many blood spaces that are relatively empty when the organ is flaccid but fill with blood and distend when the penis is erect. The penis and scrotum are referred to as the *external genitalia* of the male.

Reflex centers in the spinal cord order the contraction of the smooth muscle tissue in the prostate gland, followed by the contraction of skeletal muscle in the pelvic floor. This provides the force needed for **ejaculation** (e-jak"u-la'shun), the expulsion of semen through the urethra to the outside.

The Spermatozoa

Spermatozoa are tiny individual cells. They are so small that at least 200 million are contained in the average ejaculation. Spermatozoa are continuously manufactured in the testes. They develop within the seminiferous tubules with the aid of special cells called **Sertoli,** or "nurse," **cells.** These cells help nourish and protect the developing spermatozoa.

The individual sperm cell has an oval head that is largely a nucleus containing chromosomes. Covering the head like a cap is the **acrosome** (ak'ro-some), which contains enzymes that help the spermatozoon penetrate the ovum. The whiplike tail (flagellum) enables the sperm cell to make its way through the various passages until it reaches the ovum of the female. A middle region contains many mitochondria to provide energy for movement (Fig. 21-2). Out of the millions of spermatozoa in an ejaculation, only one, if any, fertilizes the ovum. The remainder of the spermatozoa live only a few hours, up to a maximum of 3 days.

≡ Hormonal Control of Male Reproduction

The activities of the testes are under the control of two hormones produced by the anterior pituitary gland (hypophysis). One of these, **FSH** (follicle-stimulating hormone), stimulates the Sertoli cells and promotes the formation of spermatozoa. Testosterone is also needed in this process. The other hormone is **LH** (luteinizing hormone), called **ICSH** (interstitial cell–stimulating hormone) in males. It stimulates the

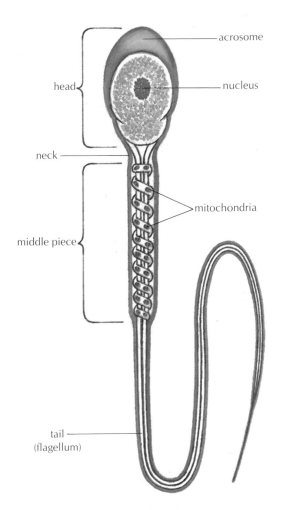

Figure 21-2. *Diagram of a human spermatozoon showing major structural features. (Chaffee EE, Lytle IM: Basic Physiology and Anatomy, 4th ed, p 549. Philadelphia, JB Lippincott, 1980)*

interstitial cells to produce testosterone. These pituitary hormones are named for their activity in female reproduction, although they are chemically the same in both males and females.

You may recall from Chapter 11 that the pituitary gland is regulated by a region of the brain just above it called the *hypothalamus.* Starting at puberty, the hypothalamus begins to secrete hormones that trigger the release of FSH and LH. These hormones are secreted continuously in the male. In a typical homeostatic pattern, the activity of the hypothalamus is in turn regulated by a negative feedback mechanism involving testosterone. As the level of testosterone in the blood increases, the hypothalamus secretes less

releasing hormone; as the level of testosterone decreases, the hypothalamus secretes more releasing hormone (see Fig. 11-2).

The Effects of Aging on Male Reproduction

A gradual decrease in the production of testosterone and spermatozoa begins as early as age 20 and continues throughout life. Secretions from the prostate and seminal vesicles decrease in amount and become less viscous. In a few men (under 10%) spermatozoa remain late in life, even to age 80.

☰ Disorders of the Male Reproductive System

Infertility

Infertility means significantly lower than normal ability to reproduce. If the inability is complete, the condition is termed **sterility.** The proportion of infertile marriages due to defects involving the male has been estimated variously from 40% to 50%. The tubules of the testes are very sensitive to x-rays, infections, toxins, and malnutrition, all of which bring about degenerative changes. Such damage may cause a decrease in the numbers of spermatozoa produced, leading to a condition called **oligospermia** (ol″i-go-sper′me-ah). Adequate numbers of spermatozoa are required to disperse the coating around the ovum in order that one sperm can fertilize it. Absence of or an inadequate number of male sex cells is a significant cause of infertility.

Intentional sterilization of the male may be accomplished by an operation called a **vasectomy** (vah-sek′to-me). In this procedure a portion of the ductus deferens on each side is removed and the cut end closed to keep the spermatozoa from reaching the urethra. These tiny cells are absorbed without injury. The vasectomized male retains the ability to produce hormones and all other seminal secretions, as well as the ability to perform the sex act, but no fertilization can occur.

Cryptorchidism

Cryptorchidism (krip-tor′ki-dizm), which means "hidden testes," is a disorder characterized by failure of the testes to descend into the scrotum. Unless corrected in childhood, this condition results in sterility. Undescended testes also are particularly subject to tumor formation. Most testes that are undescended at birth descend spontaneously by age 1. Surgical correction is the usual remedy in the remaining cases.

Inguinal Hernia

Hernia (her'ne-ah), or rupture, refers to the abnormal protrusion of an organ, or part of an organ, through the wall of the cavity in which it is normally contained. Hernias most often occur where there is a weak area in the abdominal wall, such as over the inguinal canal. In this region of the lower abdomen, the testis pushes its way through the muscles and connective tissues of the abdominal wall, carrying with it the blood vessels and other structures that will form the spermatic cord. In the normal adult this area is fairly well reinforced with connective tissue, and there is no direct connection between the abdominal cavity and the scrotal sac. However, like some other regions in which openings permit the passage of various structures to and from the abdominal cavity, this area constitutes a weak place at which a hernia may occur.

Infections

Infections of various kinds may involve the male reproductive organs, but by far the most common is **gonorrhea**. This disease manifests itself by a discharge from the urethra, which may be accompanied by burning and pain, especially during urination. The infection may travel along the mucous membrane into the prostate gland and into the epididymis; if both sides are affected and enough scar tissue is formed to destroy the tubules, sterility may result.

An unpleasant, persistent infection called **genital herpes** is the second most common venereal disease. Caused by a virus that is usually transmitted by sexual contact, this disorder is characterized by fluid-filled vesicles (blisters) on and around the genital organs.

Another important venereal disease is **syphilis**, which is caused by a spirochete (*Treponema pallidum*). Because syphilis spreads quickly in the blood stream, it is regarded as a systemic disorder. (See Table 1 of Appendix 3.)

Other infectious agents that sometimes invade the reproductive organs include the tubercle bacillus

and various staphylococci. The testes may be involved in mumps, with a resulting **orchitis** (or-ki'tis), or inflammation of the testes.

Tumors

Tumors may develop in the male reproductive organs, most commonly the prostate, and are quite common in elderly men. Such growths may be benign or malignant. Both cause such pressure on the urethra that urination becomes difficult, and back pressure often causes destruction of kidney tissue, as well as permitting stagnation of urine in the bladder with a resulting tendency to infection. The prostate, or parts of it, should be removed early to prevent serious damage to the urinary system.

Cancer of the prostate is a common disorder in men over 50. It is frequently detected as a nodule during rectal examination. Surgical treatment very early in the disease is associated with the best prognosis. Additional therapy involves irradiation of the pelvic lymph nodes. Unfortunately, this cancer frequently spreads to the bones with a fatal outcome.

Phimosis

Phimosis (fi-mo'sis) is a tightness of the foreskin (prepuce) such that it cannot be drawn back. This may be remedied through circumcision, by which part or all of the foreskin is removed. This operation is often done on very young male infants as a routine measure, either for hygienic reasons or because of religious principles.

The Female Reproductive System

The Ovaries

In the female the counterparts of the testes are the two **ovaries**, where the female sex cells, or **ova**, are formed. The ovaries are small, somewhat flattened oval bodies measuring about 4 cm (1.6 inches) in length, 2 cm (0.8 inch) in width, and 1 cm (0.4 inch) in depth. Like the testes, the ovaries descend, but only as far as the pelvic portion of the abdomen. Here, they are held in place by ligaments that attach them to the uterus and the body wall (Fig. 21–3).

The outer layer of each ovary is made of a single layer of epithelium. Beneath this layer the ova are

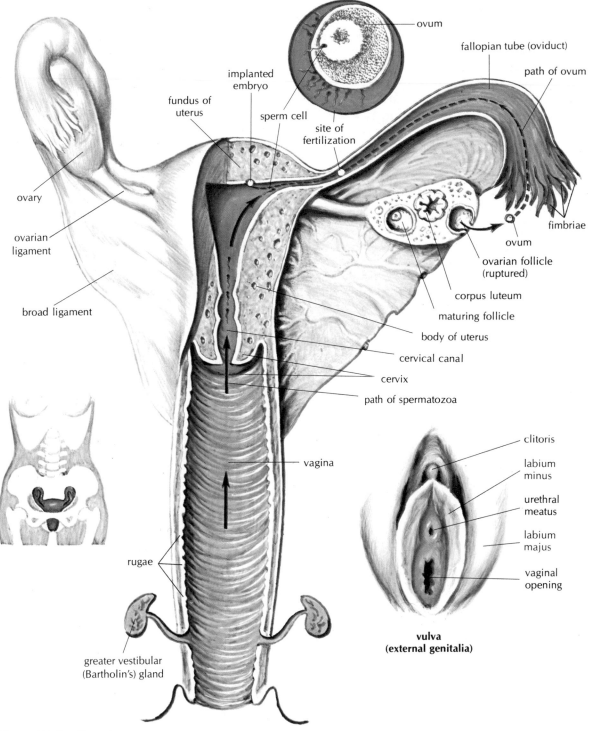

Figure 21-3. *Female reproductive system.*

produced. The ova begin a complicated process of maturation, or "ripening," which takes place in small sacs called **ovarian** (o-va′re-an) **follicles** (fal′e-kls). The cells of the ovarian follicle walls secrete estrogen. When an ovum has ripened, the ovarian follicle ruptures, and the ovum is discharged from the surface of the ovary and makes its way to the nearest **oviduct** (o′vi-dukt). The oviducts are two tubes, one of which is in the vicinity of each ovary. The rupture of a follicle allowing the escape of the egg cell is called **ovulation** (ov″u-la′shun).

The ovaries of a newborn female contain a large number of potential ova. Each month during the reproductive years, several ripen, but usually only one is released. Once this ovum has been expelled, the follicle is transformed into a solid glandular mass called the **corpus luteum** (lu′te-um), which means "yellow body." This structure secretes both estrogen and progesterone. Normally, the corpus luteum shrinks and is replaced by scar tissue. When a pregnancy occurs, this structure remains active. Often as a result of normal ovulation, the corpus luteum will persist and form a small ovarian cyst (fluid-filled sac). This condition usually resolves without treatment.

The Oviducts

The egg-carrying tubes of the female reproductive system are also known as **uterine** (u′ter-in) **tubes**, or **fallopian** (fah-lo′pe-an) **tubes**. They are small, muscular structures, nearly 12.5 cm (5 inches) long, extending from a point near the ovaries to the uterus (womb). There is no direct connection between the ovaries and these tubes. The ova are swept into the oviducts by a current in the peritoneal fluid produced by the small, fringelike extensions called **fimbriae** (fim′bre-e) that are located at the edges of the abdominal openings of the tubes.

Unlike the spermatozoon, the ovum cannot move by itself. Its progress through the oviduct toward the uterus is dependent on the sweeping action of cilia in the lining of the tubes as well as on peristalsis of the tubes. It takes about 5 days for an ovum to reach the uterus from the ovary.

The Uterus

The organ to which the fallopian tubes lead is the **uterus** (u′ter-us), and it is within this structure that the fetus grows until it is ready to be born.

The uterus is a pear-shaped, muscular organ about 7.5 cm (3 inches) long, 5 cm (2 inches) wide, and 2.5 cm (1 inch) deep. The upper portion rests on the upper surface of the urinary bladder; the lower portion is embedded in the pelvic floor between the bladder and the rectum. The upper portion, which is the larger, is called the body, or **corpus**; the lower, smaller part is the **cervix** (ser′viks), or neck. The small, rounded part above the level of the tubal entrances is known as the **fundus** (fun′dus) (see Fig. 21-3). The cavity inside the uterus is shaped somewhat like a capital **T**, but it is capable of changing shape and dilating as the fetus develops. The cervix leads to the **vagina** (vah-ji′nah), the lower part of the birth canal, which opens to the outside of the body.

The lining of the uterus is a specialized epithelium known as **endometrium** (en-do-me′tre-um), and it is this layer that is involved in menstruation.

The Vagina

The vagina is a muscular tube about 7.5 cm (3 inches) long connecting the uterine cavity with the outside. It receives the cervix, which dips into the upper vagina in such a way that a circular recess is formed, giving rise to areas known as **fornices** (for′ne-sez). The deepest of these spaces, behind the cervix, is called the **posterior fornix** (for′niks) (Fig. 21-4). This recess in the posterior vagina is separated from the lowest part of the peritoneal cavity by a rather thin layer of tissue, so that abscesses or tumor cells in the peritoneal cavity can sometimes be detected by vaginal examination.

The lining of the vagina is a wrinkled mucous membrane something like that found in the stomach. The folds (rugae) permit enlargement so that childbirth usually does not tear the lining. In addition to being a part of the birth canal, the vagina is the organ that receives the penis during sexual intercourse. A fold of membrane called the **hymen** may sometimes be found at or near the vaginal (vaj′i-nal) canal opening.

The Greater Vestibular Glands

Just above and to each side of the vaginal opening are the mucus-producing **greater vestibular** (ves-tib′u-lar), or **Bartholin's, glands**. These glands open into an area near the vaginal opening known as the **vestibule**. They may become infected, then painfully swollen,

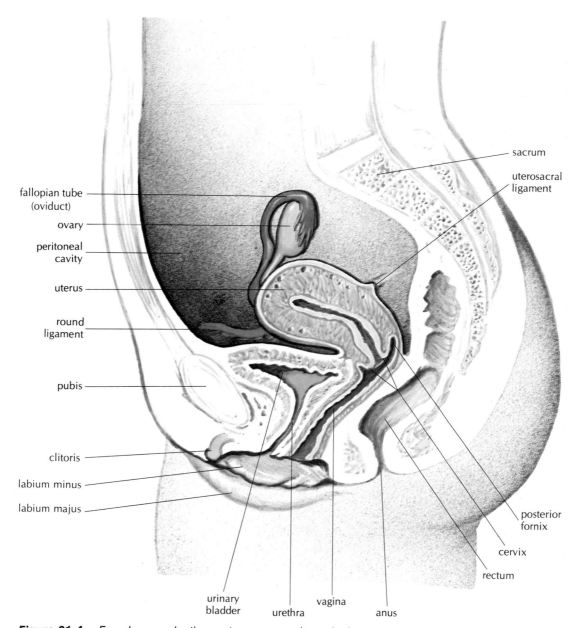

Figure 21-4. *Female reproductive system, as seen in sagittal section.*

and finally, abscessed. A surgical incision to promote drainage may be required.

The Vulva and the Perineum

The external parts of the female reproductive system form the **vulva** (vul′vah), which includes two pairs of lips, or **labia** (la′be-ah); the **clitoris** (kli′to-ris), which is a small organ of great sensitivity; and related struc-

tures. Although the entire pelvic floor in both the male and female is properly called the **perineum** (per″i-ne′um), those who care for pregnant women usually refer to the limited area between the vaginal opening and the anus as the perineum. To prevent the pelvic floor tissues from being torn during childbirth, as often happens, the physician may cut the mother's perineum just before her infant is born and then repair this clean cut immediately after childbirth; such an operation is called an **episiotomy** (e-piz″e-ot′o-me).

≡ The Menstrual Cycle

In the female, as in the male, reproductive function is controlled by hormones from the pituitary gland as regulated by the hypothalamus. Female activity differs, however, in that it is cyclic, that is, shows regular patterns of increases and decreases in hormone levels. These changes are regulated by hormonal feedback.

The length of the menstrual cycle varies between 22 and 45 days in normal women, but 28 days is taken as an average, with the first day of menstrual flow being considered the first day of the cycle (Fig. 21-5).

At the start of each cycle, under the influence of FSH produced by the pituitary, a follicle begins to develop in the ovary. This follicle produces increasing amounts of **estrogen** as the ovum matures. (*Es-*

Figure 21-5. *Summary of events in an average 28-day menstrual cycle.*

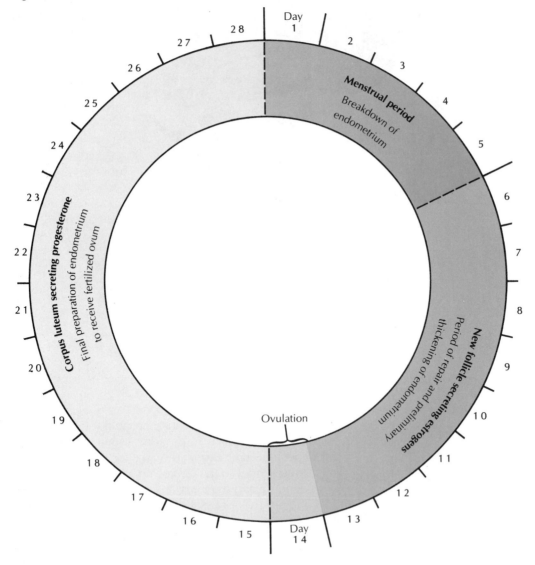

trogen is the term used for a group of related hormones, the most active of which is estradiol.) The estrogen is carried in the bloodstream to the uterus, where it starts preparing the endometrium for a possible pregnancy. This preparation includes thickening of the endometrium and elongation of the glands that produce the uterine secretion. Estrogen in the blood also acts as a feedback messenger to inhibit the release of FSH and stimulate the release of LH from the pituitary (see Fig. 11-2).

About 1 day before ovulation, there is a sharp rise in LH. This hormone causes ovulation and transforms the ruptured follicle into the corpus luteum. The corpus luteum produces some estrogen and large amounts of **progesterone**. Under the influence of these hormones, the endometrium continues to thicken, the glands and blood vessels increasing in size. The rising levels of estrogen and progesterone feed back to inhibit the release of FSH and LH from the pituitary. During this time the ovum makes its journey to the uterus by way of the oviduct. If the ovum is not fertilized while passing through the uterine tube, it dies within 2 to 3 days and then disintegrates.

If fertilization does not occur, the corpus luteum degenerates and the levels of estrogen and progesterone decrease. Without the hormones to support growth, the endometrium degenerates. Small hemorrhages appear in this lining, producing the bleeding known as **menstrual flow**. Bits of endometrium break away and accompany the flow of blood. The average duration of this discharge is 2 to 6 days.

Before the flow ceases, the endometrium begins to repair itself through the growth of new cells. The low levels of estrogen and progesterone allow the release of FSH from the anterior pituitary. This causes a new ovum to begin to ripen within the ovaries, and the cycle begins anew.

The activity of ovarian hormones as negative feedback messengers is the basis of the contraceptive (birth control) pill. These pills contain estrogen and progesterone given in sequence or together. The hormones act to inhibit the release of FSH and LH from the pituitary, resulting in a menstrual period but no ovulation. The pill is highly effective in preventing conception. However, it may have some side-effects. Smoking greatly increases the risk of serious side-effects from the pill, particularly in women over 30. All women taking birth control pills should be examined by a physician every 6 months.

Disorders of the Female Reproductive System

Leukorrhea

A nonbloody vaginal discharge, usually whitish in color, is called **leukorrhea** (loo″ko-re′ah). In many cases it is merely the colorless mucus produced by the cervical glands; these glands produce more mucus during ovulation than at other times during the cycle. Leukorrhea is not a disease, but it can be a sign of irritation or infection involving the cervix or vagina. A common causative organism is a protozoan called *Trichomonas* (trik″o-mo′nas) *vaginalis*. There may be other causes, and a microscopic examination of the discharge should be done to establish the diagnosis. Tight, nonabsorbent clothing makes this condition worse.

Menstrual Disorders

Absence of menstrual flow is known as **amenorrhea** (ah-men″o-re′ah). This condition can be symptomatic of such a disorder as insufficient hormone secretion or congenital abnormality of the reproductive organs. Psychologic factors often play a part in cessation of the menstrual flow. For example, any significant change in a woman's general state of health, or a change in her pattern of living, such as a shift in working hours, can cause her to miss a period. The most common cause of amenorrhea (except, of course, for the menopause) is pregnancy.

Dysmenorrhea (dis″men-o-re′ah) means painful or difficult menstruation, and in young women it may be due to immaturity of the uterus. Dysmenorrhea is frequently associated with cycles in which ovulation has occurred. Often the pain can be relieved by drugs that block prostaglandins, since some prostaglandins are known to cause painful uterine contractions. In many cases women have been completely relieved of menstrual cramps by their first pregnancies. Apparently, enlargement of the cervical openings remedies the condition. Artificial dilation of the cervical openings may alleviate dysmenorrhea for several months. Often such health measures as sufficient rest, a well-balanced diet, and appropriate exercises remedy the disorder. During the attack, the application of heat over the abdomen usually relieves the pain, just as it may ease other types of muscular cramps.

Premenstrual syndrome (PMS), also called **premenstrual tension**, is a condition in which nervousness, irritability, and depression precede the menstrual period. It is thought to be due to fluid retention in various tissues, including the brain. Sometimes a low-salt diet and appropriate medication for 2 weeks before the menses prevent this disorder. This treatment may also avert dysmenorrhea. PMS treatment centers in some areas of the United States are proving helpful for many women.

Abnormal uterine bleeding includes excessive menstrual flow, too-frequent menstruation, and nonmenstrual bleeding. Any of these may cause serious anemias and deserve careful medical attention. Nonmenstrual bleeding may be an indication of a tumor, possibly cancer.

Benign Tumors

Fibroids, which are more correctly called *myomas* (see Chap. 4), are common tumors of the uterus. Studies indicate that about 50% of women who reach the age of 50 have one or more of these growths in the walls of the uterus. Very often these tumors are small, and usually they remain benign and produce no symptoms. They develop between puberty and the menopause and ordinarily stop growing after a woman has reached the age of 50. In some cases these growths interfere with pregnancy, and in a patient under 40, the surgeon may simply remove the tumor and leave the uterus fairly intact. Normal pregnancies have occurred after such surgery.

Fibroids may become so large that pressure on adjacent structures causes grave disorders. In some cases invasion of blood vessels near the uterine cavity causes serious hemorrhages. For these and other reasons, it may be necessary to remove the entire uterus or a large part of it. Surgical removal of the uterus is called a **hysterectomy** (his″te-rek′to-me).

Malignant Tumors

Cancer of the breast is the most commonly occurring malignant disease in women. The tumor is usually a painless, movable mass that is often noticed by the woman and all too frequently ignored. However, in recent years there has been increasing emphasis on the importance of regular self-examination of the breasts. Any lump, no matter how small, should be reported to a physician immediately. For years the

surgical treatment of this disease has been a **radical mastectomy** (mas-tek′to-me), a procedure that involves total removal of the affected breast together with removal of the axillary lymph nodes and muscles on the chest wall. Current research indicates that much more conservative treatment can be curative. In certain cases a lump removal (lumpectomy), along with irradiation and other appropriate treatment, is giving excellent results.

The most common cancer of the female reproductive organs is cancer of the endometrium (the lining of the uterus). This type of cancer usually affects women during or after the menopause. It is seen most frequently in women who have had few pregnancies, abnormal bleeding, or cycles in which ovulation did not occur. Symptoms include an abnormal discharge or irregular bleeding. The usual methods of treatment include surgery and irradiation. Early, aggressive treatment of this, as of all cancers, can save the patient's life.

Ovarian cancer is a leading cause of cancer deaths in women. Breast cancer metastasizes to the ovaries more than to any other site. In addition to secondary growths, primary ovarian tumors are quite common. Although most ovarian cysts are not malignant, they should always be investigated for possible malignant change. Ovarian malignancies tend to progress rapidly, so that careful staging (see Chap. 4) is important if a patient's life is to be saved. Ovarian cancer is the second most common reproductive system cancer in the female, usually occurring in women between the ages of 40 and 65. Early surgery, irradiation, and especially chemotherapy have proved to be effective in many cases.

Cancer of the cervix, the third most common cancer of the female reproductive system, is most frequent in women from 30 to 50 years of age. Appropriate screening allows the discovery and treatment of many early cases. Although no specific cause has been identified, statistics indicate that the risk of development of cervical cancer is strongly increased by various factors, such as first sexual intercourse at an early age, many sexual partners, and genital herpes infection. The decline in the death rate from this type of cancer is directly related to use of the **Papanicolaou** (pap″ah-nik″o-la′oo) **test**, also known as the Pap test or Pap smear. The Pap smear is a microscopic examination of cells obtained from scrapings of the cervix and swabs of the cervical canal. All women should be encouraged to have this test every year.

Even girls under 18 should be tested if they are sexually active.

Figures on the incidences of the various types of cancer should not be confused with the death rates for each type. Owing to education of the public and increasingly better methods of diagnosis and treatment, some forms of cancer have a higher cure rate than others. For example, cancer of the breast appears much more often in women than does cancer of the lung, but more women now die each year from lung cancer than from breast cancer.

Infections

The common venereal diseases that involve the male reproductive system also attack the female genital organs (Fig. 21-6); the most common are gonorrhea and genital herpes. Syphilis also occurs in women, and the fetus of an untreated syphilitic mother may be stillborn; an infant born alive may have highly infectious lesions of the palms or the soles as well as other manifestations of the disease.

Salpingitis (sal-pin-ji′tis) means "inflammation of a tube." However, the term is used most often to refer to disease of the uterine tubes. Most cases of infection of the uterine tubes are caused by gonorrhea, but other bacteria can also bring it about. Salpingitis may cause sterility by obstructing the tubes, thus preventing the passage of ova.

Pelvic inflammatory disease (PID) is due to extension of gonorrheal or other infections from the reproductive organs into the pelvic cavity, and it often involves the peritoneum. (See the *red arrow* pathway in Fig. 21-6.)

Toxic shock syndrome (TSS), a serious bacterial infection, is usually due to certain staphylococci. It has been associated with the use of tampons, especially the superabsorbent type. Many women have a tendency to leave superabsorbent tampons in place for long periods of time, and they provide an excellent growth medium for certain types of bacteria. Women are advised to change tampons every 6 hours and to use sanitary napkins during the night. Toxic shock syndrome may also occur in men, but the causes are unknown.

Infertility

Infertility is much more difficult to diagnose and evaluate in the female than in the male. Whereas a microscopic examination of properly collected seminal fluid may be all that is required to determine the presence of abnormal or too-few spermatozoa in the male, no such simple study can be made in the female. Infertility in women, as in men, may be relative or absolute. Causes of female infertility include infections, endocrine disorders, psychogenic factors, and abnormalities in the structure and function of the reproductive organs themselves. In all cases of apparent infertility, the male partner should be investigated first, since the procedures for determining lack of fertility in the male are much simpler and less costly than those in the female, as well as being essential for the evaluation.

A woman may be sterilized surgically by a procedure called **tubal ligation**, in which both uterine tubes are cut and tied, preventing fertilization of the ovum.

≡ Pregnancy

First Stages of Pregnancy

When semen is deposited in the vagina, the many spermatozoa immediately wriggle about in all directions, some traveling into the uterus and oviducts. Some dissolve the coating surrounding the ovum, so that when a later spermatozoon encounters the ovum, it can penetrate the cell membrane of the ovum. The result of the union of these two sex cells is a single cell with the full human chromosome number of 46. This new cell, called a **zygote** (zi′gote), can divide and grow into a new individual. The zygote divides rapidly into two cells and then four cells, and soon a ball of cells is formed. During this time, the ball of cells is traveling toward the uterine cavity, pushed along by the cilia and by the peristalsis of the tube.

Development and Functions of the Placenta

After reaching the uterus, the little ball of cells burrows into the greatly thickened uterine lining, where it is soon completely covered and implanted. Following **implantation**, a group of cells within the ball becomes an **embryo** (em′bre-o). The outer cells form projections, called **villi**, that invade the uterine wall and maternal blood channels (venous sinuses). This eventually leads to the formation of the **placenta** (plah-sen′tah), a flat, circular organ that consists of a

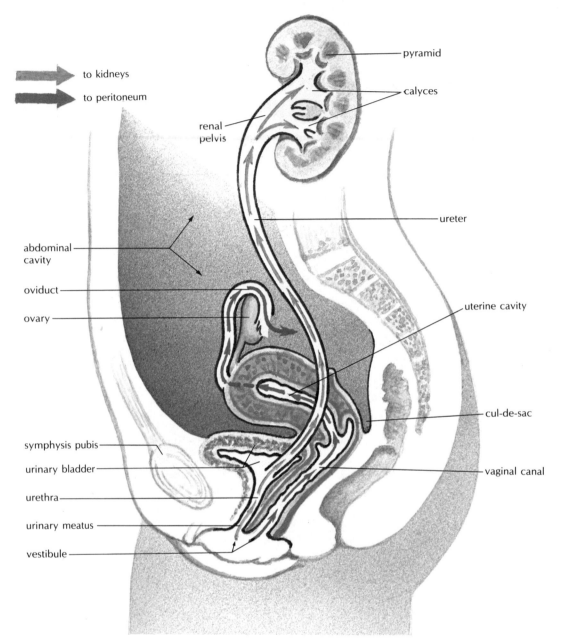

to kidneys

to peritoneum

pyramid

calyces

renal pelvis

ureter

abdominal cavity

oviduct

ovary

uterine cavity

cul-de-sac

symphysis pubis

urinary bladder

vaginal canal

urethra

urinary meatus

vestibule

Figure 21-6. *Pathway of infection from outside to the peritoneum and into the urinary system.*

spongy network of blood-filled lakes and capillary-containing villi. The embryo, later called the *fetus,* is connected to the developing placenta by a stalk of tissue that eventually becomes the **umbilical** (um-bil′i-kal) **cord**. The cord contains two arteries that carry blood from the fetus to the placenta and one vein that carries blood from the placenta to the fetus

(Fig. 21-7). The placenta serves as the organ of nutrition, respiration, and excretion for the embryo through exchanges that occur between the blood of the embryo and the blood of the mother across the capillaries of the villi.

Another function of the placenta is endocrine in nature. Beginning soon after implantation, some of

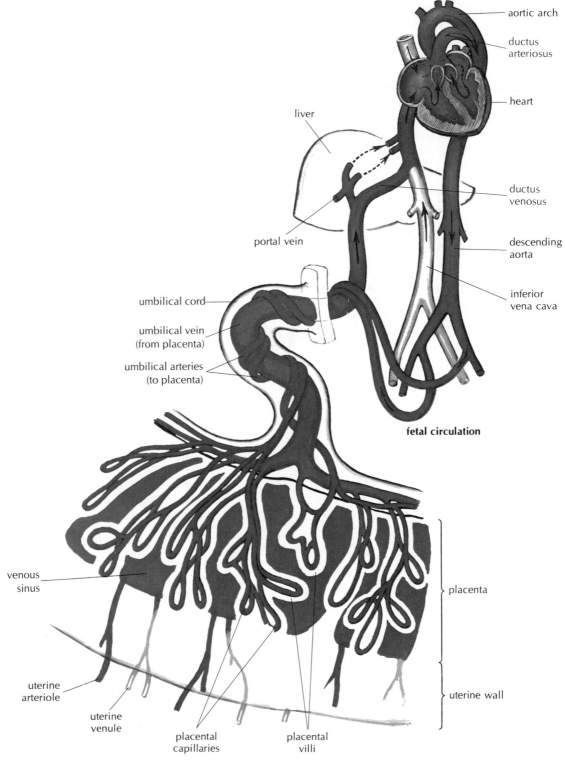

Figure 21-7. *Fetal circulation and placenta.*

the embryonic cells produce a hormone called **chorionic gonadotropin** (ko″re-on′ik gon″ah-do-tro′pin). This hormone stimulates the corpus luteum of the ovary, prolonging its life span (to 11 or 12 weeks) and causing it to secrete increasing amounts of progesterone and estrogen. Progesterone is essential for the maintenance of pregnancy. It promotes endometrial secretion to nourish the embryo, and it decreases the ability of the uterine muscle to contract, thus preventing the embryo from being expelled from the body.

During pregnancy progesterone also helps prepare the breasts for the secretion of milk. Estrogen promotes enlargement of the uterus and breasts. By the 11th or 12th week of pregnancy, the corpus luteum is no longer needed; by this time, the placenta itself can secrete adequate amounts of progesterone and estrogen.

As the pregnancy progresses, the hormones secreted by the placenta prepare the breasts for lactation, cause changes that prepare the body for delivery

Figure 21-8. *Development of an embryo into a fetus.*

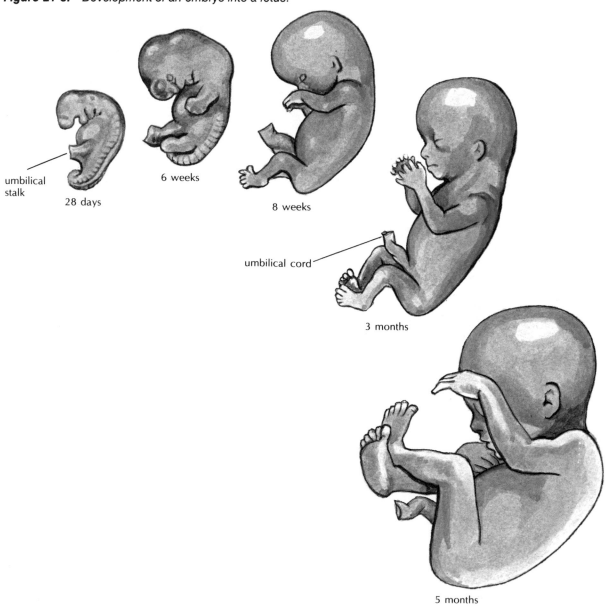

umbilical stalk

28 days

6 weeks

8 weeks

umbilical cord

3 months

5 months

such as relaxation of ligaments, and promote the storage of nutrients required for lactation.

Development of the Embryo

Embryology (em″bre-ol′o-je) is the study of the development of the embryo. Among the first organs to develop in the embryo are the heart and the brain. By the end of the first month, the embryo is about 0.62 cm (0.25 inches) long, with four small swellings at the sides called **limb buds**, which will develop into the four extremities. At this time the heart produces a prominent bulge at the front of the embryo. By the end of the second month, the embryo takes on an appearance that is recognizably human. The developing individual is called an *embryo* until the third month (Fig. 21-8).

The Fetus

From the beginning of the third month until birth, the developing individual is referred to as a **fetus** (fe′tus). During this period, the organ systems continue to grow and mature. By the end of the fourth month, the fetus is almost 15 cm (6 inches) long, and its external genitalia are sufficiently developed to reveal its sex. By the seventh month, the fetus is usually about 35 cm (14 inches) long and weighs about 1.1 kg (2.4 lbs). At the end of pregnancy, the normal length of the fetus is 45 cm to 56 cm (18–22.5 inches), and the weight varies from 2.7 kg to 4.5 kg (6–10 lb).

The **amniotic** (am-ne-ot′ik) **sac**, which is filled with a clear liquid known as **amniotic fluid**, surrounds the fetus and serves as a protective cushion for it. Popularly called the *bag of waters,* the amniotic sac ruptures at birth. During development the skin of the fetus is protected by a layer of cheeselike material called **vernix** (ver′niks) **caseosa** (ka′se-o-sa). See Figure 21-9.

The Mother

The total period of pregnancy, from fertilization of the ovum to birth, is about 280 days. During this period, the mother must supply all the food and oxygen for the fetus and eliminate its waste materials. To support the additional demands of the growing fetus, the mother's metabolism changes markedly, with increased demands being made on several organ systems:

1 The heart pumps more blood to supply the needs of the uterus and its contents.
2 The lungs provide more oxygen to supply the fetus by increasing the rate and depth of respiration.
3 The kidneys excrete nitrogenous wastes from the fetus as well as from the mother's body.
4 Nutritional needs are increased to provide for the growth of maternal organs (uterus and breasts) and growth of the fetus, as well as for preparation for labor and the secretion of milk.

Nausea and vomiting are common discomforts in early pregnancy. The specific cause is not known, but these symptoms may be due to the great changes in hormone levels that occur at this point. The nausea and vomiting usually last for only a few weeks. Frequency of urination and constipation are often present during the early stages of pregnancy and then usually disappear. They may reappear late in pregnancy as the head of the fetus drops from the abdominal region down into the pelvis, pressing on the rectum and the urinary bladder.

Childbirth

The mechanisms that trigger the beginning of uterine contractions are still unknown. However, it is recognized that the uterine muscle becomes increasingly sensitive to oxytocin (from the pituitary gland) late in pregnancy. Once labor is started, stimuli from the cervix and vagina produce reflex secretion of this hormone, which in turn increases the uterine contractions.

The process by which the fetus is expelled from the uterus is known as **labor** and **delivery**; it also may be called **parturition** (par″tu-rish′un). It is divided into four stages:

1 The **first stage** begins with the onset of regular contractions of the uterus. With each contraction, the cervix becomes thinner and the opening larger. Rupture of the amniotic sac may occur at any time, with a gush of fluid from the vagina.
2 The **second stage** begins when the cervix is completely dilated and ends with the delivery of the baby. This stage involves the passage of the fetus, usually head first, through the cervical canal and the vagina to the outside.
3 The **third stage** begins after the child is born and

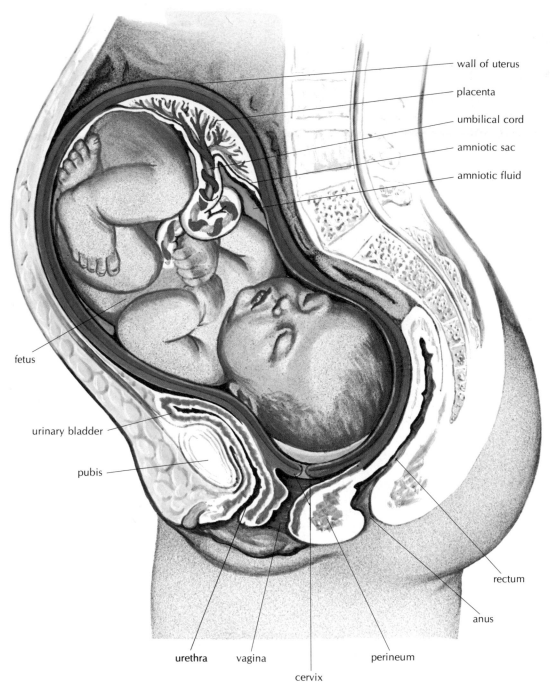

Figure 21-9. *Midsagittal section of a pregnant uterus.*

ends with the expulsion of the **afterbirth**. The afterbirth includes the placenta, the membranes of the amniotic sac, and the umbilical cord, except for a small portion remaining attached to the baby's **umbilicus** (um-bil′i-kus), or navel.

4 The **fourth stage** begins with the expulsion of the afterbirth and constitutes a period in which bleeding is controlled. Contraction of the uterine muscle acts to close off the blood vessels leading to the placental site.

The Mammary Glands and Lactation

The **mammary glands,** or the breasts of the female, are accessories of the reproductive system. They are designed to provide nourishment for the baby after its birth, and the secretion of milk at this time is known as **lactation** (lak-ta'shun).

The mammary glands are constructed in much the same manner as the sweat glands. Each of these glands is divided into a number of lobes composed of glandular tissue and fat, and each lobe is further subdivided. The secretions from the lobes are conveyed through **lactiferous** (lak-tif'er-us) **ducts,** all of which converge at the nipple (Fig. 21-10).

The mammary glands begin developing during puberty, but they do not become functional until the end of a pregnancy. A hormone called **prolactin** (PRL), produced by the anterior lobe of the pituitary, stimulates the secretory cells of the mammary glands. The first of the mammary gland secretions is a thin liquid called **colostrum** (ko-los'trum). It is nutritious but has a somewhat different composition from milk. Secretion of milk begins within a few days and can continue for several months as long as milk is frequently removed by the suckling baby or by pumping.

The digestive tract of the newborn baby is not ready for the usual mixed diet of an adult. Mother's milk is more desirable for the young infant than milk from other animals for several reasons, some of which are listed below:

1 Infections that may be transmitted by foods exposed to the outside air are avoided by nursing.
2 Both breast milk and colostrum contain maternal antibodies that help protect the baby against pathogens.
3 The proportions of various nutrients and other substances in human milk are perfectly suited to the human infant. Substitutes are not exact imitations of human milk. Nutrients are present in

Figure 21-10. *Section of the breast.*

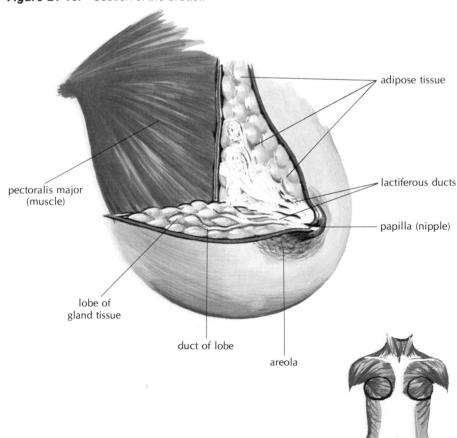

pectoralis major
(muscle)

adipose tissue

lactiferous ducts

papilla (nipple)

lobe of
gland tissue

duct of lobe

areola

more desirable amounts if the mother's diet is well balanced.

4 The psychologic and emotional benefits of nursing are of infinite value to both the mother and the infant.

Multiple Births

Until recently, statistics indicated that twins occurred in about 1 of every 80 to 90 births, varying somewhat in different countries. Triplets occurred much less frequently, usually once in several thousand births, while quadruplets occurred very rarely indeed. The birth of quintuplets represented a historic event unless the mother had taken fertility drugs. Now these fertility drugs, usually gonadotropins, are given quite frequently, and the number of multiple births has increased significantly. Multiple fetuses tend to be born prematurely and therefore have a high death rate. However, better care of infants and newer treatments have resulted in more living multiple births than ever.

Twins originate in two different ways and on this basis are divided into two groups:

1 **Fraternal twins** are formed as a result of the fertilization of two different ova by two spermatozoa. Two completely different individuals, as distinct from each other as brothers and sisters of different ages, are produced. Each fetus has its own placenta and surrounding sac.

2 **Identical twins** develop from a single zygote formed from a single ovum fertilized by a single spermatozoon. Obviously, they are always the same sex and carry the same inherited traits. Sometime during the early stages of development the embryonic cells separate into two units. Usually there is a single placenta, although there must be a separate umbilical cord for each individual.

Other multiple births may be fraternal, identical, or combinations of these. The tendency to multiple births seems to be hereditary.

≡ Disorders of Pregnancy

Ectopic Pregnancy

A pregnancy that develops in a location outside the uterine cavity is said to be an **ectopic** (ek-top′ik) **pregnancy**, *ectopic* meaning "out of normal place."

The most common type is the **tubal ectopic pregnancy**, in which the embryo grows in the uterine tube. This structure, which is not designed by nature for pregnancy, is not able to expand to contain the growing embryo and soon ruptures. The ruptured tube causes internal hemorrhage, and prompt surgical removal of the affected tube is required to save the mother's life.

Placenta Previa

The placenta is usually attached to the upper part of the uterus. In **placenta previa** (pre′via) the placenta becomes attached at or near the internal opening of the cervix. The normal softening and dilation of the cervix that occur in later pregnancy will separate part of the placenta from its attachment. The result will be painless bleeding and interference with the fetal oxygen supply. Somtimes placenta previa necessitates **cesarean** (se-zar′re-an) **section**, which is delivery of the fetus by way of an incision made in the abdominal wall and the wall of the uterus.

Placental Abruption

Sometimes the placenta separates from the wall of the uterus prematurely, often after the 20th week of pregnancy, causing hemorrhage. This disorder, known as **abruptio placentae** (ab-rup″she-o plah-sen′te), occurs most often in women over 35 who have had several pregnancies (multigravidas). This is a common cause of bleeding during the second half of pregnancy and may require the termination of pregnancy to save the mother's life.

The Use of Ultrasound

A valuable diagnostic tool that avoids the use of undesirable x-rays is a form of vibrational energy called *ultrasound*. By this method soft tissues can be visualized and such abnormalities as ectopic pregnancies and placenta previa can be accurately delineated. The relatively inexpensive ultrasound equipment has been found useful in detecting abnormalities of the fetus as well as tumors and other disorders of the reproductive system.

Toxemia of Pregnancy

Toxemia of pregnancy is a serious, often life-threatening disorder that can develop in the latter part of pregnancy. The causes of this disorder are unknown.

However, it is most common in women whose nutritional state is poor and who have received little or no health care during pregnancy. Symptoms include hypertension, protein in the urine (proteinuria), general edema, and sudden weight gain. If the condition remains untreated, convulsions, kidney failure, and finally death of both mother and infant can occur.

Lactation Disturbances

Disturbances in lactation may be due to a variety of reasons, including the following:

1 Malnutrition or anemia, which may prevent lactation entirely
2 Emotional disturbances, which may affect lactation (as they may other glandular activities)
3 Abnormalities of parts of the mammary glands or injuries to these organs, which may cause interference with their functioning
4 **Mastitis** (mas-ti′tis), which means "inflammation of the breast," and which makes nursing inadvisable

Live Births and Fetal Deaths

The duration, or average term, of a human pregnancy is 9 calendar months, 10 lunar months, or 40 weeks. However, a pregnancy may end before that time.

The term **live birth** is used if the baby breathes or shows any evidence of life such as heartbeat, pulsation of the umbilical cord, or movement of voluntary muscles.

An **immature** or **premature** infant is one born before the organ systems are mature. Infants born before the 37th week of gestation or weighing less than 2500 grams (5.5 lb) are considered preterm.

Loss of the fetus is classified according to the duration of the pregnancy:

1 The term **abortion** refers to loss of the embryo or fetus before the 20th week or weight of about 500 grams (1.1 lb). This loss can be either spontaneous or induced.
 a **Spontaneous abortions** occur naturally with no interference. The most common causes are related to an abnormality of the embryo or fetus. Other causes include abnormality of the mother's reproductive organs, infections, or chronic disorders such as kidney disease or hypertension. **Miscarriage** is the lay term for spontaneous abortions.
 b **Induced abortions** occur as a result of artificial or mechanical interruption of pregnancy. This classification includes **criminal abortions**, which are performed illegally and which are the cause of many unnecessary deaths among pregnant women. **Therapeutic abortions** are abortions performed by physicians as a form of treatment for a variety of reasons. With more liberal use of this type of abortion, there has been a dramatic decline in the incidence of death related to illegal abortion, particularly among poor people.

2 The term **fetal death** refers to loss of the fetus after the eighth week of pregnancy. **Stillbirth** refers to the delivery of an infant that is lifeless.

Immaturity is a leading cause of death in the newborn. After the 20th week of pregnancy, the fetus is considered **viable**, that is, able to live outside the uterus. A fetus expelled before the 28th week or a weight of 1000 grams (2.2 lb) has less than a 50% chance of survival. One born at a point closer to the full 40 weeks stands a much better chance of survival. Increasing numbers of immature infants are being saved owing to the advances in neonatal intensive care.

Postpartum Disorders

Puerperal Infection
Childbirth-related deaths are often due to infections. **Puerperal** (pu-er′per-al) **infections** (those related to childbirth) were once the cause of death in as many as 10% to 12% of women going through labor. Cleanliness and sterile techniques have improved the chances of avoiding such endings of pregnancies. Nevertheless, in the United States, puerperal infection still develops in about 6% of maternity patients. Antibiotics have dramatically improved the chances of recovery of both the mother and the child.

Choriocarcinoma
A very malignant tumor that is made of placental tissue is the **choriocarcinoma** (ko″re-o-kar″si-no′mah). It spreads rapidly, and if the patient isn't treated, it may be fatal within 3 to 12 months. With the use of modern chemotherapy, the outlook for cure is very good. If metastases have developed, irradiation and other forms of treatment may be necessary.

The Menopause

The **menopause** (men'o-pawz), often called *change of life,* is that period at which menstruation ceases altogether. It ordinarily occurs between the ages of 45 and 55 and is caused by a normal decline in ovarian function. The ovary becomes chiefly scar tissue and no longer produces ova or appreciable amounts of estrogen. Eventually the uterus, oviducts, vagina, and vulva all become somewhat atrophied.

Although the menopause is an entirely normal condition, its onset sometimes brings about effects that are temporarily disturbing. The decrease in estrogen levels can cause such nervous symptoms as irritability, "hot flashes," and dizzy spells.

Although long a subject of controversy, the use of estrogen replacement therapy for menopausal women is now generally considered to be safe under strict supervision by a physician. Estrogen therapy has proved effective in alleviating hot flashes and the sensitivity of a thinning atrophic vaginal mucosa. Some women may require hormone therapy to pre-vent or halt osteoporosis (see Chap. 7). The longer the duration of hormone treatment, the greater is the risk of cancer of the uterus (endometrial cancer); reducing the dosages and the duration of the therapy reduces the risks. Other factors that must be considered involve the risk of thrombosis and embolism, which is highest in women who smoke. A patient who has a family history of cancer of the breast or of the uterus should avoid estrogen therapy.

Contraception

The steady increase in world population has gone hand in hand with efforts to find safer, more effective, and less expensive methods of birth control. **Contraception** is defined as the use of artificial methods to prevent fertilization of the ovum or implantation of the fertilized ovum. Table 21-1 presents a brief description of the main contraceptive methods currently in use, along with some advantages and disadvantages of each. The list is given in rough order of decreasing effectiveness.

Table 21-1 Main Methods of Contraception Currently in Use

Method	Description	Advantages	Disadvantages
Vasectomy/tubal ligation	Cutting and tying of tubes carrying gametes	Is nearly 100% effective; involves no chemical or mechanical devices	Is not usually reversible; surgery may have side-effects
Birth control pill	Estrogen and progesterone used to prevent ovulation	Is highly effective; requires no last-minute preparation	Has side-effects, especially in smokers
Intrauterine device (IUD)	Small device inserted into uterus to prevent implantation	Requires no last-minute preparation or drugs	Has side-effects; may cause sterility; may be lost accidentally
Diaphragm (with spermicide)	Rubber cap that fits over cervix and prevents entrance of sperm	Does not affect physiology	Must be inserted before intercourse and left in place 6–8 hours; may be damaged or poorly fitting
Vaginal sponge	Sponge impregnated with spermicide that fits over cervix	Is easily available; requires no special fitting; is effective for 24 hours	Causes irritation; may be difficult to remove
Condom	Sheath that fits over erect penis and prevents release of semen	Is easily available; does not affect physiology; protects against venereal disease (VD)	Must be applied just before intercourse; may slip or tear
Spermicide alone	Chemicals used to kill sperm	Is easily available; does not affect physiology	Causes irritation; must be used just before intercourse
Rhythm	Avoidance of intercourse for 3 days before and 3 days after ovulation to avoid fertilization	Involves no surgery, mechanical devices, drugs, or hormones; agrees with some religions	Is difficult to follow; requires that female's menstrual cycle be regular; has a high failure rate

Summary

I **Structure of reproductive tract**
A Primary organs—gonads
  1 Testes in male; ovaries in female
  2 Germ cells (sperms and eggs)—produced in gonads by meiosis, which reduces chromosome number from 46 to 23
B Accessory organs—ducts and exocrine glands

II **Male reproductive system**
A Structure
  1 Testes
    a Products
      (1) Spermatozoa—produced in seminiferous tubules
        (a) Head—mainly nucleus
        (b) Middle region—has mitochondria
        (c) Tail—for locomotion
        (d) Acrosome—covers head (aids in penetration of ovum)
      (2) Testosterone—produced in interstitial cells (between tubules)
        (a) Development of spermatozoa
        (b) Production of secondary sex characteristics
  2 Ducts
    a Epididymis—stores spermatozoa until ejaculation
    b Ductus deferens—transports spermatozoa
    c Ejaculatory duct—receives secretions from seminal vesicles
    d Urethra—carries semen through penis
  3 Penis—copulatory organ
  4 Scrotum—sac that contains testes
B Semen
  1 Functions
    a Nourishment and transportation of spermatozoa
    b Lubrication of reproductive tract
    c Neutralization of female reproductive tract
  2 Formation
    a Seminal vesicles
    b Prostate
    c Bulbourethral glands
C Hormonal control of reproduction
  1 Hypothalamus—produces releasing hormone, causing anterior pituitary to release FSH and LH
  2 FSH—stimulates formation of spermatozoa
  3 LH (ICSH)—stimulates production of testosterone
  4 Testosterone—regulates continuous hormone production by acting as negative feedback messenger to hypothalamus
D Disorders
  1 Infertility—decreased ability to reproduce
    a Sterility—complete inability to reproduce
  2 Cryptorchidism—failure of testes to descend into scrotum
  3 Inguinal hernia—caused by weakness in inguinal canal
  4 Infections
    a Gonorrhea—main venereal disease
    b Others—genital herpes, syphilis
  5 Tumors

III **Female reproductive tract**
A Structure
  1 Ovaries—produce ova and hormones
  2 Oviducts—carry ovum to uterus by means of cilia in lining and by peristalsis
  3 Uterus—site for development of fertilized egg
    a Endometrium—lining of uterus
    b Cervix—narrow region at bottom
  4 Vagina—canal for copulation, birth, menstrual flow
    a Hymen—membrane that covers opening of vagina
    b Greater vestibular glands—secrete mucus
  5 Vulva—external female genitalia
    a Labia—two pairs of liplike tissue
    b Clitoris—sensitive tissue
B Menstrual cycle
  1 First hormone is FSH from anterior pituitary, which starts ripening of ovum within follicle
  2 Production of estrogen by follicle
    a Development of endometrium for possible pregnancy
    b Feedback to hypothalamus to inhibit FSH and start production of LH
  3 LH—surge occurs 24 hours before ovulation
    a Ovulation—caused by LH on day 14 of 28-day cycle

  b Conversion of follicle to corpus luteum by LH

 4 Production of progesterone (and some estrogen) by corpus luteum

  a Continued development of endometrium

  b Feedback to inhibit release of LH

 5 No fertilization

  a Degeneration of corpus luteum

  b Drop in hormone levels

  c Menstruation

C Disorders

 1 Leukorrhea—vaginal discharge; sign of irritation or infection

 2 Menstrual disorders

  a Amenorrhea—absence of menstrual flow

  b Dysmenorrhea—painful or difficult menstruation

  c Premenstrual syndrome

 3 Malignant tumors—cancer of breast, endometrium, ovary, cervix most common

 4 Infections

  a Salpingitis—inflammation of uterine tubes

  b Pelvic inflammatory disease

  c Toxic shock syndrome

 5 Infertility

IV **Pregnancy**

A Fertilization

 1 Uterine tube—place of fertilization of ovum

 2 Zygote (fertilized egg)—begins to divide

 3 Embryo (developing egg)—travels into uterus and implants

B Early pregnancy

 1 Placenta

  a Formation—formed by cells around embryo and lining of uterus; connected to embryo by umbilical cord

  b Functions

   (1) Provision of nourishment to embryo

   (2) Gas exchange with embryo

   (3) Removal of waste from embryo

   (4) Production of chorionic gonadotropin—maintains corpus luteum until 11–12 weeks of pregnancy

 2 Amniotic sac—fluid-filled sac around embryo that serves as protective cushion

 3 Embryo—becomes fetus after third month

C Childbirth—four stages

D Lactation—prolactin stimulates flow of milk in mammary glands

 1 Advantages—reduces infections, provides best form of nutrition, antibodies, emotional satisfaction

E Multiple births—incidence increased because of fertility drugs

F Disorders of pregnancy and delivery

 1 Ectopic pregnancy—pregnancy outside of uterus

 2 Placenta previa—improper attachment of placenta to uterus

 3 Placental abruption—separation of placenta from uterus

 4 Others—toxemia, infection, choriocarcinoma

G Abortion—loss of embryo or fetus before week 20 of pregnancy; may be spontaneous or induced

 1 Fetal death—loss of fetus after 8 weeks of pregnancy

V **Menopause**—cessation of menstruation

A Characteristics

 1 Degeneration of reproductive organs

 2 Possibility of disturbing side-effects

 3 Increased risk of osteoporosis

B Therapy—estrogen replacement

VI **Contraception**—use of methods to prevent fertilization or implantation of ovum

Questions for Study and Review

1 In what fundamental respect does reproduction in some single-celled animals such as the ameba differ from that in most animals?

2 Name the sex cells of both the male and the female.

3 Name all the parts of the male reproductive system and describe the function of each.

4 What is cryptorchidism? Why does this condition cause sterility?

5 Name and describe a disorder of the male reproductive system that is common in elderly men. What are some other effects of aging in the male?

6 Name the principal parts of the female reproductive system and describe the function of each.

7 Describe the process of ovulation.

8 Beginning with the first day of the menstrual flow, describe the events of one complete cycle, including the role of the various hormones.

9 Distinguish between dysmenorrhea and amenorrhea.

10 What is a Pap test? Why is it important?

11 What are the most common malignant diseases in women? For early detection, what should a woman do at regular intervals?

12 What are the two most common cancers of the uterus?

13 What are some causes of infertility in both males and females?

14 Distinguish among the following: zygote, embryo, fetus.

15 Name two auxiliary structures that are designed to serve the fetus. What is their origin and what are their functions?

16 Is blood in the umbilical arteries relatively low or high in oxygen? in the umbilical vein?

17 Describe some of the changes that take place in the mother's body during pregnancy.

18 What is the major event of each of the four stages of labor and delivery?

19 List some of the advantages associated with breastfeeding a baby.

20 Define *ectopic pregnancy; placenta previa; abortion* (two categories); *premature,* or *preterm, infant.*

21 What is the menopause? What causes it? What are some of the changes that take place in the body as a result?

22 What are the values of estrogen replacement therapy after menopause? What are some of the dangers of such therapy?

22

Heredity and Hereditary Diseases

Behavioral Objectives

After careful study of this chapter, you should be able to:

Briefly describe the mechanism of gene function

Explain the difference between dominant and recessive genes

Describe a carrier of a genetic trait

Define meiosis and explain the function of meiosis in reproduction

Explain how sex is determined in humans

Describe what is meant by the term sex linked and list several sex-linked traits

List several factors that may influence the expression of a gene

Define mutation

Differentiate among congenital, genetic, and hereditary disorders and give several examples of each

List several factors that may produce genetic disorders

Define karyotype and explain how karyotypes are used in genetic counseling

Briefly describe several methods used to treat genetic disorders

Selected Key Terms

The following terms are defined in the glossary:

amniocentesis
carrier
chromosome
congenital
dominant
gene
genetics
heredity
karyotype
meiosis
mutation
pedigree
progeny
recessive
sex linked
trait

Often we are struck by the resemblance of a baby to one or both of its parents, yet rarely do we stop to consider *how* various traits are transmitted from parents to offspring. This subject—heredity—has fascinated humans for thousands of years; the Old Testament contains numerous references to heredity (although, of course, the word was unknown in biblical times). However, it was not until the 19th century that methodic investigation into heredity was begun. At that time an Austrian monk, Gregor Mendel, discovered through his experiments with garden peas that there was a precise pattern in the appearance of differences among parents and their progeny. Mendel's most important contribution to the understanding of heredity was the demonstration that there are independent units of hereditary influence. Later, these independent units were given the name *genes*.

Mechanism of Gene Function

The primary action of each gene is to control the manufacture of a specific protein. Remember that DNA—deoxyribonucleic acid, the genetic material—controls the formation of RNA (ribonucleic acid) in the nucleus (see Chap. 3). RNA in turn travels into the cytoplasm and controls the manufacture of the special class of proteins called *enzymes*. Because enzymes promote all of the chemical reactions that take place in a cell, the genes control all of the cell's activities.

Genes and Chromosomes

Genes are contained in the threadlike chromosomes within the nucleus of each cell. As described in Chapter 3, chromosomes are composed mainly of DNA. When body cells divide by the process of mitosis, these chromosomes are duplicated and distributed to the daughter cells such that each daughter cell gets exactly the same kind and number of chromosomes as were in the original cell. Each chromosome (aside from the Y chromosome, which determines sex) may carry thousands of genes, and each gene carries the code for a specific trait (characteristic). These traits constitute the physical, biochemical, and physiologic makeup of every cell in the body.

Every body cell in humans contains 46 chromosomes. These chromosomes exist in pairs. One member of each pair was received at the time of fertilization from the father of the offspring, and one was received from the mother. These paired chromosomes, except for the pair that determines sex, are alike in size and appearance and carry genes for the same traits. Thus, the genes for each trait exist in pairs.

Dominant and Recessive Genes

Another of Mendel's discoveries was that genes can be either dominant or recessive. A **dominant** gene is one that expresses its effect in the cell regardless of whether the gene at the same site on the matching chromosome is the same as or different from the dominant gene. The gene need be received from only one parent in order to be expressed in the offspring. The effect of a **recessive** gene will not be evident unless the gene at that site in the matching chromosome in the pair is also recessive. Thus, a recessive trait will appear only if the genes for that trait are received from both parents. For example, genes for dark eyes are dominant, whereas genes for light eyes are recessive. Light eyes will appear in the offspring only if genes for light eyes are received from both parents.

Clearly, a recessive gene will not be expressed if it is present in the cell together with a dominant gene. However, it can be passed on to offspring and may thus appear in future generations. An individual who shows no evidence of a trait but has a recessive gene for that trait is described as a **carrier** of the gene.

Distribution of Chromosomes to Offspring

The reproductive cells (ova and spermatozoa) are produced by a special process of cell division called **meiosis**. Recall from Chapter 21 that this process divides the chromosome number in half so that each reproductive cell has 23 chromosomes. Moreover, the division occurs in such a way that each cell receives one member of each chromosome pair that was present in the original cell. Either member of the original pair may be included in a given germ cell. Thus, the maternal and paternal sets of chromosomes get mixed up and redistributed at this time, leading to increased variety within the population.

Sex Determination

The two chromosomes that determine the sex of the offspring, unlike the other 22 pairs of chromosomes, are not matched in size and appearance. The female X chromosome is larger than other chromosomes and carries genes for other characteristics in addition to that for sex. The male Y chromosome is smaller than other chromosomes and mainly determines sex. A female has two X chromosomes in each body cell; a male has one X and one Y. By the process of meiosis, each male sperm cell receives either an X or a Y chromosome, whereas every egg cell can have only an X chromosome. If a sperm with an X chromosome fertilizes an ovum, the resulting infant will be female; if a sperm with a Y chromosome fertilizes an ovum, the resulting infant will be male (Fig. 22-1).

Sex-linked Traits

Any trait that is carried on a sex chromosome is said to be sex linked. Since the Y chromosome carries few traits aside from sex determination, most sex-linked

Figure 22-1. *If an X chromosome from a male unites with an X chromosome from a female, the child is female; if a Y chromosome from a male unites with an X chromosome from a female, the child is male.*

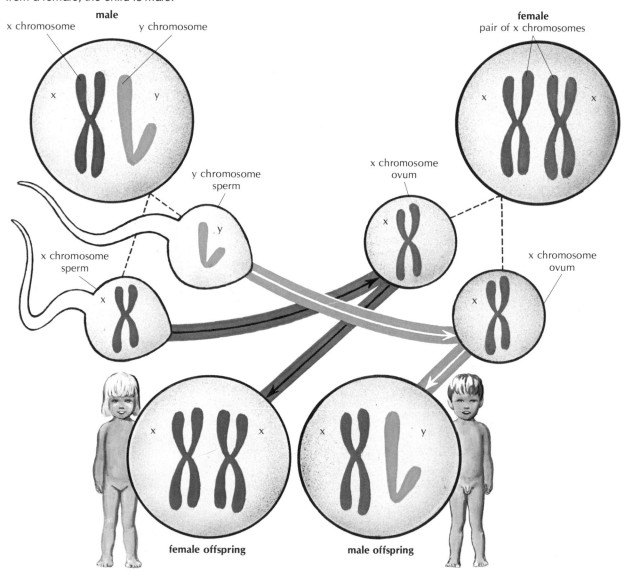

traits are carried on the X chromosome and are described as *X-linked*. Examples are hemophilia, certain forms of baldness, and red–green color blindness. Sex-linked traits appear almost exclusively in males. The reason for this is that most of these traits are recessive, and if a recessive gene is located on the X chromosome in a male it cannot be masked by a matching dominant gene. Thus, a male who has only one recessive gene for the trait will exhibit the characteristic, whereas a female must have two recessive genes to show the trait.

Hereditary Traits

Some simple, observable hereditary traits are skin, eye, and hair color and body build. Also inherited are less specific traits, such as height and weight, life span, and susceptibility to disease. Some human traits, including many genetic diseases, are determined by single pairs of genes; most, however, are the result of two or more gene pairs acting together in what is termed **multifactorial inheritance**. This accounts for the great variations in such characteristics as skin color, height, and weight, all of which are determined by several gene pairs.

Gene Expression

The effect or expression of a gene may be influenced by a variety of factors, including the sex of the individual and the presence of other genes. For example, the genes for certain types of baldness and certain types of color-blindness may be inherited by either males or females, but the traits appear mostly in males under the effects of male sex hormone.

Environment also plays a part in the expression of genes. One inherits a potential for a given size, for example, but one's actual size is additionally influenced by such factors as nutrition, development, and general state of health. The same is true of lifespan and susceptibility to diseases.

Gene Mutation

As a rule, chromosomes replicate exactly during cell division. Occasionally, however, for reasons not yet clearly understood, the genes or chromosomes change. This change may be in a single gene or in the number of chromosomes. Alternatively, it may consist of chromosomal breakage, in which there is loss or rearrangement of gene fragments. Such changes are termed genetic **mutations**. Mutations may occur spontaneously or may be induced by some agent, such as ionizing radiation or chemicals, described as **mutagenic**.

If the mutation occurs in an ovum or a sperm cell involved in reproduction, the altered trait will be inherited by the offspring. The vast majority of harmful mutations never are expressed because the affected fetus dies and is spontaneously aborted. Most mutations are so inconsequential that they have no visible effect. Beneficial mutations tend to survive and spread throughout a population.

Genetic Diseases

Advances in genetic research have made it possible to identify the causes of many hereditary disorders and to develop methods of genetic screening. Persons who are "at risk" for having a child with a genetic disorder, as well as fetuses and newborns in whom the presence of an abnormality may be suspected, can have chromosome studies done to identify genetic abnormalities.

Congenital vs. Hereditary Diseases

Before we discuss hereditary diseases, we need to distinguish them from other congenital diseases. To illustrate, let us assume that two infants are born within seconds in adjoining delivery rooms of the same hospital. It is noted that one infant has a clubfoot, a condition called *talipes* (tal'i-pes); the second infant has a rudimentary extra finger attached to the fifth finger of each hand, a condition called *polydactyly* (pol-y-dac'tyl-y). Are both conditions hereditary? both congenital? Is either hereditary? We can answer these questions by defining the key terms, *congenital* and *hereditary*. *Congenital* means existing from the time of birth; *hereditary* means genetically transmitted or transmissible. Thus, one condition may be both congenital and hereditary; another, congenital yet not hereditary.

Hereditary conditions are usually congenital; many genetic disorders are evident at birth or soon thereafter. However, certain inherited disorders, such as adult polycystic kidney and Huntington's chorea, a nervous disorder, do not manifest themselves until about midlife (40 to 50 years of age). In the case of our earlier examples, the clubfoot is congenital, but not hereditary, having resulted from severe distortion of the developing extremities during intra-uterine growth; the extra fingers are hereditary, a familial trait that appears in another relative, a grandparent perhaps, or a parent, and that is evident at the time of birth.

Although causes of congenital deformities and birth defects often are not known, some are known and could be prevented. For example, certain infections and toxins may be transmitted from the mother's blood by way of the placenta to the circulation of the fetus. Some of these cause serious developmental disorders in affected babies. German measles (rubella) is a contagious viral infection that is ordinarily a mild disease, but if maternal infection occurs during the first 3 or 4 months of pregnancy, the fetus has a 40% chance of developing defects of the eye (cataracts), of the ear (deafness), and of the brain and heart. Infection can be prevented by appropriate immunizations.

Ionizing radiation and various toxins may damage the genes, but the disorders they produce are not hereditary. Environmental agents, such as mercury and some chemicals used in industry (for example, certain phenols and PCB), as well as some drugs, notably LSD, are known to disrupt genetic organization.

Intake of alcohol and cigarette smoking by a pregnant woman often cause growth retardation and low birth weight in her infant. Smaller than normal infants do not do as well as babies of average weight. Some congenital heart defects have been associated with a condition called *fetal alcohol syndrome*. Total abstinence from alcohol and cigarettes is strongly recommended during pregnancy.

Examples of Genetic Diseases

Any disorders that involve the genes may be said to be genetic, but in some cases they are not hereditary, that is, passed from parent to offspring. Nonhereditary genetic disorders may begin during maturation of the sex cells or even during development of the embryo.

The best known example of a genetic disorder that is not inherited is the most common form of **Down's syndrome**, which results from the presence of an extra chromosome per cell. The disorder is usually recognizable at birth by the afflicted child's distinctive facial features. The face is round, with close-set eyes that slant upward at the outside. The head is small and grows at an unusually slow rate. The nose is flat, the tongue is large and protruding, and the muscles and joints are lax. Intellectual function is imparied in Down's children; however, the amount of skill they can gain depends on the severity of the disease and their family and school environments. Down's syndrome is usually not inherited, although there is a hereditary form of the disorder. In most cases, both parents are normal, as are the child's siblings. The likelihood of having a baby with Down's syndrome increases dramatically in women past the age of 35, and may be the result of defects in germ cells due to age.

Most genetic diseases are **familial** or **hereditary**; that is, they are passed on from parent to child by way of the spermatozoa and ova. In the case of a dominant trait, one parent usually carries the abnormal gene that gives rise to the disorder, as is the case in Huntington's chorea. The disturbance appears in the parent and any of the offspring who receive the defective gene. If the trait is a recessive one, as is the case in the majority of inheritable disorders, a defective gene must come from each parent. Important inheritable diseases that are carried as recessive traits include diabetes mellitus, cystic fibrosis, and sickle cell anemia.

We said earlier, that genes control the production of specific enzymes. In the case of **PKU, or phenyl-ketonuria** (fen″il-ke″to-nu′re-ah), the lack of a certain enzyme prevents the proper metabolism of **phenyl-alanine** (fen″il-al′ah-nin), one of the common amino acids. The phenylalanine accumulates in the infant's blood. If the condition remains untreated, it leads to mental retardation before the age of 2 years. PKU screening is done routinely on newborn infants.

Sickle cell disease is described in Chapter 12, where it is stated that the disease is found almost exclusively in members of the black race. By contrast, **cystic fibrosis** is most common in members of the Caucasian race; in fact, it is possibly the most frequently inherited disease in white populations. It is characterized by excessively viscid (thickened) secretions of the linings of the bronchi, the intestine, and the ducts of the pancreas. Such secretions in the ducts of the pancreas prevent the flow of pancreatic juice to the small intestine. Obstruction and blockage of these vital organs follows, in association with frequent respiratory infections, with uncontrollable intestinal losses, particularly of fats (and the vitamins these fats carry), as well as massive salt loss. Treatment includes oral administration of pancreatic enzymes and special pulmonary exercises. Cystic fibrosis was once a fatal disease in children and adolescents, but now, with appropriate care, life expectancies are extending into the third decade.

Another group of heritable muscle disorders is known collectively as the **progressive muscular atrophies.** *Atrophy* means wasting due to decrease in the size of a normally developed part. The absence of normal muscle movement in the infant proceeds within a few months to extreme weakness of the respiratory muscles, until ultimately the infant is unable to breathe adequately. Most afflicted babies die within several months. The name *floppy baby syndrome,* as the disease is commonly called, provides a vivid description of its effects.

Albinism is an inherited disorder that is carried by recessive genes. It is of particular interest because of the easily recognizable appearance it lends to the affected person. The skin and hair color are strikingly white and do not darken with age. The skin is abnormally sensitive to sunlight and may appear wrinkled. Albinos are especially susceptible to skin cancer and to some severe visual disturbances, such as myopia and abnormal sensitivity to light (photophobia).

Other inherited disorders include **osteogenesis** (os″teo-jen′e-sis) **imperfecta,** or brittle bones, in which multiple fractures may occur during and shortly after fetal life, and a disorder of skin, muscles, and bones called **neurofibromatosis** (nu″ro-fi″bro-mah-to′sis). In the latter condition multiple masses, often on stalks (pedunculated), grow along nerves all over the body.

≡ Treatment and Prevention of Genetic Diseases

The list of genetic diseases is so lengthy that many pages of this book would be needed simply to enumerate them. Moreover, the list continues to grow as sophisticated research techniques and advances in biology make it clear that various diseases whose causes did not used to be understood are now known to be genetic—some hereditary, others not. Can we identify which are inherited genetic disorders and which are due to environmental factors? Can we prevent the occurrence of any of them?

Genetic Counseling

It is possible to prevent genetic disorders in many cases and even to treat some of them. The most effective method of preventing genetic disease is through genetic counseling, a specialized field of health care. Genetic counseling centers use a team approach of medical, nursing, laboratory, and social service professionals to advise and care for the clients.

The Family History

An accurate and complete family history of both prospective parents is necessary. It includes information about relatives with respect to age, onset of a specific disease, health status, and cause of death. The families' ethnic origins may be relevant, since some genetic diseases have a definite relationship to certain ethnic groups. Hospital and physician records are studied, as are photographs of family members. The ages of the prospective parents is a factor, as is parental or ancestral relationship (for example, marriage between first cousins). The complete, detailed family history, or tree, is called a **pedigree.** Pedigrees are used to determine the pattern of inheritance of a genetic disease within a family. They may also indicate whether a given member of the family is a carrier of the disease.

Karyotype

Abnormalities in the number of chromosomes and some abnormalities within the chromosomes can be detected by analysis of the **karyotype** (kar′eo-type), a word derived from *karyon,* which means "nucleus." A karyotype is produced by the growth of certain cells in a special medium and arrest of cell division at the stage called *metaphase.* The chromosomes, visible under the microscope, are then photographed, and the photographs are cut out and arranged in groups according to their size and form (Fig. 22-2). Abnormalities in the number and structure of chromosomes—called *chromosomal errors*—can thereby be detected. Special stains are used to reveal certain changes in fine structure within the chromosomes.

A technique that enables the geneticist to prepare a karyotype of an unborn fetus is **amniocentesis** (am″ne-o-sen-te′sis). During this procedure, a small

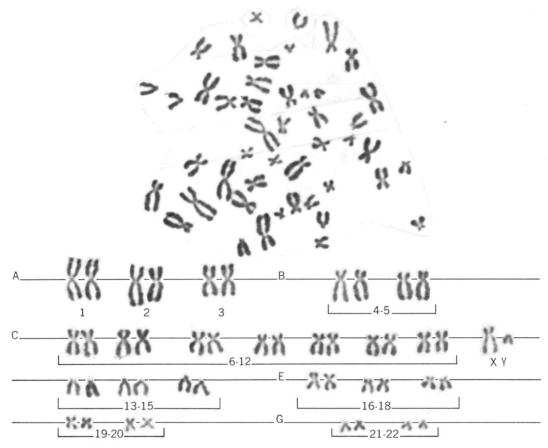

A _____ 1   2   3   B _____ 4-5 _____

C _____ 6-12 _____ X Y

_____ 13-15 _____ E _____ 16-18 _____

_____ 19-20 _____ G _____ 21-22 _____

Figure 22-2. (Top) *Metaphase spread. Chromosomes of a normal male photographed during metaphase when they have doubled and are ready to divide. (Bottom) Karyotype. The chromosomes from the metaphase spread, above, arranged in matching pairs according to size and other characteristics. (Courtesy of Kenneth L. Garver, M.D., and Angela M. Ciocio, Ph.D. In Chaffee EE, Lytle IM: Basic Physiology and Anatomy, 4th ed, p 562. Philadelphia, JB Lippincott, 1980)*

amount of amniotic fluid, which surrounds the fetus and is often referred to as the *waters,* is withdrawn. Fetal skin cells in the amniotic fluid are removed, grown (cultured), and separated for study. A karyotype is prepared, and the chromosomes are examined. The amniotic fluid is also analyzed for biochemical abnormalities. With these methods almost 200 genetic diseases can be detected before birth.

A newer method for obtaining fetal cells for study involves sampling of the chorionic villi through the cervix. The chorionic villi are hairlike projections of the membrane that surrounds the embryo in early pregnancy. The method is called **chorionic villus sampling.** Samples may be taken between 8 and 10 weeks of pregnancy, and the cells obtained may be

analyzed immediately. In contrast, amniocentesis cannot be done before the 14th to 16th week of pregnancy, and test results are not available for about 2 weeks.

Counseling the Prospective Parents

Armed with all the available pertinent facts, as well as with special knowledge of the recurrence risk rate, the counselor is equipped to inform the prospective parents of their possibility of having genetically abnormal offspring. The couple may then elect to have no children, to have an adoptive family, to undergo sterilization, to terminate the pregnancy, or to accept the risk.

Progress in Medical Treatment

The mental and physical ravages of many genetic diseases are largely preventable, provided the diseases are diagnosed and treated early in the individual's life. Some of these diseases respond well to dietary control. One such disease, called *maple syrup urine disease,* responds to very large doses of thiamine along with control of the intake of certain amino acids. The disastrous effects of Wilson's disease, in which abnormal accumulations of copper in the tissue cause tremor, rigidity, uncontrollable stagger, and finally extensive liver damage, can be prevented by a combination of dietary and drug therapy.

Phenylketonuria is perhaps the best-known example of dietary management of inherited disease. If the disorder is undiagnosed and untreated, 98% of affected patients will be severely mentally retarded by 10 years of age; in contrast, if the condition is diagnosed and treated before the baby reaches the age of 6 months and treatment is maintained until age 10, mental deficiency will be prevented or at least minimized. A simple blood test for PKU is now done routinely immediately after birth in hospitals throughout the United States. The test should be repeated 24 to 48 hours after the infant has received protein.

Klinefelter's (kline′fel-terz) **syndrome,** which occurs in about 1 in 600 males, is a common cause of underdevelopment of the gonads with resulting infertility. Victims of this disorder have abnormal sex chromosome patterns, usually an extra X chromosome. Instead of the typical male XY pattern, the cells contain an XXY combination owing to failure of the sex chromosomes to separate during cell division. Treatment of this disorder includes the use of hormones and pyschotherapy.

As couples tend to have smaller families, concern about the health and well-being of each newborn infant increases. Hence, we can anticipate greatly improved methods of screening, diagnosis and treatment of genetic diseases. There have been reports of fetuses being treated with vitamins or hormones following prenatal diagnosis of a genetic disorder. Far in the future lies the possibility of treating or correcting genetic disorders through genetic engineering. For the present, it is important to educate the public about the availability of screening methods for both parents and offspring. People should also be made aware of the possible genetic effects of radiation, drugs, and other toxic substances.

Summary

I **Mechanism of gene function**—genes control manufacture of enzymes in cytoplasm of cell

II **Genes and chromosomes**
  A Genes—contained in chromosomes within nucleus
    1 Dominant gene—always expressed
    2 Recessive gene—expressed only if gene received from both parents
      a Carrier—person with recessive gene that is not apparent but can be passed to offspring
  B Chromosomes—46 in each human body cell
    1 Pairs—matched in size and appearance; one member of each pair from each parent
    2 X and Y chromosomes—determine sex
  C Meiosis—form of cell division
    1 Production of sex cells
    2 Halving of chromosome number from 46 to 23
    3 Separation of maternal and paternal chromosomes into different daughter cells
  D Sex chromosomes—females XX, males XY
    1 X chromosome—larger than others; carries traits in addition to sex determination
    2 Sex-linked traits—appear mostly in males
      a Hemophilia
      b Baldness
      c Red–green color blindness

III **Hereditary traits**—genes determine physical, biochemical, and physiologic characteristics of every cell
  A Traits determined by single gene pairs
  B Traits determined by multiple gene pairs (multifactorial inheritance)
    1 Height
    2 Weight
    3 Skin color
    4 Susceptibility to disease
  C Factors affecting gene expression
    1 Sex
    2 Presence of other genes
    3 Environment

D Mutation—change in genes or chromosomes; may be passed to offspring if occurs in germ cells

  1 Mutagenic agents

   a Ionizing radiation

   b Drugs

   c Toxins

   d Chemicals

IV Genetic diseases

 A Congenital disorders—present at birth; may or may not be hereditary

 B Examples

  1 Down's syndrome—results from extra chromosome

  2 PKU (phenylketonuria)—inability to metabolize phenylalanine

  3 Cystic fibrosis—common in white populations

  4 Progressive muscular atrophies

  5 Albinism—lack of pigment

  6 Others: Huntington's chorea, sickle cell anemia, osteogenesis imperfecta, neurofibromatosis

V Treatment and prevention

 A Genetic counseling

  1 Family history to establish pedigree

  2 Karyotype—analysis of chromosomes

   a Amniocentesis—withdrawal of amniotic fluid

   b Chorionic villus sampling—newer method

  3 Counseling of prospective parents about risks

 B Progress in medical treatment

  1 Dietary control—maple syrup urine disease, Wilson's disease, PKU

  2 Hormone therapy—Klinefelter's disease

  3 Fetal therapy

Questions for Study and Review

1 How many chromosomes are there in a human body cell? in a human sex cell?

2 What process results in the distribution of chromosomes to the offspring?

3 What sex chromosomes are present in a male? in a female?

4 From which parent does a male child receive an X-linked gene?

5 Explain how two normal parents can give birth to a child with a recessive hereditary disease.

6 Explain the great variation in the color of skin, hair, and eyes in humans.

7 Explain how a hereditary disease can suddenly appear in a family with no history of the disease.

8 A baby is born with syphilis. Is this congenital or hereditary? Why?

9 List several mutagenic agents.

10 Could a karyotype be used to diagnose Down's syndrome? Klinefelter's syndrome?

11 How is an amniocentesis performed and what can be learned from it?

12 How is a pedigree used in genetic counseling?

13 What is PKU and how should this disease be treated?

14 What are some characteristics of albinism and what are the risks associated with this disorder?

15 What heritable disorder is most common among black persons and how does it manifest itself?

16 What is the most common heritable disease among white persons and what are some of its symptoms?

Suggestions for Further Study

Anderson L et al: Nutrition in Health and Disease, 17th ed. Philadelphia, JB Lippincott, 1982

Anderson WA, Fuller K: Pathology, 10th ed. St Louis, CV Mosby, 1980

Ayala FJ, Kiger JA Jr.: Modern Genetics, 2nd ed. Menlo Park, CA, Benjamin-Cummings, 1984

Bellanti JA: Immunology: Basic Processes, 2nd ed. Philadelphia, WB Saunders, 1985

Bevelander G, Ramsley J: Essentials of Histology, 8th ed. St Louis, CV Mosby, 1979

Brunner LS, Suddarth DS: Textbook of Medical-Surgical Nursing, 5th ed. Philadelphia, JB Lippincott, 1984

Brunner LS, Suddarth DS: The Lippincott Manual of Nursing Practice, 4th ed. Philadelphia, JB Lippincott, 1986

Burton GW: Microbiology for the Health Sciences, 2nd ed. Philadelphia, JB Lippincott, 1983

Carter S et al: Principles of Cancer Treatments. New York, McGraw-Hill, 1982

Creasy WA: Cancer. An Introduction. New York, Oxford University Press, 1981

Crouch JE: Essential Human Anatomy. Philadelphia, Lea & Febiger, 1982

Crouch JE: Functional Human Anatomy, 4th ed. Philadelphia, Lea & Febiger, 1985

DeGroot LJ et al: Endocrinology. New York, Grune & Stratton, 1979

di Fiore M: Atlas of Human Histology, 5th ed. Philadelphia, Lea & Febiger, 1981

Frenay A: Understanding Medical Terminology, 7th ed. St Louis, Catholic Hospital Association, 1984

Fuerst R: Microbiology in Health and Disease, 15th ed. Philadelphia, WB Saunders, 1983

Ganong WF: Review of Medical Physiology, 12th ed. Los Altos, CA, Lange Medical Publications, 1985

Garb S: Laboratory Tests in Common Use, 6th ed. New York, Springer-Verlag, 1976

Gever LN et al (eds): Nurse's Reference Library: Drugs, 2nd ed. Springhouse, PA, Springhouse Corporation, 1984

Gilbert E, Huntington R: An Introduction to Pathology. New York, Oxford University Press, 1978

Goldberger E: A Primer of Water, Electrolyte and Acid–Base Syndromes, 6th ed. Philadelphia, Lea & Febiger, 1980

Goodhart RS, Shils ME: Modern Nutrition in Health and Disease, 6th ed. Philadelphia, Lea & Febiger, 1980

Guyton AC: Human Physiology and Mechanisms of Disease, 3rd ed. Philadelphia, WB Saunders, 1982

Guyton AC: Anatomy and Physiology. Philadelphia, WB Saunders, 1985

Ham AW, Cormack D: Histology, 8th ed. Philadelphia, JB Lippincott, 1979

Hamilton H (ed): Neoplastic Disorders. Springhouse, PA, Springhouse Corporation, 1985

Hamilton H, Rose MB (eds): Nurse's Reference Library: Diagnostics. Springhouse, PA, Springhouse Corporation, 1983

Hamilton H, Rose MB (eds): Nurse's

Reference Library: Diseases. Springhouse, PA, Springhouse Corporation, 1983

Hamilton HK, Rose MB (eds): Nurse's Reference Library: Procedures. Springhouse, PA, Springhouse Corporation, 1982

Haskel CM: Cancer Treatment, 2nd ed. Philadelphia, WB Saunders, 1985

Hole JW Jr.: Human Anatomy and Physiology, 3rd ed. Dubuque, Wm C Brown, 1984

Holum JR: Elements of General and Biological Chemistry, 6th ed. New York, John Wiley & Sons, 1983

Jawetz E, Melnick JL, Adelberg EA: Review of Medical Microbiology, 16th ed. Los Altos, CA, Lange Medical Publications, 1984

Kapff CT, Jandl HJ: Blood: Atlas & Sourcebook of Hematology. Boston, Little, Brown & Co., 1981

King EM, Wieck L, Dyer M: Illustrated Manual of Nursing Techniques, 2nd ed. Philadelphia, JB Lippincott, 1981

Kozier B, Erb G: Fundamentals of Nursing: Concepts and Procedures, 2nd ed. Reading, MA, Addison-Wesley, 1983

Krause MV, Mahan LK: Food, Nutrition and Diet Therapy, 7th ed. Philadelphia, WB Saunders, 1984

Merrell DJ: Ecological Genetics. Minneapolis, University of Minnesota Press, 1981

Metheny NM: Snively WD: Nurses' Handbook of Fluid Balance, 4th ed. Philadelphia, JB Lippincott, 1983

Nagle JJ: Heredity and Human Affairs, 3rd ed. St Louis, CV Mosby, 1983

Naval Education and Training Program: The Metric System; America Measures Up. Washington, DC, United States Superintendent of Documents, 1979

Nicksic E: The Plus and Minus of Fluids and Electrolytes. Reston, VA, Reston Publishing Co, 1981

Pansky B: Review of Gross Anatomy, 4th ed. London, Macmillan, 1979

Rakel RF (ed): Conn's Current Therapy. Philadelphia, WB Saunders, 1985

Rodman MJ, Smith DW: Pharmacology and Drug Therapy in Nursing Text, 2nd ed. Philadelphia, JB Lippincott, 1979

Rothwell NV: Understanding Genetics, 3rd ed. New York, Oxford University Press, 1983

Sackheim G et al: Chemistry for the Health Sciences, 4th ed. New York, Macmillan, 1981

Smith AL: Microbiology and Pathology, 12th ed. St Louis, CV Mosby, 1980

Smith AL: Principles of Microbiology, 9th ed. St Louis, CV Mosby, 1981

Sobotta J: Atlas of Human Anatomy, 3 Vols, 11th text ed. Baltimore, Urban & Schwarzenberg, 1978

Spivak JL (ed): Fundamentals of Clinical Hematology, 2nd ed. New York, Harper & Row, 1984

Stites DP et al (eds): Basic and Clinical Immunology, 5th ed. Los Altos, CA, Lange Medical Publications, 1984

Thompson RB, Proctor SJ: A Concise Textbook of Hematology, 6th ed. Marshfield, MA, Pitman Publishing, 1984

Turek SL: Orthopaedics, 4th ed. Philadelphia, JB Lippincott, 1983

Vaughan D, Asbury T: General Ophthalmology, 10th ed. Los Altos, CA, Lange Medical Publications, 1983

Volk WA, Wheeler MF: Basic Microbiology, 5th ed. New York, Harper & Row, 1984

Vredevoe DL et al: Concepts of Oncology Nursing. Englewood Cliffs, NJ, Prentice-Hall, 1981

Weinreb EL: Anatomy and Physiology. Reading, MA: Addison-Wesley, 1984

West JB (ed): Best & Taylor's Physiological Basis of Medical Practice, 11th ed. Baltimore, MD, Williams & Wilkins, 1984

Wintrobe MM et al: Clinical Hematology, 8th ed. Philadelphia, Lea & Febiger, 1981

Wyngaarden JB, Smith LH: Cecil's Textbook of Medicine, 16th ed. Philadelphia, WB Saunders, 1982

Glossary

Abortion   Loss of an embryo or fetus before the 20th week of pregnancy

Absorption   Transfer of digested food molecules from the digestive tract into the circulation

Accommodation   Coordinated changes in the eye that enable one to focus on near and far objects

Acid   Substance that donates a proton (H^+) to another substance

Acidosis   Condition that results from a decrease in the pH of body fluids

Acrosome   Caplike structure over the head of the sperm cell that helps the sperm penetrate the ovum

Actin   One of the contractile proteins in muscle cells

Action potential   Sudden change in the electric charge on a cell membrane

Active transport   Movement of a substance into or out of the cell in a direction opposite that in which it would normally flow by diffusion

Acute   Referring to a severe but short-lived disease or condition

ADH   Antidiuretic hormone; hormone released from the posterior pituitary gland that increases the reabsorption of water in the kidneys, thus decreasing the volume of urine excreted

Adipose   Referring to a type of connective tissue that stores fat

Aerobic   Requiring oxygen

Afferent   Carrying toward a given point, such as a sensory neuron that carries nerve impulses toward the central nervous system

Albumin   Protein in blood plasma that helps maintain the osmotic pressure of the blood

Aldosterone   Hormone released by the adrenal cortex that promotes the reabsorption of sodium and water from the kidneys

Alkalosis   Condition that results from an increase in the pH of body fluids

Allergy   Tendency to react unfavorably to a certain substance that is normally harmless to most people; hypersensitivity

Alveolus (*pl.,* alveoli)   One of the millions of tiny air sacs in the lungs through which gases are exchanged between the outside air and the blood

Amniocentesis   Removal of fluid and cells from the amniotic sac for prenatal diagnostic tests

Amniotic sac   Fluid-filled sac that surrounds and cushions the developing fetus

Amphiarthrosis   Slightly movable joint

Anabolism   Metabolic conversion of small molecules into substances needed by the body

Anaerobic   Not requiring oxygen

Anastomosis   Communication between two structures such as blood vessels

Anatomy   Study of body structure

Anemia   Reduction in the amount of red cells or hemoglobin in the blood resulting in inadequate delivery of oxygen to the tissues

Aneurysm   Bulging sac in the wall of a vessel

Antagonist   Muscle that has an action opposite that of a given movement; substance that opposes the action of another substance

Antibody Substance produced in response to a specific antigen

Antigen Foreign substance that enters the body and produces an immune response

Antiserum Serum containing antibodies; given for the purpose of providing passive immunity

Aorta Large artery that carries blood out of the left ventricle of the heart

Aponeurosis Broad sheet of fibrous connective tissue that attaches muscle to bone or to other muscle

Appendicular Referring to the part of the skeleton that includes the bones of the arms, legs, shoulder girdle, and hips

Arachnoid Middle layer of the meninges

Areolar Referring to loose connective tissue

Arrhythmia Abnormal rhythm of the heartbeat

Arteriole Vessel between a small artery and a capillary

Arteriosclerosis Hardening of the arteries

Artery Vessel that carries blood away from the heart

Arthritis Inflammation of the joints

Asepsis Condition in which no pathogens are present

Astigmatism Visual defect due to an irregularity in the curvature of the cornea or the lens

Atom Fundamental unit of a chemical element

ATP Adenosine triphosphate; compound that stores energy in the cell

Atrium One of the two upper chambers of the heart

Attenuated Weakened

Autoimmunity Abnormal reactivity to one's own tissues

Autonomic Referring to the part of the nervous system that controls the action of smooth muscle, cardiac muscle, and glands; motor division of the visceral or involuntary nervous system

Axial Referring to the part of the skeleton that includes the skull, spinal column, ribs, and sternum

Axon Projection from the cytoplasm of a neuron that carries nerve impulses away from the cell body

Bacterium Type of microorganism

Base Substance that can accept a proton (H^+)

Benign Describing a tumor that does not spread

Bile Substance produced in the liver that emulsifies fats

Bradycardia Heart rate of less than 60 beats per minute

Brain stem Portion of the brain that connects the cerebrum with the spinal cord; contains the midbrain, pons, and medulla oblongata

Bronchiole One of the small subdivisions of the bronchi that branch throughout the lungs

Bronchus (*pl.,* bronchi) One of the large air tubes in the lung

Buffer Substance that prevents sharp changes in the *p*H of a solution

Bursa Small, fluid-filled sac found in an area subject to stress around bones and joints

Bursitis Inflammation of a bursa

Cancer A tumor that spreads to other tissues; a malignant neoplasm

Capillary Microscopic vessel through which exchanges take place between the blood and the tissues

Carbohydrate Simple sugar or compound made from simple sugars linked together; sugar or starch

Carcinogen Cancer-causing substance

Carrier Individual who has a gene that is not expressed but that can be passed to offspring

Cartilage Type of hard connective tissue

Catabolism Metabolic breakdown of food for simple compounds and energy

Cataract Opacity of the eye lens or lens capsule

Cecum Small pouch at the beginning of the large intestine

Cell Basic unit of life

Cell membrane Outer covering of a cell; regulates what enters and leaves the cell

Cellular respiration Series of reactions by which food is oxidized for energy within the cell

Centrifuge Instrument for separating materials in a mixture based on density

Centriole Rod-shaped body near the nucleus of a cell that functions in cell division

Cerebellum Small section of the brain located under the cerebral hemispheres; functions in coordination, balance, and muscle tone

Cerebrospinal fluid Fluid that circulates in and around the brain and spinal cord

Cerebrum Largest part of the brain; composed of the cerebral hemispheres and diencephalon

Chemoreceptor Receptor that detects chemical changes

Chemotherapy Treatment of a disease by administration of a chemical agent

Choroid Pigmented middle layer of the eye

Chromosome Dark-staining, threadlike body in the nucleus of a cell that contains the genes, which determine hereditary traits

Chronic Referring to a disease that is not severe but is continuous or recurring

Chyle Milky-appearing fluid containing fat that drains into the lymphatic system from the small intestine

Chyme Mixture of partially digested food, water, and digestive juices that forms in the stomach

Cilia Small hairlike projections from the surface of a cell

Circumduction Circular movement at a joint

Coagulation Clotting, as of blood

Cochlea Coiled portion of the inner ear that contains the organs of hearing

Collagen Flexible white protein that gives strength and resilience to connective tissue such as bone and cartilage

Colon Main portion of the large intestine

Complement Group of nonspecific blood proteins that help antibodies destroy foreign cells

Compound Substance composed of two or more chemical elements

Congenital Present at birth

Conjunctiva Membrane that lines the eyelid and covers the anterior part of the sclera

Contraception Use of artificial methods to prevent fertilization of an ovum or the implantation of a fertilized ovum

Cornea Clear forward continuation of the sclera that covers the front of the eye

Coronary Referring to the heart or to the arteries supplying blood to the heart

Corpus callosum Band of white matter at the bottom of the cerebral hemispheres

Corpus luteum Structure that develops from the follicle in the ovary after ovulation

Cortex Outer layer of an organ such as the brain or kidney

Covalent bond Chemical bond formed by the sharing of electrons between atoms

Cutaneous Referring to the skin

Cystitis Inflammation of the urinary bladder

Cytoplasm Substance that fills the cell and holds the organelles

Defecation Act of eliminating undigested waste from the digestive tract

Degeneration Breaking down, as from age, injury, or disease

Deglutition Act of swallowing

Dehydration Excessive loss of body fluid

Dendrite Projection from the cytoplasm of a neuron that carries nerve impulses toward the cell body

Dermatitis Inflammation of the skin

Dermis True skin; underlying layer of the skin

Diagnosis Identification of an illness

Dialysis Diffusion of molecules in solution through a semipermeable membrane; method for cleansing the blood of an individual with defective kidneys

Diaphragm Dome-shaped muscle under the lungs that flattens during inhalation; membrane or structure that serves to separate

Diaphysis Shaft of a long bone

Diastole Relaxation phase of the cardiac cycle

Diencephalon Region of the brain between the cerebral hemispheres and the midbrain; contains the thalamus, hypothalamus, and pituitary gland

Diffusion Movement of molecules from a region where they are in higher concentration to a region where they are in lower concentration

Digestion Process of breaking food down into small particles

Disease Abnormal state in which part or all of the body is not properly adjusted or is not capable of carrying on all of its required functions

DNA Deoxyribonucleic acid; genetic material of the cell

Dominant Referring to a gene that is always expressed if present

Duct Tube or vessel

Ductus (vas) deferens Tube that carries spermatozoa from the testis to the urethra

Duodenum First portion of the small intestine

Dura mater Outermost layer of the meninges

Echocardiograph Instrument to study the heart by means of ultrasound

Eczema Skin condition that may involve redness, blisters, pimples, scaling, and crusting

Edema Accumulation of fluid in the tissue spaces

Effector Muscle or gland that carries out a response to a stimulus

Efferent Carrying away from a given point, such as a motor neuron that carries nerve impulses away from the central nervous system

Ejaculation Expulsion of semen through the urethra

Electrocardiograph Instrument used to study the electric activity of the heart

Electrolyte Compound that forms ions in solution; substance that conducts an electric current in solution

Electron Negatively charged subatomic particle located in an orbital outside the nucleus of an atom

Element One of the substances from which all matter is made

Embolus Blood clot or other obstruction in the circulation

Embryo Developing offspring during the first 2 months of pregnancy

Emphysema Pulmonary disease characterized by dilation and destruction of the alveoli

Emulsification Breakup of fats into small particles

Endocardium Lining of the heart

Endocrine Referring to a gland that releases its secretion directly into the bloodstream

Endometrium Lining of the uterus

Endothelium Epithelium that lines the heart, blood vessels, and lymphatic vessels

Enzyme Organic catalyst; speeds up the rate of a reaction but is not changed in the reaction

Epidemic Occurrence of a disease among many people in a given region at the same time

Epidermis Outermost layer of the skin

Epiglottis Leaf-shaped cartilage that covers the larynx during swallowing

Epimysium Sheath of fibrous connective tissue that encloses a muscle

Epiphysis End of a long bone

Epithelium One of the four main types of tissue; forms glands, covers surfaces, and lines cavities

ER Endoplasmic reticulum; network of membranes in the cytoplasm of a cell

Erythema Redness

Erythrocyte Red blood cell

Erythropoietin Hormone released from the kidney that stimulates the production of red blood cells in the bone marrow

Esophagus Tube that carries food from the throat to the stomach

Estrogen Group of female sex hormones that promotes development of the uterine lining and maintains secondary sex characteristics

Etiology Study of the cause of a disease or the theory of its origin

Eustachian (auditory) tube Tube that connects the middle ear cavity to the throat

Excretion Removal and elimination of metabolic waste products from the blood

Exocrine Referring to a gland that releases its secretions through a duct

Fascia Band or sheet of fibrous connective tissue

Feedback Return of information into a system so that it can be used to regulate that system

Fertilization Union of an ovum and a spermatozoon

Fetus Developing individual from the third month of pregnancy until birth

Fever Abnormally high body temperature

Fibrin Blood protein that forms a blood clot

Fissure Deep groove

Flagellum Long whiplike projection from a cell used for locomotion

Follicle Structure in which the ovum ripens in the ovary

Fontanel "Soft spot"; area in the infant skull in which bone formation is incomplete

FSH Follicle-stimulating hormone; hormone, produced by the anterior pituitary, that stimulates development of the ova in the ovary and the spermatozoa in the testes

Fungus Type of plantlike microorganism; yeast or mold

Gamete Germ cell; ovum or spermatozoon

Gamma globulin Fraction of the blood plasma that contains antibodies

Ganglion Collection of nerve cell bodies located outside the central nervous system

Gene Hereditary unit; portion of the DNA on a chromosome

Genetic Pertaining to the genes and heredity

Glomerular filtrate Fluid and dissolved materials that leave the glomerulus and enter the kidney nephron through Bowman's capsule

Glomerulonephritis Kidney disease often resulting from antibodies to a streptococcal infection

Glomerulus Cluster of capillaries in Bowman's capsule of the nephron

Glucose Simple sugar; main energy source for the cells

Glycogen Compound, made of glucose molecules, that is stored as a glucose reserve in liver and muscle cells

Golgi apparatus System of membranes in the cell that formulates special substances

Gram Basic unit of weight in the metric system

Gray matter Nervous tissue composed of unmyelinated fibers and cell bodies

Gyrus Raised area of the cerebral cortex

Helminth Worm

Hematocrit Test that measures the volume percentage of red blood cells in whole blood

Hemoglobin Iron-containing protein in red blood cells that functions mainly to transport oxygen

Hemolysis Rupture of red blood cells

Hemorrhage Loss of blood

Hemostasis Stoppage of bleeding

Heredity Genetic transmission of characteristics from parent to offspring

Histology Study of tissues

Homeostasis State of balance within the body; maintenance of body conditions within set limits

Hormone Secretion of an endocrine gland

Hydrolysis Splitting of large molecules by the addition of water

Hypertension High blood pressure

Hypertonic Describing a solution that is more concentrated than the fluids within a cell

Hypothalamus Region of the brain that controls the pituitary (hypophysis) and maintains homeostasis

Hypothermia Abnormally low body temperature

Hypotonic Describing a solution that is less concentrated than the fluids within a cell

Hypoxia Reduced oxygen supply to the tissues

ICSH Interstitial cell–stimulating hormone. *See* LH

Immunity Power of an individual to resist or overcome the effects of a particular disease or other harmful agent

Immunization Use of a vaccine to produce immunity

Infarct Area of tissue damaged as a result of lack of blood supply caused by blockage of a vessel

Infertility Decreased ability to reproduce

Inflammation Response of tissues to injury; characterized by heat, redness, swelling, and pain

Insertion   End of a muscle attached to a movable part

Integument   Skin

Ion   Charged particle formed when an electrolyte goes into solution

Iris   Circular colored region of the eye around the pupil

Ischemia   Lack of blood supply to an area

Isometric contraction   Muscle contraction in which there is no change in muscle length but an increase in muscle tension, as in pushing against an immovable force

Isotonic   Describing a solution that has the same concentration of molecules as the fluid within a cell

Isotonic contraction   Muscle contraction in which the tone within the muscle remains the same but the muscle shortens to produce movement

Joint   Articulation; area of junction between two or more bones

Karyotype   Picture of the chromosomes arranged according to size and form

Keratin   Protein that thickens and protects the skin and makes up hair and nails

Kidney   One of the two excretory organs

Lacrimal   Referring to tears

Lacteal   Capillary of the lymphatic system that drains digested fats from the villi of the small intestine

Lactic acid   Organic acid that accumulates in muscle cells functioning without oxygen.

Larynx   Voice box; structure between the pharynx and the trachea that contains the vocal cords

Lens   Crystalline lens; biconvex structure of the eye that changes in thickness to accommodate for near and far vision

Lesion   Wound or local injury

Leukemia   Malignant blood disease

characterized by abnormal development of white blood cells

Leukocyte   White blood cell

LH   Luteinizing hormone; hormone, produced by the anterior pituitary, that induces ovulation and the formation of the corpus luteum in females; in males it is called *ICSH* and stimulates cells in the testes to produce testosterone

Lipid   Type of organic compound, one example of which is a fat

Liter   Basic unit of volume in the metric system

Lung   One of the two organs of respiration

Lymph   Fluid in the lymphatic system

Lymphadenitis   Inflammation of the lymph nodes

Lymphangitis   Inflammation of the lymphatic vessels

Lymphocyte   Agranular leukocyte that functions in immunity

Lysosome   Organelle that contains digestive enzymes

Macrophage   Large phagocytic cell that develops from a monocyte

Malignant   Describing a tumor that spreads

Malnutrition   State resulting from lack of food, lack of an essential component of the diet, or faulty use of food in the diet

Mastication   Act of chewing

Mediastinum   Region between the lungs and the organs and vessels it contains

Medulla   Inner region of an organ; marrow

Medulla oblongata   Part of the brain stem that connects the brain with the spinal cord

Megakaryocyte   Large cell that gives rise to blood platelets

Meiosis   Process of cell division that halves the chromosome number in the formation of the reproductive cells

Melanin   Pigment that gives color to skin and hair

Membrane   Thin sheet of tissue

Meninges   Three layers of fibrous membranes around the brain and spinal cord

Menopause   Time at which menstruation ceases

Mesentery   Section of the peritoneum that folds over the abdominal organs

Metabolic rate   Rate at which energy is released from food in the cells

Metabolism   Total of all life-sustaining reactions that occur in the living cell; includes catabolism and anabolism

Metastasis   Process of tumor cell spread

Meter   Basic unit of length in the metric system

Micrometer (μm)   1/1000th of a millimeter

Microorganism   Microscopic organism

Micturition   Act of urination

Midbrain   Upper portion of the brain stem

Mineral   Element; in the diet, an element needed in small amounts for health

Mitochondria   Cell organelles that manufacture ATP with the energy released from the oxidation of food

Mitosis   Type of cell division that produces two daughter cells exactly like the parent cell

Mixture   Blend of two or more substances

Molecule   Particle formed by the union of two or more atoms held together by chemical bonding; smallest subunit of a compound

Monocyte   Agranular leukocyte active in the mononuclear phagocyte system

Mucosa   Mucous membrane

Mucus   Clear, sticky fluid secreted by cells to lubricate and protect tissues

Murmur   Abnormal heart sound

Mutation   Change in a gene or a chromosome

Myalgia   Muscular pain

Myelin   Fatty material that covers

and insulates the axons of some neurons

Myocardium   Middle layer of the heart; heart muscle

Myoglobin   Compound that stores oxygen in muscle cells

Myosin   Contractile protein of muscle cells

Necrosis   Tissue death

Neoplasm   Abnormal growth of cells; a tumor

Nephron   One of the many microscopic functional units of the kidney

Nerve   Bundle of nerve fibers outside the central nervous system

Nerve impulse   Electric charge that spreads along the membrane of a neuron

Neurilemma   Thin sheath on the outside of some peripheral axons; aids in regeneration of the axon

Neuroglia   Supporting and protecting cells of the nervous system

Neuromuscular junction   Point at which a nerve fiber contacts a muscle cell

Neuron   Nerve cell

Neurotransmitter   Chemical that transmits a nerve impulse across a synapse

Neutron   Uncharged subatomic particle located in the nucleus of an atom

Neutrophil   Phagocytic granular leukocyte; polymorph or poly

Node   Small mass of tissue such as a lymph node; space between cells in the myelin sheath

Nucleotide   Building block of DNA and RNA

Nucleus   Largest organelle in the cell; contains the DNA, which directs all cell activities

Organ   Group of tissues functioning together for specific purposes

Organelle   Specialized subdivision within a cell

Organic   Referring to compounds found in living things and containing carbon, hydrogen, and oxygen

Origin   End of a muscle attached to a nonmovable part

Osmosis   Movement of water through a semipermeable membrane

Osmotic pressure   Tendency of a solution to draw water into it; is directly related to the concentration of the solution

Ossicles   Three small bones of the middle ear: malleus, incus, and stapes

Osteoblast   Bone-forming cell

Osteoclast   Cell that breaks down bone for resorption

Osteocyte   Mature bone cell; maintains bone but does not divide

Ovary   Female gonad

Ovulation   Release of an egg cell from a follicle in the ovary

Ovum   Female reproductive cell or gamete

Oxidation   Chemical breakdown of food for energy

Oxygen debt   Amount of oxygen needed to reverse the effects produced in muscles functioning without oxygen

Pacemaker   SA node of the heart; group of cells or artificial device that sets the rate of heart contraction

Parasympathetic nervous system   Craniosacral division of the autonomic nervous system

Parturition   Childbirth

Pathogen   Disease-causing organism

Pathology   Study of disease

Pathophysiology   Study of the physiologic basis of disease

Pedigree   Family history used in the study of heredity

Pericardium   Fibrous sac lined with serous membrane that surrounds the heart

Periosteum   Connective tissue membrane covering a bone

Peripheral   Located away from a center or central structure

Peristalsis   Wavelike movements in the wall of an organ or duct that propel its contents forward

Peritoneum   Serous membrane that lines the abdominal cavity and folds over the abdominal organs

*p*H   Scale that indicates the amounts of hydrogen ion (H^+) and hydroxide ion (OH^-) in solution; the scale measures the relative acidity and alkalinity (basicity) of a solution

Phagocytosis   Engulfing of large particles through the cell membrane

Pharynx   Throat; passageway between the mouth and the esophagus

Phlebitis   Inflammation of a vein

Pia mater   Innermost layer of the meninges

Pinocytosis   Intake of small particles and droplets through the cell membrane

Pituitary gland (hypophysis)   Endocrine gland located under and controlled by the hypothalamus; releases hormones that control other glands

Placenta   Structure that nourishes and maintains the developing individual during pregnancy

Plasma   Liquid portion of the blood

Plasma cell   Cell derived from a B-lymphocyte and capable of producing specific antibodies

Platelet   Cell fragment that forms a plug to stop bleeding and acts in blood clotting

Pleura   Serous membrane that lines the pleural cavity and covers the lungs

Plexus   Network of vessels or nerves

Pneumothorax   Accumulation of air in the pleural cavity

Pons   Area of the brain between the midbrain and the medulla; connects the cerebellum with the rest of the nervous system

Portal system   Venous system that carries blood to a second capillary bed before it returns to the heart

Prime mover   Muscle or set of muscles that performs a given movement

Progeny   Offspring

Progesterone   Hormone, produced

by the corpus luteum and placenta, that maintains the lining of the uterus for pregnancy

Prognosis Prediction of the probable outcome of a disease based on the condition of the patient

Proprioceptor Sensory receptor that aids in judging body position and changes in position; proprioceptors are located in muscles, tendons, and joints

Prostaglandin Group of hormones, produced by many cells of the body, that has a variety of effects

Protein Organic compound made of amino acids; all proteins contain nitrogen in addition to carbon, hydrogen, and oxygen

Proton Positively charged subatomic particle located in the nucleus of an atom

Protozoon Animal-like microorganism

Pulse Wave of increased pressure in the vessels produced by contraction of the heart

Pupil Opening in the center of the eye through which light enters

Pyrogen Substance that produces fever

Receptor Specialized cell or ending of a sensory neuron that can be excited by a stimulus; also a site in the cell membrane to which special substances (*e.g.,* hormones) may attach

Recessive Referring to a gene that is not expressed if a dominant gene for the same trait is present

Reflex Simple, rapid, involuntary response

Refraction Bending of light rays as they travel through a medium other than air

Renin Hormone released from the kidneys that acts to increase blood pressure

Resorption Loss of substance, such as bone

Respiration Exchange of oxygen and carbon dioxide between the outside air and body cells

Retina Innermost layer of the eye; contains light-sensitive cells (rods and cones)

Ribosome Small body in the cytoplasm of a cell that is active in protein manufacture

RNA Ribonucleic acid; type of nucleic acid needed for protein manufacture in the cell

Saliva Secretion of the salivary glands; moistens food and contains an enzyme that digests starch

Sclera Outermost layer of the eye made of tough connective tissue; "white" of the eye

Scrotum Sac in which the testes are suspended

Sebaceous Referring to the skin glands that secrete sebum

Sebum Oily secretion of the sebaceous glands that lubricates the skin

Semen Mixture of sperm cells and secretions from the seminal vesicles, prostate, and bulbourethral glands that is expelled from the male at ejaculation

Semicircular canal One of three bony canals in the inner ear that contain receptors for the sense of dynamic equilibrium

Septum Dividing wall, as between the chambers of the heart

Serosa Serous membrane

Serum Liquid portion of blood without clotting factors; liquid that remains after blood has clotted

Sex linked Referring to a gene carried on a sex chromosome, usually the X chromosome

Shock Pertaining to the circulation: inadequate output of blood by the heart

Sign Manifestation of a disease that can be noted by an observer

Sinusoid Enlarged capillary that serves as a blood channel

Solute Substance that is dissolved in another substance (the solvent)

Solution Mixture, the components of which are evenly distributed

Solvent Substance in which another substance (the solute) is dissolved

Spermatozoon Male reproductive cell (gamete)

Sphincter Muscular ring that regulates the size of an opening

Sphygmomanometer Device used to measure blood pressure

Spleen Lymphoid organ in the upper left region of the abdomen

Spore Resistant form of bacterium; reproductive cell in lower plants

Stenosis Narrowing of a duct or canal

Sterilization Process of killing every living microorganism on or in an object; procedure that makes an individual incapable of reproduction

Steroid Category of lipids that includes the hormones of the sex glands and the adrenal cortex

Stimulus Change in the external or internal environment that produces a response

Sudoriferous Referring to the sweat glands

Sulcus Shallow groove, as in the cortex of the cerebral hemispheres

Surfactant Substance in the alveoli that prevents their collapse by reducing surface tension of the fluids within

Suspension Mixture that must be shaken to prevent the materials distributed in the solvent from settling out

Sympathetic nervous system Thoracolumbar division of the autonomic nervous system

Symptom Evidence of disease noted by the patient

Synapse Point of junction between two neurons or between a neuron and an effector

Synarthrosis Immovable joint

Synovial Referring to a freely movable (diarthrotic) joint or to the fluid that fills the joint cavity of such a joint

System Group of organs functioning together for the same general purpose

Systemic Referring to a generalized infection or condition

Systole Contraction phase of the cardiac cycle

Tachycardia Heart rate over 100 beats per minute

Target tissue Tissue that is capable of responding to a specific hormone

Tendinitis Inflammation of tendons and their attachments

Tendon Cord of fibrous connective tissue that attaches a muscle to a bone

Testis (*pl.,* testes) Male gonad

Testosterone Male sex hormone, produced in the testes, that promotes the development of spermatozoa and maintains secondary sex characteristics

Thalamus Region of the brain located in the diencephalon; most sensory impulses pass through the thalamus on their way to the cerebral cortex

Thrombocytopenia Deficiency in the number of platelets in the blood

Thrombus Blood clot within a vessel

Thymus Endocrine gland in the upper portion of the chest that functions in immunity

Tissue Group of cells that performs a specialized function

Tone Partially contracted state of muscles

Tonsil Masses of lymphoid tissue in the region of the pharynx

Toxin Poison

Toxoid Altered toxin used to produce active immunity

Trachea Windpipe; tube that extends from the layrnx to the bronchi

Tract Bundle of nerve fibers within the central nervous system

Trait Characteristic

Transplant Organ or tissue from an animal or other human used to replace an injured or incompetent part of the body

Tympanic membrane Eardrum; membrane between the outer ear and middle ear that transmits sound waves to the bones of the middle ear

Ulcer Area of the skin or mucous membrane in which the tissues are gradually destroyed

Umbilical cord Structure that connects the fetus with the placenta; contains vessels that carry blood between the fetus and the placenta

Urea Main nitrogen-containing waste product of metabolism

Ureter One of the two tubes that carry urine from the kidney to the urinary bladder

Urethra Tube that carries urine from the urinary bladder to the outside of the body

Urinary bladder Hollow organ that stores urine until it is eliminated

Urine Liquid waste material excreted by the kidneys

Uterus Organ in which the fetus develops during pregnancy

Vaccine Substance used to produce active immunity

Valve Structure that keeps blood and lymph flowing in a forward direction in the vessels

Vasoconstriction Decrease in the diameter of a blood vessel

Vasodilation Increase in the diameter of a blood vessel

Vein Vessel that carries blood toward the heart

Vena cava One of the two large veins that carry blood into the right atrium of the heart

Venous sinus Large channel that drains deoxygenated blood

Ventilation Movement of air into and out of the lungs

Ventricle Cavity or chamber; one of the two lower chambers of the heart

Venule Vessel between a capillary and a small vein

Vestibule Part of the internal ear that contains receptors for the sense of equilibrium; any space at the entrance to a canal or organ

Villus (*pl.,* villi) Small projection in the lining of the small intestine through which digested food is absorbed

Virus Extremely small microorganism that can reproduce only within a living cell

Viscera Internal organs

Vitamin Organic compound needed in small amounts for health

White matter Nervous tissue composed of myelinated fibers

Zygote Fertilized ovum

Medical Terminology

Medical terminology, the special language of the health occupations, is based on an understanding of a relatively few basic elements. These elements—combinations of forms, roots, prefixes, and suffixes—form the foundation of almost all medical terms. A useful way to familiarize yourself with each term is to learn to pronounce it correctly and say it aloud several times. Soon it will become an integral part of your vocabulary.

The foundation of a word is the word root. Examples of word roots are *abdomin-,* referring to the belly region; and *aden-,* pertaining to a gland. A word root is often followed by a vowel to facilitate pronunciation, as in *abdomino-* and *adeno-.* We then refer to it as a "combining form." The hyphen appended to a combining form indicates that it is not a complete word; if the hyphen precedes the combining form, then it commonly appears as the terminal element or the word ending, as in *-algia,* meaning "a painful condition."

A prefix is a part of a word that precedes the word root and changes its meaning. For example, the prefix *mal-* in *malunion* means "abnormal." A suffix, or word ending, is a part that follows the word root and adds to or changes its meaning. The suffix *-rrhea* means "profuse flow" or "discharge," as in *diarrhea,* a condition characterized by excessive discharge of liquid stools.

Many medical words are compound words; that is, they are made up of more than one root or combining form. Examples of such compound words are *erythrocyte* (red blood cell) and *hydrocele* (fluid-containing sac), and many more difficult words, such as *sternoclavicular* (indicating relationship to both the sternum and the clavicle).

A general knowledge of language structure and spelling rules is also helpful in mastering medical terminology. For example, adjectives include words that end in *-al,* as in *sternal* (the noun is *sternum*), and words that end in *-ous,* as in *mucous* (the noun is *mucus*).

The following list includes some of the most commonly used word roots, combining forms, prefixes, and suffixes, as well as examples of their use.

a-, an- absent, deficient, lack of: *atrophy, anemia, anuria*

ab- away from: *abduction, aboral*

abdomin-, abdomino- belly or abdominal area: *abdominocentesis, abdominoscopy*

acou- hearing, sound: *acoustic*

acr-, acro- extreme ends of a part, especially of the extremities: *acromegaly, acromion*

actin-, actini-, actino- relationship to raylike structures or, more commonly, to light or roentgen (x-) rays, or some other type of radiation: *actiniform, actinodermatitis*

ad- (sometimes converted to *ac-, af-, ag-, ap-, as-, at-*) toward, added to, near: *adrenal, accretion, agglomerated, afferent*

aden-, adeno- gland: *adenectomy, adenitis, adenocarcinoma*

-agogue inducing, leading, stimulating: *cholagogue, galactagogue*

alge-, algo-, algesi-, pain: *algetic, algophobia, analgesic*

-algia pain, painful condition: *myalgia, neuralgia*

amb-, ambi-, ambo- both, on two sides: *ambidexterity, ambivalent*

ambly- dimness, dullness: *amblyopia*

angio- vessel: *angiogram, angiotensin*

ant-, anti- against; to prevent, suppress, or destroy: *antarthritic, antibiotic, anticoagulant*

ante- before, ahead of: *antenatal, antepartum*

antero- position ahead of or in front of (*i.e.,* anterior to) another part: *anterolateral, anteroventral*

arthr-, arthro- joint or articulation: *arthrolysis, arthrostomy, arthritis*

-ase enzyme: *lipase, protease*

-asis *see* -sis.

audio- sound, hearing: *audiogenic, audiometry, audiovisual*

aur- ear: *aural, auricle*

aut-, auto- self: *autistic, autodigestion, autoimmune*

bi- two, twice: *bifurcate, bisexual*

bio- life, living organism: *biopsy, antibiotic*

blast-, blasto-, -blast early stage, immature cell or bud: *blastula, blastophore, erythroblast*

bleph-, blephar-, blepharo- eyelid, eyelash: *blepharism, blepharitis, blepharospasm*

brachi- arm: *brachial, brachiocephalic, brachiotomy*

brachy- short: *brachydactylia, brachyesophagus*

brady- slow: *bradycardia*

bronch- windpipe or other air tubes: *bronchiectasis, bronchoscope*

bucc- cheek: *buccal*

carcin- cancer: *carcinogenic, carcinoma*

cardi-, cardia-, cardio- heart: *carditis, cardiac, cardiologist*

-cele swelling; enlarged space or cavity: *cystocele, meningocele, rectocele*

centi- relating to 100 (used in naming units of measurements): *centigrade, centimeter*

-centesis perforation, tapping: *amniocentesis, paracentesis*

cephal-, cephalo- head: *cephalalgia, cephalopelvic*

cerebro- brain: *cerebrospinal, cerebrum*

cervi- neck: *cervical, cervix*

cheil-, cheilo-, lips; brim or edge: *cheilitis, cheilosis*

cheir-, cheiro- (also written **chir-, chiro-**) hand: *cheiralgia, cheiromegaly, chiropractic*

chol-, chole-, cholo- bile, gall: *chologogue, cholecyst, cholecystitis, cholecystokinin*

chondr-, chondri-, chondrio- cartilage: *chondric, chondrocyte, chondroma*

-cid, -cide to cut, kill or destroy: *bactericidal, germicide, suicide*

circum- around, surrounding: *circumorbital, circumrenal, circumduction*

-clast break: *osteoclast*

colp-, colpo- vagina: *colpectasia, colposcope, colpotomy*

contra- opposed, against: *contraindication, contralateral*

cost-, costa-, costo- ribs: *intercostal, costosternal*

counter- against, opposite to: *counterirritation, countertraction*

crani-, cranio- skull: *cranium, craniotomy*

cry-, cryo-, crymo- low temperature: *cryalgesia, cryogenic, cryotherapy*

crypt-, crypto- hidden, concealed: *cryptic, cryptogenic, cryptorchidism*

cut- skin: *subcutaneous*

cysti-, cysto- sac, bladder: *cystitis, cystoscope*

cyt-, cyto-, -cyte cell: *cytolytic, cytoplasm*

dactyl-, dactylo- digits (usually fingers, but sometimes toes): *dactylitis, polydactyly*

de- remove: *detoxify, dehydration*

dendr- tree: *dendrite*

dento-, dent-, denti- tooth: *dentition, dentin, dentifrice*

derm-, derma-, dermo-, dermat-,

dermato- skin: *dermatitis, dermatology, dermatosis*

di-, diplo- twice, double: *dimorphism, diplopia*

dia- through, between, across, apart: *diaphragm, diaphysis*

dis- apart, away from: *disarticulation, distal*

dorsi-, dorso- back (in the human, this combining form refers to the same regions as postero-): *dorsiflexion, dorsonuchal*

-dynia pain, tenderness: *myodynia, neurodynia*

dys- disordered, difficult, painful: *dysentery, dysphagia, dyspnea*

-ectasis expansion, dilation, stretching: *angiectasis, bronchiectasis*

ecto- outside, external: *ectoderm, ectogenous*

-ectomize, -ectomy surgical removal or destruction by other means: *thyroidectomize, appendectomy*

edem- swelling: *edema*

-emia blood: *glycemia, hyperemia*

encephal-, encephalo- brain: *encephalitis, encephalogram*

end-, endo- within, innermost: *endarterial, endocardium, endothelium*

enter-, entero- intestine: *enteritis, enterocolitis*

epi- on, upon: *epicardium, epidermis*

eryth-, erythro- red: *erythema, erythrocyte*

-esthesia sensation: *anesthesia, paresthesia*

eu- well, normal, good: *euphoria, eupnea*

ex-, exo- outside, out of, away from: *excretion, exocrine, exophthalmic*

extra- beyond, outside of, in addition to: *extracellular, extrasystole, extravasation*

fasci- fibrous connective tissue layers: *fascia, fasciitis, fascicle*

-ferent to bear, to carry: *afferent, efferent*

fibr-, fibro- threadlike structures, fibers: *fibrillation, fibroblast, fibrositis*

galact-, galacta-, galacto- milk: *galactemia, galactagogue, galactocele*

gastr-, gastro- stomach: *gastritis, gastroenterostomy*

-gen an agent that produces or originates: *allergen, pathogen, fibrinogen*

-genic produced from, producing: *endogenic, pyogenic*

genito- organs of reproduction: *genitoplasty, genitourinary*

geno- a relationship to reproduction or sex: *genodermatology, genotype*

-geny manner of origin, development or production: *ontogeny, progeny*

glio-, -glia gluey material; specifically, the connective tissue of the brain: *glioma, neuroglia*

gloss-, glosso- tongue: *glossitis, glossopharyngeal*

gly-, glyco- sweet, relating to sugar: *glycemia, glycosuria*

-gnath, gnatho- related to the jaw: *prognathic, gnathoplasty*

gon- seed, knee: *gonad, gonarthritis*

-gram record, that which is recorded: *electrocardiogram, electroencephalogram*

-graph instrument for recording: *electrocardiograph, electroencephalograph*

gyn-, gyne-, gyneco-, gyno- female sex (women): *gynecology, gynecomastia, gynoplasty*

hem-, hema-, hemato-, hemo- blood: *hematoma, hematuria, hemorrhage*

hemi- one half: *hemisphere, heminephrectomy, hemiplegia*

hepat-, hepato- liver: *hepatitis, hepatogenous*

heter-, hetero- other, different: *heterogeneous, heterosexual, heterochromia*

hist-, histio- tissue: *histology, histiocyte*

homeo-, homo- unchanging, the same: *homeostasis, homosexual*

hydr-, hydro- water: *hydrolysis, hydrocephalus*

hyper- above, over, excessive: *hyperesthesia, hyperglycemia, hypertrophy*

hypo- deficient, below, beneath: *hypochondrium, hypodermic, hypogastrium*

hyster, hystero- uterus: *hysterectomy*

-ia state of: *myopia, hypochondria, ischemia*

-iatrics, -trics medical practice specialties: *pediatrics, obstetrics*

idio- self, one's own, separate, distinct: *idiopathic, idiosyncrasy*

im-, in- in, into, lacking: *implantation, inanimate, infiltration*

infra- below: *infraspinous, infracortical*

inter- between: *intercostal, interstitial*

intra- within a part or structure: *intracranial, intracellular, intraocular*

-ism state of: *hyperthyroidism*

iso- equal: *isotonic, isometric*

-itis inflammation: *dermatitis, keratitis, neuritis*

juxta- next to: *juxtaglomerular*

karyo- nucleus: *karyotype, karyoplasm*

kerat-, kerato- cornea of the eye, certain horny tissues: *keratin, keratitis, keratoplasty*

lacri- tear: *lacrimal*

lact-, lacto- milk: *lactation, lactogenic*

later- side: *lateral*

leuk-, leuko- (also written as *leuc-, leuco-*) white: *leukocyte, leukoplakia*

lig- bind: *ligament, ligature*

lith-, litho- stones (calculi): lithiasis

-logy, -ology study of: *physiology, gynecology*

lyso-, -lysis flowing, loosening, dissolution (dissolving of): *hemolysis, paralysis, lysosome*

macro- large, abnormal length: *macrophage, macroblast.* See also **-mega, megalo-**

mal- disordered, abnormal: *malnutrition, malocclusion, malunion*

malac-, malaco-, -malacia- softening: *malacoma, malacosarcosis, osteomalacia*

mast-, masto- breast: *mastectomy, mastitis*

meg-, mega-, megal-, megalo- usually or excessively large: *megacolon, megaloblast, megakaryocyte*

men-, meno- physiologic uterine bleeding: *menses, menorrhagia, menopause*

mening-, meningo- membranes covering the brain and spinal cord: *meningitis, meningocele*

mes-, mesa-, meso- middle, midline: *mesencephalon, mesoderm*

meta- change, beyond, after, over, near: *metabolism, metacarpus, metaplasia*

-meter measure: *hemocytometer, sphygmomanometer*

micro- very small: *microscope, microbiology, microabscess, micrometer*

mono- single: *monocyte, mononucleosis*

my-, myo- muscle: *myenteron, myocardium, myometrium*

myc-, mycet-, myco- fungi: *mycid, mycete, mycology, mycosis*

myel- myelo- marrow (often used in reference to the spinal cord): *myeloid, myeloblast, osteomyelitis, poliomyelitis*

nect-, necro- death, corpse: *necrosis*

neo- new, strange: *neopathy, neoplasm*

neph-, nephro- kidney: *nephrectomy, nephron*

neur-, neuro- nerve: *neuron, neuralgia, neuroma*

noct-, nocti- night: *noctambulation, nocturia, noctiphobia*

nos-, noso- disease: *nosema, nosophobia*

ocul-, oculo- eye: *oculist, oculomotor, oculomycosis*

ondont-, odonto- tooth, teeth: odontalgia, orthodontics

-oid likeness, resemblance: *lymphoid, myeloid*

olig-, oligo- few, a deficiency: *oligemia, oligospermia, oliguria*

-oma- tumor, swelling: *hematoma, sarcoma*

onych-, onycho- nails: paronychia, onychoma

oo-, ovi-, ovo- ovum, egg: *oocyte, oviduct, ovoplasm* (do not confuse with **oophor-**)

oophor-, oophoro- ovary: *oophorectomy, oophoritis, oophorocystectomy.* See also **ovar-**

ophthalm-, ophthalmo- eye: *ophthalmia, ophthalmologist, ophthalmoscope*

orth-, ortho- straight, normal: *orthopedics, orthosis*

oscillo- to swing to and fro: *oscilloscope*

oss-, osseo-, ossi-, oste-, osteo- bone, bone tissue: *osseous, ossicle, osteocyte, osteomyelitis*

-ostomy creation of a mouth or opening by surgery: *colostomy, tracheostomy*

ot-, oto- ear: *otalgia, otitis, otomycosis*

-otomy cutting into: *phlebotomy, tracheotomy*

ovar-, ovario- ovary: *ovariectomy.* See also **oophor—**

-oxia pertaining to oxygen: *hypoxia, anoxia*

para- near, beyond, apart from, beside: *paramedical, parametrium, parathyroid, parasagittal*

path-, patho-, -pathy disease, abnormal condition: *pathogen, pathognomonic, pathology, neuropathy*

ped-, pedia- child, foot: *pedialgia, pedophobia, pediatrician*

-penia lack of: *leukopenia, thrombocytopenia*

per- through, excessively: *percutaneous, perfusion*

peri- around: *pericardium, perichondrium*

-pexy fixation: *nephropexy, proctopexy*

phag-, phago- to eat, to ingest: *phage, phagocyte*

-phagia, -phagy eating, swallowing: *aphagia, dysphagia*

-phasia speech, ability to talk: *aphasia, dysphasia*

-phil, -philic to be fond of, to like (have an affinity for): *eosinophilia, hemophilia, hydrophilic*

phleb-, phlebo- vein: *phlebitis, phlebotomy*

phob-, -phobia fear, dread, abnormal aversion: *phobic, acrophobia, hydrophobia*

phot- light: *photoreceptor, photophobia*

pile-, pili-, pilo- hair, resembling hair: *pileous, piliation, pilonidal*

-plasty molding, surgical formation: *gastroplasty, kineplasty*

pleur-, pleuro- side, rib, serous membrane covering the lung and lining the chest cavity: *pleurisy, pleurotomy*

-pnea air, breathing: *dyspnea, eupnea*

pneum-, pneuma-, pneumo-, pneumon-, pneumato- lung, air: *pneumectomy, pneumograph, pneumonia*

pod-, podo- foot: *podiatry, pododynia*

-poiesis making, forming: *erythropoiesis, hematopoiesis*

polio- gray: *polioencephalitis, poliomyelitis*

poly- many: *polyarthritis, polycystic, polycythemia*

post- behind, after, following: *postnatal, postocular, postpartum*

pre- before, ahead of: *precancerous, preclinical, prenatal*

presby- old age: *presbyophrenia, presbyopia*

pro- in front of, before: *prodromal, prosencephalon, prolapse, prothrombin*

proct-, procto- rectum: *proctitis, proctocele, proctologist, proctopexy*

pseud-, pseudo- false: *pseudoarthrosis, pseudomania, pseudopod*

psych-, psycho- mind: *psychosomatic, psychotherapy*

-ptosis downward displacement, falling, prolapse: *enteroptosis, nephroptosis*

pulmo-, pulmono- lung: *pulmonic, pulmonology*

py-, pyo- pus: *pyuria, pyogenic, pyorrhea*

pyel-, pyelo- kidney pelvis: *pyelitis, pyelogram, pyelonephrosis*

rachi-, rachio- spine: *rachiceniesis, rachischisis*

radio- emission of rays or radiation: *radioactive, radiography, radiology*

re- again, back: *reabsorption, reaction, regenerate*

ren- kidney: *renal, renopathy*

retro- backward, located behind: *retrocecal, retroperitoneal*

rheo- flow of matter, or of a current of electricity: *rheology, rheoscope*

rhin-, rhino- nose: *rhinitis, rhinoplasty*

-rrhage, -rrhagia excessive flow: *hemorrhage, menorrhagia*

-rrhaphy suturing of or sewing up of a gap or defect in a part: *enterorrhaphy, perineorrhaphy*

-rrhea flow, discharge: *diarrhea, gonorrhea, seborrhea*

salping-, salpingo- tube: *salpingitis, salpingoscopy*

scler-, sclero- hardness: *scleroderma, sclerosis*

scolio- twisted, crooked: *scoliosis, scoliosometer*

-scope instrument used to look into or examine a part: *bronchoscope, cystoscope, endoscope*

semi- mild, partial, half: *semipermeable, semicoma*

sep-, septic- poison, rot, decay: *sepsis, septicemia*

-sis condition or process, usually abnormal: *dermatosis, osteoporosis*

somat-, somato- body: *somatic, somatotype*

sono- sound: *sonogram, sonography*

splanchn-, splanchno- internal organs: *splanchnic, splanchnoptosis*

sta-, stat- stop, stand still, remain at rest: *stasis, static*

sten-, steno- contracted, narrowed: *stenosis*

sthen-, stheno-, -sthenia, -sthenic strength: *asthenic, neurasthenia*

stomato- mouth: *stomatitis*

sub- under, below, near, almost: *subclavian, subcutaneous, subluxation*

super- over, above, excessive: *superego, supernatant, superficial*

supra- location above or over: *supranasal, suprarenal*

sym-, syn- with, together: *symphysis, synapse*

syring-, syringo- fistula, tube, cavity: *syringectomy, syringomyelia*

tacho-, tachy- rapid, fast, swift: *tachycardia*

tars-, tarso- eyelid, foot: *tarsitis, tarsoplasty, tarsoptosis*

-taxia, -taxis order, arrangement: *ataxia, chemotaxis, thermotaxis*

tens- stretch, pull: *extension, tensor*

therm-, thermo-, -thermy heat: *thermalgesia, thermocautery, diathermy, thermometer*

tox-, toxic-, toxico- poison: *toxemia, toxicology, toxicosis*

trache- windpipe: *trachea, tracheitis, tracheotomy*

trans- across, through, beyond: *transorbital, transpiration, transplant, transport*

tri- three: *triad, triceps*

trich-, tricho- hair: *trichiasis, trichocardia, trichosis*

-trophic, -trophy nutrition (nurture): *atrophic, hypertrophy*

-tropic turning toward, influencing, changing: *adrenotropic, gonadotropic, thyrotropic*

ultra- beyond or excessive: *ultrasound, ultraviolet, ultrastructure*

uni- one: *unilateral, uniovular, unicellular*

-uria urine: *glycosuria, hematuria, pyuria*

vas-, vaso- vessel, duct: *vascular, vasectomy, vasodilation*

viscer-, viscero- internal organs: *viscera, visceroptosis*

xero- dryness: *xeroderma, xerophthalmia, xerosis*

Appendices

≡ Appendix 1. Metric Measurements

Unit	Abbreviation	Metric equivalent	U.S. equivalent
Units of length			
Kilometer	km	1000 meters	0.62 miles; 1.6 km/mile
Meter*	m	100 cm; 1000 mm	39.4 inches; 1.1 yards
Centimeter	cm	$\frac{1}{100}$ m; 0.01 m	0.39 inches; 2.5 cm/inch
Millimeter	mm	$\frac{1}{1000}$ m; 0.001 m	0.039 inches; 25 mm/inch
Micrometer	μm	$\frac{1}{1000}$ mm; 0.001 mm	
Units of weight			
Kilogram	kg	1000 g	2.2 lb
Gram*	g	1000 mg	0.035 oz; 28.5 g/oz
Milligram	mg	$\frac{1}{1000}$ g; 0.001 g	
Microgram	μg	$\frac{1}{1000}$ mg; 0.001 mg	
Units of volume			
Liter*	l	1000 ml	1.06 qt
Deciliter	dl	$\frac{1}{10}$ l; 0.1 l	
Milliliter	ml	$\frac{1}{1000}$ l; 0.001 l	0.034 oz; 29.4 ml/oz
Microliter	μl	$\frac{1}{1000}$ ml; 0.001 ml	

*Basic unit

≣ *Appendix 2.   Celsius–Fahrenheit Temperature Conversion Scale*

Use the following formula to convert Celsius readings to Fahrenheit readings:

$$°F = 9/5°C + 32$$

For example, if the Celsius reading is 37°:

$°F = (9/5 \times 37) + 32$

$\quad = 66.6 + 32$

$\quad = 98.6°F$ (normal body temperature)

Use the following formula to convert Fahrenheit readings to Celsius readings:

$$°C = 5/9 (°F - 32)$$

For example, if the Fahrenheit reading is 68°:

$°C = 5/9 (68 - 32)$

$\quad = 5/9 \times 36$

$\quad = 20°C$ (a nice spring day)

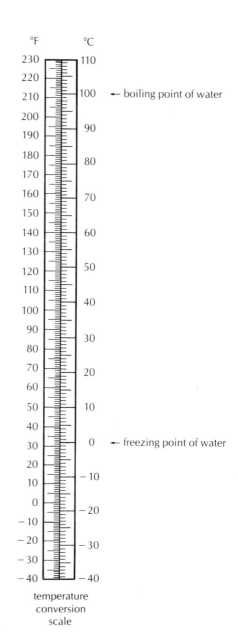

temperature
conversion
scale

≡ Appendix 3. *Typical Disease Conditions and Causative Organisms*

Table 1   Bacterial Diseases

Organism	Disease and Description
Cocci	
Neisseria gonorrhoeae (gonococcus)	Gonorrhea. Acute inflammation of mucous membranes of the reproductive and urinary tracts (with possible spread to the peritoneum in the female). Systemic infection may cause gonococcal arthritis and endocarditis. Organism also causes ophthalmia neonatorum, an eye inflammation of the newborn.
Neisseria meningitidis (meningococcus)	Epidemic meningitis. Inflammation of the membranes covering brain and spinal cord.
Streptococcus pneumoniae (*Diplococcus pneumoniae*)	Pneumonia. Inflammation of the alveoli, bronchioles, and bronchi. May be prevented by use of polyvalent pneumococcal vaccine.
Staphylococcus aureus and other staphylococci	Boils, carbuncles, impetigo, osteomyelitis, staphylococcal pneumonia, cystitis, pyelonephritis, empyema, septicemia, toxic shock, and food poisoning. Strains resistant to antibiotics are a cause of infections originating in the hospital, such as wound infections.
Streptococcus pyogenes, Streptococcus hemolyticus, and other streptococci	Septicemia, septic sore throat, scarlet fever (an acute infectious disease characterized by red skin rash, sore throat, "strawberry" tongue, high fever, enlargement of the lymph nodes), puerperal sepsis, erysipelas (an acute infection of skin occurring in lymph channels, usually of the face), streptococcal pneumonia, rheumatic fever (an inflammation of the joints, usually progressing to heart disease), subacute bacterial endocarditis (an inflammation of the heart valves), acute glomerulonephritis (inflammation of the glomeruli)
Bacilli	
Escherichia coli, Proteus bacilli, and other colon bacilli	Normal inhabitants of the colon, and usually harmless there. Cause of local and systemic infections, diarrhea (especially in children), septicemia, and septic shock. *E. coli* is the most common organism in hospital-transmitted infections.
Pseudomonas aeruginosa	Ubiquitous organism is a frequent cause of wound and urinary infections in debilitated hospitalized patients. Often found in solutions that have been standing for long periods.
Mycobacterium tuberculosis (tubercle bacillus)	Tuberculosis. Infectious disease in which the organism causes primary lesions called *tubercles.* These break down into cheeselike masses of tissue, a process known as *caseation.* Any body organ can be infected, but in adults the usual site is the lungs. Still one of the most widespread diseases in the world, tuberculosis is treated with chemotherapy; resistant strains of the bacillus have developed.
Mycobacterium leprae (Hansen's bacillus)	Leprosy. Chronic illness in which hard swellings occur under the skin, particularly of the face, causing a grotesque appearance. In one form of leprosy the nerves are affected, resulting in loss of sensation in the extremities.
Legionella pneumophila	Legionnaires' disease (pneumonia). Seen in localized epidemics, may be transmitted by air conditioning towers and by contaminated soil at excavation sites. Not spread person to person. Characterized by high fever, vomiting, diarrhea, cough, and bradycardia. Mild form of the disease called *Pontiac fever.*
Clostridium tetani	Tetanus. Acute, often fatal poisoning caused by introduction of the organism into deep wounds. Characterized by severe muscular spasms. Also called *lockjaw.*
Clostridium perfringens	Gas gangrene. Acute wound infection. Organisms cause death of tissues accompanied by the generation of gas within them.
Clostridium botulinum	Botulism. Very severe poisoning caused by eating food in which the organism has been allowed to grow and excrete its toxin. Can cause paralysis of the muscles and death from asphyxiation.
Bacillus anthracis	Anthrax. Disease acquired from animals. Characterized by a primary lesion called a *pustule.* Can develop into a fatal septicemia.

(Continued)

Table 1   Bacterial Diseases (Continued)

Organism	Disease and Description
Bacilli	
Corynebacterium diphtheriae	Diphtheria. Acute inflammation of the throat with the formation of a leathery membrane-like growth (pseudomembrane) that can obstruct air passages and cause death by asphyxiation. Toxin produced by this organism can damage heart, nerves, kidneys, and other organs. Disease preventable by appropriate vaccination.
Bordetella pertussis	Pertussis (whooping cough). Severe infection of the trachea and bronchi. The "whoop" is caused by the effort to recover breath after coughing. All children should be inoculated with appropriate vaccine.
Salmonella typhi (and others)	Salmonellosis occurs as enterocolitis, bacteremia, localized infection, or typhoid. Depending on type, presenting symptoms may be fever, diarrhea, or abscesses; complications include intestinal perforation and endocarditis. Carried in water, milk, meat, and other food.
Shigella dysenteriae (and others)	A serious bacillary dysentery. Acute intestinal infection with diarrhea (sometimes bloody); may cause dehydration with electrolyte imbalance or septicemia. Transmitted through fecal oral route or other poor sanitation.
Yersinia pestis (formerly called *Pasteurella pestis*)	Plague, the "black death" of the Middle Ages. Transmitted by fleas from infected rodents to humans. Symptoms of the most common form are swollen, infected lymph nodes or buboes. Another form may cause pneumonia. All forms may lead to a rapidly fatal septicemia.
Francisella tularensis	Tularemia, or deer fly fever. Transmitted by contact with an infected animal or bite of a tick or fly. Symptoms are fever, ulceration of the skin, and enlarged lymph nodes.
Brucella abortus (and others)	Brucellosis, or undulant fever. Disease of animals such as cattle and goats transmitted to humans through unpasteurized dairy products or undercooked meat. Acute phase of fever and weight loss; chronic disease with abscess formation and depression.

Note: The following organisms are smaller than other bacteria and vary in shape. Like viruses, they grow within cells, but they differ from viruses in that they are affected by antibiotics.

Organism	Disease and Description
Chlamydia psittaci	Psittacosis, also called *ornithosis*. Disease transmitted by various birds, including parrots, ducks, geese, and turkeys. Primary symptoms are chills, headache, and fever, more severe in older persons. The duration may be from 2 to 3 weeks, often with a long convalescence. Antibiotic drugs are effective remedies.
Chlamydia trachomatis (the same organism causes trachoma)	Lymphogranuloma venereum (LGV). Venereal disease characterized by swelling of inguinal lymph nodes and accompanied by signs of general infection. Later scar tissue forms in the genital region, possibly resulting in complete rectal stricture.
Chlamydia trachomatis	Trachoma. Common cause of blindness in underdeveloped areas of the world. Infection of the conjunctiva and cornea characterized by redness, pain, and lacrimation. Antibiotic therapy is effective if begun before there is scarring.
Chlamydia oculogenitalis	Inclusion conjunctivitis, acute eye infection. Carried in genital organs, transmitted during birth or through water in inadequately chlorinated swimming pools.
Rickettsia prowazekii	Epidemic typhus. Transmitted to humans by lice; associated with poor hygiene and war. Main symptoms are headache, hypotension, delirium, and a red rash. Frequently fatal in older persons.
Rickettsia typhi	Endemic or murine typhus. A milder disease transmitted to man from rats by fleas. Symptoms are fever, rash, headache, and cough. The disease is rarely fatal.
Rickettsia rickettsii	Rocky Mountain spotted fever. Tick-borne disease occurring throughout the United States. Symptoms are fever, muscle aches, and a rash that may progress to gangrene over bony prominences. The disease is rarely fatal.
Coxiella burnetii	Q fever. Infection transmitted from cattle, sheep, and goats to humans by contaminated dust and also carried by arthropods. Symptoms are fever, headache, chills, and pneumonitis. This disorder is almost never fatal.

(Continued)

Table 1   Bacterial Diseases (Continued)

Organism	Disease and Description
Curved, Wavy or Corkscrew Rods	
Spirilla	
Vibrio cholerae (*Vibrio comma*)	Cholera. Acute infection of the intestine characterized by prolonged vomiting and diarrhea, leading to severe dehydration, electrolyte imbalance, and in some cases death.
Spirochetes	
Treponema vincentii (formerly called *Borelia vincentii* or *Spirillum vincentii*)	Vincent's disease (trench mouth). Infection of the mouth and throat accompanied by formation of a pseudomembrane, with ulceration.
Borrelia recurrentis (and others)	Relapsing fever. Generalized infection in which attacks of fever alternate with periods of apparent recovery. Organisms spread by lice, ticks, and other insects.
Leptospira	Leptospirosis. Infection of rodents and certain domestic animals transmitted to humans by way of contaminated water or by direct contact. The organisms may penetrate the mucous membranes and broken skin. Leptospirosis causes hepatitis (with or without jaundice), nephritis, and meningitis.
Treponema pallidum	Syphilis. Infectious disease transmitted mainly by sexual intercourse. Untreated syphilis is seen in the following three stages: primary—formation of primary lesion (chancre); secondary—skin eruptions and infectious patches on mucous membranes; tertiary—development of generalized lesions (gummas) and destruction of tissues resulting in aneurysm, heart disease, and degenerative changes in brain, spinal cord and ganglia, meninges. Also a cause of intrauterine fetal death or stillbirth.
Treponema pertenue	Yaws. Tropical disease characterized by lesions of the skin and deformities of hands, feet, and face.

Table 2   Fungal Diseases

Disease	Description
Candidiasis	An infection that can involve the skin and mucous membranes. May cause diaper rash, infection of the nail beds, and infection of the mucous membranes of the mouth (thrush), throat, and vagina.
Histoplasmosis	This fungus may cause a variety of disorders, ranging from mild respiratory symptoms or enlargement of liver, spleen, and lymph nodes to cavities in the lungs with symptoms similar to those of tuberculosis.
Ringworm (tinea capitis) (tinea corporis) (tinea pedis)	Common fungal infections of the skin, many of which cause blisters and scaling with discoloration of the affected areas. All are caused by similar organisms from a group of fungi called *dermatophytes*. They are easily transmitted from person to person or by contaminated articles.
Actinomycosis	"Lumpy jaw," which occurs in cattle and humans. The organisms cause the formation of large masses of tissue, which are often accompanied by abscesses. The lungs and liver may be involved.
Blastomycosis	A general term for any infection caused by a yeastlike organism. There may be skin tumors and lesions in the lungs, bones, liver, spleen, and kidneys.
Coccidioidomycosis	Also called *San Joaquin Valley fever,* it is another systemic fungal disease. Because it often attacks the lungs, it may be mistaken for tuberculosis.

Table 3   *Viral Diseases*

Disease	Description
Chickenpox (varicella)	A usually mild infection, almost completely confined to children, characterized by blister-like skin eruptions.
Shingles (herpes zoster)	The cause of this disease is the virus of chickenpox. Herpes is a very painful eruption of blisters of the skin that follow the course of certain peripheral nerves. These blisters eventually dry up and form scabs that resemble shingles.
Cold sores (herpes simplex)	In this condition cold sores or fever blisters appear about the mouth and nose of patients with colds or other illness accompanied by fever. This condition should not be confused with herpes zoster.
Measles (rubeola)	An acute respiratory inflammation followed by fever and a generalized skin rash. Patients are prone to the development of dangerous complications, such as bronchopneumonia and other secondary infections caused by staphylococci and streptococci.
Yellow fever	An acute infectious tropical disease transmitted by the bite of an infected mosquito. The disease is marked by jaundice, severe gastrointestinal symptoms, stomach hemorrhaging, and nephritis, which may be fatal.
Infectious hepatitis	Liver inflammation caused by type A hepatitis virus. The portal of entry and exit is often, but not always, the digestive tract.
Serum hepatitis	Liver disease caused by type B hepatitis virus. It was formerly thought to be transmitted by injection into the tissue or blood, as by contaminated needles, surgical instruments, or blood specimens. It is now known that this virus may also enter by the oral route. It is a more serious and prolonged illness than is infectious hepatitis.
Poliomyelitis	An acute viral infection that may attack the anterior horns of the spinal cord, resulting in paralysis of certain voluntary muscles. The degree of permanent paralysis depends on the extent of damage sustained by the motor nerves. Three types of causative viruses are known (types 1, 2, and 3).
Rabies	An acute, fatal disease transmitted to humans through the saliva of an infected animal. Rabies is characterized by violent muscular spasms induced by the slightest sensations. Because the swallowing of water causes spasms of the throat, the disease is also called *hydrophobia* ("fear of water"). The final stage of paralysis ends in death.
Viral encephalitis	*Encephalitis* usually is understood to be any brain inflammation accompanied by degenerative tissue changes, and it can have many causes besides viruses. There are several forms of viral encephalitis (Western and Eastern epidemic, equine, St. Louis, Japanese B, etc.), some of which are known to be transmitted from birds and other animals to humans by insects, principally mosquitoes.
Mumps (epidemic parotitis)	An acute inflammation with swelling of the parotid salivary glands. Mumps can have many complications, such as orchitis (an inflammation of the testes), especially in children.
German measles (rubella)	A less severe form of measles, but especially dangerous during the first 3 months of pregnancy because the disease organism can cause heart defects, deafness, mental deficiency, and other permanent damage in the fetus.
Common cold (coryza)	A viral infection of the upper respiratory tract. Victims are highly susceptible to complications such as pneumonia and influenza.
Influenza	An epidemic viral infection, marked by chills, fever, muscular pains, and prostration. The most serious complication is bronchopneumonia caused by *Hemophilus influenzae* (a bacillus) or streptococci.
Genital herpes	An acute inflammatory disease of the genitalia, often recurring. Caused by herpes simplex II virus. A very common venereal disease.
AIDS (acquired immune deficiency syndrome)	A newly discovered fatal disease caused by human immunodeficiency virus (HIV) which infects the T-lymphocytes of the immune system. Patients develop certain forms of cancer, pneumonia, and other infections. The disease has been found in the United States among homosexuals and other limited populations.

Table 4 **Protozoal Diseases**

Organism	Disease and Description
Amebae	
Entamoeba histolytica	Amebic dysentery. Severe ulceration of the wall of the large intestine caused by amebae. Acute diarrhea may be an important symptom. This organism also may cause liver abscesses.
Ciliates	
Balantidium coli	Gastrointestinal disturbances and ulcers of the colon.
Flagellates	
Giardia lamblia	Gastrointestinal disturbances.
Trichomonas vaginalis	Inflammation and discharge from the vagina of the female. In the male it involves the urethra and causes painful urination.
Trypanosoma	African sleeping sickness. Disease begins with a high fever, followed by invasion of the brain and spinal cord by the organisms. Usually the disease ends with continued drowsiness, coma, and death.
Leishmania donovani (and others)	Kala-azar. In this disease there is enlargement of the liver and spleen, as well as skin lesions.
Sporozoa	
Plasmodium; varieties include *vivax, falciparum, malariae*	Malaria. Characterized by recurrent attacks of chills followed by high fever. Severe attacks of malaria can be fatal because of kidney failure, cerebral disorders, and other complications.
Toxoplasma gondii	Toxoplasmosis. Common infectious disease transmitted by cats and raw meat. Mild forms cause fever and enlargement of lymph nodes. Infection of a pregnant woman is a cause of fetal stillbirth or congenital damage.

Index

The letter *f* following a page number indicates a figure; the letter *t* following a page number indicates a table.